Man and the Ecosphere

Readings from
SCIENTIFIC AMERICAN

Man and the Ecosphere

with commentaries by

Paul R. Ehrlich
Stanford University

John P. Holdren
University of California
Lawrence Radiation Laboratory
Livermore

Richard W. Holm
Stanford University

W. H. Freeman and Company
San Francisco

PREFACE

Most of the topical collections of articles from SCIENTIFIC AMER-ICAN that have been published have dealt with well-defined areas of study or with subjects of contemporary scientific research. This collection, like one of its more recent predecessors (*Science, Conflict, and Society,* with introductions by Garrett Hardin), contains a wider range of subject matter: we have selected twenty-seven articles treating a variety of aspects of the growing crisis in population, resources, and environment—its history, its components, its implications. We hope that these articles, together with the commentaries that introduce them, convey a sense of the dimensions of man's impact on the ecosphere and, correspondingly, of the fundamental sociological and technological changes required to alleviate that impact while an element of choice still remains.

The articles presented here have appeared in SCIENTIFIC AMERICAN in the course of the past fifteen years. Although most of them stem from the later part of this period, the reader may in a few instances be surprised that a more recent article on a similar topic was not included instead of the one chosen. Where such choices were made, it was done in favor of readability and comprehensiveness, or to illustrate the historical development of an important theme. This may mean, of course, that a few articles may not precisely reflect the current thinking of their authors (a liability of any collection). We hope the authors—as well as the reader—will find that the result is nevertheless worthwhile: that we have managed to present the highlights of a vast and complex issue in a small space, using selections accessible to readers without specialized scientific or technical training.

Paul R. Ehrlich
John P. Holdren
Richard W. Holm

March 1971

Contents

Note on cross-references: References to articles included in this book are noted by the title of the article and the page on which it begins; references to articles that are available as offprints but are not included here are noted by the article's title and offprint number; references to articles published by SCIENTIFIC AMERICAN but which are not available as offprints are noted by the title of the article and the month and year of its publication.

Man and the Ecosphere

Optimism is a good characteristic, but if carried to an excess it becomes foolishness. . . .

Theodore Roosevelt,
Annual Message to Congress, 1907.

An ecologist must either harden his shell and make believe that the consequences of science are none of his business, or he must be the doctor who sees the marks of death in a community that believes itself well and does not want to be told otherwise.

Aldo Leopold,
Round River

The three decades since the beginning of World War II have been perhaps the most exciting in the history of science and technology. The astonishing advances in physics, chemistry, and engineering during this period comprise the latest phase of an industrial revolution that has reshaped civilization. Unfortunately, although that revolution has left practically no corner of the globe unaffected, its principal fruits have been unevenly distributed. Moreover, it has initiated a triad of problems so grave that they call into question the ultimate viability of the human enterprise itself.

The best known of these problems is, of course, the development of military technologies powerful enough to eradicate mankind; nuclear weapons obviously belong in this category, and certain biological weapons may also. The second grave problem has been the achievement and wide dissemination of various means to prolong life, many decades in advance of equally effective programs to limit births. The resulting explosive growth of the human population has rendered almost every other human problem more difficult of solution — including the inequitable distribution of the requisites of a decent existence, the politics of international competition for high-grade resources, and the impact of civilization on the environmental systems that sustain it. The third great problem — spawned by the industrial revolution and, especially, the last three decades of hectic scientific and technological activity — has been the dramatic increase in per capita human impact on the environment. Coupled with the increase in human numbers, this effect has made mankind a global ecological force — well before human understanding of the operation of the global ecosystem is sufficient to cope with such a role.

This striking dualism in contemporary science and technology —monumental achievements beside astonishing omissions and misdirection—deserves the most careful scrutiny. If the present destructive course is to be altered, we must understand not only the operational details of past and present errors, but also the way in which society's institutions, goals, and prejudices have interacted with science and technology to produce such imperfect results. Not surprisingly, the pages of SCIENTIFIC AMERICAN for the past two decades have offered a wealth of fertile material to the student of these problems.

We will not attempt to grapple here with the broad issue of science and society in all its aspects: the question of an individual scientist's responsibility for potential applications of his work, for example, is outside the intended scope of this book. Rather, the articles from SCIENTIFIC AMERICAN included here deal principally with some of the more tangible components of man's predicament: the history of his interaction with the ecosphere, his escalating demands and impact on it today, and the paucity of easy remedies.

At the same time, it is worth noting that the multitude of SCIENTIFIC AMERICAN articles *not* included here offer important insights into one of the sociopolitical underpinnings of the ecological crisis: the priorities of institutionalized science during the past few decades. For it can be seen from the pages of SCIENTIFIC AMERICAN (which, we believe, has mirrored rather accurately the interests of science and scientists) that science during this period has been dominated by "experimental" and "hard" disciplines.

More specifically, those areas in which rapid progress was made were those that seemed useful to an ever-expanding technological society. Clear-cut, usable answers seemed to flow, one after another, from laboratories. This has been the science that has attracted prestige and money. Generally, it has also been a reductionist science, which pulled things apart to see how they worked, and used the knowledge gained thereby to produce complex artifacts, and to repair (or destroy) human bodies. Science in these areas was self reinforcing, in that it obtained much of the research support that was available. It thus tended to attract the best students who, in turn, helped to produce further progress.

Partly as a result of the disproportionate support of the hard sciences, those disciplines that attempt to deal with higher levels of organization have made relatively little headway. Scientists working in these areas use a holistic, rather than a reductionist, approach, and must struggle with complex systems much less susceptible to experimental analysis than those studied by the physicist or biochemist. Disciplines sharing these difficulties include most of the behavioral sciences and such "new" fields as population biology and ecology, whose coverage in both the scientific and popular press has been extremely superficial. This has been especially unfortunate, because it has led many laymen, as well as certain "hard" scientists, to overestimate their own grasp of ecological and psychological principles.

The comparative neglect of the more complex sciences is not really surprising. After all, physics, chemistry, and mathematics get "results": nuclear weaponry, superconductors, computers, and space rockets. And other "hard" disciplines, such as biochemistry, promise results in areas high on the list of society's present priorities—for example, a cure for cancer. In contrast, the revolution of the past decade in theoretical community ecology (which deals with the nature of ecoysystem complexity) has received little attention. Theoretical ecology has not been newsworthy, by the standards of technologists and their publicists. This outlook can be traced to journalism's massive experience with the hard sciences, where success is most often a result of narrowness of outlook and monolithic dedication to detail. Because of the narrow focus of the hard scientist, and its reflection in scientific reports, many scientists, technologists, and laymen are still unaware that mankind's entire future may depend upon our understanding of the fundamental relation between complexity and stability in ecological systems.

A particularly unfortunate consequence of too narrow a view is the dangerous phenomenon of unrestrained technological optimism. In the view of the technological optimist, humanity has gained complete dominance over nature; he envisions technological solutions to all human problems. This view has spread from some scientists and engineers, through publicists, to much of the general public. In the sections that follow, it will become apparent that such optimism is hardly warranted. There is much that technology can contribute to the solution of man's problems, but it must be managed with unprecedented attention to fundamentally nontechnological constraints: the finiteness of resources, the need for ecosystem complexity, and the consequent necessity of stabilizing both human population size and per capita consumption.

I

THE ECOSPHERE AND PREINDUSTRIAL MAN

I

THE ECOSPHERE
AND
PREINDUSTRIAL MAN

Prudent men should judge of future events by what has taken place in the past, and what is taking place in the present.

Miguel de Cervantes,
Persiles and Sigismunda

INTRODUCTION

LaMont Cole's essay "The Ecosphere" provides the foundation for the discussions in this section and, indeed, for the remainder of this book. Cole's paper places man in humbling perspective, against the backdrop of natural cycles that still dwarf his own growing efforts at mobilizing energy and resources. Yet Cole, in moving from the macroscopic to the microscopic and back again—from the solar energy striking the planet, the annual evaporation from its waters, and the prodigious quantities of minerals washed annually to the sea, to the trace elements and the bacteria essential to life—manages to convey both the staggering scale of the "system" and the surprising vulnerability of its living component to disruption.

What Cole calls the "overwhelming dominance" of man within the animal community is, in effect, the central theme of this book. In a brief period of only thirteen years (from 1958, when "The Ecosphere" was published, to 1971) that dominance, in the form of man's population size, increased by more than 35 percent—from 2.7 to 3.7 billion people. If we apply some simple arithmetic to Cole's figures for plant productivity and the present rate of increase for the human population of 2 percent per annum, we are quickly led to an unsettling conclusion: If nothing else intervenes (something will!), the demands of the human population about 250 years from now will exceed what the earth can supply. This calculation assumes that *all* metabolizable plant material produced each year will be consumed directly by man, the competition of other animal species having been eliminated.

Of course, man's impact on the ecosphere entails far more than the results of his requirement for food. With his brain, with his hands, with his tools, with the energy he has harnessed in increasing quantities, man, over the millenia, has ranked as a modifier of the environment far out of proportion to his numbers. The long history of this phenomenon makes instructive reading at a time when many people believe that man's environmental impact began with the industrial revolution. Some commentators have erroneously implied that our environmental problems can be traced primarily to misuses of technology since World War II (see, for example, Barry Commoner, *The Humanist*, November–December 1970, p. 10). Such views seriously underestimate the degree to which *Homo sapiens* had altered the face of the planet before he had harnessed steam and other surrogates for muscle power.

The first big ecological change that may reasonably be attributed to our species was the extinction of large mammals toward the end of the Pleistocene epoch—roughly, thirty or forty thousand years ago.

Many paleontologists believe that primitive man developed techniques for killing large animals in great numbers. These early techniques included the use of fire, the driving of herds of animals over cliffs, and other practices not too different from those used in the more recent past by, for example, the American Indians. During the late Pleistocene, 70 percent of the large mammals of North America, for example, became extinct, along with their predators and scavengers. The Peistocene was, of course, a time of great climatic change, and there is a temptation to attribute the megafaunal extinctions to this factor. However, there are no indications that mass extinction of small animals, of plants, or of marine forms took place. Nor are there any areas in which massive extinctions of mammalian species occurred before man's arrival, which is why the extinctions have been referred to as "Pleistocene Overkill."

The depredations of our early hunting ancestors did more than alter the fauna of the planet. Large grazers and browsers have profound effects on plants, and the extermination of such animals undoubtedly influenced floristic patterns. Moreover, in using fire to help manage their food supply, hunters and food-gatherers obviously changed the botanical landscape. But these changes were minor when compared with those caused by man and his domestic animals once the agricultural revolution was well under way. Overgrazing and lumbering, for instance, were at least partly responsible for the "desertification" of much of northern Africa, and for the expansion of the great Thar Desert of western India. Heavy logging and the clearing of land for agriculture denuded many of China's watersheds, leading to destructive flooding on her rivers. Even within the borders of the United States, preindustrial men have greatly altered the landscape. Large areas of what previously was first-rate grazing land have, for example, been turned into desolate expanses of sandy desert by Navaho sheepherding.

The inception of the agricultural revolution, then, was a turning point in cultural evolution: the real beginning of trends that today might reasonably be called a journey toward oblivion. This singular event, perhaps the most significant in the history of mankind, is described in Robert Braidwood's article "The Agricultural Revolution." The importance of the transformation so carefully reconstructed for us in Braidwood's paper depends upon two factors: the resultant increase in the human population and the simplification of complex ecological systems.

First, the ability to grow food and to store it made human life more secure, and led to a slow, irregular decline in the death rate. The birthrate, however, did not decline, and the result was a pattern of accelerating population growth: It took millions of years for the human population to reach some 5 million at the time of the agricultural revolution; in the 10,000 years since then, the population has increased 700-fold. Now, the equivalent of the entire population in 8000 BC is added to the world population every month.

Second, agricultural practices tend to remove complex ecological systems and to replace them with simple ones. Forest and grassland communities, containing many different kinds of plants and animals, are displaced by fields of single crops from which man attempts to exclude other animals and plants. Unfortunately, complexity is one of the factors that makes natural ecosystems stable; simple ecosystems tend to be very unstable. As man has brought more and more of the earth under the plow, he has made the aggregate of ecological systems more unstable and thus subject to rapid and unfavorable alteration. Grazing has a related effect, greatly reducing the diversity of plants in an area until only those most unlikely to be eaten remain. Under certain conditions, such plants may have little power to hold soil, and thus a cycle of deterioration leads to the desert and wasteland conditions mentioned above.

Johannes Iversen's article "Forest Clearance in the Stone Age" explains how neolithic man—as a participant in the agricultural revolution—managed to destroy complex ecosystems with stone tools. Here is substantial evidence of man's ability to make massive inroads on his environment long before the advent of the bulldozer and DDT. There is little foundation, then, for industrial man's common assumption that nonindustrial man is a helpless waif adrift in a hostile sea of environment. The archeological evidence recorded here, and the remains of the great preindustrial farming civilizations in Yucatan, the Tigris and Euphrates valleys, Cambodia, and elsewhere, testify to the enormous capacity for changing the environment possessed by our ancestors thousands of years ago.

Of course, the man $\rightarrow$ environment relationship is really the man $\rightleftarrows$ environment relationship. While *Homo sapiens* is affecting his environment, his environment is also affecting him. It is not clear how much evolutionary change man has undergone in the 400 or so generations since the agricultural revolution, but it seems safe to say that shifting selection pressures have changed man's hereditary endowment such that his tolerance to crowding and his nutritional requirements, among other things, have been altered. The environment also affects the dynamics of human populations. Environmental changes such as wars, earthquakes, crop failures, and deterioration of farmland have had dramatic, but usually localized, retarding effects on human population growth.

Perhaps the best known of such environmental changes, and certainly one of the most dramatic, was the epidemic of bubonic plague described in William Langer's article "The Black Death," which closes this section. The origin of the plague is obscure, but its effects on the population of fourteenth century Europe are dramatically described by Langer. There are several lessons for contemporary man in the story of the Black Death. First, subtle environmental changes can make a population susceptible to epidemic disease. Crowding is clearly such a change, and the density of the human population is rising both locally and globally. Malnutrition is another, and this condition today affects perhaps two thirds of mankind. (Other aspects of man's aggravation of the problem of epidemic disease are considered in Tsutomu Watanabe's "Infectious Drug Resistance," the last article in Section III.)

Another lesson to be learned from the story of the Black Death is that great catastrophes may have profound psychological effects on human beings, effects that may influence people for generations after the event. Langer discusses such effects of the plague. A similar phenomenon is clearly visible in the history of Ireland subsequent to the Great Potato Famine, an event that followed the collapse of an unstable agricultural ecosystem. These historical phenomena should give pause to those who blithely anticipate the regeneration of civilization following a thermonuclear holocaust. Such a war—all too possible today, both technically and politically—would dwarf all past human tragedies. It would surely result in immense psychological and ecological damage, in addition to its other more immediate and obvious effects on civilization.

1

The Ecosphere

LaMONT C. COLE
April 1958

Probably I should apologize for using a coined word like "ecosphere," but it seems nicely to describe just what I want to discuss. It is intended to combine two concepts: the "biosphere" and the "ecosystem."

The great 19th-century French naturalist Jean Lamarck first conceived the idea of the biosphere as the collective totality of living creatures on the earth, and the concept has been taken up and developed in recent years by the Russian geochemist V. I. Vernadsky. The word "ecosystem" means a self-sustaining community of organisms—plants as well as animals—taken together with its inorganic environment.

Now all these are interdependent. Animal life could not exist without plants nor plants without animals, which supply them with carbon dioxide. Even the composition of the inorganic environment depends upon the cyclic activity of life. Photosynthesis by the earth's plants would remove all of the carbon dioxide from the atmosphere within a year or so if it were not returned by fires and by the respiration of animals and other consumers of plants. Similarly nitrogen-fixing organisms would exhaust all of the nitrogen in the air in less than a million years. And so on. The conclusion is that a self-sustaining community must contain not just plants, animals and nitrogen-fixers but also decomposers which can free the chemicals bound in proto-

THE AMAZON, one of whose mouths is shown in this aerial photograph, plays an important role in the earth's circulation of water. Together with the Congo it carries more than 10 per cent of the 9,000 cubic miles of water that flow into the sea every year.

plasm. It is very fortunate from our standpoint that some microorganisms have solved the biochemical trick of decomposing chitin, lignins and other inert organic compounds that tie up carbon.

A community must consist of producers or accumulators of energy (green plants), primary consumers (fungi, microorganisms and herbivores), higher-order consumers (carnivorous predators, parasites and scavengers), and decomposers that regenerate the raw materials.

Communities vary, of course, all over the world, and each ecosystem is a composite of the community and the features of the inorganic environment that govern the availability of energy and essential chemicals and the conditions that the community members must tolerate. But the system that I wish to consider here is not a local one but the largest possible ecosystem: namely, the sum total of life on earth together with the global environment and the earth's total resources. This is what I call the ecosphere. My purpose is to reach some conclusions on such questions as how much life the earth can support.

Organisms living on the face of the earth as it floats around in space can receive energy from several sources. Energy from outside comes to us as sunlight and starlight, is reflected to us as moonlight, and is brought to earth by cosmic radiation and meteors. Internally the earth is heated by radioactivity, and it is also gaining heat energy from the tidal friction that is gradually slowing our rotation. On top of this man is tapping enormous amounts of stored energy by burning fossil fuels. But all these secondary sources of energy are infinitesimal compared to our daily sunshine, which accounts for 99.9998 per cent of our total energy income.

This supply of solar energy amounts to 13×10^{23} gram-calories per year, or, if you prefer, it represents a continuous power supply at the rate of 2.5 billion billion horsepower. About one third of the incoming energy is lost at once by being reflected back to space, chiefly by clouds. The rest is absorbed by the atmosphere and the earth itself, to remain here temporarily until it is re-radiated to space as heat. During its residence on earth this energy serves to melt ice, to warm the land and oceans, to evaporate water, to generate winds and waves and currents. In addition to these activities, a ridiculously small proportion—about four hundredths of 1 per cent—of the solar energy goes to feed the metabolism of the biosphere.

Practically all of this energy enters the biosphere by means of photosynthesis. The plants use one sixth of the energy they take up from sunlight for their own metabolism, making the other five sixths available for animals and other consumers. About 5 per cent of this net energy is dissipated by forest and grass fires and by man's burning of plant products as fuel.

When an animal or other consumer eats plant protoplasm, it uses some of the substance for energy to fuel its metabolism and some as raw materials for growth. Some it discharges in broken-down form as metabolic waste products: for example, animals excrete urea, and yeast releases ethyl alcohol. And a large part of the plant material it ingests is simply indigestible and passes through the body unused. Herbivores, whether they are insects, rabbits, geese or cattle, succeed in extracting only about 50 per cent of the calories stored in the plant protoplasm. (The lost calories are, however, extractable by other consumers: flies may feed on the excretions or man himself may burn cattle dung for fuel.)

Of the plant calories consumed by an animal that eats the plant, only 20 to 30 per cent is actually built into protoplasm. Thus, since half of its consumption is lost as waste, the net efficiency of a herbivore in converting plant protoplasm into meat is about 10 to 15 per cent. The secondary consumers—i.e., meat-eaters feeding on the herbivores—do a little better. Because animal protoplasm has a smaller proportion of indigestible matter than plants have, a carnivore can use 70 per cent of the meat for its internal chemistry. But again only 30 per cent at most goes into building tissue. So the maximum efficiency of carnivores in converting one kind of meat into another is 20 per cent.

Some of the consequences of these relationships are of general interest and are fairly well known. For example, 1,000 calories stored up by the algae in Cayuga Lake can be converted into protoplasm amounting to 150 calories by small aquatic animals. In turn, smelt eating these animals produce 30 calories of protoplasm from the 150. If a man then eats the smelt, he can synthesize six calories worth of fat or muscle from the 30; if he waits for the smelt to be eaten by a trout and then eats the trout, the yield shrinks to 1.2 calories. If we were really dependent on the lake for food, we would do well to exterminate the trout and eat the smelt ourselves, or, better yet, to exterminate the smelt and live on planktonburgers. The same principles, of course, apply on land. If man is really determined to support the

largest possible populations of his kind, he will have to shorten the food chains leading to himself and, so far as practicable, turn to a vegetarian diet.

The rapid shrinkage of stored energy as it passes from one organism to another serves to make the study of natural communities a trifle more simple for the ecologist than it would otherwise be. It explains why food chains in nature rarely contain more than four or five links. Thus in our Cayuga Lake chain the trout was the third animal link and man the fourth. Chains of the same sort occur in the ocean, with, for example, a tuna or cod as the third link and perhaps a shark or a seal replacing man as the fourth link. Now if we look for the fifth link in the chain we find that it takes something like a killer whale or a polar bear to be able to subsist on seals. As to a sixth link—it would take quite a predator to make its living by devouring killer whales or polar bears.

We could, of course, trace food chains in other directions. Each species has its parasites that extort their cut of the stored energy, and these in turn support other parasites down to the point where there is not enough energy available to support another organism. Also, we should not forget the unused energy contained in the feces and urine of each animal. The organic matter in feces is often the basic resource of a food chain in which the next link may be a dung beetle or the larva of a fly.

I estimate that the maximum amount of protoplasm of all types that can be produced on earth each year amounts to 410 billion tons, of which 290 billion represent plant growth and the other 120 billion all of the consumer organisms. We see, then, that the availability of energy sets a limit to the amount of life on earth—that is, to the size of the biosphere. This energy also keeps the nonliving part of the ecosphere animated, largely through the agency of moving water, which is the single most important chemical substance in the physiology of the ecosphere.

Each year the oceans evaporate a quantity of water equivalent to an average depth of one meter. The total evaporation from land and bodies of fresh water is one sixth of the evaporation from the sea, and at least one fifth of this evaporation is from the transpiration of plants growing on land. The grand total of water evaporated annually is roughly 100,000 cubic miles, and this must be roughly the annual precipitation. The precipitation on land exceeds the evaporation by slightly over 9,000 cubic

ENERGY CYCLES of the ecosphere are powered by the sun. Land plants bind solar energy into organic compounds utilized successively (*gray arrows*) by herbivore, carnivore and scavenger; residual compounds are decomposed by bacteria. Energy fixed by microscopic sea plants through a similar "food chain" (*color arrows*). In the water cycle (*broken gray arrows*) water evaporated from the sea is precipitated on land and used by living organisms, eventually returning to the sea bearing minerals and organic matter.

miles, which therefore represents the annual runoff of water from land to sea. It is astonishing to me to note that more than one tenth of this total runoff is carried to the sea by just two rivers—the Amazon and the Congo.

Precipitation supplies nonmarine organisms with the water which they require in large quantities. Protoplasm averages at least 75 per cent water, and plants require something like 450 grams of water to produce one gram of dry organic matter. The water moving from land to sea also erodes the land surface and dissolves soluble mineral matter. It brings to the plants the chemical nutrients that they require and it tends to level the land surface and deposit the minerals in the sea. At present the continents are being worn down at an average world-wide rate of one centimeter per century. The leveling process, however, apparently has never gone on to completion on the earth. Geological uplift of the land always intervenes and brings marine sediments above sea level, where the cycle can begin again.

The rivers of the world are now washing into the seas some four billion tons of dissolved inorganic matter a year, about 400 million tons of dissolved organic matter and about five times as much undissolved matter. The undissolved matter represents destruction of the land where organisms live, but the dissolved material is of greater interest, because it includes such important chemicals as 3.5 million tons of phosphorus, 100 million tons of potassium and 10 million tons of fixed nitrogen. In order to say what these losses may mean to the biosphere we must review a few facts about the chemical composition of the earth and of organisms.

Every organism seems to require at least 20 chemical elements and probably several others in trace amounts. Some of the organisms' requirements are rather surprising. *Penicillium* is said to need traces of tungsten, and the common duckweed demands manganese and the rare earth gallium. There is a European pansy which needs high concentrations of zinc in the soil, and several plants in different parts of the world are so hungry for copper that they help prospectors to find the mineral. Many organisms have fantastic abilities to concentrate the necessary elements from dilute media. The sea-squirts have vanadium in their blood, and the liver of the edible scallop contains on a dry-weight basis one tenth of 1 per cent of cadmium, although the amount of this element in sea water is so small that it cannot be de-

tected by chemical tests.

But the exotic chemical tastes of organisms are comparatively unimportant. Their main needs can be summed up in just five words—oxygen, carbon, hydrogen, nitrogen and phosphorus, which account for more than 95 per cent of the mass of all protoplasm. Oxygen is the most abundant chemical element on earth, so we probably do not need to be concerned about any absolute deficiency of oxygen. But nitrogen is a different matter. Whereas protein, the main stuff of life, is 18 per cent nitrogen, the relative abundance of this element on the earth is only one 10,000th of the earth's mass. It is apparent that our land forms of life could not long tolerate a net annual loss of 10 million tons of fixed nitrogen to the sea. Fortunately this nitrogen loss from land is reversible, so that we can speak of a "nitrogen cycle." Organisms in the sea convert the fixed nitrogen into ammonia, a gas which can return to land via the atmosphere.

Carbon also is not in too abundant supply, for it amounts to less than three parts in 10,000 of the total mass of the earth's matter. But once again the biosphere profits from the fact that carbon can escape from the oceans as a gas—carbon dioxide. This gas goes through a complex circulation in the atmosphere, being released from the oceans in tropical regions and absorbed by the ocean waters in polar regions. Because some carbon is deposited in ocean sediments as carbonates, there is a net loss of carbon from the ecosphere. But there seems to be no danger that a shortage of this element will restrict life. The atmosphere contains 2,400 billion tons of carbon dioxide, and at least 30 times that much is dissolved in the oceans, waiting to be released if the atmosphere should become depleted. Volcanoes discharge carbon dioxide, and man is burning fossil fuels at such a rate that he has been accused of increasing the average carbon dioxide content of the atmosphere by some 10 per cent in the last 50 years. In addition, lots of limestone, which is more than 4 per cent carbon dioxide, has been pushed up from ancient seas by uplifts of the earth.

The story of phosphorus appears somewhat more alarming. This element accounts for a bit more than one tenth of 1 per cent of the mass of terrestrial matter, is enriched to about twice this level in plant protoplasm and is greatly enriched in animals, accounting for more than 1 per cent of the weight of the human body. As a constituent of nucleic

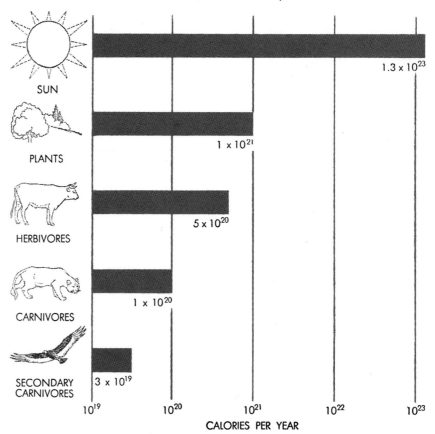

UTILIZATION OF SOLAR ENERGY decreases with each step along the food chain. These bars (on a logarithmic scale) show that plants use only .08 per cent of energy reaching the atmosphere; plant-eaters use only part of this fraction and flesh-eaters even less.

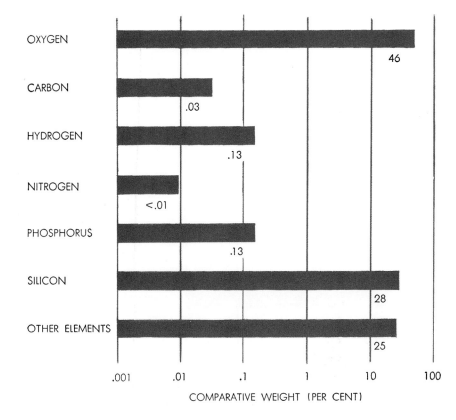

OXYGEN
46

CARBON
.03

HYDROGEN
.13

NITROGEN
<.01

PHOSPHORUS
.13

SILICON
28

OTHER ELEMENTS
25

.001   .01   .1   1   10   100

COMPARATIVE WEIGHT (PER CENT)

ESTIMATED RELATIVE ABUNDANCE of elements in the earth and its atmosphere (*above*) and in living matter (*below*) is compared in these charts; the scale is logarithmic. Silicon, with many stable compounds, is abundant on earth but rare in living organisms. Nitrogen, rare on earth, is important to life, making up as much as 18 per cent of proteins.

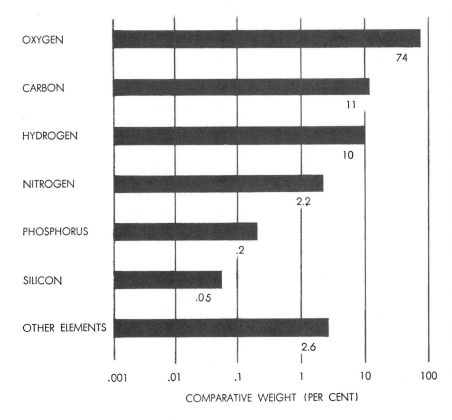

OXYGEN
74

CARBON
11

HYDROGEN
10

NITROGEN
2.2

PHOSPHORUS
.2

SILICON
.05

OTHER ELEMENTS
2.6

.001   .01   .1   1   10   100

COMPARATIVE WEIGHT (PER CENT)

acids it is indispensable for all types of life known to us. But many agricultural lands already suffer a deficiency of phosphorus, and a corn crop of 60 bushels per acre removes 10 per cent of the phosphorus in the upper six inches of fertile soil. Each year 3.5 million tons of phosphorus are washed from the land and precipitated in the seas. And unfortunately phosphorus does not escape from the sea as a gas. Its only important recovery from the sea is in the guano produced by sea birds, but less than 3 per cent of the phosphorus annually lost from the land is returned in this way.

I must agree with agriculturalists who say that phosphorus is the critical limiting resource for the functioning of the ecosphere. The supply is at least shrinking (if dwindling is too strong a word) and there seems to be no practical way of improving the situation short of waiting for the next geological cycle of uplift to bring phosphate rock above sea level. Perhaps we should also worry about other essential elements, such as calcium, potassium, magnesium and iron, which behave much like phosphorus in the metabolism of the ecosphere, but the evidence clearly indicates that if present trends continue phosphorus will be the first to run out.

This brings me to the close of a very superficial summary of some of the physiological processes of the ecosphere. There are drastic oversimplifications in this treatment; the importance of some processes may be overestimated, and others (*e.g.*, dumping sewage in rivers and oceans) may not have received enough attention. The figures for the total quantity of energy received by the earth, for total annual precipitation and for the total supply of some chemical elements may overlook the very irregular distribution of these resources in time and space. Much solar energy falls on deserts and fields of snow and ice where it cannot be used by plants, and much precipitation arrives at unfavorable seasons or in such torrents that it does more harm than good to organisms. Yet I believe that there may be some merit, both intellectual and practical, in attempting to scan the entire picture.

Our survey suggests that man may be justified in feeling some real concern about the problem of erosion. It should also make us aware of the important role played by organisms that we might otherwise ignore or even regard as pests. The dung beetles, the various scavengers and the termites and other decomposers all play important bit parts in this great production. At least six diverse groups

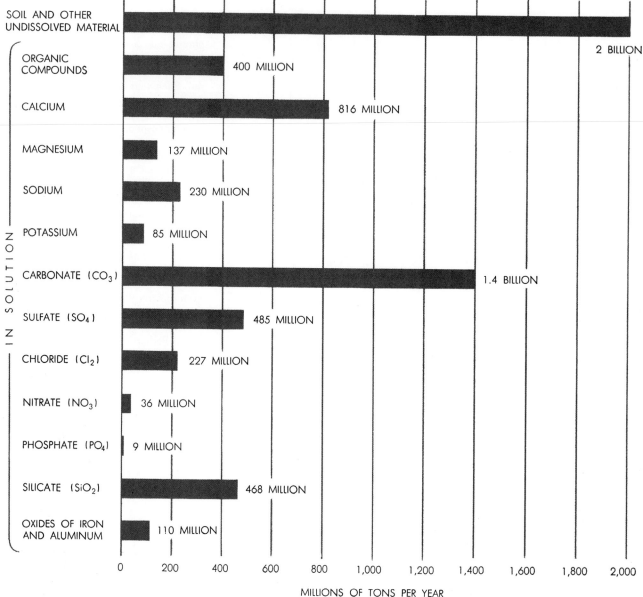

ANNUAL LOSS of minerals and organic matter washed into the sea amounts to billions of tons. Much nitrogen and carbon eventually return to the land via the atmosphere; the loss of phosphate is more serious since almost all of it remains in the oceans.

of bacteria are absolutely essential for the proper physiological functioning of the nitrogen cycle alone. Man in his carelessness would probably neither notice nor care if by some unlikely chance his radioactive fallout or one of his chemical sprays or fumes should exterminate all of the microorganisms that are capable of decomposing chitin. Yet, as we have seen, such a tragedy would eventually mean an end to life on earth.

Finally, it is interesting to ask how large a role man plays in the physiology of the ecosphere. The Statistical Office of the United Nations estimates the present human population of the earth at 2.7 billion persons. Each of these is supposed to consume at least 2,200 metabolizable kilocalories per day. This makes a total food requirement of 22×10^{14} kilocalories per year. I have estimated that all of the plant growth in the world amounts to an annual net of 5×10^{17} kilocalories, of which not more than 50 per cent is metabolizable by any primary consumer. Thus if man were to feed exclusively on plants he would require almost exactly 1 per cent of the total productivity of the earth.

To me this is a very impressive figure. There are more than one million species of animals, and when just one of these million species can corner 1 per cent of the total food resources, this form is truly in a position of overwhelming dominance. The figure becomes even more impressive when we reflect that 70 per cent of the total plant production takes place in the oceans, and that our figure for productivity includes inedible materials such as straw and lumber.

If human beings were to eat meat exclusively, the present world population would require 4 per cent of all of the flesh of primary consumers of all types that the earth could support—and this means that much of our meat would be insects and tiny crustaceans. I suspect that the human population is already so large that no conceivable technical advances could make it possible for all mankind to live on a meat diet. Speaking as one who would like to live on a meat diet, I can't see very much to be optimistic about for the future. This opinion, however, cannot be expected to alter the physiology of the ecosphere.

2

The Agricultural Revolution

ROBERT J. BRAIDWOOD
September 1960

Tool-making was initiated by pre-*sapiens* man. The first comparable achievement of our species was the agricultural revolution. No doubt a small human population could have persisted on the sustenance secured by the hunting and food-gathering technology that had been handed down and slowly improved upon over the 500 to 1,000 millennia of pre-human and pre-*sapiens* experience. With the domestication of plants and animals, however, vast new dimensions for cultural evolution suddenly became possible. The achievement of an effective food-producing technology did not, perhaps, predetermine subsequent developments, but they followed swiftly: the first urban societies in a few thousand years and contemporary industrial civilization in less than 10,000 years.

The first successful experiment in food production took place in southwestern Asia, on the hilly flanks of the "fertile crescent." Later experiments in agriculture occurred (possibly independently) in China and (certainly independently) in the New World. The multiple occurrence of the agricultural revolution suggests that it was a highly probable outcome of the prior cultural evolution of mankind and a peculiar combination of environmental circumstances. It is in the record of culture, therefore, that the origin of agriculture must be sought.

About 250,000 years ago wide-wandering bands of ancient men began to make remarkably standardized stone hand-axes and flake tools which archeologists have found throughout a vast area of the African and western Eurasian continents, from London to Capetown to Madras. Cultures producing somewhat different tools spread over all of eastern Asia. Apparently the creators of these artifacts employed general, non-specialized techniques in gathering and preparing food. As time went on, the record shows, specialization set in within these major traditions, or "genera," of tools, giving rise to roughly regional "species" of tool types. By about 75,000 years ago the tools became sufficiently specialized to suggest that they corresponded to the conditions of food-getting in broad regional environments. As technological competence increased, it became possible to extract more food from a given environment; or, to put the matter the other way around, increased "living into" a given environment stimulated technological adaptation to it.

Perhaps 50,000 years ago the mod-

AIR VIEW OF JARMO shows 3.2-acre site and surroundings. About one third of original area has eroded away. Archeologists dug the square holes in effort to trace village plan.

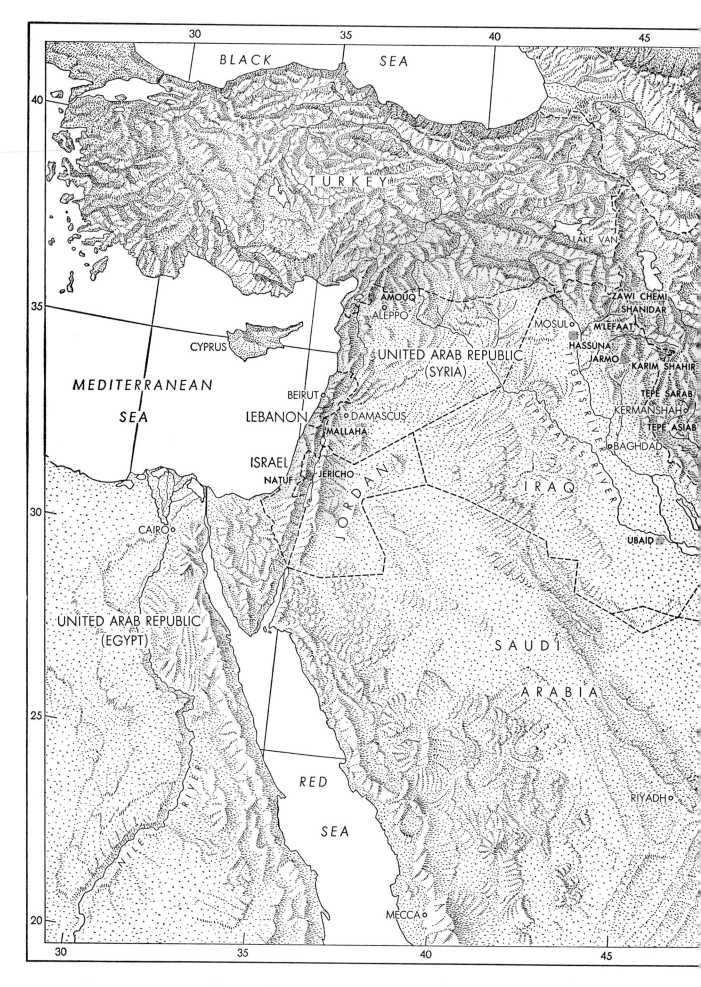

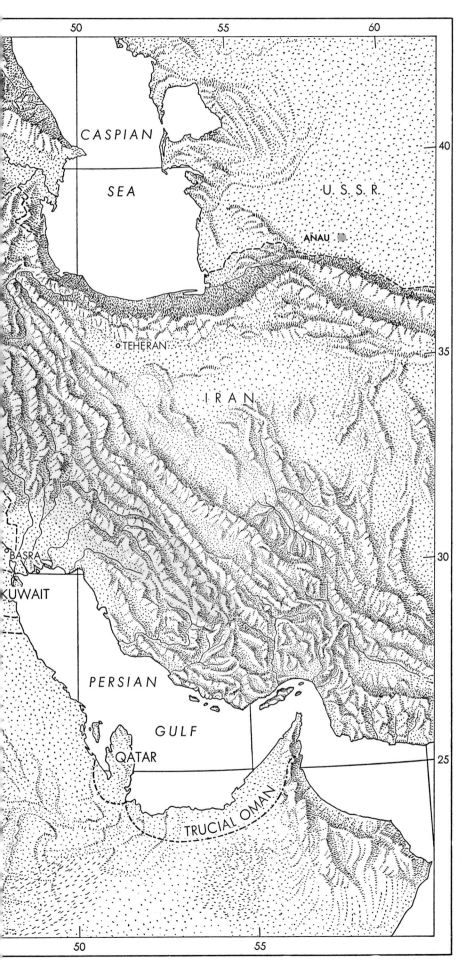

ern physical type of man appeared. The record shows concurrently the first appearance of a new genera of tools: the blade tools which incorporate a qualitatively higher degree of usefulness and skill in fabrication. The new type of man using the new tools substituted more systematic food-collection and organized hunting of large beasts for the simple gathering and scavenging of his predecessors. As time passed, the human population increased and men were able to adjust themselves to environmental niches as diverse as the tropical jungle and the arctic tundra. By perhaps 30,000 years ago they spread to the New World. The successful adaptation of human communities to their different environments brought on still greater cultural complexity and differentiation. Finally, between 11,000 and 9,000 years ago some of these communities arrived at the threshold of food production.

In certain regions scattered throughout the world this period (the Mesolithic in northwestern Europe and the Archaic in North America) was characterized by intensified food-collection: the archeological record of the era is the first that abounds in the remains of small, fleet animals, of water birds and fish, of snails and mussels. In a few places signs of plant foods have been preserved, or at least we archeologists have learned to pay attention to them. All of these remains show that human groups had learned to live into their environment to a high degree, achieving an intimate familiarity with every element in it. Most of the peoples of this era of intensified food-collecting changed just enough so that they did not need to change. There are today still a few relict groups of intensified food-collectors—the Eskimos, for example—and there were many more only a century or two ago. But on the grassy and forested uplands bordering the fertile crescent a real change was under way. Here in a climate that provided generous winter and spring rainfall, the intensified food-collectors had been accumulating a rich lore of experience with wild wheat, barley and other food plants, as well as with wild dogs,

HILLS FLANKING fertile crescent, where agricultural revolution occurred, are indicated in color. Hatched areas are probably parts of this "nuclear" zone of food-producing revolution. Sites discussed in this article are indicated by large circles. Open circles are prefarming sites; solid circles indicate that food production was known there.

goats, sheep, pigs, cattle and horses. It was here that man first began to control the production of his food.

Not long ago the proponents of environmental determinism argued that the agricultural revolution was a response to the great changes in climate which accompanied the retreat of the last glaciation about 10,000 years ago. However, the climate had altered in equally dramatic fashion on other occasions in the past 75,000 years, and the potentially domesticable plants and animals were surely available to the bands of food-gatherers who lived in southwestern Asia and similar habitats in various parts of the globe. Moreover, recent studies have revealed that the climate did not change radically where farming began in the hills that flank the fertile crescent. Environmental determinists have also argued from the "theory of propinquity" that the isolation of men along with appropriate plants and animals in desert oases started the process of domestication. Kathleen M. Kenyon of the University of London, for example, advances the lowland oasis of Jericho as a primary site of the agricultural revolution [see "Ancient Jericho," by Kathleen M. Kenyon; SCIENTIFIC AMERICAN, April, 1954].

In my opinion there is no need to complicate the story with extraneous "causes." The food-producing revolution seems to have occurred as the culmination of the ever increasing cultural differentiation and specialization of human communities. Around 8000 B.C. the inhabitants of the hills around the fertile crescent had come to know their habitat so well that they were beginning to domesticate the plants and animals they had been collecting and hunting. At slightly later times human cultures reached the corresponding level in Central America and perhaps in the Andes, in southeastern Asia and in China. From these "nuclear" zones cultural diffusion spread the new way of life to the rest of the world.

In order to study the agricultural revolution in southwestern Asia I have since 1948 led several expeditions, sponsored by the Oriental Institute of the University of Chicago, to the hills of Kurdistan north of the fertile crescent in Iraq and Iran. The work of these expeditions has been enriched by the collaboration of botanists, zoologists and geologists, who have alerted the archeologists among us to entirely new kinds of evidence. So much remains to be done, however, that we can describe in only a tentative and quite incomplete fashion how food production began. In part, I must freely admit, my reconstruction depends upon extrapolation backward from what I know had been achieved soon after 9,000 years ago in southwestern Asia.

The earliest clues come from sites of the so-called Natufian culture in Palestine, from the Kurdistan site of Zawi Chemi Shanidar, recently excavated by Ralph S. Solecki of the Smithsonian Institution, from our older excavations at Karim Shahir and M'lefaat in Iraq, and from our current excavations at Tepe Asiab in Iran [see map on preceding two pages]. In these places men appear to have moved out of caves, although perhaps not for the first time, to live in at least semipermanent communities. Flint sickle-blades occur in such Natufian locations as Mallaha, and both the Palestine and Kurdistan sites have yielded milling and pounding stones—strong indications that the people reaped and ground wild cereals and other plant foods. The artifacts do not necessarily establish the existence of anything more than intensified or specialized food-collecting. But these people were at home in a landscape in which the grains grew wild, and they may have begun to cultivate them in open meadows. Excavations of later village-farming communities, which have definitely been identified as such, reveal versions of the same artifacts that are only slightly more developed than those from Karim Shahir and other earlier sites. We are constantly finding additional evidence that will eventually make the picture clearer. For example, just this spring at Tepe Asiab we found many coprolites (fossilized excrement) that appear to be of human origin. They contain abundant impressions of plant and animal foods, and when analyzed in the laboratory they promise to be a gold mine of clues to the diet of the Tepe

SICKLE BLADES FROM JARMO are made of chipped flint. They are shown here approximately actual size. When used for harvesting grain, several were mounted in a haft of wood or bone. Other Jarmo flint tools show little advance over those found at earlier sites.

Asiab people. The nature of these "antiquities" suggests how the study of the agricultural revolution differs from the archeology of ancient cities and tombs.

The two earliest indisputable village-farming communities we have so far excavated were apparently inhabited between 7000 and 6500 B.C. They are on the inward slopes of the Zagros mountain crescent in Kurdistan. We have been digging at Jarmo in Iraq since 1948 [see "From Cave to Village," by Robert J. Braidwood; SCIENTIFIC AMERICAN, October, 1952], and we started our investigations at Tepe Sarab in Iran only last spring. We think there are many sites of the same age in the hilly-flanks zone, but these two are the only ones we have so far been able to excavate. Work should also be done in this zone in southern Turkey, but the present interpretation of the Turkish antiquities law discourages our type of "problem-oriented" research, in which the investigator must take most of the ancient materials back to his laboratory. I believe that these northern parts of the basins of the Tigris and Euphrates rivers and the Cilician area of Turkey will one day yield valuable information.

Although Jarmo and Tepe Sarab are 120 miles apart and in different drainage systems, they contain artifacts that are remarkably alike. Tepe Sarab may have been occupied only seasonally, but Jarmo was a permanent, year-round settlement with about two dozen mud-walled houses that were repaired and rebuilt frequently, creating about a dozen distinct levels of occupancy. We have identified there the remains of two-row barley (cultivated barley today has six rows of grains on a spike) and two forms of domesticated wheat. Goats and dogs, and possibly sheep, were domesticated. The bones of wild animals, quantities of snail shells and acorns and pistachio nuts indicate that the people still hunted and collected a substantial amount of food. They enjoyed a varied, adequate and well-balanced diet which was possibly superior to that of the people living in the same area today. The teeth of the Jarmo people show even milling and no marginal enamel fractures. Thanks apparently to the use of querns and rubbing stones and stone mortars and pestles, there were no coarse particles in the diet that would cause excessive dental erosion. We have calculated that approximately 150 people lived in Jarmo. The archeological evidence from the area indicates a population density of 27 people per square mile, about the same as today. Deforestation, soil deteriora-

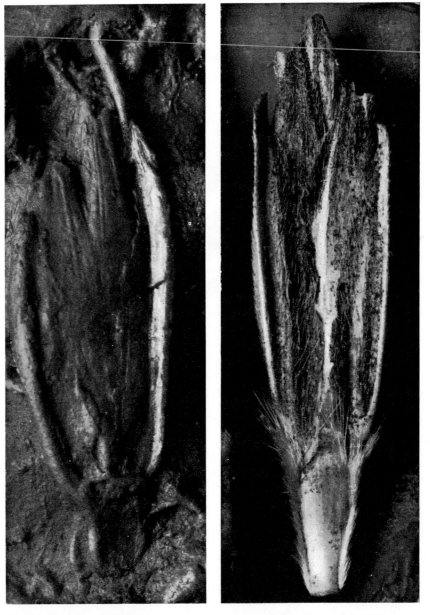

JARMO WHEAT made imprint upon clay. Cast of imprint (*left*) resembles spikelet of present-day wild wheat *Triticum dicoccoides* (*right*). Specimens are enlarged seven times.

tion and erosion, the results of 10,000 years of human habitation, tend to offset whatever advantages of modern tools and techniques are available to the present population.

Stone vessels of fine craftsmanship appear throughout all levels at Jarmo, but portable, locally made pottery vessels occur only in the uppermost levels. A few impressions on dried mud indicate that the people possessed woven baskets or rugs. The chipped flint tools of Jarmo and Tepe Sarab, in both normal and microlithic sizes, are direct and not very distant descendants of those at Karim Shahir and the earlier communities. But the two farming villages exhibit a geo-

metric increase in the variety of materials of other types in the archeological catalogue. Great numbers of little clay figurines of animals and pregnant women (the "fertility goddesses") hint at the growing nonutilitarian dimensions of life. In both communities the people for the first time had tools of obsidian, a volcanic glass with a cutting edge much sharper and harder than stone. The obsidian suggests commerce, because the nearest source is at Lake Van in Turkey, some 200 miles from Jarmo. The sites have also yielded decorative shells that could have come only from the Persian Gulf.

For an explanation of how plants and animals might have been domesticated

KERNELS OF JARMO WHEAT were carbonized in fires of ancient village. They resemble kernels of wild wheat growing in area today. They are enlarged approximately four times.

between the time of Karim Shahir and of Jarmo, we have turned to our colleagues in the biological sciences. As the first botanist on our archeological team, Hans Helbaek of the Danish National Museum has studied the carbonized remains of plants and the imprints of grains, seeds and other plant parts on baked clay and adobe at Jarmo and other sites. He believes that the first farmers, who grew both wheat and barley, could

only have lived in the highlands around the fertile crescent, because that is the only place where both plants grew wild. The region is the endemic home of wild wheat. Wild barley, on the other hand, is widely scattered from central Asia to the Atlantic, but no early agriculture was based upon barley alone.

Helbaek surmises that from the beginning man was unintentionally breeding the kind of crop plants he needed.

Wild grasses have to scatter their seeds over a large area, and consequently the seed-holding spike of wild wheat and barley becomes brittle when the plant ripens. The grains thus drop off easily. A few wild plants, however, exhibit a recessive gene that produces tough spikes that do not become brittle. The grains hang on, and these plants do not reproduce well in nature. A man harvesting wild wheat and barley would necessarily reap plants with tough spikes and intact heads. When he finally did sow seeds, he would naturally have on hand a large proportion of grains from tough-spike plants—exactly the kind he needed for farming. Helbaek points out that early farmers must soon have found it advantageous to move the wheat down from the mountain slopes, from 2,000 to 4,300 feet above sea level (where it occurs in nature), to more level ground near a reliable water supply and other accommodations for human habitation. Still, the plant had to be kept in an area with adequate winter and spring rainfall. The piedmont of the fertile crescent provides even today precisely these conditions. Since the environment there differs from the native one, wheat plants with mutations and recessive characteristics, as well as hybrids and other freaks, that were ill adapted to the uplands would have had a chance to survive. Those that increased the adaptation of wheat to the new environment would have made valuable contributions to the gene pool. Domesticated wheat, having lost the ability to disperse its seeds, became totally dependent upon man. In turn, as Helbaek emphasizes, man became the servant of his plants, since much of his routine of life now depended upon the steady and ample supply of vegetable food from his fields.

The traces and impressions of the grains at Jarmo indicate that the process of domestication was already advanced at that place and time, even though human selection of the best seed had not yet been carried far. Carbonized field peas, lentils and vetchling have also been found at Jarmo, but it is not certain that these plants were under cultivation.

Apparently farming and a settled community life were cultural prerequisites for the domestication of animals. Charles A. Reed, zoologist from the University of Illinois, has participated in the Oriental Institute expeditions to Iraq and Iran and has studied animal skeletons we have excavated. He believes that animal domestication first occurred in this area, because wild goats, sheep, cattle, pigs, horses, asses and dogs were all present

CARBONIZED BARLEY KERNELS from Jarmo, enlarged four times, are from two-row grain. The internodes attached to kernels at right indicate tough spikes of cultivated barley.

there, and settled agricultural communities had already been established. The wild goat (*Capra hircus aegagrus*, or pasang) and sheep (*Ovis orientalis*), as well as the wild ass (onager) still persist in the highlands of southwestern Asia. Whether the dog was the offspring of a hypothetical wild dog, of the pariah dog or of the wolf is still uncertain, but it was undoubtedly the first animal to be domesticated. Reed has not been able to identify any dog remains at Jarmo, but doglike figurines, with tails upcurled, show almost certainly that dogs were established in the domestic scene. The first food animal to be domesticated was the goat; the shape of goat horns found at Jarmo departs sufficiently from that of the wild animal to certify generations of domestic breeding. On the other hand, the scarcity of remains of cattle at Jarmo indicates that these animals had not yet been domesticated; the wild cattle in the vicinity were probably too fierce to submit to captivity.

No one who has seriously considered the question believes that food needs motivated the first steps in the domestication of animals. The human proclivity for keeping pets suggests itself as a much simpler and more plausible explanation. Very young animals living in the environment may have attached themselves to people as a result of "imprinting," which is the tendency of the animal to follow the first living thing it sees and hears during a critically impressionable period in its infancy [see " 'Imprinting' in Animals," by Eckhard H. Hess; SCIENTIFIC AMERICAN Offprint 416].

Young animals were undoubtedly also captured for use as decoys on the hunt. Some young animals may have had human wet nurses—a practice in some primitive tribes even today. After goats were domesticated, their milk would have been available for orphaned wild calves, colts and other creatures. Adult wild animals, particularly goats and sheep, which sometimes approach human beings in search of food, might also have been tamed.

Reed defines the domesticated animal as one whose reproduction is controlled by man. In his view the animals that were domesticated were already physiologically and psychologically pre-adapted to being tamed without loss of their ability to reproduce. The individual animals that bred well in captivity would have contributed heavily to the gene pool of each succeeding generation. When the nucleus of a herd was established, man would have automatically selected against the aggressive and un-

CLAY FIGURES from Sarab, shown half size, include boar's head (*top*), what seems to be lion (*upper left*), two-headed beast (*upper right*), sheep (*bottom left*) and boar.

"FERTILITY GODDESS" or "Venus" from Tepe Sarab is clay figure shown actual size. Artist emphasized parts of body suggesting fertility. Grooves in leg indicate musculature.

STONE PALETTES from Jarmo show that the men who lived there were highly skilled in working stone. The site has also yielded many beautifully shaped stone bowls and mortars.

JARMO IN IRAQI KURDISTAN is the site of the earliest village-farming community yet discovered. This photograph of an upper level of excavation shows foundation and paving stones. Site was occupied for perhaps 300 years somewhere around 6750 B.C.

EXCAVATION AT KARIM SHAHIR contained confused scatter of rocks brought there by ancient men and disturbed by modern plowing. This prefarming site had no clear evidence of permanent houses, but did have skillfully chipped flints and other artifacts.

POTTERY MADE AT JARMO, in contrast to the stonework, is simple. It is handmade, vegetable-tempered, buff or orange-buff in color. It shows considerable technical competence.

manageable individuals, eventually producing a race of submissive creatures. This type of unplanned breeding no doubt long preceded the purposeful artificial selection that created different breeds within domesticated species. It is apparent that goats, sheep and cattle were first husbanded as producers of meat and hides; wild cattle give little milk, and wild sheep are not woolly but hairy. Only much later did the milk- and wool-producing strains emerge.

As the agricultural revolution began to spread, the trend toward ever increasing specialization of the intensified food-collecting way of life began to reverse itself. The new techniques were capable of wide application, given suitable adaptation, in diverse environments. Archeological remains at Hassuna, a site near the Tigris River somewhat later than Jarmo, show that the people were exchanging ideas on the manufacture of pottery and of flint and obsidian projectile points with people in the region of the Amouq in Syro-Cilicia. The basic elements of the food-producing complex —wheat, barley, sheep, goats and probably cattle—in this period moved west beyond the bounds of their native habitat to occupy the whole eastern end of the Mediterranean. They also traveled as

far east as Anau, east of the Caspian Sea. Localized cultural differences still existed, but people were adopting and adapting more and more cultural traits from other areas. Eventually the new way of life traveled to the Aegean and beyond into Europe, moving slowly up such great river valley systems as the Dnieper, the Danube and the Rhone, as well as along the coasts. The intensified food-gatherers of Europe accepted the new way of life, but, as V. Gordon Childe has pointed out, they "were not slavish imitators: they adapted the gifts from the East . . . into a new and organic whole capable of developing on its own original lines." Among other things, the Europeans appear to have domesticated rye and oats that were first imported to the European continent as weed plants contaminating the seed of wheat and barley. In the comparable diffusion of agriculture from Central America, some of the peoples to the north appear to have rejected the new ways, at least temporarily.

By about 5000 B.C. the village-farming way of life seems to have been fingering down the valleys toward the alluvial bottom lands of the Tigris and Euphrates. Robert M. Adams believes that there may have been people living in the

lowlands who were expert in collecting food from the rivers. They would have taken up the idea of farming from people who came down from higher areas. In the bottom lands a very different climate, seasonal flooding of the land and small-scale irrigation led agriculture through a significant new technological transformation. By about 4000 B.C. the people of southern Mesopotamia had achieved such increases in productivity that their farms were beginning to support an urban civilization. The ancient site at Ubaid is typical of this period [see "The Origin of Cities," by Robert M. Adams; SCIENTIFIC AMERICAN Offprint 606].

Thus in 3,000 or 4,000 years the life of man had changed more radically than in all of the preceding 250,000 years. Before the agricultural revolution most men must have spent their waking moments seeking their next meal, except when they could gorge following a great kill. As man learned to produce food, instead of gathering, hunting or collecting it, and to store it in the grain bin and on the hoof, he was compelled as well as enabled to settle in larger communities. With human energy released for a whole spectrum of new activities, there came the development of specialized nonagricultural crafts. It is no accident that such innovations as the discovery of the basic mechanical principles, weaving, the plow, the wheel and metallurgy soon appeared.

No prehistorian worth his salt may end or begin such a discussion without acknowledging the present incompleteness of the archeological record. There is the disintegration of the perishable materials that were primary substances of technology at every stage. There is the factor of chance in archeological discovery, of vast areas of the world still incompletely explored archeologically, and of inadequate field techniques and interpretations by excavators. There are the vagaries of establishing a reliable chronology, of the whimsical degree to which "geobiochemical" contamination seems to have affected our radioactive-carbon age determinations. There is the fact that studies of human paleo-environments by qualified natural historians are only now becoming available. Writing in the field, in the midst of an exciting season of excavation, I would not be surprised if the picture I have presented here needs to be altered somewhat by the time that this article has appeared in print.

3

Forest Clearance in the Stone Age

JOHANNES IVERSON
March 1956

Perhaps the greatest single step forward in the history of mankind was the transition from hunting to agriculture. In the Mesolithic Age men lived by the spear, the bow and the fishing net; in the Neolithic Age they became farmers. The change came independently at different times in diverse parts of the world. Just how and when men turned to farming in Western Europe has been a subject of debate among naturalists and archaeologists for a hundred years. New methods of dating the implements of Stone Age men have recently given more factual substance to the debate. What is more, we have learned enough about the world in which they lived to test our theories about how they lived by experiment. This is a report of a set of experiments by which a group of

scientists in Denmark attempted to re-enact some aspects of the hunting-to-agriculture chapter of mankind's past.

Denmark has unearthed relics of both stages—the bone and flint implements of the Mesolithic hunters and the polished stone axes of the Neolithic farmers. And in ancient lake sediments and bogs the prehistoric tools lie in recognizable strata of pollen, that marvelous dating instrument which identifies each period by its prevailing vegetation. The pollen record, as ecologists read it, tells the following story.

Toward the end of the last ice age, when vegetation was emerging and the country was still open, hunters ranged all over Denmark. Then, as forests grew dense and reduced large game, men abandoned the forested interior and re-

treated to the coast, where they made their living by fishing and seal-hunting. This state of affairs continued for thousands of years, until man suddenly appears in the forest, hacking out a new living. Clearings are hewed in the primeval forest. Tree pollen rapidly declines in certain regions, and we find in its place a sharp rise in pollen of herbaceous plants and the emergence of cereals and new weeds, notably plantain—the plant which the Indians of North America called "the footsteps of the white man."

Very shortly a new growth of tree species which typically follow forest clearance—willow, aspen, birch—springs up. The presence of birch strongly suggests that man used fire to help clear the forest, for on fertile soil birch succeeds

STONE AXE was reconstructed by mounting the Neolithic flint head on a copy of a Neolithic haft preserved at the bottom of a bog. It was found that the full swing of the modern woodsman often chipped or broke the head. Using short, rapid strokes, the experimenters learned to fell trees more than a foot in diameter in 30 minutes. To fell small trees they chopped all the way around the trunk.

a mixed oak forest only after burning. Meanwhile the ground flora undergoes a radical and significant change. Grasses, white clover, sheep sorrel, sheep's-bit and other pasture plants take the upper hand. We can visualize cattle grazing and browsing in grassy meadows bordered by scrub forests of birch and hazel.

Finally comes a third phase. The grasses, birch and eventually hazel decline, and a big-tree forest takes over once more. Oak now is more dominant than before; elm and linden never recover the strength they had in the primeval forest.

All this seems to mean that men cleared large areas of the original forest with axes, burned over the clearings, planted small fields of cereals and used the rest for pasturing animals. Their colonization was of short duration: when the forest grew back, they moved on to clear a suitable new area. According to the pollen record, some of their settlements can scarcely have lasted more than 50 years.

Now this is a neat, tidy theory, but there are troublesome questions. Could Neolithic man really have cleared large areas of the thick primeval forest with his crude flint axes? Could he have burned off the felled trees and shrubs in his clearings? Our team of ecologists and archaeologists decided to put these questions to the test of field experiment. We obtained the needed funds and permission to clear a two-acre area in the Draved Forest of Denmark, which is a mixed oak forest like that of Neolithic times.

Two archaeologists, Jörgen Troels-Smith and Svend Jörgensen, took charge of the axe tests. They were able to obtain a number of Neolithic flint axe blades from the National Museum in Copenhagen, and a model for the wooden haft was available in the form of the famous Sigerslev hafted axe excavated from a Danish bog. In Neolithic axes, whose hafts were of ash wood, the blade was inserted in a rectangular hole in the haft [see drawing on opposite page]. Jörgensen and Troels-Smith demonstrated that if the haft was not to be split, it must not hold the blade too tightly but must leave room for a little sidewise play of the blade when it struck.

After making a number of hafted axes fitted with Stone Age man's blades, the two archaeologists, together with two professional lumberjacks, went forth into the forest in September, 1952. When the party attacked the trees, it soon became

TREES WERE BURNED by covering them with brushwood and igniting a 30-foot strip. When the strip was almost burned out, the larger logs were used to light the next one.

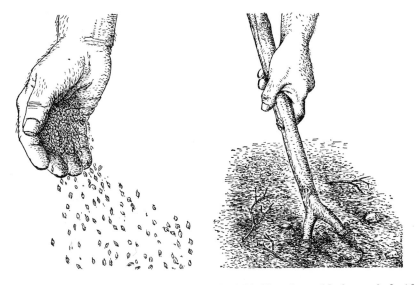

SEED WAS SOWN by hand in the still-warm ash (left). Then the seed bed was raked with a forked stick (right). The plants sown were barley and two primitive varieties of wheat.

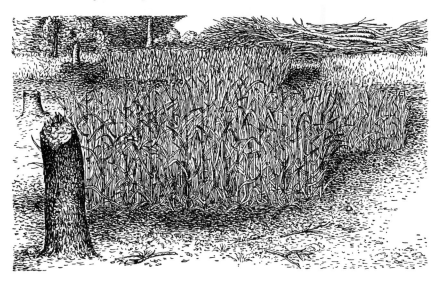

BARLEY HAD GROWN to this height six weeks after it had been sown in the ash of the burned brushwood and trees. Barley sown in plots not covered with ash grew very poorly.

apparent that the usual tree-chopping technique, in which one puts his shoulders and weight into long, powerful blows, would not do. It often shattered the edge of the delicate flint blade or broke the blade in two. The lumberjacks, unable to change their habits, damaged several axes. The archaeologists soon discovered that the proper way to use the flint axe was to chip at the tree with short, quick strokes, using mainly the elbow and wrist. Troels-Smith, working with an axe blade which had not been sharpened since the Stone Age, employed it effectively throughout the whole clearing operation without damaging it.

When the two archaeologists reached peak form, they were able to fell oak trees more than a foot in diameter within half an hour. Small trees they dropped by cutting all around the trunk; on substantial-sized ones they used the slower method of hewing through notches on the opposite sides, in order to control the direction of fall. We realized that for clearing purposes it would be advantageous to have all the trunks lying in the north-south direction; for example, the wood would dry more quickly.

In this manner we cleared the two acres of forest, letting the largest trees stand but killing them by cutting rings through the sapwood. Troels-Smith and Jörgensen concluded that Neolithic men could have cut large clearings in the

forests with their flint axes without great difficulty.

The next problem was to learn how they might have burned off their clearings. For help in this phase of the experiment we called on Kustaa Vilkuna of the University of Helsinki, who is an expert on primitive burning techniques which were still being used quite recently by farmers in the spruce forests of Finland.

Without waiting for the wood to dry, we first tested two burning methods, one modern, the other primitive. The modern method, though effective in forests of conifers, failed completely in our deciduous forest. The primitive method, how-

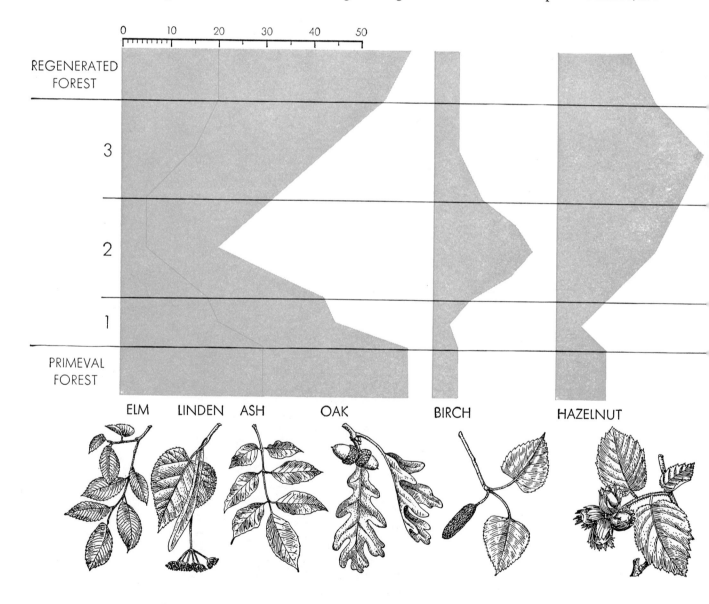

POLLEN DIAGRAM shows the effect of forest clearance on the vegetation of Denmark between about 2500 B.C. and 2300 B.C. The diagram is based on many samples of pollen taken by boring down into bogs. The width of each colored area on the diagram represents the proportion of pollen from one species in comparison to that from all others. The scale of the proportions is given at the

ever, was successful, and we proceeded to use it in the clearing in May of 1954, after the felled trees had had more than a year to dry. Brushwood and branches cut from the trees were spread over the area to be burned. Then this material was ignited along a 30-foot-wide belt by means of torches of burning birch bark attached to stakes. When the belt was well cleared, we pushed its still burning logs forward with long poles to set fire to the adjacent area. In this way we burned off the tangle of felled vegetation belt by belt. The fire was controlled carefully, day and night, to achieve an even and thorough burning of the ground. It was rather hard work, as oak wood burns slowly, but there were no serious diffi-

culties, and in three or four days the job was finished. We burned only half of the two-acre clearing, because we wished to compare the subsequent growth on burned and unburned ground.

Immediately after the burning we sowed part of the area with primitive varieties of wheat (einkorn and emmer) and naked barley. That these cereals were grown in Denmark by Neolithic man is shown by grain impressions on excavated pottery. Axel Steensberg, an expert on agricultural methods, old and new, obtained seeds of the cereals from botanical collections and directed our agriculture.

We spread the seeds on the ground, raked them in with a forked branch, and

waited for the harvest. For comparison we sowed two sets of plots—one burned and one unburned but hoed and weeded. The contrast in results was remarkable. On the unburned ground the grain scarcely grew at all. Evidently the rather acid forest soil was not suited to cereal growing. But the burned ground produced a luxuriant crop (which Steensberg harvested, in Neolithic fashion, with a flint knife and a flint sickle). The success of the cereals in this ground was due in part to sweetening of the soil by the wood-ash and the absence of competition from other vegetation, but the burning may also have created other beneficial factors, and we are now investigating this matter. In any case,

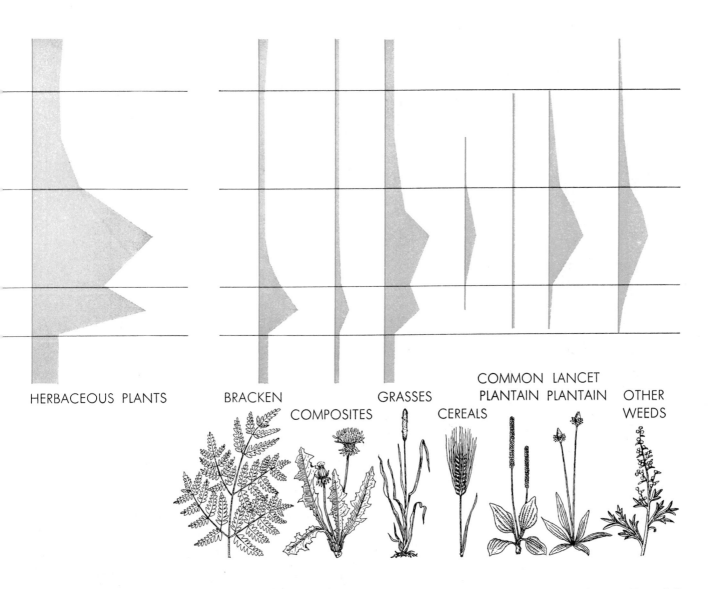

HERBACEOUS PLANTS   BRACKEN   COMPOSITES   GRASSES   CEREALS   COMMON LANCET PLANTAIN PLANTAIN   OTHER WEEDS

upper left. In the primeval forest (*colored areas below the bottom horizontal line*) the distribution of pollens was 30 per cent elm, linden and ash; 30 per cent oak; 5 per cent birch; 10 per cent hazel, and so on. During the three stages of forest clearance (*1, 2 and 3*) the distribution of pollens changed. The distribution of herb pollens is shown at the right of the break in the horizontal lines.

NEW COMMUNITY OF WILD PLANTS grew up in the parts of the clearing that had been burned over. At the left is a species of fern called bracken. Second from the left is hazel. Both of these plants had been present in the original forest. They grew up again

whatever the factors are, they are short-lived, for the second year the burned plots yielded much smaller crops.

Now, two years after the clearing and burning, we are in the process of watching developments in the early recovery of natural plant growth. The burned and unburned areas are developing quite differently.

In the area cleared of trees but unburned, events are following an unsurprising and unexciting course. The ground vegetation consists mainly of the species that grew there before the clearing, though it is growing more luxuriously because it has more sunlight. Bracken (ferns), always abundant in this part of the world, is flourishing far more richly than when it was shaded. Grasses and sedges have increased.

The burned ground, on the other

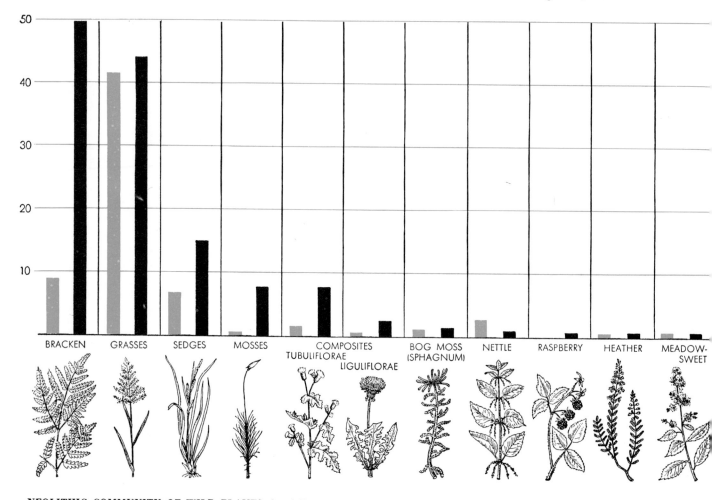

NEOLITHIC COMMUNITY OF WILD PLANTS that followed clearance and cultivation is analyzed in this pollen diagram. The colored bars indicate the amount of pollen from each plant before clearance. The black bars indicate the amount of pollen after clear-

from relatively deep roots. Third from the left are dandelions, members of a family which grows in profusion under such condi-   tions. Fourth are mosses, which had never been seen in this forest before. Their spores were blown into the clearing on the wind.

hand, is a scene of botanical revolution. Bracken is coming back here too, but most of the other old plants, having shallower roots, were killed off by the fire. In their stead we have a whole garden of new plants. Plantain has made its appearance, just as it does in the ancient pollen record after forest clearance. There is a profusion of members of the family *Compositae*, including dandelions, daisies, sow thistle and so forth. (These plants do not bulk large in the fossil pollen record, but that is understandable because they are pollinated by insects rather than by the wind.)

A particularly interesting development is the sudden appearance of mosses and their spread over large patches of the burned area. The main species have never been seen in this forest before. Their spores have flown into the clearing on the wind, and no doubt mosses came the same way to the areas burned by Neolithic man. What makes them especially significant is that certain mosses seem to be definite indicators of fire; three species have been so identified in America, and sure enough the same three appeared in our burned clearing. Since the moss phase in a burned forest must be ephemeral, moss spores in the fossil record should enable us to pinpoint the dates of forest clearance by Neolithic man and to learn whether they burned the same clearing more than once during the existence of a continuous settlement. Unfortunately the small moss spores are difficult to recognize, and analysts of the ancient pollen deposits have not counted them hitherto. We made a small test count at the site of a Neolithic forest clearing in Denmark, analyzing the layers representing the time of the clearance and the period just before. According to our fragmentary count, there was a sharp rise in general moss growth (we made no attempt to distinguish individual species) immediately after the clearance of the area [*see chart at the left*].

Our experimental clearing in the Danish forest is just beginning to pass into the second phase, when pioneer trees appear and the regeneration of the forest commences. Birch seedlings are starting to spring up in profusion; willow seedlings have appeared; and hazel, aspen and linden shoots are rising from roots that were not killed by the fire. We are looking forward to studying this gradual regeneration in the years to come, as well as to reliving the stage in Neolithic farming when men grazed their cattle on the re-emerging ground vegetation.

Meanwhile we can say that so far our experiment has confirmed the archaeological interpretation of the pollen record on several important counts. It has been demonstrated that the forest could indeed have been cleared by the primitive tools of Neolithic man, and that in the first stage at least the reviving vegetation follows a course very like that deduced from the ancient pollen layers.

Of course man's transition from hunting to farming may well have taken other paths besides the one we have traced in the Danish clearings. More than one type of agriculture may have existed simultaneously in Denmark. As a matter of fact, Troels-Smith has found evidences of a more primitive agriculture during the same period on the Danish coast, where the Middle Stone Age men apparently cleared no forests but practiced a little crude farming along with their hunting and fishing.

The Neolithic farming culture described in this article is so much more advanced, and begins so suddenly, that it seems to signal the arrival and invasion of a vigorous new people from another region.

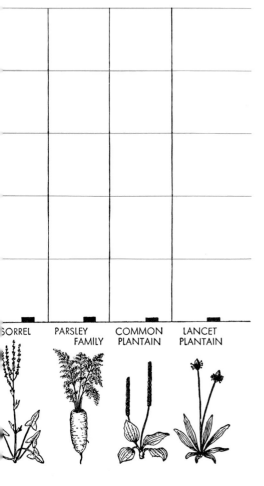

SORREL   PARSLEY FAMILY   COMMON PLANTAIN   LANCET PLANTAIN

ance. The scale at the left is based on grains of pollen per 1,000 grains of tree pollen.

4

The Black Death

WILLIAM L. LANGER
February 1964

In the three years from 1348 through 1350 the pandemic of plague known as the Black Death, or, as the Germans called it, the Great Dying, killed at least a fourth of the population of Europe. It was undoubtedly the worst disaster that has ever befallen mankind. Today we can have no real conception of the terror under which people lived in the shadow of the plague. For more than two centuries plague has not been a serious threat to mankind in the large, although it is still a grisly presence in parts of the Far East and Africa. Scholars continue to study the Great Dying, however, as a historic example of human behavior under the stress of universal catastrophe. In these days when the threat of plague has been replaced by the threat of mass human extermination by even more rapid means, there has been a sharp renewal of interest in the history of the 14th-century calamity. With new perspective, students are investigating its manifold effects: demographic, economic, psychological, moral and religious.

Plague is now recognized as a well-marked disease caused by a specific organism (*Bacillus pestis*). It is known in three forms, all highly fatal: pneumonic (attacking primarily the lungs), bubonic (producing buboes, or swellings, of the lymph glands) and septicemic (killing the victim rapidly by poisoning of the blood). The disease is transmitted to man by fleas, mainly from black rats and certain other rodents, including ground squirrels. It produces high fever, agonizing pain and prostration, and it is usually fatal within five or six days. The Black Death got its name from dark blotches produced by hemorrhages in the skin.

There had been outbreaks of plague in the Roman Empire in the sixth century and in North Africa earlier, but for some reason epidemics of the disease in Europe were comparatively rare after that until the 14th century. Some historians have suggested that the black rat was first brought to western Europe during the Crusades by expeditions returning from the Middle East. This seems unlikely: remains of the rat have been found in prehistoric sites in Switzerland, and in all probability the houses of Europe were infested with rats throughout the Middle Ages.

In any event, the 14th-century pandemic clearly began in 1348 in the ports of Italy, apparently brought in by merchant ships from Black Sea ports. It gradually spread through Italy and in the next two years swept across Spain, France, England, central Europe and Scandinavia. It advanced slowly but pitilessly, striking with deadliest effect in the crowded, unsanitary towns. Each year the epidemic rose to a peak in the late summer, when the fleas were most abundant, and subsided during the winter, only to break out anew in the spring.

The pandemic of 1348–1350 was followed by a long series of recurrent outbreaks all over Europe, coming at intervals of 10 years or less. In London there were at least 20 attacks of plague in the 15th century, and in Venice the Black Death struck 23 times between 1348 and 1576. The plague epidemics were frequently accompanied by severe outbreaks of typhus, syphilis and "English sweat"—apparently a deadly form of influenza that repeatedly afflicted not only England but also continental Europe in the first half of the 16th century.

From the 13th to the late 17th century Europe was disease-ridden as never before or since. In England the long affliction came to a climax with an epidemic of bubonic plague in 1665 that killed nearly a tenth of London's estimated population of 460,000, two-thirds of whom fled the city during the outbreak. Thereafter in western and central Europe the plague rapidly died away as mysteriously as it had come. The theories advanced to explain its subsidence are as unconvincing as those given for its rise. It was long supposed, for instance, that an invasion of Europe early in the 18th century by brown rats, which killed off the smaller black rats, was responsible for the decline of the disease. This can hardly be the reason; the plague had begun to subside decades before, and the brown rat did not by any means exterminate the black rat. More probably the answer must be sought in something that happened to the flea, the bacillus or the living conditions of the human host.

This article, however, is concerned not with the medical but with the social aspects of the Black Death. Let us begin by examining the dimensions of the catastrophe in terms of the death toll.

As reported by chroniclers of the time, the mortality figures were so incredibly high that modern scholars long regarded them with skepticism. Recent detailed and rigorously conducted analyses indicate, however, that many of the reports were substantially correct. It is now generally accepted that at least a quarter of the European population was wiped out in the first epidemic of 1348 through 1350, and that in the next 50 years the total mortality rose to more than a third of the population. The incidence of the disease and the mortality rate varied, of course, from place to place. Florence was reduced in population from 90,000 to 45,000, Siena from 42,000 to 15,000; Hamburg apparently lost almost two-thirds of its inhabitants. These estimates are borne out by accurate records that were kept in later epidemics. In Venice, for example, the Magistrato della Sanità (board of health) kept a meticulous count of the victims of a severe plague attack in 1576 and 1577; the deaths totaled 46,721 in a total estimated population of about 160,000. In 1720 Marseilles lost 40,000 of a population of 90,000, and in Messina about half of the inhabitants died in 1743.

It is now estimated that the total population of England fell from about 3.8 million to 2.1 million in the period from 1348 to 1374. In France, where the loss of life was increased by the Hundred Years' War, the fall in population was even more precipitate. In western and central Europe as a whole the mortality was so great that it took nearly two centuries for the population level of 1348 to be regained.

The Black Death was a scourge such as man had never known. Eighty per cent or more of those who came down with the plague died within two or three days, usually in agonizing pain. No one knew the cause of or any preventive or cure for the disease. The medical profession was all but helpless, and the desperate measures taken by town authorities proved largely futile. It is difficult to imagine the growing terror with which the people must have watched the inexorable advance of the disease on their community.

They responded in various ways. Almost everyone, in that medieval time, interpreted the plague as a punishment by God for human sins, but there were arguments whether the Deity was sending retribution through the poisoned arrows of evil angels, "venomous moleculae" or earthquake-induced or comet-borne miasmas. Many blamed the Jews,

accusing them of poisoning the wells or otherwise acting as agents of Satan. People crowded into the churches, appealing for protection to the Virgin, to St. Sebastian, to St. Roch or to any of 60 other saints believed to have special influence against the disease. In the streets half-naked flagellants, members of the century-old cult of flagellantism, marched in processions whipping each other and warning the people to purge themselves of their sins before the coming day of atonement.

Flight in the face of approaching danger has always been a fundamental human reaction, in modern as well as ancient times. As recently as 1830, 60,-000 people fled from Moscow during an epidemic of cholera, and two years later, when the first cases of this disease turned up in New York City, fully a fourth of the population of 220,000 took flight in

RAPHAEL'S "LA PÈSTE" ("The Plague") reflects the preoccupation of European art with plague and its consequences during the plague-ridden three centuries following the Black Death. This picture, now worn with time, is divided into two parts: night at right and day at left. Among other plague themes of artists were the dance of death and the terrors of the Last Judgment.

steamboats, stagecoaches, carts and even wheelbarrows. The plague epidemics of the 14th to 16th century of course produced even more frightened mass migrations from the towns. Emperors, kings, princes, the clergy, merchants, lawyers, professors, students, judges and even physicians rushed away, leaving the common people to shift for themselves. All who could get away shut themselves up in houses in the country.

At the same time drastic efforts were made to segregate those who were forced to remain in the towns. In an epidemic in 1563 Queen Elizabeth took refuge in Windsor Castle and had a gallows erected on which to hang anyone who had the temerity to come out to Windsor from plague-ridden London. Often when a town was hit by the plague a cordon of troops would be thrown around the town to isolate it, allowing no one to leave or enter. In the afflicted cities entire streets were closed off by chains, the sick were quarantined in their houses and gallows were installed in the public squares as a warning against the violation of regulations. The French surgeon Ambroise Paré, writing of a plague epidemic in 1568,

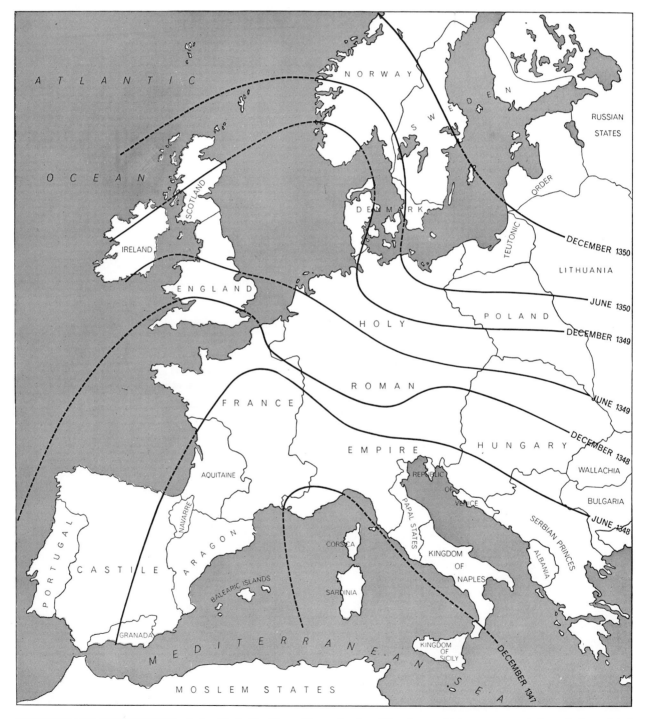

APPROXIMATE CHRONOLOGY of the Black Death's rapid sweep through Europe in the middle of the 14th century is indicated on this map, which shows the political divisions as they existed at the time. The plague, which was apparently brought from Asia by ships, obtained a European foothold in the Mediterranean in 1347; during the succeeding three years only a few small areas escaped.

reported that husbands and wives deserted each other, that parents sometimes even abandoned their children and that people went mad with terror and committed suicide.

Victims of the disease often died in the streets, as is shown in Raphael's "La Pèste," now in the Uffizi Gallery in Florence. Gravediggers were understandably scarce. For the most part those hired for the job, at fantastic wages, were criminals and tramps—men who could not be expected to draw fine distinctions between the dying and the dead. The corpses and the near corpses were thrown into carts and dumped indiscriminately into huge pits outside the town walls.

The sufferings and reactions of humanity when the plague came have been depicted vividly by writers such as Boccaccio, Daniel Defoe, Alessandro Manzoni and the late Albert Camus (in his novel *The Plague*) and by artists from Raphael and Holbein to Delacroix. Boccaccio's *Decameron*, an account of a group of well-to-do cavaliers and maidens who shut themselves up in a country house during the Black Death in Florence and sought to distract themselves with revelry and spicy stories, illustrates one of the characteristic responses of mankind to fear and impending disaster. It was most simply described by Thucydides in his report of the "Plague of Athens" in 430 B.C.:

"Men resolved to get out of life the pleasures which could be had speedily and would satisfy their lusts, regarding their bodies and their wealth alike as transitory.... No fear of gods or law of men restrained them; for, on the one hand, seeing that all men were perishing alike, they judged that piety or impiety came to the same thing, and, on the other hand, no one expected that he would live to be called to account and pay the penalty for his misdeeds. On the contrary, they believed that the penalty already decreed against them and now hanging over their heads was a far heavier one, and that before it fell it was only reasonable to get some enjoyment out of life."

From this philosophy one might also develop the rationalization that hilarity and the liberal use of liquor could ward off the plague. In any event, many people of all classes gave themselves up to carousing and ribaldry. The Reformation theologian John Wycliffe, who survived the Black Death of the 14th century, wrote with dismay of the lawlessness and depravity of the time. Everywhere, wrote chroniclers of the

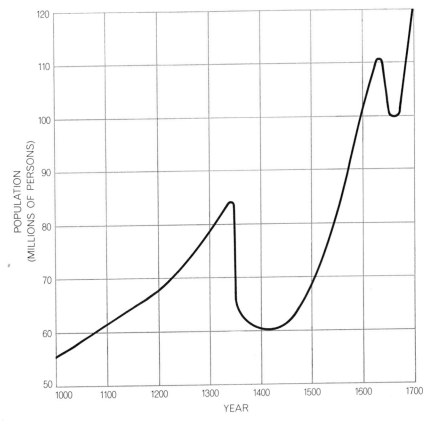

IMPACT ON POPULATION from recurrent plagues in Europe is indicated. For more than 300 years after 1347 the plagues checked the normal rise in population; sometimes, as in the 14th and 17th centuries, they resulted in sharp reductions. The figures shown on this chart derive from estimates by students of population; actual data for the period are scarce.

epidemics in London then and later, there was "drinking, roaring and surfeiting.... In one house you might hear them roaring under the pangs of death, in the next tippling, whoring and belching out blasphemies against God." Even the sober Samuel Pepys admitted to his diary that he had made merry in the shadow of death, indulging himself and his wife in a "great store of dancings." The university town of Oxford, like London, also was the scene of much "lewd and dissolute behavior."

The outbreak of an epidemic of plague was almost invariably the signal for a wave of crime and violence. As Boccaccio wrote, "the reverend authority of the laws, both human and divine, was all in a manner dissolved and fallen into decay, for lack of the ministers and executors thereof." In the midst of death, looting and robbery flourished. Burial gangs looted the houses of the dead and stripped the corpses of anything of value before throwing them into the pits. On occasion they even murdered the sick.

Just as desperation drove some to a complete abandonment of morality, it drove others, perhaps the majority, to

pathetic extravagances of religiosity or superstition. The poet George Wither noted this contrast in the London epidemic of 1625:

*Some streets had Churches full
    of people, weeping;
Some others, Tavernes had, rude-revell
    keeping;
Within some houses Psalmes
    and Hymnes were sung;
With raylings and loud scouldings
    others rung.*

Many people threw themselves on God's mercy, showered the church with gifts and made extravagant vows for the future. Others hunted down Jews and witches as the originators of the plague. The Black Death generated a startling spread of belief in witchcraft. Even as learned a scholar and theologian as John Calvin was convinced that a group of male and female witches, acting as agents of Satan, had brought the plague to Geneva. In the cult of Satanism, as in that of flagellantism, there was a strong strain of sexuality. It was believed that the women accused of being witches had intercourse with the

Devil and could strike men with sexual impotence. From the psychoanalytic point of view this belief may have stemmed from an unconscious reaction to the tremendous shrinkage of the population.

Jews and witches were not the only victims of the general panic. The wrath of the people also fell on physicians. They were accused of encouraging or helping the spread of the plague instead of checking it. Paré tells us that some of them were stoned in the streets in France. (In the 19th century physicians were similarly made scapegoats during epidemics of cholera. Some people accused them of poisoning public water supplies, at the behest of the rich, in order to kill off the excessive numbers of the poor.)

Although we have fairly accurate knowledge of the immediate effects of the great plagues in Europe—they were fully and circumstantially chronicled by many contemporary writers—it is not so easy to specify the long-term effects of the plagues. Many other factors entered into the shaping of Europe's history during and after the period of the plague epidemics. Nevertheless, there can be no doubt that the Great Dying had a profound and lasting influence on that history.

In its economic life Europe suffered a sudden and drastic change. Before the Black Death of 1348–1350 the Continent had enjoyed a period of rather rapid population growth, territorial expansion and general prosperity. After the pandemic Europe sank into a long depression: a century or more of economic stagnation and decline. The most serious disruption took place in agriculture.

For a short time the towns and cities experienced a flush of apparent prosperity. Many survivors of the epidemic had suddenly inherited substantial amounts of property and money from the wholesale departure of their relatives. They built elegant houses and went on a buying spree that made work (and high prices) for the manufacturing artisans. The churches and other public institutions, sharing in the wealth of the new rich, also built imposing and expensive structures.

The rural areas, on the other hand, virtually collapsed. With fewer people to feed in the towns and cities, the farmers lost a large part of the market for their crops. Grain prices fell precipitately. So did the farm population. Already sadly depleted by the ravages of the plague, it was now further reduced by a movement to the towns, which offered the impoverished farmers work as artisans. In spite of strenuous efforts by landlords and lords of the manor to keep the peasants on the land by law and sometimes by force, the rural population fled to the cities en masse. Thousands of farms and villages were deserted. In central Germany some 70

DESERTED ENGLISH VILLAGE, typical of many medieval communities made ghost towns by the Black Death and succeeding plagues, occupied the site shown in this aerial photograph. This site is Tusmore in Oxfordshire; most of the lines are earthworks that bounded farm enclosures behind cottages. Aerial photography has been used to locate many abandoned medieval villages.

per cent of all the farm settlements were abandoned in the period following the Black Death. (Many of these "lost" farms and villages, long overgrown, have recently been located by aerial photography.)

Farms became wilderness or pasture. Rents and land values disappeared. The minor land-owning gentry sank into poverty. In the words of the 14th-century poet Petrarch, "a vast and dreadful solitude" settled over the land. And of course in the long run the depression of agriculture engulfed the cities in depression as well.

Some authorities believe that Europe had begun to fall into a period of economic decay before the Black Death and that the epidemics only accentuated this trend. The question is certainly a complicated one. Wars and other economic forces no doubt played their part in Europe's long recession. It seems probable, however, that the decisive factor was the repeated onslaught of epidemics that depleted and weakened the population. The present consensus on the subject is that population change is a main cause of economic change rather than vice versa. Surely it must be considered significant that Europe's economic revival in the 17th and 18th centuries coincided with the disappearance of the plague and a burst of rapid population growth [see "Population," by Kingsley Davis; SCIENTIFIC AMERICAN Offprint 645].

The psychological effects of the ordeal of the plague are at least as impressive as the economic ones. For a long time it held all of Europe in an apocalyptic mood, which the Dutch historian Johan Huizinga analyzed brilliantly a generation ago in his study *The Waning of the Middle Ages*. As Arturo Castiglioni, the eminent Yale University historian of medicine, has written: "Fear was the sovereign ruler of this epoch." Men lived and worked in constant dread of disease and imminent death. "No thought is born in me that has not 'Death' engraved upon it," wrote Michelangelo.

Much of the art of the time reflected a macabre interest in graves and an almost pathological predilection for the manifestations of disease and putrefaction. Countless painters treated with almost loving detail the sufferings of Christ, the terrors of the Last Judgment and the tortures of Hell. Woodcuts and paintings depicting the dance of death, inspired directly by the Black Death, enjoyed a morbid popularity. With pitiless realism these paintings portrayed Death as a horridly grinning skeleton that seized, without warning, the prince and the peasant, the young and the old, the lovely maiden and the hardened villain, the innocent babe and the decrepit dotard.

Along with the mood of despair there was a marked tendency toward wild defiance—loose living and immoralities that were no doubt a desperate kind of reassertion of life in the presence of death. Yet the dominant feature of the time was not its licentiousness but its overpowering feelings of guilt, which arose from the conviction that God had visited the plague on man as retribution for his sins. Boccaccio, a few years after writing his *Decameron*, was overcome by repentance and a sense of guilt verging on panic. Martin Luther suffered acutely from guilt and fear of death, and Calvin, terror-stricken by the plague, fled from each epidemic. Indeed, entire communities were afflicted with what Freud called the primordial sense of guilt, and they engaged in penitential processions, pilgrimages and passionate mass preaching.

Some 70 years ago the English Catholic prelate and historian (later cardinal) Francis Gasquet, in a study entitled *The Great Pestilence*, tried to demonstrate that the Black Death set the stage for the Protestant Reformation by killing off the clergy and upsetting the entire religious life of Europe. This no doubt is too simple a theory. On the other hand, it is hard to deny that the catastrophic epidemics at the close of the Middle Ages must have been a powerful force for religious revolution. The failure of the Church and of prayer to ward off the pandemic, the flight of priests who deserted their parishes in the face of danger and the shortage of religious leaders after the Great Dying left the people eager for new kinds of leadership. And it is worth noting that most if not all of the Reformation leaders—Wycliffe, Zwingli, Luther, Calvin and others—were men who sought a more intimate relation of man to God because they were deeply affected by mankind's unprecedented ordeal by disease.

This is not to say that the epidemics of the late Middle Ages suffice to explain the Reformation but simply that the profound disturbance of men's minds by the universal, chronic grief and by the immediacy of death brought fundamental and long-lasting changes in religious outlook. In the moral and religious life of Europe, as well as in the economic sphere, the forces that make for change were undoubtedly strengthened and given added impetus by the Black Death.

II

LIMITS RARELY PERCEIVED

The problem is not shortage of data,
but rather our inability to perceive the consequences
of the information we already possess.
Jay W. Forrester,
Technology Review, January 1971

INTRODUCTION

One of the most pervasive fallacies of the twentieth century is that technological innovations will permit expansion of the carrying capacity of the earth to almost any required size. Many scientists and technicians, who should know better, have encouraged the lay public to believe that, given the funds and the time, a human population that is orders of magnitude larger than the present one can be sustained. This cheerful world view has often been reflected in professional scientific journals, as well as in more popular media (SCIENTIFIC AMERICAN not excepted). But recently, more and more articles have been appearing that lend support to a countervailing view. Some of the SCIENTIFIC AMERICAN articles that appear in this section deal with the factors that (at least ultimately) place upper limits on the size of our population. Others indicate short-term limits based on the inability of technology to provide solutions rapidly enough to keep up with the *rate* of population growth.

Edward Deevey's article "The Human Population" presents the history of the remarkable increase in man's numbers and the potential for its long continuation. It is a frightening article for several reasons. In 1960, Deevey could write: "The population, now passing 2.7 billion, is doubling itself every 50 years or so." A mere decade later, the population, now passing 3.7 billion, is doubling itself every 40 years or so. Perhaps even more alarming than the statistics themselves is the increase in pessimism among ecologists during the last decade. Deevey, a first-class ecologist, warned of the possibility of a 10- to 20-fold increase in the human population. It seems unlikely that the same discussion would be germane today, as the ecological costs of maintaining the present population of 3.7 billion people become more and more apparent. Indeed, it now seems clear that a population size smaller than that of 1970 will be necessary, if all human beings are to have a high material standard of living and if a comfortable margin for error is to be maintained against ecocatastrophes.

We cannot leave Deevey's article without calling attention to the dangers of bending over backward in order to give a completely "balanced" presentation. Specifically, Deevey felt constrained to include in his paper the views on population size of Arnold Harburger and Colin Clark. In connection with Harburger's bedraggled argument about increasing the number of geniuses, recall that human society today neglects to develop the intellect of its women, its minority groups, and the billion or so people who have grown up with protein deficiencies. In the light of that neglect, and in view of the near certainty that more people would simply aggravate the environmental suppression of genius, to suggest that more people be added to the population in order to provide more geniuses is mind-boggling indeed. Catholic economist Colin Clark believes that increased competition for resources, occasioned by continued population growth, leads to "sharpening of wits." For more realistic appraisals of the consequence of such competition, the reader is referred to Section III, *The Dimensions of Intervention.*

Roger Revelle, now Director of the Center on Population Studies at Harvard University, is an oceanographer with long experience with the trying interface of science and government. Those with serious interests in the effect of population size on the availability of food and other resources will have found Revelle an almost ubiquitous figure on the countless government panels and commissions convened to consider these matters over the past decade. His article "Water" is at once an informative survey of the subject and an illustration of the ambivalence pervading what might be called the "scientific-establishment view" of resource problems. For example, Revelle covers, in instructive detail, a wealth of obstacles to the intelligent and fruitful use of the world's water resources, and it would be difficult to improve on his concluding summary of the complexities of the water-agriculture relationship in underdeveloped countries. Yet, he writes so eloquently of what *could* be done in these difficult areas that the reader may be given the impression that the problems are in the process of being solved more or less routinely. This is not so; and giving the impression that it is, either to the public or to the government, can only delay the initiation of the unprecedented assault these problems actually require. This ambivalence, which consists in clearly recognizing the obstacles but, at the same time, glossing over their operational significance, is widespread among technological optimists.

Economics, logistics, and lead time are three components of the important and complicated distinction between what is theoretically feasible and what can and will be accomplished in practice. Thus, any number of enterprises that appear attractive on paper may prove to be too expensive, too little, and too late, particularly in the face of the present rate of population growth. One example from Revelle's article is the desalting of seawater for irrigation, about which he is, in fact, quite cautious. For a scholarly study demonstrating that desalting will make no substantial impact on world agriculture for at least two more decades, the reader may wish to consult "Desalting for Agriculture: Is it Economic?" by M. Clawson, H. Landsberg, and L. Alexander (*Science*, vol. 164, p. 1141, June 6, 1969). Another example of the detrimental relation between technological lead time and population growth is provided by the Aswan High Dam, about which most authorities are far less optimistic than Revelle. Thus, although estimates of the actual increase in the United Arab Republic's tilled acreage differ, it seems clear that population growth has outstripped the gains. There is less cultivable land per capita now than when construction on the dam began (see, for example, the books by food scientist Georg Borgstrom, *The Hungry Planet* and *Too Many*, published by Macmillan in 1965 and 1969, respectively).

The factor most underrated by the traditional analyses of population and resources is the environmental impact of technological schemes to redress the balance. Again, the Aswan High Dam project, for which Revelle held such high hopes in 1963, serves as a discouraging example. The impoundment of the Nile behind the dam has limited the nutrient flow of the river, eliminating the rich silting of the annual flood and apparently causing a decline in some of the fisheries of the eastern Mediterranean. (A recent partial recovery in the UAR catch is evidently due to the extension of their fisheries to deeper water with the aid of Soviet-supplied vessels.) Changes in the flow of the Nile have reportedly also led to salt-water intrusions in some of the richest delta land; and, as anticipated by Revelle, the new irrigation canals are spreading bilharzia, a serious schistosome parasite of humans that uses canal-dwelling snails as an intermediate host.

One might, of course, claim that the UAR would be much worse off without the dam. This is doubtful. The dam has been ballyhooed as the great hope of Egypt, distracting attention from needed improvements in UAR agriculture and, above all, from the necessity for heroic population-control measures. When the project is completed, the UAR will still be faced with a horrendous rate of population growth, and no prospect whatsoever for any suitable encore to the Aswan High Dam.

The statement in Revelle's paper that "in humid areas agriculture is limited only by the extent of good land" oversimplifies the problems of tropical agriculture. One of the most serious is that much "good land" will rapidly undergo the process of laterization, graphically described by Mary McNeil in her paper "Lateritic Soils." As she points out, the tendency of such soils to turn to rock upon cultivation is a major barrier to increasing the agricultural productivity of the tropics. This situation is potentially so serious that McNeil can write: "Because of laterite, attempts to grow more food in the Tropics may turn much of that region of the earth into wasteland."

An even less widely appreciated hazard of tropical agriculture is the absence of a severe winter. In the temperate zones, this harsh season tends to reduce populations of insects and, thus, to greatly simplify pest-control problems. The difficulty of tropical pest control is compounded because the poisonous nature of a proportionately large number of tropical plant species has led to the evolution of insects well equipped to deal with poisons. Specifically, organisms with a long evolutionary history of exposure to poisons are more likely to be in a position to evolve defenses to novel poisons than those that lack such experience. In the developed countries the petrochemical industry has fostered a simplistic reaction to pest problems: when in trouble, double the dose. If this philosophy prevails in attempts to improve and expand tropical agriculture, the absence of winter and the resistance of the pest populations will lead to unprecedented quantities of poisons in the ecosystem. (Some of the consequences may be extrapolated from data in G. M. Woodwell's article "Toxic Substances and Ecological Cycles," which is included in Section III, *The Dimensions of Intervention.*) This potential disaster, coupled with the laterization problem discussed by McNeil and the difficulties listed by Revelle in his concluding paragraphs, yield a disheartening prognosis for a revolution in tropical agriculture. Regrettably, "good land" and available water are far from enough.

It is particularly appropriate, then, that Lester Brown—one of the architects of the "Green Revolution"—emphasizes the achievement of high yields rather than the farming of virgin lands in his article "Human Food Production as a Process in the Biosphere." This paper deals effectively with many of the ecological problems associated with agriculture, and Brown's last sentence should be the motto of all those concerned with the provision of food for our burgeoning population: "The central question is no longer *Can we produce enough food?* but *What are the environmental consequences of attempting to do so?*"

There are also, of course, many economic, social and political factors that will hinder the spread of the Green Revolution. (An introduction to these may be found in Lester Brown's book *The Seeds of Change,* Praeger, 1970.) Therefore, it is not clear, at the moment, how much time to halt population growth can be "bought" by the Green Revolution, but it seems certain that it will not be more than 30 years. This is roughly one-half the time required, under the most optimistic assumptions, to significantly slow population growth through birth control.

Thus, the evidence suggests that an eventual rise in the death rate from starvation is inevitable—the only questions remaining are how large that rise will be, and in what context it will occur. Certainly, we must make a determined effort, within the constraints set by sound environmental policies, to maximize the success of the Green Revolution. The overdeveloped countries (ODCs) must also extend an unprecedented helping hand to the underdeveloped countries (UDCs). The UDCs must be helped to solve their economic problems, especially through revisions in the world trade system. Of primary importance, aid should be given in improving food storage and transportation systems, to help eliminate the tragic waste, between harvest and table, of as much as one-third of the food grown in certain areas.

Above all, ODCs must set an example by controlling their own populations, and then must give all acceptable assistance to the UDCs to help them move toward zero population growth. This necessity is clearly recognized by the foremost exponents of the Green Revolution. For example, Dr. Norman Borlaug, who received the 1970 Nobel Peace Prize for his work on developing the high-yield varieties of grain on which the Green Revolution is based, recently stated:

"I am convinced that those of us working with food and agriculture also must bring pressure on politicians, government officials and the general public to face up to and tame the monster of population growth before it is too late."

If the inevitable rise in the death rate occurs in the present context—that is, with the ODCs competing for and looting the world's resources and polluting its environment—a breakdown of international relations and a thermonuclear war seem to be probable results. If, on the other hand, the ODCs make massive efforts to take pressure off of the world's resources and extend unprecedented aid to the UDCs, we may well ride out the crisis. A logical beginning must be to develop the will and the institutions to eliminate the present gross inequities in the distribution of high-quality protein. The economic context that finds ODC chicken farmers and petfood manufacturers able to outbid the hungry peoples of the world for much of Peru's anchovy catch* is in serious need of modification.

The general problem of extracting human food from the sea is the subject of S. J. Holt's article "The Food Resources of the Ocean." His estimate of a fisheries catch of 100–200 million metric tons as a theoretical sustainable maximum is of the order of magnitude accepted by most fisheries biologists. The consensus now appears to be moving toward the lower side of the estimate, however; and it is clear that the theoretical yield cannot be reached if man continues to pollute the oceans and to overfish certain species. The consequences of present practices have been reflected in the announcement by the Food and Agriculture Organization (FAO) of the United Nations of a 3 percent absolute decline in fisheries yield in 1969. This decline, the first since 1950, came in the face of increased fisheries effort, and may well portend tragedy. While fisheries provide only about 2 percent of the world's calorie needs, the catch could, if equitably distributed, supply 23 percent of the crucial high-quality protein requirement, according to William E. Ricker (in *Resources and Man*, by the Committee on Resources and Man of the National Academy of Sciences–National Research Council, W. H. Freeman and Company, 1969, p. 106). Holt gives 10 percent as the fraction of the high-quality protein need actually being met from fisheries, although it is not clear whether he has included the growing contribution of fish meal fed to animals that are subsequently eaten by humans.

The plight of the world's poor—of which undernourishment (deficiency of calories) and malnourishment (deficiency of particular nutrients) are but two components—is detailed in David Simpson's article "The Dimensions of World Poverty." We included Simpson's paper in this section because the magnitude of the poverty problem is, in fact, a "limit rarely perceived." Mankind is performing badly in the task of providing the majority of its members with a decent

---

*Peru's annual catch, mostly anchovies, amounts to about ten million metric tons, or fifteen percent of the total world catch of fish of all kinds.

existence; the standard of living in much of the world is far from adequate. To talk of "keeping up" with population growth, therefore, is
absurd on the face of it: We must catch up before we can keep up.

Simpson points out in his opening sentence that the gap between
the poorer and richer countries is actually widening today, a fact that
deserves more widespread recognition than it has received. According
to figures compiled by the U.S. Agency for International Development, the gross national product per capita of the "developed" countries increased by 35 percent between 1960 and 1968, while that in
the "less developed" countries increased by only 23 percent in the
same period. At the lower rate, per capita GNP takes 25 years to
double. A doubling in 25 years will seem to be no progress at all to
those who start with rising expectations and a per capita GNP of
$100. Such pathetic dollar figures have little reality for citizens of
the ODCs. Simpson gives these figures substance in his discussion
of such elements of poverty as the inadequacy of housing in Calcutta
and the appallingly low number of physicians per capita in much
of Africa.

Our only criticism of this otherwise excellent article is that we
believe that Simpson underrated two important aspects of the food
problem. First, although we do not question the importance of the
logistics and economics of food distribution, "continuation of the
present trends in food production" is not as certain as Simpson implies; the reasons are, to a great extent, ecological and sociological,
as noted elsewhere in this section and in the remainder of this book.
Second, the problem of protein malnourishment—as distinct from
undernourishment, or simple calorie deficiency—should receive
more emphasis. More calories could be produced easily by increasing
the area planted to sugar beets and sugar cane. But it is high-quality
protein (generally expensive, both in economic and in ecological
terms) that is required if children are to resist disease and mature with
their intellectual capacities fully developed. It now seems certain
that mental retardation traceable to protein malnutrition in pregnant
women and young children is a major barrier against the poor helping
themselves escape their poverty.

The final article in this section is "Human Materials Production as
a Process in the Biosphere," by the noted geochemist Harrison
Brown. Brown's pioneering book, *The Challenge of Man's Future*
(Viking, 1954), emphasized energy as a fundamental raw material in
meeting the needs of a burgeoning population. That emphasis is to
be seen in the present article, where some of the relations among
energy, metals and prosperity are developed in instructive detail.
An aspect of the article worth noting is the author's ambivalence between optimism and pessimism. On the one hand, Brown identifies
the staggering problem of providing a "capital stock" of metals adequate to the needs of even the present population of today's UDCs.
Indeed, he notes, in connection with a projected demand for steel
fifty years hence, that "anything approaching such a demand would

clearly place enormous strains on the earth's resources and would greatly accentuate rivalries between nations for the earth's remaining deposits of relatively high-grade ores." Yet, in his closing paragraph, Brown writes: "Man has it in his power technologically to maintain a high level of industrial civilization, to eliminate deprivation and hunger and to control his environment for many millenniums." Is this statement consistent with the enormous difficulties identified in the body of the article?

We believe the explanation for this ambivalence lies in a distinction that, although seldom clearly stated, is crucial to the discussion of the relation of population to resources. The distinction that must be made is between the consideration of a hypothetical equilibrium and an analysis of the problem of competing rates that actually confronts us. Thus, although one can say, with Brown, that it is at least possible that an enlightened technology could support a stable population somewhat larger than today's, the environmental instabilities characteristic of simplified ecosystems may keep us from accomplishing even that. As Brown says, we may not "learn enough quickly enough."

Unfortunately, these theoretical considerations are virtually meaningless in the context of the dynamic rate problem with which we are confronted. The rate of development needed to provide *today's* population with a decent standard of living in an acceptable time is ridiculously high. The ecological errors that will be made in attempting hasty solutions may finish us, if the political stresses arising from existing inequities do not do so first. And, of course, we cannot plan only for today's population, because tomorrow's will be significantly larger.

Utopian technologies simply cannot be brought to bear in time. Rather, we must initiate unprecedented changes in the utilization and distribution of those resources that can be mobilized in the decades immediately to come, and with technology very much like today's. Thus, the debate about mining "the leanest of earth substances" does not interest us much; nor does the amount of water in the hydrologic cycle or the photosynthetic capacity of the land and seas. With respect to the problems of the next critical decades, such questions of the ultimate capacities of the earth are of no consequence.

ROMAN TOMBSTONE from the first century A.D. records the death of Cominia Tyche, aged 27 years, 11 months, 28 days. Tombstones are a source of information on life expectancy in the ancient world. Stone is in the Metropolitan Museum of Art in New York.

5

The Human Population

EDWARD S. DEEVEY, JR.
September 1960

Almost until the present turn in human affairs an expanding population has been equated with progress. "Increase and multiply" is the Scriptural injunction. The number of surviving offspring is the measure of fitness in natural selection. If number is the criterion, the human species is making great progress. The population, now passing 2.7 billion, is doubling itself every 50 years or so. To some horrified observers, however, the population increase has become a "population explosion." The present rate of increase, they point out, is itself increasing. At 1 per cent per year it is double that of the past few centuries. By A.D. 2000, even according to the "medium" estimate of the careful demographers of the United Nations, the rate of increase will have accelerated to 3 per cent per year, and the total population will have reached 6.267 billion. If Thomas Malthus's assumption of a uniform rate of doubling is naive, because it so quickly leads to impossible numbers, how long can an accelerating annual increase, say from 1 to 3 per cent in 40 years, be maintained? The demographers confronted with this question lower their eyes: "It would be absurd," they say, "to carry detailed calculations forward into a more remote future. It is most debatable whether the trends in mortality and fertility can continue much longer. Other factors may eventually bring population growth to a halt."

So they may, and must. It comes to this: Explosions are not made by force alone, but by force that exceeds restraint. Before accepting the implications of the population explosion, it is well to set the present in the context of the record of earlier human populations. As will be seen, the population curve has moved upward stepwise in response to the three major revolutions that have marked the evolution of culture [*see bottom illustration on page 52*]. The tool-using and toolmaking revolution that started the growth of the human stem from the primate line gave the food-gatherer and hunter access to the widest range of environments. Nowhere was the population large, but over the earth as a whole it reached the not insignificant total of five million, an average of .04 person per square kilometer (.1 person per square mile) of land. With the agricultural revolution the population moved up two orders of magnitude to a new plateau, multiplying 100 times in the short span of 8,000 years, to an average of one person per square kilometer. The increase over the last 300 years, a multiplication by five, plainly reflects the first repercussions of the scientific-industrial revolution. There are now 16.4 persons per square kilometer of the earth's land area. It is thus the release of restraint that the curve portrays at three epochal points in cultural history.

But the evolution of the population size also indicates the approach to equilibrium in the two interrevolutionary periods of the past. At what level will the present surge of numbers reach equilibrium? That is again a question of restraint, whether it is to be imposed by the limitations of man's new command over his environment or by his command over his own nature.

The human generative force is neither new nor metabiological, nor is it especially strong in man as compared to other animals. Under conditions of maximal increase in a suitable environment empty of competitors, with births at maximum and deaths negligible, rats can multiply their numbers 25 times in an average generation-time of 31 weeks. For the water flea *Daphnia*, beloved by ecologists for the speedy answers it gives, the figures are 221 times in a generation of 6.8 days. Mankind's best efforts seem puny by contrast: multiplication by about 1.4 times in a generation of 28 years. Yet neither in human nor in experimental populations do such rates continue unchecked. Sooner or later the births slow down and the deaths increase, until—in experiments, at any rate—the growth tapers off, and the population effectively saturates its space. Ecologists define this state (of zero rate of change) as equilibrium, without denying the possibility of oscillations that average out to zero, and without forgetting the continuous input of energy (food, for instance) that is needed to maintain the system.

Two kinds of check, then, operate to limit the size of a population, or of any living thing that grows. Obviously the environment (amount of space, food or other needed resources) sets the upper limit; sometimes this is manipulatable, even by the population itself, as when it exploits a new kind of food in the same old space, and reaches a new, higher limit. More subtly, populations can be said to limit their own rates of increase. As the numbers rise, female fruit-flies, for example, lay fewer eggs when jostled by their sisters; some microorganisms battle each other with antibiotics; flour beetles accidentally eat their own defenseless eggs and pupae; infectious diseases spread faster, or become more virulent, as their hosts become more numerous. For human populations pestilence and warfare, Malthus's "natural restraints," belong among these devices for self-limitation. So, too, does his "moral restraint," or voluntary birth control. Nowadays a good deal of attention is being given, not only to voluntary methods,

YEARS AGO	CULTURAL STAGE	AREA POPULATED	ASSUMED DENSITY PER SQUARE KILOMETER	TOTAL POPULATION (MILLIONS)
1,000,000	LOWER PALEOLITHIC		.00425	.125
300,000	MIDDLE PALEOLITHIC		.012	1
25,000	UPPER PALEOLITHIC		.04	3.34
10,000	MESOLITHIC		.04	5.32
6,000	VILLAGE FARMING AND EARLY URBAN		1.0 .04	86.5
2,000	VILLAGE FARMING AND URBAN		1.0	133
310	FARMING AND INDUSTRIAL		3.7	545
210	FARMING AND INDUSTRIAL		4.9	728
160	FARMING AND INDUSTRIAL		6.2	906
60	FARMING AND INDUSTRIAL		11.0	1,610
10	FARMING AND INDUSTRIAL		16.4	2,400
A.D. 2000	FARMING AND INDUSTRIAL		46.0	6,270

but also to a fascinating new possibility: mental stress.

Population control by means of personality derangement is probably a vertebrate patent; at least it seems a luxury beyond the reach of a water flea. The general idea, as current among students of small mammals, is that of hormonal imbalance (or stress, as defined by Hans Selye of the University of Montreal); psychic tension, resulting from overcrowding, disturbs the pituitary-adrenal system and diverts or suppresses the hormones governing sexuality and parental care. Most of the evidence comes from somewhat artificial experiments with caged rodents. It is possible, though the case is far from proved, that the lemming's famous mechanism for restoring equilibrium is the product of stress; in experimental populations of rats and mice, at least, anxiety has been observed to increase the death rate through fighting or merely from shock.

From this viewpoint there emerges an interesting distinction between crowding and overcrowding among vertebrates; overcrowding is what is perceived as such by members of the population. Since the human rate of increase is holding its own and even accelerating, however, it is plain that the mass of men, although increasingly afflicted with mental discomfort, do not yet see themselves as overcrowded. What will happen in the future brings other questions. For the present it may be noted that some kind of check has always operated, up to now, to prevent populations from ex-

ceeding the space that contains them. Of course space may be non-Euclidean, and man may be exempt from this law.

The commonly accepted picture of the growth of the population out of the long past takes the form of the top graph on the next page. Two things are wrong with this picture. In the first place the basis of estimates, back of about A.D. 1650, is rarely stated. One suspects that writers have been copying each other's guesses. The second defect is that the scales of the graph have been chosen so as to make the first defect seem unimportant. The missile has left the pad and is heading out of sight—so it is said; who cares whether there were a million or a hundred million people around when Babylon was founded? The difference is nearly lost in the thickness of the draftsman's line.

I cannot think it unimportant that (as I calculate) there were 36 billion Paleolithic hunters and gatherers, including the first tool-using hominids. One begins to see why stone tools are among the commonest Pleistocene fossils. Another 30 billion may have walked the earth before the invention of agriculture. A cumulative total of about 110 billion individuals seem to have passed their days, and left their bones, if not their marks, on this crowded planet. Neither for our understanding of culture nor in terms of man's impact upon the land is it a negligible consideration that the patch of ground allotted to every person now alive may have been the lifetime habitat of 40 predecessors.

These calculations exaggerate the truth in a different way: by condensing into single sums the enormous length of prehistoric time. To arrive at the total of 36 billion Paleolithic hunters and gatherers I have assumed mean standing populations of half a million for the Lower Paleolithic, and two million for the Middle and Upper Paleolithic to 25,000 years ago. For Paleolithic times there are no archeological records worth considering in such calculations. I have used some figures for modern hunting tribes, quoted by Robert J. Braidwood and Charles A. Reed, though they are not guilty of my extrapolations. The assumed densities per square kilometer range from a tenth to a third of those estimated for eastern North America before Columbus came, when an observer would hardly have described the woods as full of Indians. (Of course I have excluded any New World population from my estimates prior to the Mesolithic climax of the food-gathering and hunting phase of cultural evolution.) It is only

because average generations of 25 years succeeded each other 39,000 times that the total looms so large.

For my estimates as of the opening of the agricultural revolution, I have also depended upon Braidwood and Reed. In their work in Mesopotamia they have counted the number of rooms in buried houses, allowing for the areas of town sites and of cultivated land, and have compared the populations so computed with modern counterparts. For early village-farmers, like those at Jarmo, and for the urban citizens of Sumer, about 2500 B.C., their estimates (9.7 and 15.4 persons per square kilometer) are probably fairly close. They are intended to apply to large tracts of inhabited country, not to pavement-bound clusters of artisans and priests. Nevertheless, in extending these estimates to continentwide areas, I have divided the lower figure by 10, making it one per square kilometer. So much of Asia is unirrigated and nonurban even today that the figure may still be too high. But the Maya, at about the same level of culture (3,000 or 4,000 years later), provide a useful standard of comparison. The present population of their classic homeland averages .6 per square kilometer, but the land can support a population about a hundred times as large, and probably did at the time of the classic climax. The rest of the New World, outside Middle America, was (and is) more thinly settled, but a world-wide average of one per square kilometer seems reasonable for agricultural, pre-industrial society.

For modern populations, from A.D. 1650 on, I have taken the estimates of economic historians, given in such books as the treatise *World Population and Production*, by Wladimir S. and Emma S. Woytinsky. All these estimates are included in the bottom graph on the next page. Logarithmic scales are used in order to compress so many people and millennia onto a single page. Foreshortening time in this way is convenient, if not particularly logical, and back of 50,000 years ago the time-scale is pretty arbitrary anyway. No attempt is made to show the oscillations that probably occurred, in glacial and interglacial ages, for example.

The stepwise evolution of population size, entirely concealed in graphs with arithmetic scales, is the most noticeable feature of this diagram. For most of the million-year period the number of hominids, including man, was about what would be expected of any large Pleistocene mammal—scarcer than

POPULATION GROWTH, from inception of the hominid line one million years ago through the different stages of cultural evolution to A.D. 2000, is shown in the chart on the opposite page. In Lower Paleolithic stage, population was restricted to Africa (*colored area on world map in third column*), with a density of only .00425 person per square kilometer (*fourth column*) and a total population of only 125,000 (*column at right*). By the Mesolithic stage, 10,000 years ago, hunting and food gathering techniques had spread the population over most of the earth and brought the total to 5,320,-000. In the village farming and early urban stage, population increased to a total of 86,500,000 and a density of one person per square kilometer in the Old World and .04 per square kilometer in the New World. Today the population density exceeds 16 persons per square kilometer, and pioneering of the antarctic continent has begun.

horses, say, but commoner than elephants. Intellectual superiority was simply a successful adaptation, like longer legs; essential to stay in the running, of course, but making man at best the first among equals. Then the food-gatherers and hunters became plowmen and herdsmen, and the population was boosted by about 16 times, between 10,000 and 6,000 years ago. The scientific-industrial revolution, beginning some 300 years ago, has spread its effects much faster, but it has not yet taken the number as far above the earlier base line.

The long-term population equilibrium implied by such base lines suggests

something else. Some kind of restraint kept the number fairly stable. "Food supply" offers a quick answer, but not, I think, the correct one. At any rate, a forest is full of game for an expert mouse-hunter, and a Paleolithic man who stuck to business should have found enough food on two square kilometers, instead of 20 or 200. Social forces were probably more powerful than mere starvation in causing men to huddle in small bands. Besides, the number was presumably adjusted to conditions in the poorest years, and not to average environments.

The main point is that there were ad-

justments. They can only have come about because the average female bore two children who survived to reproduce. If the average life span is 25 years, the "number of children ever born" is about four (because about 50 per cent die before breeding), whereas a population that is really trying can average close to eight. Looking back on former times, then, from our modern point of view, we might say that about two births out of four were surplus, though they were needed to counterbalance the juvenile death toll. But what about the other four, which evidently did not occur? Unless the life expectancy was very much less

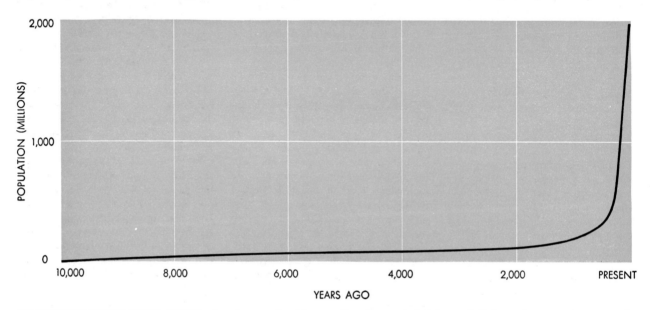

ARITHMETIC POPULATION CURVE plots the growth of human population from 10,000 years ago to the present. Such a curve suggests that the population figure remained close to the base line for an indefinite period from the remote past to about 500 years ago, and that it has surged abruptly during the last 500 years as a result of the scientific-industrial revolution.

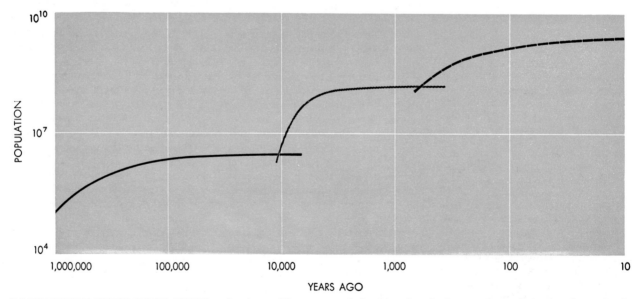

LOGARITHMIC POPULATION CURVE makes it possible to plot, in a small space, the growth of population over a longer period of time and over a wider range (from 10^4, or 10,000, to 10^{10}, or 10 billion, persons). Curve, based on assumptions concerning relationship of technology and population as shown in chart on page 80, reveals three population surges reflecting toolmaking or cultural revolution (*solid line*), agricultural revolution (*gray line*) and scientific-industrial revolution (*broken line*).

than I have assumed (and will presently justify), some degree of voluntary birth control has always prevailed.

Our 40 predecessors on earth make an impressive total, but somehow it sounds different to say that nearly 3 per cent of the people who have ever lived are still around. When we realize that they are living twice as long as their parents did, we are less inclined to discount the revolution in which we are living. One of its effects has just begun to be felt: The mean age of the population is increasing all over the world. Among the more forgivable results of Western culture, when introduced into simpler societies, is a steep drop in the death rate. Public-health authorities are fond of citing Ceylon in this connection. In a period of a year during 1946 and 1947 a campaign against malaria reduced the death rate there from 20 to 14 per 1,000. Eventually the birth rate falls too, but not so fast, nor has it yet fallen so far as a bare replacement value. The natural outcome of this imbalance is that acceleration of annual increase which so bemuses demographers. In the long run it must prove to be temporary, unless the birth rate accelerates, for the deaths that are being systematically prevented are premature ones. That is, the infants who now survive diphtheria and measles are certain to die of something else later on, and while the mean lifespan is approaching the maximum, for the first time in history, there is no reason to think that the maximum itself has been stretched. Meanwhile the expectation of life at birth is rising daily in most countries, so that it has already surpassed 70 years in some, including the U. S., and probably averages between 40 and 50.

It is hard to be certain of any such world-wide figure. The countries where mortality is heaviest are those with the least accurate records. In principle, however, mean age at death is easier to find out than the number of children born, the frequency or mean age at marriage, or any other component of a birth rate. The dead bones, the court and parish records and the tombstones that archeology deals with have something to say about death, of populations as well as of people. Their testimony confirms the impression that threescore years and ten, if taken as an average and not as a maximum lifetime, is something decidedly new. Of course the possibilities of bias in such evidence are almost endless. For instance, military cemeteries tend to be full of young adult males. The hardest bias to allow for is the deficiency of in-

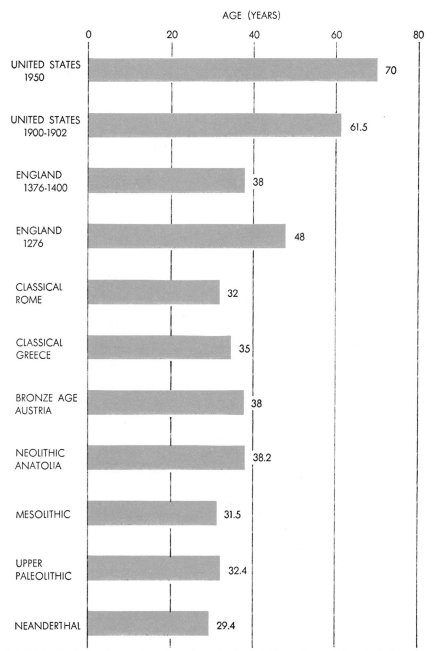

LONGEVITY in ancient and modern times is charted. From time of Neanderthal man to 14th century A.D., life span appears to have hovered around 35 years. An exception is 13th-century England. Increase in longevity partly responsible for current population increase has come in modern era. In U.S. longevity increased about 10 years in last half-century.

fants and children; juvenile bones are less durable than those of adults, and are often treated less respectfully. Probably we shall never know the true expectation of life at birth for any ancient people. Bypassing this difficulty, we can look at the mean age at death among the fraction surviving to adolescence.

The "nasty, brutish and short" lives of Neanderthal people have been rather elaborately guessed at 29.4 years. The record, beyond them, is not one of steady improvement. For example, Neolithic farmers in Anatolia and Bronze Age Austrians averaged 38 years, and even the

Mesolithic savages managed more than 30. But in the golden ages of Greece and Rome the life span was 35 years or less. During the Middle Ages the chances of long life were probably no better. The important thing about these averages is not the differences among them, but their similarity. Remembering the crudeness of the estimates, and the fact that juvenile mortality is omitted, it is fair to guess that human life-expectancy at birth has never been far from 25 years— 25 plus or minus five, say—from Neanderthal times up to the present century. It follows, as I have said, that about half

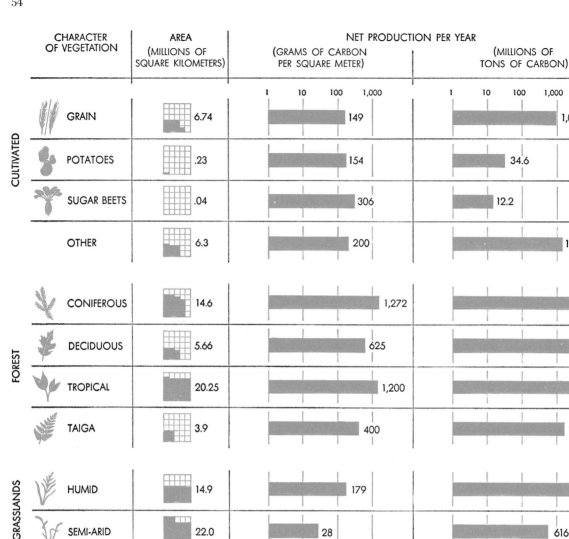

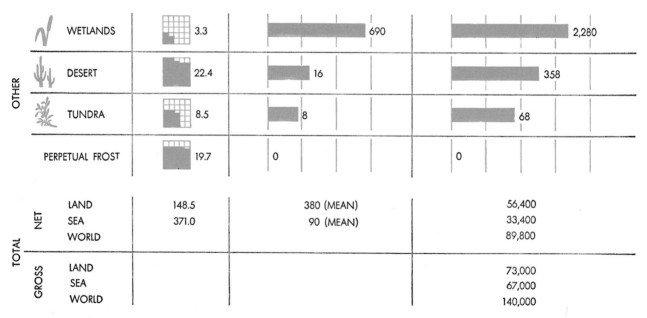

CHARACTER OF VEGETATION		AREA (MILLIONS OF SQUARE KILOMETERS)	NET PRODUCTION PER YEAR (GRAMS OF CARBON PER SQUARE METER)	NET PRODUCTION PER YEAR (MILLIONS OF TONS OF CARBON)
CULTIVATED	GRAIN	6.74	149	1,000
CULTIVATED	POTATOES	.23	154	34.6
CULTIVATED	SUGAR BEETS	.04	306	12.2
CULTIVATED	OTHER	6.3	200	1,260
FOREST	CONIFEROUS	14.6	1,272	18,600
FOREST	DECIDUOUS	5.66	625	3,540
FOREST	TROPICAL	20.25	1,200	24,400
FOREST	TAIGA	3.9	400	1,560
GRASSLANDS	HUMID	14.9	179	2,670
GRASSLANDS	SEMI-ARID	22.0	28	616
OTHER	WETLANDS	3.3	690	2,280
OTHER	DESERT	22.4	16	358
OTHER	TUNDRA	8.5	8	68
OTHER	PERPETUAL FROST	19.7	0	0
TOTAL NET	LAND	148.5	380 (MEAN)	56,400
TOTAL NET	SEA	371.0	90 (MEAN)	33,400
TOTAL NET	WORLD			89,800
TOTAL GROSS	LAND			73,000
TOTAL GROSS	SEA			67,000
TOTAL GROSS	WORLD			140,000

PRODUCTION OF ORGANIC MATTER per year by the land vegetation of the world—and thus its ultimate food-producing capacity—is charted in terms of the amount of carbon incorporated in organic compounds. Cultivated vegetation (*top left*) is less efficient than forest and wetlands vegetation, as indicated by the uptake of carbon per square meter (*third column*), and it yields a smaller over-all output than forest, humid grasslands and wetlands vegetation (*fourth column*). The scales at top of third and fourth columns are logarithmic. Land vegetation leads sea vegetation in efficiency and in net and gross tonnage (*bottom*). The difference between the net production and gross production is accounted for by the consumption of carbon in plant respiration.

the children ever born have lived to become sexually mature. It is not hard to see why an average family size of four or more, or twice the minimum replacement rate, has come to seem part of a God-given scheme of things.

The 25-fold upsurge in the number of men between 10,000 and 2,000 years ago was sparked by a genuine increase in the means of subsistence. A shift from animal to plant food, even without agricultural labor and ingenuity, would practically guarantee a 10-fold increase, for a given area can usually produce about 10 times as much plant as animal substance. The scientific-industrial revolution has increased the efficiency of growing these foods, but hardly, as yet, beyond the point needed to support another 10 times as many people, fewer of whom are farmers. At the present rate of multiplication, without acceleration, another 10-fold rise is due within 230 years. Disregarding the fact that developed societies spend 30 to 60 times as much energy for other purposes as they need for food, one is made a little nervous by the thought of so many hungry mouths. Can the increase of efficiency keep pace? Can some of the apparently ample energy be converted to food as needed, perhaps at the cost of reducing the size of Sunday newspapers? Or is man now pressing so hard on his food supply that another 10-fold increase of numbers is impossible?

The answers to these questions are not easy to find, and students with different viewpoints disagree about them. Richard L. Meier of the University of Michigan estimates that a total of 50 billion people (a 20-fold increase, that is) can be supported on earth, and the geochemist Harrison Brown of the California Institute of Technology will allow (reluctantly) twice or four times as many. Some economists are even more optimistic; Arnold C. Harberger of the University of Chicago presents the interesting notion that a larger crop of people will contain more geniuses, whose intellects will find a solution to the problem of feeding *still* more people. And the British economist Colin Clark points out that competition for resources will sharpen everyone's wits, as it always has, even if the level of innate intelligence is not raised.

An ecologist's answer is bound to be cast in terms of solar energy, chlorophyll and the amount of land on which the two can interact to produce organic carbon. Sources of energy other than the sun are either too expensive, or nonrenewable or both. Land areas will continue for a very long time to be the places where food is grown, for the sea is not so productive as the land, on the average. One reason, sometimes forgotten, is that the plants of the sea are microscopic algae, which, being smaller than land plants, respire away a larger fraction of the carbon they fix. The culture of the fresh-water alga *Chlorella* has undeniable promise as a source of human food. But the high efficiencies quoted for its photosynthesis, as compared with agricultural plants, are not sustained outdoors under field conditions. Even if Chlorella (or another exceptionally efficient producer, such as the water hyacinth) is the food plant of the future, flat areas exposed to sunlight will be needed. The 148.5 million square kilometers of land will have to be used with thoughtful care if the human population is to increase 20-fold. With a population of 400 per square kilometer (50 billion total) it would seem that men's bodies, if not their artifacts, will stand in the way of vital sunshine.

Plants capture the solar energy impinging on a given area with an efficiency of about .1 per cent. (Higher values often quoted are based on some fraction of the total radiation, such as visible light.) Herbivores capture about a 10th of the plants' energy, and carnivores convert about 10 per cent of the energy captured by herbivores (or other carnivores). This means, of course, that carnivores, feeding on plants at second hand, can scarcely do so with better than 1 per cent efficiency ($1/10 \times 1/10$ equals $1/100$). Eugene I. Rabinowitch of the University of Illinois has calculated that the current crop of men represents an ultimate conversion of about 1 per cent of the energy trapped by land vegetation. Recently, however, I have re-examined the base figure—the efficiency of the land-plant production—and believe it should be raised by a factor of three or four. The old value came from estimates made in 1919 and in 1937. A good deal has been learned since those days. The biggest surprise is the high productivity of forests, especially the forests of the Temperate Zone.

If my new figures are correct, the population could theoretically increase by 30 or 40 times. But man would have to displace all other herbivores and utilize all the vegetation with the 10 per cent efficiency established by the ecological rule of tithes. No land that now supports greenery could be spared for nonagricultural purposes; the populace would have to reside in the polar regions, or on artificial "green isles in the sea, love"—scummed over, of course, by 10 inches of Chlorella culture.

The picture is doubtless overdrawn. There is plenty of room for improvement in present farming practice. More land could be brought under cultivation if a better distribution of water could be arranged. More efficient basic crops can be grown and used less wastefully. Other sources of energy, notably atomic energy, can be fed back into food production to supplement the sun's rays. None of these measures is more than palliative, however; none promises so much as a 10-fold increase in efficiency; worse, none is likely to be achieved at a pace equivalent to the present rate of doubling of the world's population. A 10-fold, even a 20-fold, increase can be tolerated, perhaps, but the standard of living seems certain to be lower than today's. What happens then, when men perceive themselves to be overcrowded?

The idea of population equilibrium will take some getting used to. A population that is kept stable by emigration, like that of the Western Islands of Scotland, is widely regarded as sick—a shining example of a self-fulfilling diagnosis. Since the fall of the death rate is temporary, it is those two or more extra births per female that demand attention. The experiments with crowded rodents point to one way they might be corrected, through the effect of anxiety in suppressing ovulation and spermatogenesis and inducing fetal resorption. Some of the most dramatic results are delayed until after birth: litters are carelessly nursed, deserted or even eaten. Since fetuses, too, have endocrine glands, the specter of maternal transmission of anxiety now looms: W. R. Thompson of Wesleyan University has shown that the offspring of frustrated mother mice are more "emotional" throughout their own lives, and my student Kim Keeley has confirmed this.

Considered abstractly, these devices for self-regulation compel admiration for their elegance. But there is a neater device that men can use: rational, voluntary control over numbers. In mentioning the dire effects of psychic stress I am not implying that the population explosion will be contained by cannibalism or fetal resorption, or any power so naked. I simply suggest that vertebrates have that power, whether they want it or not, as part of the benefit—and the price—of being vertebrates. And if the human method of adjusting numbers to resources fails to work in the next 1,000 years as it has in the last million, subhuman methods are ready to take over.

6

Water

ROGER REVELLE

September 1963

*Did you ever hear of Sweet Betsy
   from Pike
Who crossed the wide prairie with her
   lover Ike?
The alkali desert was burning and bare
And Ike got disgusted with everything
   there.
They reached California with sand
   in their eye,
Saying, "Good-by Pike County, we'll
   stay till we die."*

This bleary and partly unprintable ballad of the 1850's marks the time when most Americans first became aware of the problems of water in national development. In northern Europe, where most of their ancestors had lived, there had always been plenty of water; in the eastern U.S., where they had learned to farm, abundant rain supplied all the water needs of their crops. But when the pioneers crossed the Missouri River, they came to an arid country where water was more precious than land: its presence meant life, its absence death.

Today water problems are part of the national consciousness, and most Americans are aware that the future development of their country is intimately related to the wise use of water resources. The same obviously holds true for the less developed countries. The water problems of the U.S. and the poorer countries are fundamentally similar, but they also differ in significant ways.

Water is both the most abundant and the most important substance with which man deals. The quantities of water required for his different uses vary over a wide range. The amount of drinking water needed each year by human beings and domestic animals is of the order of 10 tons per ton of living tissue. Industrial water requirements for washing, cooling and the circulation of materials range from one to two tons per ton of product in the manufacture of brick to 250 tons per ton of paper and 600 tons per ton of nitrate fertilizer. Even the largest of these quantities is small compared with the amounts of water needed in agriculture. To grow a ton of sugar or corn under irrigation about 1,000 tons of water must be "consumed," that is, changed by soil evaporation and plant transpiration from liquid to vapor. Wheat, rice and cotton fiber respectively require about 1,500, 4,000 and 10,000 tons of water per ton of crop.

When we think of water and its uses, we are concerned with the volume of flow through the hydrologic cycle; hence the most meaningful measurements are in terms of volume per unit time: acre-feet per year, gallons per day, cubic feet per second. An acre-foot is 325,872 gallons, the amount of water required to cover an acre of land to a depth of a foot. Eleven hundred acre-feet a year is approximately equal to a million gallons a day, or 1.5 cubic feet per second. A million gallons a day fills the needs of 5,000 to 10,000 people in a city; 1,100 acre-feet a year is enough to irrigate 250 to 300 acres of farmland.

The total amount of rain and snow falling on the earth each year is about 380 billion acre-feet: 300 billion on the ocean and 80 billion on the land. Over the ocean 9 per cent more water evaporates than falls back as rain. This is balanced by an equal excess of precipitation over evaporation on land; consequently the volume of water carried to the sea by glaciers, rivers and coastal springs is close to 27 billion acre-feet per year. About 13 billion acre-feet is carried by 68 major river systems from a drainage area of 14 billion acres. Somewhat less than half the runoff of liquid water from the land to the ocean is carried by thousands of small rivers flowing across coastal plains or islands; the area drained is about 11 billion acres, but part of this is desert with virtually no runoff.

Eight billion acres on the continents drain into inland seas, lakes or playas. This includes most of the earth's six billion acres of desert and also such relatively well-watered areas as the basins of the Volga, Ural, Amu Darya and Syr Darya rivers, which transport several hundred million acre-feet of water each year into the Caspian and Aral seas. The remainder of the land surface, about four billion acres, is covered by glaciers.

Even agriculture, man's principal consumer of water, takes little of the available supply. A billion acre-feet per year —less than 4 per cent of the total river flow—is used to irrigate 310 million acres of land, or about 1 per cent of the land area of the earth. Roughly 10 billion acre-feet of rainfall and snowfall is evaporated and transpired each year from the remaining three billion acres of the earth's cultivated lands and thus helps to grow mankind's food and fiber. Most river waters flow to the sea almost unused by man, and more than half of the water evaporating from the continents—

MULTIPURPOSE DAM at Watts Bar, Tenn., appears in the aerial photograph on the opposite page. The blue lake at left is formed where the dam halts the Tennessee River. Spilled back to river depth beyond the dam, the water regains a slate-gray hue. The turbulent area at lower right is caused by the flow of water through the square-capped hydroelectric generators. At bottom cente. is a power-distribution station. At top is the lock that enables shipping to pass the dam. The ribs in the dam are spill-ways, which here are closed. They can adjust the lake level to help control flooding.

58

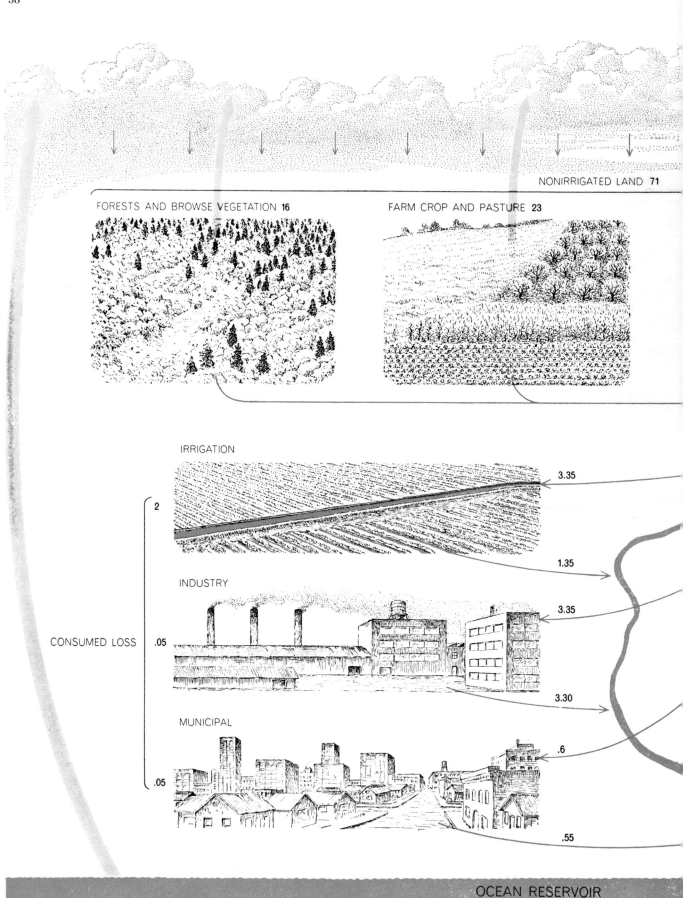

NONIRRIGATED LAND **71**

FORESTS AND BROWSE VEGETATION **16**

FARM CROP AND PASTURE **23**

IRRIGATION

3.35

2

1.35

CONSUMED LOSS

INDUSTRY

3.35

.05

3.30

MUNICIPAL

.6

.05

.55

OCEAN RESERVOIR

HYDROLOGIC CYCLE for the U.S. shows the fraction of annual precipitation used in a highly developed nation. Twenty-nine per cent of the rainfall arrives at the oceans (*bottom*) via stream flow; 71 per cent falls on various types of nonirrigated land, returning

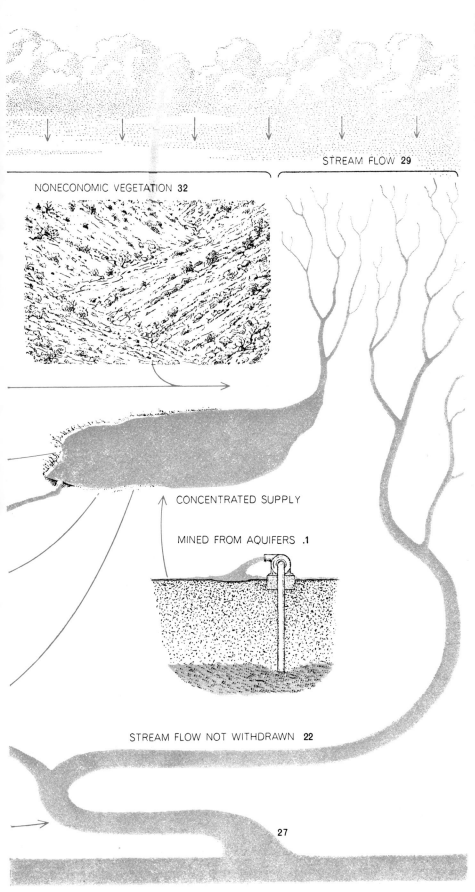

STREAM FLOW 29

NONECONOMIC VEGETATION 32

CONCENTRATED SUPPLY

MINED FROM AQUIFERS .1

STREAM FLOW NOT WITHDRAWN 22

27

directly to the atmosphere (*top*) by transpiration and evaporation. Water withdrawn for irrigation, industry and municipal use is shown at left to constitute only 7.3 per cent of total.

particularly that part of the evaporation taking place in the wet rain forests and semihumid savannas of the Tropics—plays little part in human life.

Although it is not usually reckoned as such in economic statistics, water can be considered a raw material. In the U.S. the production of raw materials has a minor role in the total economy, and water costs are small even when compared with those of other raw materials. The cost of all the water used by U.S. householders, industry and agriculture is around $5 billion a year: only 1 per cent of the gross national product. The less developed countries, where raw materials are a major component of the economy, cannot afford water prices that would be acceptable in the U.S.

In the U.S. water costs $10 to $20 an acre-foot, compared with wholesale prices of $22,000 an acre-foot for petroleum, $100,000 an acre-foot for milk and $1 million an acre-foot (not counting taxes) for bourbon whiskey. The largest tanker ever built can hold less than $1,000 worth of water. Yet Americans use so much water—about 1,700 gallons a day per capita—that capital costs for water development are comparable to other kinds of investment. Although the water diverted from streams and pumped from the ground is equivalent to only about 7 per cent of the rain and snow falling on the U.S., this is still an enormous quantity: 200 times more than the weight of any other material used except air. The annual capital expenditure for water structures in the U.S.—dams, community and industrial water works, sewage-treatment plants, pipelines and drains, irrigation canals, river-control structures and hydroelectric works—is about $10 billion.

One of the most critical water problems of the U.S. is represented by the vast water-short region of the Southwest and the high Western plains. In some parts of the Southwest water stored underground is being mined at an alarmingly high rate, and new sources must soon be found to supply even the present population. The average annual supply of controllable water in the entire region is 76 million acre-feet. If agriculture continued to develop at the present rate, 98 to 131 million acre-feet would be required by the year 2000. Provided that the neighboring water-surplus regions could be persuaded to share their abundance, this deficit could be met by long-distance transportation of 22 to 55 million acre-feet per year. But the annual cost would be $2 billion to $4 billion, or

$60 to $100 per acre-foot of water, including amortization of capital costs of $30 billion to $70 billion. The cost per acre-foot would be too high for most agriculture, although not too high for municipal, industrial and recreational needs.

Nathaniel Wollman of the University of New Mexico and his colleagues have shown that the average value added to the economy of the Southwest through the use of water in irrigation is only $44 to $51 an acre-foot, whereas the value gained from recreational uses could be about $250 an acre-foot and from industrial uses $3,000 to $4,000 an acre-foot. Because the quantities of water consumed by city-dwellers and their industries are much less than those in agriculture, the arid Western states would not require such a vast increase in future supply if they shifted from a predominantly agricultural to a predominantly industrial economic base.

The value of water in the water-short regions of the U.S. that are in a phase of rapid economic development increases more rapidly than the cost. Even high-cost water is a small burden on the gross product of a predominantly industrial and urban economy, and high water costs are only a small economic disadvantage. This is easily overcome if other

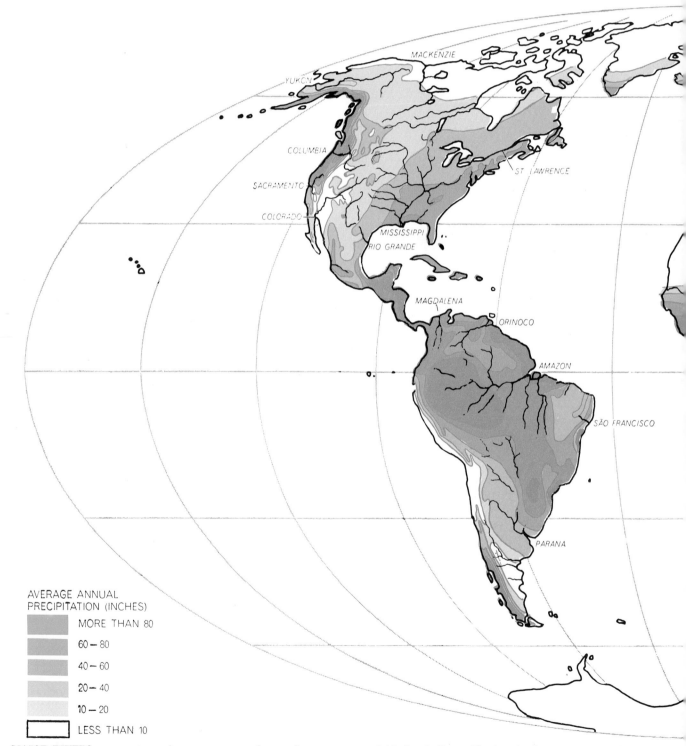

AVERAGE ANNUAL
PRECIPITATION (INCHES)

MORE THAN 80

60 – 80

40 – 60

20 – 40

10 – 20

LESS THAN 10

MAJOR RIVERS carry water to the oceans at rate of more than 11 billion acre-feet every year, but even in the U.S. less than a quarter of this flow is diverted by man for his own purposes. Key at lower left distinguishes areas by amount of precipitation they

conditions, such as climate, happen to be propitious.

Throughout the country favorable benefit-to-cost ratios can usually be attained from relatively high-cost multi-purpose water developments for city residents, industry, irrigation agriculture, the oxidation and dispersal of municipal and industrial wastes, the generation of hydroelectric power, pollution control, fish and wildlife conservation, navigation, recreation and flood control.

In the less developed countries water development by itself does not produce much added value for the present economy. Municipal and industrial water requirements are much smaller than they are in the U.S., and the immediate water needs are chiefly for agriculture, which calls for about the same amount of water in any warm region. Most of these countries have a low-yielding subsistence agriculture that brings in very little cash per acre-foot of water, and their farmers can afford to pay only a few dollars per acre-foot. Development of water resources must be accompanied by other measures to raise agricultural yields per acre-foot and per man-hour, and in general to increase the economic value of water.

One means of coping with water problems in both the U.S. and the less de-

receive each year. Several regions where the average annual precipitation is less than 10 inches (*white*) can be seen to lie close to large rivers. Plans for overcoming the aridity of Egypt and central Russia call for giant dams on the Nile and the Ob.

veloped countries is to improve the present rather low efficiency of water use. Here much could be done by effective research. For example, about half the water provided for irrigation is lost in transport, and less than half the water that reaches the fields is utilized by plants.

New mulching methods are already being applied to reduce evaporation from soil surfaces, thereby making more water available for transpiration by the plants. Through research on the physiology of water uptake and transport in plants, and on plant genetics, transpiration could probably be lowered without a proportional reduction in growth. Development of salt-tolerant crops would reduce the amounts of irrigation water needed to maintain low salt concentrations in the solution around the plant

roots. The loss of water by seepage from irrigation canals and percolation from fields would be lowered by the development of better linings for canals and better irrigation practices. Losses from canals would also be reduced if we could learn how to control useless water-loving plants that suck water through the canal banks and transpire it to the air.

In arid regions the runoff from a large area must be concentrated to provide water for a relatively small fraction of the land, and techniques are needed to increase the proportion of total precipitation that can be concentrated. Development of such techniques requires research on means of increasing the runoff from mountain areas (for example, by reducing evaporation from snow fields and modifying the plant cover in order to

reduce transpiration) and on methods for accelerating the rate of recharge of valley aquifers.

Finally, water problems could be dealt with by steps that—in contrast to those seeking to make better use of existing supplies—sought to increase the total volume of fresh water. Here research moves on two fronts: attempts to modify precipitation patterns by exerting control over weather and climate, and development of more economical methods of converting sea water or brackish water to fresh water. The ability to control weather and climate, even to a small degree, would be of the greatest importance to human beings everywhere. Whether or not a measure of control can be obtained will remain uncertain until we understand the natural proc-

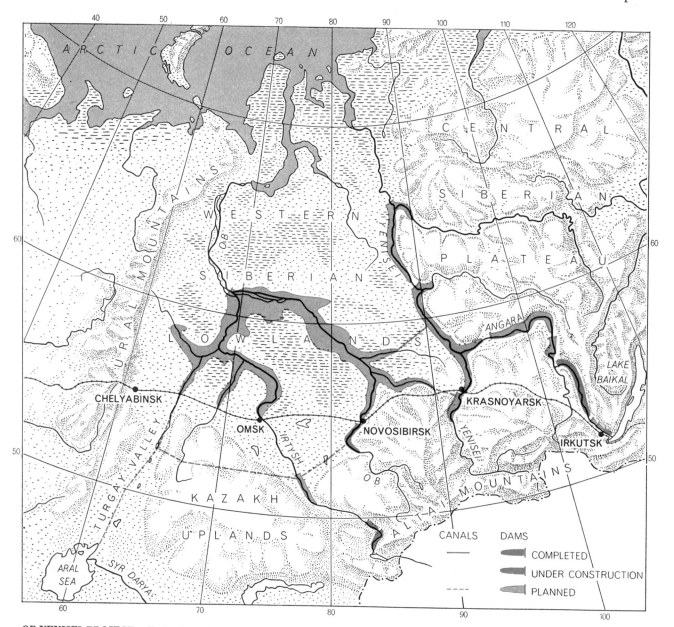

OB-YENISEI PROJECT calls for huge dam on the Ob, creating an inland sea five-sixths the size of Italy. Canal would link Ob and Yenisei rivers so that 12.5 per cent of the water now flowing unused to the Arctic would irrigate the central Soviet steppes.

esses in the atmosphere much better than we do now. As for desalination, this could be accomplished more economically than at present if the amount of energy required to separate water and salt could be reduced or the cost of energy lowered. Research on the properties of water, salt solutions, surfaces and membranes is fundamental to the desalination problem. So is research aimed at lowering energy costs.

We know too little to be able to make more than a rough appraisal of the potentialities of water-resources development for agriculture in the less developed countries. The modern technology of irrigation engineering, drainage, sanitation and agricultural practice is quite different from that which determined patterns of land and water use in the past. At the same time technology is almost completely lacking for expanding productive agriculture in the areas of most abundant water and almost unused land: the humid Tropics. Our concern should be not only to find ways of increasing total production in order to feed and clothe the world's expanding human population but also to raise production per farm worker, that is, to raise living standards. A world-wide strategy for development of land and water will require a careful analysis of existing knowledge, region by region, together with field surveys and experimental research in each region by experienced and imaginative specialists.

In humid areas agriculture is limited only by the extent of good land; in arid lands water is the absolute limiting factor. Unless climates can be modified or sea water can be cheaply converted and economically transported, the area of arable land in the arid zone will always exceed the available water. At present, however, neither surface nor underground waters are fully utilized, either for double-cropping in presently cultivated lands or for bringing new land under cultivation.

In addition to improving the utilization of water and increasing agricultural yields other problems that contributed to the destruction of desert civilizations in the past must still be overcome in arid land development. Among them is the fact that the spreading of water over large areas provides a fertile ground for human diseases, such as malaria and bilharzia, and for plant pests. Egyptian records show an average of one plague every 11 years. Uncontrollable malaria might well have been the cause of the mysterious disappearance of the great civilization of the cities Mohenjo-Daro and Harappa, which flourished 4,500

WATERLOGGED FIELDS near Sargodha in Pakistan reflect leaky canal system and inadequate drainage. Cultivated plots can be seen under water in center of photograph. When it evaporates, the water will deter renewed cultivation by leaving salts in topsoil.

SALINE FIELDS stand out against darker cultivated land in this aerial photograph. The related problems of waterlogging and salt accumulation in the soil have made five million acres of West Pakistan's irrigated farmland either impossible or unprofitable to cultivate.

years ago in the Indus valley of Pakistan.

Soil drainage in a nearly level flood plain is very difficult and is usually neglected, with the result that the water table comes close to the surface and drowns the roots of most crop plants. Water rises through the soil by capillary action and evaporates, leaving an accumulation of salt that poisons the plants. The related disasters of waterlogging and salinity may have caused the ruin of the Babylonian civilization in the valley of the Tigris-Euphrates, and they are a frightening menace today in West Pakistan.

Another threat is the conflict between the sedentary farmers of the plain and nomadic herdsmen. The present-day Powindahs of West Pakistan remind us of this ancient conflict. In our own West

the feuds between cattlemen and farmers are still a vivid memory.

In considering the possibilities of agricultural development in the world's arid lands one thinks first of the famous rivers that have played so large a role in human history: among them the Nile, the Indus and its tributaries and the Tigris-Euphrates.

For thousands of years the Egyptians carried out irrigation by allowing the Nile waters during flood stage to spread in ponded basins broadly over the delta and the valley. When the flood subsided, the basin banks were cut and the ponded water flowed back to the river. The Nile and the sun were said to be the prime farmers of Egypt. It was thought that the river's silt, deposited during the annual flood, fertilized the soil. Sun-

drying and -cracking, during the fallow season before the flood, deeply furrowed the soil and killed off weeds and microorganisms, making plowing unnecessary. The flood arrived in July, reached its height in September and subsided quickly. The fields were sown in early winter with wheat, barley, beans, onions, flax and clover. Summer crops were grown only on the river levees and in areas that contained a shallow water table, where water could be lifted by hand from the river banks or from wells. High floods left the basins pestilential morasses that brought plagues and epidemics. Low floods brought famine.

During the past 140 years this ancient system has been transformed. In 1820 Egypt had reached a nadir, with a population of only 2.5 million and with three

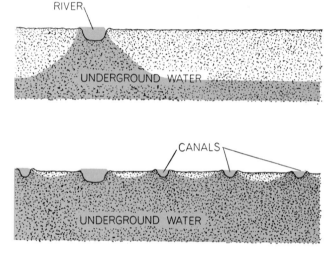

LACK OF DRAINAGE has caused the underground water table to rise disastrously in parts of Pakistan. Before construction of leaky canals, water approached ground level only near rivers. Now water table in many areas is high enough to drown crop roots.

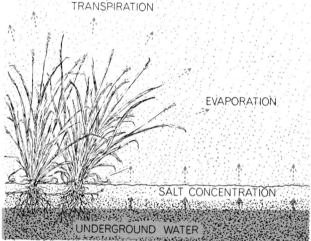

SALT ACCUMULATES on topsoil in two ways. Underground water rises by capillary action, lifting dissolved salts that will be left behind after evaporation. If farmer uses thin layer of water to irrigate topsoil, it will evaporate before percolating down.

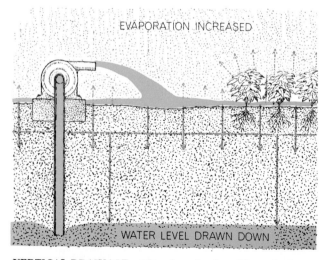

VERTICAL DRAINAGE might solve related problems of salinity and waterlogging. Pumped through cased well from underground table, as illustrated here, enough water could reach surface for salts to percolate down beneath topsoil before full evaporation occurs.

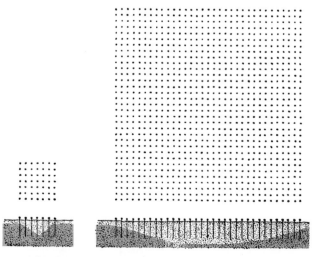

LARGE-SCALE PROJECT will be required to lower the water table. Drainage of a field of one million acres (*right*) could negate seepage from adjacent land. But pumping out a small field (*left*) would have no appreciable effect on underground water level.

million cultivated acres. This date marked the beginning of perennial canal irrigation and widespread planting of summer crops, including cotton, corn, rice and sugar cane as well as the traditional winter crops. Low dams called barrages were built across the river; the water backed up behind these structures was diverted through large new canals that flowed the year round. By 1955–1956 the cultivated area had increased to 5.7 million acres and the intensity of cultivation to 177 per cent; that is, more than 10 million acres of crops were harvested. Salinity and waterlogging became serious menaces in the early part of this century, but they have been fairly well controlled by an extensive drainage system. Chemical fertilizers are used in large amounts and crop yields per acre are high, even though the Nile silt no longer settles on the fields but is deposited back of the barrages. Sufficient food is grown to feed the present population of 27 million. From the standpoint of crop yields per acre, although not per man, Egypt is a developed country.

The average annual flow of the Nile is 72 million acre-feet, but it is occasionally as high as 105 million acre-feet or as low as 36 million. If all the average flow could be utilized, it would be enough to irrigate 12 to 15 million acres on a year-round basis. At present the area of irrigated land in Egypt is less than half that. During the flood season much of the water flows to the sea unused, and during the rest of the year a shortage of surface and underground water limits the size of the cultivated area.

Now the construction of the Aswan High Dam promises to bring the river under complete control. The dam will have a storage capacity of 105 million acre-feet, equal to the highest annual flow during the past century. There will no longer be a Nile flood; the tamed river will become simply a huge feeder canal for irrigation. With the average of 55 million acre-feet per year available to Egypt (17 million acre-feet from the reservoir is allocated to the Sudan), it will be possible to increase the cultivated area in the delta and the valley floor by 2.2 million acres, or nearly 40 per cent, and to convert .7 million acres from flood to perennial irrigation. Hydroelectric power generation of more than a million kilowatts will make power available for pump drainage, which may increase crop production by 20 per cent, and for the manufacture of chemical fertilizers. The electric power will also be used to lift water to the desert margins of the valley, where it is

hoped that an additional one to two million acres can be brought under the plow. If all these benefits can be realized, total agricultural production in Egypt can be increased by 90 per cent, enough to feed almost twice the present population and at the same time provide crops for export.

When Alexander the Great pushed his tired armies eastward some 2,300 years ago, they came at last to an old desert civilization on the banks of the mightiest river they had ever seen. The Aryans, who had preceded Alexander by 1,000 years, did not give the river a name; they called it simply the Indus, which was their word for river, and they named the subcontinent they had invaded "India": the land of the river.

The Indus and its five tributaries of the Punjab, together with the flat plain through which they flow, are one of the major natural resources of the earth. In the Punjab and Sind regions of West Pakistan 30 million persons dwell on the plain; 23 million make their living from farming it. They produce most of the food and fiber that feed and clothe nearly 50 million people.

The rivers carry more than twice the flow of the Nile. Half this water is diverted into a highly developed system of irrigation canals and is used to irrigate some 23 million acres—by far the largest single irrigated region on earth. Underneath the northern part of the plain lies a huge reservoir of fresh ground water, equal in volume to 10 times the annual flow of the rivers.

In spite of the great potentialities of the plain, the fact is that poverty and hunger, not well-fed prosperity, are today the common lot of the people of West Pakistan. These afflictions are nowhere more desperately evident than in the farming villages of the countryside. In a country of farmers food must be imported to provide the most meager of diets; the gap between food production and the number of mouths to be fed is widening.

The problem of agriculture in West Pakistan is both a physical and a human one. It is a problem of land, water and people and of the interactions among them. One of its aspects is the waterlogging and salt accumulation in the soil, caused by poor drainage in the vast, nearly flat plain, that are slowly destroying the fertility of much of the irrigated land. The area of canal-irrigated and cultivated land already seriously damaged by waterlogging and salinity is close to five million acres, or about 18 per cent of the gross sown area. Three

other difficulties also beset agriculture: shortage of irrigation water, problems of land tenure and poor farming practices.

Although crops can be grown throughout the year, and both a winter and a summer growing season are traditional, the irrigation canals lose so much water by seepage that the amount carried to the fields is sufficient to irrigate only about half the land during each season. Even so, the crops are inadequately irrigated, particularly in summer. Much of the cropped area receives insufficient water to prevent salt accumulation.

Many of the farmers are sharecropping tenants who have little incentive to increase production. Nearly all of them struggle with small and widely separated plots that multiply the difficulties of efficient use of irrigation water and farm animals and gravely inhibit change in traditional practices.

In West Pakistan we have the wasteful paradox of a great and modern irrigation system pouring its water onto lands cultivated as they were in the Middle Ages. Plowing is done by a wooden plow of ancient design, pulled by undernourished bullocks. Unselected seeds are sown broadcast. Pakistan uses only a hundredth as much fertilizer per acre as Egypt.

Careful investigation shows that in most of the Punjab the problems of waterlogging and salinity could be cured, and at the same time adequate water could be supplied to the crops, by sinking fields of large wells to pump the underground water and spread it on the cultivated lands. Part of the pumped water would be carried off by evaporation and transpiration and part would percolate back into the ground, in the process washing the salt out of the soil.

If the well fields are too small in area, lateral infiltration of underground water from the surrounding land will be large compared with the rate at which the pumped water can evaporate, and the process of dewatering will be retarded or completely inhibited. For this and other reasons each Punjab project area should be about a million acres in size.

Removal of salt and provision of additional water are necessary, but by no means sufficient, measures to raise agriculture in West Pakistan from its desperate poverty. Equally essential are chemical fertilizers, higher-yielding seeds, pest control, credit and marketing facilities, and above all incentives and knowledge to adopt better farming practices. The job cannot be done all at once; it is necessary to concentrate on project areas of manageable size. Initial capital costs for a million-acre project in the Punjab would be of the order of $55 million, including costs of wells and electrification, nitrogen-fertilizer plants, pest-control facilities and filling of administrative, educational and research pipelines.

In the Sind region initial capital costs would be considerably higher, probably between $130 million and $165 million per million acres. That is largely because the underground water in most of the Sind is too salty to be used for irrigation, and drainage is therefore a more difficult matter than in the Punjab.

After a few years the minimum net increase in crop value in each million-acre project in the Punjab could be $55 million to $60 million a year, equal to the capital costs and to twice the present gross production, excluding livestock. In the Sind the net increase, including livestock, could probably be at least equal to the present output.

The same interrelated problems of water, land and people that afflict the Indus plain also exist in the valley of the Tigris-Euphrates, but on a much smaller scale. Salty soil is found over large areas; because of waterlogging it is possible to cultivate only about a third of the seven million acres of irrigated land each year. The remainder is left fallow and unirrigated to dry out the subsoil and to build up a little soil nitrogen. Great damage was done long ago when the ancient canal systems were destroyed and the land was depopulated by waves of nomadic invaders. But the nomads merely hastened the salt accumulation and waterlogging that were the seeds of destruction. These had begun centuries earlier as a result of inadequate drainage and inability to control floods.

If the flow of the Tigris-Euphrates could be fully utilized, through combined development of surface and ground water, and if the soils were adequately leached and drained, the irrigated area cultivated each year could be increased to 10 to 12 million acres. If greater water usage were combined with perennial cropping, better farming practices and the application of chemical fertilizers, total agricultural production could be raised at least fivefold.

The largest opportunities for expansion of the area of irrigated arid and semiarid lands exist in the U.S.S.R. Between 1950 and 1960, 15 million acres in the neighborhood of the Black and Caspian seas were provided with irrigation water from the Volga, Dnieper, Amu Darya and Syr Darya rivers. The total flow of these rivers is more than 300 million acre-feet, sufficient, under the cold-winter and warm-summer cli-

mate of the steppes, to supply all the water needed to irrigate 70 to 100 million acres.

Because of the relatively advanced economic level of the country, large multipurpose water developments in the U.S.S.R. are economically feasible, and a high percentage of the capital invested goes for power, transportation, industrial water supplies and flood control.

Soviet engineers have outlined a plan to build an immense dam on the Ob River, creating an inland sea five-sixths the size of Italy, and to dig a canal connecting the Yenisei with the Ob above the dam [see illustration on page 62]. The impounded waters would be transported through a giant system of canals, rivers and lakes to the Aral Sea and thence by canal to the Caspian Sea. Several hundred million acre-feet of water that now goes to waste each year in the Arctic Ocean would be conserved. This water would be used to irrigate 50 million acres of crop lands and a somewhat larger area of pasture in arid western Siberia and Kazakhstan. Accompanying hydroelectric power installations would have a capacity of more than 70 million kilowatts. Major storage, irrigation and hydroelectric works are also under construction or planned in the northern Caucasus and in the Azerbaijan, Georgian and Armenian Soviet Socialist republics. These will bring additional tens of millions of acres under irrigation.

In some parts of the arid zone both surface and ground water are so scarce that it is difficult to see how irrigation agriculture can be developed to support the rapidly expanding population. In the Maghreb countries of North Africa—Tunisia, Algeria and Morocco—there is probably not enough water in the region north of the Sahara to irrigate more than 3.5 million acres of land, yet the combined population of these three countries is already 26 million (equal to Egypt's) and will double in 20 to 25 years. Elaborate systems of dry farming have been developed in the Maghreb; for example, the planting of olive trees far apart in light, sandy soils that catch and hold the nighttime dew. With this technique it has been possible to grow olive and other fruit trees on more than a million acres in Tunisia. In the long run it may be necessary to employ most of the available water in the Maghreb countries for industrial purposes, because these can provide a tenfold to hundredfold higher marginal value for water than agriculture can.

A new possibility for water development has recently been opened, how-

ever. During the past few years evidence has been obtained that large areas in the Sahara may be underlain by an enormous lake of fresh water. In some places the water-bearing sands are 3,000 feet thick, and they appear to extend for at least 500 miles south of the Atlas Mountains and perhaps eastward into Tunisia and Libya. If this evidence is correct, the amount of useful water may be very large indeed—of the order of 100 billion acre-feet, sufficient to irrigate many millions of acres for centuries.

In general the possibilities of expanding the area of irrigated land in the arid zone outside the U.S.S.R. are not large when measured in numbers of acres. But crop yields under irrigation in the arid lands are high and assured if all the factors of agricultural production are properly applied. In fact, irrigation agriculture in arid regions can be successful only if it is intensive and high-yielding; it is costly to construct and maintain drainage systems that will keep the water table from rising too close to the surface, and to provide enough water on each acre to leach the salts out of the soil. In hot, arid lands some kinds of irrigation agriculture can be so productive that very expensive irrigation water, such as could be produced by sea-water desalination, may soon become economical.

Much greater possibilities (and also greater difficulties) exist for agricultural expansion in the regions of savanna climate, which are characterized by an annual cycle of heavy rainfall during one season, followed by drought the remainder of the year, and by warm weather at all seasons. In Africa, for example, many millions of what are now barren acres could be brought under irrigated cultivation, provided that interested farmers could be found, in the neighborhood of the great bend of the Niger River in former French West Africa, in the basin of the Rufiji River of Tanganyika and near Lake Kyoga in Uganda. Similarly, in the area extending from India east through Burma, Thailand and Vietnam to the northern Philippines, air temperature and solar radiation are suitable for year-round crop growth, and water and land are the limiting factors [see "The Mekong River Plan," by G. F. White; SCIENTIFIC AMERICAN, April 1963].

In the lower basin of the Ganges and Brahmaputra rivers, comprising East Pakistan and the Indian states of Bengal, Bihar and Assam, some 140 million people live on 70 million cultivated acres. The basic resources of soil and water are grossly underutilized in this land of ancient civilization, extreme present poverty and strong population pressure. Each year the rivers carry about a billion acre-feet to the Bay of Bengal, and in the process they flood most of the countryside. Yet only one crop is grown a year. The land is left idle half the year because of the shortage of water and there is a lack of useful occupation for the people six to eight months of the year. Agricultural practices are adjusted to the rhythm of the monsoon.

The opportunities for increasing production are enormous in this region of land shortage and overabundant water. Through surface and underground storage of a portion of the flood waters, water could be provided for three crops each year over more than half of the cultivable area in the alluvial plain, and a considerable additional area could receive sufficient water for two crops. An assured year-round water supply would also provide favorable conditions for intensive use of fertilizers, higher-yielding plant varieties and better farming practices, which could result in a tripling of yields per crop and per acre for cereals, pulses (the edible seeds of leguminous plants such as peas and beans) and oilseeds.

A well-fed livestock industry could be developed in addition to improvements in field crops, and a balanced diet, instead of the present completely inadequate one, could be provided for twice the present population. Expansion of agricultural production here, based on irrigation, would raise few basic problems of land and settlement, but it would require a reorientation of thinking regarding patterns of land and water use. Because of the enormous volumes of water involved and the flatness of the alluvial basin, the cost of water storage and distribution and of flood control and drainage would be high, but the returns through increased farm and livestock production could be several times higher than the cost. The yields per worker must also be increased, however, and a large degree of industrialization accomplished if the project is to finance itself.

Development of water resources is not an end in itself. The investment can be justified only if it leads to higher agricultural or industrial production, or in other ways to an increase of human well-being. To gain these objectives water development must be accompanied by other actions needed to use the water effectively. This is well illustrated in agriculture. One of the basic principles of agricultural science is the principle of interaction: the concurrent use of all the factors of production on the same parcel of land, which will give a much larger harvest than if these factors are used separately on different parcels. Adequate water and water at the right time are essential if seeds of a particular crop variety planted in a given soil are to yield a good crop. But a much larger crop is possible if seeds of a higher-yield variety are planted. This potential increase in the harvest will be realized, however, only if the soil contains sufficient plant nutrients. Usually nitrogen fertilizers and phosphate fertilizers must be added in large amounts to provide the maximum yield. Increased soil fertility will be drained off by weeds unless these are rigorously controlled, and an eager host of insect pests and plant diseases will fight to share the crop with the farmer unless he can combat them with pest-control measures. Improved seed varieties planted without adequate water, abundant fertilizer and rigorous pest control may not do even as well as the traditionally planted varieties. The potentialities for double- or triple-cropping in a perennial irrigation system cannot be achieved if the farmers do not have tractors and efficient tools to enable them to prepare their fields in the short interval between harvest and planting.

To meet the cost of new irrigation systems the farmer must produce much more per acre-foot of water than he has in the past, and this can be done only if all the factors of production are made available to him and if he is taught how to use them effectively. The human, educational, social and institutional problems of bringing the necessary knowledge to millions of farmers are immense. The task of remaking methods of production that are intimately tied to ways of living and of overcoming institutional and political resistance to change is more difficult than any of the engineering problems. Illiteracy, malnutrition and disease; poverty so harsh that the farmer does not dare risk innovation because failure will mean starvation; small and fragmented farm holdings; land-rental and taxation systems that destroy incentive; extreme difficulties in obtaining a farm loan promptly at a reasonable interest rate; poor marketing and storage systems; administrative inefficiency and corruption; the shortage of trained teachers and farm advisers; inadequate government services for agricultural research, education and extension and for control of water-borne diseases—all must be overcome if investments in water resources in the developing countries are to produce really beneficial results.

7

Lateritic Soils

MARY McNEIL
November 1964

In the year 1860 a French naturalist named Henri Mouhot, struggling through the jungles of Indochina in search of plant species, came on a clearing in the tangled wilderness about 150 miles north of Pnompenh, the present capital of Cambodia. Looking up at the sky, he was astonished to see, standing out above the treetops, the sculptured towers of an ancient temple. It proved to be one of the remains of a "lost" civilization that had ruled the area from the ninth to the 16th century. Near the temple was a great walled city, Angkor Thom, with other superb edifices. The wooden parts of these structures had long since rotted away, but the walls, floors, stairs, towers and works of sculpture still stood virtually untouched by time. They were built of sandstone and the extraordinarily durable material known as laterite.

Laterite is a mineral-rich earth that, when exposed to air, turns into a brick-like form of rock (its name comes from the Latin word for brick). It has been an important building material since prehistoric times. Ancient roads were constructed of laterite, and it is still used for highways in parts of southeast Asia and Africa. In modern Thailand many public buildings are built at least in part of laterite. And many communities in India and Africa still rely on laterite, as early man did, as a source of iron.

Paradoxically this interesting and useful material may have been one of the principal reasons for the disappearance of the Khmer civilization that built the city of Angkor Thom. Laterites and lateritic soils are disastrous handicaps to agriculture. Today they are known to be major obstacles to the development of many of the underdeveloped countries. Because of laterite, attempts to grow more food in the Tropics may turn much of that region of the earth into wasteland. Laterite is a grave danger to projects such as the flood-control program for the Mekong Valley of southeast Asia [see "The Mekong River Plan," by Gilbert F. White; SCIENTIFIC AMERICAN, April, 1963]. Unless the laterite problem is dealt with, flood control might actually reduce, instead of improve, the food productivity of such areas.

Let us look more closely at this material. It has been a subject of much controversy among geologists and soil scientists. The two groups define laterite somewhat differently. The geologist thinks of laterites primarily as rock or earth aggregates with a high content of iron, aluminum, nickel or manganese. The soil scientist is concerned with the minerals as components of the soil, particularly with the way their role in the soil is affected by weathering and leaching. This article will discuss mainly the "laterization" of soil.

A lateritic soil is rich in iron and aluminum, low in silica and chemically acidic. It is usually red or yellow—a reflection of its high iron and/or aluminum content. Laterized soils occur most commonly in the tropical belt between the latitudes of 30 degrees North and 30 degrees South. High temperature and heavy rainfall, at least during part of the year, are basic causes of laterization.

The nature of a lateritic soil can be seen in its profile, or cross section. All soils consist of distinct layers, and soil scientists generally describe them in terms of three main "horizons," labeled *A*, *B* and *C*. In ordinary soils the top layer, horizon *A*, usually contains considerable amounts of organic material, silica, bases and undecomposed minerals; horizon *B* holds an accumulation of material that has leached down from *A*, and horizon *C* is composed of transitional parent rock that is in the process of breaking down into soil through physical and chemical weathering. Lateritic soil shows a radically different picture [*see bottom illustration on page 69*]. Most of the organic material has been broken down and leached out of horizon *A;* the silica and bases also are leached away, and the layer is largely depleted of potassium, calcium, phosphorus and other elements required by plants. The result is that the *A* horizon is composed in large part of oxides of iron, aluminum and other minerals. Below this, the *B* horizon is often either thin or completely missing, and the *C* horizon also may have failed to develop. The soil is so porous that most of the decomposed material has been washed away.

Laterization is a function of the soil climate, which in turn is closely related to the atmospheric climate. The thorough leaching of the soil is primarily due to heavy rainfall, but other tropical conditions play their part. The dampness and high temperature combine to produce a luxuriant growth of bacteria, insects, earthworms and other organisms that break down the organic material and also aerate the soil. The oxygen of the air, permeating this porous soil, oxidizes its iron and aluminum. (It is fortunate that laterization is almost entirely limited to the high-rainfall Tropics and even there is held in check by protective vegetation; if it were not, the earth's atmosphere would soon be denuded of oxygen. All the oxygen in the atmosphere would be used up if only a small percentage of the ferrous iron estimated to be in the earth's rocks were oxidized to ferric iron.)

As a result of laterization vast areas of the earth's soil have been converted into deposits of bauxite (aluminum ore) and into hematite and limonite ores of iron. At the same time laterization has also operated to reduce the high-rainfall tropical regions to near-desert conditions from the standpoint of the agricultural quality of their soil. At first thought this generalization may seem unbelievable. Are not the lush jungles, rain forests and savannas of the Tropics plain signs of the fertility of their soil? Actually this lushness is deceptive; it is created only by the abundance of moisture and belies an essential poverty of the soil. Even soil scientists have not found it easy to accept this conclusion, but there is now abundant proof of it. That the tropical forests and grass-

lands cover some of the earth's most inhospitable and unproductive soils has been demonstrated by attempts to wrest cultivated crops from them. Put to the plow, these lands yield an amazingly small return and soon become completely infertile, as we shall see. Indeed, once a lateritic field has been laid bare to the air, it may even harden into stony laterite such as the brick of the temples of Angkor Thom.

Soil laterization has been taking place at the earth's surface since the Paleozoic era at least, and probably throughout geologic time. In the Amazon basin of Brazil there are accumulations of lateritic soil 70 feet thick. Deposits such as these are truly fossil soils that provide a record of the soil's various stages of evolution and of the changes in climate, vegetation, topography and geologic processes that took place during their history. In the Brazilian profile we can see all the phases of development of laterite, from its origin as a soil from the parent rock to its final transformation into the vast deposits of bauxite, manganese, iron and new rock that now cover about 1,000 square miles of the basin.

Laterite deposits have been found as far north as Ireland, indicating that it once had a more tropical climate. In many areas of the world—South America, Central America, Africa, Australia, India, southeast Asia—the strata of exposed hillsides show layers of laterite capping various types of underlying rock (igneous, metamorphic and sedimentary). In most cases it looks as if the lateritic soil or laterite once covered a great plain or basin and sections of the deposit were later raised by uplifts of the earth's surface that formed hills and plateaus.

Whatever the details of its history may be, it is clear that the laterization of the soil throughout the tropical belt is still taking place and that the intervention of man now threatens to accelerate the process on a large scale. The ambitious plans to increase food production in the Tropics to meet the pressure of the rapid rise in population have given too little consideration to the laterization problem and the measures that will have to be undertaken to overcome it.

In the past nature has provided a measure of control over the process by virtue of forest and jungle growth,

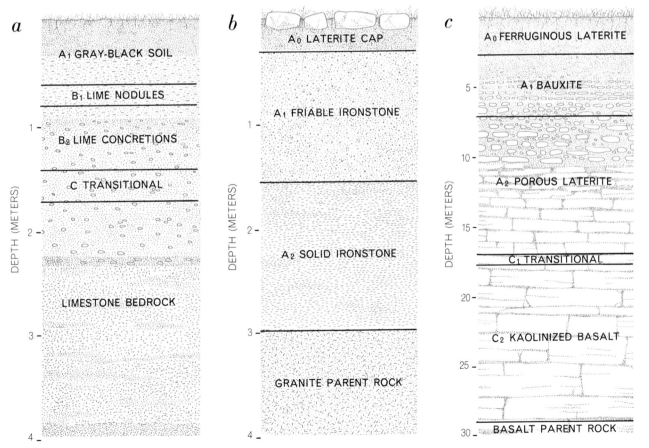

SOIL PROFILES contrast a typical Temperate Zone soil (a), as found in northern India, with lateritic soils as found in Dahomey, West Africa (b), and in southern India (c). Letters at left identify the principal soil horizons, or layers, as usually classified by soil experts. Temperate Zone soils normally have organic material in horizon A; in lateritic soils that material has been leached away.

which tends to insulate the soil from the eroding effects of the tropical climate and thereby slows down the soil's degeneration. Some of the development plans in underdeveloped areas now call for removing that protective cover to clear the land for agriculture. A recent venture in Brazil vividly illustrates the possible results.

At Iata, an equatorial wonderland in the heart of the Amazon basin, the Brazilian government set up an agricultural colony. Earthmoving machinery wrenched a clearing from the forest and

crops were planted. From the beginning there were ominous signs of the presence of laterite. Blocks of ironstone stood out on the surface in some places; in others nodules of the laterite lay just below a thin layer of soil. What had appeared to be a rich soil, with a promising cover of humus, disintegrated after the first or second planting. Under the equatorial sun the iron-rich soil began to bake into brick. In less than five years the cleared fields became virtually pavements of rock. Today Iata is a drab, despairing colony that testifies eloquent-

ly to the formidable problem laterite presents throughout the Tropics.

The small country of Dahomey, adjoining Nigeria in tropical West Africa, had a similar experience on a wholesale scale. There the replacement of forests by plantations resulted in deep leaching of the soil and converted large areas into brick in about 60 years. In an equatorial rain forest there is little growth of vegetation on the dark forest floor, and humus fails to accumulate in the soil. Small clearings in such a forest for the "milpa" type of farming, com-

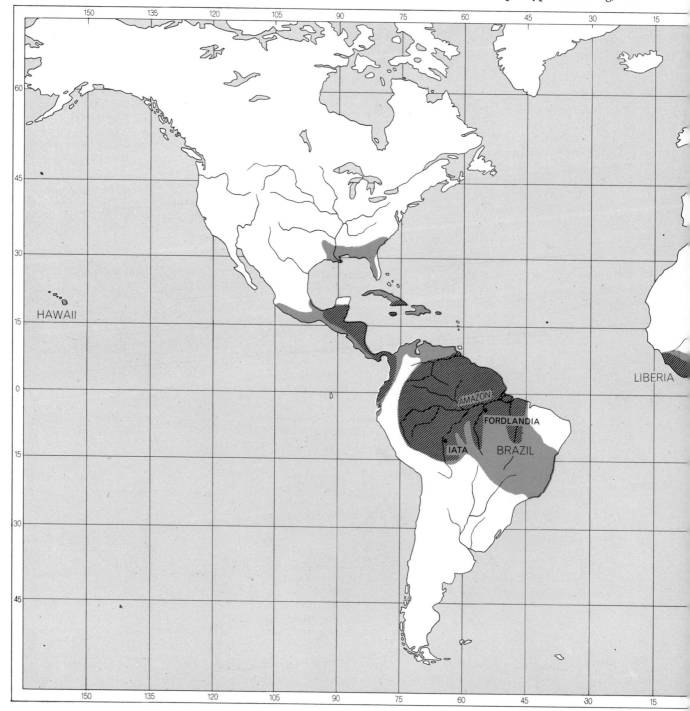

EXTENT OF LATERIZATION is indicated by the colored areas on this map. Laterization is mostly confined to tropical and sub-

tropical regions. Rain forests, shown by hatching, deter hardening of laterite by insulating the soil somewhat from the effects of tropi-

mon among forest people all over the world, will exhaust the soil within a year or two. After the clearing is abandoned a jungle-type growth of shrubs, vines and low trees may take over. This happens, however, only where the clearings are comparatively small. Large areas that have been cleared for plantation cultivation are often permanently lost to agriculture after a few crop cycles have worn out the soil.

Going back further in history one can see how important a part laterite must have played in the economies of ancient civilizations in the Tropics. The Khmer civilization in Cambodia may well have perished primarily because of the poverty of the lateritic soil. In Central America the Mayas, contemporaries of the Khmers, who depended greatly on the milpa system of agriculture, were forced to abandon their cities and move north into Mexico; perhaps the reason was the low productivity of the lateritic soil in their old kingdom.

In more modern times the British, French and Dutch colonial empires managed to maintain plantation economies in the Tropics by careful attention to the needs of the soil on an empirical basis. From experience their colonial experts learned to provide the necessary fertilizers, to rotate crops and to move the plantations to new sites every few years. Unfortunately, when they gave up their colonies, the experts went home and the newly independent nations were left with few trained people who knew how to deal with the soil. Cuba is a classic example of the necessity for careful and knowledgeable

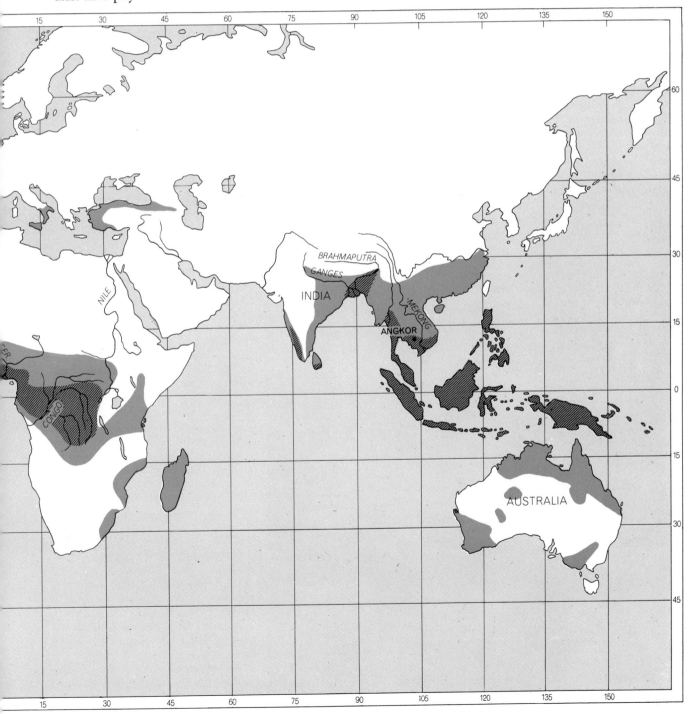

cal climate. Removal of forests, as in efforts to expand agricultural production, tends to quicken laterization, which in turn impairs

agriculture. Such an evolution has occurred at Iata in Brazil, where the government undertook to establish an agricultural colony.

soil management. Long dependent on its great sugar plantations, the island must contend with a lateritic soil of essentially low fertility that will not produce much more than two successive stands of cane on a given tract. The yields of its plantations will steadily decline unless it finds ways to conserve the island's soil.

The advanced nations now concerned with helping the underdeveloped nations of the Tropics must give serious thought to the laterite problem. If Peace Corps workers attempt to apply the agricultural methods of the U.S. corn belt to Nigeria, or Soviet agriculturists transport the methods of the Ukraine to Cuba, they may well precipitate disaster. Deep plowing of the lateritic soil would probably accelerate leaching and strip the soil of all productivity in short order. The opening up of vast tracts to cultivation, in order to make efficient use of tractors and other modern farming machinery, might lead quickly to the baking of these large expanses into brick by exposing the soil to the action of the sun and wind. And the large river-valley plans now projected for many acres—the Mekong River system of southeast Asia, the Amazon basin of Brazil, the Ganges and Brahmaputra valleys of India, the Niger River of Nigeria, the Volta River of Ghana—might lead to devastation of a more subtle kind.

The Mekong Valley has managed, in spite of conditions strongly favoring laterization of the soil, to sustain a productive agriculture: it is part of Asia's famous "rice bowl." The situation must be credited to an act of God, however, rather than to man's efforts. Each year the growing of crops depletes the highly leached soil of this rainy valley. But then in the monsoon season the overflowing rivers of the system flood the land and replenish it with a new layer of silt. Thus nature continues to renew the soil year after year and keep it reasonably fertile. The designers of the Mekong River Plan must now consider what will happen when they stop the annual floods. Plainly they will have to find a substitute for nature's annual replenishment of the soil. The same is true of most of the other tropical river-control projects, in India, Africa, South America and elsewhere.

Nigeria is a particularly good example of the kind of challenge laterite presents. Northern Nigeria, the most densely populated part of the country, is a high plateau; many geologists believe it is a remnant of an uplifted plain that

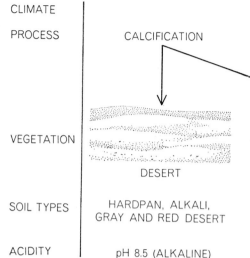

CLIMATE

PROCESS   CALCIFICATION

VEGETATION

DESERT

SOIL TYPES   HARDPAN, ALKALI,
                GRAY AND RED DESERT

ACIDITY   pH 8.5 (ALKALINE)

SPECTRUM OF SOILS ranges from dry to wet and alkaline to acidic. The method of formation is indicated by the arrows; the

covered most of Africa in Tertiary or early Quaternary times. Much of the Nigerian plateau now contains a cap of laterite, which is covered with a thin veneer of soil in some places and shows outcrops of ironstone in others. Only in the valleys of streams and other eroded beds are there deposits of soil sufficiently fertile to support intensive agriculture. The southern part of Nigeria likewise does not look very promising for the large-scale growing of crops. That area consists mainly of a tropical rain forest that could not be turned into agricultural land without destroying its productivity.

Yet Nigeria will have to depend basically on agricultural exports to raise the capital for the development of industry and a better standard of living. Its main hope seems to lie in control of the Niger River and its delta in such a way that a bed of alluvium will be built up. With careful management and the addition of necessary minerals, the reclaimed land could become a fertile agricultural bowl.

Ghana is even more handicapped agriculturally than Nigeria. Thousands of square miles of its area are covered with an almost continuous sheet of laterite, much of it in the form of bauxite. Like Nigeria, Ghana has a large river, the Volta, which by careful management might produce an arable basin for the growing of food.

Aside from efforts to develop a more arable soil, the tropical forests themselves could be exploited more effectively than they have been, in Africa and elsewhere. Several countries have shown that cacao trees (which yield co-

LATERITE CONSTRUCTION appears in the temple of Angkor Wat near Angkor Thom, a major city of the ancient Khmer civilization in what is now Cambodia. Laterite on exposure to air turns into a bricklike form of rock still widely used for construction.

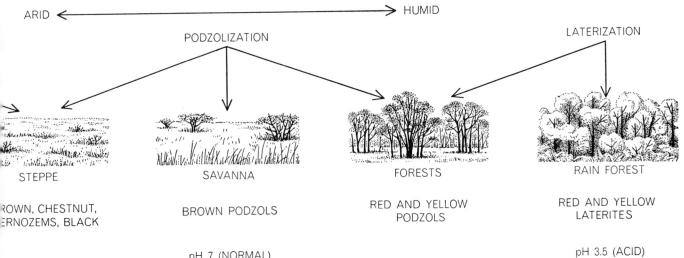

ARID ⟷ HUMID

PODZOLIZATION   LATERIZATION

STEPPE   SAVANNA   FORESTS   RAIN FOREST

BROWN, CHESTNUT, ERNOZEMS, BLACK   BROWN PODZOLS   RED AND YELLOW PODZOLS   RED AND YELLOW LATERITES

pH 7 (NORMAL)   pH 3.5 (ACID)

characteristic soil of steppes, for example, is produced through a combination of calcification, which is an accumulation of hardened carbonates, and podzolization, which is a leaching of the upper layers. Lateritic soils usually lack a hardened layer of accumulated carbonates. Weathering under certain conditions of soil climate, which are found in the Tropics, produces lateritic soil.

coa and chocolate) can be a most profitable crop; the planting of teak in the monsoon forests of Asia has been extraordinarily successful; Fordlandia in Brazil and the Firestone Rubber Company in Liberia are now carrying on experiments on the possibility of developing profitable rubber-tree plantations in the equatorial forests. It has also been urged that the savannas of the Tropics, whose lateritic soils would quickly deteriorate if plowed up for cash crops, could be turned by careful management and fertilization into large ranches and pastures for meat animals.

Laterites are not, of course, an unmitigated evil. In the form of bauxite and other economically exploitable metal ores they are a valuable natural resource. In a world that is increasingly concerned about the problem of feeding the multiplying human population, however, it is time to give intensive consideration to how to prevent the laterization of the soil from becoming a major liability.

A generation ago an American geologist, T. H. Holland, remarked that "laterization might be added to the long list of tropical diseases from which not even the rocks are safe." It is no longer a disease of minor proportions. Nor will this disease be easy to cure. The campaign against it will have to include the mapping of the world's laterized areas, research and experiments in the reclamation of lateritic soils and application of the knowledge that is already available, with the United Nations taking the lead in extending this information and help to the tropical countries. There is no single, simple formula for handling the problem of lateritic soil; each situation has to be studied and treated with an individual prescription. The encouraging fact is that the strategy and technology of agriculture have attained a high level of capability in dealing with difficult problems. What can be accomplished in one such area—where the problem is aridity rather than lateritic soil—is beautifully demonstrated by the flowering of the Negev desert in Israel.

8

Human Food Production as a Process in the Biosphere

LESTER R. BROWN
September 1970

Throughout most of man's existence his numbers have been limited by the supply of food. For the first two million years or so he lived as a predator, a herbivore and a scavenger. Under such circumstances the biosphere could not support a human population of more than 10 million, a population smaller than that of London or Afghanistan today. Then, with his domestication of plants and animals some 10,000 years ago, man began to shape the biosphere to his own ends.

As primitive techniques of crop production and animal husbandry became more efficient the earth's food-producing capacity expanded, permitting increases in man's numbers. Population growth in turn exerted pressure on food supply, compelling man to further alter the biosphere in order to meet his food needs. Population growth and advances in food production have thus tended to be mutually reinforcing.

It took two million years for the human population to reach the one-billion mark, but the fourth billion now being added will require only 15 years: from 1960 to 1975. The enormous increase in the demand for food that is generated by this expansion in man's numbers, together with rising incomes, is beginning to have disturbing consequences. New signs of stress on the biosphere are reported almost daily. The continuing expansion of land under the plow and the evolution of a chemically oriented modern agriculture are producing ominous alterations in the biosphere not just on a local scale but, for the first time in history, on a global scale as well. The natural cycles of energy and the chemical elements are clearly being affected by man's efforts to expand his food supply.

Given the steadily advancing demand for food, further intervention in the biosphere for the expansion of the food supply is inevitable. Such intervention, however, can no longer be undertaken by an individual or a nation without consideration of the impact on the biosphere as a whole. The decision by a government to dam a river, by a farmer to use DDT on his crops or by a married couple to have another child, thereby increasing the demand for food, has repercussions for all mankind.

The revolutionary change in man's role from hunter and gatherer to tiller and herdsman took place in circumstances that are not well known, but some of the earliest evidence of agriculture is found in the hills and grassy plains of the Fer-

tile Crescent in western Asia. The cultivation of food plants and the domestication of animals were aided there by the presence of wild wheat, barley, sheep, goats, pigs, cattle and horses. From the beginnings of agriculture man naturally favored above all other species those plants and animals that had been most useful to him in the wild. As a result of this favoritism he has altered the composition of the earth's plant and animal populations. Today his crops, replacing the original cover of grass or forest, occupy some three billion acres. This amounts to about 10 percent of the earth's total land surface and a considerably larger fraction of the land capable of supporting vegetation, that is, the area excluding deserts, polar regions and higher elevations. Two-thirds of the cultivated cropland is planted to cereals. The area planted to wheat alone is 600 million acres—nearly a million square miles, or an area equivalent to the U.S. east of the Mississippi. As for the influence of animal husbandry on the earth's animal populations, Hereford and Black Angus cattle roam the Great Plains, once the home of an estimated 30 to 40 million buffalo; in Australia the kangaroo has given way to European cattle; in Asia the domesticated water buffalo has multiplied in the major river valleys.

Clearly the food-producing enterprise has altered not only the relative abundance of plant and animal species but also their global distribution. The linkage of the Old and the New World in the 15th century set in motion an exchange of crops among various parts of the world that continues today. This exchange greatly increased the earth's capacity to sustain human populations, partly because some of the crops trans-

EXPERIMENTAL FARM in Brazil, one of thousands around the world where improvements in agricultural technology are pioneered, is seen as an image on an infrared-sensitive film in the aerial photograph on the opposite page. The reflectance of vegetation at near-infrared wavelengths of .7 to .9 micron registers on the film in false shades of red that are proportional to the intensity of the energy. The most reflective, and reddest, areas (*bottom*) are land still uncleared of forest cover. Most of the tilled fields, although irregular in shape, are contour-plowed. Regular patterns (*left and bottom right*) are citrus-orchard rows. The photograph was taken by a National Aeronautics and Space Administration mission in cooperation with the Brazilian government in a joint study of the assessment of agricultural resources by remote sensing. The farm is some 80 miles northwest of São Paulo.

ported elsewhere turned out to be better suited there than to their area of origin. Perhaps the classic example is the introduction of the potato from South America into northern Europe, where it greatly augmented the food supply, permitting marked increases in population. This was most clearly apparent in Ireland, where the population increased rapidly for several decades on the strength of the food supply represented by the potato. Only when the potato-blight organism (*Phytophthora infestans*) devastated the potato crop was population growth checked in Ireland.

The soybean, now the leading source of vegetable oil and principal farm export of the U.S., was introduced from China several decades ago. Grain sorghum, the second-ranking feed grain in the U.S. (after corn), came from Africa as a food store in the early slave ships. In the U.S.S.R. today the principal source of vegetable oil is the sunflower, a plant that originated on the southern Great Plains of the U.S. Corn, unknown in the Old World before Columbus, is now grown on every continent. On the other hand, North America is indebted to the Old World for all its livestock and poultry species with the exception of the turkey.

To man's accomplishments in exploiting the plants and animals that natural evolution has provided, and in improving them through selective breeding over the millenniums, he has added in this century the creation of remarkably productive new breeds, thanks to the discoveries of genetics. Genetics has made possible the development of cereals and other plant species that are more tolerant to cold, more resistant to drought, less susceptible to disease, more responsive to fertilizer, higher in yield and richer in protein. The story of hybrid corn is only one of many spectacular examples. The breeding of short-season corn varieties has extended the northern limit of this crop some 500 miles.

Plant breeders recently achieved a historic breakthrough in the development of new high-yielding varieties of wheat and rice for tropical and subtropical regions. These wheats and rices, bred by Rockefeller Foundation and Ford Foundation scientists in Mexico and the Philippines, are distinguished by several characteristics. Most important, they are short-statured and stiff-strawed, and are highly responsive to chemical fertilizer. They also mature earlier. The first of the high-yielding rices, IR-8, matures in 120

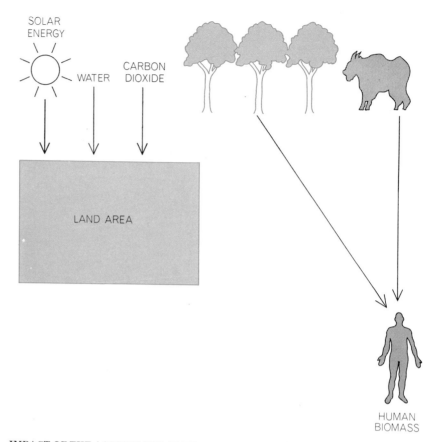

IMPACT OF THE AGRICULTURAL REVOLUTION on the human population is outlined in these two diagrams. The diagram at left shows the state of affairs before the invention of agriculture: the plants and animals supported by photosynthesis on the total land area could support a human population of only about 10 million. The diagram at right shows

days as against 150 to 180 days for other varieties.

Another significant advance incorporated into the new strains is the reduced sensitivity of their seed to photoperiod (length of day). This is partly the result of their cosmopolitan ancestry: they were developed from seed collections all over the world. The biological clocks of traditional varieties of cereals were keyed to specific seasonal cycles, and these cereals could be planted only at a certain time of the year, in the case of rice say at the onset of the monsoon season. The new wheats, which are quite flexible in terms of both seasonal and latitudinal variations in length of day, are now being grown in developing countries as far north as Turkey and as far south as Paraguay.

The combination of earlier maturity and reduced sensitivity to day length creates new opportunities for multiple cropping in tropical and subtropical regions where water supplies are adequate, enabling farmers to harvest two, three and occasionally even four crops per year. Workers at the International Rice Research Institute in the Philippines regularly harvest three crops of rice per

year. Each acre they plant yields six tons annually, roughly three times the average yield of corn, the highest-yielding cereal in the U.S. Thousands of farmers in northern India are now alternating a crop of early-maturing winter wheat with a summer crop of rice, greatly increasing the productivity of their land. These new opportunities for farming land more intensively lessen the pressure for bringing marginal land under cultivation, thus helping to conserve precious topsoil. At the same time they increase the use of agricultural chemicals, creating environmental stresses more akin to those in the advanced countries.

The new dwarf wheats and rices are far more efficient than the traditional varieties in their use of land, water, fertilizer and labor. The new opportunities for multiple cropping permit conversion of far more of the available solar energy into food. The new strains are not the solution to the food problem, but they are removing the threat of massive famine in the short run. They are buying time for the stabilization of population, which is ultimately the only solution to the food crisis. This "green revolution"

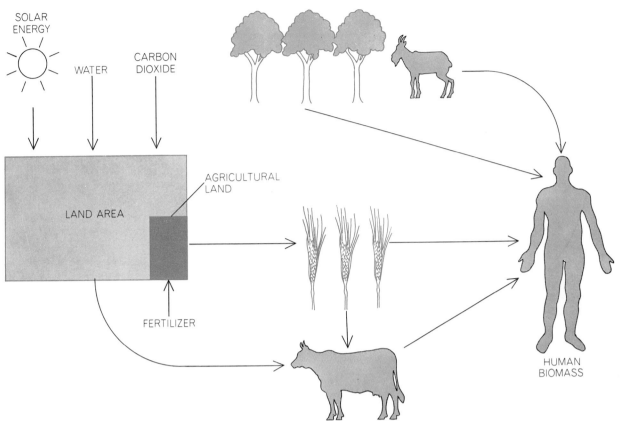

the state of affairs after the invention of agriculture. The 10 percent of the land now under the plow, watered and fertilized by man, is the primary support for a human population of 3.5 billion. Some of the agricultural produce is consumed directly by man; some is consumed indirectly by first being fed to domestic animals. Some of the food for domestic animals, however, comes from land not under the plow (*curved arrow at bottom left*). Man also obtains some food from sources other than agriculture, such as fishing.

may affect the well-being of more people in a shorter period of time than any technological advance in history.

The progress of man's expansion of food production is reflected in the way crop yields have traditionally been calculated. Today the output of cereals is expressed in yield per acre, but in early civilizations it was calculated as a ratio of the grain produced to that required for seed. On this basis the current ratio is perhaps highest in the U.S. corn belt, where farmers realize a four-hundred-fold return on the hybrid corn seed they plant. The ratio for rice is also quite high, but the ratio for wheat, the third of the principal cereals, is much lower, possibly 30 to one on a global basis.

The results of man's efforts to increase the productivity of domestic animals are equally impressive. When the ancestors of our present chickens were domesticated, they laid a clutch of about 15 eggs once a year. Hens in the U.S. today average 220 eggs per year, and the figure is rising steadily as a result of continuing advances in breeding and feeding. When cattle were originally domesticated, they probably did not produce more than 600 pounds of milk per year,

barely enough for a calf. (It is roughly the average amount produced by cows in India today.) The 13 million dairy cows in the U.S. today average 9,000 pounds of milk yearly, outproducing their ancestors 15 to one.

Most such advances in the productivity of plant and animal species are recent. Throughout most of history man's efforts to meet his food needs have been directed primarily toward bringing more land under cultivation, spreading agriculture from valley to valley and continent to continent. He has also, however, invented techniques to raise the productivity of land already under cultivation, particularly in this century, when the decreasing availability of new lands for expansion has compelled him to turn to a more intensive agriculture. These techniques involve altering the biosphere's cycles of energy, water, nitrogen and minerals.

Modern agriculture depends heavily on four technologies: mechanization, irrigation, fertilization and the chemical control of weeds and insects. Each of these technologies has made an important contribution to the earth's in-

creased capacity for sustaining human populations, and each has perturbed the cycles of the biosphere.

At least as early as 3000 B.C. the farmers of the Middle East learned to harness draft animals to help them till the soil. Harnessing animals much stronger than himself enabled man to greatly augment his own limited muscle power. It also enabled him to convert roughage (indigestible by humans) into a usable form of energy and thus to free some of his energy for pursuits other than the quest for food. The invention of the internal-combustion engine and the tractor 5,000 years later provided a much greater breakthrough. It now became possible to substitute petroleum (the product of the photosynthesis of aeons ago) for oats, corn and hay grown as feed for draft animals. The replacement of horses by the tractor not only provided the farmer with several times as much power but also released 70 million acres in the U.S. that had been devoted to raising feed for horses.

In the highly mechanized agriculture of today the expenditure of fossil fuel energy per acre is often substantially greater than the energy yield embodied in the food produced. This deficit in the output is of no immediate consequence, because the system is drawing on energy in the bank. When fossil fuels become scarcer, man will have to turn to some other source of motive energy for agriculture: perhaps nuclear energy or some means, other than photosynthesis, of harnessing solar energy. For the present and for the purposes of agriculture the energy budget of the biosphere is still favorable: the supply of solar energy—both the energy stored in fossil fuels and that taken up daily and converted into food energy by crops—enables an advanced nation to be fed with only 5 percent of the population directly employed in agriculture.

The combination of draft animals and mechanical power has given man an enormous capacity for altering the earth's surface by bringing additional land under the plow (not all of it suited for cultivation). In addition, in the poorer countries his expanding need for fuel has forced him to cut forests far in excess of their ability to renew themselves. The areas largely stripped of forest include mainland China and the subcontinent of India and Pakistan, where much of the population must now use cow dung for fuel. Although statistics are not available, the proportion of mankind using cow dung as fuel to prepare meals may

far exceed the proportion using natural gas. Livestock populations providing draft power, food and fuel tend to increase along with human populations, and in many poor countries the needs of livestock for forage far exceed its self-renewal, gradually denuding the countryside of grass cover.

As population pressure builds, not only is more land brought under the plow but also the land remaining is less suited to cultivation. Once valleys are filled, farmers begin to move up hillsides, creating serious soil-erosion problems. As the natural cover that retards runoff is reduced and soil structure deteriorates, floods and droughts become more severe.

Over most of the earth the thin layer of topsoil producing most of man's food is measured in inches. Denuding the land of its year-round natural cover of grass or forest exposes the thin mantle of life-sustaining soil to rapid erosion by wind and water. Much of the soil ultimately washes into the sea, and some of it is lifted into the atmosphere. Man's actions are causing the topsoil to be removed faster than it is formed. This unstable relationship between man and the land from which he derives his subsistence obviously cannot continue indefinitely.

Robert R. Brooks of Williams College, an economist who spent several years in India, gives a wry description of the process occurring in the state of Rajasthan, where tens of thousands of acres of rural land are being abandoned yearly because of the loss of topsoil: "Overgrazing by goats destroys the desert plants which might otherwise hold the soil in place. Goatherds equipped with sickles attached to 20-foot poles strip the leaves of trees to float downward into the waiting mouths of famished goats and sheep. The trees die and the soil blows away 200 miles to New Delhi, where it comes to rest in the lungs of its inhabitants and on the shiny cars of foreign diplomats."

Soil erosion not only results in a loss of soil but also impairs irrigation systems. This is illustrated in the Mangla irrigation reservoir, recently built in the foothills of the Himalayas in West Pakistan as part of the Indus River irrigation system. On the basis of feasibility studies indicating that the reservoir could be expected to have a lifetime of at least 100 years, $600 million was invested in the construction of the reservoir. Denuding and erosion of the soil in the watershed, however, accompanying a rapid growth of population in the area, has already washed so much soil into the reservoir that it is now expected to be completely filled with silt within 50 years.

A historic example of the effects of man's abuse of the soil is all too plainly visible in North Africa, which once was the fertile granary of the Roman Empire and now is largely a desert or near-desert whose people are fed with the aid of food imports from the U.S. In the U.S. itself the "dust bowl" experience of the 1930's remains a vivid lesson on the folly of overplowing. More recently the U.S.S.R. repeated this error, bringing 100 million acres of virgin soil under the plow only to discover that the region's rainfall was too scanty to sustain continuous cultivation. Once moisture reserves in the soil were depleted the soil began to blow.

Soil erosion is one of the most pressing and most difficult problems threatening the future of the biosphere. Each year it is forcing the abandonment of millions of acres of cropland in Asia, the Middle East, North Africa and Central America. Nature's geological cycle continuously produces topsoil, but its pace is far too slow to be useful to man. Someone once defined soil as rock on its way to the sea. Soil is produced by the weathering of rock and the process takes several centuries to form an inch of topsoil. Man is managing to destroy the topsoil

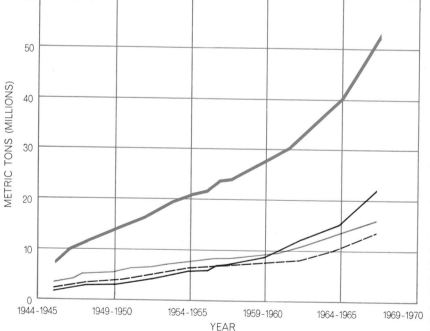

FERTILIZER CONSUMPTION has increased more than fivefold since the end of World War II. The top line in the graph (*color*) shows the tonnage of all kinds of fertilizers combined. The lines below show the tonnages of the three major types: nitrogen (*black*), now the leader, phosphate (*gray*) and potash (*broken line*). Figures, from the most recent report by the UN Food and Agriculture Organization, omit fertilizer consumption in China.

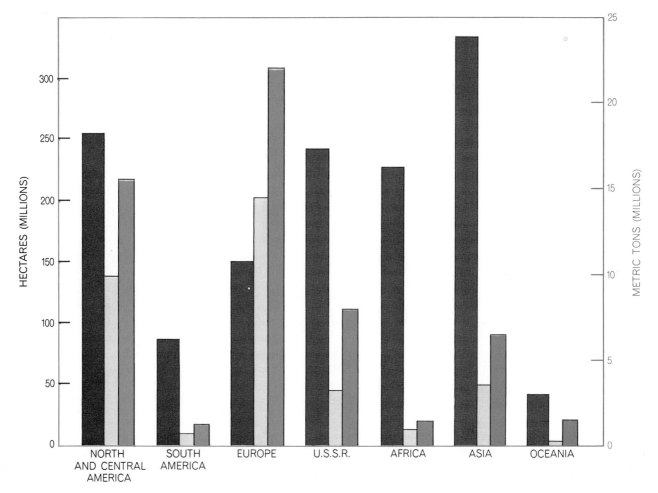

TONS OF FERTILIZER used in seven world areas are compared with the amount of agricultural land in each area. Two tonnages are shown in each instance: the amount used in 1962–1963 (*light color*) and the amount used in 1967–1968 (*solid color*). The great-est use of fertilizer occurs in Europe, the least fertilized area is Africa and the greatest percentage increase in the period was in Australia and New Zealand. Figures, from the Food and Agriculture Organization, omit China, North Korea and North Vietnam.

in some areas of the world in a fraction of this time. The only possible remedy is to find ways to conserve the topsoil more effectively.

The dust-bowl era in the U.S. ended with the widespread adoption of conservation practices by farmers. Twenty million acres were fallowed to accumulate moisture and thousands of miles of windbreaks were planted across the Great Plains. Fallow land was alternated with strips of wheat ("strip-cropping") to reduce the blowing of soil while the land was idle. The densely populated countries of Asia, however, are in no position to adopt such tactics. Their food needs are so pressing that they cannot afford to take large areas out of cultivation; moreover, they do not yet have the financial resources or the technical skills for the immense projects in reforestation, controlled grazing of cattle, terracing, contour farming and systematic management of watersheds that would be required to preserve their soil.

The significance of wind erosion goes far beyond the mere loss of topsoil. As other authors in this issue have observed, a continuing increase in particulate matter in the atmosphere could affect the earth's climate by reducing the amount of incoming solar energy. This particulate matter comes not only from the technological activities of the richer countries but also from wind erosion in the poorer countries. The poorer countries do not have the resources for undertaking the necessary effort to arrest and reverse this trend. Should it be established that an increasing amount of particulate matter in the atmosphere is changing the climate, the richer countries would have still another reason to provide massive capital and technical assistance to the poor countries, joining with them to confront this common threat to mankind.

Irrigation, which agricultural man began to practice at least as early as 6,000 years ago, even earlier than he harnessed animal power, has played its great role in increasing food production by bringing into profitable cultivation vast areas that would otherwise be unusable or only marginally productive. Most of the world's irrigated land is in Asia, where it is devoted primarily to the production of rice. In Africa the Volta River of Ghana and the Nile are dammed for irrigation and power purposes. The Colorado River system of the U.S. is used extensively for irrigation in the Southwest, as are scores of rivers elsewhere. Still to be exploited for irrigation are the Mekong of southeastern Asia and the Amazon.

During the past few years there has been an important new irrigation development in Asia: the widespread installation of small-scale irrigation systems on individual farms. In Pakistan and India, where in many places the water table is close to the surface, hundreds of thousands of tube wells with pumps have been installed in recent years. Interestingly, this development came about partly as an answer to a problem that had been presented by irrigation itself.

Like many of man's other interventions in the biosphere, his reshaping of the hydrologic cycle has had unwanted side effects. One of them is the raising of the water table by the diversion of river water onto the land. Over a period of time the percolation of irrigation water downward and the accumulation of this water underground may gradually raise the water table until it is within a few feet or even a few inches of the surface. This not only inhibits the growth of plant roots by waterlogging but also results in the surface soil's becoming salty as water evaporates through it, leaving a concentrated deposit of salts in the upper few inches. Such a situation developed in West Pakistan after its fertile plain had been irrigated with water from the Indus for a century. During a visit by President Ayub to Washington in 1961 he appealed to President Kennedy for help: West Pakistan was losing 60,-000 acres of fertile cropland per year because of waterlogging and salinity as its population was expanding 2.5 percent yearly.

This same sequence, the diversion of river water into land for irrigation, followed eventually by waterlogging and salinity and the abandonment of land,

had been repeated many times throughout history. The result was invariably the decline, and sometimes the disappearance, of the civilizations thus intervening in the hydrologic cycle. The remains of civilizations buried in the deserts of the Middle East attest to early experiences similar to those of contemporary Pakistan. These civilizations, however, had no one to turn to for foreign aid. An interdisciplinary U.S. team led by Roger Revelle, then Science Adviser to the Secretary of the Interior, studied the problem and proposed among other things a system of tube wells that would lower the water table by tapping the ground water for intensive irrigation. Discharging this water on the surface, the wells would also wash the soil's salt downward. The stratagem worked, and the salty, waterlogged land of Pakistan is steadily being reclaimed.

Other side effects of river irrigation are not so easily remedied. Such irrigation has brought about a great increase in the incidence of schistosomiasis, a disease that is particularly prevalent in the river valleys of Africa and Asia. The disease is produced by the parasitic larva of a blood fluke, which is harbored by aquatic snails and burrows into the flesh

of people standing in water or in water-soaked fields. The Chinese call schistosomiasis "snail fever"; it might also be called the poor man's emphysema, because, like emphysema, this extremely debilitating disease is environmentally induced through conditions created by man. The snails and the fluke thrive in perennial irrigation systems, where they are in close proximity to large human populations. The incidence of the disease is rising rapidly as the world's large rivers are harnessed for irrigation, and today schistosomiasis is estimated to afflict 250 million people. It now surpasses malaria, the incidence of which is declining, as the world's most prevalent infectious disease.

As a necessity for food production water is of course becoming an increasingly crucial commodity. The projected increases in population and in food requirements will call for more and more water, forcing man to consider still more massive and complex interventions in the biosphere. The desalting of seawater for irrigation purposes is only one major departure from traditional practices. Another is a Russian plan to reverse the flow of four rivers currently flowing northward and emptying into the Arctic Ocean. These rivers would be diverted southward into the semiarid lands of southern Russia, greatly enlarging the irrigated area of the U.S.S.R. Some climatologists are concerned, however, that the shutting off of the flow of relatively warm water from these four rivers would have far-reaching implications for not only the climate of the Arctic but also the climatic system of the entire earth.

The growing competition for scarce water supplies among states and among various uses in the western U.S. is also forcing consideration of heroic plans. For example, a detailed engineering proposal exists for the diversion of the Yukon River in Alaska southward across Canada into the western U.S. to meet the growing need for water for both agricultural and industrial purposes. The effort would cost an estimated $100 billion.

Representing an even greater intervention in the biosphere is the prospect that man may one day consciously alter the earth's climatic patterns, shifting some of the rain now falling on the oceans to the land. Among the steps needed for the realization of such a scheme are the construction of a comprehensive model of the earth's climatic system and the development of a computational facility capable of simulating

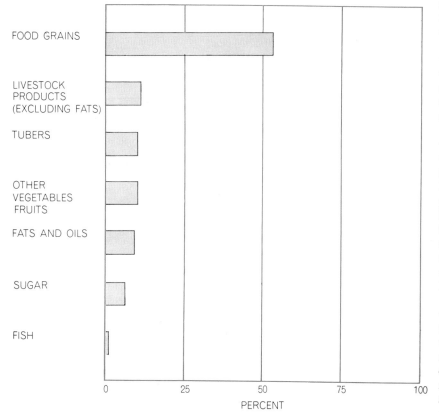

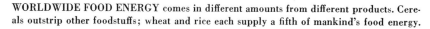

WORLDWIDE FOOD ENERGY comes in different amounts from different products. Cereals outstrip other foodstuffs; wheat and rice each supply a fifth of mankind's food energy.

and manipulating the model. The required information includes data on temperatures, humidity, precipitation, the movement of air masses, ocean currents and many other factors that enter into the weather. Earth-orbiting satellites will doubtless be able to collect much of this information, and the present generation of advanced computers appears to be capable of carrying out the necessary experiments on the model. For the implementation of the findings, that is, for the useful control of rainfall, there will of course be a further requirement: the project will have to be managed by a global and supranational agency if it is not to lead to weather wars among nations working at cross purposes. Some commercial firms are already in the business of rainmaking, and they are operating on an international basis.

The third great technology that man has introduced to increase food production is the use of chemical fertilizers. We owe the foundation for this development to Justus von Liebig of Germany, who early in the 19th century determined the specific requirements of nitrogen, phosphorus, potassium and other nutrients for plant growth. Chemical fertilizers did not come into widespread use, however, until this century, when the pressure of population and the disappearance of new frontiers compelled farmers to substitute fertilizer for the expansion of cropland to meet growing food needs. One of the first countries to intensify its agriculture, largely by the use of fertilizers, was Japan, whose output of food per acre has steadily risen (except for wartime interruptions) since the turn of the century. The output per acre of a few other countries, including the Netherlands, Denmark and Sweden, began to rise at about the same time. The U.S., richly endowed with vast farmlands, did not turn to the heavy use of fertilizer and other intensive measures until about 1940. Since then its yields per acre, assisted by new varieties of grain highly responsive to fertilizer, have also shown remarkable gains. Yields of corn, the production of which exceeds that of all other cereals combined in the U.S., have nearly tripled over the past three decades.

Experience has demonstrated that in areas of high rainfall the application of chemical fertilizers in conjunction with other inputs and practices can double, triple or even quadruple the productivity of intensively farmed soils. Such levels of productivity are achieved in Japan and the Netherlands, where farmers apply up to 300 pounds of plant nutrients per acre per year. The use of chemical fertilizers is estimated to account for at least a fourth of man's total food supply. The world's farmers are currently applying 60 million metric tons of plant nutrients per year, an average of nearly 45 pounds per acre for the three billion acres of cropland. Such application, however, is unevenly distributed. Some poor countries do not yet benefit from the use of fertilizer in any significant amounts. If global projections of population and income growth materialize, the production of fertilizer over the remaining three decades of this century must almost triple to satisfy food demands.

Can the projected demand for fertilizer be met? The key ingredient is nitrogen, and fortunately man has learned how to speed up the fixation phase of the nitrogen cycle [see "The Nitrogen Cycle," by C. C. Delwiche, page 69]. In nature the nitrogen of the air is fixed in the soil by certain microorganisms, such as those present in the root nodules of leguminous plants. Chemists have now devised various ways of incorporating nitrogen from the air into inorganic compounds and making it available in the form of nitrogen fertilizers. These chemical processes produce the fertilizer much more rapidly and economically than the growing of leguminous-plant sources such as clover, alfalfa or soybeans. More than 25 million tons of nitrogen fertilizer is now being synthesized and added to the earth's soil annually.

The other principal ingredients of chemical fertilizer are the minerals potassium and phosphorus. Unlike nitrogen, these elements are not replenished by comparatively fast natural cycles. Potassium presents no immediate problem; the rich potash fields of Canada alone are estimated to contain enough potassium to supply mankind's needs for centuries to come. The reserves of phosphorus, however, are not nearly so plentiful as those of potassium. Every year 3.5 million tons of phosphorus washes into the sea, where it remains as sediment on the ocean floor. Eventually it will be thrust above the ocean surface again by geologic uplift, but man cannot wait that long. Phosphorus may be one of the first necessities that will prompt man to begin to mine the ocean bed.

The great expansion of the use of fertilizers in this century has benefited mankind enormously, but the benefits are not unalloyed. The runoff of chemical fertilizers into rivers, lakes and underground waters creates two important hazards. One is the chemical pollution of drinking water. In certain areas in Illinois and California the nitrate content of well water has risen to a toxic

EXPERIMENTAL PLANTINGS at the International Rice Research Institute in the Philippine Republic are seen in an aerial photograph. IR-8, a high-yield rice, was bred here.

RUINED FARM in the "dust bowl" area of the U.S. in the 1930's is seen in an aerial photograph. The farm is near Union in Terry County, Tex. The wind has eroded the powdery, drought-parched topsoil and formed drifts among the buildings and across the fields.

level. Excessive nitrate can cause the physiological disorder methemoglobinemia, which reduces the blood's oxygen-carrying capacity and can be particularly dangerous to children under five. This hazard is of only local dimensions and can be countered by finding alternative sources of drinking water. A much more extensive hazard, profound in its effects on the biosphere, is the now well-known phenomenon called eutrophication.

Inorganic nitrates and phosphates discharged into lakes and other bodies of fresh water provide a rich medium for the growth of algae; the massive growth of the algae in turn depletes the water of oxygen and thus kills off the fish life. In the end the eutrophication, or overfertilization, of the lake slowly brings about its death as a body of fresh water, converting it into a swamp. Lake Erie is a prime example of this process now under way.

How much of the now widespread eutrophication of fresh waters is attributable to agricultural fertilization and how much to other causes remains an open question. Undoubtedly the runoff of nitrates and phosphates from farmlands plays a large part. There are also other important contributors, however. Considerable amounts of phosphate, coming mainly from detergents, are discharged into rivers and lakes from sewers carrying municipal and industrial wastes. And there is reason to believe that in some rivers and lakes most of the

nitrate may come not from fertilizers but from the internal-combustion engine. It is estimated that in the state of New Jersey, which has heavy automobile traffic, nitrous oxide products of gasoline combustion, picked up and deposited by rainfall, contribute as much as 20 pounds of nitrogen per acre per year to the land. Some of this nitrogen washes into the many rivers and lakes of New Jersey and its adjoining states. A way must be found to deal with the eutrophication problem because even in the short run it can have damaging effects, affecting as it does the supply of potable water, the cycles of aquatic life and consequently man's food supply.

Recent findings have presented us with a related problem in connection with the fourth technology supporting man's present high level of food production: the chemical control of diseases, insects and weeds. It is now clear that the use of DDT and other chlorinated hydrocarbons as pesticides and herbicides is beginning to threaten many species of animal life, possibly including man. DDT today is found in the tissues of animals over a global range of life forms and geography from penguins in Antarctica to children in the villages of Thailand. There is strong evidence that it is actually on the way to extinguishing some animal species, notably predatory birds such as the bald eagle and the peregrine falcon, whose capacity for using calcium is so impaired by DDT that the shells of their eggs are too thin

to avoid breakage in the nest before the fledglings hatch. Carnivores are particularly likely to concentrate DDT in their tissues because they feed on herbivores that have already concentrated it from large quantities of vegetation. Concentrations of DDT in mothers' milk in the U.S. now exceed the tolerance levels established for foodstuffs by the Food and Drug Administration.

It is ironic that less than a generation after 1948, when Paul Hermann Müller of Switzerland received a Nobel prize for the discovery of DDT, the use of the insecticide is being banned by law in many countries. This illustrates how little man knows about the effects of his intervening in the biosphere. Up to now he has been using the biosphere as a laboratory, sometimes with unhappy results.

Several new approaches to the problem of controlling pests are now being explored. Chemists are searching for pesticides that will be degradable, instead of long-lasting, after being deposited on vegetation or in the soil, and that will be aimed at specific pests rather than acting as broad-spectrum poisons for many forms of life. Much hope is placed in techniques of biological control, such as are exemplified in the mass sterilization (by irradiation) of male screwworm flies, a pest of cattle that used to cost U.S. livestock producers $100 million per year. The release of 125 million irradiated male screwworm flies weekly in the U.S. and in adjoining areas of Mexico (in a cooperative effort with the Mexican government) is holding the fly population to a negligible level. Efforts are now under way to get rid of the Mexican fruit fly and the pink cotton bollworm in California by the same method.

Successes are also being achieved in breeding resistance to insect pests in various crops. A strain of wheat has been developed that is resistant to the Hessian fly; resistance to the corn borer and the corn earworm has been bred into strains of corn, and work is in progress on a strain of alfalfa that resists aphids and leafhoppers. Another promising approach, which already has a considerable history, is the development of insect parasites, ranging from bacteria and viruses to wasps that lay their eggs in other insects. The fact remains, however, that the biological control of pests is still in its infancy.

I have here briefly reviewed the major agricultural technologies evolved to meet man's increasing food needs, the problems arising from them and some possible solutions. What is the present balance sheet on the satisfaction of human food needs? Although man's food supply has expanded several hundredfold since the invention of agriculture, two-thirds of mankind is still hungry and malnourished much of the time. On the credit side a third of mankind, living largely in North America, Europe, Australia and Japan, has achieved an adequate food supply, and for the remaining two-thirds the threat of large-scale famine has recently been removed, at least for the immediate future. In spite of rapid population growth in the developing countries since World War II, their peoples have been spared from massive famine (except in Biafra in 1969–1970) by huge exports of food from the developed countries. As a result of two consecutive monsoon failures in India, a fifth of the total U.S. wheat crop was shipped to India in both 1966 and 1967, feeding 60 million Indians for two years.

Although the threat of outright famine has been more or less eliminated for the time being, human nutrition on the global scale is still in a sorry state. Malnutrition, particularly protein deficiency, exacts an enormous toll from the physical and mental development of the young in the poorer countries. This was dramatically illustrated when India held tryouts in 1968 to select a team to represent it in the Olympic games that year. Not a single Indian athlete, male or female, met the minimum standards for qualifying to compete in any of the 36

track and field events in Mexico City. No doubt this was partly due to the lack of support for athletics in India, but poor nutrition was certainly also a large factor. The young people of Japan today are visible examples of what a change can be brought about by improvement in nutrition. Well-nourished from infancy, Japanese teen-agers are on the average some two inches taller than their elders.

Protein is as crucial for children's mental development as for their physical development. This was strikingly shown in a recent study extending over several years in Mexico: children who had been severely undernourished before the age of five were found to average 13 points lower in I.Q. than a carefully selected control group. Unfortunately no amount of feeding or education in later life can repair the setbacks to development caused by undernourishment in the early years. Protein shortages in the poor countries today are depreciating human resources for at least a generation to come.

Protein constitutes the main key to human health and vigor, and the key to the protein diet at present is held by grain consumed either directly or indirectly (in the form of meat, milk and eggs). Cereals, occupying more than 70 percent of the world's cropland, provide 52 percent of man's direct energy intake. Eleven percent is supplied by livestock products such as meat, milk and eggs, 10 percent by potatoes and other tubers, 10 percent by fruits and vegetables, 9 percent by animal fats and vegetable oils, 7 percent by sugar and 1 percent by fish. As in the case of the total quantity of the individual diet, however, the composition of the diet varies greatly around the world. The difference is most marked in the per capita use of grain consumed directly and indirectly.

The two billion people living in the poor countries consume an average of about 360 pounds of grain per year, or about a pound per day. With only one pound per day, nearly all must be consumed directly to meet minimal energy requirements; little remains for feeding to livestock, which may convert only a tenth of their feed intake into meat or other edible human food. The average American, in contrast, consumes more than 1,600 pounds of grain per year. He eats only about 150 pounds of this directly in the form of bread, breakfast cereal and so on; the rest is consumed indirectly in the form of meat, milk and eggs. In short, he enjoys the luxury of the highly inefficient animal conversion

of grain into tastier and somewhat more nutritious proteins.

Thus the average North American currently makes about four times as great a demand on the earth's agricultural ecosystem as someone living in one of the poor countries. As the income levels in these countries rise, so will their demand for a richer diet of animal products. For the increasing world population at the end of the century, which is expected to be twice the 3.5 billion of today, the world production of grain would have to be doubled merely to maintain present consumption levels. This increase, combined with the projected improvement in diet associated with gains in income over the next three decades, could nearly triple the demand for grain, requiring that the food supply increase more over the next three decades than it has in the 10,000 years since agriculture began.

There are ways in which this pressure can be eased somewhat. One is the breeding of higher protein content in grains and other crops, making them nutritionally more acceptable as alternatives to livestock products. Another is the development of vegetable substitutes for animal products, such as are already available in the form of oleomargarine, soybean oil, imitation meats and other replacements (about 65 percent of the whipped toppings and 35 percent of the coffee whiteners now sold in U.S. supermarkets are nondairy products). Pressures on the agricultural ecosystem would thus drive high-income man one step down in the food chain to a level of more efficient consumption of what could be produced by agriculture.

What is clearly needed today is a cooperative effort—more specifically, a world environmental agency—to monitor, investigate and regulate man's interventions in the environment, including those made in his quest for more food. Since many of his efforts to enlarge his food supply have a global impact, they can only be dealt with in the context of a global institution. The health of the biosphere can no longer be separated from our modes of political organization. Whatever measures are taken, there is growing doubt that the agricultural ecosystem will be able to accommodate both the anticipated increase of the human population to seven billion by the end of the century and the universal desire of the world's hungry for a better diet. The central question is no longer "Can we produce enough food?" but "What are the environmental consequences of attempting to do so?"

9

The Food Resources of the Ocean

S. J. HOLT
September 1969

I suppose we shall never know what was man's first use of the ocean. It may have been as a medium of transport or as a source of food. It is certain, however, that from early times up to the present the most important human uses of the ocean have been these same two: shipping and fishing. Today, when so much is being said and written about our new interests in the ocean, it is particularly important to retain our perspective. The annual income to the world's fishermen from marine catches is now roughly $8 billion. The world ocean-freight bill is nearly twice that. In contrast, the wellhead value of oil and gas from the seabed is barely half the value of the fish catch, and all the other ocean mineral production adds little more than another $250 million.

Of course, the present pattern is likely to change, although how rapidly or dramatically we do not know. What is certain is that we shall use the ocean more intensively and in a greater variety of ways. Our greatest need is to use it wisely. This necessarily means that we use it in a regulated way, so that each ocean resource, according to its nature, is efficiently exploited but also conserved. Such regulation must be in large measure of an international kind, particularly insofar as living resources are concerned. This will be so whatever may be the eventual legal regime of the high seas and the underlying bed. The obvious fact about most of the ocean's living resources is their mobility. For the most part they are lively animals, caring nothing about the lines we draw on charts.

The general goal of ecological research, to which marine biology makes an important contribution, is to achieve an understanding of and to turn to our advantage all the biological processes that give our planet its special character. Marine biology is focused on the prob-

lems of biological production, which are closely related to the problems of production in the economic sense. Our most compelling interest is narrower. It lies in ocean life as a renewable resource: primarily of protein-rich foods and food supplements for ourselves and our domestic animals, and secondarily of materials and drugs. I hope to show how in this field science, industry and government need each other now and will do so even more in the future. First, however, let me establish some facts about present fishing industries, the state of the art governing them and the state of the relevant science.

The present ocean harvest is about 55 million metric tons per year. More than 90 percent of this harvest is finfish; the rest consists of whales, crustaceans and mollusks and some other invertebrates. Although significant catches are reported by virtually all coastal countries, three-quarters of the total harvest is taken by only 14 countries, each of which produces more than a million tons annually and some much more. In the century from 1850 to 1950 the world catch increased tenfold—an average rate of about 25 percent per decade. In the next decade it nearly doubled, and this rapid growth is continuing [*see illustration on page 89*]. It is now a commonplace that fish is one of the few major foodstuffs showing an increase in global production that continues to exceed the growth rate of the human population.

This increase has been accompanied

by a changing pattern of use. Although some products of high unit value as luxury foods, such as shellfish, have maintained or even enhanced their relative economic importance, the trend has been for less of the catch to be used directly as human food and for more to be reduced to meal for animal feed. Just before World War II less than 10 percent of the world catch was turned into meal; by 1967 half of it was so used. Over the same period the proportion of the catch preserved by drying or smoking declined from 28 to 13 percent and the proportion sold fresh from 53 to 31 percent. The relative consumption of canned fish has hardly changed but that of frozen fish has grown from practically nothing to 12 percent.

While we are comparing the prewar or immediate postwar situation with the present, we might take a look at the composition of the catch by groups of species. In 1948 the clupeoid fishes (herrings, pilchards, anchovies and so on), which live mainly in the upper levels of the ocean, already dominated the scene (33 percent of the total by weight) and provided most of the material for fish meal. Today they bulk even larger (45 percent) in spite of the decline of several great stocks of them (in the North Sea and off California, for example). The next most important group, the gadoid fishes (cod, haddock, hake and so on), which live mainly on or near the bottom, comprised a quarter of the total in 1948. Although the catch of these fishes has continued to increase absolutely, the

SCHOOL OF FISH is spotted from the air at night by detecting the bioluminescent glow caused by the school's movement through the water. As the survey aircraft flew over the Gulf of Mexico at an altitude of 3,500 feet, the faint illumination in the water was amplified some 55,000 times by an image intensifier before appearing on the television screen seen in the photograph on the opposite page. The fish are Atlantic thread herring. Detection of fish from the air is one of several means of increasing fishery efficiency being tested at the Pascagoula, Miss., research base of the U.S. Bureau of Commercial Fisheries.

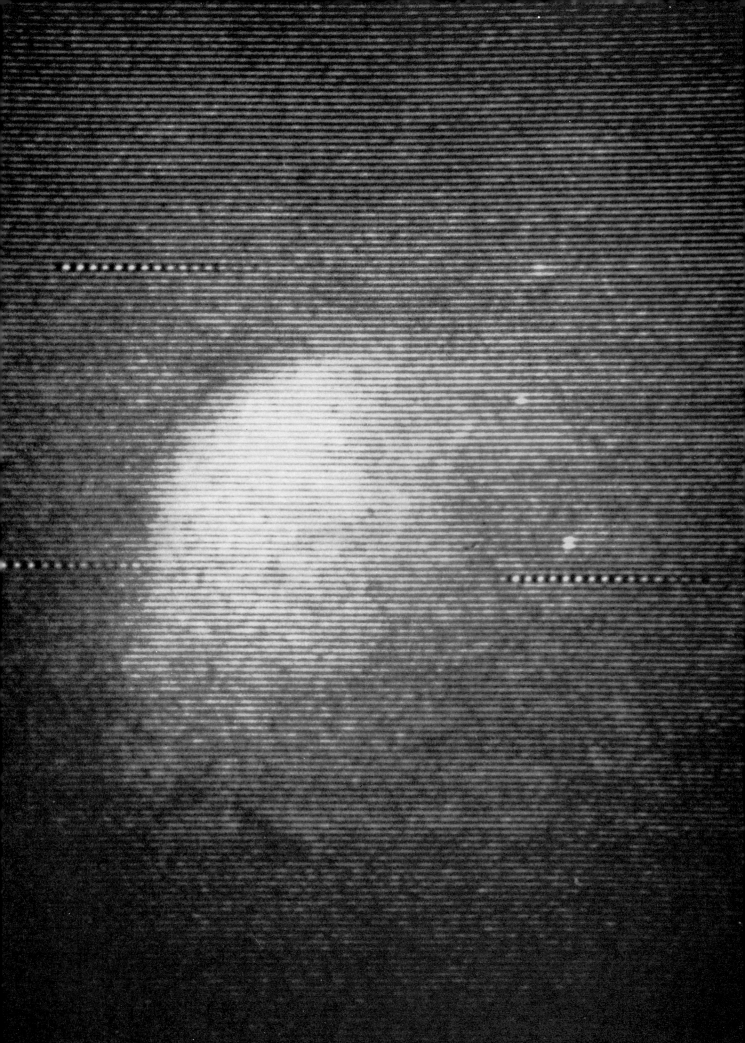

proportion is now reduced to 15 percent. The flounders and other flatfishes, the rosefish and other sea perches and the mullets and jacks have collectively stayed at about 15 percent; the tunas and mackerels, at 7 percent. Nearly a fifth of the total catch continues to be recorded in statistics as "Unsorted and other"—a vast number of species and groups, each contributing a small amount to a considerable whole.

The rise of shrimp and fish meal production together account for another major trend in the pattern of fisheries development. A fifth of the 1957 catch was sold in foreign markets; by 1967, two-fifths were entering international trade and export values totaled $2.5 billion.

Furthermore, during this same period the participation of the less developed countries in the export trade grew from a sixth to well over 25 percent. Most of these shipments were destined for markets in the richer countries, particularly shrimp for North America and fish meal for North America, Europe and Japan. More recently several of the less developed countries have also become importers of fish meal, for example Mexico and Venezuela, South Korea and the Republic of China.

The U.S. catch has stayed for many years in the region of two million tons, a low figure considering the size of the country, the length of the coastline and the ready accessibility of large resources

on the Atlantic, Gulf and Pacific seaboards. The high level of consumption in the U.S. (about 70 pounds per capita) has been achieved through a steady growth in imports of fish and fish meal: from 25 percent of the total in 1950 to more than 70 percent in 1967. In North America 6 percent of the world's human population uses 12 percent of the world's catch, yet fishermen other than Americans take nearly twice the amount of fish that Americans take from the waters most readily accessible to the U.S.

There has not been a marked change in the broad geography of fishing [see illustration on these two pages]. The Pacific Ocean provides the biggest

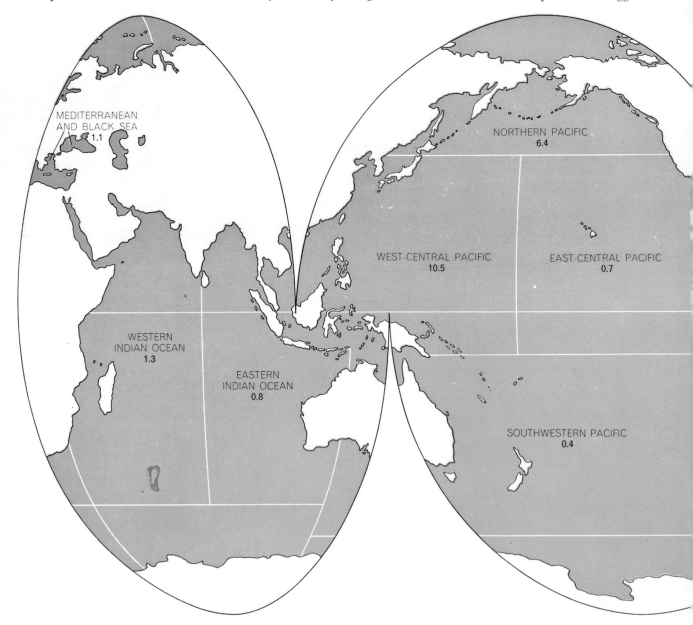

MAJOR MARINE FISHERY AREAS are 14 in number: two in the Indian Ocean (left), five in the Pacific Ocean (center) and six in the Atlantic (right). Due to the phenomenal expansion of the Peru fishery, the total Pacific yield is now a third larger than the Atlantic total. The bulk of Atlantic and Pacific catches, however, is still taken well north of the Equator. The Indian Ocean, with a

share (53 percent) but the Atlantic (40 percent, to which we may add 2 percent for the Mediterranean) is yielding considerably more per unit area. The Indian Ocean is still the source of less than 5 percent of the catch, and since it is not a biologically poor ocean it is an obvious target for future development. Within the major ocean areas, however, there have been significant changes. In the Pacific particular areas such as the waters off Peru and Chile and the Gulf of Thailand have rapidly acquired importance. The central and southern parts of the Atlantic, both east and west, are of growing interest to more nations. Although, with certain exceptions, the traditional fisheries in the colder waters of

the Northern Hemisphere still dominate the statistics, the emergence of some of the less developed countries as modern fishing nations and the introduction of long-range fleets mean that tropical and subtropical waters are beginning to contribute significantly to world production.

Finally, in this brief review of the trends of the past decade or so we must mention the changing importance of countries as fishing powers. Peru has become the leading country in terms of sheer magnitude of catch (although not of value or diversity) through the development of the world's greatest one-species fishery: 10 million tons of anchovies per year, almost all of which is reduced to meal [*see illustration on page 91*].

The U.S.S.R. has also emerged as a fishing power of global dimension, fishing for a large variety of products throughout the oceans of the world, particularly with large factory ships and freezer-trawlers.

At this point it is time to inquire about the future expectations of the ocean as a major source of protein. In spite of the growth I have described, fisheries still contribute only a tenth of the animal protein in our diet, although this proportion varies considerably from one part of the world to another. Before such an inquiry can be pursued, however, it is necessary to say something about the problem of overfishing.

A stock of fish is, generally speaking, at its most abundant when it is not being exploited; in that virgin state it will include a relatively high proportion of the larger and older individuals of the species. Every year a number of young recruits enter the stock, and all the fish—but particularly the younger ones—put on weight. This overall growth is balanced by the natural death of fish of all ages from disease, predation and perhaps senility. When fishing begins, the large stock yields large catches to each fishing vessel, but because the pioneering vessels are few, the total catch is small.

Increased fishing tends to reduce the level of abundance of the stock progressively. At these reduced levels the losses accountable to "natural" death will be less than the gains accountable to recruitment and individual growth. If, then, the catch is less than the difference between natural gains and losses, the stock will tend to increase again; if the catch is more, the stock will decrease. When the stock neither decreases nor increases, we achieve a sustained yield. This sustained yield is small when the stock is large and also when the stock is small; it is at its greatest when the stock is at an intermediate level—somewhere between two-thirds and one-third of the virgin abundance. In this intermediate stage the average size of the individuals will be smaller and the age will be younger than in the unfished condition, and individual growth will be highest in relation to the natural mortality.

The largest catch that on the average can be taken year after year without causing a shift in abundance, either up or down, is called the maximum sustainable yield. It can best be obtained by leaving the younger fish alone and fishing the older ones heavily, but we can also get near to it by fishing moderately, taking fish of all sizes and ages. This

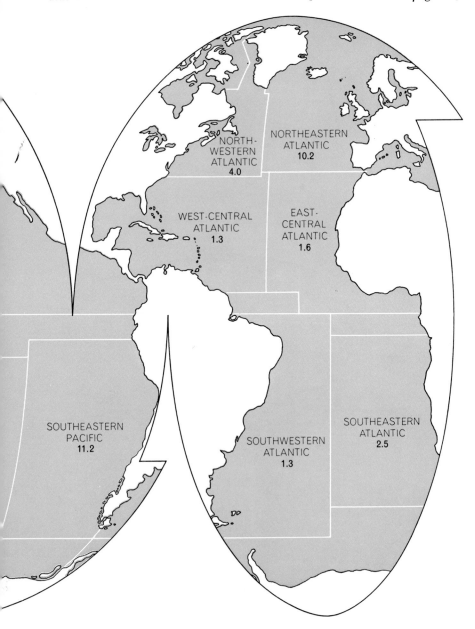

total catch of little more than two million metric tons, live weight, is the world's major underexploited region. The number below each area name shows the millions of metric tons landed during 1967, as reported by the UN Food and Agriculture Organization.

phenomenon—catches that first increase and then decrease as the intensity of fishing increases—does not depend on any correlation between the number of parent fish and the number of recruits they produce for the following generation. In fact, many kinds of fish lay so many eggs, and the factors governing survival of the eggs to the recruit stage are so many and so complex, that it is not easy to observe any dependence of the number of recruits on the number of their parents over a wide range of stock levels.

Only when fishing is intense, and the stock is accordingly reduced to a small fraction of its virgin size, do we see a decline in the number of recruits coming in each year. Even then there is often a wide annual fluctuation in this number. Indeed, such fluctuation, which causes the stock as a whole to vary greatly in abundance from year to year, is one of the most significant characteristics of living marine resources. Fluctuation in number, together with the considerable variation in "availability" (the change in the geographic location of the fish with respect to the normal fishing area), largely account for the notorious riskiness of fishing as an industry.

For some species the characteristics of growth, natural mortality and recruit-

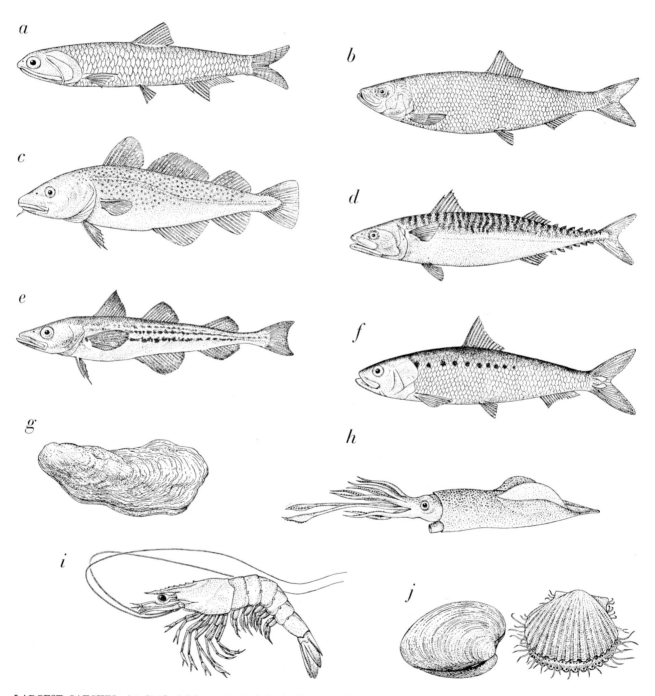

LARGEST CATCHES of individual fish species include the five fishes shown here (left). They are, according to the most recent detailed FAO fishery statistics (1967), the Peruvian anchoveta (a), with a catch of more than 10.5 million metric tons; the Atlantic herring (b), with a catch of more than 3.8 million tons; the Atlantic cod (c), with a catch of 3.1 million tons; the Alaska walleye pollack (d), with a catch of 1.7 million metric tons, and the South African pilchard (e), with a catch of 1.1 million tons. No single invertebrate species (right) is harvested in similar quantities. Taken as a group, however, various oyster species (f) totaled .83 million tons in 1967; squids (g), .75 million tons; shrimps and prawns (h), .69 million tons; clams and cockles (i), .48 million tons.

ment are such that the maximum sustainable yield is sharply defined. The catch will decline quite steeply with a change in the amount of fishing (measured in terms of the number of vessels, the tonnage of the fleet, the days spent at sea or other appropriate index) to either below or above an optimum. In other species the maximum is not so sharply defined; as fishing intensifies above an optimum level the sustained catch will not significantly decline, but it will not rise much either.

Such differences in the dynamics of different types of fish stock contribute to the differences in the historical development of various fisheries. If it is unregulated, however, each fishery tends to expand beyond its optimum point unless something such as inadequate demand hinders its expansion. The reason is painfully simple. It will usually still be profitable for an individual fisherman or ship to continue fishing after the *total* catch from the stock is no longer increasing or is declining, and even though his own rate of catch may also be declining. By the same token, it may continue to be profitable for the individual fisherman to use a small-meshed net and thereby catch young as well as older fish, but in doing so he will reduce both his own possible catch and that of others in future years. Naturally if the total catch is declining, or not increasing much, as the amount of fishing continues to increase, the net economic yield from the fishery—that is, the difference between the total costs of fishing and the value of the entire catch—will be well past its maximum. The well-known case of the decline of the Antarctic baleen whales provides a dramatic example of overfishing and, one would hope, a strong incentive for the more rational conduct of ocean fisheries in the future.

There is, then, a limit to the amount that can be taken year after year from each natural stock of fish. The extent to which we can expect to increase our fish catches in the future will depend on three considerations. First, how many as yet unfished stocks await exploitation, and how big are they in terms of potential sustainable yield? Second, how many of the stocks on which the existing fisheries are based are already reaching or have passed their limit of yield? Third, how successful will we be in managing our fisheries to ensure maximum sustainable yields from the stocks?

The first major conference to examine the state of marine fish stocks on a global basis was the United Nations Scientific Conference on the Conservation and Utilization of Resources, held in 1949 at Lake Success, N.Y. The small group of fishery scientists gathered there concluded that the only overfished stocks at that time were those of a few high-priced species in the North Atlantic and North Pacific, particularly plaice, halibut and salmon. They produced a map showing 30 other known major stocks they believed to be underfished. The situation was reexamined in 1968. Fishing on half of those 30 stocks is now close to or beyond that required for maximum yield. The fully fished or overfished stocks include some tunas in most ocean areas, the herring, the cod and ocean perch in the North Atlantic and the anchovy in the southeastern Pacific. The point is that the history of development of a fishery from small beginnings to the stage of full utilization or overutilization can, in the modern world, be compressed into a very few years. This happened with the anchovy off Peru, as a result of a massive local fishery growth, and it has happened to some demersal, or bottom-dwelling, fishes elsewhere through the large-scale redeployment of long-distance trawlers from one ocean area to another.

It is clear that the classical process of fleets moving from an overfished area to another area, usually more distant and less fished, cannot continue indefinitely. It is true that since the Lake Success

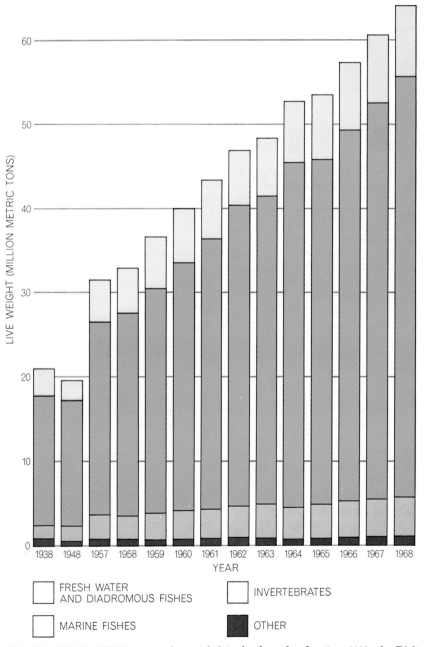

WORLD FISH CATCH has more than tripled in the three decades since 1938; the FAO estimate of the 1968 total is 64 million metric tons. The largest part consists of marine fishes. Humans directly consume only half of the catch; the rest becomes livestock feed.

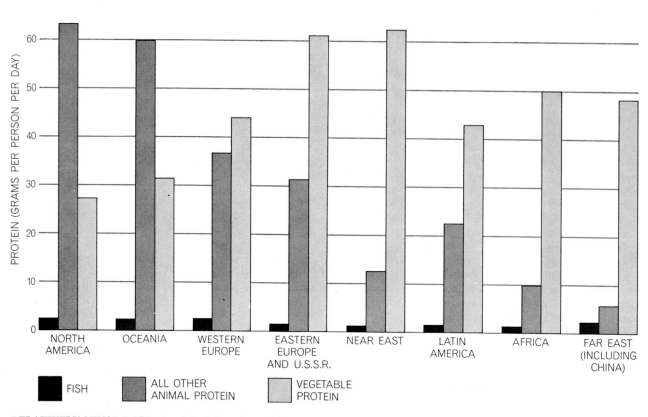

RELATIVELY MINOR ROLE played by fish in the world's total consumption of protein is apparent when the grams of fish eaten per person per day in various parts of the world (*left column in* *each group*) is compared with the consumption of other animal protein (*middle column*) and vegetable protein (*right column*). The supply is nonetheless growing more rapidly than world population.

meeting several other large resources have been discovered, mostly in the Indian Ocean and the eastern Pacific, and additional stocks have been utilized in fishing areas with a long history of intensive fishing, such as the North Sea. In another 20 years, however, very few substantial stocks of fish of the kinds and sizes of commercial interest and accessible to the fishing methods we know now will remain underexploited.

The Food and Agriculture Organization of the UN is now in the later stages of preparing what is known as its Indicative World Plan (IWP) for agricultural development. Under this plan an attempt is being made to forecast the production of foodstuffs in the years 1975 and 1985. For fisheries this involves appraising resource potential, envisioning technological changes and their consequences, and predicting demand. The latter predictions are not yet available, but the resource appraisals are well advanced. With the cooperation of a large number of scientists and organizations estimates are being prepared in great detail on an area basis. They deal with the potential of known stocks, both those fished actively at present and those

exploited little or not at all. Some of these estimates are reliable; others are naturally little more than reasonable guesses. One fact is abundantly clear: We still have very scrappy knowledge, in quantitative terms, of the living resources of the ocean. We can, however, check orders of magnitude by comparing the results of different methods of appraisal. Thus where there is good information on the growth and mortality rates of fishes and measures of their numbers in absolute terms, quite good projections can be made. Most types of fish can now in fact virtually be counted individually by the use of specially calibrated echo sounders for area surveys, although this technique is not yet widely applied. The size of fish populations can also be deduced from catch statistics, from measurements of age based on growth rings in fish scales or bands in fish ear stones, and from tagging experiments. Counts and maps of the distribution of fish eggs in the plankton can in some cases give us a fair idea of fish abundance in relative terms. We can try to predict the future catch in an area little fished at present by comparing the present catch with the catch in another area that has similar oceanographic char-

acteristics and basic biological productivity and that is already yielding near its maximum. Finally, we have estimates of the food supply available to the fish in a particular area, or of the primary production there, and from what we know about metabolic and ecological efficiency we can try to deduce fish production.

So far as the data permit these methods are being applied to major groups of fishes area by area. Although individual area and group predictions will not all be reliable, the global totals and subtotals may be. The best figure seems to be that the potential catch is about three times the present one; it might be as little as twice or as much as four times. A similar range has been given in estimates of the potential yield from waters adjacent to the U.S.: 20 million tons compared with the present catch of rather less than six million tons. This is more than enough to meet the U.S. demand, which is expected to reach 10 million tons by 1975 and 12 million by 1985.

Judging from the rate of fishery development in the recent past, it would be entirely reasonable to suppose that the maximum sustainable world catch of between 100 and 200 million tons could be reached by the second IWP target date, 1985, or at least by the end of the century. The real question is whether or not this will be economically worth the effort. Here any forecast is, in my view, on soft ground. First, to double the catch we have to more than double the amount of fishing, because the stocks decline in abundance as they are exploited. Moreover, as we approach the global maximum more of the stocks that are lightly fished at present will be brought down to intermediate levels. Second, fishing will become even more competitive and costly if the nations fail to agree, and agree soon, on regulations to cure overfishing situations. Third, it is quite uncertain what will happen in the long run to the costs of production and the price of protein of marine origin in relation to other protein sources, particularly from mineral or vegetable bases.

In putting forward these arguments I am not trying to damp enthusiasm for the sea as a major source of food for coming generations; quite the contrary. I do insist, however, that it would be dangerous for those of us who are interested in such development to assume that past growth will be maintained along familiar lines. We need to rationalize present types of fishing while preparing ourselves actively for a "great leap forward." Fishing as we now know it will need to be made even more efficient; we shall need to consider the direct use of the smaller organisms in the ocean that mostly constitute the diet of the fish we now catch; we shall need to try harder to improve on nature by breeding, rearing and husbanding useful marine animals and cultivating their pasture. To achieve this will require a much larger scale and range of scientific research, wedded to engineering progress; expansion by perhaps an order of magnitude in investment and in the employment of highly skilled labor, and a modified legal regime for the ocean and its bed not only to protect the investments but also to ensure orderly development and provide for the safety of men and their installations.

To many people the improvement of present fishing activities will mean increasing the efficiency of fishing gear and ships. There is surely much that could be done to this end. We are only just beginning to understand how trawls, traps, lines and seines really work. For example, every few years someone tries a new design or rigging for a deep-sea trawl, often based on sound engineering and hydrodynamic studies. Rarely do these "improved" rigs catch more than the old ones; sometimes they catch much

less. The error has been in thinking that the trawl is simply a bag, collecting more or less passive fish, or at least predictably active ones. This is not so at all. We really have to deal with a complex, dynamic relation between the lively animals and their environment, which includes in addition to the physical and biological environment the fishing gear itself. We can expect success in understanding and exploiting this relation now that we can telemeter the fishing gear, study its hydrodynamics at full scale as well as with models in towing tanks, monitor it (and the fish) by means of underwater television, acoustic equipment and divers, and observe and experiment with fish behavior both in the sea and in large tanks. We also probably have something to learn from studying, before they become extinct, some kinds of traditional "primitive" fishing gear still used in Asia, South America and elsewhere—mainly traps that take advantage of subtleties of fish behavior observed over many centuries.

Successful fishing depends not so much on the size of fish stocks as on their concentration in space and time. All fishermen use knowledge of such concentrations; they catch fish where they have

gathered to feed or to reproduce, or where they are on the move in streams or schools. Future fishing methods will surely involve a more active role for the fishermen in causing the fish to congregate. In many parts of the world lights or sound are already used to attract fish. We can expect more sophistication in the employment of these and other stimuli, alone and in combination.

Fishing operations as a whole also depend on locating areas of concentration and on the efficient prediction, or at least the prompt observation, of changes in these areas. The large stocks of pelagic, or open-sea, fishes are produced mainly in areas of "divergencies," where water is rising from deeper levels toward the surface and hence where surface waters are flowing outward. Many such areas are the "upwellings" off the western coasts of continental masses, for example off western and southwestern Africa, western India and western South America. Here seasonal winds, currents and continental configurations combine to cause a periodic enrichment of the surface waters.

Divergencies are also associated with

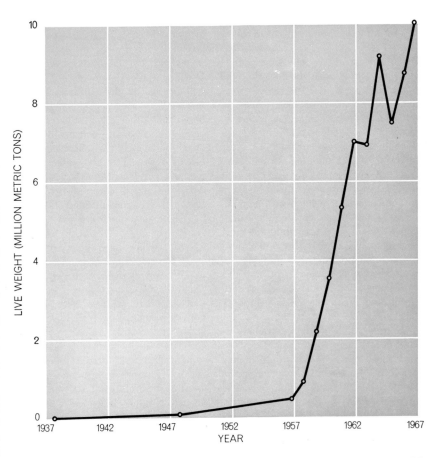

EXPLOSIVE GROWTH of the Peruvian anchoveta fishery is seen in rising number of fish taken between 1938 and 1967. Until 1958 the catch remained below half a million tons. By 1967, with more than 10.5 million tons taken, the fishery sorely needed management.

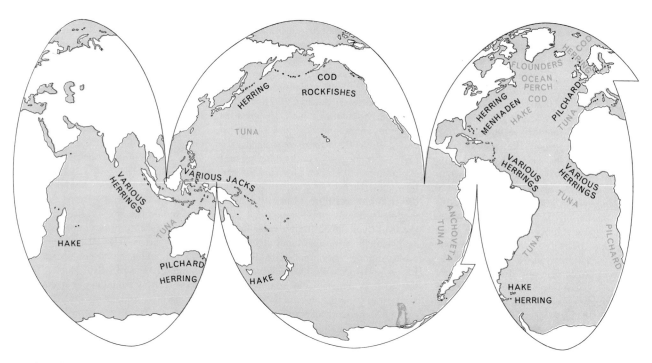

EXPLOITATION OF FISHERIES during the past 20 years is evident from this map, which locates 30 major fish stocks that were thought to be underfished in 1949. Today 14 of the stocks (*color*) are probably fully exploited or in danger of being overfished.

certain current systems in the open sea. The classical notion is that biological production is high in such areas because nutrient salts, needed for plant growth and in limited supply, are thereby renewed in the surface layers of the water. On the other hand, there is a view that the blooming of the phytoplankton is associated more with the fact that the water coming to the surface is cooler than it is associated with its richness in nutrients. A cool-water regime is characterized by seasonal peaks of primary production; the phytoplankton blooms are followed, after a time lag, by an abundance of herbivorous zooplankton that provides concentrations of food for large schools of fish. Fish, like fishermen, thrive best not so much where their prey are abundant as where they are most aggregated. In any event, the times and places of aggregation vary from year to year. The size of the herbivore crop also varies according to the success of synchronization with the primary production cycle.

There would be great practical advantage to our being able to predict these variations. Since the weather regime plays such a large part in creating the physical conditions for high biological production, the World Weather Watch, under the auspices of the World Meteorological Organization, should contribute much to fishery operations through both long-range forecasting and better short-term forecasting. Of course our interest is not merely in atmospheric forecasts,

nor in the state of the sea surface, but in the deeper interaction of atmosphere and ocean. Thus, from the point of view of fisheries, an equal and complementary partner in the World Weather Watch will be the Integrated Global Ocean Station System (IGOSS) now being developed by the Intergovernmental Oceanographic Commission. The IGOSS will give us the physical data, from networks of satellite-interrogated automatic buoys and other advanced ocean data acquisition systems (collectively called ODAS), by which the ocean circulation can be observed in "real time" and the parameters relevant to fisheries forecast. A last and much more difficult link will be the observation and prediction of the basic biological processes.

So far we have been considering mainly the stocks of pelagic fishes in the upper layers of the open ocean and the shallower waters over the continental shelves. There are also large aggregations of pelagic animals that live farther down and are associated particularly with the "deep scattering layer," the sound-reflecting stratum observed in all oceans. The more widespread use of submersible research vessels will tell us more about the layer's biological nature, but the exploitation of deep pelagic resources awaits the development of suitable fishing apparatus for this purpose.

Important advances have been made in recent years in the design of pelagic trawls and in means of guiding them in

three dimensions and "locking" them onto fish concentrations. We shall perhaps have such gear not only for fishing much more deeply than at present but also for automatically homing on deep-dwelling concentrations of fishes, squids and so on, using acoustic links for the purpose. The Indian Ocean might become the part of the world where such methods are first deployed on a large scale; certainly there is evidence of a great but scarcely utilized pelagic resource in that ocean, and around its edge are human populations sorely in need of protein. The Gulf of Guinea is another place where oceanographic knowledge and new fishing methods should make accessible more of the large sardine stock that is now effectively exploited only during the short season of upwelling off Ghana and nearby countries, when the schools come near the surface and can be taken by purse seines.

The bottom-living fishes and the shellfishes (both mollusks and crustaceans) are already more fully utilized than the smaller pelagic fishes. On the whole they are the species to which man attaches a particularly high value, but they cannot have as high a global abundance as the pelagic fishes. The reason is that they are living at the end of a longer food chain. All the rest of ocean life depends on an annual primary production of 150 billion tons of phytoplankton in the 2 to 3 percent of the water mass into which light penetrates and photosynthesis can occur. Below this "photic" zone dead and dying organisms sink as a continual rain of organic matter and are eaten or decompose. Out in the deep ocean little, if any, of this organic matter reaches the bottom, but nearer land a substantial quantity does; it nourishes an entire community of marine life, the benthos, which itself provides food for animals such as cod, ocean perch, flounder and shrimp that dwell or visit there.

Thus virtually everywhere on the bed of the continental shelf there is a thriving demersal resource, but it does not end there. Where the shelf is narrow but primary production above is high, as in the upwelling areas, or where the zone of high primary production stretches well away from the coast, we may find considerable demersal resources on the continental slopes beyond the shelf, far deeper than the 200 meters that is the average limiting depth of the shelf itself. Present bottom-trawling methods will work down to 1,000 meters or more, and it seems that, at least on some slopes, useful resources of shrimps and bottom-dwelling fishes will be found even down to 1,500 meters. We still know very little about the nature and abundance of these resources, and current techniques of acoustic surveying are not of much use in evaluating them. The total area of the continental slope from, say, 200 to 1,500 meters is roughly the same as that of the entire continental shelf, so that when we have extended our preliminary surveys there we might need to revise our IWP ceiling upward somewhat.

Another problem is posed for us by the way that, as fishing is intensified throughout the world, it becomes at the same time less selective. This may not apply to a particular type of fishing operation, which may be highly selective with regard to the species captured. Partly as a result of the developments in processing and trade, and partly because of the decline of some species, however, we are using more and more of the species that abound. This holds particularly for species in warmer waters, and also for some species previously neglected in cool waters, such as the sand eel in the North Sea. This means that it is no longer so reasonable to calculate the potential of each important species stock separately, as we used to do. Instead we need new theoretical models for that part of the marine ecosystem which consists of animals in the wide range of sizes we now utilize: from an inch or so up to several feet. As we move toward fuller utilization of all these animals we shall need to take proper account of the interactions among them. This will mean devising quantitative methods for evaluating the competition among them for a common food supply and also examining the dynamic relations between the predators and the prey among them.

These changes in the degree and quality of exploitation will add one more dimension to the problems we already face in creating an effective international system of management of fishing activities, particularly on the high seas. This system consists at present of a large number—more than 20—of regional or specialized intergovernmental organizations established under bilateral or multilateral treaties, or under the constitution of the FAO. The purpose of each is to conduct and coordinate research leading to resource assessments, or to promulgate regulations for the better conduct of the fisheries, or both. The organizations are supplemented by the 1958 Geneva Convention on Fishing and Conservation of the Living Resources of the High Seas. The oldest of them, the International Council for the Exploration of the Sea, based in Copenhagen and concerned particularly with fishery research in the northeastern Atlantic and the Arctic, has had more than half a century of activity. The youngest is the International Commission for the Conservation of Atlantic Tunas; the convention that establishes it comes into force this year.

For the past two decades many have hoped that such treaty bodies would ensure a smooth and reasonably rapid approach to an international regime for ocean fisheries. Indeed, a few of the organizations have fair successes to their credit. The fact is, however, that the fisheries have been changing faster than the international machinery to deal with them. National fishery research budgets and organizational arrangements for guiding research, collecting proper statistics and so on have been largely inadequate to the task of assessing resources. Nations have given, and continue to give, ludicrously low-level support to the bodies of which they are members, and the bodies themselves do not have the powers they need properly to manage the fisheries and conserve the resources. Add to this the trend to high mobility and range of today's fishing fleets, the problems of species interaction and the growing number of nations at various stages of economic development participating in international fisheries, and the regional bodies are indeed in trouble! There is some awareness of this, yet the FAO, having for years been unable to give adequate financial support to the fishery bodies it set up years ago in the Indo-Pacific area, the Mediterranean and the southwestern Atlantic, has been pushed, mainly through the enthusiasm of its new intergovernmental Committee on Fisheries, to establish still other bodies (in the Indian Ocean and in the east-central and southeastern Atlantic) that will be no better supported than the ex-

RUSSIAN FACTORY SHIP *Polar Star* lies hove to in the Barents Sea in June, 1968, as two vessels from its fleet of trawlers unload their catch for processing. The worldwide activities of the Russian fishing fleet have made the U.S.S.R. the third-largest fishing nation.

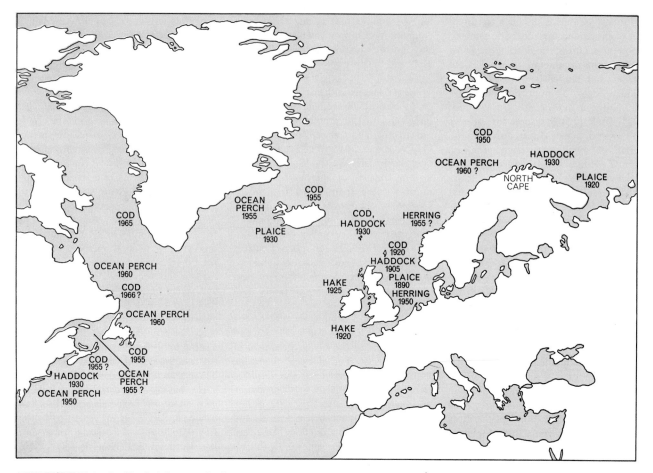

OVERFISHING in the North Atlantic and adjacent waters began some 80 years ago in the North Sea, when further increases in fishing the plaice stock no longer produced an increase in the catch of that fish. By 1950 the same was true of North Sea cod, haddock and herring, of cod, haddock and plaice off the North Cape and in the Barents Sea, of plaice, haddock and cod south and east of Iceland and of the ocean perch and haddock in the Gulf of Maine. In the period between 1956 and 1966 the same became true of ocean perch off Newfoundland and off Labrador and of cod west of Greenland. It may also be true of North Cape ocean perch and Labrador cod.

isting ones. A grand plan to double the finance and staff of the FAO's Department of Fisheries (including the secretariats and working budgets of the associated regional fishery bodies) over the six-year period 1966–1971, which member nations endorsed in principle in 1965, will be barely half-fulfilled in that time, and the various nations concerned are meanwhile being equally parsimonious in financing the other international fishery bodies.

Several of these bodies are now facing a crucial, and essentially political, problem: How are sustainable yields to be shared equitably among participating nations? It is now quite evident that there is really no escape from the paramount need, if high yields are to be sustained; this is to limit the fishing effort deployed in the intensive fisheries. This could be achieved by setting total quotas for each species in each type of fishery, but this only leads to an unseemly scramble by each nation for as large a share as possible of the quota. This can only be avoided by agreement on national al-

locations of the quotas. On what basis can such agreement be reached? On the historical trends of national participation? If so, over what period: the past two years, the past five, the past 20? On the need for protein, on the size or wealth of the population or on the proximity of coasts to fishing grounds? Might we try to devise a system for maximizing economic efficiency in securing an optimum net economic yield? How can this be measured in an international fishery? Would some form of license auction be equitable, or inevitably loaded in favor of wealthy nations? The total number or tonnage of fishing vessels might be fixed, as the United Kingdom suggested in 1946 should be done in the North Sea, but what flags should the ships fly and in what proportion? Might we even consider "internationalizing" the resources, granting fishing concessions and using at least a part of the economic yield from the concessions to finance marine research, develop fish-farming, police the seas and aid the participation of less developed nations?

Some of my scientific colleagues are optimistic about the outcome of current negotiations on these questions, and indeed when the countries participating are a handful of nations at a similar stage of economic and technical development, as was the case for Antarctic whaling, agreement can sometimes be reached by hard bargaining. What happens, however, when the participating countries are numerous, widely varying in their interests and ranging from the most powerful nations on earth to states most newly emerged to independence? I must confess that many of us were optimistic when 20 years ago we began proposing quite reasonable net-mesh regulations to conserve the young of certain fish stocks. Then we saw these simple—I suppose oversimple—ideas bog down in consideration of precisely how to measure a mesh of a particular kind of twine, and how to take account of the innumerable special situations that countries pleaded for, so that fishery research sometimes seemed to be becoming perverted from its earlier clarity and broad perspective.

Apprehension and doubt about the ultimate value of the concept of regulation through regional commissions of the present type have, I think, contributed to the interest in recent years in alternative regimes: either the "appropriation" of high-seas resources to some form of international "ownership" instead of today's condition of no ownership or, at the other extreme, the appropriation of increasingly wide ocean areas to national ownership by coastal states. As is well known, a similar dialectic is in progress in connection with the seabed and its mineral resources. Either solution would have both advantages and disadvantages, depending on one's viewpoint, on the time scale considered and on political philosophy. I do not propose to discuss these matters here, although personally I am increasingly firm in the conclusion that mankind has much more to gain in the long run from the "international" solution, with both seabed and fishery resources being considered as our common heritage. We now at least have a fair idea of what is economically at stake.

Here are some examples. The wasted effort in capture of cod alone in the northeastern Atlantic and salmon alone in the northern Pacific could, if rationally deployed elsewhere, increase the total world catch by 5 percent. The present catch of cod, valued at $350 million per year, could be taken with only half the effort currently expended, and the annual saving in fishing effort would amount to $150 million or more. The cost of harvesting salmon off the West Coast of North America could be reduced by three-quarters if management policy permitted use of the most efficient fishing gear; the introduction of such a policy would increase net economic returns by $750,000 annually.

The annual benefit that would accrue from the introduction and enforcement of mesh regulations in the demersal fishery—mainly the hake fishery—in the east-central Atlantic off West Africa is of the order of $1 million. Failure to regulate the Antarctic whaling industry effectively in earlier years, when stocks of blue whales and fin whales were near their optimum size, is now costing us tens of millions of dollars annually in loss of this valuable but only slowly renewable resource. Even under stringent regulation this loss will continue for the decades these stocks will need to recover. Yellowfin tuna in the eastern tropical Pacific are almost fully exploited. There is an annual catch quota, but it is not allocated to nations or ships, with the classic inevitable results: an increase in the catching capacity of fleets, their use in shorter and

shorter "open" seasons and an annual waste of perhaps 30 percent of the net value of this important fishery.

Such regulations as exist are extremely difficult to enforce (or to be seen to be enforced, which is almost as important). The tighter the squeeze on the natural resources, the greater the suspicion of fishermen that "the others" are not abiding by the regulations, and the greater the incentive to flout the regulations oneself. There has been occasional provision in treaties, or in *ad hoc* arrangements, to place neutral inspectors or internationally accredited observers aboard fishing vessels and mother ships (as in Antarctic whaling, where arrangements were completed but never implemented!). Such arrangements are exceptional. In point of fact the effective supervision of a fishing fleet is an enormously difficult undertaking. Even to know where the vessels are going, let alone what they are catching, is quite a problem. Perhaps one day artificial satellites will monitor sealed transmitters compulsorily carried on each vessel. But how to ensure compliance with minimum landing-size regulations when increasing quantities of the catch are being processed at sea? With factory ships roaming the entire ocean, even the statistics reporting catches by species and area can become more rather than less difficult to obtain.

Some of these considerations and pessimism about their early solution have, I think, played their part in stimulating other approaches to harvesting the sea.

One of these is the theory of "working back down the food chain." For every ton of fish we catch, the theory goes, we might instead catch say 10 tons of the organisms on which those fish feed. Thus by harvesting the smaller organisms we could move away from the fish ceiling of 100 million or 200 million tons and closer to the 150 billion tons of primary production. The snag is the question of concentration. The billion tons or so of "fish food" is neither in a form of direct interest to man nor is it so concentrated in space as the animals it nourishes. In fact, the 10-to-one ratio of fish food to fish represents a use of energy—perhaps a rather efficient use—by which biomass is concentrated; if the fish did not expend this energy in feeding, man might have to expend a similar amount of energy—in fuel, for example—in order to collect the dispersed fish food. I am sure the technological problems of our using fish food will be solved, but only careful analysis will reveal whether or not it is better to turn fish food, by way of fish meal, into chickens or rainbow trout than to harvest the marine fish instead.

There are a few situations, however, where the concentration, abundance and homogeneity of fish food are sufficient to be of interest in the near future. The best-known of these is the euphausiid "krill" in Antarctic waters: small shrimplike crustaceans that form the main food of the baleen whales. Russian investigators and some others are seriously charting krill distribution and production, relating them to the oceanographic features of the Southern Ocean, experiment-

JAPANESE MARICULTURE includes the raising of several kinds of marine algae. This array of posts and netting in the Inland Sea supports a crop of an edible seaweed, *Porphyra*.

AUSTRALIAN MARICULTURE includes the production of some 60 million oysters per year in the brackish estuaries of New South Wales. The long racks in the photograph have been exposed by low tide; they support thousands of sticks covered with maturing oysters.

ing with special gear for catching the krill (something between a mid-water trawl and a magnified plankton net) and developing methods for turning them into meal and acceptable pastes. The krill alone could produce a weight of yield, although surely not a value, at least as great as the present world fish catch, but we might have to forgo the whales. Similarly, the deep scattering layers in other oceans might provide very large quantities of smaller marine animals in harvestable concentration.

An approach opposite to working down the food chain is to look to the improvement of the natural fish resources, and particularly to the cultivation of highly valued species. Schemes for transplanting young fish to good high-seas feeding areas, or for increasing recruitment by rearing young fish to viable size, are hampered by the problem of protecting what would need to be quite large investments. What farmer would bother to breed domestic animals if he were not assured by the law of the land that others would not come and take them as soon as they were nicely fattened? Thus mariculture in the open sea awaits a regime of law there, and effective management as well as more research.

Meanwhile attention is increasingly given to the possibilities of raising more fish and shellfish in coastal waters, where the effort would at least have the protection of national law. Old traditions of shellfish culture are being reexamined,

and one can be confident that scientific bases for further growth will be found. All such activities depend ultimately on what I call "productivity traps": the utilization of natural or artificially modified features of the marine environment to trap biological production originating in a wider area, and by such a biological route that more of the production is embodied in organisms of direct interest to man. In this way we open the immense possibilities of using mangrove swamps and productive estuarine areas, building artificial reefs, breeding even more efficient homing species such as the salmon, enhancing natural production with nutrients or warm water from coastal power stations, controlling predators and competitors, shortening food chains and so on. Progress in such endeavors will require a better predictive ecology than we now have, and also many pilot experiments with corresponding risks of failure as well as chances of success.

The greatest threat to mariculture is perhaps the growing pollution of the sea. This is becoming a real problem for fisheries generally, particularly coastal ones, and mariculture would thrive best in just those regions that are most threatened by pollution, namely the ones near large coastal populations and technological centers. We should not expect, I think, that the ocean would not be used at all as a receptacle for waste—it is in some ways so good for such a purpose: its large volume, its deep holes, the hydrolyzing, corrosive and biologically degrading

properties of seawater and the microbes in it. We should expect, however, that this use will not be an indiscriminate one, that this use of the ocean would be internationally registered, controlled and monitored, and that there would be strict regulation of any dumping of noxious substances (obsolete weapons of chemical and biological warfare, for example), including the injection of such substances by pipelines extending from the coast. There are signs that nations are becoming ready to accept such responsibilities, and to act in concert to overcome the problems. Let us hope that progress in this respect will be faster than it has been in arranging for the management of some fisheries, or in a few decades there may be few coastal fisheries left worth managing.

I have stressed the need for scientific research to ensure the future use of the sea as a source of food. This need seems to me self-evident, but it is undervalued by many persons and organizations concerned with economic development. It is relatively easy to secure a million dollars of international development funds for the worthy purpose of assisting a country to participate in an international fishery or to set up a training school for its fishermen and explore the country's continental shelf for fish or shrimps. It is more difficult to justify a similar or lesser expenditure on the scientific assessment of the new fishery's resources and the investigation of its ocean environment. It is much more difficult to secure even quite limited support for international measures that might ensure the continued profitability of the new fishery for all participants.

Looking back a decade instead of forward, we recall that Lionel A. Walford of the U.S. Fish and Wildlife Service wrote, in a study he made for the Conservation Foundation: "The sea is a mysterious wilderness, full of secrets. It is inhabited only by wild animals and, with the exception of a few special situations, is uncultivated. Most of what we know about it we have had to learn indirectly with mechanical contrivances to probe, feel, sample, fish." There are presumably fewer wild animals now than there were then—at least fewer useful ones—but there seems to be a good chance that by the turn of the century the sea will be less a wilderness and more cultivated. Much remains for us and our children to do to make sure that by then it is not a contaminated wilderness or a battlefield for ever sharper clashes between nations and between the different users of its resources.

10

The Dimensions of World Poverty

DAVID SIMPSON
November 1968

The economic gulf that has divided the poorer countries of the world from the richer countries is rapidly widening. Whereas the affluent nations continue to become richer, the impoverished nations continue to increase in population without raising their food production fast enough to reach a state of self-sustaining growth. Even though there have been recent gains in their agricultural production, and even if one makes the most optimistic assumptions about the programs instituted to limit the growth of populations, the prospect remains bleak. It is highly probable that for at least the next 20 years most of the people in the world will continue to exist at the margin of subsistence.

Where is poverty the most serious? How many people are critically deprived of food and the other necessities of life? In this review of the available evidence concerning world poverty I shall attempt to answer these questions, concluding with some proposals as to what can be done about the groups that are critically underfed.

There is no single statistical indicator by which one can distinguish people who are seriously deprived from those who are merely poor. One can make only rough estimates based on a number of indicators, all of them crude. The justification for using such necessarily uncertain statistics is that, in Gunnar Myrdal's words, "it is better to paint with a wide brush of unknown thickness than to leave the canvas blank."

The measure of a country's material progress that has been most widely adopted is per capita national income, which is to say the net value of goods and services produced by a nation within one year per head of population. As a comparative measure of the standard of living or of the degree of well-being, it nonetheless has at least three weaknesses. The first is the difficulty of measurement: A comparison between the national incomes of two countries essentially involves valuing two bundles of goods. Inasmuch as similar goods have different prices depending on the country, two answers are possible according to which set of prices is used in the valuation. The second weakness is more fundamental: The satisfactions that people in different societies gain from similar goods are not comparable. It is argued that even if a Burmese peasant and an American housewife consumed similar goods at the same prices, and the American consumed 40 times as much as the Burmese, it would not follow that the American was 40 times better off. Finally, per capita income is an average measure; it cannot reflect the distribution of income within a country.

In spite of these shortcomings per capita income can be defended as an indicator of the level of output of goods and services within a country, and indeed it is widely used as such. Even when the estimate of income can only be crude, it nevertheless reveals differences in the order of magnitude of the incomes of the rich and the poor regions of the world. Thus on the basis of figures for 1965 (or the most recent year available) the average per capita income of the poorest region of Latin America is more than twice that of the poorer regions of Asia and Africa. The countries of Europe have average incomes that are 10 times greater than those of the poorer regions of Asia and Africa; in Oceania national incomes are larger by a factor of 14 and in North America they are larger by a factor of 28. It should be mentioned, however, that the way these estimates are prepared tends to overstate the differences between the richest and the poorest regions of the world.

It is clear that within continents there is considerable variation between regions and countries. South Asia and Indonesia have much lower incomes than East Asia or West Asia. The average income of the North African region is more than twice that of eastern and southern Africa. On both continents there are rich countries such as Japan, Singapore, Israel, Cyprus, Libya and the Republic of South Africa, whose average incomes approach European levels or even surpass them.

If we regard per capita income as a first approximation to the identification of the poorest regions of the world, it indicates that these regions include eastern, northeastern, southern, western and central Africa together with South and Southeast Asia and Indonesia. This impression is confirmed when one ranks the countries of the world whose average incomes are less than $300 per head according to relative wealth, dividing them into four classes.

First of all are countries with the lowest average incomes, namely a range from $30 to $79 per head. Of the 22 countries, 17 are African and account for more than half of the continent's population, or about 167 million people. In this class there are only five Asian countries: Afghanistan, Burma, Laos, Nepal and Yemen, with a population totaling less than 60 million.

The next income class ($80 to $99) is important because it includes India, Indonesia and Pakistan, the three major countries of South Asia, whose population amounts to almost 700 million.

In the third class ($100 to $199) fall China, most of the Arab countries and four countries of Latin America (Bolivia, Ecuador, Honduras and Paraguay). The estimate of the per capita income of China is extremely uncertain, but I feel reasonably confident in placing China within this range.

The fourth and relatively highest income range ($200 to $299) includes Iran, Turkey, the Philippines and Brazil but only two African countries, Ghana and Rhodesia. The countries in this range could be described as being on the threshold of economic development: all the countries in the range below them

($100 to $199) are clearly not developed, whereas Cuba, Costa Rica, Portugal and Yugoslavia, whose incomes fall in the range above them ($300 to $399), clearly are.

It would be unwise to propose any single value of per capita income above which a country can be judged to have passed out of the stage of economic backwardness or underdevelopment, both because of the uncertainty of the estimates and the variation in circumstances among countries. If a line must nevertheless be drawn for practical purposes, then $300 would appear to be a reasonable level at which to draw it. Whereas there are many countries clustered below $300, there are relatively few spread

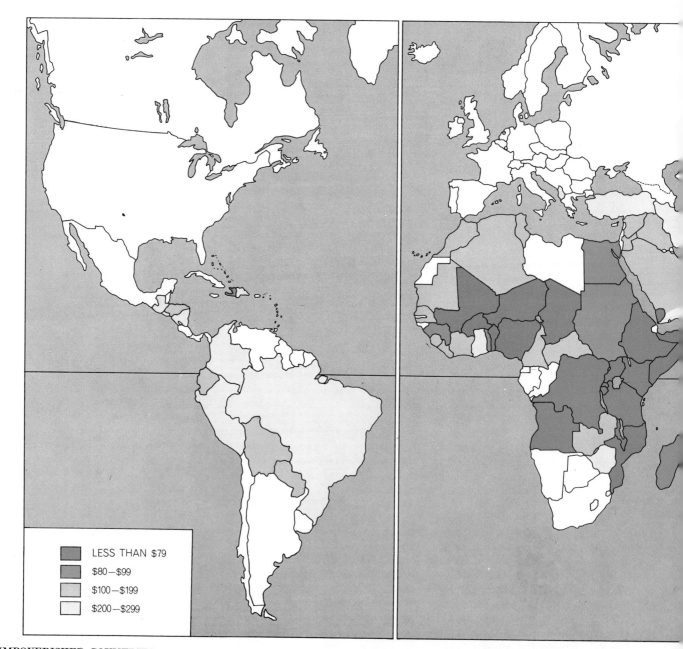

LESS THAN $79
$80—$99
$100—$199
$200—$299

IMPOVERISHED COUNTRIES are grouped according to their average per capita income for 1965 (or the most recent year available). Estimates have not been made for some of the smaller countries. The income and population of the larger countries

over the wide range of incomes between $300 and $700. About 2.1 billion people, or 64 percent of the world's population, live in countries whose average income is less than $300, and almost 1.9 billion of these people live in countries whose average income falls below $200. A world poverty line at $300 is of course far below the level at which the poverty line would be drawn in the richer regions of the world. Taking four people as the average number in an American family, the simple U.S. poverty line works out at $750 per head.

An interesting characteristic of the countries with incomes less than $300, which we shall now call the low-income countries, is that their distribution in terms of population is extremely skewed. About 67 percent of the people in this group live in only four countries: China, India, Indonesia and Pakistan. At the other end of the scale, 50 small countries of Africa, Asia and Latin America account for less than .6 percent of the people in the group. These facts alone suggest that there are no simple universal prescriptions for economic development.

As an index of the economic progress of the low-income countries, the level of per capita income is of course less important than the rate of its growth. Estimates of the annual growth rates of per capita income are available for only a few of these countries. Statisticians at the United Nations have, however, estimated the average growth rate of per capita income (at constant prices) of developing, or poorer, countries as a group. During the 1950's their growth rate was 2.3 percent, and it dropped slightly to 2.2 percent during the period from 1960 to 1964. The corresponding figures for the developed countries were 2.7 percent and 3.7 percent, thus the widening gap between rich and poor. Naturally these averages conceal a wide variety of experience in different countries. Per capita income actually dropped in Morocco, Haiti and Syria in the 1950's and in Guyana and Uruguay from 1960 to 1965. On the other hand, the annual rate of growth of per capita income was 4.3 percent in Burma in the 1950's and 3.5 percent in Iran between 1960 and 1965. Over the same two periods the incomes of India and Nigeria grew modestly but steadily, whereas Pakistan moved from an annual growth rate of .6 percent in the 1950's to a rate of 3.2 percent in the 1960's.

It should be remembered that a growing per capita income is quite compatible with a simultaneous increase in the absolute number of people in the country who are subsisting at the lowest income level. The statistics used in the calculation of the level and rate of growth of income are national averages. For an appreciation of the extent of poverty within a country a knowledge of the distribution of income is essential. Unfortunately the available statistics of income distribution in the low-income countries are seriously limited in both quantity and quality. The most thorough analyst of these data, Simon Kuznets of Harvard University, draws the conclusion that the upper-income groups in the countries below the $300 line receive a larger share of total income than their counterparts in the rich countries do; below the top-income groups there is a greater equality in the distribution.

If we interpret poverty to mean sustained deprivation, then per capita income is not necessarily the best measure, and it is certainly not the only measure, of such poverty. It is possible, for example, to envision a society that has a very low per capita income as a result of a low level of material production but at the same time is not seriously deprived of the basic necessities of life: food, shelter, clothing and reasonable conditions of health. What precisely constitutes sustained deprivation or serious poverty is a matter that could be discussed at length. Fortunately such a discussion is unnecessary, because the number of statistical indicators that are relevant to any rea-

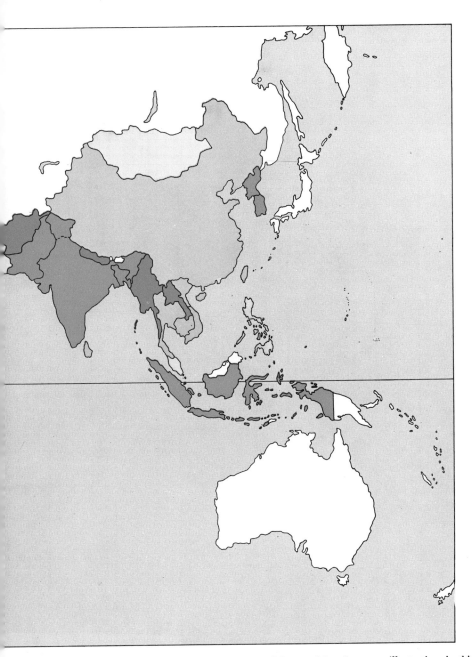

are listed on the next two pages. The data used here and in subsequent illustrations in this article are based on statistics of United Nations agencies and estimates of the author.

sonable definition of serious poverty and also are actually available is quite limited. It is therefore simpler to consider these indicators in turn and to allow the impression of poverty to be formed by them.

As far as the lack of shelter is concerned, the available quantitative evidence does not allow us to draw any conclusions that are relevant to our purpose. We know the average number of inhabitants per room for some segments of the population, but we do not know the number of inhabitants per square foot. A country with a high proportion of dwellings without electricity or without a piped-in water supply can be considered poor, but this does not necessarily represent serious hardship. Dwellings are not easily comparable from country to country, and needs vary. Similar considerations apply to the availability of clothing as a measure of poverty.

In the cities of the poorer countries there is of course dramatic and visible evidence of the qualitative inadequacy of housing. The population of such cities as Nairobi, Calcutta, Caracas, Bogotá and São Paulo is growing faster than the rate at which even rudimentary housing facilities can be provided. A recent account of housing conditions in Calcutta illustrates the magnitude of the problem there. The 1966 development plan of the Calcutta Metropolitan Planning Organisation states that adequate housing is "not within the bounds of feasible achievement over a 25-year period." The

COUNTRY	INCOME PER CAPITA (U.S. DOLLARS)	POPULATION (MILLIONS)
AFGHANISTAN	47	15.7
ALBANIA	239	1.9
ALGERIA	195	11.9
ANGOLA	56	5.2
ARGENTINA	740	22.4
AUSTRALIA	1,620	11.4
AUSTRIA	970	7.3
BELGIUM	1,406	9.5
BOLIVIA	144	3.7
BRAZIL	217	82.2
BRUNEI	1,395	.1
BULGARIA	691	8.2
BURMA	56	24.7
BURUNDI	38	3.2
CAMBODIA	112	6.1
CAMEROON	104	5.2
CANADA	1,825	19.6
CENTRAL AFRICAN REPUBLIC	123	1.4
CEYLON	130	11.2
CHAD	60	3.3
CHILE	515	8.6
CHINA	147	700.0
COLOMBIA	237	18.1
CONGO (KINSHASA)	66	15.6
COSTA RICA	353	1.4
CUBA	319	7.6
CYPRUS	623	0.6
CZECHOSLOVAKIA	1,482	14.2
LAOS	59	2.6
LEBANON	204	2.4
LIBERIA	148	1.0
LIBYA	636	1.6
MADAGASCAR	83	6.4
MALAWI	38	3.9
MALAYA	257	8.0
MALI	57	4.6
MAURITANIA	106	1.1
MEXICO	412	42.7
MONGOLIA	250	1.1
MOROCCO	174	13.3
MOZAMBIQUE	40	7.0
NEPAL	66	10.1
NETHERLANDS	1,265	12.3
NEW ZEALAND	1,706	2.6
NICARAGUA	298	1.7
NIGER	78	3.3
NIGERIA	63	57.5
NORWAY	1,453	3.7
PAKISTAN	89	102.9
PANAMA	425	1.2
PARAGUAY	186	2.0
PERU	218	11.7
PHILIPPINES	219	32.3
POLAND	904	31.5
PORTUGAL	351	9.2
PUERTO RICO	959	2.6
RHODESIA	206	4.3

WEALTH OF NATIONS is expressed in annual income per head of population. The impoverished countries, those with per capita income less than $300 (*color*), are seen to be predominant. Countries with a population under one million are omitted from this dimensions of the problem are so enormous that the plan does not anticipate the provision of houses but rather the construction of open-sided sheds to serve as shelters. One estimate suggests that 77 percent of the families in Calcutta at present have less than 40 square feet (an area a little more than six feet square) of living space per person. Nevertheless, the problem of housing in the cities may be not so much a problem of shelter as a problem of sanitation, and therefore of disease. In cities such as Calcutta the lack of housing means that the spread of disease in the slum areas is literally uncontrollable.

The problem of disease in the poorer countries is inextricably linked to other social conditions: lack of sanitation, lack of food and lack of medical facilities. It would therefore seem that the incidence of particular diseases would be a useful indicator of levels of poverty. Although diseases such as hookworm, trachoma and malaria, respiratory diseases (tuberculosis, whooping cough), intestinal diseases (typhoid, dysentery, gastroenteritis) and deficiencies arising from malnutrition (kwashiorkor, anemia, goiter, beriberi, rickets) are known to be prevalent in some of the poorer countries, there is no reliable evidence of their incidence. The reason is that the countries require notification of only a limited number of illnesses and the reporting of these is incomplete. It is of interest, however, that the global incidence of malaria, a disease that is prevalent in tropical Africa, East Asia and South America, has been esti-

SAUDI ARABIA	125	6.8
SENEGAL	149	3.5
SIERRA LEONE	123	2.4
SINGAPORE	508	1.9
SOMALIA	48	2.5
SOUTH AFRICA	509	20.3
SPAIN	594	31.6
SUDAN	90	13.5
SWEDEN	2,046	7.7
SWITZERLAND	1,928	5.9
SYRIA	156	5.3
TAIWAN	185	12.4
TANZANIA	64	10.8
THAILAND	105	30.6
TOGO	82	1.6
TUNISIA	179	4.4
TURKEY	244	31.2
UGANDA	77	7.6
U.S.S.R.	1,195	231.0
UNITED ARAB REPUBLIC	96	29.6
UNITED KINGDOM	1,451	54.6
U.S.	2,893	194.6
UPPER VOLTA	35	4.9
URUGUAY	537	2.7
VENEZUELA	745	8.7
VIETNAM, NORTH	113	19.0
VIETNAM, SOUTH	113	16.1
YEMEN	36	5.0
YEMEN, SOUTH	246	1.1
YUGOSLAVIA	319	19.5
ZAMBIA	174	3.7

DOMINICAN REPUBLIC	212	3.6
ECUADOR	183	5.2
EL SALVADOR	236	2.9
ETHIOPIA	42	22.6
FINLAND	1,399	4.6
FRANCE	1,436	48.9
GERMANY, EAST	1,458	17.1
GERMANY, WEST	1,447	59.0
GHANA	245	7.7
GREECE	566	8.6
GUATEMALA	281	4.4
GUINEA	83	3.5
HAITI	80	4.4
HONDURAS	194	2.3
HONG KONG	291	3.7
HUNGARY	1,031	10.1
INDIA	86	486.8
INDONESIA	85	104.5
IRAN	211	24.8
IRAQ	193	8.2
IRELAND	783	2.9
ISRAEL	1,067	2.6
ITALY	883	51.6
IVORY COAST	188	3.8
JAMAICA	407	1.8
JAPAN	696	98.0
JORDAN	179	2.0
KENYA	77	9.3
KOREA, NORTH	88	12.1
KOREA, SOUTH	88	28.4
KUWAIT	3,184	0.5

chart and subsequent ones; exceptions here are Brunei, Cyprus and Kuwait, whose high incomes in relation to nearby countries illustrate the variation in wealth within geographic regions. There are fewer poor countries in Latin America than in Africa and Asia.

mated to be about 140 million cases per year, from which result just under a million deaths per year.

Perhaps the most useful single index of the health conditions prevailing in a community is the infant death rate. Deaths, unlike illnesses, are usually reported, at least in towns, and the death of children under the age of one year reflects a multitude of diseases and the entire spectrum of social and economic conditions. Currently the highest infant mortality rate is that of Cameroon, which has 137.2 infant deaths per 1,000 live births; for comparison the average rate in North America and western Europe is fewer than 25 deaths per 1,000 live births. These figures are national averages, and one would expect the rates in particular localities to be much higher. For example, in a recent year the infant mortality rate in the state of Alagoas in northeastern Brazil was 266.9. On the whole, infant mortality is higher in African countries than it is in most Asian countries. What may be surprising is that the rate in many Latin-American countries is higher than it is in Asian countries; Chile, Ecuador, Peru and Guatemala, all with rates close to 100, are the outstanding examples.

Another indication of the extent of poverty in a country is the number of inhabitants per physician. Whereas Indonesia and all the African countries except those in the north have more than 30,000 inhabitants per physician, South, East and West Asia have 6,000 people or fewer for each physician. The differences

between individual countries are great: in thousands of population per physician Upper Volta has 63, Niger 65, Ethiopia 69 and Rwanda 97; yet countries with only slightly higher levels of per capita income, such as Burma, Pakistan, India and South Korea, have figures of 11.7, 6.2, 5.8 and 2.7 respectively. With the exception of Haiti all the Latin-American countries have rates lower than 5.2, and the rates of most of them are less than 3.0, as are those of North America and Europe. This indicator thus underlines the impression created by the others, namely that the impoverished countries of Africa are worse off than their Asian counterparts, and that the impoverished Latin-American countries are in general much better off than their Asian counterparts.

Let us now consider one other measure of poverty: nutrition. If there is one form of deprivation in the interdependent pattern of poverty that could be described as fundamental, it is the deprivation of food. Hunger weakens an individual's resistance to disease, lowering his ability to perform work, and therefore his ability to provide himself and his family with food for the future. The most widespread nutritional diseases arise from the lack of calories and the lack of protein. Whereas calorie deficiency (undernutrition) is due to an insufficient quantity of food, protein deficiency (a form of malnutrition) reflects the inadequate quality of a diet. Since proteins are one source of calories (the others are

fats and cereals), a diet that contains enough proteins is also likely to provide enough calories. The reverse is not true. Calorie deficiency, then, is much less common than protein deficiency but much more serious.

Since calorie deficiency is precisely measurable, at least in principle, and also the mark of sustained deprivation of food, it is potentially a good indicator of the existence of serious poverty. A deficiency of calories, however, means a shortage of supply in relation to requirement, and in the measurement of both supply and requirement there are ambiguities. During the several stages between the production of food in the poorer countries and its consumption by an individual there is wastage varying from 20 to 50 percent of the calorie content. The estimate of calorie supply therefore depends on the stage at which the estimate has been made, and on the allowance that has been made for losses at later stages. On the other hand, the definition of the number of calories required varies according to the weight, sex, age and other characteristics of the individual, including the intensity of his activity and the climate in which he is working. Even the standard requirement for a reference individual, worked out by the Food and Agriculture Organization (FAO), has been revised (downward) over the years (inspiring the remark that physiology is "even more inexact a science than economics").

In spite of these recognized difficulties, the FAO has estimated calorie supplies by country and calorie requirements by region, and these data upset the hierarchy of poverty established by the previous indicators. They show the lowest-calorie regions to be not in Africa but in Asia and in parts of Latin America. Almost 1.8 billion people live in the calorie-deficient regions and 1.6 billion of these people are in Asia. As we shall see, this does not mean that so large a number of people are suffering from undernutrition, nor does it mean that we can ignore the possibility of undernutrition in the calorie-surplus regions. In order to reach an estimate of the number of people who are suffering from calorie deficiency, one must first know something about the distribution of calories within countries.

The problem of the distribution of food within a country has a space dimension and a time dimension. The movement of food from the food-surplus regions of a country to the food-deficit regions may be restricted by lack of

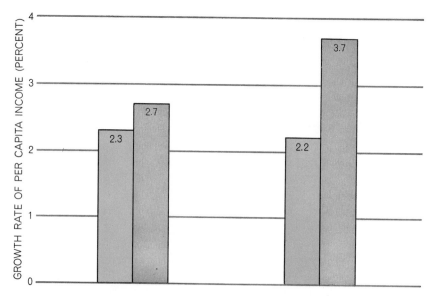

DIFFERENTIAL INCOME GROWTH indicates a widening economic gap between the poorer countries of the world (color) and the richer countries (gray). The average per capita income of the poorer nations actually grew somewhat more rapidly during the 1950's (left) than from 1960 to 1964 (right). Constant prices were used in estimating income growth.

transportation facilities, by political difficulties or both. Within regions the distribution of food is obviously limited by the distribution of purchasing power; even if a distribution to households in proportion to each household's needs were somehow ensured, there is no guarantee of an appropriate distribution within the household. Indeed, in many impoverished societies custom dictates that those who require the most calories (women of childbearing age, children aged one to four and adolescents) receive less than their requirement and the adult male receives more than his requirement.

An unequal distribution of calories over a period of time arises from inadequate methods of storage, so that the "hungry months" before harvest are a familiar feature of poor societies. Again, a harvest may fail in one year, or a succession of years, leading to a temporary drop in the food supply below the level of requirements. The availability of food grains in India is estimated to have fallen from 19 ounces per head per day in 1965 to 16.5 in 1966.

Putting together the results of household-diet surveys of India, Pakistan, Ceylon and Burma, and certain hypothetical distributions of calorie requirements for these countries, P. V. Sukhatme made a pioneering estimate of the numbers of people in the world who suffer from calorie deficiency. He put the total figure at between 300 and 500 million. It is important to emphasize that these figures refer only to the numbers suffering from undernutrition as distinct from protein deficiency. Sukhatme estimates the number of the latter to be between a third and half of the world's population.

W here are the 300 million or more people in the world who are undernourished? For the reasons given above, their number and location vary from year to year as circumstances change. Nonetheless, one can use such indicators as child mortality (age one to four years), not to be confused with infant mortality (from birth to one year), and crop yields

INFANT DEATH RATES (birth to one year) reflect social and economic conditions and thus are an index of poverty. The average rate in North America and western Europe is fewer than 25 deaths per 1,000 live births. Rates for Algeria, Brazil, Burma and Nigeria refer only to towns. The death rate of Bantu infants in South Africa is not known.

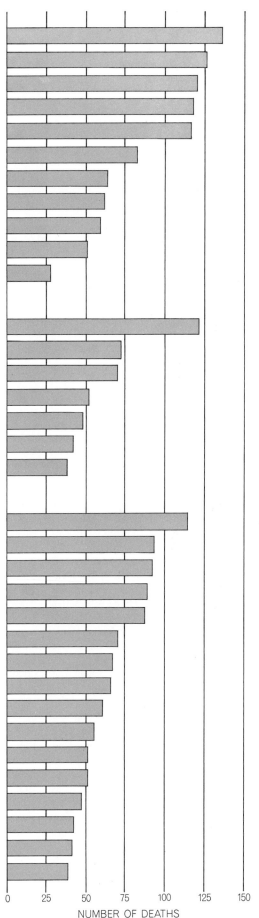

AFRICA
CAMEROON
TOGO
SOUTH AFRICA (ASIATIC-WHITE)
ALGERIA
UNITED ARAB REPUBLIC
MOZAMBIQUE
GUINEA
NIGERIA
SOUTH AFRICA (ASIATIC)
MADAGASCAR
SOUTH AFRICA (WHITE)

ASIA
BURMA
INDIA
PHILIPPINES
CEYLON
MALAYA
JORDAN
THAILAND

LATIN AMERICA
CHILE
ECUADOR
PERU
GUATEMALA
COLOMBIA
BRAZIL
DOMINICAN REPUBLIC
COSTA RICA
MEXICO
ARGENTINA
NICARAGUA
PUERTO RICO
VENEZUELA
PANAMA
JAMAICA
CUBA

0   25   50   75   100   125   150
NUMBER OF DEATHS
(PER THOUSAND LIVE BIRTHS)

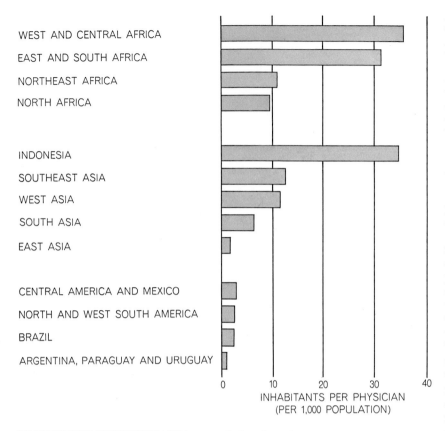

WEST AND CENTRAL AFRICA

EAST AND SOUTH AFRICA

NORTHEAST AFRICA

NORTH AFRICA

INDONESIA

SOUTHEAST ASIA

WEST ASIA

SOUTH ASIA

EAST ASIA

CENTRAL AMERICA AND MEXICO

NORTH AND WEST SOUTH AMERICA

BRAZIL

ARGENTINA, PARAGUAY AND URUGUAY

0   10   20   30   40

INHABITANTS PER PHYSICIAN
(PER 1,000 POPULATION)

PROPORTION OF PHYSICIANS in a population also indicates the level of poverty. In this breakdown rich countries are omitted, as are China, Ghana, North Korea, North Vietnam, Somalia, South Yemen, Yemen and part of Rhodesia. There are fewer than 1,000 people per physician in Australia, Europe, New Zealand, North America and the U.S.S.R.

per acre to identify some of the more critical areas. Child-mortality rates are particularly sensitive to protein and calorie deficiency.

Any estimate of the total number and distribution of the underfed in the world must lean heavily on the assumptions that are made about China, a country for which little reliable information has been available for the past 10 years. Sukhatme estimated that 20 percent of the population of China (some 140 million people) were undernourished, but this fraction appears rather high if one considers food production in China in 1965. The total cereal production per head of population appears to have been almost 50 percent higher in China than in India in that year, and one also expects there to be a more equal distribution of food in China. For these reasons it would seem unrealistic to suggest that more than 100 million people are undernourished in China, and the true figure might be nearer 50 million.

There is no reason to doubt Sukhatme's estimate that 25 percent of the population of India and Pakistan is underfed. A careful nutrition survey of East Pakistan recently carried out by the

Office of International Research of the U.S. National Institutes of Health discovered that "46 percent of the households studied had an inadequate calorie intake." Hence India and Pakistan together could account for between 100 to 150 million of the undernourished of the world. Indonesia, where Java is a critical area, might provide about 20 million more people, and the rest of Asia—East, Southeast and West—perhaps another 20 million. In Africa there may be about 40 million underfed people. West Africa and Ethiopia are the most serious areas, although the high child-mortality rate in West Africa may reflect a deficiency of protein rather than of calories. In Latin America the hungriest areas would appear to be in Guatemala, Honduras, Bolivia and Ecuador and in northeastern Brazil. Taken together, these areas could account for the remaining 20 million people.

The evidence we have reviewed suggests that hunger is primarily an Asian problem, and that more than two-thirds of the people in the world who are undernourished are to be found in four countries: India, Pakistan, China and Indonesia. On the other hand, material

poverty and health conditions appear to be worse in African countries. As we have seen, 17 countries, representing more than half the population of Africa, are in the very lowest income range. All the indicators suggest that, with the exception of one or two countries or areas within countries, Latin America is much better off than either of the other two continents.

It would be inappropriate to conclude this review of world poverty without commenting on the prospects for its alleviation. What can be done?

If we take hunger as the most urgent form of poverty, then the prospects of achieving a solution range from the euphoric to the cataclysmic. The difference between the two extreme views—that there is a world food surplus and that famine is just around the corner—turns on the question of distribution. The world's calorie supply slightly exceeds the world's calorie requirement. Given the continuation of present trends in food production, a worldwide food shortage is improbable. In this sense it is true to say that there is a world food surplus. This fact, however, is of little comfort to the low-calorie countries if their rate of food production cannot keep pace with their food requirements, and if balance-of-payment considerations place a limit on the amount of food they can import from the high-calorie countries. Similarly, a country's total food production may be growing fast enough to meet total requirements, but maldistribution may mean that grave food shortages can be expected in certain regions. In many respects the food problem is really a distribution problem rather than a production problem. Nonetheless, it may be easier to achieve increases in production than improvements in distribution.

It would be fair to say of the national and international plans designed to increase food production in the low-calorie countries that they have concentrated on long-run solutions. This is so because it is recognized that a significant increase in agricultural production presupposes changes in habits and attitudes, which can seldom be altered rapidly. The production of food in these countries is not expected to match their nutritional requirements for 15 to 25 years. The programs to control the growth of populations must also be classed as long-run solutions. It has been estimated that even if current birth-control programs are extremely successful, the overall food requirements of the low-calorie countries in 1985 will be at most 11 percent lower.

Nor do official plans usually provide for any change in the present distribution pattern of food supplies. Yet in the absence of any deliberate policy of redistribution it is clear that still larger total supplies would be necessary to ensure nutritionally adequate diets to major sections of the population. V. M. Dandekar goes so far as to suggest that in India the average daily intake of calories would have to be 3,000 or more if "the usual inequalities in the distribution of essential food supplies among individuals are to be allowed for." For most of the low-calorie countries the achievement of such an average level of calorie intake is much more than 20 years away.

Thus according to current development plans there appears to be no prospect of a solution to the problem of hunger for 20 years at the very least. Given the resources that are at the disposal of the rich countries, it seems quite unreasonable to condemn at least 300 million people to wait 20 years for their hunger to be satisfied. What is required to complement the long-run development strategy is a short-term program to alleviate the most extreme cases of hunger and other forms of poverty. Such a program might include three features: first, surveys of the health and nutritional status of the populations in the poorest areas of the world to establish priorities and requirements; second, food given to women and children either at schools or clinics (or both) in exchange for their attendance at instruction on elementary points of nutrition and hygiene; third, food given to men in exchange for work on projects yielding some immediate and visible return, such as improving the supply and distribution of water.

Such a program could not be more than a holding operation, but it would have two clear advantages. By feeding those who normally have the least food in relation to their needs (women and children), it would reduce the long-run food production requirement, because fewer calories would be needed to lift the lower end of the population distribution free from the level of undernutrition. Furthermore, a program of this kind would be less likely to encounter the current political resistance to transfer of resources from the rich countries to the poor ones. From the point of view of the donor country each unit of aid would have visible and immediate results; from the recipient country's point of view there would be no interference in its long-run development strategy.

There are of course many organizations, both official and voluntary, that already carry out functions such as those I have proposed. These activities are, however, only a drop in an ocean of need. The major objection to giving these proposals a systematic basis is the problem of administration: one recoils instinctively at the prospect of still another international-aid bureaucracy, yet some administration is essential to organize the transport and distribution of food and medicine. One possible solution might be to use the most effective organization already existing in each country; in many countries this might be the armed forces.

A further objection is that such a scheme would never work because of its low political priority: in the areas of serious poverty people are literally too weak to protest. Unless some such scheme is put into effect, however, there seems to be little prospect of making any reduction in the number of people suffering from serious poverty in the world during the next 20 years.

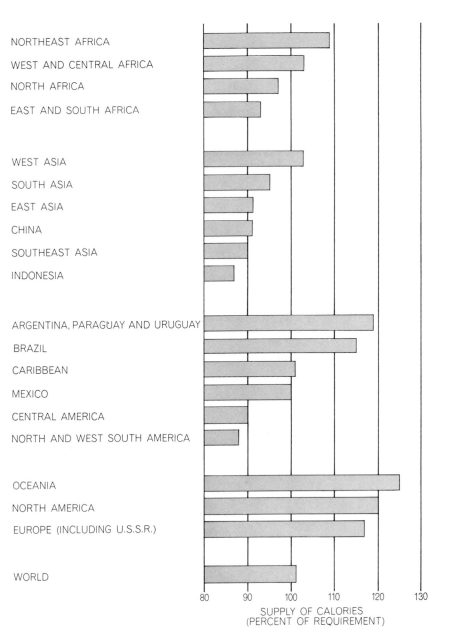

CALORIE PROVISIONS, in proportion to need, are another rough indicator of poverty (but one that does not tell how calories are distributed within a population). Almost 1.8 billion people live in calorie-deficient countries, 1.6 billion of these people in Asia. Oceania is chiefly Australia and New Zealand. Regions of Africa and Asia do not include rich countries.

11

Human Materials Production as a Process in the Biosphere

HARRISON BROWN
September 1970

The materials used by man for tools, shelter and clothing have traditionally been both organic (for example wood and natural fiber) and inorganic (stone, including glass and ceramics, and metals). To this classification we now add synthetic materials, which are mostly made from what are called in another connection fossil fuels. The organic materials are of course products of the biosphere, and assuming appropriate levels of use and sensible management they are self-renewing. The inorganic materials are the product of extremely slow processes in the lithosphere, and are hence not self-renewing in the human scheme of things. Yet the increasing need for such materials—mainly metals, stone and concrete—is one of the outstanding features of advancing societies. Moreover, the fact that inorganic materials are for the most part not recycled creates a pressing need for their disposal. These demands present men with numerous difficult choices, many of which inevitably involve the functioning of the biosphere.

For the greater part of the two million years or so of human existence man's need for materials was modest. With the

COPPER IS MINED at the Twin Buttes mine of the Anaconda Company near Tucson. The conspicuous hole in the photograph on the opposite page was made by removing some 236 million tons of overburden and rock to get at the ore lying between 600 and 800 feet below the surface of the ground. The ore has a copper content of about .5 percent and is considered to be a low-grade ore. Since copper is not highly abundant in the lithosphere but is extensively used, the trend has been toward mining low-grade ores.

adoption of each technological innovation that improved the chances of human survival, however, the need for materials increased in both absolute and per capita terms. For example, the controlled use of fire, which increased the variety of things that could be eaten and extended man's environment, created a substantial demand for firewood. Here, of course, a material was being used as fuel, but the development of tools that improved the efficiency of hunting and food gathering and protected men against predators created demands for materials in the strict sense: the right kinds of stone or of plant or animal substance.

With the invention of agriculture the need for materials increased considerably. The new technology made it possible for thousands of people to be supported by the produce of land that formerly could support only one person. Moreover, it was no longer necessary for everyone to be involved in food production. Farmers were able to grow a surplus of food to support nonfarmers. Until relatively recent times this surplus was never large, amounting to perhaps 5 percent, but it meant that some people could devote their energies to occupations other than farming. It was the surplus of food that made possible the emergence of cities and the evolution of the great civilizations of antiquity.

The oldest civilizations came into existence in regions that had ample areas of arable land and adequate supplies of water. Cities could become large only if they could draw on the agricultural surpluses of vast farmlands. Since water transport was by far the easiest way to ship foodstuffs in ancient times, the earliest civilizations and the first large cities

came into being in the valleys of the great rivers such as the Tigris and the Euphrates, the Nile, the Indus and the Yellow River. With the emergence of major urban centers increasingly elaborate technologies were developed, and they in turn led to the need for larger per capita quantities of raw materials such as stone, wood, clay, fiber and skin. (The ancient urban centers also confronted a problem that continues today: the disposal of garbage and rubbish. Scavenger birds, such as the kites of modern Calcutta, were probably essential elements in the system of processing garbage, but even so life must have been unsanitary, unsightly and odoriferous, at least for the great masses of the poor. The evidence suggests the prevalence of high mortality rates. Many ancient cities appear to have been literally buried in their own rubbish.)

Until the development of metal technology men appear to have used renewable resources such as wood at rates that were small compared with the rates of renewal. The consumption of nonrenewable resources such as stone was also small, particularly in comparison with the nearly infinite availability of resources with respect to the demand.

Copper was the first metal to come into widespread use on a substantial scale. In actuality copper is not very abundant in the lithosphere, but the metal can be won easily from its ore. The reduction temperature is fairly low, so that smelting can be accomplished in a simple furnace. Once the technology of extracting copper was developed the use of the metal became widespread in the ancient civilizations and the demand for the ore grew rapidly.

In this situation the high-grade deposits of ore close to the ancient urban centers were soon used up. Egypt, for example, quickly depleted her own copper reserves and had to develop an elaborate network of trade routes that enabled her to import copper from as far away as the British Isles and Scandinavia. Even so, high-grade ores of copper were uncommon enough to preclude widespread use of the metal. Copper did make possible a number of new technologies, but farmers, who were by far the greater proportion of society, were almost unaffected. Their implements continued to be made of stone, clay, wood and leather.

Gold is considerably easier to extract from its ore than copper; often the "ore" is metallic gold itself. As one might expect, therefore, the use of gold appears to predate the use of copper by a considerable span of time. Gold, however, is one of the rarest metals in nature, so that its ores are extremely scarce. Its rarity precluded its widespread use, except in small quantities for ornament.

Iron is considerably more abundant in the lithosphere than copper, but it is a much more difficult metal to win from the ore. The reduction temperature is high, and furnaces capable of attaining it were not developed until about 1100 B.C. The new high-temperature technology appeared first in the Middle East and quickly spread westward. The widespread availability of the ore made it possible for metal to be used on an unprecedented scale. New tools of iron helped to transform Europe from a land of dense forests to a fertile cropland.

One of the primary limitations to economic development in the ancient empires was the lack of ability to concentrate large quantities of energy. Insofar as it could be done at all it was usually accomplished by mobilizing gangs of men and to a lesser extent by the use of work animals. Use of the water mill and the windmill spread slowly. Only in sea transport was the wind used even with moderate effectiveness on a large scale as a prime mover. Remarkable as the Roman engineers were, they were limited by the concentration of energy they could mobilize. They went about as far as engineers could in the absence of a steam engine.

The development of a practical steam engine had to await the convergence of a series of developments in England in the late 17th century and the early 18th century. The island entered the Iron Age richly endowed with iron ore. Forests were also abundant, and the trees were used to produce charcoal, which in turn was used to reduce the iron oxide to the metal. These resources enabled England to become a major supplier of metallic iron for the world.

As iron production expanded English trees were consumed faster than they grew. Eventually the depletion of wood for charcoal threatened the entire iron industry. Clearly a substitute for charcoal was needed. The most likely one was coal, which existed abundantly on the island. Unfortunately, although coal can be used to reduce iron ore to the metal, the impurities in it render the metallurgical properties of the iron quite unsatisfactory.

The Darby family, which owned a substantial iron industry, spent many years attempting to transform coal into a substance suitable for the reduction of iron. Eventually a successful process was developed. It was based on the discovery that volatile impurities could be driven off by heating coal under suitable conditions. The resulting product, called coke, yielded metallic iron of satisfactory quality.

Here was a development—the linking of coal to iron—second only to agriculture in its importance to man. The new development led to a rapid expansion of the iron industry. Even more significant, it led directly to the development of the steam engine, which gave man for the first time a means of concentrating enormous quantities of inanimate energy.

Coal, iron and the steam engine gave rise to the Industrial Revolution, which spread from England to Europe and then to the U.S., the U.S.S.R. and most recently to Japan. Why did it start in the 18th century in England and not several centuries earlier in Rome? The Romans in many ways were the better engineers, and yet the harnessing of steam eluded them.

It is interesting to speculate on the role that random natural processes have played in cultural evolution. What would the course of history have been if copper had been as abundant as iron or if iron could be reduced from its ore as easily as copper? Perhaps the Iron Age would have started in the third millennium B.C. Suppose the Roman iron industry had run out of wood in the second century. Would there have been a linking of coal to iron and would the steam engine have emerged some 1,500 years earlier than it did? Such questions are diverting, but they cannot be answered with anything better than guesses.

The most important characteristics of

BLAST FURNACE for smelting iron in the 18th century was depicted in Diderot's *Encyclopédie*. The reason for the furnace's lo-

cation near a wooded area was the need for charcoal, which is what the horses in the background are carrying. In England the consumption of charcoal virtually exhausted the supply of trees before the technique of making coke from coal was developed. A furnace of this type might produce some two tons of iron a day. In the foreground a freshly produced pig, No. 289, is being weighed.

110

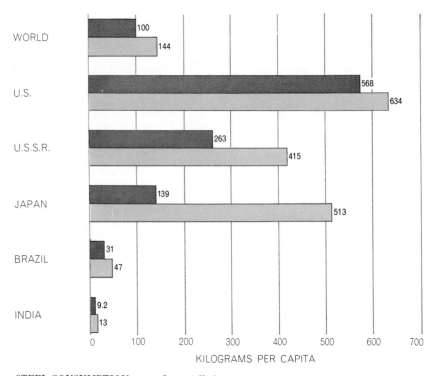

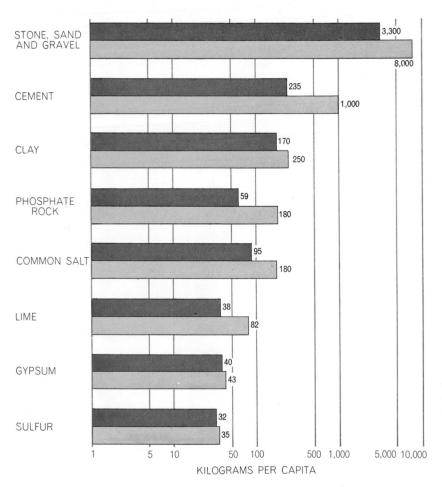

STEEL CONSUMPTION rose substantially but unevenly in the world and five major countries between 1957 (gray) and 1967 (color). The units are kilograms per person per year.

BASIC MATERIALS other than metal were produced in greatly increased amounts in the U.S. in 1967 (color) as compared with 1949 (gray). Units are kilograms per capita.

the Industrial Revolution have been rapid change and rapid increases in rates of change. Since the beginnings of the epoch mankind has seen the emergence of almost innumerable technological innovations that have competed with existing ways of doing things and have further released men from physical labor. It is now generally recognized that technological innovation has been a prime contributing factor to economic growth, perhaps equaling the combined effect of the classical factors of land, labor and capital.

Successful innovations have driven many older technologies to extinction and have resulted in higher productivity, greater consumption of energy, increased demand for raw materials, accelerated flow of materials through the economy and increased quantities of metals and other substances in use per capita. The history of industrial development abounds with examples.

In 1870 horses and mules were the prime source of power on U.S. farms. One horse or mule was required to support four human beings—a ratio that remained almost constant for many decades. Had a national commission been asked at that time to forecast the horse and mule population in 1970, its answer probably would have depended on whether its consultants were of an economic or a technological turn of mind. Had they been "economists," they would in all likelihood have estimated the 1970 horse and mule population at more than 50 million. Had they been "technologists," they would have recognized that steam had already been harnessed to industry and to ground and ocean transport. They would have recognized further that it would be only a matter of time before steam would be the prime source of power on the farm. It would have been difficult for them to avoid the conclusion that the horse and mule population would decline rapidly.

In fact, steam power appeared on the farm in about 1875 and spread rapidly. Had it not been for the introduction of the internal-combustion engine shortly after the turn of the century, steam power alone would have driven the horse off the farm. The internal-combustion engine, which was unforeseen in 1875, succeeded in driving off both the horse and the steam combine. Today the horse population is little more than 1.5 million, and most of the horses cannot in any real sense be regarded as work animals.

A second example of technological competition was the introduction of the steam-powered iron ship. In a period of only 30 years (1870 to 1900) the composition of the United Kingdom's merchant marine was transformed from 90 percent wooden sailing ships to 90 percent iron ships powered by steam. This technological transformation resulted in a greatly enhanced ability to transport goods rapidly and inexpensively over long distances. It also resulted in a greatly increased demand for iron and coal.

In the modes of intercity transportation in the U.S. one can see a dramatic sequence of competitions. In the first years of this century nearly all passenger traffic between cities was carried by the railroads. By 1910 the private car was competing seriously, and by 1920 the automobile was accounting for more passenger-miles between cities than the railroads were. Since World War II the airplane has competed with both the railroad and the automobile for intercity traffic. The combined impact of the automobile and the airplane has come close to putting railroads out of the passenger business. In the decade of the 1970's the airplane will probably make serious inroads on intercity automobile traffic as well. The net result of these changes, as with others, has been increased expenditure of energy and increased demand for materials in both absolute and per capita terms.

Levels of steel production and consumption are among the most useful indicators of worldwide technological and economic change. In the 19th century England became the dominant producer and consumer of steel, later being replaced by Germany. After World War I the U.S. became the largest industrial power, and steel production rose rapidly. In 1900 per capita steel production in the U.S. reached 140 kilograms, and by 1910 it was up to 300 kilograms. The level exceeded 400 kilograms during World War I, and during World War II it rose to 600 kilograms. Since World War II the picture has changed: although total steel production has continued to rise, the annual per capita level has changed little, averaging about 550 kilograms.

Per capita steel consumption has risen since World War II, but the rise has been slow. The difference between production and consumption has been made up by an increase in imports. In 1967 U.S. steel consumption was 634 kilograms per capita.

Although this is at present the highest per capita level of steel consumption in the world, the U.S. is being overtaken rapidly by other countries. Levels of consumption in much of western Europe and in Japan, Czechoslovakia, East Germany, the U.S.S.R. and Australia are now close to the U.S. level, and the rates of growth are such that Japan will overtake the U.S. quite soon. The per capita level of steel consumption in the U.S.S.R. will probably equal that of the U.S. within another decade. The worldwide rate of increase in per capita steel consumption from 1957 to 1967 was 44 percent, compared with the U.S. rate of 12 percent and the Japanese rate of 270 percent [see top illustration on page 110]. In view of the fact that virtually all elements of economic growth correlate reasonably well with per capita steel consumption, it is useful to inquire into the future levels of consumption in the U.S. and the rest of the world.

Consumption of metals other than iron can conveniently be stated in terms of steel consumption. When this is done, it becomes apparent that the consumption levels of certain metals, such as copper, zinc and lead, have remained remarkably constant over the past 50 years in spite of rapidly changing technologies. Consumption of certain other metals, such as tin, has been decreasing with respect to steel as a result of decreasing availability of ore and the development of substitutes. Consumption levels of the light metals, such as aluminum, are rising. Although these metals are still much less used than steel is, they will increasingly supplant steel for certain purposes.

If all the metallic iron that has been produced in the U.S. were still in ex-

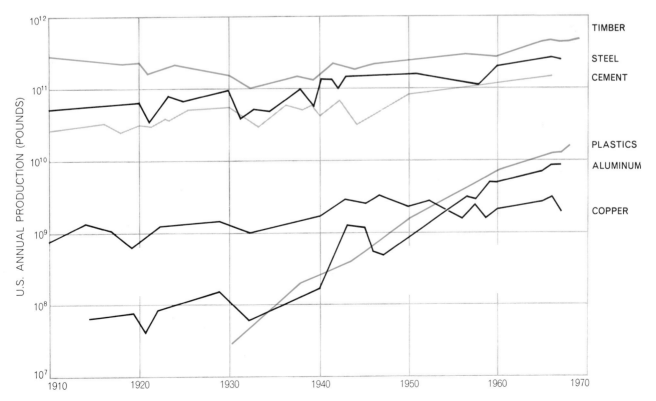

TREND IN CONSUMPTION of key materials is traced. The production of timber is usually reckoned in terms of board feet or cubic feet. For purposes of comparability it has been stated here in pounds, assuming an average density of 35 pounds per cubic foot.

istence, there would now be in use some 15 tons of steel per capita. In actuality a great deal of the steel produced has disappeared as a result of junking, production losses, corrosion and other causes. Analysis of production figures and losses suggests that the amount of steel now in use is some 9.4 metric tons of steel per capita. The greater part of it is in the form of structural materials such as heavy structural shapes and pilings, nails and staples, galvanized sheet metal and wire fence. About 8 percent of the steel, or 750 kilograms per person, is in the form of private automobiles, trucks and buses.

Of the roughly 600 kilograms of new steel consumed annually per capita in the U.S. about a third is returned to the furnaces as plant scrap, which is created as a result of the production of standard shapes and forms such as beams, sheet, pipe and wire. Therefore about 410 kilograms of the new steel enters the inventory of steel in use. At the same time about 350 kilograms of steel becomes obsolete or is lost as a result of corrosion and other processes. Of this some 140 kilograms (about 40 percent) is recovered and returned to the steel furnaces in the form of junked automobiles and other worn-out iron and steel products. The balance, corresponding to some 210 kilograms, is lost, probably never to be recovered. Some of it is dissipated widely; much of it is buried in dumps. During the course of the year the steel inventory increases by about 80 kilograms per capita, or somewhat less than 1 percent.

The mean lifetime of steel products varies enormously. Whereas an item such as a can may be in use for only a few weeks or months, steel in motor vehicles is in use on the average for about 10 years. Steel in ships may be in use for about 25 years. Steel structural shapes such as girders and concrete reinforcement may be in use for 50 years or more. The mean lifetime of all steel in use appears to be some 25 to 30 years.

Similar considerations apply to other metals. They are extracted, introduced into the national inventory and eventually lost or recycled as scrap. The mean lifetime of most of them appears to be shorter than that of steel.

Although the quantities of metal in use and the volumes of metalliferous ore that must be dug up and processed to support a human being in our society are large, the quantities of nonmetals consumed each year loom even larger and are increasing extremely rapidly [*see bottom illustration on page 110*].

Between 1949 and 1967 the per capita consumption of stone, sand and gravel in the U.S. rose some 2.5 times to about eight tons per capita. For cement the rise was by a factor of four to one ton per capita. In the same period the per capita consumption of phosphate rock rose by a factor of three and that of ordinary salt by a factor of two. All together, in order to support one individual in our society, something like 25 tons of materials of all kinds must be extracted from the earth and processed each year. This quantity seems certain to increase considerably in the years ahead.

The use of synthetic plastics is now increasing with impressive speed. Total world production of these materials now exceeds in both volume and weight the production of copper and aluminum combined. The production of synthetic fibers is now about half the combined production of cotton and wool. The relative rates of growth suggest that the output of such fibers will exceed that of cotton and wool within a short time.

Between 1945 and 1965 the price of polyethylene dropped by about 75 per-

cent while the price of steel tripled. Already polyethylene is less expensive than steel on a volume basis, although per unit of strength it remains some 15 times more expensive than steel. It is quite possible, however, that before long fiber-glass laminates will compete seriously with steel for structural purposes.

The overall figures suggest that the U.S. now has in use for every person about 150 kilograms each of copper and lead, well over 100 kilograms of aluminum, some 100 kilograms of zinc and perhaps 20 kilograms of tin. To meet the need for raw materials and the products derived from them the nation transports almost 15,000 ton-kilometers of freight per capita per year. Each person travels on the average each year some 8,500 kilometers between cities, makes more than 700 telephone calls and receives nearly 400 pieces of mail. There is now a ratio of almost one private automobile for every two people. In order to accomplish all the mining, production and distribution the American people spend energy at a rate equivalent to the burning

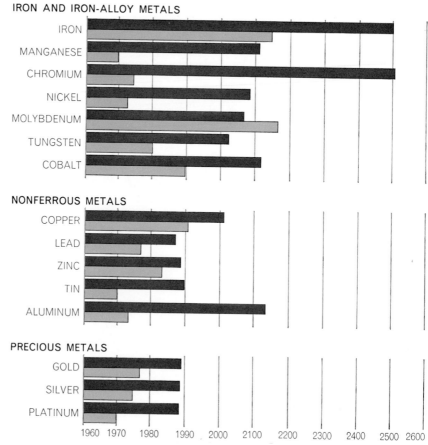

LIFETIMES OF METAL RESERVES are indicated for the world (*gray*) and the U.S. (*color*). These rough estimates are based on the assumption that the utilization of metals will continue to increase with population growth and rising per capita demand. They take into account, however, that new reserves will be discovered by exploration or created by innovation. It is estimated U.S. demands will increase four and a half times by the year 2000.

of about 10 tons of coal annually per person or about 16 tons of coal per ton of steel consumed or about one ton of coal per ton of steel in use. A convenient rule of thumb is that we must burn about one ton of coal each year, or its equivalent in some other source of energy, to keep one ton of steel in use.

Clearly man has become a major geologic force. The amount of rock and earth he moves each year in the present industrialized regions of the world is already prodigious and will continue to grow because of rising population levels, increasing demand from the industrialized nations and the gradual decline in grades of raw materials. If one adds to these requirements the fantastically high demand that would arise if the development process were to be accelerated in the poor countries, the total potential demand staggers the imagination. If the entire human population were to possess the average per capita level of metal characteristic of the 10 richest nations, all the present mines and factories in the world would have to be operated for more than 60 years just to produce the capital, assuming no losses.

Given an eventual world population of 10 billion, which is probably a conservative estimate, and a per capita steel inventory of 20 tons, some 200 billion tons of iron would have to be extracted from the earth. The task would require 400 years at current rates of extraction. Anything approaching such a demand would clearly place enormous strains on the earth's resources and would greatly accentuate rivalries between nations for

the earth's remaining deposits of relatively high-grade ores. Most of the industrialized nations already import a substantial fraction of their raw materials. Japan is almost completely dependent on imports. Whereas the U.S. imported in 1950 only 8 percent of the iron ore that it consumed, the figure today is more than 35 percent.

At present the world can be divided into two major groups of steel consumers. The first group consists of about 680 million people, living in 18 nations, who consume steel at rates varying between 300 and 700 kilograms annually per capita. The total consumption of this group comes to about 420 million tons of steel per year. The second group consists of 1,400 million people, living in 13 nations, who consume steel at rates varying between 10 and 25 kilograms annually per capita. The total consumption of this group comes to 27 million tons of steel per year. An additional 400 million people live under circumstances that are still poorer, and 440 million more live under circumstances intermediate between those of the rich and the poor. The distribution of per capita energy consumption follows a similar pattern, as does the distribution of per capita income.

The slowness of the development process and the magnitude of the task the poor countries face can be gauged by the fact that with existing production facilities the poorer group (not the poorest one) would need about 500 years to produce the per capita quantity of steel in use now characteristic of the

U.S. Although production levels in the poorer group are increasing fairly rapidly (close to 50 percent per decade on a per capita basis), many decades will be required, even in the absence of any major upheaval, before the amounts of steel in use can enable those nations to feed, clothe and house their populations adequately.

What goes into a system must eventually come out. As I have noted, somewhat less than 4 percent of the steel inventory in the U.S. is exuded annually into the environment, and only about 40 percent of this amount is recovered. As the grades of resources dwindle and locations for dumping solid wastes become more difficult to find, the economic and social pressure for more substitution, more attention to priorities of use of scarce materials and more efficient cycling will increase.

It is clear that various metals can substitute for one another, and that plastics can substitute for a number of metals. Aluminum already substitutes for copper in many roles, as copper and nickel now replace silver in coinage. Synthetic crystals come increasingly into use. All these techniques can be pushed a good deal farther than they have been up to now.

Improved efficiency of cycling is desirable for all solid wastes not only to lower the rate of depletion of high-grade resources but also to reduce the injurious effects of such wastes on the biosphere. The quantities of wastes are becoming substantial. They now amount to nearly one ton per year per person, of which

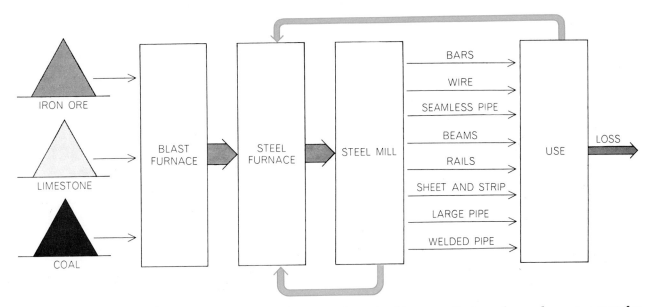

FLOW OF MATERIALS through the biosphere is depicted using steel as an example. Of the steel produced from iron ore, about a third is recycled immediately in the form of scrap left over from the production of beams, wire and other shapes. Two-thirds enters the national inventory. During each year, however, a somewhat smaller amount of steel becomes obsolete. About 40 percent of it is recycled in the form of scrap. The remainder is lost as a result of such factors as wear, corrosion and disposal through junking.

about a third consists of packaging materials. In 1968, for example, the average American threw away almost 300 cans, 150 bottles and about 140 kilograms of paper. The quantities are increasing rapidly on both an absolute and a per capita basis. Properly cycled, they could provide raw materials for the glass, steel, aluminum and plastics industries.

From a purely technological point of view man could in principle live comfortably on a combination of his own trash and the leanest of earth substances. Already, for example, copper ore containing only .4 percent copper is being processed. If the need arose, copper could be extracted from ore that is considerably leaner than .4 percent. Eventually man could, if need be, extract his metals from ordinary rock. A ton of granite contains easily extractable uranium and thorium equivalent to about 15 tons of coal, plus all the elements necessary to perpetuate a highly technological civilization. Such a way of life would create new problems, because under those circumstances man would become a geologic force transcending by orders of magnitude his present effect on the earth. Per capita energy consumption would come to the equivalent of perhaps 100 tons of coal per year, and there might be some 100 tons of steel in use per person. The world would be quite different from the present one, but there is no reason a priori why it would necessarily be unpleasant.

Man has it in his power technologically to maintain a high level of industrial civilization, to eliminate deprivation and hunger and to control his environment for many millenniums. His main danger is that he will not learn enough quickly enough and that he will not take adequate measures in time to forestall situations that will be very unpleasant indeed.

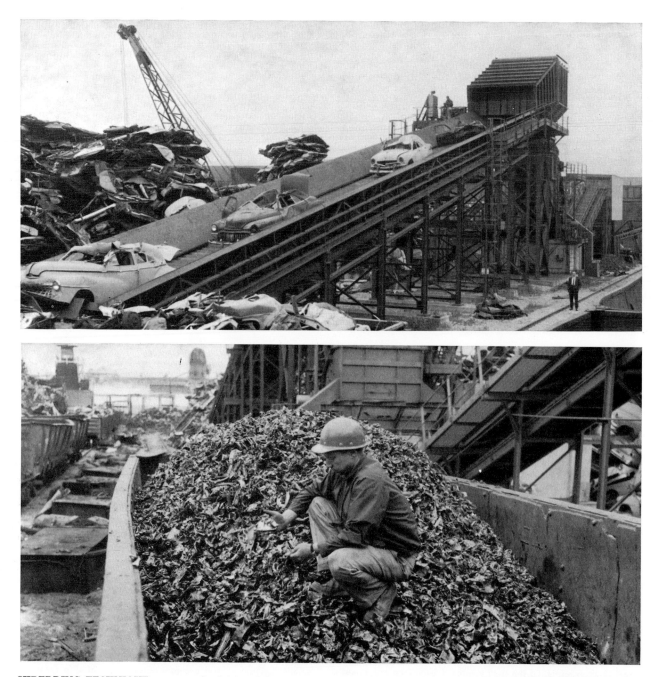

SHREDDING TECHNIQUE was recently developed for turning worn-out or wrecked automobiles into scrap that can be recycled to steel furnaces. At top stripped automobile bodies are being fed into the shredder; the product that emerges is shown at bottom.

III

THE DIMENSIONS OF INTERVENTION

THE DIMENSIONS
OF INTERVENTION

*It should be obvious that the possible action
of all such substances [lead, mercury, insecticides,
defoliants] on the tenuous and geochemically inefficient
green mantle of the earth demands intense study
if life is to continue in the biosphere.*

G. Evelyn Hutchinson,
SCIENTIFIC AMERICAN, September 1970

INTRODUCTION

Unfortunately, the word "environment" still conveys to many people an image resembling an advertisement for cigarettes — sparkling streams, snow-covered peaks, and green expanses of meadow sprinkled with wildflowers. In this context, pollution is a pile of discarded beer cans detracting from the view. A more sophisticated (but still inadequate) perspective embraces environmental problems — such as air and water pollution, noise, and the loss of open space — as nuisances that contribute to the deteriorating quality of life. But missing still, evidently, is a widespread consciousness of environment as the entire complex of factors that supports, shapes, and incorporates life itself. Without this consciousness, general recognition of the seriousness of existing and impending environmental threats is impossible, and the drastic action required to avert or ameliorate them will never take place.

The articles in this section offer two sorts of contributions to the development of the ecological awareness we need so desperately. The first is a grasp of the foundations, the implications, and the extent of some of the problems that have become widely known, at least by name: pesticides, air pollution, eutrophication, radiation, and thermal pollution. The second contribution is an illustration of the dimensions of man's impact on the ecosphere in the form of less publicized — but no less serious — perturbations: the changing carbon dioxide balance, the modifications of urban climates, and the alteration of the epidemiological environment. These articles form a necessarily limited sampling of valid environmental concerns, but we believe they more than adequately illustrate a rather ominous proposition: In a great many areas, man's capacity to intervene significantly in the processes of the ecosphere far overshadows his meager ability to predict the exact results of that intervention.

Few papers have made a greater contribution to ecological awareness than George M. Woodwell's "Toxic Substances and Ecological Cycles." The underlying theme of the paper is Woodwell's systematic refutation of what we call "the myth of dilution." This is the notion that pouring one pound of poison into a billion pounds of ocean, atmosphere, or soil automatically and instantaneously yields one part per billion as the concentration to be dealt with. Woodwell illustrates the dangerous inaccuracy of this proposition by explaining his own classic work (with Charles F. Wurster, Jr., and Peter A. Isaacson) on the concentration of pesticide residues in the food web of a Long Island estuary. The author also describes a number of studies sponsored by the U. S. Atomic Energy Commission on the behavior of radioactive isotopes in the ecosystem. Taken together, the various investigations yield a consistent and disturbing set of conclusions: (1) that such factors as wind, water movement, and animal migration spread toxic substances over enormous areas of the earth's surface (this is the grain of truth in the myth of dilution, although the processes are neither instantaneous nor uniform); (2) that the food webs through which energy passes from plants to herbivores to carnivores may reconcentrate the pollutants to astonishing and dangerous levels; and (3) that where and when these levels will be reached in the food web, in any given case, defies prediction because of the enormous number of variable factors that may be operative.

Woodwell raises several other points that appear again and again in considerations of man's impact on the ecosphere. The first is our consistent tendency to underestimate the hazard associated with toxic substances. This tendency is frequently compounded by the time lag between the contamination and the appearance of harmful results, as in Woodwell's example of the iodine-131 hazard. Also underestimated in many evaluations of environmental risks is the potential for the destructive synergism of pollutants—that is, two or more pollutants, acting together, may produce a destructive effect that exceeds the sum of the effects expected if the pollutants act separately. See, for example, Woodwell's discussion of food-web destruction by pesticides coupled with over-fertilization of aquatic systems by sewage and agricultural runoff.

Altogether, man's record of pooh-poohing hazards that ultimately prove to be real (pesticides, radioactivity, and heavy metals, to name only a few) would seem to argue for conservatism in the setting and enforcing of standards to protect man and his environment from wholesale poisoning. Woodwell's reference to the recognition of the hazards of DDT 25 years ago is a significant commentary on the protestation of innocence now so often heard: "How could we have known?" Unfortunately, the well-warranted conservatism is still not in evidence in the agencies empowered to act in these matters. Perhaps part of the near paralysis of our regulatory agencies can be explained by the misconception attacked by Woodwell when he writes: "The mere fact that conspicuous mortality is not observed is no assurance of safety." We must abandon the notion that piles of dead bodies, whether of pelicans or people, are the only symptoms worthy of alarm and of corrective action. If we do not, there will be piles of bodies eventually, but they may appear only after the erosion of the ecosystem is irreversible.

A number of Woodwell's general points are visible in a different context in Walsh McDermott's earlier paper "Air Pollution and Public Health." The principal issue here is the difficulty of assessing the consequences of prolonged exposure to low levels of substances that, at high concentrations in short exposures, are deadly. Again, the assumption on the part of industry and its regulators has all too often been that the absence of a countable number of corpses signifies

safety. Convincing data on low-level effects are extraordinarily difficult to obtain. To be convincing, statistical studies require large
numbers of subjects, and the effects of a host of other variables, both
hereditary and environmental, must be sorted out. Because even the
composition and concentration of air pollutants breathed by a particular population is often not accurately known, it is easy to see that
linking air pollution to disease conclusively is a far more difficult
task than, say, linking smoking to disease. The reader may recall how
long it took to verify the relation of cigarette smoking to respiratory and cardiovascular disease, as well as the desperate propaganda
campaign waged by the tobacco industry to deny the reality of that
relation.

Unfortunately, then, the burden of proof in many environmental
conflicts still rests with the public. In part, this is because there are
known economic costs associated with cleaning up pollution, but the
public-health costs associated with doing less are, as yet, unquanti-
fied. As McDermott puts it, "the responsible public health official
needs better evidence to justify the social cost of control measures."

Since McDermott's paper was written, of course, some of the
needed evidence has come in. One of the better analyses of recent
data, together with an attempt to deduce a dollar value for the public health benefit of a 50 percent reduction in air pollution, is the
paper "Air Pollution and Human Health," by Lave and Seskin (*Science,* vol. 169, pp. 723–732, August 21, 1970). The authors of that
article put a lower limit of $2 billion on the value of a 50 percent
reduction, but they do not comment on the probable cost of achieving
such a decrease. While their work demonstrates a seemingly indisputable association between air pollution and various disease and
death rates, it does not attempt to settle the controversy, mentioned
by McDermott, about whether air pollution initiates disease or merely
aggravates existing conditions.

A point of historical interest is McDermott's mention of 150 parts
per million (ppm) as the concentration of carbon monoxide (CO)
"that would represent a hazard." This figure supports Woodwell's
conclusion that we traditionally underestimate hazards, revising
"permissible concentrations" steadily downward as our knowledge
grows. Specifically, since McDermott wrote his article, studies on
humans have shown impairment of visual acuity upon exposure to
50 ppm of CO for only 50 minutes, psychomotor impairment upon
intermittent exposure to 100 ppm, and cardiovascular changes in
subjects with heart disease exposed to only 30 ppm for periods of
8 hours. Another point on which ten years of hindsight permits a
mild criticism of McDermott's paper is the ranking of various sources
of pollutants—automobiles, industry, and so forth. If one ranks according to the volume of emissions, as did McDermott and as many
observers still do today, the automobile is the dominant culprit. But
improved knowledge of the physiological effects of specific pollutants now permits at least a rough attempt at a more sophisticated

approach: The hazard is computed by multiplying the volume of the pollutant by its relative toxicity. By this measure, industry takes over first place easily, largely because the sulfur dioxide emitted in abundance from coal- and oil-fired power stations is so much more toxic than the carbon monoxide, hydrocarbons, and oxides of nitrogen produced by automobiles.

In other areas, time has shown McDermott's insight to be very good indeed. One such item is the nonexhaust contributions to automotive air pollution "in the form of pulverized rubber and asphalt, generated by abrasion of tires upon streets." Certain constituents of synthetic rubber, the polychlorinated biphenyls (PCBs), are now known to resemble the chlorinated hydrocarbon pesticides in toxicity, persistence, and propensity to be concentrated in food chains. Like many particulates, pulverized asphalt may well be carcinogenic. Asbestos particles from brake linings, a nonexhaust pollutant not mentioned by McDermott, appear to be implicated in the increasing incidence of a form of lung cancer once restricted to workers in the asbestos industry.

Finally, McDermott saw the need for, and advocated, "a citizens' movement in the environmental-pollution field like the conservation movement of Theodore Roosevelt's day." Today's readers scarcely need reminding that just such a movement has developed. In some areas, this movement has already made important progress in shifting the burden of proof, in matters of public health and safety, to the polluters and their promoters. Supporters of the status quo have begrudged every constructive step and have successfully blocked many. For example, the 1970 ballot proposition in California to divert a portion of gasoline-tax revenues to pollution control efforts and rapid transit was rejected at the polls, owing to a campaign of opposition heavily financed by major oil companies. These interests will not be beaten down without still more data and more public concern—the same goals that Walsh McDermott was urging in 1961.

"The Aging Great Lakes," by Charles F. Powers and Andrew Robertson, is yet another demonstration that there is more to pollution than filth. The authors state their central message plainly: "The ill effect of pollution is not limited to the circumstance that it renders the waters unclean. Pollution also hastens the degeneration and eventual extinction of the lakes as bodies of water." There is little to brighten this disquieting message in the paragraphs that follow. Perhaps the only "good" news is that Lake Erie is not yet dead—it is merely in the advanced stages of a premature and man-induced senility. Above all, it is important to remember that the accelerated eutrophication process described by Powers and Robertson is in progress in lakes all over the nation, while many of the components of the process are in operation in our rivers, bays, and estuaries, as well. The steady deterioration of our environment in the form of such unspectacular but insidious phenomena is among the most underrated aspects of the ecological crisis.

Yet another subtly destructive environmental threat is radiation, concerning which some relevant information was also presented in the article by Woodwell. A bitter controversy over the public health aspects of radiation exposure is raging as the decade of the 1970s begins. An up-to-date, authoritative survey of this subject is needed. Nevertheless, it is instructive to regard this issue in the perspective of Nobel Laureate George W. Beadle's 1959 article, "Ionizing Radiation and the Citizen." Most of Beadle's basic points concerning the effects of radiation and the philosophy of setting standards are still valid today. The emphasis, however, has changed from weapons tests in the historical context of 1959 to a range of proposed or actual peaceful uses of atomic energy in the 1970s. Yet in today's debate over quantitative standards, some long-valid qualitative judgments occasionally seem to have been swept aside, much to the dismay and frustration, we suspect, of the scientists who initiated the present controversy.

As Beadle points out, for example, nearly all mutations are harmful; and we assume that *any* dose of radiation, however small, causes some mutations. It must only be added that, since 1959, enzymatic repair of some kinds of defects in DNA, which constitute mutations, has been demonstrated (see, for example, "The Repair of DNA," by Hanawalt and Haynes, SCIENTIFIC AMERICAN Offprint 1061), but the extent to which repair of radiation-induced mutations can be relied upon is unknown. Moreover, prudence still requires the possibly pessimistic assumption that the life-shortening and carcinogenic effects of radiation persist in proportion to even the lowest doses. Thus, Beadle's conclusion must stand: ". . . every reasonable effort should be made to reduce the levels of ionizing radiation to which man is exposed to the lowest level that can reasonably be attained."

The catch, of course, is in the word "reasonable." Today, in an obvious conflict of interest, the regulators empowered to interpret what is "reasonable" in matters relating atomic energy to public health are also charged with the promotion of this technology—the Atomic Energy Commission, however well intentioned its members and advisers may be, has incompatible roles. Not surprisingly, then, critics of nuclear power fear that the promoter-regulators of the AEC will find it "unreasonable" to demand expenditures for reduced emissions if no deaths can be conclusively proved to have resulted from emission levels theretofore considered safe. This is a version of the "conspicuous mortality" problem cited by Woodwell, and Beadle has some important comments about it. He points out, for example, that "from the beginning of man's experience with ionizing radiation, he has consistently underestimated its hazards." He also notes that an experiment that shows no statistically significant effect of radiation at some level does not prove that the effect does not exist; it often merely means that the sample was too small for the effect to be unequivocally identified, or that the effect was masked by other variables. This is part of the reason we have so consistently underestimated risks.

It is most important, Beadle insists, that we not "postpone decisions until we have final and complete answers." We must act on the basis of the best information we have, augmented in matters of public health by a liberal dose of caution, for the answers will *never* be final and complete. We must beware of procrastinators in every field, who respond to the need for action only with clarion calls for more research. It should be more widely recognized that to "postpone decisions" means to make a decision in favor of the status quo.

The discharge of waste heat into local bodies of water, a problem associated with the use of nuclear reactors to generate electricity, has received—somewhat inappropriately—nearly as much public attention as has radiation. Heat is discharged by any steam-electric power station, but nuclear plants have often been singled out because they discharge into aquatic systems more heat per unit of useful output than do their fossil-fueled counterparts. This particular aspect of the very general thermal pollution problem is treated by John R. Clark in "Thermal Pollution and Aquatic Life." Clark raises many instructive points: the importance of temperature as a controlling biological variable; the various factors that place increased demand on dissolved oxygen as water temperature rises, thus diminishing the capacity of the water to absorb waste; and the deceptive nature of increases in animal growth rate in warmer water (many aquatic animals grow more slowly but achieve larger size in colder water). Special emphasis should be given to the possibility, raised and illustrated by Clark at several points in his article, that thermal pollution may participate in destructive synergisms with other threats to our aquatic systems—sewage, chemicals, agricultural runoff, and the destruction of wetlands.

On the technological side, Clark is appropriately cautious in discussing the possibilities of putting the waste heat of powerplants to constructive use. The temperature of the effluent, while uncomfortably high in the perspective of the environment, is uneconomically low for most industrial and commercial purposes. Although Clark does not say so, there are circumstances in which the thermal effluent could be useful for space heating in nearby buildings. But this would require locating the power plants in metropolitan areas, which, at least in the case of nuclear reactors, seems imprudent for reasons of safety. As Clark Points out, perhaps the best way to avoid thermal pollution of our waters is to discharge the waste heat into the atmosphere; and perhaps the least offensive way to do this is by means of the dry cooling tower. It is particularly important to note how inexpensive this would actually be, the protests of the utility companies notwithstanding. Clark gives a figure of 2.6 percent of the consumer's power cost, although other estimates go as high as 10 percent. But even the latter figure should be no cause for complaint in a country such as the United States, where power is so cheap we squander it on "no-frost" refrigerators, garish neon signs, and the manufacture of aluminum beer cans and oversized automobiles.

The relative ease with which we might lift the thermal burden from our waters is deceptive; the more basic thermal pollution problem that looms in the future is, by contrast, utterly intractable. The laws of thermodynamics insist that all the energy we use, as well as the fraction wasted in the generation process, must ultimately be dissipated as heat. Thus, the electricity that cooks, lights, air conditions, and drives streetcars is converted into heat near the point of consumption. So, also, is the energy from the gasoline that drives our automobiles, and the coal and oil that provide heat for many industrial processes. The discharge of this heat into the atmosphere, from which it is ultimately radiated away into space, is already a substantial perturbation of the energy balance in metropolitan areas. (This problem is discussed later in this section in William P. Lowry's article "The Climate of Cities.")

The heat from man's activities could assume regional climatological significance in such areas as the west coast of the United States within 30–40 years. If present trends persist unchecked, it could have continental and global significance within 70–100 years. The possible sensitivity of the global meteorological system to strong local perturbations may, of course, make even these estimates too optimistic. It is to be emphasized that no scientific breakthroughs will free us from such difficulties: Anyone who may be awaiting the overthrow of the laws of thermodynamics is advised not to hold his breath. Furthermore, technological approaches to other forms of pollution will themselves have a cost in energy, thus contributing to the ultimate thermal problem. In the long run, the only solution is the stabilization of both the number of consumers of energy and their per capita consumption.

Like heat, carbon dioxide has not been considered an important pollutant until recently. Although CO_2 is produced in prodigious quantities by respiration, the combustion of fossil fuels, and many other processes, its acute toxicity is very low indeed. Clean, dry air contains 318 ppm of CO_2, and adverse effects on human health are not known to occur below 10,000 ppm. As we have already noted, however, a working definition of pollution must encompass more than outright toxicity. If we broaden our definition of pollutants to include substances introduced into the environment in quantities sufficient to alter natural cycles or processes significantly, then CO_2 certainly qualifies. The quantities produced in connection with man's activities have already perturbed the carbon cycle in a detectable way and have, in all probability, influenced global climate. The status of this interesting problem, as of 1959, is summarized in "Carbon Dioxide and Climate," by Gilbert N. Plass.

In 1971, most of the essentials of Plass's discussion remain valid, and it forms an instructive and readable introduction to the topic. However, the intensive study that the CO_2 question and related matters have received since 1959 has led to refinements in several aspects of our knowledge. First, the cumulative increase in the atmospheric concentration of CO_2, as of 1960, is now judged to have been about 8 percent, rather than the 13 percent given by Plass. Of the total amount of CO_2 injected by man, only 40–50 percent has remained in the atmosphere. Plass's diagram of the CO_2 balance should show perhaps 4 billion more tons entering the ocean than leaving it. Second, Plass's calculation of the associated temperature increase employed a heat balance for the Earth's surface, rather than for the surface-atmosphere system. A numerical calculation that includes vertical convection as well as radiative processes in the atmosphere has since become available. It leads to an estimated temperature increase due to accumulated CO_2 of 1.4°F by the year 2000 (all other factors being constant), rather than the 3.6°F predicted by Plass. (Readers interested in pursuing these details further should consult *Global Effects of Environmental Pollution*, edited by S. F. Singer, Springer-Verlag, 1970.) Work is in progress on still more elaborate models to determine the effect of CO_2 on the latitudinal distribution of surface temperature over the globe. Because of the complexity of the "atmospheric heat engine" that actually governs climate, the complete effects of CO_2 defy intuitive prediction. (See "The Energy Cycle of the Earth," by Abraham H. Oort, SCIENTIFIC AMERICAN, September 1970.) It is to be emphasized that differential heating effects could be far more serious than a postulated mean increase of 1.4°F would seem to imply.

The primitive state of our knowledge of these vital matters is underscored by one additional development since Plass's article was written. It is now generally agreed that the warming trend that had been taking place since the middle of the nineteenth century was reversed about 1940. Since that time, the mean global surface temperature has actually been decreasing. During the same period, the CO_2 content of the atmosphere has continued to increase. Thus, if CO_2 was, in fact, responsible for the observed warming prior to 1940, it is certainly now being dominated by some other effect. It has been suggested that rising particulate loads in the atmosphere have caused the temperature decrease by reflecting back into space an increasing fraction of incident solar energy. There is no doubt that the turbidity (that is, the dustiness) of the atmosphere has been increasing in recent decades, but there is considerable dispute as to the relative contributions of agriculture, urban agglomerations, and the action of volcanoes. Although Plass was concerned with the CO_2 from volcanoes, the prevailing view today seems to be that the injection of volcanic ash into the stratosphere is more important. Finally, because particulate matter can absorb as well as reflect radiation, depending on such presently unknown factors as the size distribution of the particles, it must be admitted that the entire matter is still unresolved. Some people seem reassured because science cannot accurately predict the exact direction and consequences of man-induced climatic changes. We, in contrast, are apprehensive about human intervention in global processes about which man understands very little and upon which he is utterly dependent for survival.

Today, man's impact on climate is dramatic and conclusively demonstrable only in the vicinity of his cities. The multiplicity of factors with which he brings such changes about, and the awesome complexity of the problem, even on this small scale, are highlighted in William P. Lowry's article "The Climate of Cities." Although not all of the climatic consequences of substituting cities for open country are now necessarily adverse, the potential for larger changes should be considered ominous. Most of the contributing factors—the changes in the surface materials, increased surface roughness due to structures, the generation of heat, the disposition of moisture, the presence of contaminants in the air—will increase in spatial extent, intensity, or both, as populations grow and urbanization and industrialization proceed apace. Lowry himself identifies the critical possibility that the combined effects could cause "large-scale changes of climate over entire continents." In this connection, we should perhaps emphasize more than he does that such changes could well be far more serious than a simple spreading of today's urban climates. For, as we have already suggested in our discussion of the CO_2 and thermal problems, thresholds for instability may exist: Local perturbations of sufficient scale could trigger disproportionate fluctuations or semipermanent changes on a continental or even global scale. The consequences for planetary agriculture, in particular, could be catastrophic.

A facet of man's interaction with the ecosphere that has received far less attention than climate, or indeed than any of the other problems enumerated here so far, is his effect upon the epidemiological environment. It could prove to be more important than any of the other facets and, unlike many of them, could assert itself unmistakably at virtually any time. Such alarming notions are often disparaged by those who believe that modern medicine has made plagues and epidemics things of the past. Unfortunately, this belief is not supported by the facts. The generation of dangerous new strains of disease organisms by mutation is related to the size of the host population. The probability that such a strain will flourish and spread is related to population density, population mobility, and the general level of public health. The population of the world today is unrivalled in history for its size and density. Malnutrition and inadequate sanitary conditions are appallingly widespread, and potential carriers of disease of every description move routinely and in substantial numbers from continent to continent in matters of hours. We need not go far afield to find examples of the inadequacy of "modern medicine" in the face of epidemic conditions. The Asian influenza epidemic of 1968 killed relatively few people only because the virus happened to be nonfatal to people otherwise in good health, not because of public health measures. Far deadlier viruses, which easily could become scourges without precedent in the population at large, have, on more than one occasion, been contained to research workers largely by good luck.

Yet another unsettling aspect of the epidemiological situation is the widespread appearance of drug-resistant strains of bacteria. That such resistance can appear through a process much faster than mutation and selection is explained by Tsutomu Watanabe in "Infectious Drug Resistance." The title aptly describes the process—the resistance itself spreads among the bacteria like an infection. The introduction and concluding paragraphs are "must" reading, even for those who do not wish to tackle the rather technical biochemical details. Watanabe emphasizes that the threat of this dangerous phenomenon to public health is amplified by certain of man's activities in medicine, agriculture, and food processing. These include "shotgun" treatment of infections with antibiotic drugs, the use of antibiotics in livestock feeds to promote fattening and control disease, and the treatment of meat and other foods with antibiotics and synthetic drugs as preservatives. According to Watanabe, this little-known aspect of man's tendency to lace his environment with chemicals could have dramatic consequences. Resistance to antibiotics can be transferred from one kind of bacterium to another. Such transfers have already resulted in outbreaks of diarrhea in infants. It should also seriously be considered, that, if chloramphenicol is used to treat cattle, we may create strains of bacteria that can transfer their resistance to typhoid bacteria. This would, in effect, render useless the most important treatment for typhoid in man. Watanabe writes: "Unless we put a halt to the prodigal use of antibiotics and synthetic drugs we may soon be forced back into the preantibiotic era of medicine."

As we noted at the outset, the papers presented in this section do not cover all of man's detrimental interactions with the ecosphere, or even all of those currently thought to be important. It should be apparent by now that new knowledge regularly brings with it an awareness of new threats, while it occasionally diminishes our estimation of others. Some of the problems that will be judged most serious five or ten years hence are perhaps being overlooked entirely today. The MIT-sponsored "Williamstown study" in the summer of 1970 (*Man's Impact on the Global Environment*, MIT Press, 1970) emphasized four classes of environmental problems judged to be of global importance. Two of these classes—CO_2 and particulates in the atmosphere, and persistent pesticides throughout the ecosystem—are covered in articles in this section. The other two—the contamination of the environment with heavy metals such as mercury and lead, and oil introduced into the oceans—have not at this writing been treated in depth in SCIENTIFIC AMERICAN. (The direct effects of lead on human health are considered in "Lead Poisoning," by J. Julian Chisolm, Jr., SCIENTIFIC AMERICAN, February 1971. Unfortunately, the article does not deal with the potential effects of the accumulation of lead in the ecosystem as a whole.) While not pretending completeness, then, we nevertheless trust that our selections convey a sense of the extent and the gravity of man's intervention in the life-support systems of the planet.

12

Toxic Substances and Ecological Cycles

GEORGE M. WOODWELL
March 1967

The vastness of the earth has fostered a tradition of unconcern about the release of toxic wastes into the environment. Billowing clouds of smoke are diluted to apparent nothingness; discarded chemicals are flushed away in rivers; insecticides "disappear" after they have done their job; even the massive quantities of radioactive debris of nuclear explosions are diluted in the apparently infinite volume of the environment. Such pollutants are indeed diluted to traces—to levels infinitesimal by ordinary standards, measured as parts per billion or less in air, soil and water. Some pollutants do disappear; they are immobilized or decay to harmless substances. Others last, sometimes in toxic form, for long periods. We have learned in recent years that dilution of persistent pollutants even to trace levels detectable only by refined techniques is no guarantee of safety. Nature has ways of concentrating substances that are frequently surprising and occasionally disastrous.

We have had dramatic examples of one of the hazards in the dense smogs that blanket our cities with increasing frequency. What is less widely realized is that there are global, long-term ecological processes that concentrate toxic substances, sometimes hundreds of thousands of times above levels in the environment. These processes include not only patterns of air and water circulation but also a complex series of biological mechanisms. Over the past decade detailed studies of the distribution of both radioactive debris and pesticides have revealed patterns that have surprised even biologists long familiar with the unpredictability of nature.

Major contributions to knowledge of these patterns have come from studies of radioactive fallout. The incident that triggered worldwide interest in large-scale radioactive pollution was the hydrogen-bomb test at Bikini in 1954 known as "Project Bravo." This was the test that inadvertently dropped radioactive fallout on several Pacific islands and on the Japanese fishing vessel *Lucky Dragon*. Several thousand square miles of the Pacific were contaminated with fallout radiation that would have been lethal to man. Japanese and U.S. oceanographic vessels surveying the region found that the radioactive debris had been spread by wind and water, and, more disturbing, it was being passed rapidly along food chains from small plants to small marine organisms that ate them to larger animals (including the tuna, a staple of the Japanese diet).

The U.S. Atomic Energy Commission and agencies of other nations, particularly Britain and the U.S.S.R., mounted a large international research program, costing many millions of dollars, to learn the details of the movement of such debris over the earth and to explore its hazards. Although these studies have been focused primarily on radioactive materials, they have produced a great deal of basic information about pollutants in general. The radioactive substances serve as tracers to show the transport and concentration of materials by wind and water and the biological mechanisms that are characteristic of natural communities.

One series of investigations traced the worldwide movement of particles in the air. The tracer in this case was strontium 90, a fission product released into the earth's atmosphere in large quantities by nuclear-bomb tests. Two reports in 1962 —one by S. Laurence Kulp and Arthur R. Schulert of Columbia University and the other by a United Nations committee— furnished a detailed picture of the travels of strontium 90. The isotope was concentrated on the ground between the latitudes of 30 and 60 degrees in both hemispheres, but concentrations were five to 10 times greater in the Northern Hemisphere, where most of the bomb tests were conducted.

It is apparently in the middle latitudes

FOREST COMMUNITY is an integrated array of plants and animals that accumulates and reuses nutrients in stable cycles, as indicated schematically in black. DDT participates in parallel cycles (*color*). The author measured DDT residues in a New Brunswick forest in which four pounds per acre of DDT had been applied over seven years. (Studies have shown about half of this landed in the forest, the remainder dispersing in the atmosphere.) Three years after the spraying, residues of DDT were as shown (in pounds per acre).

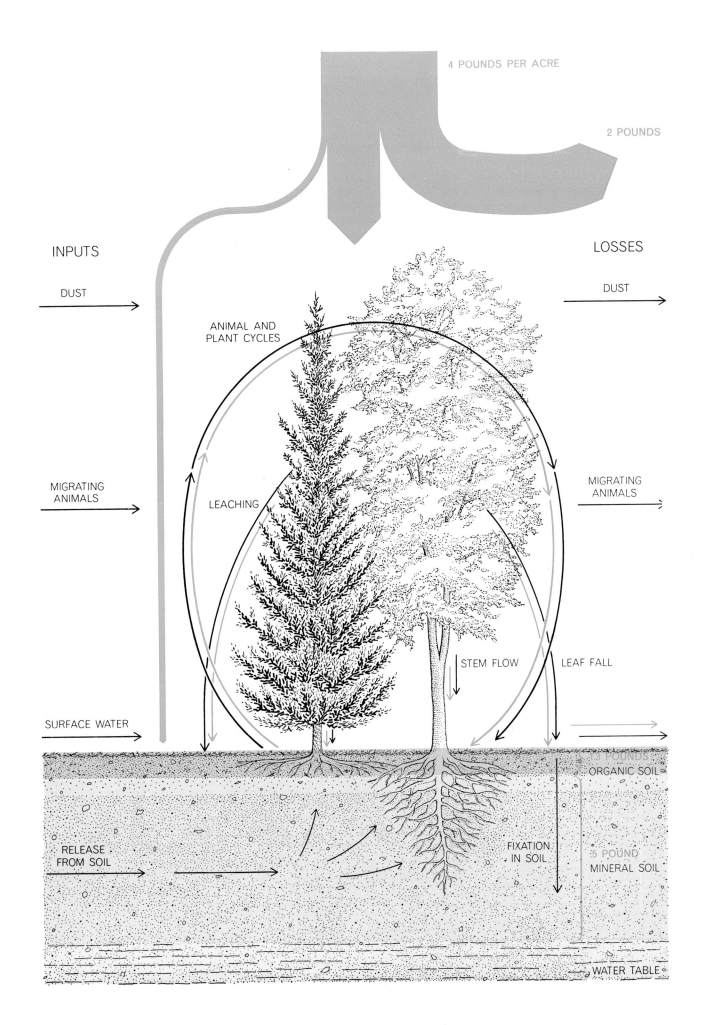

4 POUNDS PER ACRE

2 POUNDS

INPUTS

DUST

ANIMAL AND
PLANT CYCLES

MIGRATING
ANIMALS

LEACHING

SURFACE WATER

LOSSES

DUST

MIGRATING
ANIMALS

STEM FLOW

LEAF FALL

ORGANIC SOIL

RELEASE
FROM SOIL

FIXATION
IN SOIL

5 POUND
MINERAL SOIL

WATER TABLE

that exchanges occur between the air of upper elevations (the stratosphere) and that of lower elevations (the troposphere). The larger tests have injected debris into the stratosphere; there it remains for relatively long periods, being carried back into the troposphere and to the ground in the middle latitudes in late winter or spring. The mean "half-time" of the particles' residence in the stratosphere (that is, the time for half of a given injection to fall out) is from three months to five years, depending on many factors, including the height of the injection, the size of the particles, the latitude of injection and the time of year. Debris injected into the troposphere has a mean half-time of residence ranging from a few days to about a month. Once airborne, the particles may travel rapidly and far. The time for one circuit around the earth in the middle latitudes varies from 25 days to less than 15. (Following two recent bomb tests in China fallout was detected at the Brookhaven National Laboratory on Long Island respectively nine and 14 days after the tests.)

Numerous studies have shown further that precipitation (rain and snowfall) plays an important role in determining where fallout will be deposited. Lyle T. Alexander of the Soil Conservation Service and Edward P. Hardy, Jr., of the AEC found in an extensive study in Clallam County, Washington, that the amount of fallout was directly proportional to the total annual rainfall.

It is reasonable to assume that the findings about the movement and fallout of radioactive debris also apply to other particles of similar size in the air. This conclusion is supported by a recent report by Donald F. Gatz and A. Nelson Dingle of the University of Michigan, who showed that the concentration of pollen in precipitation follows the same pattern as that of radioactive fallout. This observation is particularly meaningful because pollen is not injected into the troposphere by a nuclear explosion; it is picked up in air currents from plants close to the ground. There is little question that dust and other particles, including small crystals of pesticides, also follow these patterns.

From these and other studies it is clear that various substances released into the air are carried widely around the world and may be deposited in concentrated form far from the original source. Similarly, most bodies of water—especially the oceans—have surface currents that may move materials five to 10 miles a day. Much higher rates, of course, are found in such major oceanic currents as

the Gulf Stream. These currents are one more physical mechanism that can distribute pollutants widely over the earth.

The research programs of the AEC and other organizations have explored not only the pathways of air and water transport but also the pathways along which pollutants are distributed in plant and animal communities. In this connection we must examine what we mean by a "community."

Biologists define communities broadly to include all species, not just man. A natural community is an aggregation of a great many different kinds of organisms, all mutually interdependent. The basic conditions for the integration of a community are determined by physical characteristics of the environment such as climate and soil. Thus a sand dune supports one kind of community, a freshwater lake another, a high mountain still another. Within each type of environment there develops a complex of organisms that in the course of evolution becomes a balanced, self-sustaining biological system.

Such a system has a structure of interrelations that endows the entire community with a predictable developmental pattern, called "succession," that leads toward stability and enables the community to make the best use of its physical environment. This entails the development of cycles through which the community as a whole shares certain resources, such as mineral nutrients and energy. For example, there are a number of different inputs of nutrient elements into such a system. The principal input is from the decay of primary minerals in the soil. There are also certain losses, mainly through the leaching of substances into the underlying water table. Ecologists view the cycles in the system as mechanisms that have evolved to conserve the elements essential for the survival of the organisms making up the community.

One of the most important of these cycles is the movement of nutrients and energy from one organism to another along the pathways that are sometimes called food chains. Such chains start with plants, which use the sun's energy to synthesize organic matter; animals eat the plants; other animals eat these herbivores, and carnivores in turn may constitute additional levels feeding on the herbivores and on one another. If the lower orders in the chain are to survive and endure, there must be a feedback of nutrients. This is provided by decay organisms (mainly microorganisms) that break down organic debris

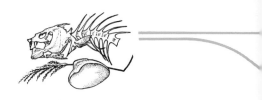

ORGANIC DEBRIS
MARSH 13 POUNDS PER ACRE
BOTTOM .3 POUND PER ACRE

CLADOPHORA .08

PLANKTON .04

MARSH PLANTS
SHOOTS .33
ROOTS 2.80

FOOD WEB is a complex network through which energy passes from plants to herbivores and on to carnivores within a biologi-

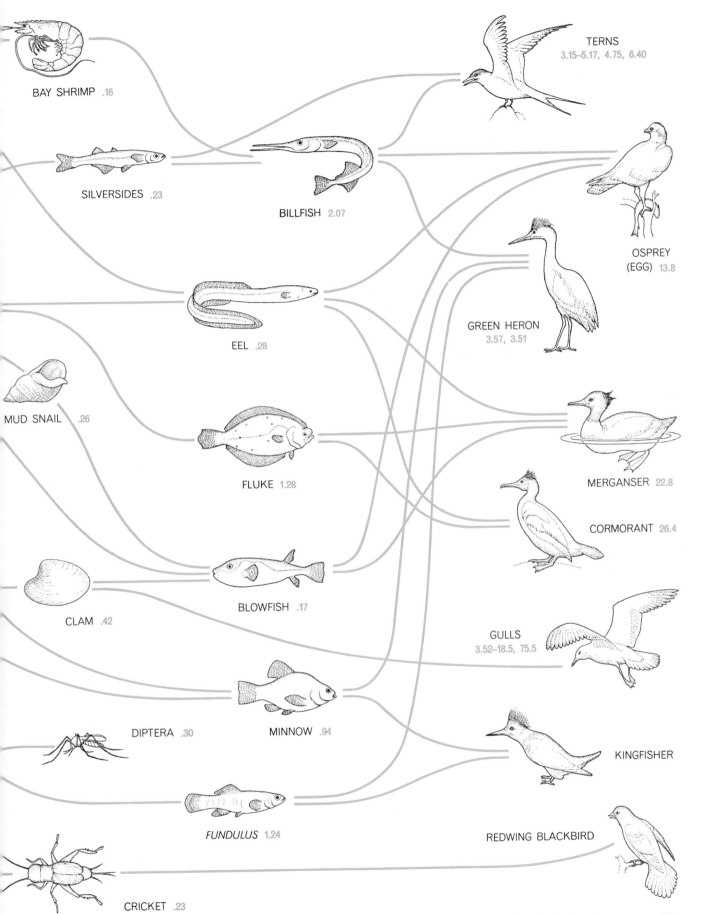

BAY SHRIMP .16

TERNS
3.15–5.17, 4.75, 6.40

SILVERSIDES .23

BILLFISH 2.07

OSPREY
(EGG) 13.8

EEL .28

GREEN HERON
3.57, 3.51

MUD SNAIL .26

FLUKE 1.28

MERGANSER 22.8

CORMORANT 26.4

CLAM .42

BLOWFISH .17

GULLS
3.52–18.5, 75.5

DIPTERA .30

MINNOW .94

KINGFISHER

FUNDULUS 1.24

REDWING BLACKBIRD

CRICKET .23

cal community. This web showing some of the plants and animals in a Long Island estuary and along the nearby shore was developed by Dennis Puleston of the Brookhaven National Laboratory. Numbers indicate residues of DDT and its derivatives (in parts per million, wet weight, whole-body basis) found in the course of a study made by the author with Charles F. Wurster, Jr., and Peter A. Isaacson.

into the substances used by plants. It is also obvious that the community will not survive if essential links in the chain are eliminated; therefore the preying of one level on another must be limited.

Ecologists estimate that such a food chain allows the transmission of roughly 10 percent of the energy entering one level to the next level above it, that is, each level can pass on 10 percent of the energy it receives from below without suffering a loss of population that would imperil its survival. The simplest version of a system of this kind takes the form of a pyramid, each successively higher population receiving about a tenth of the energy received at the level below it.

Actually nature seldom builds communities with so simple a structure. Almost invariably the energy is not passed along in a neatly ordered chain but is spread about to a great variety of organisms through a sprawling, complex web of pathways [see illustration on preceding two pages]. The more mature the community, the more diverse its makeup and the more complicated its web. In a natural ecosystem the network may consist of thousands of pathways.

This complexity is one of the principal factors we must consider in investigating how toxic substances may be distributed and concentrated in living communities. Other important basic factors lie in the nature of the metabolic process. For example, of the energy a population of organisms receives as food, usually less than 50 percent goes into the construction of new tissue, the rest being spent for respiration. This circumstance acts as a concentrating mechanism: a substance not involved in respiration and not excreted efficiently may be concentrated in the tissues twofold or more when passed from one population to another.

Let us consider three types of pathway for toxic substances that involve man as the ultimate consumer. The three examples, based on studies of ra-

dioactive substances, illustrate the complexity and variety of pollution problems.

The first and simplest case is that of strontium 90. Similar to calcium in chemical behavior, this element is concentrated in bone. It is a long-lived radioactive isotope and is a hazard because its energetic beta radiation can damage the mechanisms involved in the manufacture of blood cells in the bone marrow. In the long run the irradiation may produce certain types of cancer. The route of strontium 90 from air to man is rather direct: we ingest it in leafy vegetables, which absorbed it from the soil or received it as fallout from the air, or in milk and other dairy products from cows that have fed on contaminated vegetation. Fortunately strontium is not usually concentrated in man's food by an extensive food chain. Since it lodges chiefly in bone, it is not concentrated in passing from animal to animal in the same ways other radioactive substances may be (unless the predator eats bones!).

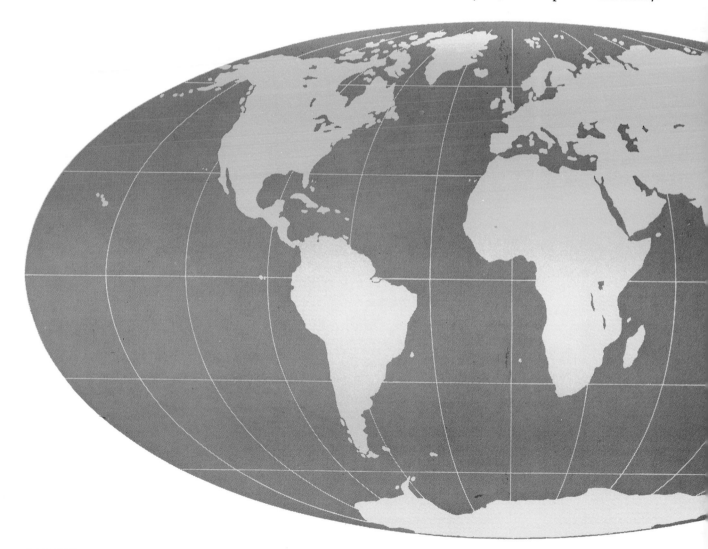

FALLOUT is distributed around the earth by meteorological processes. Deposits of strontium 90, for instance, are concentrated between 30 and 60 degrees north, as shown by depth of color on the map and by the curve (right). Points on the chart represent individual samples. The data are from a study made in 1963 and 1964 by Robert J. List and colleagues in several U.S. agencies. Such

Quite different is the case of the radioactive isotope cesium 137. This isotope, also a fission product, has a long-lived radioactivity (its half-life is about 30 years) and emits penetrating gamma rays. Because it behaves chemically like potassium, an essential constituent of all cells, it becomes widely distributed once it enters the body. Consequently it is passed along to meat-eating animals, and under certain circumstances it can accumulate in a chain of carnivores.

A study in Alaska by Wayne C. Hanson, H. E. Palmer and B. I. Griffin of the AEC's Pacific-Northwest Laboratory showed that the concentration factor for cesium 137 may be two or three for one step in a food chain. The first link of the chain in this case was lichens growing in the Alaskan forest and tundra. The lichens collected cesium 137 from fallout in rain. Certain caribou in Alaska live mainly on lichens during the winter, and caribou meat in turn is the principal diet of Eskimos in the same areas. The investigators found that caribou had accumulated about 15 micromicrocuries of cesium radioactivity per gram of tissue in their bodies. The Eskimos who fed on these caribou had a concentration twice as high (about 30 micromicrocuries per gram of tissue) after eating many pounds of caribou meat in the course of a season. Wolves and foxes that ate caribou sometimes contained three times the concentration in the flesh of the caribou. It is easy to see that in a longer chain, involving not just two animals but several, the concentration of a substance that was not excreted or metabolized could be increased to high levels.

A third case is that of iodine 131, another gamma ray emitter. Again the chain to man is short and simple: The contaminant (from fallout) comes to man mainly through cows' milk, and thus the chain involves only grass, cattle, milk and man. The danger of iodine 131 lies in the fact that iodine is concentrated in the thyroid gland. Although iodine 131 is short-lived (its half-life is only about eight days), its quick and localized concentration in the thyroid can cause damage. For instance, a research team from the Brookhaven National Laboratory headed by Robert Conard has discovered that children on Rongelap Atoll who were exposed to fallout from the 1954 bomb test later developed thyroid nodules.

The investigations of the iodine 131 hazard yielded two lessons that have an important bearing on the problem of pesticides and other toxic substances released in the environment. In the first place we have had a demonstration that the hazard of the toxic substance itself often tends to be underestimated. This was shown to be true of the exposure of the thyroid to radiation. Thyroid tumors were found in children who had been treated years before for enlarged thymus glands with doses of X rays that had been considered safe. As a result of this discovery and studies of the effects of iodine 131, the Federal Radiation Council in 1961 issued a new guide reducing the permissible limit of exposure to ionizing radiation to less than a tenth of what had previously been accepted. Not the least significant aspect of this lesson is the fact that the toxic effects of such a hazard may not appear until long after the exposure; on Rongelap Atoll 10 years passed before the thyroid abnormalities showed up in the children who had been exposed.

The second lesson is that, even when the pathways are well understood, it is almost impossible to predict just where toxic substances released into the environment will reach dangerous levels. Even in the case of the simple pathway followed by iodine 131 the eventual destination of the substance and its effects on people are complicated by a great many variables: the area of the cow's pasture (the smaller the area, the less fallout the cow will pick up); the amount and timing of rains on the pasture (which on the one hand may bring down fallout but on the other may wash it off the forage); the extent to which the cow is given stored, uncontaminated feed; the amount of iodine the cow secretes in its milk; the amount of milk in the diet of the individual consumer, and so on.

If it is difficult to estimate the nature and extent of the hazards from radioactive fallout, which have been investigated in great detail for more than a decade by an international research program, it must be said that we are in a poor position indeed to estimate the hazards from pesticides. So far the

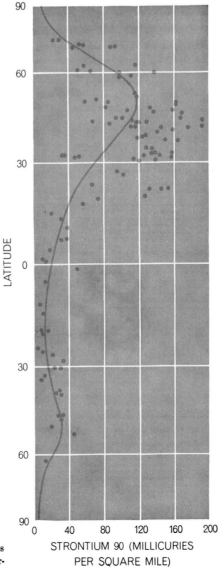

LATITUDE

STRONTIUM 90 (MILLICURIES PER SQUARE MILE)

studies have not been made for pesticides but it appears that DDT may also be carried in air and deposited in precipitation.

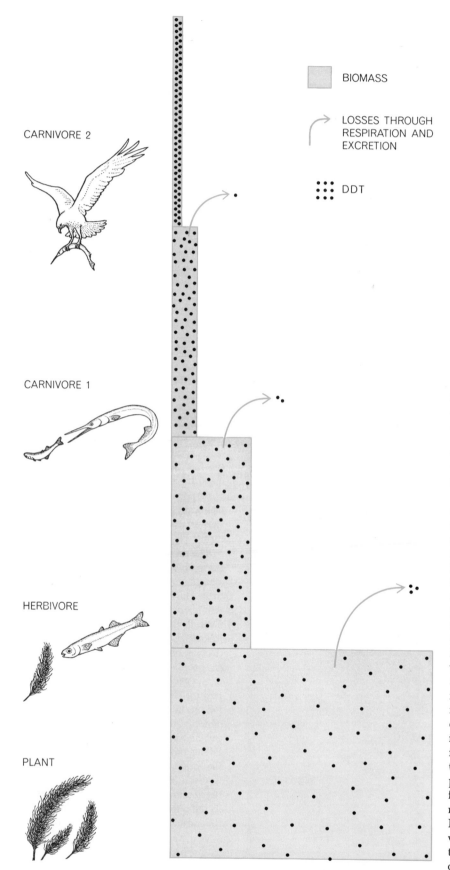

BIOMASS

LOSSES THROUGH
RESPIRATION AND
EXCRETION

DDT

CARNIVORE 2

CARNIVORE 1

HERBIVORE

PLANT

CONCENTRATION of DDT residues being passed along a simple food chain is indicated schematically in this diagram. As "biomass," or living material, is transferred from one link to another along such a chain, usually more than half of it is consumed in respiration or is excreted (*arrows*); the remainder forms new biomass. The losses of DDT residues along the chain, on the other hand, are small in proportion to the amount that is transferred from one link to the next. For this reason high concentrations occur in the carnivores.

amount of research effort given to the ecological effects of these poisons has been comparatively small, although it is increasing rapidly. Much has been learned, however, about the movement and distribution of pesticides in the environment, thanks in part to the clues supplied by the studies of radioactive fallout.

Our chief tool in the pesticide inquiry is DDT. There are many reasons for focusing on DDT: it is long-lasting, it is now comparatively easy to detect, it is by far the most widely used pesticide and it is toxic to a broad spectrum of animals, including man. Introduced only a quarter-century ago and spectacularly successful during World War II in controlling body lice and therefore typhus, DDT quickly became a universal weapon in agriculture and in public health campaigns against disease-carriers. Not surprisingly, by this time DDT has thoroughly permeated our environment. It is found in the air of cities, in wildlife all over North America and in remote corners of the earth, even in Adélie penguins and skua gulls (both carnivores) in the Antarctic. It is also found the world over in the fatty tissue of man. It is fair to say that there are probably few populations in the world that are not contaminated to some extent with DDT.

We now have a considerable amount of evidence that DDT is spread over the earth by wind and water in much the same patterns as radioactive fallout. This seems to be true in spite of the fact that DDT is not injected high into the atmosphere by an explosion. When DDT is sprayed in the air, some fraction of it is picked up by air currents as pollen is, circulated through the lower troposphere and deposited on the ground by rainfall. I found in tests in Maine and New Brunswick, where DDT has been sprayed from airplanes to control the spruce budworm in forests, that even in the open, away from trees, about 50 percent of the DDT does not fall to the ground. Instead it is probably dispersed as small crystals in the air. This is true even on days when the air is still and when the low-flying planes release the spray only 50 to 100 feet above treetop level. Other mechanisms besides air movement can carry DDT for great distances around the world. Migrating fish and birds can transport it thousands of miles. So also do oceanic currents. DDT has only a low solubility in water (the upper limit is about one part per billion), but as algae and other organisms in the water absorb the substance in fats, where it is highly soluble, they make room for more DDT to be dissolved into the water. Accordingly water that never contains more than a trace of DDT can continuously transfer it from deposits on the bottom to organisms.

DDT is an extremely stable compound that breaks down very slowly in the environment. Hence with repeated spraying the residues in the soil or water basins accumulate. Working with Frederic T. Martin of the University of Maine, I found that in a New Brunswick forest where spraying had been discontinued in 1958 the DDT content of the soil increased from half a pound per acre to 1.8 pounds per acre in the three years between 1958 and 1961. Apparently the DDT residues were carried to the ground very slowly on foliage and decayed very little. The conclusion is that DDT has a long half-life in the trees and soil of a forest, certainly in the range of tens of years.

Doubtless there are many places in the world where reservoirs of DDT are accumulating. With my colleagues Charles F. Wurster, Jr., and Peter A. Isaacson of the State University of New York at Stony Brook, I recently sampled a marsh along the south shore of Long Island that had been sprayed with DDT for 20 years to control mosquitoes. We found that the DDT residues in the upper layer of mud in this marsh ranged up to 32 pounds per acre!

We learned further that plant and animal life in the area constituted a chain that concentrated the DDT in spectacular fashion. At the lowest level the plankton in the water contained .04 part per million of DDT; minnows contained one part per million, and a carnivorous scavenging bird (a ring-billed gull) contained about 75 parts per million in its tissues (on a whole-body, wet-weight basis). Some of the carnivorous animals in this community had concentrated DDT by a factor of more than 1,000 over the organisms at the base of the ladder.

A further tenfold increase in the concentrations along this food web would in all likelihood result in the death of many of the organisms in it. It would then be impossible to discover why they had disappeared. The damage from DDT concentration is particularly serious in the higher carnivores. The mere fact that conspicuous mortality is not observed is no assurance of safety. Comparatively low concentrations may inhibit reproduction and thus cause the species to fade away.

That DDT is a serious ecological hazard was recognized from the beginning of its use. In 1946 Clarence Cottam and

LOCATION	ORGANISM	TISSUE	CONCENTRATION (PARTS PER MILLION)
U.S. (AVERAGE)	MAN	FAT	11
ALASKA (ESKIMO)			2.8
ENGLAND			2.2
WEST GERMANY			2.3
FRANCE			5.2
CANADA			5.3
HUNGARY			12.4
ISRAEL			19.2
INDIA			12.8–31.0
CALIFORNIA	PLANKTON		5.3
CALIFORNIA	BASS	EDIBLE FLESH	4–138
CALIFORNIA	GREBES	VISCERAL FAT	UP TO 1,600
MONTANA	ROBIN	WHOLE BODY	6.8–13.9
WISCONSIN	CRUSTACEA		.41
WISCONSIN	CHUB	WHOLE BODY	4.52
WISCONSIN	GULL	BRAIN	20.8
MISSOURI	BALD EAGLE	EGGS	1.1–5.6
CONNECTICUT	OSPREY	EGGS	6.5
FLORIDA	DOLPHIN	BLUBBER	ABOUT 220
CANADA	WOODCOCK	WHOLE BODY	1.7
ANTARCTICA	PENGUIN	FAT	.015–.18
ANTARCTICA	SEAL	FAT	.042–.12
SCOTLAND	EAGLE	EGGS	1.18
NEW ZEALAND	TROUT	WHOLE BODY	.6–.8

DDT RESIDUES, which include the derivatives DDD and DDE as well as DDT itself, have apparently entered most food webs. These data were selected from hundreds of reports that show DDT has a worldwide distribution, with the highest concentrations in carnivorous birds.

Elmer Higgins of the U.S. Fish and Wildlife Service warned in the *Journal of Economic Entomology* that the pesticide was a potential menace to mammals, birds, fishes and other wildlife and that special care should be taken to avoid its application to streams, lakes and coastal bays because of the sensitivity of fishes and crabs. Because of the wide distribution of DDT the effects of the substance on a species of animal can be more damaging than hunting or the elimination of a habitat (through an operation such as dredging marshes). DDT affects the entire species rather than a single population and may well wipe out the species by eliminating reproduction.

Within the past five years, with the development of improved techniques for detecting the presence of pesticide residues in animals and the environment, ecologists have been able to measure the extent of the hazards presented by DDT and other persistent general poisons. The picture that is emerging is not a comforting one. Pesticide residues have now accumulated to levels that are catastrophic for certain animal populations, particularly carnivorous birds. Furthermore, it has been clear for many years that because of their shotgun effect these weapons not only attack the pests but also destroy predators and competitors that normally tend to limit proliferation of the pests. Under exposure to pesti-

cides the pests tend to develop new strains that are resistant to the chemicals. The result is an escalating chemical warfare that is self-defeating and has secondary effects whose costs are only beginning to be measured. One of the costs is wildlife, notably carnivorous and scavenging birds such as hawks and eagles. There are others: destruction of food webs aggravates pollution problems, particularly in bodies of water that receive mineral nutrients in sewage or in water draining from heavily fertilized agricultural lands. The plant populations, no longer consumed by animals, fall to the bottom to decay anaerobically, producing hydrogen sulfide and other noxious gases, further degrading the environment.

The accumulation of persistent toxic substances in the ecological cycles of the earth is a problem to which mankind will have to pay increasing attention. It affects many elements of society, not only in the necessity for concern about the disposal of wastes but also in the need for a revolution in pest control. We must learn to use pesticides that have a short half-life in the environment—better yet, to use pest-control techniques that do not require applications of general poisons. What has been learned about the dangers in polluting ecological cycles is ample proof that there is no longer safety in the vastness of the earth.

13

Air Pollution and Public Health

WALSH McDERMOTT
October 1961

The first sign of a city visible from an airplane on a fine day is the thick brownish haze that envelops it. While still in the air one asks: "How can anyone go on breathing that stuff?" On the ground, however, people do not notice anything unusual. They blame the weather for "just another gray day" and go right on breathing.

Air pollution has nonetheless begun to arouse the concern of the public and of public officials. An increasing number of cities in this country have been recording an increasing frequency of days of severe "smog." The attendant irritation of the eyes and ruination of nylon stockings are taken as evidence that the pollutants cannot be good for the health. In Los Angeles, the most notably afflicted community, the prohibiting of domestic trash-burning has already improved the visibility of the mountains that crowd that city against the sea; local industries have been persuaded and compelled to minimize their contribution to the smog, and the compulsory installation of exhaust-pipe "afterburners" and crankcase "blow-by" scavengers on all automobiles in the state at the end of the year promises to reduce the atmospheric concentration of the substances most positively identified with eye irritation. Other communities are beginning to follow suit, and it appears that the effort to reduce the emissions from automobiles may soon become nationwide. The Secretary of Health, Education and Welfare, Abraham A.

Ribicoff, has asked the automotive industry to agree to the installation of pollution-abating devices as standard equipment on all 1964 vehicles and has threatened to ask Congress for a law requiring such installation.

Whether air pollution is to be endured as a nuisance or suppressed by vigorous civic action, it must be reckoned as an unpleasant and expensive consequence of urban and industrial civilization. But is air pollution in fact a menace to public health? The first place to look for damage by unclean air would be the body surfaces exposed to air: the skin, which is hardy and mainly covered by clothing, and the respiratory passages, which are not covered at all. There is evidence that a commonplace disorder of the bronchial tubes and lungs—chronic bronchitis and emphysema—is showing an alarming increase in some places. At the same time, it cannot be said that any particular atmospheric pollutant is the cause of bronchitis-emphysema or other bronchopulmonary disease, in the legal or scientific sense of the term.

If something is happening to the public health from the widespread pollution of the air, it must be happening to large numbers of people. Yet it must be something that goes on undramatically in its individual manifestations; otherwise it would attract public notice as an "epidemic." Fortunately the mysteriously lethal fogs that settled on the Meuse Valley in Belgium in 1930, on Donora, Pa., in 1948 and on London

in 1952 remain isolated episodes. On those occasions, strangely, there was no recorded increase in the atmospheric concentration of the usual pollutants; the increase in the death rate involved chiefly the aged and those with a history of pulmonary disorder. But if a substance or mixture of substances present in low concentration can be highly injurious to certain particularly susceptible people after only a few days' exposure, how can one know that two or three decades of exposure to the same low doses will not be injurious to many more people? Such questions are not unknown in public health research. With respect to air pollution the answer is that there is as yet no solid evidence that it is a serious threat to the "healthy" (meaning those without lung damage); there are, however, ominous portents that it may be such a threat.

Most of the pollutants get into the air as a result of burning. Though city dwellers seldom light their own fires nowadays, their daily lives still depend on the process of combustion. The spotless electric stove ultimately derives its heat from the burning of coal, and something has to be burned to make the television set function. In most cities the garbage is burned; sometimes it is burned twice, in the back yard and on the city dump. Automobiles are highly mobile "burners" throughout their active lifetime, and when they are outmoded, they too end up on the pyre. In short,

LOS ANGELES SMOG is the result primarily of hydrocarbons and nitrous oxides from automobile exhaust, chemically changed by exposure to sunlight and trapped by the city's frequent "thermal inversions," which interfere with normal vertical air movements. The top photograph shows downtown Los Angeles on a clear day. The same area is seen (*middle*) as a light smog builds up against the inversion layer and (*bottom*) on a day of heavier smog.

the energy of civilization is supplied by burning, and most of its debris is likewise burned.

The final products of a completed combustion are water and carbon dioxide, which in the amounts involved in urban life would be entirely harmless. In general, however, fuel and debris are only partially burned, and a wide variety of chemical substances are thrown off into the air. Some of this material is visible smoke, made up of particulate matter, including particles that one can see and feel, such as fly ash or soot. Some of the material entering the air is invisible, composed of complex chemicals, and it is these substances that seem to represent the greater menace to health.

Chemical analysis divides the polluted atmospheres of the world's cities into two major types: the London type, composed principally of sulfur compounds from the burning of coal; and the Los Angeles type, composed principally of petroleum products, known loosely as hydrocarbons. Given the commitment to automobile transportation, all the cities in this country suffer to some degree from air pollution by hydrocarbons; where coal is burned for power and domestic space-heating, the air may in addition be polluted with sulfur compounds.

Outside of Los Angeles, however, the term "smog" is usually a misnomer when applied to the prevailing haze; the physics of the true Los Angeles smog is somewhat different from that of the more common London fog. As shown in 1951 by A. J. Haagen-Smit of the California Institute of Technology, the hydrocarbons and nitrous oxides given off by the combustion of petroleum are at first neither visible nor irritating. But when these substances are exposed to sunlight for an hour or so, they undergo important chemical changes, yielding ozone and other reactive compounds. These products of photochemistry are the ones that irritate the eyes. As they undergo further chemical change some of them produce the characteristic haze. In the Los Angeles smog, therefore, it is sunlight acting chemically on petroleum products that obscures the blue sky, whereas in most cities of the country it is a plain London type of fog that traps the pollutants and suspends them in the air. In each case the end result—the irritation of certain cells of the body—is probably much the same.

The automobile owes its supremacy as a source of air pollution to the inefficiency with which it burns its fuel. The U.S. consumer expects his automobile engine to start instantly in all kinds of weather and accelerate rapidly with no engine knock. To meet these requirements manufacturers build large motors with a high compression ratio that operate best on high-octane gasoline, a fuel that burns with low efficiency except under optimum operating conditions. Hydrocarbons escape both through the exhaust and as vapors from the fuel tank and carburetor vents. Emission through the tail pipe varies considerably, depending somewhat on engine size and faithfulness of upkeep. It is highest during low-speed driving such as occurs twice each day at rush hour on the parkways. On a hot day in traffic the emission from the carburetor and fuel tank approximates that of the tail pipe.

According to Leslie A. Chambers, research director of the Los Angeles Air Pollution Control District, the daily output of every 1,000 operating automobiles in an urban community burdens the air with 3.2 tons of carbon monoxide, 400 to 800 pounds of organic vapors (that is, hydrocarbons) and 100 to 300 pounds of nitrous oxides, plus smaller amounts of sulfur and other chemicals. The hydrocarbons and nitrous oxides are highly important. To what extent the 3.2 tons of carbon monoxide are a menace is not known, but this is beginning to cause concern. In general, except in such closed surroundings as a household garage, the carbon monoxide given off to the air does not usually rise above the 150 parts per million that would represent a hazard. Since carbon monoxide does not change its chemical form in the air, measurement of its presence there provides a good index of the volume of automobile exhaust being poured into the atmosphere at a given moment.

The automobile makes a further contribution to air pollution in the form of highly pulverized rubber and asphalt, generated by abrasion of tires upon streets. This aspect of the situation has not been studied in much detail, but there is reason to believe that contamination from rubber and asphalt is appreciable.

In metropolitan regions all over the country municipal installations, households, industrial plants and automobiles (to list them in ascending order of rank as sources of pollution) give off approximately the same combination and relative volume of chemicals to the air. Whether the contamination becomes a community problem at any one time depends on population density and the weather. The strong breezes that attend the movement of great air masses over the continent regularly bring fresh air into most U.S. cities, and in the absence of breezes the air may be cleaned by updrafts that dilute and carry away both the smoke and the vaporized chemicals. Not infrequently these natural ventilation processes fail, and there may be no movement of air over a particular area for a matter of hours and sometimes days. One mechanism that stops air movement is the "thermal inversion." Ordinarily the air is warmer at the ground and colder above; indeed, the updrafts so essential for air cleansing arise from this temperature gradient. In

MAN-MADE HAZE lies in a layer over New York City on an otherwise clear day. Skyscrapers protrude above the smog, which is held down by a thermal inversion. A thin haze like this obscures vision only at some distance, and residents may be quite unaware of it.

a thermal inversion a layer of warm air forms at higher altitude and traps a layer of cold air at the ground. When an inversion roofs over the atmosphere of a heavily populated region, the same air must accumulate a much higher concentration of pollutants. This can happen in almost any season of the year to most of the cities in this country; it is the chronic situation in Los Angeles.

Los Angeles suffers from its smogs not because its natives are unusually careless but because there are so many of them in a place where the cleansing of the air is so frequently interrupted. There six million people with three million cars burn 5.5 million gallons of gasoline each day on a narrow strip of sunny seacoast backed up by mountains. Ther-

mal inversions occur about 100 days each year. The Los Angeles case may seem extreme, and it is the extreme at this moment. But two of the three factors that prevail there—rapid population growth and heavy hydrocarbon emission—are not peculiar to Los Angeles. The third factor—thermal inversion—can come into play elsewhere as well. What has happened to Los Angeles, therefore, is already happening to certain other urban regions and may have considerable future significance for the nation as a whole.

The facts about air pollution are plain enough. But when it comes to assessing the effects of unclean air on the public health, the ground becomes uncertain.

What British physicians call chronic bronchitis and its complications is now the leading cause of death in men over 45 in that country and the fourth leading cause of death for the population as a whole. For reasons related to the nature and course of the disease, the corresponding figures for chronic bronchitis-emphysema in the U.S. cannot be stated exactly, but it appears to be on the increase. It is not enough, however, merely to show that the incidence of pulmonary disease has been rising along with pollution. The conscientious investigator must seek out the chain of cause and effect. And the responsible public health official needs better evidence to justify the social cost of control measures.

Until recently chronic bronchitis-em-

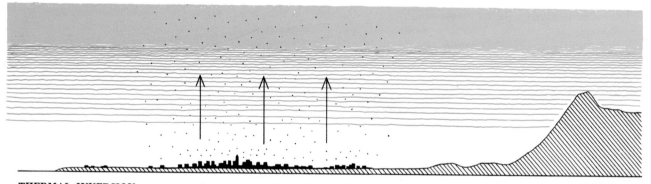

THERMAL INVERSION, common in Los Angeles, is the main meteorological factor in smog formation. Except in an inversion, air temperature decreases with height (*darker tones indicate cooler air*); the warm surface air rises, carrying pollutants away.

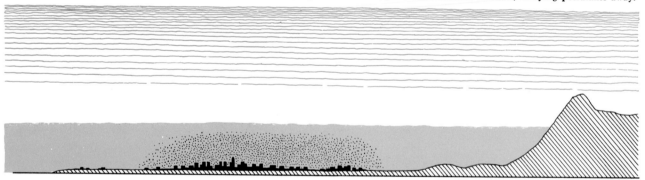

INVERSION SETS IN when cool sea air moves in under warm desert air and is trapped. The normal temperature gradient is reversed in the inversion layer, the base of which (*at the surface in this drawing*) forms a lid over the city, concentrating pollutants.

INVERSION PERSISTS until the weather changes, as when the warm air is high enough to permit the cool sea air to escape and carry away the accumulated smog. Thermal inversions occur in Los Angeles about 100 days a year, but they are also common elsewhere.

physema has been considered a rather "dull" disease by medical students and young physicians, and research on the subject has been correspondingly neglected in university circles. The chronic cough and progressive loss of breathing function may be completely incapacitating and lead eventually to failure of the heart. But the course of the disease is usually quite prolonged and undramatic, and not much can be done about it.

The aspect of the disease referred to under the heading of emphysema involves its effect on the millions of tiny air sacs in the lungs, where the transfer of oxygen to the blood takes place. In emphysema several of these tiny sacs merge to form a larger sac, just as small bubbles coalesce into larger bubbles. The single larger sac, of course, offers less surface area for respiratory gas-exchange than the half-dozen or so smaller sacs from which it is formed. This emphysema process occurs throughout both lungs, eventually causing severe impairment of the individual's ability to breathe. The situation is further aggravated by a narrowing of the tiny branches of the bronchial tree through which the air passes on its way to the individual breathing unit. The narrowing may be due to a spasm or it may be permanent. This is the "bronchitis" part of chronic bronchitis-emphysema [see illustration on page 145]. Whether the bronchitis represents the cart or the horse is a matter of ter of amiable scientific controversy. In William Osler's day emphysema was attributed to "airway resistance" and as such was regarded as an occupational disease of trombone players—individuals who certainly have to breathe out against resistance!

When the emphysema has become sufficiently advanced throughout the lungs, a heavy load is thrown on the heart, which now must pump the same volume of blood through the far fewer channels available in the greatly reduced air-sac lining of the lung. From this extra work the heart enlarges and eventually fails. Recent research indicates that the cause of the cardiac failure is not quite so simple, but this type of heart disease has been recognized for more than a century as *cor pulmonale*, or pulmonary heart.

Just how the disease gets its start is not known. The process apparently begins one or two decades before symptoms of breathlessness are first noticed. Since the bronchi are in direct communication with the outside air, they are exposed to everything in it. Fortunately

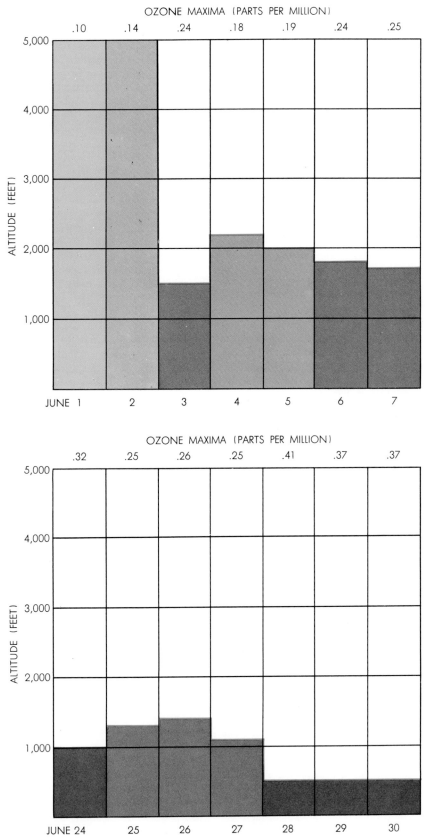

HEIGHT OF INVERSION BASE affects smog density; ordinarily the lower the base, the worse the smog. These charts relate inversion base altitude in the Los Angeles area in the first and last weeks of June, 1961, with smog density as measured by the ozone maximum in the area. The height of the bars indicates the inversion altitude on each day, and the tone of color used for each bar shows the smog density (*darker tones represent higher ozone concentrations*). Actual daily ozone values are given at the top of the charts.

the lining of the bronchi has a considerable capacity for restoration after acute damage, as the convalescent from a bout of influenza is grateful to discover. In some cases, however, presumably as a result of a steady irritation of the bronchi and breathing sacs, minute damage to the tissues becomes irreversible. Once this happens a circular process begins. The slightly damaged bronchopulmonary structures are less able to operate the mechanisms that normally protect the essentially clean lung from the microorganisms in the nose and throat. Both the lung and the bronchi tend to become repeatedly infected. Each infection damages the tissue still further, eventually producing the full bronchitis-emphysema.

A hereditary susceptibility may be involved, and it may be that the disease represents a fundamental aging process. Men are three to five times more frequently affected than women; both the illness rate and the death rate go up sharply after 45, death being caused by heart failure or pneumonia.

It is not difficult to conceive of a role for air pollution in the disease process. Both the hydrocarbon and the sulfuric compounds are highly irritating, and the bronchi are continuously exposed to them during periods of high pollution. Natural exposure to either type of smog and experimental exposure to low concentrations of smog constituents have produced tissue damage in plants and in cultures of animal cells and scarring of the lungs of laboratory animals. Plant damage in California has occurred in a noticeable swath bordering highways; ozone effects on growing tobacco leaves have been noted in Connecticut. Mary O. Amdur and her colleagues at the Harvard University School of Public Health have shown that inhalation of small amounts of the sulfur components of smog causes interference with the free passage of air in and out of the lungs of guinea pigs and normal humans. Effects of this type, if recurrent, would definitely aggravate bronchitis-emphysema and might actually initiate it. Some authorities suspect that two or more components of smog may act synergistically in the lung to cause damage that might not result from exposure to any one of them. So far, however, there is no direct evidence that continued exposure to urban air can start the disease. On the other hand, once the process does get its start, there is excellent evidence that both kinds of urban smog influence it adversely.

Bronchitis-emphysema is considerably more common among city dwellers than country people. There is some indication, however, that the advantages of country living can be canceled by cigarette smoking, which is, in effect, a portable form of air pollution. In Great Britain it has been shown that the larger the city, the higher the incidence of bronchitis-emphysema. D. D. Reid of the London School of Hygiene and Tropical Medicine was able to find, in careful studies of the absenteeism and permanent disability rates of post-office workers in Greater London, that the workers employed indoors have considerably lower rates than the postmen who worked almost exclusively outdoors. He also showed that the postmen who work in the central and northeastern sections, where air pollution is highest, have a bronchitis rate almost twice that of the men who delivered the mail in the cleaner parts of the city.

Hurley L. Motley and his associates at the University of Southern California School of Medicine have made detailed studies of 100 patients with various grades of chronic bronchitis and emphysema, first when they were breathing ordinary Los Angeles air and then when they were breathing air from which the chemical pollutants had been removed by charcoal filters. They reported that in the purer air the patients showed a striking improvement in lung function, those with the greatest disability showing the most progress. Significantly, several days of breathing pure air were needed before any change became detectable. This suggests that the effect of the contaminants on damaged bronchopulmonary tissues is less transient than those produced by smoking a cigarette, for example.

The aggravation of chronic bronchitis-emphysema by air pollution has been most drastically demonstrated in the few epidemics of acute illness attributed to air pollution. In the cases of the Donora "disaster" and the London episode of 1952 the evidence is decisive. The air at Donora, on a bend of the Monongahela River with high hills on all sides, must take up the smoke and fume of blast furnaces, steel mills, sulfuric acid mills and slag-processing plants. In October, 1948, a thermal inversion occurred over most of the U.S., including the Donora basin. There the usual smog, instead of lifting each day at noon as was its custom, remained unabated. By the third day of constant smog, 5,910 persons were reported ill. More than 60 per cent of the inhabitants 65 and older were affected, and almost half of these were seriously ill. In all, 20 persons died, 17

of the deaths occurring on the third day of unremitting smog. Then a heavy rain fell, the smog disappeared and the epidemic stopped immediately. In London in 1952 there was an "excess" mortality of 4,000 to 5,000 persons during one week. The deaths in both London and Donora occurred almost exclusively among those with previous bronchopulmonary disease. Indeed, the veteran bronchitis patients in the London clinics served almost as the canaries that miners once carried to detect noxious gases: they noted discomfort six to 12 hours before it was evident to others that an episode of smog was at hand.

The smog in these two situations was of the sulfur type, but there is no reason to doubt that a hydrocarbon smog could have the same effect. Perhaps the most significant finding is that no single smog component in either disaster was present in a higher concentration than usual. This may merely reflect faulty analysis of what may have been rapidly changing situations. But the finding points to the ugly conclusion that the same smog breathed by everyone a day or two at a time without immediate or apparent ill effect may be highly injurious to sub-

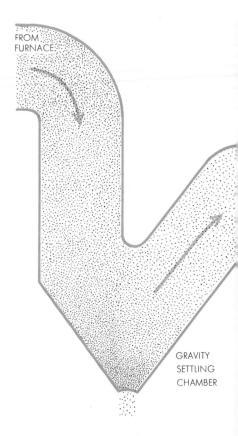

INDUSTRIAL DISCHARGE can be cleaned up appreciably by elaborate installations of the type diagramed here. Exhaust from furnaces enters at the left, where some of the heavy particles settle out because of

stantial numbers of people when it is breathed continuously for only a few days more.

Even more disquieting is the subsequent experience of those involved in the Donora disaster. Before the episode residents of Donora appeared to have the same health status as people in the rest of the country. In the first nine years thereafter, however, those who became ill and recovered showed a higher mortality and incidence of illness than those who were present but unaffected at the time of the smog. To some extent this difference can be taken as reflecting the adverse effect of the smog on those with damage to their lungs and hearts anteceding the disaster. This is not the whole story; even those Donora residents who had no history of heart disease prior to the dark days of 1948 but became ill in this period of smog have had a higher subsequent illness rate.

The deferred consequences of the Donora episode are among the scanty pieces of epidemiological evidence that contaminated air may actually initiate disease in man. In this connection the recent experience with an asthma-like

disease observed in Yokohama deserves mention. "Yokohama asthma" has become one of the major causes of illness among the personnel of the U.S. armed forces and their dependents in the Tokyo-Yokohama region. Those afflicted obtain prompt relief when moved short distances from this region. Even going up in an airplane 5,000 feet gives complete relief, only to be followed by a return of the symptoms within minutes of landing at the airport. Evidence is accumulating that permanent damage can occur if the illness is prolonged. Harvey W. Phelps and his associates in the U.S. Army Medical Corps have noted that the incidence of the disease is limited to a heavily industrialized area where conditions are ideal for the formation and retention of smog, and that increase in the attack rate can be correlated with an increase in the smog. A similar disease that appears to be correlated with atmospheric contamination has been reported in New Orleans.

One other observation suggests that urban air is related to bronchopulmonary disease. This has to do with the type of lung cancer so closely related to cigarettes. It is known that this form

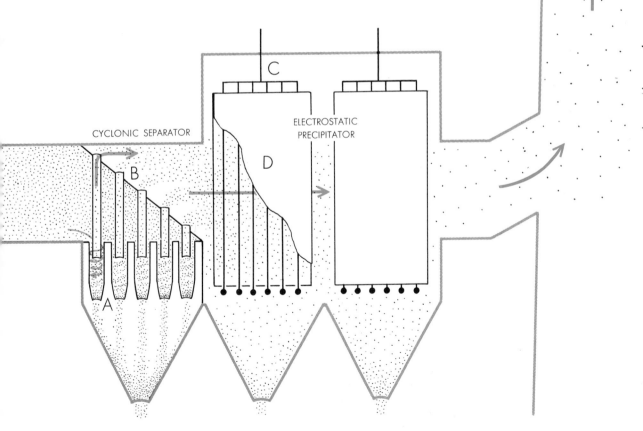

gravity. Entering the cyclonic separator, the smoke is forced downward into a series of cylinders (*A*) past vanes that whirl it rapidly; centrifugal force throws some of the suspended particles out to the walls of the cylinders, and the partially cleaned gas moves up through collecting tubes (*B*) and on to the electro-

static precipitator. Here a powerful electric field is established between discharge electrodes (*weighted wires, C*) and collecting electrodes (*plates, D*). The gas passing through the field is ionized; the ions attach themselves to ash particles, which are in turn charged and attracted to the collecting electrode, later to be removed.

of lung cancer is significantly less frequent in rural areas than in cities. But in the country, where cigarettes are a threat to barns, smoking is a less universal habit. To isolate the effect of urban air on smokers one should have the figures on groups of cigarette smokers who have moved en masse from city to country. Something of the sort is supplied by British emigration to New Zealand. The incidence of lung cancer is reported to be higher among cigarette smokers who lived their first 40 years in Great Britain than among smokers born and brought up in New Zealand. Essentially similar results have been reported for British emigrants to South Africa.

In view of the increasing pollution of the urban atmosphere and with the Donora episode in mind, it would be well to know how large a portion of the population has had a history of bronchitis-emphysema and other forms of pulmonary damage. The figures are scattered and uncertain. In the California State Board of Public Health survey of 1954–1955, bronchitis and asthma were found to be among the 10 most frequent-

ly disabling chronic diseases, accounting for 6 per cent of the total days of disability. In 1957, for the country as a whole, emphysema ranked second among the diseases in men for whom disability was allowed under the Social Security Act. During the past decade the California death rate from emphysema has risen 400 per cent, from 1.5 per 100,000 in 1950 to 5.8 per 100,000 in 1957. Presumably some portion of this increase represents better diagnosis reflecting increased medical interest, but it may also be taken as indicating a rising incidence of the disease. Quite aside from any possible role of smog in actual initiation of the disease, the number of people with chronic bronchitis-emphysema is bound to increase. The reason for this is that our population contains a steadily expanding pool of people who have weathered acute bronchopulmonary illnesses. Only 25 years ago almost one of three people with the commonest forms of bacterial pneumonia would succumb to it. Today the fatality rate of the disease would be 1 or 2 per cent.

Large numbers of people are, therefore, alive today in all age groups who would not have been alive in the days before antimicrobial therapy. So long as all goes well, they may show no signs of ill health. But when something untoward happens, as when the air fails to clean

itself, they can become seriously ill and may die.

Some idea of the number of people who are in special danger from smog may be had from the recent experience with Asian influenza. This country had its certified epidemic of Asian influenza in the autumn of 1957, "certified" in the sense that the disease was then front-page news. What is not generally known is that more people in the U.S. died as a result of Asian influenza after that epidemic than during it. These deaths were reflected in two peaks of excess mortality: one in the first three months of 1958, the other in the first three months of 1960. Indeed, in the course of the 1960 wave of influenza 26,000 excess deaths were recorded, a larger toll than that of the 1957 epidemic that had been so widely publicized. In large measure these 26,000 excess deaths were those of people with damaged bronchopulmonary structures or chronic heart disease. Speaking broadly, these are the same people who are in danger of serious illness from continued exposure to heavily contaminated air. It is true that they can be protected against the risk of influenza by vaccination. But how can they avoid continued damage from polluted air?

The control of environmental contamination—whether of air, water or food—raises formidable problems. The

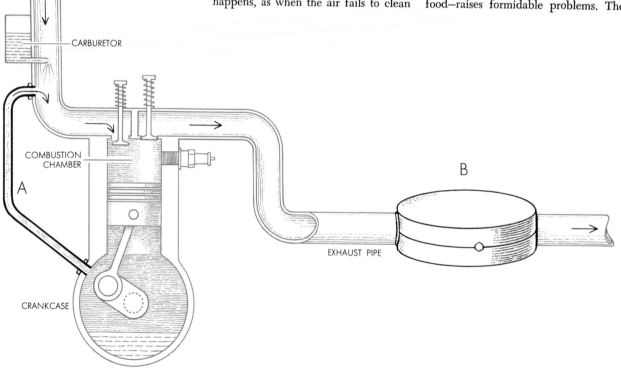

AUTOMOBILE EXHAUST is a large contributor to air pollution. Two devices have been developed to cut down this source. One is a "blow-by" pipe (*A*), which takes unburned gases from the crank-case back to the combustion chambers. The other is an "after-burner" (*B*), a special muffler that oxidizes carbon monoxide and unburned fuel in the exhaust gases through a catalytic process.

contamination is not the work of evil men or even slovenly neighbors, as were the contaminations of 50 years ago. Today's contaminations are the impersonal consequences of a highly industrialized society. Corrective measures must inevitably set up tremors across the whole delicate network of that society. Public health officials alone cannot be expected to secure the acquiescence of the host of private and public interests, businessmen, public officials, consumers and taxpayers in the considerable expense and effort that is necessarily involved. What is needed is a citizens' movement in the environmental-pollution field like the conservation movement of Theodore Roosevelt's day. The plant manager is reluctant to raise the factory smokestack 50 feet if nothing is done about the open burning at the city dump, and the city manager faces the same problem in reverse. A citizens' movement is needed, above all, to secure the cooperation of citizens—in minimizing pollution by automobile, for example, by proper engine maintenance. An aroused public opinion has brought the establishment of air-pollution control boards in a number of communities across the country, some of them interstate. In New York and Los Angeles these boards operate laboratories and have access to enforcement powers.

The formulation of effective public policy on the problem of air pollution requires an expanded research effort. For some years the U.S. Public Health Service has conducted a modest program of high quality, covering the sources and control of pollution at its Robert A. Taft Sanitary Engineering Center, in Cincinnati, Ohio, and seeking epidemiological data through community surveys such as are now in progress in New Orleans, La., and Nashville, Tenn. This work has gathered new impetus from the establishment of the Division of Environmental Health as one of the major operating units of the Public Health Service, with its own Environmental Health Center to be set up alongside the Service's other great research institutes. As a result one may now anticipate a quickening of interest in this field among medical scientists in the universities. The literature should soon show the data so much needed on the prevalence of bronchitis-emphysema and pulmonary heart disease. With an adequate estimate of the cost to health of air pollution, the public will be in a better position to assume and allocate the social cost of cleaning up the country's urban atmosphere.

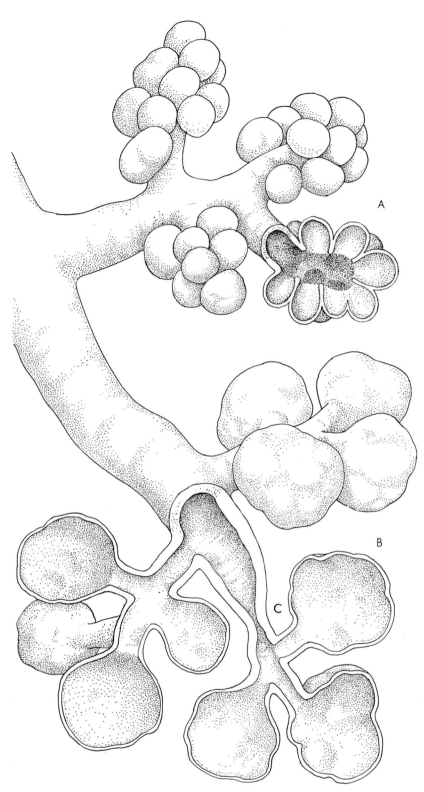

BRONCHITIS-EMPHYSEMA is a chronic lung disease that is apparently aggravated by air pollution. In the normal lung the air passes through the bronchial tubes to enter millions of alveoli (A), tiny cells in which the oxygen is transferred to the blood. In a diseased lung the walls of many of the alveoli break down (B), causing a reduction in the amount of membrane available to carry out the oxygen transfer. At the same time there is a narrowing of the smallest branches of the bronchial tree (C), further restricting air exchange.

14

The Aging Great Lakes

CHARLES F. POWERS AND ANDREW ROBERTSON
November 1966

The five Great Lakes in the heartland of North America constitute the greatest reservoir of fresh water on the surface of the earth. Lake Superior, with an area of 31,820 square miles (nearly half the area of New England), is the world's largest freshwater lake; Lake Huron ranks fourth in the world, Lake Michigan fifth, Lake Erie 11th and Lake Ontario 13th. Together the five lakes cover 95,200 square miles and contain 5,457 cubic miles of water. They provide a continuous waterway into the heart of the continent that reaches nearly 2,000 miles from the mouth of the St. Lawrence River to Duluth at the western tip of Lake Superior.

The Great Lakes are obviously an inestimable natural resource for the development of the U.S. and Canada. They supply vast amounts of water for various needs: drinking, industrial uses and so forth. They serve as a transportation system linking many large inland cities to one another and to the sea. Their falls and rapids generate huge supplies of hydroelectric power. Their fish life is a large potential source of food. And finally, they serve as an immense playground for human relaxation, through boating, swimming and fishing.

The settlements and industries that have grown up around this attractive resource are already very substantial. Although less than 3.5 percent of the total U.S. land area lies in the Great Lakes basin, it is the home of more than 13.5 percent of the nation's population (and about a third of Canada's population). In the southern part of the basin, from Milwaukee on the west to Quebec on the east, is a string of cities that is approaching the nature and dimensions of a megalopolis. Many economists believe the Great Lakes region is likely to become the fastest-growing area in the U.S. Their forecast is based mainly on the fact that whereas most other regions of the country are experiencing increasing shortages of water, the Great Lakes area enjoys a seemingly inexhaustible supply.

Unfortunately the forecast is now troubled by a large question mark. The viability of this great water resource is by no means assured. Even under natural conditions the life of an inland lake is limited. It is subject to aging processes that in the course of time foul its waters and eventually exhaust them. The Great Lakes are comparatively young, and their natural aging would not be a cause for present concern, since the natural processes proceed at the slow pace of the geological time scale. The aging of these lakes is now being accelerated tremendously, however, by man's activities. Basically the destructive agent is pollution. The ill effect of pollution is not limited to the circumstance that it renders the waters unclean. Pollution also hastens the degeneration and eventual extinction of the lakes as bodies of water.

These conclusions are based on recent extensive studies of the Great Lakes by a number of universities and governmental agencies in the U.S. and Canada. Employing various research techniques, including those of oceanography, the studies have produced new basic knowledge about the natural history and ecology of the Great Lakes and recent major changes that have occurred in them.

The natural aging of a lake results from a process called "eutrophication," which means biological enrichment of its water. A newly formed lake begins as a body of cold, clear, nearly sterile water. Gradually streams from its drainage basin bring in nutrient substances, such as phosphorus and nitrogen, and the lake water's increasing fertility gives rise to an accumulating growth of aquatic organisms, both plant and animal. As the living matter increases and organic deposits pile up on the lake bottom, the lake becomes smaller and shallower, its waters become warmer, plants take root in the bottom and gradually take over more and more of the space, and their remains accelerate the filling of the basin. Eventually the lake becomes a marsh, is overrun by vegetation from the surrounding area and thus disappears.

As a lake ages, its animal and plant life changes. Its fish life shifts from forms that prefer cold water to those that do better in a warmer, shallower environment; for example, trout and whitefish give way to bass, sunfish and perch. These in turn are succeeded by frogs, mud minnows and other animals that thrive in a marshy environment.

The natural processes are so slow that

PROCESS OF EXTINCTION that is the destiny of all lakes is seen in action in the aerial photograph on the opposite page. Cattaraugus Creek, a stream that forms the boundary between Erie and Chautauqua counties in New York, enters Lake Erie at this point southwest of Buffalo. (North is to the right.) The stream is not polluted but it carries silt and nutrients. The silt acts to fill the lake; the nutrients feed various forms of plant life that encroach on the shallows and add to the accumulation of bottom deposits. The aging process, which eventually converts every lake into dry land, is greatly accelerated when, as in the case of America's Great Lakes, human and industrial wastes are added to the normal runoff load.

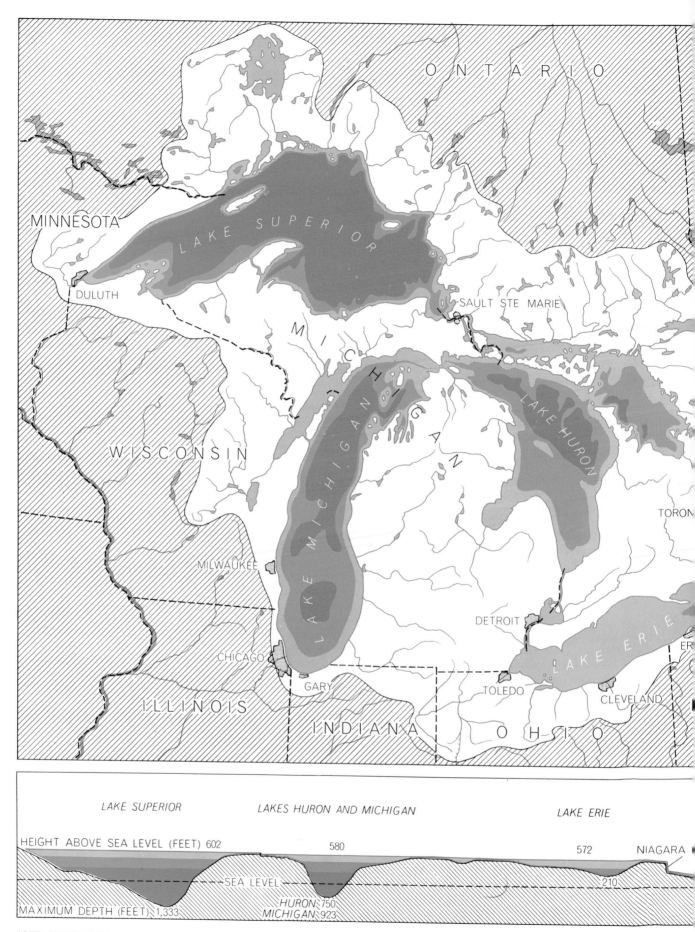

ONTARIO

MINNESOTA

LAKE SUPERIOR

DULUTH

SAULT STE MARIE

M I C H I G A N

WISCONSIN

LAKE HURON

LAKE MICHIGAN

MILWAUKEE

TORON

DETROIT

CHICAGO

LAKE ERIE

GARY

ILLINOIS

TOLEDO

ER

CLEVELAND

INDIANA

O H I O

LAKE SUPERIOR　　　*LAKES HURON AND MICHIGAN*　　　　*LAKE ERIE*

HEIGHT ABOVE SEA LEVEL (FEET) 602　　　　580　　　　572　　NIAGARA

SEA LEVEL　　　　　　　　　210

MAXIMUM DEPTH (FEET) 1,333　　HURON 750
MICHIGAN 923

AMERICAN GREAT LAKES comprise the world's largest fresh-water reservoir. Their drainage area (*white*) is not big enough to counteract the loss of lake water through discharge and evaporation but the lakes' level is kept stable by the inflow of groundwater and capture of the rain and snow that fall on 95,200 square **miles** of water surface. Superior (*left*) is the deepest of the five and Erie the shallowest (*vertical scale of profile is exaggerated*). Erosion will have destroyed the escarpment forming Niagara Falls 25,000

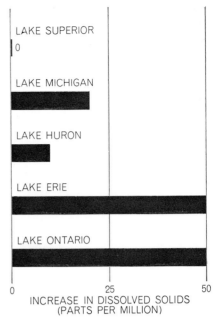

INCREASE IN DISSOLVED SOLIDS (PARTS PER MILLION)

INDEX OF POLLUTION is provided by the extent to which the lakes' content of dissolved solids has increased in the past 50 years. Lake Superior shows no increase, and the modest increase for Lake Huron is attributable to its receipt of Lake Michigan water, which is more heavily polluted. Lake Erie's major cities and its small volume of water account for its rising solids content. Lake Ontario's pollution is a combination of what is received from Lake Erie and what the cities along its shores contribute.

years from now; Lake Erie will then empty, leaving little more than a marshy stream to channel water from the upper lakes into Lake Ontario and on to the Atlantic Ocean.

the lifetime of a lake may span geological eras. Its rate of aging will depend on physical and geographic factors such as the initial size of the lake, the mineral content of the basin and the climate of the region. The activities of man can greatly accelerate this process. Over the past 50 years it has become clear that the large-scale human use of certain lakes has speeded up their aging by a considerable factor. A particularly dramatic example is Lake Zurich in Switzerland: the lower basin of that lake, which receives large amounts of human pollution, has gone from youth to old age in less than a century. In the U.S. similarly rapid aging has been noted in Lake Washington at Seattle and the Yahara lake chain in Wisconsin.

When the European explorers of North America first saw the Great Lakes, the lakes were in a quite youthful stage: cold, clear, deep and extremely pure. In the geological sense they are indeed young—born of the most recent ice age. Before the Pleistocene their present sites were only river valleys. The advancing glaciers deepened and enlarged these valleys; after the glaciers began to retreat some 20,000 years ago the scoured-out basins filled with the melting water. The succeeding advances and retreats of the ice further deepened and reshaped the lakes until the last melting of the ice sheet left them in their present form.

The land area drained by the Great Lakes (194,039 square miles) is relatively small: it is only about twice the area of the lakes themselves, whereas the ratio for most other large lakes is at least six to one. The drainage alone is not sufficient to replace the water lost from the Great Lakes by evaporation and discharge into the ocean by way of the St. Lawrence. Thanks to their immense surface area, however, their capture of rainfall and snowfall, supplemented by inflow of groundwater, maintains the lakes at a fairly stable level. The level varies somewhat, of course, with the seasons (it is a foot to a foot and a half higher in summer than in winter) and with longer-range fluctuations in rainfall. Prolonged spells of abnormal precipitation or drought have raised or lowered the level by as much as 10 feet, thereby causing serious flooding along the lake shores or leaving boat moorings high and dry.

The five lakes differ considerably from one another, not only in surface area but also in the depth and quality of their waters. Lake Superior averages

487 feet in depth, whereas shallow Lake Erie averages only 58 feet. There is also a large difference in the lakes' altitude: Lake Superior, at the western end, stands 356 feet higher above sea level than Lake Ontario at the eastern extreme. Most of the drop in elevation occurs in the Niagara River between Lake Erie and Lake Ontario. At Niagara Falls, where the river plunges over the edge of an escarpment, the drop is 167 feet. This escarpment, forming a dam across the eastern end of Lake Erie, is continuously being eroded away, and it is estimated that in 25,000 years it will be so worn down that Lake Erie will be drained and become little more than a marshy stream.

The lakes are all linked together by a system of natural rivers and straits. To this system man has added navigable canals that today make it possible for large ocean-going ships to travel from the Atlantic to the western end of Lake Superior. Hundreds of millions of tons of goods travel up and down the Great Lakes each year, and on the U.S. side alone there are more than 60 commercial ports. The Sault Ste Marie Canal (the "Soo"), which connects Lake Su-

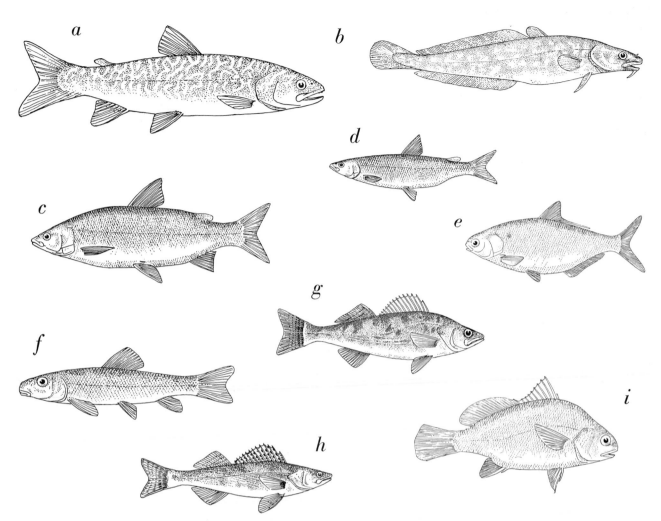

OLDER FISH POPULATION of the Great Lakes includes seven fishes that have nearly disappeared in the past two decades. Among them are the lakes' two largest species, the lake trout (a) and the burbot (b), and four smaller but economically important fishes, the whitefish (c), its close relative the chub, or lake herring (d), the walleye (g) and its close relative the blue pike (*not illustrated*). All six, as well as the sucker (f), have been victims of the parasitic sea lamprey, a fish that was confined to Lake Ontario until completion of the Welland Canal in 1932. Other indigenous fishes illustrated are the gizzard shad (e), the sauger (h) and the sheepshead (i).

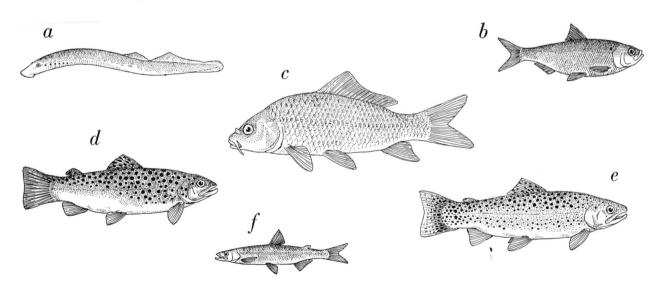

INTRUSIVE FISH POPULATION, responsible for disrupting the previous ecological balance of the four upper Great Lakes, are of two classes: those introduced by man and those that have entered on their own. The lamprey (a) is one of the voluntary intruders, as is the alewife (b), which also entered the upper lakes from Lake Ontario via the Welland Canal. Not a predator of adult fishes, the alewife nonetheless threatens the indigenous fish population. It feeds on these fishes' eggs and also consumes much of the other available food. Species introduced by man are the European carp (c) and brown trout (d), the rainbow trout (e) and the smelt (f).

perior and Lake Huron, carries a greater annual tonnage of shipping than the Panama Canal. Other major man-made links in the system are the Welland Canal, which bypasses the Niagara River's falls and rapids to connect Lake Erie and Lake Ontario, and the recently completed St. Lawrence Seaway, which makes the St. Lawrence River fully navigable from Lake Ontario to the Atlantic Ocean.

One of the first signs that man's activities might have catastrophic effects on the natural resources of the Great Lakes came as an inadvertent result of the building of the Welland Canal. The new channel allowed the sea lamprey of the Atlantic, which had previously been unable to penetrate any farther than Lake Ontario, to make its way into the other lakes. The lamprey is a parasite that preys on other fishes, rasping a hole in their skin and sucking out their blood and other body fluids. It usually attacks the largest fish available. By the 1950's it had killed off nearly all the lake trout and burbot (a relative of the cod that is also called the eelpout) in Lake Huron, Lake Michigan and Lake Superior. The lamprey then turned its attention to smaller species such as the whitefish, the chub (a smaller relative of the whitefish), the blue pike, the walleye and the sucker. Its depredations not only destroyed a large part of the fishing industry of the Great Lakes but also brought radical changes in the ecology of these lakes.

Since the late 1950's U.S. and Canadian agencies have been carrying on a determined campaign to eradicate the lamprey, using a specific larvicide to kill immature lampreys in streams where the species spawns [see "The Sea Lamprey," by Vernon C. Applegate and James W. Moffett; SCIENTIFIC AMERICAN, April, 1955]. This program has succeeded in cutting back greatly the lamprey population in Lake Superior; it is now being applied to the streams feeding into Lake Michigan and will be extended next to Lake Huron. Efforts have already been started to reestablish a growing lake-trout population in Lake Superior.

Meanwhile a second invader that also penetrated the lakes through the Welland Canal has become prominent. This fish is the alewife, a small member of the herring family. The alewife, which ranges up to about nine inches in length, does not attack adult fishes, but it feeds on their eggs and competes with their young for food. In the past decade it has

multiplied so rapidly that it is now the dominant fish species in Lake Huron and Lake Michigan and seems to be on the way to taking over Lake Superior.

Recently attempts have been made to convert the alewives from a liability to an asset. The Pacific coho, or silver salmon, has been introduced into Lake

Superior and Lake Michigan on an experimental basis. This fish should thrive feeding on the alewife and yet be protected from its depredations, because the eggs and young of the coho are found in tributary streams the alewives do not frequent. Other fishes such as the Atlantic striped bass are being con-

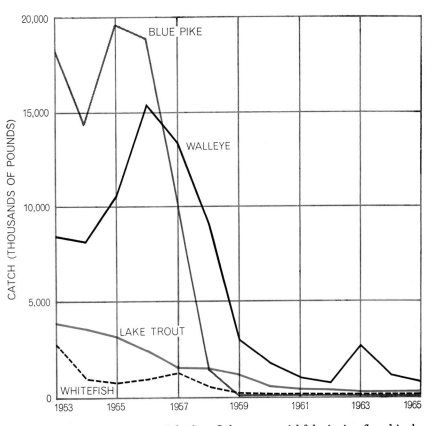

STEADY DROP in productivity of the Great Lakes commercial fisheries is reflected in the numbers of three species taken in Lake Erie (*black*) and one taken in Lake Superior (*color*) between 1953 and 1965. The lake-trout catch in Lake Michigan once rivaled Lake Superior's; from 1941 through 1946 it averaged more than six million pounds. The decline then began to be significant. Within a decade the Lake Michigan fishery ceased to yield lake trout.

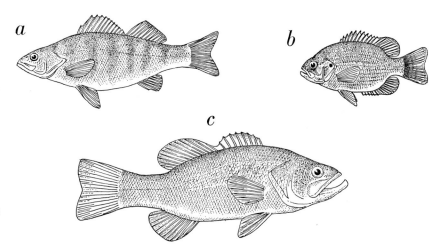

SUCCESSOR POPULATION of Great Lakes fishes when the lakes reach old age will probably include species that inhabit the lakes' shallow waters today. Among these are the yellow perch (*a*), the kind of sunfish known as rock bass (*b*) and the largemouth bass (*c*).

sidered for introduction to supplement the coho.

The introduction of a new fish into a lake is always an unpredictable matter. It may, as in the accidental admission of the lamprey and the alewife, disrupt the ecological balance with disastrous results. Even when the introduction is made intentionally with a favorable prognosis, it frequently does not work out according to expectations. The carp, prized as a food fish in many countries of Europe, was stocked in the Great Lakes many years ago and has established itself in all the lakes except Lake Superior. Commercial and sport fishermen in these lakes, however, have come to regard the carp as a nuisance. North Americans generally consider it inedible, chiefly because they have not learned how to prepare and cook it prop-

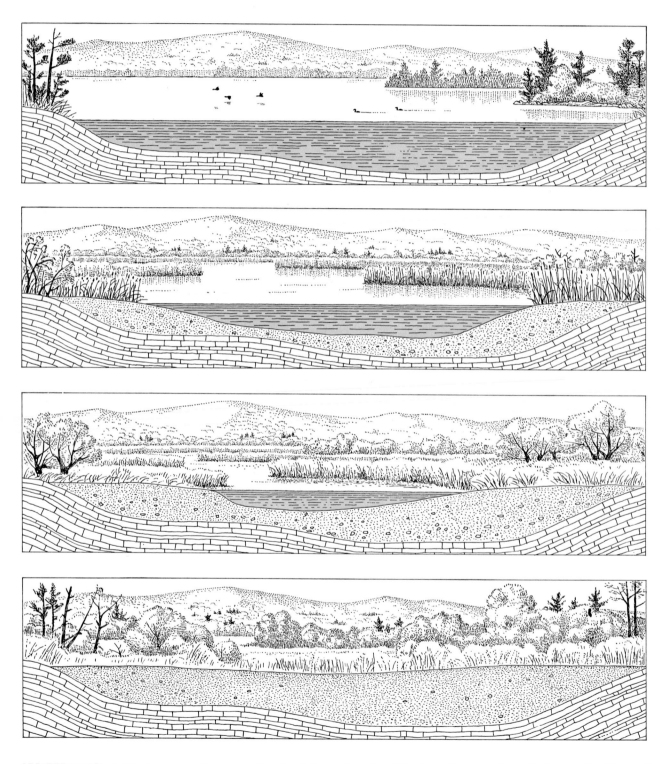

OBLITERATION of a lake is a process that starts at the edge of the water (*top*): a few bog-adapted conifers rise in a forest of hardwoods. Next the debris of shallow-water plants turns the lake margin into marsh that is gradually invaded by mosses and bog plants, bog-adapted bushes and trees such as blueberry and willow, and additional conifers. Eventually the lake, however deep, is entirely filled with silt from its tributaries and with plant debris. In the final stage (*bottom*) the last central bog soon grows up into forest.

erly. On the other hand, the smelt, introduced into the upper lakes from Lake Ontario early in this century, has become prized by fishermen and is taken in large numbers in the Great Lakes today. What effect it will eventually have on the ecology of the lakes remains to be seen.

The Great Lakes are so young that, biologically speaking, they must be considered in a formative stage. So far only a few species of fishes have been able to invade them and adapt to their specialized environment, particularly in their deep waters. As time goes on, more species will arrive in the lakes and evolve into forms specially adapted to the environmental conditions. Lake Baikal in Siberia, a very large and ancient body of fresh water, offers a good illustration of such a history: it has developed a well-diversified and distinctive population of aquatic animals including a freshwater seal. As diversity in the Great Lakes increases, it will become less and less likely that the arrival or disappearance of one or two species (such as the lake trout and burbot) will result in any profound alteration of the ecological balance.

Pollution, however, is a decidedly different factor. Its effects are always drastic—and generally for the worse. This is clearly evident in Lake Erie, the most polluted of the Great Lakes. The catch of blue pike from this lake dropped from 18,857,000 pounds in 1956 to less than 500 pounds in 1965, and that of the walleye fell from 15,405,000 pounds in 1956 to 790,000 pounds in 1965. There was also a sharp decline in lake herring, whitefish and sauger (a small relative of the walleye). While these most desirable fishes decreased, there were rises in the catch of sheepshead (the freshwater drum), carp, yellow perch and smelt. Other signs in the lake gave evidence of an environment increasingly unfavorable for desirable fish; among these were the severe depletion of oxygen in the bottom waters, the disappearance of mayfly larvae (a fish food), which used to be extremely abundant in the shallow western end of the lake, and spectacular growths of floating algae—a certain sign of advanced age in a lake.

Lake Erie receives, to begin with, the grossly polluted water of the Detroit River, into which 1.6 billion gallons of waste are discharged daily from the cities and industries along the riverbanks. To this pollution an enormous amount is added by the great urban and

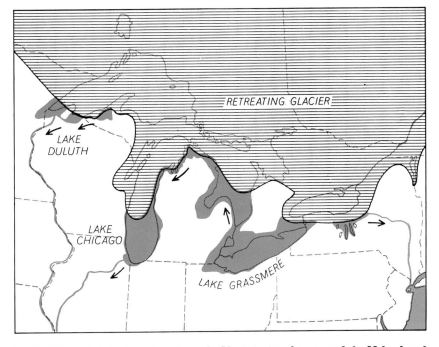

YOUNG LAKES drained southward, via the Mississippi to the west and the Mohawk and Hudson to the east, during the last glacial retreat of the Pleistocene some 10,000 years ago.

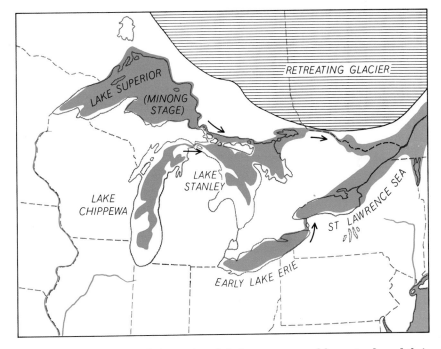

MATURING LAKES altered the southward drainage pattern and began to channel their waters eastward into the prehistoric St. Lawrence Sea as the glacial retreat continued.

industrial complex around the lake itself. A recent study of the Detroit River by the U.S. Public Health Service showed that its waters contain large quantities of sewage bacteria, phenols, iron, oil, ammonia, chlorides, nitrogen compounds, phosphates and suspended solids. Similar waste materials are discharged into the lake by the steel, chemical, refining and manufacturing plants along the lake. Pollution is par-

ticularly serious in Lake Erie because of the lake's shallowness; its volume of water is too small to dilute the pollutants effectively. Over the past 50 years the concentrations of major contaminants in the Lake Erie waters have increased sharply.

Many of the industrial wastes, notably phenols and ammonia, act as poisons to the fish and other animal life in the lake. Solid material settles to the bottom and smothers bottom-dwelling organisms. Moreover, some of the solids decompose and in doing so deplete the water of one of its most vital constituents: dissolved oxygen. Algae, on the other hand, thrive in the polluted waters, particularly since the sewage wastes contain considerable amounts of the plant-fertilizing elements nitrogen and phosphorus. The algae contribute to the depletion of oxygen (when they die and decay), give the lake water disagreeable tastes and odors and frustrate the attempts of water-purifying plants to filter the water.

In addition to Lake Erie, the southern end of Lake Michigan has also become seriously polluted. Interestingly the city of Chicago, the dominant metropolis of this area, apparently does not contribute substantially to the lake pollution; it discharges its sewage into the Mississippi River system instead of the lake. The main discharge into Lake Michigan comes from the large industrial concentration—steel mills, refineries and other establishments—clustered along its southern shores. The Public Health Service has found that the lake water in this area contains high concentrations of inorganic nitrogen, phosphate, phenols and ammonia.

Apart from the southern end, most of the water of Lake Michigan is still of reasonably good quality. In Lake Ontario, although it receives a considerable discharge of wastes, the situation is not yet as serious as in Lake Erie because Ontario's much larger volume of water provides a higher dilution factor. Lake Huron, bordered by a comparatively small population, so far shows only minor pollution effects, and Lake Superior almost none. Nevertheless, the growth of the entire region and the spreading pollution of the lakes and their tributary waters make the long-range outlook disquieting. Already the quality of the waters over a considerable portion of the lake system has greatly deteriorated, and many bathing beaches must be closed periodically because of pollution.

It is clear that in less than 150 years man has brought about changes in the Great Lakes that probably would have taken many centuries under natural conditions. These changes, shortening the usable life of the lakes, seem to be accumulating at an ever increasing rate. We still know far too little about the complicated processes that are under way or about what measures are necessary to conserve this great continental resource. Obviously the problem calls for much more study and for action that will not be too little and too late. No doubt the Great Lakes will be there for a long time to come; they are not likely to dry up in the foreseeable future. But it will be tragic irony if one day we have to look out over their vast waters and reflect bitterly, with the Ancient Mariner, that there is not a drop to drink. To realize that this is not an unthinkable eventuality we need only remind ourselves of the water crisis in New York City, where water last year had to be drastically rationed while billions of gallons in the grossly polluted Hudson River flowed uselessly by the city.

15

Ionizing Radiation and the Citizen

GEORGE W. BEADLE
September 1959

In a few short years the science and technology of nuclear physics have come to affect the lives of all men. It is abundantly clear that the nuclear age is attended by unprecedented new risks and hazards.

By far the greatest hazard, as everyone knows, is the threat of nuclear war. Nuclear weapons could bring civilization to a catastrophic end. Yet no one seems able to find a workable formula for avoiding this danger that is at once foolproof and acceptable to all nations. To many men the complete abolition of nuclear weapons is the only sure solution. This must remain an unrealistic hope until ways are found for extending

the ban to armed conflict itself. What is to prevent nations that have not renounced war from rebuilding their armories of nuclear weapons?

In their failure to settle their differences by peaceable agreement the major nations are engaged in a mad nuclear arms race. Each hopes to deter potential enemies by the threat of instantaneous and annihilating retaliation. All know the danger of the game. None of the nations appears to see how to stop in a manner that will guarantee security for all.

Meanwhile the hazard of nuclear armament becomes progressively more grave. Existing weapons are more widely

dispersed, and the responsibility for using them is delegated to lower ranks of command. The risk of accident or poor judgment increases correspondingly. In the recent report issued by the American Academy of Arts and Sciences (*The Nth Country Problem: A World-Wide Survey of Nuclear Weapons Capabilities*) it is made clear that at least a dozen nations, in addition to the Big Three, have economic resources and manpower sufficient to arm themselves with these weapons. Will they not be tempted to enter the race in increasing numbers for national prestige if not for defense? Can they be dissuaded by any real hope of a just and effective solution? Failing this,

UNITED NATIONS SCIENTIFIC COMMITTEE on the Effects of Atomic Radiation meets periodically. A U. S. representative at this March, 1959, session was Shields Warren (*at left, chin in hand*), who guided study of casualties at Hiroshima and Nagasaki.

can they be convinced that they will be better off if they do not join the competition? It is true that capability of small-scale retaliation is a highly vulnerable intermediary position along the road to full retaliatory power. But will this argument carry conviction, coming from nations that have already arrived at the latter stage, or think they have?

The only practicable solution may lie in a pedestrian step-by-step approach. Certainly the present attempts to effect a permanent ban on the testing of nuclear weapons deserve full support, if only because this is the sole first step that appears to have a reasonable chance of acceptance.

Termination of the tests, which have increased exponentially in number for 14 years, will eliminate one nuclear hazard. The hazard of fallout is quantitatively

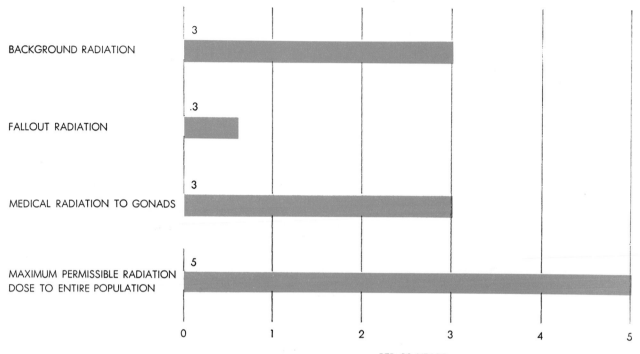

ESTIMATED RADIATION DOSE for average U. S. resident during reproductive years is represented by top three bars. Fallout estimate applies only if nuclear weapons tests cease. Permissible dose at bottom is in addition to medical and background doses.

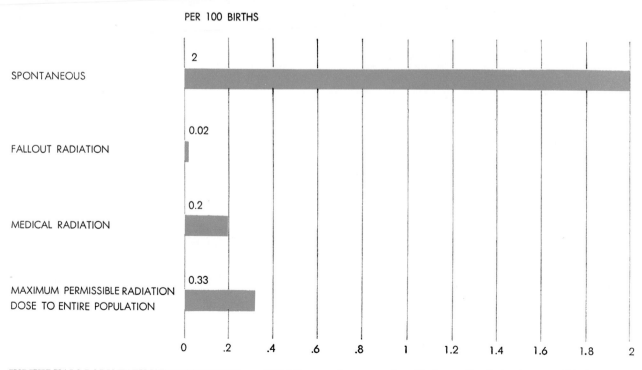

INDIVIDUALS BORN WITH NEW MUTATIONS, per 100 births, and causes of mutations are charted at left. At far right are totals of new mutations. Background radiation is responsible for some of the spontaneous mutations. All the figures on this chart are very

small but qualitatively large, because of its embarassing moral aspects. In addition, the mere fact of agreement will encourage negotiation on other issues.

But even if we succeed in taking this step and all the ones that must follow to achieve permanent peace, we will by no means be done with the hazards of radiation. We will have greatly reduced the risk of exposing large segments of the world population to high-level radiation. But there will remain the delayed effects of fallout and the increasingly important hazards of the peacetime uses of radiation. Power-reactor accidents may occur, as they already have; the radioactive by-products and spent fuels of reactors will need to be contained and safely disposed of; radiation and radioisotopes will be finding wider use in technology as well as in scientific and industrial research. The medical profession must continue its evaluation of the risks attending diagnostic and therapeutic irradiation of patients and its efforts to reduce these risks to the essential minimum.

What are the hazards to health of ionizing radiation and how great are they in given situations? After the millions of words that have been written and spoken there remain much uncertainty and confusion in public understanding. Why is it not possible to give simple answers to straightforward questions?

We are told at various times and by investigators of repute that fallout does no biological harm; that there is some damage but that it is negligible with respect to our defense needs; that present fallout levels, by producing several hundred thousand genetic mutations per generation on a world-wide basis, do enormous biological harm. Whom shall we believe?

We read in a reputable scientific journal that present and foreseeable levels of strontium 90 in human bone are unlikely to produce a single case of leukemia. But in another issue of the same journal we find it argued that the concentration of strontium 90 may already be approaching harmful levels in the bones of some individuals and may well be responsible for hundreds of new cases of leukemia in the next generation. Is there a "right" answer?

Should school children be given annual X-ray examinations? The truck continues to make its rounds and many schools still request its services. Do the advantages outweigh the risks?

In occupational exposure to ionizing radiation, is there a zone of greater danger as exposure approaches "permissible" levels? "Permissible" implies no risk, but the maximum permissible occupational exposure is several hundred times larger than fallout exposure per given period. Is this not inconsistent with the statement that even low exposure—as from fallout—produces mutations?

To arrive at sensible assessments of radiation hazards it is necessary to understand the reason for the conflict in opinion and information. Such assessments are imperative; the health and survival of hundreds of thousands of individuals are at stake. As for succeeding generations, if we now seriously underestimate genetic hazards, the harm that is done will persist, in some degree, for centuries to come. Nor can we postpone decisions until we have final and complete answers.

It is not in the nature of science to give final and complete answers. The probability is that there will always be diverse, tentative or contradictory answers to fundamental scientific questions. The best that can be hoped is that responsible citizens will make a greater effort to understand the knowledge at our disposal at any given time and to comprehend the social implications of this knowledge.

To place our present knowledge of ionizing radiation in the perspective of public policy, it will be useful to summarize here the biological aspects of the situation.

Whole-body exposure of man to penetrating ionizing radiation in large doses of 400 to 600 or more Roentgen (abbreviated r) units delivered over a short period of hours or days causes cell and tissue damage so extensive that successful repair may be impossible. Death results within days or weeks, the interval depending on the exposure. On the other hand, the same amount of radiation received over a much longer time, say months or years, permits such recovery processes as the replacement of cells by the division of still-viable cells and the successful resorption and elimination of breakdown products. Consequently the individual may survive and show little direct evidence of injury.

The chance of death after exposure to lethal radiation doses may be greatly reduced by certain therapeutic measures now under development. Of these the replacement of blood-cell-forming tissues by means of bone-marrow transplantation is one of the most promising. Nonlethal doses of something like 100 r units given at one time produce immediate damage, but it is to a considerable extent reparable. Such symptoms as change in the number and proportion of blood cells of various types, subcutaneous bleeding and loss of hair provide means of estimating exposure where this is not otherwise known.

In experimental animals, the mouse for example, sublethal doses of radiation appreciably reduce the life span. It is almost certain that this also occurs in man. Most investigators agree that there is no threshold below which ionizing radiation has no effect on living matter. On the other hand, some believe that there may be a minimum effective dose or dose rate for particular effects such as life-shortening, as John F. Loutit points out in his article "Ionizing Radition and the Whole Animal." [SCIENTIFIC AMERICAN, September 1959.] Unfortunately the quantitative relation between the degree of exposure and the reduction in longevity is difficult to determine even in experimental animals. If the relation is linear—that is, directly and simply proportional to exposure—down to low levels of radiation, and if the reduction of longevity in man is proportionately the same as in the mouse, the life-span reduction per r of total-body exposure could be something like one to 10 days.

In mice and in men heavy radiation-exposure increases the incidence of various forms of cancer. Radiologists and heavily irradiated survivors at Hiroshima

IN U. S. PER YEAR PER 4,000,000 TOTAL BIRTHS	IN WORLD PER YEAR PER 80,000,000 TOTAL BIRTHS	IN WORLD. PER GENERATION PER 2,400,000,000 TOTAL BIRTHS
80,000	1,600,000	48,000,000
800	16,000	480,000
8,000	160,000	4,800,000
13,000	270,000	8,000,000

rough estimates, and are subject to at least a five-fold uncertainty in either direction.

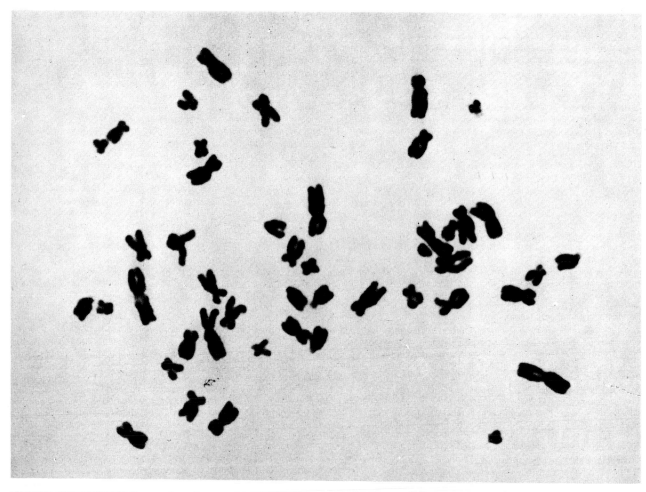

HUMAN CHROMOSOMES are enlarged some 2,000 diameters in this photomicrograph made by J. H. Tjio and T. T. Puck at University of Colorado Medical Center. The chromosomes are from a female body cell grown in tissue culture. There are 46 of them.

and Nagasaki, for example, show an incidence of leukemia 10 or more times higher than that of roughly comparable but unexposed individuals. Here again the exact relation between dose and incidence is not known; measurements are subject to large sampling errors. Even in mice the data are ambiguous. It may well be that the relation differs for different types of malignant disease. The most pessimistic assumption holds that the relation of disease to exposure is linear down to the lowest possible doses, and that the effect of intermittent and slowly delivered radiation is strictly cumulative. If this is the case, the probability that a person will develop leukemia appears to be approximately one in one million for each r of exposure per year. There is some evidence that prenatal exposure results in an even higher incidence of leukemia per r during the childhood years.

In several respects the genetic hazard is the most difficult and serious aspect of the problem of radiation. Genetic mutations are almost always harmful. Transmitted to descendants, they may express themselves over many successive generations.

It is now almost certain that in all cellular organisms (and in some viruses) molecules of deoxyribonucleic acid (DNA) bear the primary hereditary directions for the numerous processes that interact in development and function. Thus in man the DNA molecules in the chromosomes of the fertilized egg-cell are believed to carry the specifications by which the egg cell grows into an individual.

These specifications are "written" in a kind of molecular code; its basic symbols are the four kinds of units called nucleotides. Genetic directions are somehow spelled out by the sequence of these units, of which there are about 200 million in the 46 chromosomes of a human body-cell. Each grouping of 1,000 or so units of DNA is called a gene; each gene "tells" the body how to conduct some vital function; for example, how to assemble the proper amino acids (from the 20-odd kinds available) in the proper sequence to make an essential protein constituent of hemoglobin.

The individual's total DNA code is multiplied many times in the course of his life cycle and is ultimately passed on to the next generation. The details of this replication process are beginning to be understood; in fact, the process will proceed under relatively simple conditions in a test tube. Its precision is high. The probability of a genetically significant and easily detectable mistake during the 20 to 40 successive replications per generation is estimated at about one in a million for each gene. If there are 10,000 kinds of genes (an estimate subject to a large error), the chance that there will be a mistake of any kind in a given egg or sperm is only about one in 100.

Such mistakes are, like typographical errors, changes in the sequences of symbols in the code. The replications of DNA molecules is purely mechanical; therefore a sequence of incorrect symbols will be replicated as faithfully as if it were a correct sequence. Errors of this sort—

mutations—are not repaired except by the rare reversal of the process by which they occurred. There is no proofreader in the system. And such errors are likely to lead to significant errors of development or function; for example, defective hemoglobin. Since there are many ways to make hemoglobin incorrectly and only one way, or possibly a few ways, to make it correctly, mutations are much more likely to be deleterious than neutral or favorable.

If the mutant genes are replicated faithfully, with no correcting mechanism in the system, they should accumulate progressively generation after generation. Why then do species not mutate themselves out of existence? The answer is that natural selection rejects those individuals in whom deleterious mutations occur. Selection is a kind of inspector that discards the bad sets of specifications. This rejection of unfavorable mutations has been called "genetic death" by H. J. Muller. In man it may occur in many ways: death in the embryonic stage, death near or after birth, death prior to reproduction, failure to produce an average number of offspring, or failure to reproduce at all. L. S. Penrose of the University College London has estimated that in Europe and the U.S. the members of a given generation are the offspring of only 50 per cent of the members of the preceding generation. Thus "genetic death" may not mean literal premature death of individuals; it may, and frequently does, mean elimination of a particular line of descent on the instalment plan over many generations, without anyone being quite aware that it is happening.

The genes of all species, including man, are subject to varying rates of "spontaneous" mutation of which we do not know the cause. There are many ways, however, to increase the frequency of mutation, among them high temperatures, a variety of chemical treatments, and high-energy radiation. Ionizing radiation sufficiently penetrating to reach sperm and egg cells or their precursors is a particularly effective way of increasing mutation.

We may now summarize with some assurance the genetic hazard of radiation as follows: Radiation-induced mutations, like other mutations, however induced, are mostly deleterious. Under a given set of conditions, mutations appear to be induced in linear proportion to exposure; thus there is probably no threshold below which radiation will produce no mutations. Since there is no repair mechanism, once the mutation process is complete, mutations induced at different times will tend to accumulate in a line of descent until this tendency is just counterbalanced by natural selection. Ultimately, therefore, each new deleterious mutation must be compensated for by genetic death in the Muller sense.

From data on mice, fruit flies and other organisms it is estimated that the level of exposure of sperm and egg cells or their precursors to ionizing radiation sufficient to double the spontaneous mutation rate probably lies between 10 and 100 r. Taking 30 r, the geometric mean, as a reasonable guess for the doubling dose in man, it is possible to estimate in a very rough way the number of mutations for various levels of exposure to radiation.

If there is one spontaneous mutation in each 100 egg or sperm cells per generation, as suggested above, there will be two such mutations in every 100 individuals. Exposure to 30 r would double this. The exposure from fallout to date is liberally estimated at a cumulative .3 r in the 30 years of the average human reproductive lifetime. According to this estimate, fallout would increase the spontaneous-mutation rate by 1 per cent. The mutation rate calculated in a similar way for medical radiation runs considerably higher: at 10 per cent of the spontaneous rate, as shown in the bottom chart on pages 156 and 157. The maximum permissible occupational exposure allows for an increase of more than 50 per cent over the spontaneous rate. It should be emphasized that these are exceedingly rough estimates and may be too high or too low by a factor of five or more.

Although most geneticists will agree that the foregoing statements about radiation-induced mutations are reasonably well established, and that the estimates of the number of new mutations resulting from given amounts of radiation are at least plausible guesses, there remain many unanswered questions. For example, are malignant diseases the result of mutation in ordinary body cells, as contrasted with those that occur in germ cells? Although there is sufficient circumstantial evidence to convince many geneticists that some malignant diseases are the result of mutations in body cells, the answer is in most cases not positively known. Until recently no effective techniques were available for the genetic investigation of body cells. In whatever way malignant diseases arise, however, there is no doubt that high levels of radiation induce them effectively. As for low levels of exposure, the question of exact relation of exposure to incidence must remain open until better data are available.

A difficult question is: What is the magnitude of the burden added to society by a given increase in mutation rate? Suppose, for example, that fallout were to add 5,000 to 120,000 additional mutations and perhaps five to 40 additional deaths from leukemia in each generation in the U.S. What would this mean in terms of social burden?

The answer is not known. Perhaps it cannot be, for social burden consists of diverse components that cannot be summed. The cost of caring for a mentally defective person in an institution may be calculable in dollars, but how does one assess the unhappiness and mental anguish of the victim and the victim's family? Furthermore, even though we have some notion of the manner in which genetic deaths occur, and even if we could evaluate them in terms of social burden, we still could not arrive at a proper accounting, because we do not know in what relative proportions the various kinds of genetic deaths occur. It is also important to remember that the more considerate of its unfit individuals a society becomes, the greater will be the burden of a given mutation rate. On the other hand, there is a correction of unknown magnitude for coincidental elimination of two or more unexpressed mutations in single individuals who merely fail to reproduce. What we do know with some confidence is that the social burden of mutation will be increased by radiation in approximate proportion to the increase in mutation.

In view of these uncertainties about the harmful effects of exposure to low levels of radiation, is it possible to arrive at safe "permissible" upper limits of exposure for such groups as industrial workers, X-ray technicians and the public at large? If there is no threshold, the answer is clearly that it is impossible to establish any "safe" exposure other than zero, in the sense of having eliminated all risk. The best alternative is to establish permissible levels for which risks are below specified levels. This is exactly what the various commissions and committees responsible for setting permissible exposures attempt to do. The task is not an easy one, for adequate data are difficult to obtain even with animals.

A recent study by Carol W. Buck of the University of Western Ontario will serve to illustrate some of the difficulties. Let us suppose that the relation of leukemia to radiation is linear at all levels, and that for each r of total-body exposure the annual increase in deaths from this disease is one for every million individuals. This is a value that appears reasonable for high levels of exposure. If a population were exposed prior to age 30 to an average of five r above the natural and medical background, how many individuals would have to be observed to establish a statistically significant increase in leukemia?

The answer is six million people, and they would have to be observed for a period of at least a year. In this number there would be, on the average, 30 new cases of leukemia each year attributable to the five r. This additional number, over and above the 200 cases expected without those added by radiation, would be just statistically significant. To be certain that the added radiation was responsible, there would of course have to be a control rate based on an unirradiated population similarly observed and comparable in all other respects. Even if one observed a smaller population for a correspondingly longer time, say 600,-000 people for 10 years, the difficulties in meeting these requirements in human populations are formidable. They are so great that the study has not been done at this level of radiation even with an animal as favorable as the mouse.

It is obvious that we cannot for a long time arrive at better than the roughest kind of approximation in establishing permissible exposures. Right now it is difficult to see how we can improve on what the International Commission on Radiological Protection has done. This agency defines the maximum permissible dose for an individual as "that dose, accumulated over a long period of time or resulting from a single exposure, which in the light of present knowledge carries a negligible probability or severe somatic or genetic injury." It recommends that the total permissible genetic dose prior to age 30 "to the whole population from all sources additional to the natural background should not exceed five r plus the lowest practicable contribution from medical exposure."

Buck's calculations show how difficult it would be to establish whether this level of radiation to the general population would increase the incidence of leukemia by as many as five cases per million persons per year. If the entire population of the U.S. were to be exposed for generations to the maximum permissible level, it would be exceedingly difficult to exclude the possibility that the incidence of leukemia would increase by as many as 850 cases per year, or 50,000 per generation.

In addition to these difficulties, it should be remembered that ionizing radiation cannot be detected by the unaided human senses. Furthermore, overt signs of its harmful effects are often delayed for many years.

From the beginning of man's experience with ionizing radiation he has consistently underestimated its hazards. In fact, the tendency has been to underestimate not only the effects of a given exposure but often the amount of exposure as well. The exposures due to medical radiation have often been found to exceed estimates. And more recently there has been underestimation of the radiation from strontium 90 and carbon 14, two of the biologically most significant radioisotopes produced in tests of nuclear weapons. Permissible exposures have been revised downward repeatedly. Have we now reached the end? Many informed persons think not.

Incomplete knowledge thus plays a large part in public confusion and misunderstanding. It is easy to see why a qualified invesigator inclined to look at the matter in the most favorable light could reasonably say that the number of persons genetically affected by fallout per year in the U.S. population might be less than 200; that the majority of these might be counterbalanced by such factors as early embryonic deaths and slight reductions in fertility; that genetic deaths of this kind would be largely undetected, even in individual cases; that the added social burden could be negligibly small. He might reason: Why worry until more compelling evidence requires it?

At the other extreme an equally qualified worker could easily feel obligated to emphasize the least favorable possibility: that fallout might well be producing as many as 800 or more new mutations per year in the U.S., or 400,000 or more per generation on a world-wide basis. On this basis he could well argue that the fallout hazard is by no means an unimportant problem for society.

It is clear that the tendency to take one or the other of these extreme positions with regard to genetic and other hazards will be strongly influenced by attitudes toward the problem of world peace. The individual who is convinced that national defense through massive build-up of nuclear weapons is at the moment the only tenable safe position will be likely to regard the development and testing of such weapons to be of such overriding importance that the uncertain, unmeasurable and possibly small damage to the population seems of relatively little importance. In contrast, another individual who is convinced that

the only completely safe position will be attained through nuclear disarmament, and that we must get on with it immediately, tends to look for all possible arguments against nuclear weapons and will therefore be likely to cite the grimmer estimates.

There is no effortless way for the concerned citizen to arrive at an opinion. He must consider all aspects of the problem—risk of nuclear war included—hear all arguments, weigh all evidence and hope to arrive at a conclusion that makes sense to him. The scientist with special knowledge has a responsibility to make the facts available in as objective a manner as possible. As a citizen he has the obligation to help interpret them in terms of public policy.

The area of scientific confusion regarding radiation hazards can of course be greatly reduced by the direct procedure of adding to present knowledge. This work now engages many investigators in government agencies, industry and academic institutions. The process can and should be speeded up in all reasonable ways. Additional manpower is needed and, above all, new ideas. For example, the application of the techniques of microbiology to human-cell populations *in vivo* and *in vitro* promises a new approach to questions about human genetics. Existing manpower can be used to better advantage and at little additional expense.

Members of the medical profession are in an especially favorable position for learning about human genetics. Collectively they have occasion each year to examine millions of individuals. Unfortunately most physicians are not sufficiently well prepared to ask the right questions and make the right observations to add to the store of genetic knowledge of man. With only a little effort they could be equipped for the task. For example, medical records as kept by private practitioners, by clinics and by hospitals could be enormously improved from the standpoint of their genetic information.

In the long run more nearly adequate genetic training in medical schools will be the answer. Entirely aside from radiation hazards, this is necessary and desirable; it is increasingly apparent that the relative importance of genetic diseases is great and will become greater as other diseases are conquered. Already some 160,000 infants are born each year in the U.S. with significant genetic defects, many of which constitute important medical problems.

For these reasons census procedures

and records should also be revised to encompass genetic data. A pilot study is now under way in Canada, designed to find out how this might best be done. There is every reason for other nations to consider such actions.

It is well known that unambiguous communication is difficult even among investigators in the same scientific discipline. This is true especially in the area of radiation hazards, where probability arguments are so often involved. Since the incidences of radiation damage are often very low, the evaluation of their significance usually involves statistical methods of the most sophisticated kind. Scientists, who should understand statistics, have been known to be confused about them.

Consider a specific example. Shortly after World War II geneticists were asked whether long-term studies of the survivors of the bombing of Hiroshima and Nagasaki should be made to see if evidence of genetic damage could be found. Simple preliminary calculations suggested that significant results would be hard to obtain. On the assumption that man is about as mutable per unit of radiation as the fruit fly or mouse, the detectable genetic effects would be near the borderline of statistical significance—maybe just over, maybe just under. Despite this and other difficulties the study was made, for there was both a clear obligation and an opportunity to add significantly to knowledge of the genetic hazards of radiation.

The results were pretty much as predicted: There were at first no demonstrable effects that were statistically significant. What did this mean to laymen—and, it should be added, to some scientists? The result was often taken to mean that there was no effect. The correct interpretation was that from this study alone it could not at the time be said whether the effect was zero, or as great as that expected in mice, or at a level between the two. We are not in any way justified in concluding that radiation is less effective in producing mutations in man than in mice. The data do indicate that the genes of man are not more sensitive than those of the mouse by any large amount, and that is gratifying to know.

World-wide radioactive contamination by the testing of nuclear weapons makes moral problems of a new kind. It has not previously been possible for any one nation to alter the global environment in a manner clearly harmful to other nations. A nation accused of such contamination is naturally reluctant to face the issue squarely. The temptation is rather to avoid the issue by alleging that the harm does not exist or that it is insignificantly small. Once significant harm is admitted. the issue can no longer be evaded, for morality is qualitative, not quantitative.

During war, standards shift. Mutual harm is then inflicted in the name of self-defense or rightful causes. Neutrals inadvertently caught between belligerents may then accept injury that would not otherwise be tolerated. There is a close analogy in the case of individuals. Society permits individuals to commit acts in self-defense that would not otherwise go unpunished. Again, innocent bystanders may be hurt in the process.

A large portion of the confusion that arises in disagreements about nuclear weapons results from failure of the adversaries to make clear whether they are arguing on the basis of a peacetime or wartime moral standard. Which moral standard is applicable during a cold war? Does the potential enemy follow the same standard? Although attempts to define moral standards may not help in arriving at final agreement, they may nevertheless establish that the basic issue is not one of science at all.

What should the citizen conclude about ionizing radiation? Having heard what the scientist has to say about it, and having checked a few references to be sure that what he has been told is good science, he might find the following considerations decisive in his thinking: Ionizing radiation has always been with us and will be for all foreseeable time. Our genetic system is probably well adjusted by natural selection to normal background-radiation. Added radiation will increase the frequency of mutations; most of these will be harmful. Exposure to radiation in large amounts will increase malignant disease; small amounts may possibly do the same, in proportionately lesser degree. In view of these potentially harmful effects every reasonable effort should be made to reduce the levels of ionizing radiation to which man is exposed to the lowest levels that can reasonably be attained.

As to fallout from nuclear-weapons tests, the citizen will conclude that it contributes in a small way to world-wide levels of radiation. For this reason alone the tests should be discontinued, or conducted in such a way as not to lead to atmospheric contamination. Additionally, as a hopeful first step toward a final solution of the problem of nuclear war, every possible effort should be made to discontinue the tests altogether.

Medical radiation, if properly used, is of great benefit to man. The citizen will accordingly support the investigation of ways to reduce the exposure, especially to the gonads of persons who may still reproduce, without sacrifice of clearly established diagnostic or therapeutic benefits. Radiologists estimate that progress in this direction can be expected before many years to reduce medical radiation to the gonads by a factor of five to 10—perhaps to an average value for the entire population of .5 r per reproductive generation. For the same reason exposure from industrial and experimental radiation sources should be held at minimum levels. This means that adequate shielding must be engineered into power reactors and other sources of radiation. Safe, permanent methods of waste disposal can and must be developed.

If all reasonable measures are taken, it does not seem an unreasonable hope that present levels of radiation exposure in the U.S. can be appreciably reduced —perhaps to an average level of less than one r above natural background.

With the millennium—when the citizenry has achieved sophistication in science, when wars have been abolished, when populations are stabilized at levels compatible with food supplies, when medicine has conquered the last infectious disease and corrected most genetic ailments—it may at last become essential to take a hard look at man's long-term evolutionary past and his prospects for the future.

Painful questions will have to be asked. It may become important, for example, to determine whether conquest through war, with subsequent replacement of one population by another, has been important in man's evolution. Did the conquerors differ genetically from the conquered? If so, was the effect favorable for the species (assuming that man will by then have arrived at some sensible definition of "favorable")? For the same reasons it may become essential to ask whether man's evolution has been held back because his system of controlling populations has made insufficient provision for natural selection.

Finally. assuming that medicine will have become highly successful in circumventing genetic death, will the net effect of medical practice have been unfavorable to the genetic capital of mankind? It is not inconceivable that by asking such questions man may one day find himself in the paradoxical position of searching for wiser and more humane ways than he now knows to counteract the undesirable evolutionary effects of too much success.

16

Thermal Pollution and
Aquatic Life

JOHN R. CLARK
March 1969

Ecologists consider temperature the primary control of life on earth, and fish, which as cold-blooded animals are unable to regulate their body temperature, are particularly sensitive to changes in the thermal environment. Each aquatic species becomes adapted to the seasonal variations in temperature of the water in which it lives, but it cannot adjust to the shock of abnormally abrupt change. For this reason there is growing concern among ecologists about the heating of aquatic habitats by man's activities. In the U.S. it appears that the use of river, lake and estuarine waters for industrial cooling purposes may become so extensive in future decades as to pose a considerable threat to fish and to aquatic life in general. Because of the potential hazard to life and to the balance of nature, the discharge of waste heat into the natural waters is coming to be called thermal pollution.

The principal contributor of this heat is the electric-power industry. In 1968 the cooling of steam condensers in generating plants accounted for about three-quarters of the total of 60,000 billion gallons of water used in the U.S. for industrial cooling. The present rate of heat discharge is not yet of great consequence except in some local situations; what has aroused ecologists is the ninefold expansion of electric-power production that is in prospect for the coming years with the increasing construction of large generating plants fueled by nuclear energy. They waste 60 percent more energy than fossil-fuel plants, and this energy is released as heat in condenser-cooling water. It is estimated that within 30 years the electric-power industry will be producing nearly two million megawatts of electricity, which will require the disposal of about 20 million billion B.T.U.'s of waste heat per day. To carry off that heat by way of natural waters would call for a flow through power plants amounting to about a third of the average daily freshwater runoff in the U.S.

The Federal Water Pollution Control

HEATED EFFLUENT from a power plant on the Connecticut River is shown in color thermograms (*opposite page*), in which different temperatures are represented by different hues. At the site (*above*) three large pipes discharge heated water that spreads across the river at slack tide (*top thermogram*) and tends to flow downriver at ebb tide (*bottom*). An infrared camera made by the Barnes Engineering Company scans the scene and measures the infrared radiation associated with the temperature at each point in the scene (350 points on each of 180 horizontal lines). Output from an infrared radiometer drives a color modulator, thus changing the color of a beam of light that is scanned across a color film in synchrony with the scanning of the scene. Here the coolest water (*black*) is at 59 degrees Fahrenheit; increasingly warm areas are shown, in three-degree steps, in blue, light blue, green, light green, yellow, orange, red and magenta. The effluent temperature was 87 degrees. A tree (*dark object*) appears in lower thermogram because the camera was moved.

NUCLEAR POWER PLANT at Haddam on the Connecticut River empties up to 370,000 gallons of coolant water a minute through a discharge canal (*bottom*) into the river. In this aerial thermogram, made by HRB-Singer, Inc., for the U.S. Geological Survey's

Administration has declared that waters above 93 degrees Fahrenheit are essentially uninhabitable for all fishes in the U.S. except certain southern species. Many U.S. rivers already reach a temperature of 90 degrees F. or more in summer through natural heating alone. Since the waste heat from a single power plant of the size planned for the future (some 1,000 megawatts) is expected to raise the temperature of a river carrying a flow of 3,000 cubic feet per second by 10 degrees, and since a number of industrial and power plants are likely to be constructed on the banks of a single river, it is obvious that many U.S. waters would become uninhabitable.

A great deal of detailed information is available on how temperature affects the life processes of animals that live in the water. Most of the effects stem from the impact of temperature on the rate of metabolism, which is speeded up by heat in accordance with the van't Hoff principle that the rate of chemical reaction increases with rising temperature. The acceleration varies considerably for particular biochemical reactions and in different temperature ranges, but gener-

ally speaking the metabolic rate doubles with each increase of 10 degrees Celsius (18 degrees F.).

Since a speedup of metabolism increases the animal's need for oxygen, the rate of respiration must rise. F. E. J. Fry of the University of Toronto, experimenting with fishes of the salmon family, found that active fish increased their oxygen consumption as much as fourfold as the temperature of the water was raised to the maximum at which they could survive. In the brown trout the rate of oxygen consumption rose steadily until the lethal temperature of 79 degrees F. was reached; in a species of lake trout, on the other hand, the rate rose to a maximum at about 60 degrees and then fell off as the lethal temperature of 77 degrees was approached. In both cases the fishes showed a marked rise in the basal rate of metabolism up to the lethal point.

The heart rate often serves as an index of metabolic or respiratory stress on the organism. Experiments with the crayfish (*Astacus*) showed that its heart rate increased from 30 beats per minute at a water temperature of 39 degrees F. to 125 beats per minute at 72 degrees and then slowed to a final 65 beats per min-

ute as the water approached 95 degrees, the lethal temperature for this crustacean. The final decrease in heartbeat is evidence of the animal's weakening under the thermal stress.

At elevated temperatures a fish's respiratory difficulties are compounded by the fact that the hemoglobin of its blood has a reduced affinity for oxygen and therefore becomes less efficient in delivering oxygen to the tissues. The combination of increased need for oxygen and reduced efficiency in obtaining it at rising temperatures can put severe stress even on fishes that ordinarily are capable of living on a meager supply of oxygen. For example, the hardy carp, which at a water temperature of 33 degrees F. can survive on an oxygen concentration as low as half a milligram per liter of water, needs a minimum of 1.5 milligrams per liter when the temperature is raised to 95 degrees. Other fishes can exist on one to two milligrams at 39 degrees but need three to four milligrams merely to survive at 65 degrees and five milligrams for normal activity.

The temperature of the water has pronounced effects on appetite, digestion and growth in fish. Tracer experiments

Water Resources Division, temperature is represented by shades of gray. The hot effluent (*white*) is at about 93 degrees F.; ambient river temperature (*dark gray*) is 77 degrees. The line across the thermogram is a time marker for a series of absolute measurements.

with young carp, in which food was labeled with color, established that they digest food four times as rapidly at 79 degrees F. as they do at 50 degrees; whereas at 50 degrees the food took 18 hours to pass through the alimentary canal, at 79 degrees it took only four and a half hours.

The effects of temperature in regulating appetite and the conversion of the food into body weight can be used by hatcheries to maximize fish production in terms of weight. The food consumption of the brown trout, for example, is highest in the temperature range between 50 and 66 degrees. Within that range, however, the fish is so active that a comparatively large proportion of its food intake goes into merely maintaining its body functions. Maximal conversion of the food into a gain in weight occurs just below and just above that temperature range. A hatchery can therefore produce the greatest poundage of trout per pound of food by keeping the water temperature at just under 50 degrees or just over 66 degrees.

It is not surprising to find that the activity, or movement, of fish depends considerably on the water temperature.

By and large aquatic animals tend to raise their swimming speed and to show more spontaneous movement as the temperature rises. In many fishes the temperature-dependent pattern of activity is rather complex. For instance, the sockeye salmon cruises twice as fast in water at 60 degrees as it does in water at 35 degrees, but above 60 degrees its speed declines. The brook trout shows somewhat more complicated behavior: it increases its spontaneous activity as the temperature rises from 40 to 48 degrees, becomes less active between 49 and 66 degrees and above 66 degrees again goes into a rising tempo of spontaneous movements up to the lethal temperature of 77 degrees. Laboratory tests show that a decrease in the trout's swimming speed potential at high temperatures affects its ability to feed. By 63 degrees trout have slowed down in pursuing minnows, and at 70 degrees they are almost incapable of catching the minnows.

That temperature plays a critical role in the reproduction of aquatic animals is well known. Some species of fish spawn during the fall, as temperatures drop; many more species, however,

spawn in the spring. The rising temperature induces a seasonal development of their gonads and then, at a critical point, triggers the female's deposit of her eggs in the water. The triggering is particularly dramatic in estuarine shellfish (oysters and clams), which spawn within a few hours after the water temperature reaches the critical level. Temperature also exerts a precise control over the time it takes a fish's eggs to hatch. For example, fertilized eggs of the Atlantic salmon will hatch in 114 days in water at 36 degrees F. but the period is shortened to 90 days at 45 degrees; herring eggs hatch in 47 days at 32 degrees and in eight days at 58 degrees; trout eggs hatch in 165 days at 37 degrees and in 32 days at 54 degrees. Excessive temperatures, however, can prevent normal development of eggs. The Oregon Fish Commission has declared that a rise of 5.4 degrees in the Columbia River could be disastrous for the eggs of the Chinook salmon.

Grace E. Pickford of Yale University has observed that "there are critical temperatures above or below which fish will not reproduce." For instance, at a temperature of 72 degrees or higher the banded sunfish fails to develop eggs. In the case of the carp, temperatures in the range of 68 to 75 degrees prevent cell division in the eggs. The possum shrimp *Neomysis,* an inhabitant of estuaries, is blocked from laying eggs if the temperature rises above 45 degrees. There is also the curious case of the tiny crustacean *Gammarus,* which at temperatures above 46 degrees produces only female offspring.

Temperature affects the longevity of fish as well as their reproduction. D'Arcy Wentworth Thompson succinctly stated this general life principle in his classic *On Growth and Form:* "As the several stages of development are accelerated by warmth, so is the duration of each and all, and of life itself, proportionately curtailed. High temperature may lead to a short but exhausting spell of rapid growth, while the slower rate manifested at a lower temperature may be the best in the end." Thompson's principle has been verified in rather precise detail by experiments with aquatic crustaceans. These have shown, for example, that *Daphnia* can live for 108 days at 46 degrees F. but its lifetime at 82 degrees is 29 days; the water flea *Moina* has a lifetime of 14 days at 55 degrees, its optimal temperature for longevity, but only five days at 91 degrees.

Other effects of temperature on life processes are known. For example, a century ago the German zoologist Karl Möbius noted that mollusks living in cold waters grew more slowly but attained larger size than their cousins living in warmer waters. This has since been found to be true of many fishes and other water animals in their natural habitats.

Fortunately fish are not entirely at the mercy of variations in the water temperature. By some process not yet understood they are able to acclimate themselves to a temperature shift if it is moderate and not too sudden. It has been found, for instance, that when the eggs of largemouth bass are suddenly transferred from water at 65 or 70 degrees to water at 85 degrees, 95 percent of the eggs perish, but if the eggs are acclimated by gradual raising of the temperature to 85 degrees over a period of 30 to 40 hours, 80 percent of the eggs will survive. Experiments with the possum shrimp have shown that the lethal temperature for this crustacean can be raised by as much as 24 degrees (to a high of 93 degrees) by acclimating it through a series of successively higher temperatures. As a general rule aquatic animals can acclimate to elevated temperatures faster than they can to lowered temperatures.

Allowing for maximum acclimation (which usually requires spreading the gradual rise of temperature over 20 days), the highest temperatures that most fishes of North America can tolerate range from about 77 to 97 degrees F. The direct cause of thermal death is not known in detail; various investigators have suggested that the final blow may be some effect of heat on the nervous system or the respiratory system, the coagulation of the cell protoplasm or the inactivation of enzymes.

Be that as it may, we need to be concerned not so much about the lethal temperature as about the temperatures that may be *unfavorable* to the fish. In the long run temperature levels that adversely affect the animals' metabolism, feeding, growth, reproduction and other vital functions may be as harmful to a fish population as outright heat death.

Studies of the preferred, or optimal, temperature ranges for various fishes have been made in natural waters and in the laboratory [*see illustration on page 168*]. For adult fish observed in nature the preferred level is about 13 degrees F. below the lethal temperature on the average; in the laboratory, where the experimental subjects used (for convenience) were very young fish, the preferred level was 9.5 degrees below the lethal temperature. Evidently young fish need warmer waters than those that have reached maturity do.

The optimal temperature for any water habitat depends not only on the preferences of individual species but also on the well-being of the system as a whole. An ecological system in dynamic balance is like a finely tuned automobile engine, and damage to any component can disable or impair the efficiency of the entire mechanism. This means that if we are to expect a good harvest of fish, the temperature conditions in the water medium must strike a favorable balance for all the components (algae and other plants, small crustaceans, bait fishes and so on) that constitute the food chain producing the harvested fish. For example, above 68 degrees estuarine eelgrass does not reproduce. Above 90 degrees there is extensive loss of bottom life in rivers.

So far there have been few recorded instances of direct kills of fish by thermal pollution in U.S. waters. One recorded kill occurred in the summer of 1968 when a large number of menhaden acclimated to temperatures in the 80's became trapped in effluent water at 93 to 95 degrees during the testing of a new power plant on the Cape Cod Canal. A very large kill of striped bass occurred

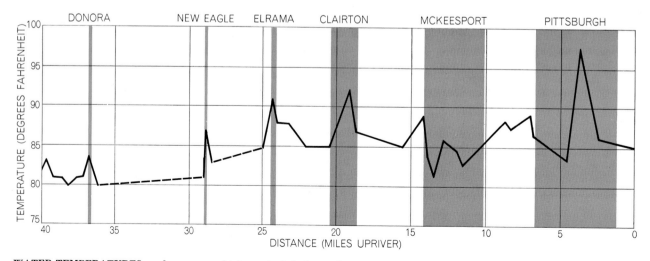

WATER TEMPERATURES can become very high, particularly in summer, along rivers with concentrated industry. The chart shows the temperature of the Monongahela River, measured in August, along a 40-mile stretch upriver from its confluence with the Ohio.

in the winter and early spring of 1963 at the nuclear power plant at Indian Point on the Hudson River. In that instance the heat discharge from the plant was only a contributing factor. The wintering, dormant fish, attracted to the warm water issuing from the plant, became trapped in its structure for water intake, and they died by the thousands from fatigue and other stresses. (Under the right conditions, of course, thermal discharges benefit fishermen by attracting fish to discharge points, where they can be caught with a hook and line.)

Although direct kills attributable to thermal pollution apparently have been rare, there are many known instances of deleterious effects on fish arising from natural summer heating in various U.S. waters. Pollution by sewage is often a contributing factor. At peak summer temperatures such waters frequently generate a great bloom of plankton that depletes the water of oxygen (by respiration while it lives and by decay after it dies). In estuaries algae proliferating in the warm water can clog the filtering apparatus of shellfish and cause their death. Jellyfish exploding into abundant growth make some estuarine waters unusable for bathing or other water sports, and the growth of bottom plants in warm waters commonly chokes shallow bays and lakes. The formation of hydrogen sulfide and other odorous substances is enhanced by summer temperatures. Along some of our coasts in summer "red tides" of dinoflagellates occasionally bloom in such profusion that they not only bother bathers but also may poison fish. And where both temperature and sewage concentrations are high a heavy toll of fish may be taken by proliferating microbes.

This wealth of evidence on the sensitivity of fish and the susceptibility of aquatic ecosystems to disruption by high temperatures explains the present concern of biologists about the impending large increase in thermal pollution. Already last fall 14 nuclear power plants, with a total capacity of 2,782 megawatts, were in operation in the U.S.; 39 more plants were under construction, and 47 others were in advanced planning stages. By the year 2000 nuclear plants are expected to be producing about 1.2 million megawatts, and the nation's total electricity output will be in the neighborhood of 1.8 million megawatts. As I have noted, the use of natural waters to cool the condensers would entail the heating of an amount of water equivalent to a third of the yearly freshwater runoff in the U.S.; during low-flow periods in summer the requirement would be 100 percent of the runoff. Obviously thermal pollution of the waters on such a scale is neither reasonable nor feasible. We must therefore look for more efficient and safer methods of dissipating the heat from power plants.

One might hope to use the heated water for some commercial purpose. Unfortunately, although dozens of schemes have been advanced, no practicable use has yet been found. Discharge water is not hot enough to heat buildings. The cost of transmission rules out piping it to farms for irrigation even if the remaining heat were enough to improve crop production. More promising is the idea of using waste heat in desalination plants to aid in the evaporation process, but this is still only an idea. There has also been talk of improving the efficiency of sewage treatment with waste heat from power plants. Sea farm-

ing may offer the best hope of someday providing a needed outlet for discharges from coastal power plants; pilot studies now in progress in Britain and the U.S. are showing better growth of fish and shellfish in heated waters than in normal waters, but no economically feasible scheme has yet emerged. It appears, therefore, that for many years ahead we shall have to dispose of waste heat to the environment.

The dissipation of heat can be facilitated in various ways by controlling the passage of the cooling water through the condensers. The prevailing practice is to pump the water (from a river, a lake or an estuary) once through the steam-condensing unit, which in a 500-megawatt plant may consist of 400 miles of one-inch copper tubing. The water emerging from the unit has been raised in temperature by an amount that varies from 10 to 30 degrees F., depending on the choice of manageable factors such as the rate of flow. This heated effluent is then discharged through a channel into the body of water from which it was taken. There the effluent, since it is warmer and consequently lighter than the receiving water, spreads in a plume over the surface and is carried off in the direction of the prevailing surface currents.

The ensuing dispersal of heat through the receiving water and into the atmosphere depends on a number of natural factors: the speed of the currents, the turbulence of the receiving water (which affects the rate of mixing of the effluent with it), the temperature difference between the water and the air, the humidity of the air and the speed and direction of the wind. The most variable and most important factor is wind: other things being equal, heat will be dissipated from

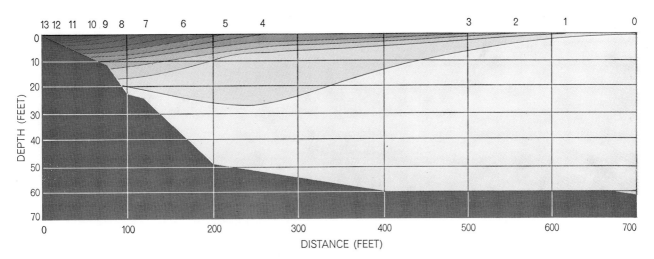

HOT-WATER "PLUME" that would result from an Indian Point nuclear power plant mixes with cooler Hudson River as shown by the one-degree contour lines. This section across the river shows temperature structure that was predicted by engineering studies.

the water to the air by convection three times faster at a wind speed of 20 miles per hour than at a wind speed of five miles.

In regulating the rate of water flow through the condenser one has a choice between opposite strategies. By using a rapid rate of flow one can spread the heat through a comparatively large volume of cooling water and thus keep down the temperature of the effluent; conversely, with a slow rate of flow one can concentrate the heat in a smaller volume of coolant. If it is advantageous to obtain good mixing of the effluent with the receiving water, the effluent can be discharged at some depth in the water rather than at the surface. The physical and ecological nature of the body of water will determine which of these strategies is best in a given situation. Where the receiving body is a swift-flowing river, rapid flow through the condenser and dispersal of the low-temperature effluent in a narrow plume over the water surface may be the most effective way to dissipate the heat into the atmosphere. In the case of a still lake it may be best to use a slow flow through the condenser so that the comparatively small volume of effluent at a high tem-

perature will be confined to a small area in the lake and still transfer its heat to the atmosphere rapidly because of the high temperature differential. And at a coastal site the best strategy may be to discharge an effluent of moderate temperature well offshore, below the ocean-water surface.

There are many waters, however, where no strategy of discharge will avail to make the water safe for aquatic life (and where manipulation of the discharge will also be insufficient to avoid dangerous thermal pollution), particularly where a number of industrial and power plants use the same body of water for cooling purposes. It therefore appears that we shall have to turn to extensive development of devices such as artificial lakes and cooling towers.

Designs for such lakes have already been drawn up and implemented for plants of moderate size. For the 1,000-megawatt power plant of the future a lake with a surface area of 1,000 to 2,000 acres would be required. (A 2,000-acre lake would be a mile wide and three miles long.) The recommended design calls for a lake only a few feet deep at one end and sloping to a depth of 50

feet at the other end. The water for cooling is drawn from about 30 feet below the surface at the deep end and is pumped through the plant at the rate of 500,000 gallons per minute, and the effluent, 20 degrees higher in temperature than the inflow, is discharged at the lake's shallow end. The size of the lake is based on a pumping rate through the plant of 2,000 acre-feet a day, so that all the water of the lake (averaging 15 feet in depth) is turned over every 15 days. Such a lake would dissipate heat to the air at a sufficient rate even in prolonged spells of unfavorable weather, such as high temperature and humidity with little wind.

Artificial cooling lakes need a steady inflow of water to replace evaporation and to prevent an excessive accumulation of dissolved material. This replenishment can be supplied by a small stream flowing into the lake. The lake itself can be built by damming a natural land basin. A lake complex constructed to serve not only for cooling but also for fishing might consist of two sections: the smaller one, in which the effluent is discharged, would be stocked with fishes tolerant to heat, and the water from this basin, having been cooled by exposure to

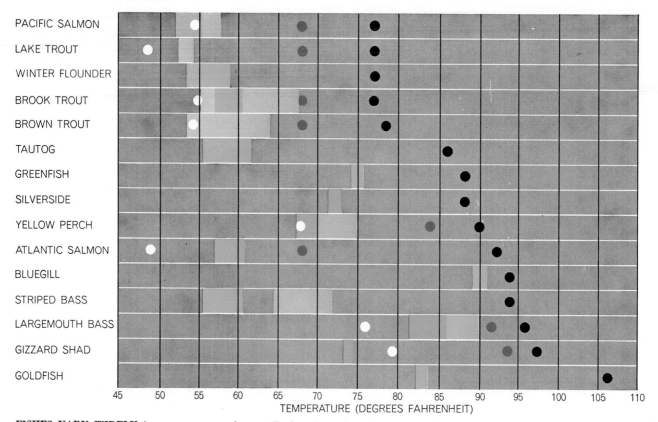

FISHES VARY WIDELY in temperature preference. Preferred temperature ranges are shown here for some species for which they have been determined in the field (*dark colored bands*) and, generally for younger fish, in the laboratory (*light color*). The chart also indicates the upper lethal limit (*black dot*) and upper limits recommended by the Federal Water Pollution Control Administration for satisfactory growth (*colored dot*) and spawning (*white dot*). Temperatures well below lethal limit can be in stress range.

the air, would then flow into a second and larger lake where other fishes could thrive.

In Britain, where streams are small, water is scarce and appreciation of aquatic life is high, the favored artificial device for getting rid of waste heat from power plants has been the use of cooling towers. One class of these towers employs the principle of removing heat by evaporation. The heated effluent is discharged into the lower part of a high tower (300 to 450 feet) with sloping sides; as the water falls in a thin film over a series of baffles it is exposed to the air rising through the tower. Or the water can be sprayed into the tower as a mist that evaporates easily and cools quickly. In either case some of the water is lost to the atmosphere; most of it collects in a basin and is pumped into the waterway or recirculated to the condensers. The removal of heat through evaporation can cool the water by about 20 degrees F.

The main drawback of the evaporation scheme is the large amount of water vapor discharged into the atmosphere. The towers for a 1,000-megawatt power plant would eject some 20,000 to 25,000 gallons of evaporated water per minute—an amount that would be the equivalent of a daily rainfall of an inch on an area of two square miles. On cold days such a discharge could condense into a thick fog and ice over the area in the vicinity of the plant. The "wet" type of cooling tower may therefore be inappropriate in cold climates. It is also ruled out where salt water is used as the coolant: the salt spray ejected from a single large power plant could destroy vegetation and otherwise foul the environment over an area of 160 square miles.

A variation of the cooling-tower system avoids these problems. In this refinement, called the "dry tower" method, the heat is transferred from the cooling water, through a heat exchanger something like an enormous automobile radiator, directly to the air without evaporation. The "dry" system, however, is two and a half to three times as expensive to build as a "wet" system. In a proposed nuclear power plant to be built in Vernon, Vt., it is estimated that the costs of operation and amortization would be $2.1 million per year for a dry system and $800,000 per year for a wet system. For the consumer the relative costs would amount respectively to 2.6 and 1 percent of the bill for electricity.

The public-utility industry, like other industries, is understandably reluctant to incur large extra expenses that add sub-

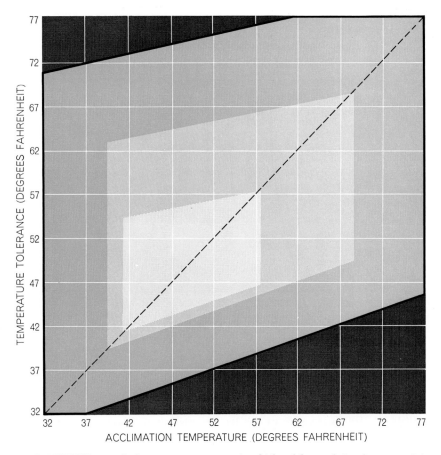

ACCLIMATION extends the temperature range in which a fish can thrive, but not indefinitely. For a young sockeye salmon acclimated as shown by the horizontal scale, spawning is inhibited outside the central (*light color*) zone and growth is poor outside the second zone (*medium color*); beyond the outer zone (*dark color*) lie the lethal temperatures.

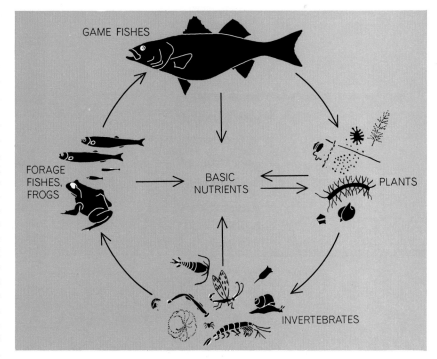

AQUATIC ECOSYSTEM is even more sensitive to temperature variation than an individual fish. A single game-fish species, for example, depends on a food chain involving smaller fishes, invertebrates, plants and dissolved nutrients. Any change in the environment that seriously affects the proliferation of any link in the chain can affect the harvest of game fish.

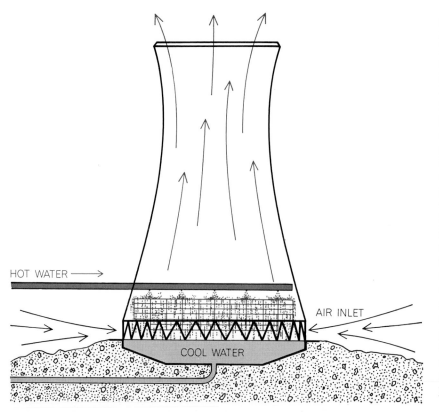

HOT WATER ——→

AIR INLET

COOL WATER

COOLING TOWER is one device that can dissipate industrial heat without dumping it directly into rivers or lakes. This is a "wet," natural-draft, counterflow tower. Hot water from the plant is exposed to air moving up through the chimney-like tower. Heat is removed by evaporation. The cooled water is emptied into a waterway or recirculated through the plant. In cold areas water vapor discharged into the atmosphere can create a heavy fog.

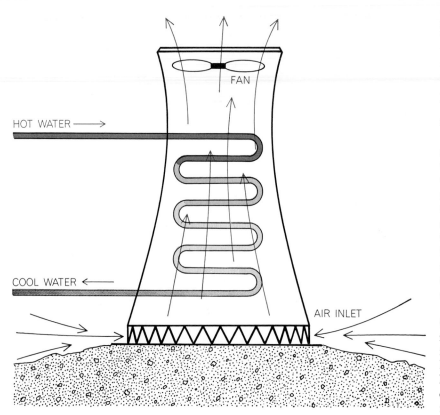

FAN

HOT WATER ——→

COOL WATER ←——

AIR INLET

"DRY" COOLING TOWER avoids evaporation. The hot water is channeled through tubing that is exposed to an air flow, and gives up its heat to the air without evaporating. In this mechanical-draft version air is moved through the tower by a fan. Dry towers are costly.

stantially to the cost of its product and services. There is a growing recognition, however, by industry, the public and the Government of the need for protecting the environment from pollution. The Federal Water Pollution Control Administration of the Department of the Interior, with help from a national advisory committee, last year established a provisional set of guidelines for water quality that includes control of thermal pollution. These guidelines specify maximum permissible water temperatures for individual species of fish and recommend limits for the heating of natural waters for cooling purposes. For example, they suggest that discharges that would raise the water temperature should be avoided entirely in the spawning grounds of cold-water fishes and that the limit for heating any stream, in the most favorable season, should be set at five degrees F. outside a permitted mixing zone. The size of such a zone is likely to be a major point of controversy. Biologists would limit it to a few hundred feet, but in one case a power group has advocated 10 miles.

It appears that the problem of thermal pollution will receive considerable attention in the 91st Congress. Senator Edward M. Kennedy has proposed that further licensing of nuclear power-plant construction be suspended until a thorough study of potential hazards, including pollution of the environment, has been made. Senator Edmund S. Muskie's Subcommittee on Air and Water Pollution of the Senate Committee on Public Works last year held hearings on thermal pollution in many parts of the country.

Thermal pollution of course needs to be considered in the context of the many other works of man that threaten the life and richness of our natural waters: the discharges of sewage and chemical wastes, dredging, diking, filling of wetlands and other interventions that are altering the nature, form and extent of the waters. The effects of any one of these factors might be tolerable, but the cumulative and synergistic action of all of them together seems likely to impoverish our environment drastically.

Temperature, Gordon Gunter of the Gulf Coast Research Laboratory has remarked, is "the most important single factor governing the occurrence and behavior of life." Fortunately thermal pollution has not yet reached the level of producing serious general damage; moreover, unlike many other forms of pollution, any excessive heating of the waters could be stopped in short order by appropriate corrective action.

POWER PLANT being completed by the Tennessee Valley Authority on the Green River in Kentucky will be the world's largest coal-fueled electric plant. Its three wet, natural-draft cooling towers, each 437 feet in height and 320 feet in diameter at ground level, will each have a capacity of 282,000 gallons of water a minute, which they will be able to cool through a range of 27.5 degrees.

INDUSTRIAL PLANTS of various kinds can use towers to cool process water. These two five-cell cooling towers were built by the Marley Company for a chemical plant. They are wet, mechanical-draft towers of the cross-flow type: a fan in each stack draws air in through the louvers, across films of falling water and then up. The towers cool 120,000 gallons a minute through a 20-degree range.

17

Carbon Dioxide and Climate

GILBERT N. PLASS
July 1959

The theories that explain worldwide climate change are almost as varied as the weather. The more familiar ones attribute changes of climate to Olympian forces that range from geological upheavals and dust-belching volcanoes to long-term variations in the radiation of the sun and eccentricities in the orbit of the earth. Only the so-called carbon dioxide theory takes account of the possibility that human activities may have some effect on climate. This theory suggests that in the present century man is unwittingly raising the temperature of the earth by his industrial and agricultural activities.

Even the carbon dioxide theory is not new; the basic idea was first precisely stated in 1861 by the noted British physicist John Tyndall. He attributed climatic temperature-changes to variations in the amount of carbon dioxide in the atmosphere. According to the theory, carbon dioxide controls temperature because the carbon dioxide molecules in the air absorb infrared radiation. The carbon dioxide and other gases in the atmosphere are virtually transparent to the visible radiation that delivers the sun's energy to the earth. But the earth in turn reradiates much of the energy in the invisible infrared region of the spectrum. This radiation is most intense at wavelengths very close to the principal absorption band (13 to 17 microns) of the carbon dioxide spectrum. When the carbon dioxide concentration is sufficiently high, even its weaker absorption bands become effective, and a greater amount of infrared radiation is absorbed [*see illustration on next page*]. Because the carbon dioxide blanket prevents its escape into space, the trapped radiation warms up the atmosphere.

A familiar instance of this "greenhouse" effect is the heating-up of a closed automobile when it stands for a while in the summer sun. Like the atmosphere, the car's windows are transparent to the sun's visible radiation, which warms the upholstery and metal inside the car; these materials in turn re-emit some of their heat as infrared radiation. Glass, like carbon dioxide, absorbs some of this radiation and thus traps the heat, and the temperature inside the car rises.

Water vapor and ozone, as well as carbon dioxide, have this effect because they too absorb energy in the infrared region. But the climatic effects due to carbon dioxide are almost entirely independent of the amount of these other two gases. For the most part their absorption bands occur in different regions of the spectrum. In addition, nearly all water vapor remains close to the ground, while carbon dioxide diffuses more evenly through the atmosphere. Thus throughout most of the atmosphere carbon dioxide is the main factor determining changes in the radiation flux.

The 2.3×10^{12} (2,300 billion) tons of carbon dioxide in the earth's present atmosphere constitute some .03 per cent of its total mass. The quantity of carbon dioxide in the atmosphere is determined by the amounts supplied and withdrawn from three other great reservoirs: oceans, rocks and living organisms. The oceans contain some 1.3×10^{14} tons of carbon dioxide—about 50 times as much as the air. Some of the gas is dissolved in the water, but most of it is present in carbonate compounds. The oceans exchange about 200 billion tons of carbon dioxide with the atmosphere each year. When the equilibrium is disturbed, the oceans may engulf or disgorge billions of additional tons of carbon dioxide. This puts a damper on the fluctuations in the carbon dioxide content of the atmosphere: when the atmospheric concentration rises, the oceans tend to absorb much of the excess; when it falls, the oceanic reservoir replenishes it.

Both the atmosphere and the oceans continuously exchange carbon dioxide with rocks and with living organisms. They gain carbon dioxide from the volcanic activity that releases gases from the earth's interior and from the respiration and decay of organisms; they lose carbon dioxide to the weathering of rock and the photosynthesis of plants. As these processes change pace, the content of carbon dioxide in the atmosphere also changes, shifting the radiation balance and raising or lowering the earth's temperature.

Of course during any particular geologic era other factors may influence climate. Nonetheless let us examine some of the known facts of geological history and see how many can be explained in terms of variation in the carbon dioxide content of the atmosphere.

Studies of rock strata reveal that for the past billion years most of the world has had a tropical climate. Every 250 million years or so this tropical spell is broken by relatively short glacial periods which bury a substantial portion of the earth under ice sheets. These cool periods last several million years, during which the glaciers retreat and advance many times as the temperature rises and falls. During the last 620,000 years of the current glacial epoch, for example, deep ocean sediments show 10 distinct temperature cycles. The carbon dioxide theory may well account for these temperature fluctuations.

A decline in the carbon dioxide concentration in the atmosphere-ocean system—and a period of decline in worldwide temperature—may be induced by a number of developments. The rate of volcanic activity could slow down as the rate of rock weathering increased, or an especially flourishing mantle of vegetation could take up huge quantities of carbon dioxide and form new coal beds and other organic deposits in marshy areas. After a geologically short time, the adjustment of the atmosphere-ocean equilibrium to the leaner supply of carbon dioxide could bring the atmospheric concentration down to .015 per cent, half its present value. Calculations show that a 50-per-cent decrease in the amount of carbon dioxide in the air will lower the average temperature of the earth 6.9 degrees Fahrenheit.

We can be reasonably sure that such a sharp drop in temperature would cause glaciers to spread across the earth. As the ice sheets grow, the oceans shrink; at the height of glacial periods ice sheets contain 5 to 10 per cent of the oceans' waters. The glaciers contain little carbon dioxide, however, because ice can hold very small amounts of carbonates compared to the same volume of sea water. The shrunken oceans thus accumulate an excess of carbon dioxide which they must release to the atmosphere in order to return to equilibrium. And so the cycle draws to a close: As carbon dioxide returns to the atmosphere, the earth's temperature rises and the ice melts away. The oceans fill to their former levels, reabsorb the carbon dioxide they had released, and a new glacial epoch begins.

So long as the total amount of carbon dioxide in the atmosphere-ocean system does not change, such a cycle of temperature oscillation will tend to repeat itself. The period of the complete cycle would be determined primarily by the

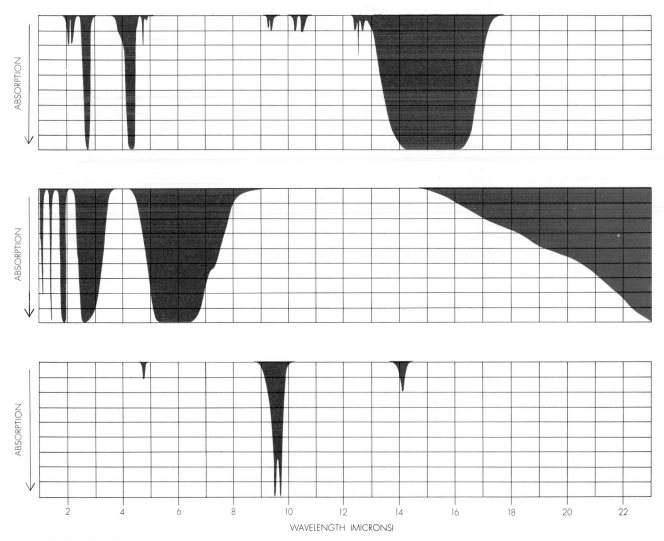

INFRARED ABSORBERS in the earth's atmosphere include carbon dioxide (*top*) water vapor (*center*) and ozone (*bottom*). Spectral charts of their absorption in the infrared region show that these gases warm the earth by preventing its infrared radiation from escaping into space. Carbon dioxide influences climate because it has a broad absorption band at wavelengths (13 to 17 microns) near the wavelengths at which the earth's infrared radiation is most intense. Water vapor and ozone can also influence climate.

time required for an ice sheet to form, grow to maximum size and melt away. Estimates indicate that this should take about 50,000 years, in agreement with the observed time for the cycle. Other time factors in the cycle, such as the period required for the ocean-atmosphere system to come to equilibrium after a change in its carbon dioxide concentration, are probably much shorter. The system never quite reaches equilibrium, however, because the freezing and melting of glaciers is out of phase with the fluctuation of carbon dioxide in the atmosphere. Glaciers are slow to form and slow to melt, so for thousands of years during the earth's recovery from an ice age the cold winds from melting glaciers continue to chill the earth.

The mechanism here proposed to explain the cycle of glaciation does not depend in any way upon the particular numbers assumed for illustrative purposes. Such oscillations will occur whenever the temperature during one phase of the cycle falls low enough to cause ice sheets to grow and during another phase rises high enough to cause them to melt. A change in the comparatively small volume of carbon dioxide in the atmosphere provides ample leeway to swing the temperature past either extreme. The oscillation is reinforced by the accompanying change in the earth's humidity. A colder atmosphere holds less water vapor, and so further reduces the atmospheric absorption of infrared radiation emitted by the earth's surface. At the same time, however, the earth's cloud cover thickens and precipitation increases despite the reduction in the water-vapor burden of the atmosphere. The top of a cloud is cooled by the radiation of heat into space; when there is less carbon dioxide in the atmosphere, cloud tops lose more heat energy and thus become colder. With a steeper temperature gradient there is increased convection within the cloud. The result is larger clouds and more precipitation. Moreover, since the cloud cover reflects the sun's visible radiation back into space, less solar energy reaches the earth, and the temperature falls still lower.

The geological record indicates that the huge capacity of the biosphere to store and turn over carbon dioxide has also had its effect upon climatic change. We know that plants borrow 60 billion tons of carbon dioxide yearly for photosynthesis. Under present conditions the organic world repays nearly all of this debt each year via respiration and decay. The formation of new fossil fuel

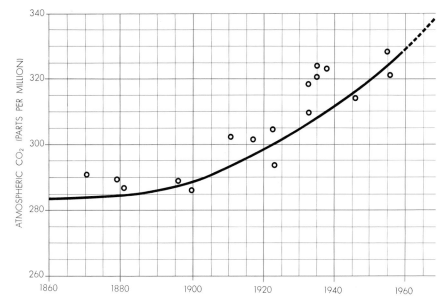

RISING CARBON DIOXIDE CONCENTRATION in the atmosphere during the present century is due to man's increased burning of fossil fuels and greater agricultural activities. The data on which this chart and the one below are based were compiled by G. S. Callendar.

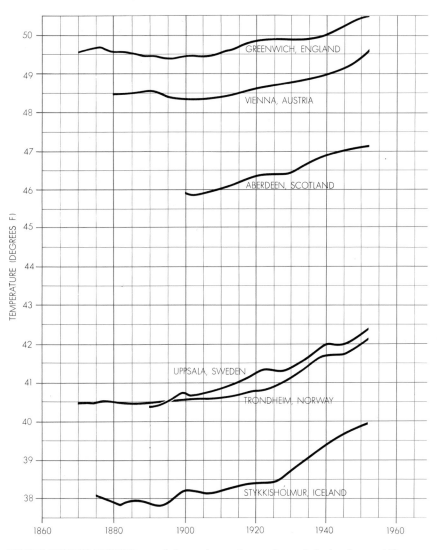

RISING TEMPERATURES recorded at various points on the earth during the past 100 years parallel the increase in atmospheric carbon dioxide plotted in this chart. The yearly mean temperatures shown were averaged over previous 30 years to remove short-term fluctuations.

deposits withholds at most only 100 million tons of carbon dioxide, or less than .2 per cent of the annual amount used for photosynthesis. At one time, however, the withdrawals were much larger. During the Carboniferous period, when most of the coal and oil deposits were formed, about 10^{14} tons of carbon dioxide were withdrawn from the atmosphere-ocean system. This staggering loss must have dropped the earth's temperature to chilly levels indeed; it is not surprising that the gigantic glaciers that moved across the earth after this period were perhaps the most extensive in history.

The present capacity of plants to consume carbon dioxide in photosynthesis gives us an interesting clue to the carbon dioxide content of the atmosphere in bygone ages. Plants are almost perfectly adapted to the spectral range and intensity of the light they receive, yet they grow far more rapidly and luxuriantly in an atmosphere that contains five to 10 times the present carbon dioxide concentration; in fact, florists sometimes release tankfuls of carbon dioxide in greenhouses to promote plant growth. The present carbon dioxide concentration in the atmosphere must therefore be unusually low. Apparently plant evolution was keyed to some much higher concentration in the atmosphere of the geologic past. This hypothesis is also supported by the known fact that the earth's climate was warmer during most of geologic time; presumably the atmosphere then contained a much higher percentage of carbon dioxide.

Much of the carbon dioxide in the atmospheres of past geologic epochs now lies buried in the carbon dioxide reservoir of the earth itself. The earth's hot springs and volcanoes pour about 100 million tons of carbon dioxide back into the atmosphere per year. The earth in turn recaptures approximately the same amount each year by the weathering of rocks. But this equilibrium is upset during periods of mountain-building. In fact, the carbon dioxide theory provides an essential link to explain the timing of the last two glacial epochs with respect to the mountain-building periods that preceded them.

At least several million years intervened between the climax of these mountain-building episodes and the formation of the great ice sheets. If glaciation was brought on only by the elevation of the land or by the slight darkening of the sky with the dust of volcanoes, there should have been no

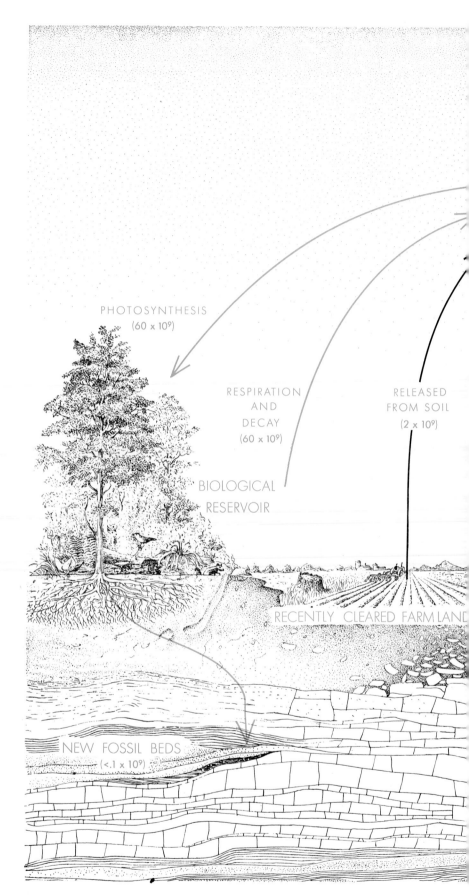

CARBON DIOXIDE BALANCE results from the equilibrium of natural processes that continuously increase and decrease the atmospheric carbon dioxide concentration. The numbers in parentheses after the name of a process indicate the number of tons of carbon

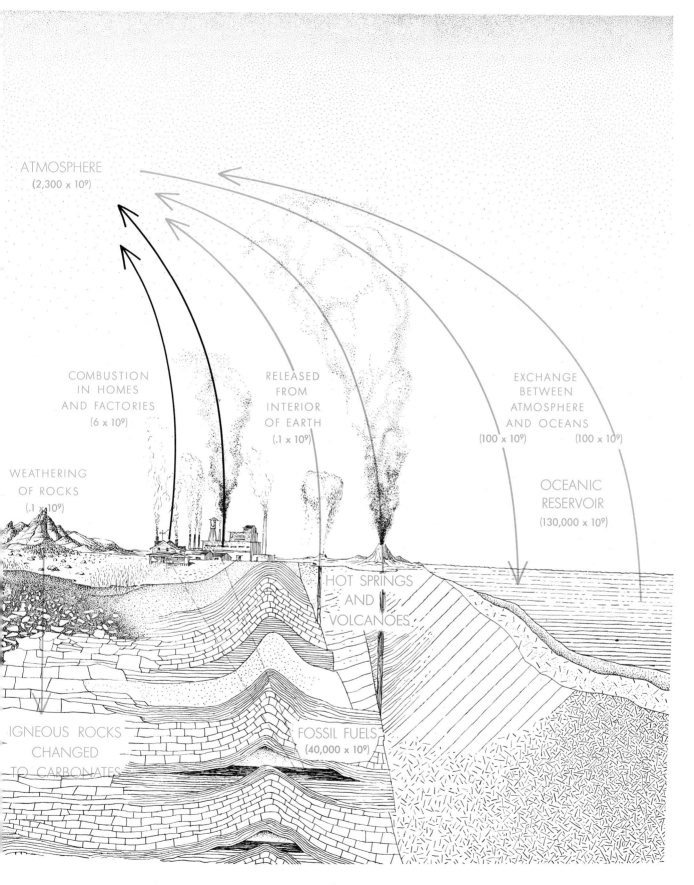

ATMOSPHERE
(2,300 x 10⁹)

COMBUSTION
IN HOMES
AND FACTORIES
(6 x 10⁹)

RELEASED
FROM
INTERIOR
OF EARTH
(.1 x 10⁹)

EXCHANGE
BETWEEN
ATMOSPHERE
AND OCEANS
(100 x 10⁹)   (100 x 10⁹)

WEATHERING
OF ROCKS
(.1 x 10⁹)

OCEANIC
RESERVOIR
(130,000 x 10⁹)

HOT SPRINGS
AND
VOLCANOES

IGNEOUS ROCKS
CHANGED
TO CARBONATES

FOSSIL FUELS
(40,000 x 10⁹)

dioxide being used in that process each year. Vast quantities of carbon dioxide are stored in the three great natural reservoirs: the earth, the oceans and the biosphere. These reservoirs can hoard carbon dioxide or release it to the atmosphere, depending on equilibrium conditions. The black arrows indicate the artificial processes by which man adds carbon dioxide to the atmosphere.

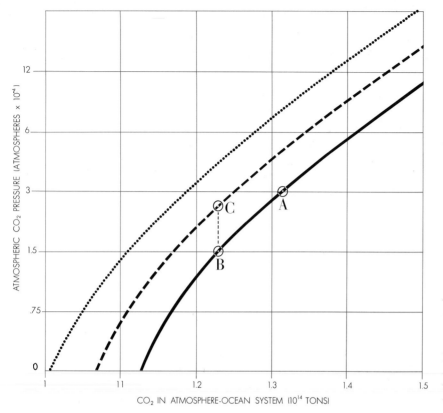

ATMOSPHERE-OCEAN SYSTEM will change the surface temperature of the earth if its equilibrium is disrupted. The three curves here show how this equilibrium shifts when the oceans contain 100 per cent (*solid line*), 95 per cent (*broken line*) and 90 per cent (*dotted line*) of their present volume of water. If the total carbon dioxide content of the system drops only 7 per cent, the equilibrium shifts from point A, its present value, to point B. Such a change would cut the atmospheric carbon dioxide pressure to half its present value, bringing on a possible glacial epoch. As the glaciers grow, the oceans shrink; at the height of a glacial period the ice sheets contain from 5 to 10 per cent of the oceans' waters. With the oceans reduced to 95 per cent of their present volume, the equilibrium would shift to point C, because the shrunken oceans would be forced to release some of their carbon dioxide to the air. Then the temperature rises, glaciers melt and the cycle begins anew.

great time lag before the onset of the glaciers. But these upheavals exposed large quantities of igneous rock to the chemical action of the minute amounts of atmospheric carbon dioxide dissolved in the rain water that washed over them. Over millions of years the weathering of the rock trapped vast quantities of carbon dioxide from the air. With the atmospheric concentration reduced sufficiently, the temperature fell, permitting the young mountains to provide natural birthplaces for the glaciers that then crept across the earth.

Some periods of mountain-building have not produced glaciers. In these periods the output of carbon dioxide from volcanoes, which are especially active during the early stages of mountain-building, might have balanced the carbonate consumption of the newly exposed rocks In fact, a landscape teeming with active volcanoes could easily release more carbon dioxide than the rocks could possibly absorb, so the temperature of the earth would rise sufficiently to prevent the expansion of glaciers.

The geological effects of volcanic action, coal formation or any other local disturbance of the carbon dioxide concentration are not restricted to the area in which they occur. If the amount of carbon dioxide in one hemisphere of the earth rises or falls sharply, the concentration in the other hemisphere changes rather quickly. In less than a few decades the concentration in both hemispheres becomes identical. According to the carbon dioxide theory, this rapid diffusion helps to explain the fact that glaciers advance and retreat simultaneously in both hemispheres.

During the past century a new geological force has begun to exert its effect upon the carbon dioxide equilibrium of the earth. By burning fossil fuels man dumps approximately six billion tons of carbon dioxide into the atmosphere each year. His agricultural activities release two billion tons more. Grain fields and pastures store much smaller quantities of carbon dioxide than the forests they replace, and the cultivation of the soil permits the vast quantities of carbon dioxide produced by bacteria to escape into the air.

Not all of this eight billion tons of surplus carbon dioxide remains in the atmosphere. Plants remove some of it. When the atmospheric concentration rises, plants use more carbon dioxide for photosynthesis. In a few years, however, the increase in the rate of photosynthesis is balanced by advances in the rate of respiration and decay processes. The net result is only a slight increase in the carbon dioxide content of the biosphere.

Most of the carbon dioxide added to the atmosphere by human activities will ultimately be absorbed by the oceans. To predict the effect of human activities upon climate we must calculate just how rapidly this happens. Recent studies make it appear that the volume of carbon dioxide dissolved in the oceans comes to equilibrium with the carbon dioxide pressure of the atmosphere in about 1,000 years, and that the oceans take up about half of any carbon dioxide added to the air. Over a longer period of time, perhaps several thousand years, the oceans take up much larger additional quantities of carbon dioxide in carbonate compounds before the system again reaches equilibrium. These equilibrium rates are quite significant, because they will govern the temperature of the earth as long as man burns large amounts of fossil fuels.

We have only to extrapolate existing records of temperature and fossil-fuel consumption to predict the climate of the future. Quite accurate records of the amount of fossil fuel consumed in the world each year show that in the past 100 years man has added about 360 billion tons of carbon dioxide to the atmosphere. As a result the atmospheric concentration has increased by about 13 per cent. The carbon dioxide theory predicts that such an increase should raise the average temperature of the earth one degree F. This is almost exactly the average increase recorded all over the world during the past century! If fuel consumption continues to increase at the present rate, we will have sent more than a trillion tons of carbon dioxide into the air by the year 2000. This should raise the earth's average temperature 3.6 degrees.

In less than 1,000 years, if consumption continues to increase at the current rate, we will have exhausted the currently known reserves of coal and oil. By that time we will have multiplied the carbon dioxide tonnage of the air 18 times. When the ocean-atmosphere system comes back to equilibrium, the concentration of carbon dioxide in the air will be 10 times greater than it is today, and the earth will be 22 degrees warmer. In another few thousand years, when the carbonate content of the oceans has reached equilibrium, the concentration will still be four times greater than it is today. The earth's temperature will then fall to about 12.5 degrees above its present average.

Meanwhile the carbon dioxide content of the oceans will have doubled. This raises an incidental question about the welfare of sea organisms. We know that an increase in carbon dioxide concentration increases the acidity of water, and that many marine animals are extremely sensitive to changes in acidity. However, if the carbon dioxide content of the air were to increase sevenfold, the acidity (pH) of sea water would not rise more than .5 above its present value. Thus changes in carbon dioxide concentration, which have such a profound effect on climate, will probably not disturb future marine life. Perhaps only man will be uncomfortable.

We shall be able to test the carbon dioxide theory against other theories of climatic change quite conclusively during the next half-century. Since we now can measure the sun's energy output independent of the distorting influence of the atmosphere, we shall see whether the earth's temperature trend correlates with measured fluctuations in solar radiation. If volcanic dust is the more important factor, then we may observe the earth's temperature following fluctuations in the number of large volcanic eruptions. But if carbon dioxide is the most important factor, long-term temperature records will rise continuously as long as man consumes the earth's reserves of fossil fuels.

MAN UPSETS THE BALANCE of natural processes by adding billions of tons of carbon dioxide to the atmosphere each year. Most of this carbon dioxide is released by the burning of fossil fuels in homes and factories, such as these plants in Youngstown, Ohio. Like the smoke in the photograph, the carbon dioxide released in this manner diffuses rapidly throughout the atmosphere.

18

The Climate of Cities

WILLIAM P. LOWRY
August 1967

It is widely recognized that cities tend to be warmer than the surrounding countryside, and one is reminded almost daily by weather forecasts such as "low tonight 75 in the city and 65 to 70 in the suburbs." Exactly what accounts for the difference? Meteorological studies designed to answer such questions have now been made in a number of cities. Much work remains to be done, but one thing is clear. Cities differ from the countryside not only in their temperature but also in all other aspects of climate.

By climate is meant the net result of several interacting variables, including temperature, the amount of water vapor in the air, the speed of the wind, the amount of solar radiation and the amount of precipitation. The fact that the variables do not usually change in the same way in a city as they do in the open country nearby can often be measured directly in differences of temperature, humidity, precipitation, fog and wind speed between a city and its environs. It is also apparent in such urban phenomena as persistent smog, the earlier blooming of flowering plants and longer periods free of frost.

The city itself is the cause of these differences. Its compact mass of buildings and pavement obviously constitutes a profound alteration of the natural landscape, and the activities of its inhabitants are a considerable source of heat. Together these factors account for five basic influences that set a city's climate apart from that of the surrounding area.

The first influence is the difference between surface materials in the city and in the countryside. The predominantly rocklike materials of the city's buildings and streets can conduct heat about three times as fast as it is conducted by wet, sandy soil. This means that the city's materials can accept more heat energy in less time, even though it takes roughly a third more energy to heat a given amount of rock, brick or concrete to a certain temperature than to heat an equal amount of soil. The temperature of soil at the warmest time of the day may be higher than that of a south-facing rock wall, but the temperature three or four inches below the surface will probably be higher in the wall. At the end of a day the rocky material will have stored more heat than an equal volume of soil.

Second, the city's structures have a far greater variety of shapes and orientations than the features of the natural landscape. The walls, roofs and streets of a city function like a maze of reflectors, absorbing some of the energy they receive and directing much of the rest to other absorbing surfaces [see top illustration on page 182]. In this way almost the entire surface of a city is used for accepting and storing heat, whereas in a wooded or open area the heat tends to be stored in the upper parts of plants.

Since air is heated almost entirely by contact with warmer surfaces rather than by direct radiation, a city provides a highly efficient system for using sunlight to heat large volumes of air. In addition, the city's many structures have a braking effect on the wind, thereby increasing its turbulence and reducing the amount of heat it carries away.

Third, the city is a prodigious generator of heat, particularly in winter, when heating systems are in operation. Even in summer, however, the city has many sources of heat that the countryside either lacks or has in far smaller numbers. Among them are factories, vehicles and even air conditioners, which of course must pump out hot air in order to produce their cooling effect.

Fourth, the city has distinctive ways of disposing of precipitation. If the precipitation is in the form of rain, it is quickly removed from the surface by drainpipes, gutters and sewers. If it is snow, much of it is cleared from the surface by plows and shovels, and significant amounts are carried away. In the country much precipitation remains on the surface or immediately below it; the water is thus available for evaporation, which is of course a cooling process powered by heat energy. Because there is less opportunity for evaporation in the city, the heat energy that would have gone into the process is available for heating the air.

Finally, the air in the city is different

HEAT PATTERNS in the lower Manhattan area of New York City on a summer day are shown by infrared photography. In the photographs, which were made with a Barnes thermograph, the lightest areas are the warmest and the darkest are the coolest. The view above shows the buildings at about 11:00 A.M. and the view below at about 3:30 P.M. The day was sunny but hazy; the temperature in the city during the time covered by the photographs was about 75 degrees Fahrenheit. The storage of heat by buildings affects a city's climate.

in that it carries a heavy load of solid, liquid and gaseous contaminants. About 80 percent of the solid contaminants are in the form of particles that are small enough to remain suspended for several days in still air. Although these particles collectively tend to reflect sunlight, thereby reducing the amount of heat reaching the surfaces, they also retard the outflow of heat. The gaseous contaminants, which usually have a greater total mass than the solid ones, come primarily from the incomplete combustion of fuels. One of the principal gases in many cities is sulfur dioxide; when this gas is dissolved under the appropriate meteorological conditions in cloud droplets or raindrops, it is oxidized to form dilute sulfuric acid.

Let us consider how these five influences act over a period of time on the climate of a large city. Our hypothetical city lies in an area of flat or gently rolling countryside and has no large bodies of water nearby. The day is a Sunday, so that no substantial amounts of fuel are being used for industrial purposes. It is a summer day, with clear skies and light winds.

As the sun rises it shines equally on city and country. The sunlight strikes the flat, open country at a low angle; much of it is reflected from the surface. The many vertical walls of the city, however, are almost perpendicular to the sun's rays. In spite of the fact that when the sun is low in the sky its rays are less intense because they must pass through more of the earth's atmosphere, the walls begin almost at once to absorb heat. In the country little heat is being absorbed, even in the sunlit areas.

Later in the day the rural areas begin to respond more like the city. The sun has risen high enough for its radiation to impinge on the surface more directly and with less reflection. The air outside the city begins to warm rapidly. The city has already been warming for some time, however, and so it has a large lead toward the day's maximum temperature.

The warm air in the city concentrates near the city's center of mass. Toward midmorning the air in the center begins to rise. Being warmer at each level than the air at the same level in the surrounding countryside, the city air continues to rise in a gentle stream flowing upward from the center. The air that rises must be replaced; hence a flow from the rural areas into the city begins in the layers near the ground. The air from the country must also be replaced, and gradually a slow circulation is established. Air

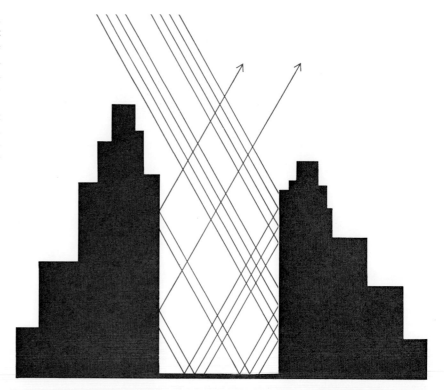

SHAPE AND ORIENTATION OF SURFACES in a city have a strong bearing on the climate. Vertical walls tend to reflect solar radiation toward the ground instead of the sky. Rocklike materials also store heat, so that the city often becomes warmer than its environs.

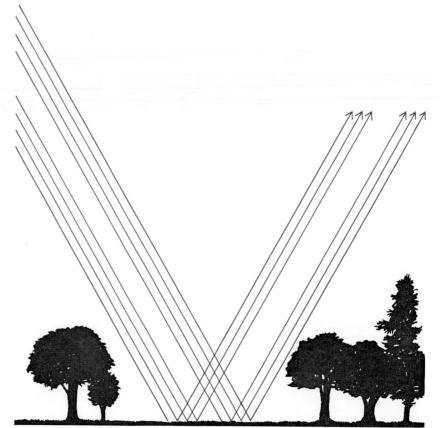

RADIATION IN COUNTRYSIDE tends to be reflected back to the sky because the countryside has fewer vertical surfaces than the city. Toward midday, however, when the sun's rays are perpendicular to the ground, city and country temperatures may be about the same.

TEMPERATURE DISTRIBUTION in San Francisco on a spring evening is depicted by means of isotherms, which are lines of equal temperature. The shading ranges from the most densely built-up areas (*dark*) through less dense sections to open country (*light*).

EMISSIONS OF HEAT from an automobile with its engine idling appear in an infrared photograph made with a Barnes thermograph. Bright area below the car is pavement, which was in direct sunlight. Vehicles are a major source of heat production in a city.

moves into the center of the city in the lower layers, rises in the central core, flows outward again at a higher altitude and as it cools settles down over the open country to complete the cycle.

Near midday the sunlight strikes the open country still more directly, and the difference in temperature between city and country becomes quite small. Now the air rising over the city is not appreciably warmer than the surrounding air, so that in the early afternoon the cycle of circulation is considerably weakened. As the afternoon progresses, however, a situation similar to that of the early morning develops. The sun sinks, its rays striking the open country at a lower and lower angle; an increasing proportion of its radiation is reflected. During this time the walls in the city are still intercepting the sun's radiation quite directly. The difference in temperature between city and country begins to increase again, and the circulation of air rising over the city and sinking outside it is reinvigorated. Just before sunset the circulation is fairly strong, but it weakens again as darkness falls. At about this time one would be likely to find the temperature at a weather station outside the city (such as at an airport) lower than the temperature at the downtown weather office.

During the night the surfaces that radiate their warmth to the sky most rapidly are the streets and the rooftops. If much of the rooftop area of the city is at about the same height, there will be a strong tendency for a cool layer of air to be formed at that level. With cool air at the rooftops now lying below warmer air just above it, a rather stable stratification of air develops, and any tendency for upward movement of warm air in the spaces between buildings is inhibited.

The overall situation now is that the rural area is cooling rapidly and the city area is cooling slowly. Heat is being removed from the fields by light winds and by almost unobstructed radiation to the night sky. In the city, however, pockets of air are trapped. They cannot move upward, and they are still receiving heat from the release of energy stored in the walls of the buildings during the day. Through the night both the city and the countryside will continue to cool, but by dawn the city is still likely to be four or five degrees warmer than its surroundings.

Early Monday morning the factories in the city begin to put forth heat, smoke and gases. Automobiles, trucks and buses start to emit large quantities

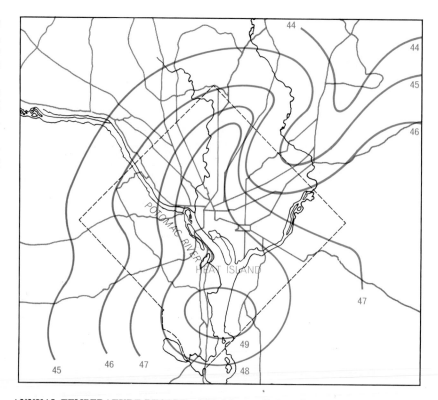

ANNUAL TEMPERATURE RECORD of Washington, D.C., and its environs gives the average of annual minimum temperatures for the period 1946–1960. The areas inside closed isotherms constitute what is known as the heat island. Here as in other cities the island is associated with the most densely built-up part of the urban complex. This map and the one below are based on data obtained by Clarence A. Woollum of the U.S. Weather Bureau.

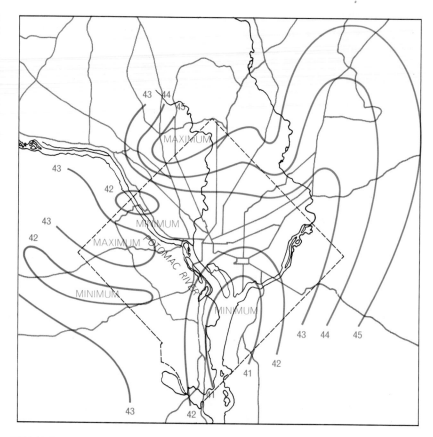

RECORD OF PRECIPITATION in the Washington area covers the same 15 years as the temperature record. Both topography and the existence of the city affect precipitation.

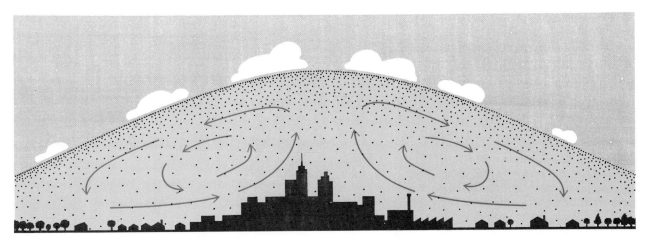

DUST DOME takes shape periodically over large cities because of the particles of dust and smoke that enter the air as a result of activities in the city. Air tends to rise over the warmer central part of the city and to settle over the cooler environs, so that a circulatory system develops. Dome is likely to persist, significantly affecting the city's climate, until a strong wind or a heavy rain carries it away.

of heat and fumes. Even stoves in kitchens constitute a source of heat that cannot be neglected. Artificial heating and air pollution thus become meteorologically significant as the day begins.

As before, the early sun starts to warm the city's walls and streets, and heat begins to accumulate in the downtown area. Today, however, there is a difference because of the heat being added to the system by the tall chimneys of factories. Ordinarily air rising to the height of the chimney tops would have had a chance to cool, but now it receives more heat at that level and will probably rise higher above the city than it did on Sunday. Moreover, the column of air now carries a freight of particles of dust and smoke. The smallest particles will fall only after they have been carried away from the rising column of air and out over the suburbs. Other particles will remain suspended over the city all day.

Over a long period of time the con-

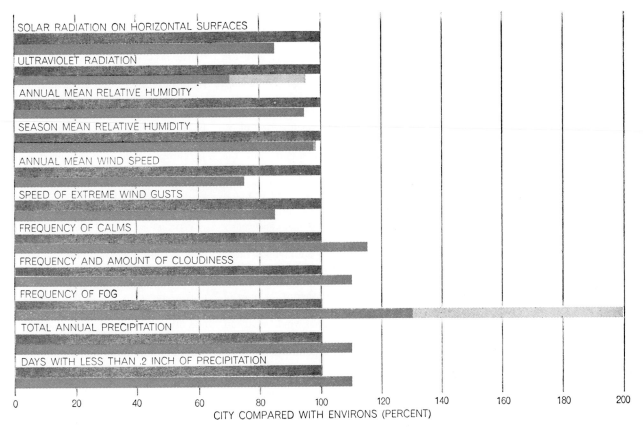

MAJOR DIFFERENCES IN CLIMATE between a city (*color*) and its environs (*gray*) are set out in terms of the percentage by which the city has more or less of each climatic variable during a year than is experienced in the countryside. For example, the city receives 5 percent less ultraviolet radiation than the countryside in summer, 30 percent less in winter; frequency of fog in city is 30 percent higher in summer and 100 percent higher in winter. Findings were made by Helmut E. Landsberg of the University of Maryland.

tinuous introduction and movement of particles creates a dome-shaped layer of haze over the city. This structure, variously called the "dust dome" and the "haze hood," has long been characteristic of large cities, although in recent years the general dirtiness of the air has made the dome harder to distinguish from its surroundings than it was several decades ago. Nonetheless, it still has a marked effect on the city's climate.

At night, as the particles in the dome cool, they can become nuclei on which the moisture in the air condenses as fog. The phenomenon occurs over cities in the middle latitudes when conditions are precisely right. The first layers of fog will usually form near the top of the dome, where the particles cool most rapidly by radiation; the blanket becomes thicker by downward growth until it reaches the ground as smog. This extra covering of water droplets over the city further retards nighttime cooling. Fog helps to perpetuate the dust dome by preventing the suspended particles from moving upward out of the system. Thus one day's contribution of solid contaminants will remain in the air over the city to be added to the next day's.

In the absence of a strong wind or a heavy rain to clear away the dust dome, the haze becomes denser each day. In winter, since less and less sunshine penetrates the dome to warm the city naturally, more and more fuel is burned to make up the difference. The combustion contributes further to the processes that build up smog. It is in this gradual but inexorable way that the smog problem has attained serious dimensions in many large cities.

In sum, a city's effect on its own climate is complex and far-reaching. Helmut E. Landsberg of the University of Maryland, who until recently was director of climatology in the U.S. Weather Bureau, has drawn up a balance sheet showing the net effect of the variables [*see bottom illustration on preceding page*]. Among other things, he has concluded that cities in the middle latitudes receive 15 percent less sunshine on horizontal surfaces than is received in surrounding rural areas and that they receive 5 percent less ultraviolet radiation in summer and 30 percent less in winter. Landsberg's figures also show that the city, compared with the countryside, has a 6 percent lower annual mean relative humidity, 10 percent more precipitation, 10 percent more cloudiness, 25 percent lower mean annual wind speed and 30

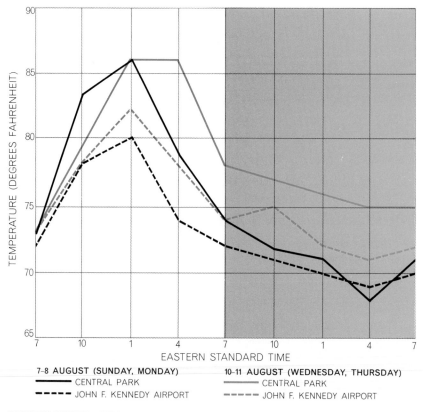

TEMPERATURE DIFFERENCES appear in readings at a weather station in New York City and one at an airport in the environs for two 24-hour periods in August, 1966. The graph begins at 7:00 A.M. for each period. Temperature differences are often less pronounced on weekends than on weekdays because fewer of a city's heat sources are operating on weekends.

percent more fog in summer and 100 percent more in winter.

T. J. Chandler, director of the London Climatic Survey, has compiled a number of records for the London area. He has found that over a period of 30 years the average maximum temperatures in the city, the suburbs and the surrounding countryside were respectively 58.3, 57.6 and 57.2 degrees and the average minimums 45.2, 43.1 and 41.8 degrees. His figures also show that over the period the city had consistently less sunshine than its environs did.

Some of these broad findings merit closer consideration. The patterns of temperature in a city can be shown on maps by drawing isotherms, or lines of equal temperature, for various times. Under a great variety of wind, cloud and sunshine conditions isotherm maps all show the highest temperatures clustered near the center of the city, with lower temperatures appearing radially toward the suburbs and the countryside. The resulting pattern of isotherms suggests the term "heat island" for the warmest area [*see top illustration on page 184*]. The term is used regularly by meteorologists to describe this major feature of a city's climate.

The heat island has been observed in many cities, some large and some small, some near water and some not, some with hills and some with none. How, then, can one be sure that the heat island, and thus the city climate itself, is really attributable to the works of man? J. Murray Mitchell, urban climatologist in the U.S. Weather Bureau, has considered the question and found three kinds of evidence that the city climate is caused by the city itself.

First, cities exhibit the heat island whether they are flat like Indianapolis or built on hills like San Francisco. Hence topography cannot explain the heat-island pattern. Second, temperature records averaged by day of the week show marked differences between Sundays and other days. Since many of the heat-creating processes distinctive to cities are inactive on Sundays, it is evident that those man-made processes account for the heat island. Finally, Mitchell has carefully examined the population and temperature records of a number of cities and found that the size of the heat island and the difference in temperature between it and surrounding areas increase as population does.

Another fact to be noted about tem-

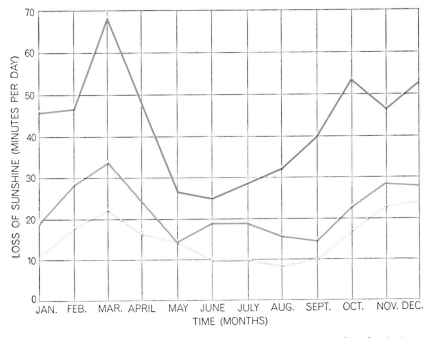

LOSS OF BRIGHT SUNSHINE in London compared with areas surrounding the city is expressed in terms of minutes per day for each month. The figures show the city's average loss during the period 1921 to 1950. London area's districts are represented by the dark line at top, the inner suburbs by the middle line and the outer suburbs by the bottom line.

peratures is that the maximum difference between city and countryside appears to be about 10 to 15 degrees Fahrenheit, regardless of the size of the city. Chandler has found this to be the case in London, which has a population of eight million; my colleagues and I have found the same in Corvallis, Ore., which has a population of about 20,000.

Chandler's figures for the loss of sunlight in London show larger losses in winter, when the sun is low, than in summer, when sunlight takes a shorter path through the atmosphere. The amount of reduction increases markedly toward the center of the city, showing both the greater depth of the dust dome and the greater density of pollutants

there. Part of the reduction of sunlight in London and other cities can be laid to the fact that a city tends to be more cloudy than its environs. Warm air rising over the center of the city provides a mechanism for the formation of clouds on many days when clouds fail to form in the country.

The frequency of fogs during the winter has to do with the greater relative reductions in sunshine during the winter months. One cannot simply say, however, that the greater frequency of fog explains the reduced total of sunshine. A feedback process is involved. Once fog forms, a weak sun has most of its energy reflected from the top of the fog layer. Little of the energy penetrates the fog to warm the city, and so the fog

tends to perpetuate itself until the climatic situation changes.

Another connection between winter and the higher frequency of fog arises from the low temperatures. After an incursion of cold arctic air the residents of the city increase their rate of fuel consumption. The higher consumption of fuel produces more particulate pollutants and more water vapor. The air above a city is usually quite stagnant following the arrival of a cold wave, and thus the stage is set for the generation of fog. Lacking ventilation, the city's atmosphere fills with smoke, dirt and water vapor. The particles of smoke and dirt act as nuclei for the condensation of the water vapor. Because the water is shared among a large number of nuclei, the air contains a large number of small water droplets. Such a size distribution of water droplets forms a persistent fog, and the fog retards warming of the city. Retarded warming prolongs the need for extra heating. Only another change of air mass will relieve the situation. This chain of events has been associated with nearly every major disaster resulting from air pollution.

Reduction of visual range by smoke alone is not regularly recorded in cities. It is recorded at airports, however, and Landsberg has been able to use data from the Detroit City Airport, which is near the center of the city, and Wayne County Airport, which is in a more rural area, to deduce something about climatic differences between a city and the nearby countryside. The records indicate that a city will have, in the course of a year, 10 times more hours in which smoke restricts visibility to a mile or less than will be experienced in rural areas.

Contrary to what one might think, this situation may be improving somewhat. Robert Beebe of the U.S. Weather Bureau recently studied records of the visual range at the major municipal airports that did not change either their location or their schedule of weather observation between 1945 and 1965. He found that the number of times when smoke reduces horizontal visibility at the airports is less now than it was in 1945. The change might be explained by efforts to control air pollution, resulting in reduced concentrations of smoke and in changes in the size and character of smoke particles.

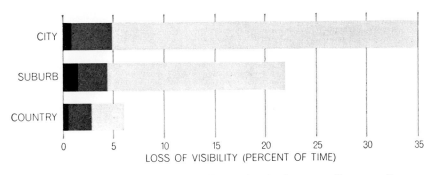

FOG IN PARIS has cut visibility more in the city than in the surrounding areas. Data are for winter and show the percent of time when visibility was reduced to between one mile and a quarter-mile by light fog (light), a quarter-mile to 300 feet by moderate fog (medium) and less than 300 feet by dense fog (dark). In the summer there were far fewer days of fog.

The differences in moisture and precipitation between a city and its environs are somewhat contradictory. During periods without rain the relative scarcity of water for evaporation in the city results in a reduced concentration of water vapor in the air. Expressed as relative humidity, the difference gives the city a reduction of 6 percent in the annual average of the countryside, of 2 percent in the winter average and of 8 percent in the summer.

Even though the city is somewhat drier than its environs, on the days when rain or snow falls there is likely to be more in the city than in the countryside. The difference amounts to 10 percent in a year. It builds up mostly as an accumulation of small increments on drizzly days, when not much precipitation falls anywhere in the area. On such days the updrafts over the warm city provide enough extra lift so that the clouds there produce a slightly higher amount of precipitation.

Perhaps the catalogue of differences I have cited will leave the reader thinking that the city climate offers no advantages over the country climate. Actually there are several, including lower heating bills, fewer days with snow and a longer gardening season. Landsberg has estimated that a city has about 14 percent fewer days with snow than the countryside. The season between the last freeze in the spring and the first freeze in the fall may be three or four weeks longer in the city than in the countryside.

Both the advantages and the disadvantages of city climate testify to the fact that the city's climate is distinctly different from the countryside's. Every major aspect of climate is changed, if only slightly, by an urban complex. The differences in a small city may be only occasional; in a large city every day is different climatically from what it would have been if the city were not there.

Fuller understanding of the climatic changes created by a city may make it possible to manage city growth in such a way that the effect of troublesome changes will be minimal. Perhaps the changes can even be made beneficial. Several organizations are accumulating climatological data on cities. I have already mentioned the London Climatic Survey. Similar work is in progress in the U.S. Environmental Science Services Administration, at the University of California at Los Angeles, at New York University and in the research laboratories of the Travelers Insurance Company. Meteorologists in those organizations are driving instrumented automobiles, flying instrumented aircraft and operating hundreds of ground stations to obtain weath-

er data. Although the studies are aimed primarily at understanding the meteorological problems of air pollution, other aspects of the local modification of climate by cities will be better understood as a result.

What may be even more important is the possibility of ascertaining the potential of extensive urbanization for

causing large-scale changes of climate over entire continents. The evidence is not yet substantial enough to show that urbanization does cause such changes, but it is sufficient to indicate that the possibility cannot be ignored. The acquisition of more knowledge about the climate of cities may in the long run be one of the keys to man's survival.

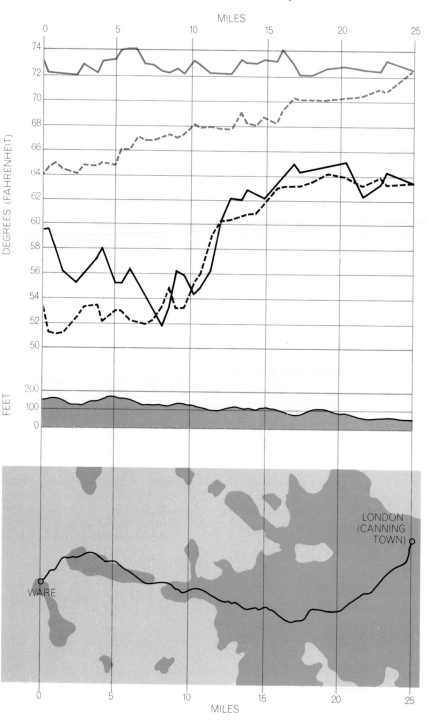

TEMPERATURE TRAVERSES between the Canning Town section of London and the community of Ware 25 miles north were made on a June day (color) and night (black) by T. J. Chandler of the London Climatic Survey. In each case he made an outbound trip (solid line) and an inbound one (broken line). Dark shading at bottom shows heavily built-up areas.

19

Infectious Drug Resistance

TSUTOMU WATANABE
December 1967

The advent of sulfonamide drugs and antibiotics brought with it the promise that bacterial disease might be brought under control, but that promise has not been fulfilled. Although many infections respond dramatically to chemotherapy, tuberculosis, dysentery and typhoid fever continue to be endemic in many parts of the world; cholera and plague erupt periodically; staphylococcal infections persist in the most advanced medical centers. One major reason is that the disease organisms have developed resistance to the drugs.

Until recently it was assumed that the appearance of drug-resistant bacteria was the result of a predictable process: the spontaneous mutation of a bacterium to drug resistance and the selective multiplication of the resistant strain in the presence of the drug. In actuality a more

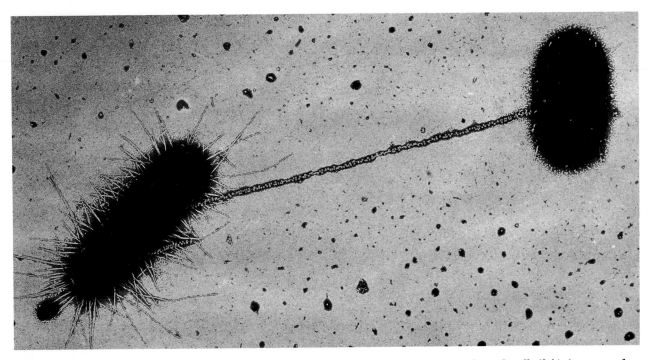

R FACTOR, the particle that imparts infectious drug resistance, is transferred from one bacterial cell to another by conjugation. The various forms of conjugation are thought to be effected by way of thin tubules called pili. In this electron micrograph made by Charles C. Brinton, Jr., and Judith Carnahan of the University of Pittsburgh a male *Escherichia coli* cell (*left*) is connected to a female bacterium of the same species by an F pilus, which shows as a thin white line in the negatively stained preparation. Numerous spherical bacterial viruses, or phages, adhere to the F pilus. The cells have been magnified about 20,000 diameters.

190

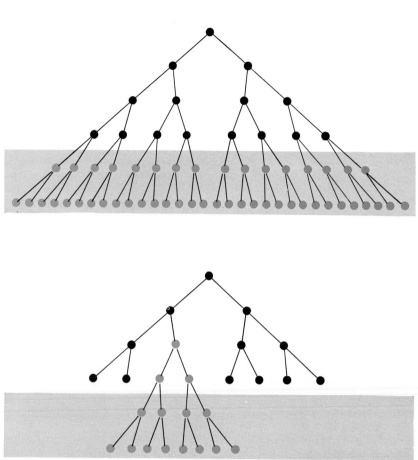

DRUG RESISTANCE involves a change in the genetic material of a bacterial cell. The change from drug-sensitive cell (*black*) to drug-resistant cell (*color*) is not induced by the presence of the drug (*light color*), as was once thought (*top*). It is the result of a spontaneous mutation that gives rise to cells that survive in the drug environment (*bottom*).

ominous phenomenon is at work. It is called infectious drug resistance, and it is a process whereby the genetic determinants of resistance to a number of drugs are transferred together and at one stroke from a resistant bacterial strain to a bacterial strain, of the same species or a different species, that was previously drug-sensitive, or susceptible to the drug's effect. Infectious drug resistance constitutes a serious threat to public health. Since its discovery in Japan in 1959 it has been detected in many countries. It affects a number of bacteria, including organisms responsible for dysentery, urinary infections, typhoid fever, cholera and plague, and each year it is found to confer resistance to more antibacterial agents. (What may be a related form of transmissible drug resistance has been discovered in staphylococci and may be responsible for "hospital staph" infections.) Quite aside from its importance to medicine, the study of infectious drug resistance is making significant contributions to microbial genetics by illuminating the complex and little understood relations among viruses, genes and

the particles called episomes that lie somewhere between them.

If an antibacterial drug is added to a liquid culture of bacteria that are sensitive to the drug, after a while all the cells in the culture are found to be resistant to the drug. Once it was thought that the drug must somehow have induced the resistance. What has actually happened, of course, is that a few cells in the original culture were already resistant; these cells survive and their daughter cells multiply when the sensitive majority of bacteria succumb to the drug [*see illustration above*]. The resistance was not induced by the drug but was the result of a spontaneous mutation. Bacteria, like higher organisms, have chromosomes incorporating the genetic material, and from time to time a gene—perhaps one controlling drug resistance—undergoes a mutation. The mutation of a drug-sensitivity gene occurs only once in 10 million to a billion cell divisions, and when it occurs it alters a cell's sensitivity to one particular drug or perhaps two related drugs.

In 1955 a Japanese woman recently returned from Hong Kong came down with a stubborn case of dysentery. When the causative agent was isolated, it turned out to be a typical dysentery bacillus of the genus *Shigella*. This shigella was unusual, however. It was resistant to four drugs: sulfanilamide and the antibiotics streptomycin, chloramphenicol and tetracycline. In the next few years the incidence of multiply drug-resistant shigellae in Japan increased, and there were a number of epidemics of intractable dysentery.

The familiar process of mutation and selection could not explain either this rapid increase in multiple resistance or a number of other findings concerning the dysentery epidemics. For one thing, during a single outbreak of the disease resistant shigellae were isolated from some patients and sensitive shigellae of exactly the same type from other patients. Even the same patient might yield both sensitive and resistant bacteria of the same type. Moreover, the administration of a single drug, say chloramphenicol, to patients harboring a sensitive organism could cause them to excrete bacteria that were resistant to all four drugs. Then it was found that many of the patients who harbored drug-resistant shigellae also harbored strains of the relatively harmless colon bacillus *Escherichia coli* that were resistant to the four drugs. It was impossible, on the other hand, to obtain multiple resistance in the laboratory by exposing sensitive shigellae or *E. coli* to any single drug; multiply resistant mutants could be obtained only after serial selections with each drug in turn, and these mutants, unlike the ones taken from sick patients, multiplied very slowly.

Taken together, these characteristics of the resistant shigellae suggested to Tomoichiro Akiba of Tokyo University in 1959 that resistance to the four drugs might be transferred from multiply resistant *E. coli* to sensitive shigellae within a patient's digestive tract. Akiba's group and a group headed by Kunitaro Ochiai of the Nagoya City Higashi Hospital thereupon confirmed the possibility by transferring resistance from resistant *E. coli* to sensitive shigellae—and from resistant shigellae to sensitive *E. coli*—in liquid cultures. Other investigators demonstrated the same kind of transfer in laboratory animals and eventually in human volunteers. Clearly a new kind of transferable drug resistance had been discovered. What, then, was the mechanism of transfer? There were three known mechanisms of genetic transmission in bacteria that had to be considered as possibilities.

One was transformation, which involves "naked" deoxyribonucleic acid (DNA), the stuff of genes. DNA can be extracted from a donor strain of bacteria and added to a culture of a recipient strain; some of the extracted genes may "recombine," or replace homologous genes on chromosomes of the recipient bacteria, thus transferring a mutation from the donor to the recipient [see top illustration below]. In this way, for example, streptomycin-sensitive bacteria can become streptomycin-resistant.

Transformation occurs in a number of different bacteria, and it can occur spontaneously as well as experimentally. Because only small fragments of DNA are taken up by bacteria in transformation, however, it is seldom that more than two different drug-resistance genes are transferred together. It requires optimal laboratory conditions, moreover, for transformation to occur at a significant frequency, and such conditions are not likely to prevail in nature.

Another mechanism of gene transmission is transduction, in which genes are

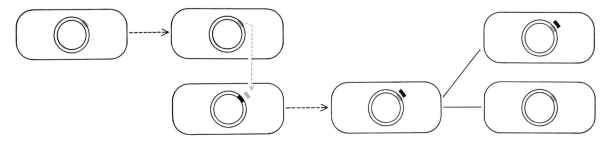

TRANSFORMATION is a form of genetic transmission in which deoxyribonucleic acid (DNA) extracted or excreted from a donor cell (top) enters a recipient cell (bottom) and is incorporated into its chromosome. In this way a mutated gene (color) controlling resistance to a drug may be transferred to a drug-sensitive cell, replacing a homologous gene, which is unable to replicate and dies out.

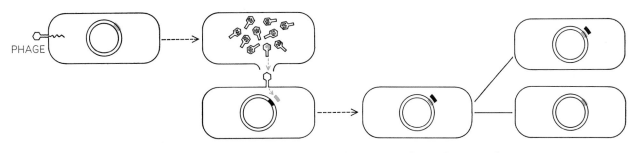

TRANSDUCTION is effected by phage, or bacterial virus. Phage DNA enters a cell (left) and directs the synthesis of new phage, killing the cell (second from left). A bit of bacterial DNA (color), perhaps a mutated gene that causes drug resistance, may be incorporated inside a newly formed phage, be carried to a sensitive cell (bottom) and "recombine," or replace a gene on the chromosome.

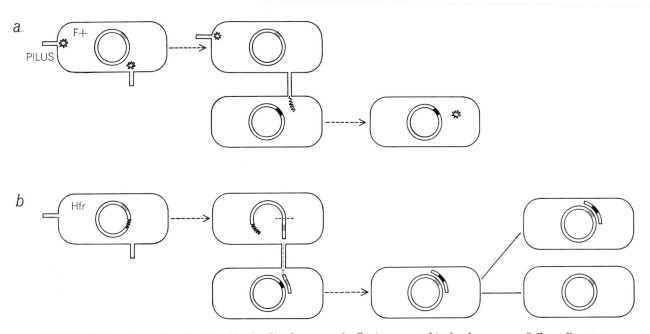

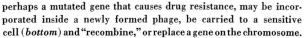

SEXUAL MATING is a form of conjugation. If a fertility factor (F) is in the cytoplasm of a male (F⁺) cell (a), it is transferred alone through a pilus to a female (F⁻) cell. In an Hfr cell (b) the F is incorporated in the chromosome. Cell-to-cell contact causes part or all of the chromosome, perhaps including a mutation for drug resistance (color), to pass to a female cell and recombine.

carried from one bacterial cell to another by infecting phages, or bacterial viruses. Transduction occurs when a phage, reproducing inside a cell by taking over the cell's synthesizing machinery, incorporates a bit of the bacterial chromosome within its protein coat "by mistake." When the phage subsequently infects a second cell, the bacterial genes it carries may recombine with homologous genes on the second cell's chromosome. The phage in effect acts as a syringe to bring about what in transformation is accomplished by the movement of naked DNA [see middle illustration on preceding page]. Transduction takes place in a variety of bacteria, but at a very low frequency. Genes for resistance can be transduced like other genes, but it is unlikely that more than two resistance genes could be transferred together because the small transducing phage can carry only a short segment of bacterial chromosome.

The third type of genetic transmission in bacteria is conjugation: a direct contact between two cells during which genetic material passes from one cell to the other. Transfer by conjugation occurs primarily from male to female cells of certain groups of bacteria. The male bacteria carry a fertility factor, the F factor, that is ordinarily located in the cytoplasm of the cell but may become integrated into the chromosome. When the F is cytoplasmic, the male cells are called F^+. In such cells the F is readily transferred to female (F^-) cells by conjugation, but it is transferred alone. When the F factor is integrated into the bacterial chromosome, it serves to "mobilize" the chromosome. That is, the chromosome, which in bacteria forms a closed loop, opens and portions of it can pass by conjugation to a female cell, recombine with the female chromosome and thereby endow the female bacterium with traits from the male. Because this transfer occurs with a high frequency in male cells with an integrated F, such cells are called Hfr, for "high frequency of recombination" [see bottom illustration on preceding page].

The F factor is what is generally called an episome: a genetic element that may or may not be present in a cell, that when present may exist autonomously in the cytoplasm or may be incorporated into the chromosome, and that is neither essential to the cell nor damaging to it. An episome is something like a virus without a coat; indeed, some bacterial viruses can become "temperate" and exist as harmless episomes inside certain bacterial cells [see "Viruses

and Genes," by François Jacob and Elie L. Wollman; SCIENTIFIC AMERICAN Offprint 89].

Until recently the actual route of transfer was not known. In 1964 Charles C. Brinton, Jr., of the University of Pittsburgh and his colleagues proposed that the F factor or the F-mobilized chromosome passes from one cell to the other through a thin tubular appendage, the F pilus, that is formed on both F^+ and Hfr cells by the presence of the F factor. Another kind of pilus, the Type 1 pilus, is seen on female cells as well as male cells, but the two can be distinguished: the F pilus is the site of infection by certain phages, and so the phages cluster along the F pili, marking them clearly in electron micrographs [see top and middle illustrations on page 195].

If a male chromosome transferred to a female cell by conjugation carries drug-resistance genes, these genes may be incorporated into the female chromosome. Experiments with sexual mating showed that drug-resistance genes are in fact sometimes scattered along bacterial chromosomes. Rather long segments—sometimes the entire length—of the chromosome can be transferred in sexual mating, and so it is possible for several resistance genes to be transferred in a single mating event.

In 1960 we took up the study of the resistant shigellae in my laboratory at the Keio University School of Medicine. It soon became clear that the mechanism of transfer of multiple resistance was not transformation, because sensitive strains were not made resistant by DNA extracted from the resistant bacteria. It was not transduction, because it could not ordinarily be effected by cell-free filtrates of the resistant cultures.

There was strong evidence that some form of conjugation must be responsible. Microscopic examination of a mixed culture of sensitive and resistant bacteria revealed pairing between the different kinds of cells. When a mixed liquid culture was agitated in a blender to break off any cell-to-cell contact, and the culture was then diluted to prevent further pairing, the transfer of resistance ceased. If the mechanism of resistance transfer was conjugation, however, it was not the familiar process of sexual mating. For one thing, it occurred between F^- cells. Moreover, two observations showed that unlike the transmission of traits by sexual mating the transfer did not involve the chromosome itself. First, we noted that known chromosomal traits of certain strains, such as the inability to syn-

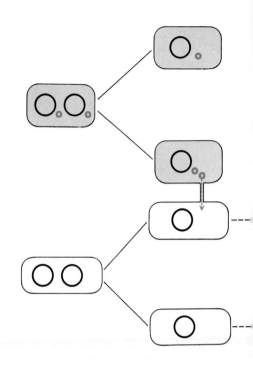

INFECTIOUS DRUG RESISTANCE, another form of conjugation, involves transfer of the R (resistance) factor. A cell of a re-

thesize particular substances, were not usually transferred along with the drug-resistance traits. Second, we noted that the recipient cells became resistant immediately after the transfer occurred, whereas chromosomal drug resistance is ordinarily expressed only after the original drug-sensitivity genes have been lost in the course of cell division through the process known as segregation.

We concluded that the factor responsible for infectious drug resistance was an extrachromosomal element, which we called the R factor (for "resistance"). A number of experiments have confirmed the cytoplasmic nature of these factors. They are obtained by bacteria only by infection from other R-factor-carrying cells, never by spontaneous mutation. They can be eliminated from cells by treatment with acridine dyes; F factors can be eliminated in the same way when they are in the cytoplasm of F^+ cells but not when they are incorporated into the

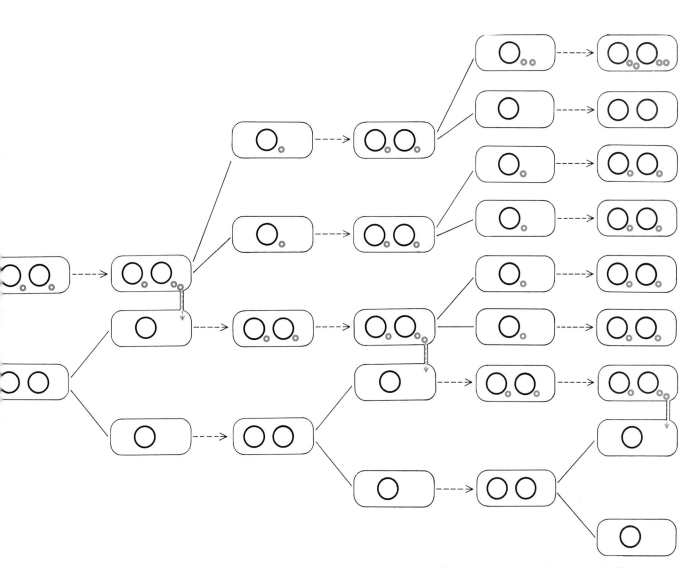

sistant strain (*light color*) comes in contact with one of a sensitive strain (*white*); one of its *R* factors (*color*) replicates and a copy passes through a pilus to the sensitive recipient. The procedure is repeated as cells come in contact. In the course of cell division an *R* factor is sometimes lost. The diagram is highly schematic; the actual sequence of replication and transfer is not established.

chromosome of *Hfr* cells. Finally, consider what happens when one adds a small number of bacteria with *R* factor to a culture of drug-sensitive cells. There is a rapid increase in the relative number of drug-resistant cells; in 24 hours or so the culture is almost completely resistant. This must be owing to the rapid infectious spread of *R* factors to the once sensitive bacteria, because it occurs at a much faster rate than the overall growth of the culture [*see top illustration on next page*]. Since chromosome replication is synchronized with cell division, the *R* factor must be replicating faster than the chromosomes and must therefore replicate outside the chromosome, in the cytoplasm.

Although the *R* factor is usually located in the cytoplasm, in rare instances it is integrated into the chromosome, and when that happens it is transferred together with some chromosomal genes. Such behavior suggests that the *R* factor,

like the *F* factor, is episomal in nature. Both of them may be of selective advantage to the cells in which they exist, the *F* factor by making for genetic variability and the *R* factor of course by providing drug resistance. When they are not providing an advantage, they at least do the host cells no harm; they are symbionts rather than harmful parasites. Their behavior is similar to that of a temperate, or nonvirulent, phage, and it may be that both are descended from bacterial viruses. Unlike viruses, they cannot exist at all outside the cell; they are obligatory intracellular symbionts with even less biological function than viruses, which are usually considered to be on the borderline between living and nonliving matter.

There is a further major point of similarity between the *F* and the *R* factor, and that is their method of transfer. In London, Naomi Datta of the Royal

Postgraduate Medical School, A. M. Lawn of the Lister Institute of Preventive Medicine and Elinor Meynell of the Medical Research Council observed in 1965 that most *R* factors induce the formation of pili that are shaped like *F* pili and attract the same phages as *F* pili: apparently they *are F* pili [*see bottom illustration on page 195*]. When bacteria that have such pili and are able to transmit multiple resistance are severely agitated in a blender, the pili are sheared off. Such "shaved" cells are unable to transfer the *R* factor; later, when the *F* pili have been regenerated, the cells are once again infectious. It now appears that both *R* factors and any chromosomal genes mobilized by *R* factors are transferred by the *F* pili or another closely related kind of pili.

The big difference between the transfer of *F* factors and the transfer of *R* factors is in the frequency with which they occur. In a mixed culture of male

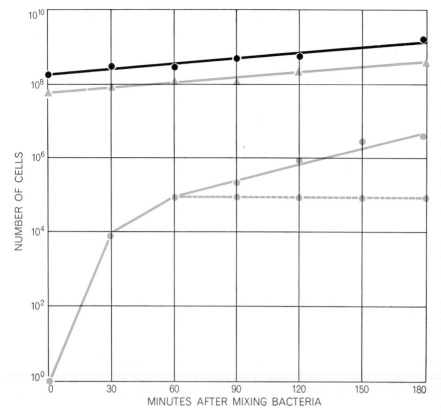

TIME COURSE of *R*-factor transfer is shown. Equal volumes of cells of a donor *E. coli* strain infected with *R* factors (*triangles*) and of an initially sensitive recipient strain (*black dots*) were mixed. Sampling at intervals traced the increase in the number of resistant *E. coli* (*colored dots*). After one hour some of the culture was removed, agitated to break off cell-to-cell contact and diluted to prevent pairing. In the diluted culture there was no increase in the number of resistant cells (*broken line*), indicating that conjugation was the mechanism of transfer. The data are from David H. Smith of the Harvard Medical School.

percent. (If this were not the case, *R* factors could hardly multiply so rapidly in a newly infected culture.) They lose this high competence after several cell-division cycles. The explanation seems to be that most *R* factors form a "repressor" substance that somehow inhibits the formation of *F* pili. Cells that are newly infected with such *R* factors contain no repressor, and so *F* pili are initially induced at a high frequency. Later, as the repressor accumulates, the formation of the pili is inhibited.

It is now possible to describe what happens when bacteria with the *R* factor come into contact with a population of drug-sensitive bacteria [*see illustration on preceding two pages*]. A few *R* factors are transmitted by conjugation from donor cells bearing pili into the cytoplasm of recipient cells, which immediately become resistant. The transfer process is repeated from cell to cell, and the normal process of cell division also contributes to the rapid proliferation of multiple resistance in the recipient population. From time to time an *R* factor is lost. Both the rate of transfer and the rate of loss vary in different strains of bacteria and *R* factors, thus accounting in part for the fact that naturally occurring multiple resistance is much more common in some bacteria that are susceptible to infectious drug resistance than in others.

For several years we have been seeking to map the various elements of an *R* factor as one maps the genes of a chromosome. To do this we capitalize on the fact that although *R* factors are not normally transferred by transduction, it is possible to transduce them under carefully controlled conditions. If we grow large phages in a culture of bacteria with *R* factors, a few of the phages pick up entire *R* factors and are capable of transferring them to recipient cells. If we use small phages, there is room for only part of the *R* factor to be incorporated inside their protein coats and transduced. Some of the transduced particles impart drug resistance but lack the ability to replicate or to be transferred by conjugation; others lack determinants of one or more of the multiple drug resistances. By calculating the frequency with which various segments of the *R* factor are transduced together, we can determine their relative distance from one another and so visualize the structure of the *R* factor we are studying.

The map is not yet conclusive, but we think the factor is circular and that it has a segment—the resistance-transfer factor, or RTF—that controls replication

and female bacteria the transfer of nearly 100 percent of the *F* factors or *F*-mobilized chromosome, as the case may be, occurs within an hour. In a culture of drug-resistant (donor) and drug-sensitive (recipient) bacteria, on the other hand, only 1 percent or less of the donor cells transfer their *R* factors in an hour. The low frequency of transfer is due to the relative scarcity of cells with *F* pili in a culture of bacteria carrying *R* factors. Bacteria that have newly acquired the *R* factor, on the other hand, can transfer it at a very high frequency—almost 100

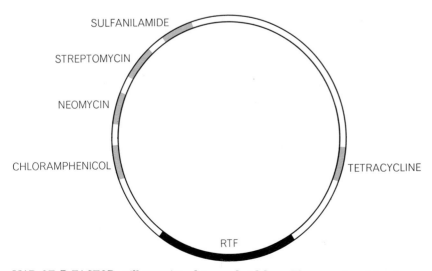

MAP OF *R* FACTOR, still tentative, shows a closed loop. There are five determinants (*color*) of resistance to five different drugs. There is also a determinant, the resistance-transfer factor (*black*), that controls the ability of the *R* factor to replicate and be transferred.

and transferability, as well as segments determining resistance to each of five types of drug [see *bottom illustration on opposite page*]. We have suggested that the R factors originate when a resistance-transfer factor picks up resistance genes from some bacterial chromosome and that the two then form a single episomal unit. E. S. Anderson and M. J. Lewis of the Central Public Health Laboratory in London have advanced a different view. They consider that the resistance-transfer factor and the set of resistance determinants exist as two separate units, which on occasion become associated to form R factors.

Since R factors are self-replicating units, carry genetic information and can recombine with bacterial chromosomes, it is safe to assume that they are composed of DNA. This is confirmed by the fact that R factors, like nucleic acids in general, are inactivated by ultraviolet radiation and by the decay of incorporated radioactive phosphorus. At the Walter Reed Army Institute of Research and at Keio, Stanley Falkow, R. V. Citarella, J. A. Wohlhieter and I were able to isolate the DNA of R factors by density-gradient centrifugation. A first attempt to separate R-factor DNA from that of E. coli was unsuccessful, suggesting that the densities of the two DNA's are very similar. We then selected as the host cell the bacterium *Proteus mirabilis,* which was known to have a DNA of unusually low density and to be subject to infectious drug resistance.

When DNA extracted from *Proteus* carrying the R factor is centrifuged in a solution of cesium chloride, two satellite bands of DNA appear in addition to the band characteristic of the bacterial DNA [see illustration on next page]. These bands disappear if the *Proteus* loses its R factors spontaneously or if they are eliminated by the acridine dye treatment, and so we conclude that the bands do represent the R-factor DNA. Analysis of this fraction by column chromatography shows that it is typical double-strand DNA. It is possible that R factors contain components other than DNA, but this is not likely in view of the fact that entire factors are transduced and transducing phages incorporate only DNA.

The original finding that infectious drug resistance affected four unrelated drugs implied that some factor was altering the cell membrane, reducing its permeability and thereby barring all the drugs from their normal sites of action inside the cell. The finding that there are separate resistance determinants for the various drugs, however, indicated that

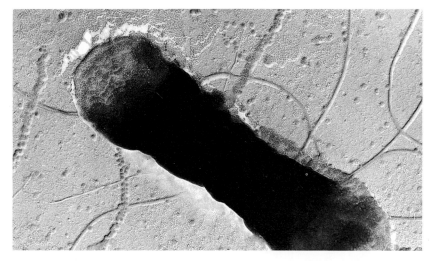

MALE BACTERIUM, an *E. coli* **infected with phage, has** *F* **pili.** They are thin fibers, here hidden below the spherical phage particles. The thin fibers without phages are Type 1 pili and the thick fibers are flagella. The preparation has been enlarged about 30,000 diameters.

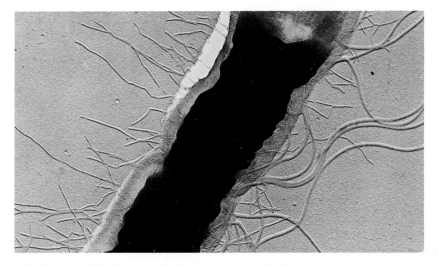

FEMALE *E. COLI,* which lacks the *F* factor, also lacks *F* pili. It does have both the Type 1 pili and flagella, which are organelles of locomotion for the cell. The electron micrograph, like the others on this page, was made by Toshihiko Arai in the author's laboratory.

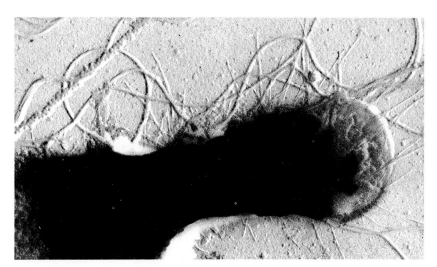

E. COLI **WITH** *R* **FACTOR,** although a female cell, does carry an *F* pilus, the phage-covered fiber at top left. It also has Type 1 pili and flagella. The most common type of *R* factor initially induces the formation of *F* pili, but it also tends to repress them later.

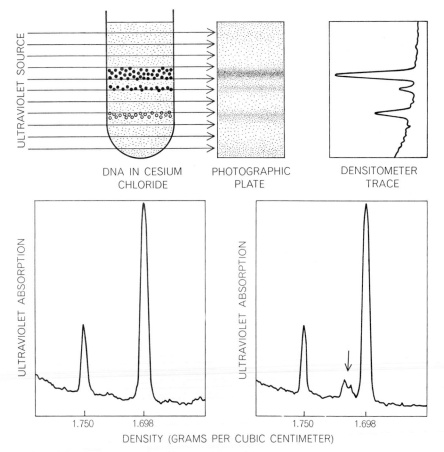

DNA IN CESIUM
CHLORIDE

PHOTOGRAPHIC
PLATE

DENSITOMETER
TRACE

DENSITY (GRAMS PER CUBIC CENTIMETER)

R-FACTOR DNA is isolated by density-gradient centrifugation. DNA from *Proteus* cells is suspended in a cesium chloride solution and spun in a high-speed centrifuge. The cesium chloride establishes a density gradient and the DNA forms bands in the solution according to its density. The DNA pattern is photographed in ultraviolet, which is absorbed by DNA, and the photograph is scanned by a densitometer (*top*). The densitometer trace derived from *Proteus* without R factor (*bottom left*) shows a band at 1.698 grams per cubic centimeter that is characteristic of *Proteus* DNA and a reference band at 1.750. The trace from *Proteus* with R factor (*right*) has extra bands (*arrow*) at 1.710 and 1.716, representing R-factor DNA.

each determinant had its own mode of action. Permeability may be involved in the case of some drugs, but it is now clear that other processes are at work. S. Okamoto and Y. Suzuki of the National Institute of Health in Japan and Mrs. Datta and P. Kontomichalou in Britain have shown that bacteria bearing various R factors synthesize particular enzymes that inactivate specific drugs, thereby rendering them harmless to the bacteria.

The public health threat posed by infectious drug resistance is measured by the range of bacterial hosts it affects, the number of drugs to which it imparts resistance and the prevalence of certain practices in medicine, agriculture and food processing that tend to favor its spread. R factors can be transferred not only to shigellae but also to *Salmonella*, one species of which causes typhoid fever; to *Vibrio cholerae*, the agent of cholera; to the plague bacillus

Pasteurella pestis and to *Pseudomonas aeruginosa*, which causes chronic purulent infections. In addition, more than 90 percent of the agents of urinary tract infections, including *E. coli, Klebsiella, Citrobacter* and *Proteus,* now carry R factors.

(These organisms are all gram-negative bacteria; R factors seem not to be transferable to the gram-positive bacteria, which include streptococci and staphylococci. A somewhat similar form of transmissible resistance has been discovered in staphylococci, however. There are cytoplasmic genes, or plasmids, in some staphylococci that determine the production of penicillinase, an enzyme that inactivates penicillin. Richard P. Novick of the Public Health Research Institute in New York and Stephen I. Morse of Rockefeller University recently showed that these plasmids can be transduced to drug-sensitive staphylococci both in the test tube and

in laboratory animals. The actual clinical importance of this process remains to be determined.)

The R factors seem to be acquiring resistance genes for an increasing number of antibiotics. The original factors, it will be remembered, imparted resistance to sulfanilamide, streptomycin, chloramphenicol and tetracycline. In 1963 G. Lebek of West Germany discovered a factor that causes resistance to these four drugs and also to the neomycin-kanamycin group of antibiotics. In 1965 Mrs. Datta and Kontomichalou reported a new determinant of resistance to aminobenzyl penicillin (ampicillin). In 1966 H. W. Smith and Sheila Halls of the Animal Health Trust in Britain found factors imparting resistance to the synthetic antibacterial drug furazolidone. This year David H. Smith of the Harvard Medical School reported R-factor-controlled resistance to gentamycin and spectinomycin. We must assume that additional drug-resistance determinants will appear and proliferate as new antibiotics come into use.

This is implicit in the mechanism of infectious resistance. R factors are common in *E. coli*, which are often present in the intestinal tracts of human beings and animals. When a person or an animal becomes infected with a susceptible disease organism, the R factor is readily transferred to the new population. Although the frequency of transfer of R factors is not high even in the laboratory, and is reduced by the presence of bile salts and fatty acids in the intestine, recipient bacteria bearing the R factor are given a selective advantage as soon as drug therapy begins, and they soon predominate.

In addition to being ineffective and helping to spread resistance, "shotgun" treatment of an infection with drugs to which it is resistant causes undesirable side effects. It is therefore important to culture the causative agent, determine its drug-resistance pattern and institute treatment with a drug to which it is not resistant; that is the only way to combat the multiple-resistance strains. As more is learned about the R factor, new forms of therapy may be developed—possibly utilizing the acridine dyes, which attack drug-resistant as well as sensitive cells and can also eliminate R factors from cells.

In many parts of the world antibiotics are routinely incorporated in livestock feeds to promote fattening and are also used to control animal diseases. Anderson and Mrs. Datta have shown clearly that the presence of antibiotics in livestock exerts a strong selective pressure in favor of organisms—particularly salmonellae—with R factors and plays an important role in the spread of infectious resistance. Meat and other foodstuffs are also treated with antibiotics and synthetic drugs as preservatives in many countries, and this too may help to spread R factors and carry them to man. Unless we put a halt to the prodigal use of antibiotics and synthetic drugs we may soon be forced back into the preantibiotic era of medicine.

One final note. Typhoid, cholera and plague bacilli are obviously much more difficult to combat if they are resistant to drug therapy. There are grounds for believing that the military in some countries are investigating the potentialities of R factors as weapons of bacteriological warfare.

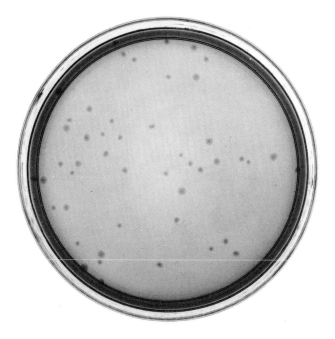
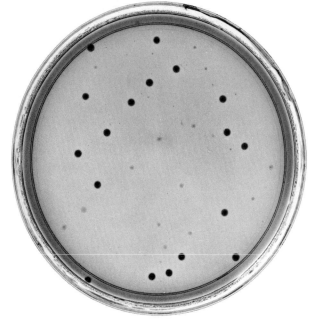

SENSITIVITY TEST conducted in Smith's laboratory at Harvard demonstrates infectious drug resistance. A culture of *Salmonella typhimurium* with an R factor controlling resistance to four drugs is mixed with drug-sensitive *E. coli*. A portion of the mixed culture is immediately plated on a medium containing the drugs (*left*). Only *Salmonella* colonies (*gray*) appear. After the mixed culture has incubated, the plating procedure is repeated, and now *E. coli* colonies (*black*) grow as well (*right*): the R factor was transferred.

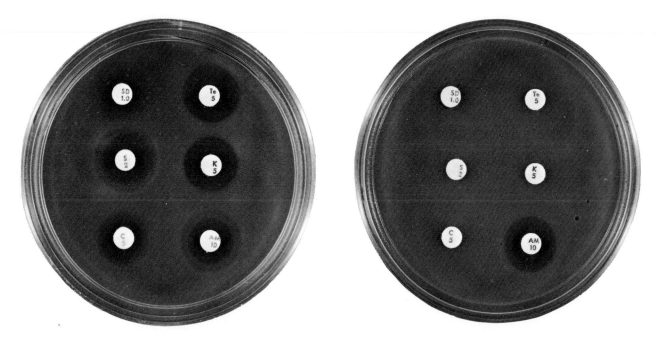

SIMILAR TEST is performed with filter-paper disks impregnated with six drugs: sulfadiazine (*SD*), tetracycline (*Te*), streptomycin (*S*), kanamycin (*K*), chloramphenicol (*C*) and ampicillin (*AM*). A culture of *E. coli* was at first sensitive to all six, as shown by the dark zones around each disk where the bacteria have been killed (*left*). After the culture was incubated with a strain of *Klebsiella*, taken from a patient, that was resistant to all the drugs but ampicillin, the *E. coli* too were resistant to all but ampicillin (*right*).

IV

ON MANAGEMENT AND BUYING TIME

IV

ON MANAGEMENT
AND BUYING TIME

*No matter how effective and sound are social, economic
and ecological considerations in the development process,
benefits will be negated and overrun by the spiraling
human pressures on the environment.*

Gunnar Myrdal,
quoted in *Environment*, January–February 1969

INTRODUCTION

The pessimistic picture presented in these pages so far should not be misconstrued. We do not contend that man's manipulation of his environment must invariably yield unfortunate results, nor do we deny that the needed economic and sociological changes must be accompanied and supported by massive (but enlightened) technological enterprises. We do insist, however, that even the best technology, by itself, will be far from sufficient to extricate man from his present predicaments; its use must be regarded primarily as a means of buying time in which to resolve fundamental economic, sociological, and biological problems. Among these are the stabilization of population, the reduction of consumption in the overdeveloped nations, the equitable distribution of the requisites of a decent life, and the recognition of man's position as part of, rather than lord over, nature. To persuade humanity that salvation can be achieved through technology alone is to postpone confrontation of these basic problems and surely, therefore, to sabotage the human enterprise.

The philosophical task of the technologist does not end with recognition of the more fundamental, nontechnical problems. Within the technological sphere, he must seek the optimum allocation of his efforts among many possible approaches, and he must strive to minimize adverse side effects, both short-term and long-term. This mind-boggling task has recently been dubbed "technology assessment." It is treated by Harvey Brooks and Raymond Bowers (representing a much larger panel of scholars convened by the National Academy of Sciences) in their article "The Assessment of Technology." This article raises many vital issues, but the weakness of its recommendations for institutionalizing the process of assessment is a tragic disappointment.

The authors note, at the outset, the flaw in conventional "cost-benefit" analyses: Those who make the decisions and receive the benefits are not necessarily the same people who bear the brunt of the costs. Their article also mentions the dangers of the present "crisis mentality," in which lack of adequate planning and outright disinterest in problems of less than critical proportions leaves us stumbling, in something of a societal daze, from one problem to another. Their discussions of the importance of reversibility as a criterion for judging potential environmental damage, the role of the legal system in providing a framework for change, and the necessity of separating the promotional and regulatory functions of government agencies, all deserve careful attention.

The burden-of-proof argument—or "burden of uncertainty," as the authors call it—is also vital, but it is unnecessarily diluted here with equivocal language. The technologists must not simply "gather evidence," they must demonstrate beyond reasonable doubt that the harmful effects of the schemes that they propose are justified by the benefits, and that these effects are less harmful than those of alternative means to achieve the same goals. The implication that the misuse of pesticides persisted so long because their possible harmful effects were not perceived in time is not justified: Many biologists perceived the dangers and communicated them to the government ten to twenty-five years ago. Obviously, implementing the burden-of-proof ideal entails more than securing good information. It requires an institutional framework that will insure that sound technical advice will be heeded.

Here, then, is the great weakness in the case that Brooks and Bowers present: their claim that the needed institution for technology assessment should be empowered only to recommend, *not to act or intervene*. Thus, in fear of stultifying "the delicate mechanisms of innovation," they would guarantee the impotence of the still-conceptual assessment mechanism. Under their restrictions, whatever mechanism emerges will inevitably be as useless as the Commission on Obscenity and Pornography, the Kerner Commission, and the President's Ad Hoc Panel on the SST. Good advice will continue to be ignored, while *a priori* judgments and the power of vested interests will continue to dominate decisions.

The next four articles in this section deal with some of the philosophies and technologies of land use and agriculture. These articles illustrate many of the general points we have just discussed concerning assessment and buying time. Together with the readings in Sections I–III, they also convey some of the difficulties inherent in "managing" ecosystems whose operations are only dimly understood. In "The Reclamation of a Man-Made Desert," Walter Lowdermilk gives an enthusiastic view of the potential for correcting yesterday's blunders with sound management today. Israel certainly provides the classic example of "making the desert bloom," and we would like to believe, with Lowdermilk, that this proves for all dwellers on poor soil that ". . . the land can be reclaimed and that increase in the food supply can overtake the population increase. . . ." Unfortunately, from the evidence at hand, this conclusion can be reached only by a mighty stretch of the imagination. The pattern of overgrazing and poor cultivation practices implicated in the creation of Israel's desert has been repeated all over the world. Although Lowdermilk does not say so, today's continuing losses on the boundaries of Africa's Sahara and India's Great Thar Desert alone probably outweigh the world's isolated gains from reclamation. Without question, Israel's agricultural achievements are a monument to industriousness, perseverance, and sound management. But it is only wishful thinking to surmise that the accomplishments of this well fed, virtually 100 percent literate, highly motivated population can be duplicated across the underdeveloped world. Note also that Israel is an industrial nation with full access to the fossil-fuel "subsidy" without which modern agriculture is impossible. Even in Israel, we are inclined to hedge somewhat our tribute to sound management. The measures described by Lowdermilk for the control of salination of the soil have yet to stand the test of time; this problem continues to plague the agriculture of irrigated arid lands throughout the world.

Some of the tenets of the managment philosophy expressed by R. Merton Love in "The Rangelands of the Western United States" are admirable. For example, he recognizes that such traditional "enemies" of man as brushfires serve a useful purpose, and he wishes to accommodate "in harmony" the various demands on our western open spaces. (What must be understood by everyone is that "harmony" may require excluding some activities altogether.) But the article, as a whole, serves to mirror the most dangerous and bankrupt aspects of the modern development-management mentality.

Love writes on his first page that ". . . the balance is on man's side; if his activities did not help nature more than they hurt, the land could not support the great world population it does today." As everyone should know, the bulk of that population is "supported" only in abject poverty, and many of the techniques that are applied to provide even that support are eroding the long-term capability of the planet to support any population at all. The fundamental misunderstanding that permeates most of Love's article seems to be the confusion between quality and yield and, more specifically, the belief that to increase the latter, by whatever means, is to "improve on nature." But "nature" does not optimize for yield; she optimizes, in some general sense, for stability. To do otherwise is, in the long run, fatal.

To an unfortunate degree, man's successes at increasing his consumption have been achieved at the expense of ecosystem diversity and, therefore, stability. Such behavior should probably be regarded as transient—eventually, the note will come due. The difficulty of maintaining the monocultures of plants that supply man with the bulk of his diet is acknowledged in this article, but the author's statement that man "has found it possible to maintain such systems indefinitely" is unfounded. The intensive use of the inorganic fertilizers and persistent pesticides that supports today's high-yield agriculture is historically unprecedented. As we have noted repeatedly, such practices have already had effects so ominous that the prospect of their long continuation can only be viewed with horror. And for a classic example of the catastrophic failure of a monoculture, one need only consider the Irish Potato Famine of the last century.

Love's article concludes with the quotation of a statement by Stephen H. Spurr, dean of the School of Graduate Studies at the University of Michigan: "We should be positive and not negative, we should be active and not passive, we should be wilderness managers and not conservationists." We feel obliged to offer a rebuttal: We should be careful (as befits the stakes) and not rash; we should be humble (as befits our limitations) and not arrogant; we should leave something unmanaged, for wilderness contains answers we have not yet learned to seek.

With Christopher Pratt's illuminating article "Chemical Fertilizers," we shift our attention from the general philosophy of land management to the operational aspects of agriculture. Perhaps the most important aspect of this article is the discussion of the "law of diminishing returns" as it applies to fertilizer use. That is, at high levels of use, the additional yield per unit of fertilizer applied decreases rapidly. This pattern is certain to aggravate the ecological problems associated with inorganic fertilizers. As desperate attempts are made to double and redouble productivity to "keep pace with population growth," the concomitant fertilizer input could easily, say, triple and triple again. Pratt, unfortunately, does not discuss the ecological costs of such behavior. They include the serious disruption of the nitrogen and phosphorus cycles, which is already reflected in the eutrophication of lakes, streams, and bays in agricultural regions, and in the contamination of groundwater supplies. (For further distressing details on this subject, the reader may consult *Global Effects of Environmental Pollution*, edited by S. F. Singer, Springer-Verlag, 1970.)

Even more dangerous than the excessive use of fertilizer in today's high-yield agriculture is the accompanying barrage of broadcast poisons. One of the most constructive contributions that technology could make toward the solution of problems of the interaction of man and the ecosphere would be the development and implementation of sounder methods of pest control. The promise of one such approach is discussed by Carroll Williams in his article "Third Generation Pesticides." The two outstanding features of the pest-control substances he describes are their specificity and the relative inability of the target insects to develop resistance to them. The specificity of these substances to insects is important because other animal populations, including man, would be unaffected by them. It is hoped that substances specific to a single *species* of insect can be developed. With such chemicals, the pests' natural enemies, whose help we so desperately need in the battle for control, would be spared.

The contrast with present practices is obvious. Encouraged by the petrochemical industry, today's farmer often aggravates his pest problems and increases his dependence on chemicals by exterminating beneficial insects with broad-spectrum poisons such as dieldrin, aldrin, and Azodrin. It is worth repeating here that attempts to farm the tropics may stimulate even greater pesticide abuses than any heretofore experienced, owing both to the greater natural resistance of tropical pest populations and to the absence of a harsh winter season. This prospect makes it all the more urgent that enlightened research, such as that described by Williams, be heavily funded.

Energy is the prime mover of technology and a central ingredient of man's impact on the ecosphere. Thus, on the one hand, means to generate energy cheaply and in abundance figure prominently in technological schemes to bring prosperity to the impoverished peoples of the world. On the other hand, the environmental costs of today's energy budget move ecologists and conservationists to view massive projected increases in energy consumption with horror.

The dilemma seems particularly acute with respect to electric power, consumption of which is increasing in the United States more than twice as fast as the energy budget as a whole. It is clear, first of all, that no means of generating electricity is without its liabilities. Unexploited hydroelectric sites are in short supply, and their development compromises other values. The burning of fossil fuels pollutes the air and squanders a limited resource perhaps better saved for other uses (such as lubrication, the manufacture of synthetic materials, and protein culture). Present-day nuclear fission plants also rely on a fuel that is in limited supply, and they generate an enormous burden of radioactive wastes which must be infallibly contained and then indefinitely interred. Geothermal power is available only in certain localities, the total exploitable amount is small compared with current world energy consumption, and the underground reservoirs of superheated water, which provide the power, will be depleted after perhaps fifty years of use. Under present economic assumptions, other sources, such as solar power, do not appear to be serious contenders.

For the developed countries, at least, a possible short-term solution is available; it requires changing the economic assumptions. At a cost, fossil-fuel power plants can be made cleaner and nuclear plants safer. At a cost, even solar power could be exploited on a large scale. If the necessary measures doubled or tripled the cost of electricity, it is hard to see what truly unacceptable consequences would follow. Certainly, demand would fall, to the consternation of utilities, which have traditionally used advertising to boost consumption artificially. But it does not follow, as the conventional wisdom goes, that our "standard of living" would drop if the consumption of electricity did. Electricity (and indeed energy in general) is so cheap today that, as already noted, we squander it on the manufacture of aluminum beer cans and oversized automobiles, on space heating and air conditioning for poorly insulated homes, and in a host of other frivolous and inefficient activities. Many of them have little to do with any objectively defined standard of living.

The "need" for cheap electricity for innovative and useful industrial processes also depends on one's economic assumptions. For example, recycling steel and aluminum requires much less energy than winning the metal from ore. A significant increase in the cost of energy would therefore increase the economic attractiveness of recycling relative to the processing of new ore. The energy cost at which such processes as the gassification or liquefaction of coal become feasible depends on the price of the products. Our wasteful use of fossil fuels and many other raw materials of commerce and industry suggests that these things are badly underpriced today. If all the costs of our present habits of consumption—including the quantifiable costs of depletion and environmental degradation—are brought into the balance sheets, the more realistic prices that result will render obsolete most of today's notions about feasible and infeasible processes.

Obviously, such an approach to energy problems in the developed countries presupposes the existence of institutions capable of buffering the impact on the poor. This is a difficult problem, but we are certainly rich enough (and, it is hoped, clever enough) to manage it. In a related way, energy supply and demand in today's underdeveloped countries poses complicated questions. The need for energy to create the requisites of a decent existence is beyond dispute, and it would be inappropriate for overdeveloped countries to claim now that UDC energy consumption must level off for environmental reasons. Still, energy is only one of many ingredients of development—one can say that energy is a necessary but far from sufficient condition for prosperity. Moreover, energy accounts for only a small fraction of the *cost* of development. (It has been argued that, at present prices, the yearly capital investment needed to maintain typical power-consuming industries is on the order of 100 times the cost of the power itself.) We therefore suggest that the cost of energy is not the limiting factor in the development process today, and that it would not be so even if energy were considerably more expensive. Indeed, it is clear, for a host of reasons, that achieving increases in UDC standards of living at any meaningful rate will be a gargantuan task whether energy is "dirt cheap" or not (see, for example, *Population/ Resources/Environment*, by Paul R. Ehrlich and Anne H. Ehrlich, W. H. Freeman and Company, 1970). Real progress will require, among other things, the diversion of consumption of energy and materials from frivolous uses in the United States (and, to a lesser extent, in Europe, the USSR, and Japan) to necessity-oriented uses in the UDCs.

Obviously, such economic and behavioral changes as can be achieved will not avert entirely the question of how best to produce power. It is to be hoped that the demand for power can be stabilized in the ODCs soon, but this is not a reasonable prospect for the UDCs for a much longer time. In both cases, the means by which even a stabilized demand can be sustained in the long run, with an absorbable impact on the environment, is a crucial issue. The three alternatives that meet the basic requirement of virtually inexhaustible fuel supply are solar power, controlled thermonuclear fusion, and nuclear-fission breeder reactors. All three have liabilities at the present time. Solar power is expensive (even though the "fuel" is free), because elaborate technology is needed to compensate for the energy's low concentration and irregular distribution in space and time. Fission-breeder reactors pose problems of safety and waste disposal. (For a discussion of some technical aspects of breeders—a discussion that tries, however, to be more reassuring than is presently warranted in the matter of safety—see "Fast Breeder Reactors," by Glenn T. Seaborg and Justin L. Bloom, SCIENTIFIC AMERICAN, November 1970.) Finally, controlled thermonuclear fusion has not yet been conclusively demonstrated to be technologically feasible. And, contrary to popular belief, it is not obvious that power from either breeder reactors or fusion reactors will be particularly cheap; although fuel costs would be low, capital costs could be high enough to erase this advantage.

In our opinion, the priorities of the Federal Government in energy research do not reflect the relative importance of the liabilities just mentioned. Today, the U.S. government spends $200 million per year on breeder reactors, $30 million per year on controlled fusion, and nothing on solar power. Apparently, the only justification for the neglect of solar power is the outworn economic considerations mentioned in the foregoing paragraphs. This scandalous situation should be rectified. A compelling case can also be made for upgrading the support for controlled fusion, and William C. Gough and Bernard J. Eastlund have done so in "The Prospects of Fusion Power." This article is an outstanding successor to a distinguished series of SCIENTIFIC AMERICAN articles on fusion—including those by R. F. Post, December 1957 (available as SCIENTIFIC AMERICAN Offprint 236); Lyman Spitzer, Jr., October 1958 (SCIENTIFIC AMERICAN Offprint 246); T. K. Fowler and R. F. Post, December 1966; and F. F. Chen, July 1967. It surveys with commendable comprehensiveness the important advances of recent years in approaching the "break even" point in a controlled fusion device. Moreover, Gough and Eastlund offer thought-provoking discussions of the role of energy in man's future, and of the relative environmental costs of fusion and fission power. Without agreeing with everything in Gough and Eastlund's paper, we endorse it heartily as an important and scholarly contribution to the needed debate on energy supply, demand, and priorities.

It has been suggested with increasing frequency in some quarters that the population problem in the world in general and in the United States in particular is most often only a distribution problem. More specifically, it is argued that "pollution" is mainly the result of the concentration of too large a fraction of our population in urban areas. The implication is that population-related problems can be made to vanish by cleverly managing the way in which people distribute themselves. This proposition has at least three important flaws. The first is the assumption that population size and patterns of distribution are unrelated variables. The fallacy of this notion is exposed by Kingsley Davis in his article "The Urbanization of the Human Population." He emphasizes that distribution problems are driven by population growth itself. He writes that the dream of redistribution "would eventually obliterate the distinction between urban and rural, but at the expense of the rural." He also notes that, although the urbanization that accompanied industrialization in today's developed countries served useful purposes (for example, consolidating agricultural holdings, increasing capitalization, and improving efficiency), urbanization in the underdeveloped countries today is exacerbating already staggering sociological problems. (For a discussion of such problems attending the Green Revolution, see *Seeds of Change*, by Lester R. Brown, Praeger, 1970.)

The second flaw in the redistribution argument originates in the belief that urban air and water pollution are the only, or at least the most serious, population-related threats. In reality, of course, there are many grave problems that depend on how many people there are and on what they consume, but not, in any important way, on how they are distributed. Included in this category are the depletion of high-grade resources, the ecological consequences of agriculture, much of the environmental impact of power production, and the poisoning of global ecosystems with substances as diverse as lead, mercury, and the toxic constitutents of synthetic rubber. The seriousness of these essentially distribution-independent problems is of course compounded by the phenomena described in the articles and accompanying commentary in Sections II and III of this book. These include destructive synergisms, the potential for triggering environmental instabilities, the existence of thresholds in the capacity of an ecosystem to absorb abuse, and the time lag between some kinds of environmental insults and the appearance of their consequences.

The third shortcoming of redistribution is that such a policy would, in many cases *increase* environmental stresses. Many "underpopulated" regions are that way because they are deficient in the requisites of civilized existence: power, water, employment opportunities, agricultural potential, and high-capacity transportation networks to supply missing necessities and amenities from elsewhere. The economic and environmental costs of making these essentials available in new and relatively inhospitable areas may far exceed the costs of supporting the same increment of population in areas already densely inhabited. Consider, for example, the environmental impact of attempting to supply power and water to the vast spaces of the American Southwest.

We do not suggest, of course, that the costs of absorbing an increment of population growth are low under *any* circumstances. The serious sociological problems of our present urban areas seem especially unlikely to be resolved if the size of the unit to be "managed" continues to grow without limit. Moreover, technological "fixes" that reduce per capita contributions to urban air and water pollution, among other ills, will inevitably be cancelled by long continued population growth. Finally, the law of diminishing returns mentioned in connection with Pratt's article on fertilizers appears to be operating on a much broader front. As we move to lower-grade mineral ores, the amount of energy consumed and the waste material created to obtain a pound of metal increases dramatically. As water "needs" exceed local supplies, ever more heroic and environmentally destructive water-movement projects are required. As population growth forces more complete pollution control per capita, the costs in dollars and energy skyrocket.

It becomes increasingly clear that there are no easy solutions to the problems posed by man's growing intervention in the ecosphere that supports him. Indeed, there are no purely technical solutions at all. This is not to say that the enlightened application of technology cannot ameliorate many of these problems—it can and it must. But technology cannot relieve the burden of grappling with the deeper, nontechnological questions: the necessity of achieving the stable population size consistent with a finite system, and the development of economic and political restraints on behavior inconsistent with a fragile one.

It is difficult for citizens of this technological age to accept the concept that some problems exist for which there are no technological solutions. It strikes us as highly significant that the avoidance of nuclear war—a problem even more immediate and compelling than the others considered in these pages—seems also to belong to this class. That case is made persuasively, and certainly authoritatively, by Herbert F. York in "Military Technology and National Security." We offer his paper as the conclusion to this book of readings because we believe that even man's short-term survival hinges on the acceptance of its message: The search for national security through technology alone is the pursuit of the impossible. We believe that the search for a primarily technological route to prosperity, opportunity, and a viable ecosystem is as futile and, in the longer term, as assuredly fatal.

20

The Assessment of Technology

HARVEY BROOKS AND RAYMOND BOWERD
February 1970

Technological developments in the U.S. arise and evolve out of a multiplicity of decisions in industry, government and the marketplace. When individuals, corporations and public agencies consider exploiting or opposing a particular development, they attempt to project the potential gains and losses to themselves, and their decision usually turns on what they believe will maximize the gains and minimize the losses. This system has created an economy of great strength and versatility, but it also gives rise to troublesome imbalances that are evident in such phenomena as polluted air and deteriorating cities.

The difficulty is that self-interested analyses of the kind usually made are likely to ignore important implications of particular choices for sectors of society other than those represented in the initial decisions. In their pursuit of benefits for themselves or the segment of the public that they represent, those who make the relevant decisions often have little incentive, responsibility or authority to consider the possibility that a technological application might have undesirable consequences. For the same reasons they may fail to pursue technological opportunities that, from a broader perspective, might clearly deserve exploitation.

Rising concern over the imbalances that result has led to a number of proposals to create what is plainly lacking in the economy: a mechanism whereby the broad social effects of exploiting or restricting a technological development could be considered and effectively expressed. Among the proposals is a bill that Representative Emilio Q. Daddario of Connecticut, chairman of the Subcommittee on Science, Research and Development of the Committee on Science and Astronautics of the U.S. House of Representatives, has introduced "as a stimulant to discussion." The bill would establish a Technology Assessment Board "to provide a method for identifying, assessing, publicizing and dealing with the implications and effects of applied research and technology."

At the request of the Daddario subcommittee both the National Academy of Sciences and the National Academy of Engineering convened panels to examine the problem of assessing technology. One of us (Brooks) was chairman of the panel established by the National Academy of Sciences, and the other (Bowers) was a member of the panel; the other members are listed in the box below. This article summarizes the panel's report, *Technology: Processes of Assessment and Choice.*

At the outset it should be emphasized that the panel began with (and retained) the conviction that the advances of technology have yielded benefits that on the whole vastly outweigh the injuries they have caused. The reader should bear this attitude in mind as he considers what may seem to be a catalogue of technological deficiencies—

EDITOR'S NOTE

In addition to the authors of this article the members of the panel convened by the National Academy of Sciences to study the assessment of technology were Hendrik W. Bode of Harvard University; Edward C. Creutz of Gulf General Atomic, Inc.; A. Hunter Dupree of Brown University; Ralph W. Gerard of the University of California at Irvine; Norman Kaplan of Northeastern University; Milton Katz of Harvard University; Melvin Kranzberg of Case Western Reserve University; Hans H. Landsberg of Resources for the Future, Inc.; Gene M. Lyons of Dartmouth College; Louis H. Mayo of George Washington University; Gerard Piel of SCIENTIFIC AMERICAN; Herbert A. Simon of Carnegie-Mellon University; Cyril S. Smith of the Massachusetts Institute of Technology; Morris Tanenbaum of Western Electric, and Dael Wolfle of the American Association for the Advancement of Science. Laurence H. Tribe of Harvard University served as executive director of the panel.

instances where the technological developments chosen for exploitation now seem to have been needlessly injurious to certain social or environmental interests; instances where alternative technologies could have achieved comparable objectives at lower social cost; instances where technological developments were accompanied by inadequate or inappropriate systems of supporting institutions and technological or legal safeguards. If it appears that the panel was, to borrow an expression of a member of the panel, "quick to lament the fallen sparrow, but slow to celebrate the fall of 'Typhoid Mary,'" the reason was not that we overlooked the benefits of technology but that our mission was to explore how such benefits might be achieved with less injury to the society and the environment.

Indeed, although political attention appears to be focused now on the negative effects of technology, the panel believed an effective system of assessing technology would as often stimulate the development and application of desirable new technologies and underemployed ones as it would give warning of possibly harmful side effects. Many of the problems that are identified as undesirable results of technological development can also be seen as the result of failure to develop or apply technologies that would have mitigated the undesired effects. A scheme for the manufacture of housing units at low cost could have counteracted the deterioration of housing; improved systems of controlling air traffic would have forestalled the problem of crowded airways, and better design of power plants would have made a significant impact on the problem of air pollution.

The panel also believed an effective system of assessing technology would strengthen rather than weaken technological innovation, and could shield it from the capricious political action that will surely result if the nation moves from one social or environmental crisis to another in the absence of adequate planning. Already one can see that a number of efforts at applying technology—the routing of interstate highways, the location of airports and power plants and the development of larger and faster airplanes—are encountering unanticipated public resistance, at substantial cost not only to technology but also to the public in the form of postponed benefits. Since the progress of science in recent years has greatly broadened the spectrum of technological possibilities, the nation is in a position to choose among many technological paths to a given objective. Thus two important aspects of technology assessment are the evaluation of alternate means to the same end and a comparison of their social and economic costs.

Choices between alternative technologies are partly economic and political decisions. In our opinion it is neither feasible nor desirable to develop an assessment mechanism that would circumvent the political processes or the push and pull in the marketplace that are crucial in the accommodation of the conflicts of interest and values that must arise. We view assessment as one of many inputs to the system of private and public decisions that together shape the growth of technology and direct its integration into human life.

One can approach the problem of assessing technology in a number of ways. A standard commonly raised is that technology should be in "the public

INTERSTATE ROUTE 80, which is the light-colored road running horizontally across the center of this aerial photograph, was planned as a limited-access route between New York and San Francisco but is interrupted in Paterson, N.J., 10 miles west of New York, because of disagreement over the course it should take through the heavily urban area. Opposition to the interstate high-interest" or should maximize the "net gain to society." Such phrases have the merit of brevity and the appearance of objectivity, but it is far from clear that they convey any operationally useful meaning.

Almost without exception, technological developments will affect some people or interests beneficially and others adversely. There is no accepted arithmetic wherewith one can neatly subtract the pains from the pleasures in order to arrive at a net index of social desirability. How are the interests of suburban commuters and the residents of central cities to be balanced in the evaluation of urban transport systems? How should the future needs of radio astronomy be weighed against the present uses of television in allocating the electromagnetic spectrum? How are the desires of conservationists to be balanced against the economic needs of local industry? Because there are many values other than economic efficiency but the buyer and seller rarely confront them in their transactions, the idea of attempting to compute net social benefits is useful only as a rough first approach.

Another consideration is that a basic

way system has arisen in a number of cities because of conflict of interest between urban residents and convenience of motorists.

principle of decision-making should be to maintain the greatest practicable latitude for future action. Other things being equal, the technological projects that should be favored are the ones that leave maximum room for maneuver. The reversibility of an action should thus be counted as a major benefit, its irreversibility as a major cost.

Policy-making should therefore reflect the fact, for example, that pollution of a lake is more difficult to reverse than pollution of a river, or that the disposal of municipal wastes in streams may create an overload that is harder to reverse than disposal on land would be. (The recycling of wastes, which has only begun to be considered on a large scale, provides a major opportunity for lowering the irreversibility of the disposal process.) The construction of dams and reservoirs, which fill up with silt and hence have a finite life, precludes the possibility of using the same sites for waterworks when waterworks may be more urgently needed.

Another approach is to consider where the burden of uncertainty should fall when the consequences of a contemplated action can only be surmised and when its costs and benefits cannot be clearly assessed. Historically the burden has tended to fall on those who challenge the wisdom of a technological trend. The usual presumption has been that such a trend ought to be allowed to continue as long as it can be expected to yield a profit for those who are exploiting it, and that any harmful consequences that might ensue either will be manageable or will not be serious enough to warrant a decision to interfere with the technology. So it was, for example, that drilling rights were leased to oil companies operating in the Santa Barbara Channel without sufficient consideration of the possible effects of massive oil leakage near the coast and with inadequate preventive measures to minimize the damages; that vast quantities of chemicals have been released into the biosphere with little attention to their potential hazard; that the number of internal-combustion automobiles has been allowed to mount steadily with only sporadic efforts to study alternatives that would entail less pollution and crowding, and that repeated decisions have been made to proceed with a supersonic transport although the problem of sonic boom has yet to be solved.

The panel believed there should be limits on the extent to which any major technology is allowed to proliferate or to stagnate without the gathering of evidence on the possible harmful effects and on the relative merits of alternatives. The nation's experience with certain chemical pesticides is strongly suggestive. Although the pesticides have undoubtedly prevented a great many deaths from starvation and disease, it is now apparent that they have also inflicted unintended but widespread losses of fish and wildlife, and it is increasingly suspected that they are causing injury to man. The experience suggests that carefully designed experiments in the early days might have influenced the technology of pesticides before the nation was so committed to certain forms of pest control as to make any significant alteration of the technology extremely difficult. Knowledge has advanced to the point where, in spite of many uncertainties, it is possible to predict at least some of the ecological effects of building another Aswân Dam or opening a sea-level canal through the Isthmus of Panama, or the effects of paving and housing on the reflectivity of the earth's surface, or the effects of high-altitude aircraft exhaust on the radiation balance of the earth. The panel saw an obligation to undertake the necessary research and monitoring at the earliest possible stages of development.

All these considerations—the questions concerning the general welfare, the preservation of options and the burden of uncertainty—reflect a lack of constituencies potent enough to inject diffuse and poorly articulated interests into the decision-making process. Here one encounters not only the lack of effective voices in opposition to a potentially harmful technology but also the problem of finding support for a potentially desirable technology that is opposed by vested interests. When a faster or cheaper building technique might affect alignments in the construction industry, for example, one can rely on opposition from those interests but not on organized advocacy from residents of the ghetto who might benefit from cheaper housing. The difficulty lies not with groups that perceive their interests to be affected but rather with the representation of groups for whom the consequences are less obvious and more remote. The panel was convinced that more must be done to give all affected interests effective representation in the crucial processes of decision.

The existing processes of technology assessment are diffused throughout the society in both the private and the governmental sectors. In the private sec-

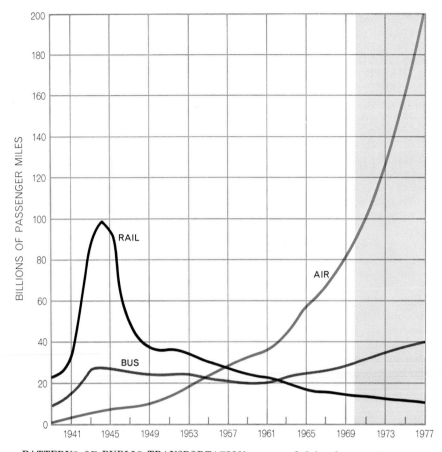

PATTERNS OF PUBLIC TRANSPORTATION are recorded for the past 30 years and projected to 1977 on the basis of information assembled by the National Academy of Engineering. The chart covers domestic intercity travel by railroad, bus and airplane.

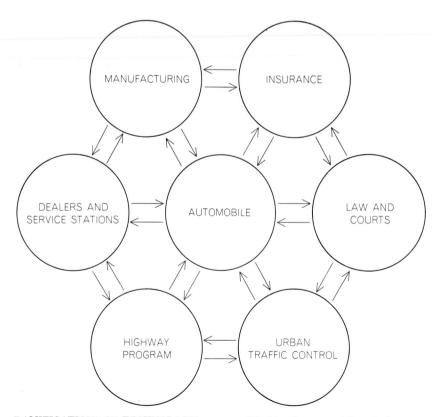

RAMIFICATIONS OF TECHNOLOGY are exemplified by the automobile, which represents a system of social and technological activities with a combined effect on the environment. The elements of the system also interact, as indicated by the arrows between circles.

tor technology assessment takes place whenever a business enterprise contemplates an investment that would introduce a new technology or expand or modify its use of an existing technology. In the larger industrial enterprises the assessment takes place in connection with research and development. Assessment is also done by the investment companies and banks to which business enterprises turn for capital.

Whether or not the assessors are aware of the fact, the existing legal order infuses their calculations. It determines which of the anticipated costs and benefits are taken into account by the enterprise and which are ignored. A power company, for example, that contemplates the installation of a new generating station will treat the fuel to be consumed as a cost but not the smoke that may pollute the surrounding air or the waste products that may be discharged into nearby streams. Pollution of the community's air or streams is not legally charged against the company; it is a social cost and not a cost to the enterprise. The legal system can change this relationship by laws or court decisions that put on the company the burden previously borne by the public in the form of air or water pollution.

The assessment of technology that is done by governmental agencies is also profoundly affected by the legal system. The predominant mission of each agency, as set forth in the law, determines its pattern of assessing technology. Weather modification provides an example. The Bureau of Reclamation looks for ways to increase rainfall in the dry Western states. The Department of Agriculture, mainly concerned with reducing crop losses, sponsors research in suppressing storm damage. The Federal Aviation Administration is interested in ways to dissipate fogs that hang over airports. None of these agencies considers the total effects. In the case of regulatory agencies, limitations by law often prevent the agency from considering the complete problem.

Within the set of governmental and market processes the initial assessment of the costs and benefits of alternative technologies is normally undertaken by those who seek to exploit them. As a result the frame of reference is often quite limited. Although such groups as professional societies and conservation organizations may add inputs to the evaluation, the assessment is usually based on the contending interests of those who already recognize their stake in the technology and are prepared to enter the public arena to defend their position. In

213

KENNEDY INTERNATIONAL AIRPORT near New York has only one major road (*top center*) for ground traffic, and there is no rail service between the airport and the city. The question is wheth- er, with the increasing number of flights and the introduction of "jumbo jets" carrying more than 350 passengers, the ground facili- ties will match the sophisticated technology of the airport itself.

all but a few cases, usually when Congress takes a special interest, no other assessment occurs. The central question asked is what will the technology do for the economic and institutional interests of those who want to exploit it or to the interests of those with a stake in competing technologies. If the technology leads to social problems, they are usually recognized only when they have reached serious proportions and generated acute public concern.

The achievement of a better system for assessing technology faces major obstacles. The society is ill equipped to handle conflicting interests. It does not know how to value in a quantitative way such goals as a clean environment and the preservation of future choices. Analytical tools are primitive, and crucial knowledge is often missing.

Projections of the impact of technology are limited by failure or inadequacy of imagination, particularly in forecasting cumulative effects of scale. For example, the number of television sets in the U.S. rose from 100,000 in 1948 to a million a year later and 50 million a decade later. The social and psychological consequences of such an explosive growth are hard to contemplate, let alone predict.

The history of asbestos demonstrates the effects of scale in one of its most insidious forms. Asbestos is so diversely useful that it has found its way into every automobile, train, airplane, factory and home and thence into human lungs, where, remaining as indestructible as it is in nature, it can cause grave disease. So too with the proliferation of automobiles: as recently as 1958 an authoritative book on the consequences of

the automobile failed to mention atmospheric pollution.

A closely related problem has resulted from the failure to foresee the supporting systems that new technologies would demand. One can fly from London to New York in six hours and then encounter difficulties getting from the airport to the city because the roads are often crowded and there is no rail service between the city and the major airports. Courts of law have huge backlogs, in large part because of litigation involving automobile-accident claims.

Political and jurisdictional problems also abound. When a city discharges untreated sewage into a river without consideration of the effect on communities downstream, or a nation engages in a cloud-seeding experiment or conducts a nuclear test without concern for its effects on other countries, the reason is

TECHNOLOGICAL DEVELOPMENTS foreseen by panelists consulted by the Institute for the Future are charted, with developments in the physical sciences at left and developments in the biological sciences at right. Each polygon represents estimates made

that a decision-making unit smaller than the area affected by the decision tends to view the effects as someone else's problem. There is also artificial narrowness of jurisdiction. The Army recently denied permission for a private dredging-and-filling operation in navigable waters of Florida, responding to the argument of health and conservation agencies that the project would injure fish and wildlife. A Federal court overturned the decision on the ground that the law makes interference with navigation the only basis for refusing permission to dredge and fill.

Our conclusion was that the best place to begin the formidable task of improving the assessment of technology is the Federal Government, which is already deeply involved in the support and regulation of technology. If the Fed-

eral Government can point the way to more responsible management of technological change, it will have accomplished no mean task; if it cannot, little more can be expected of other institutions in the society.

In recommending new Federal mechanisms for supplementing and broadening the present means of assessing technology, we were mindful of several principles that ought to guide the new procedure. To maintain its credibility among diverse interests, a new mechanism for assessing technology must adopt as neutral a stance as possible. For this reason it should not have policy-making authority, regulatory powers or responsibility for promoting any particular technology. Unlike the Atomic Energy Commission, for example, it should not be charged with advancing reactor technology and at the same time pro-

moting radiation safety. Unlike the Federal Aviation Administration, the new mechanism should not be entrusted with the realization of a supersonic transport. Unlike the Public Health Service, it must not be held responsible for protecting the public from hazardous drugs. To give it responsibilities of this kind would clearly generate internal conflicts of interest.

A governmental institution assessing technology must also be sensitive to the dangers of the process. The major danger is that the institution could stultify the delicate mechanisms of technological innovation by magnifying risks or ignoring the possibility of finding solutions. If innovation is discouraged, the cure may be worse than the disease. Hence the new entity must be given no authority to screen or "clear" new technological undertakings. In short, it

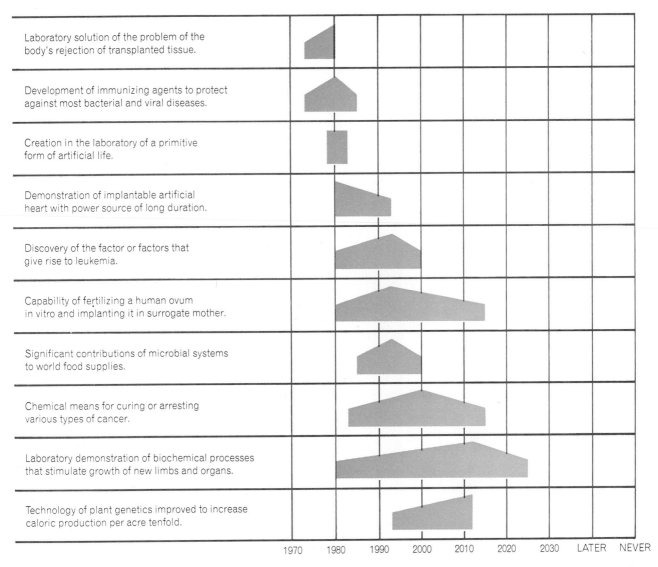

by half of the group; estimates by the quarter of the panel that foresaw an earlier date and the quarter that chose a later one are ex-

cluded. Peak of each polygon indicates the median date when the panelists foresaw a 50 percent chance that the event would occur.

should be empowered to study and recommend but not to act; it must be able to evaluate but not to sponsor or prevent.

At the same time, any new assessment mechanism must be influential. It would have no hope of materially affecting public policy unless it were located close to the centers of political power. Accordingly there must be a close relation between some component of the new mechanism and the President, and some component of the new mechanism must be linked closely to Congress. The new entity must be designed to supplement, coordinate and improve the multiplicity of existing mechanisms rather than to supersede them. We rejected the concept of a highly centralized process of technology assessment as being unworkable in practice and even dangerous in principle.

With these considerations in mind the panel recommended the creation of a constellation of organizations that would have components located strategically in both the executive and the legislative branch of the Government and would constitute both a focus and a forum for technology-assessment activities throughout government and the private sector. For the executive branch the recommendation is that the President's Office of Science and Technology be expanded and given the authority to collect information on technology assessment, make an annual report on priorities in the area, initiate conferences and prepare policy papers. This office would review specific assessments carried out by other agencies but would confine the review to an evaluation of the criteria, procedures and evidence used and the adequacy of the representation of potentially affected interests. The Office of Science and Technology would cooperate with a new Technology Assessment Division of the National Science Foundation, which would award contracts and grants for the assessment of specific developments and for research on methods of assessment. Most of the work would be done in nongovernmental agencies such as universities, independent research organizations and industry.

For Congress the recommendation is the creation of either a Joint Congressional Committee on Technology Assessment or a Technology Assessment Office that would be an arm of Congress analogous to the Legislative Reference Service or the General Accounting Office. In either case the principal functions of the mechanism would be to provide Congress with better access to the professional judgments it needs in considering assessments of technology and to provide within or close to Congress a forum for the assessment activities of individuals or groups operating outside present government and industrial institutions. Existing committees of Congress do not seem promising in these respects because of fragmentation by jurisdictional divisions and internal rivalries.

The panel considered and rejected the idea of an independent Federal commission. Such a body would have the advantage of freedom from political interference, but the separation of the assessment process from the center of political decisions seemed too high a price to pay.

One major matter that received little attention from the panel is the assessment of military technology. The reason was its special character: military technology is strongly conditioned by the interpretation of intelligence, and much of the technological information is classified. Control over the flow of this information, however, is effectively in the hands of people who assess technology only in terms of national security, viewed in the narrowest sense. Our panel was convinced of the importance of establishing some mechanism for the assessment of military technology by a group of experts having the requisite security clearance but without direct responsibility for national security. Presumably such a group could bring broader social, political and environmental considerations to bear on the assessment of military technology.

Our panel was convinced that, however our specific recommendations might be viewed, some form of constructive action to improve the assessment of technology is imperative and that it cannot be long delayed without increasing the difficulty of implementation and diminishing the prospects of success. The future of technology holds great promise for mankind if greater thought and effort are devoted to its development. If society persists in its present course, however, the future holds great peril, whether from the uncontrolled effects of technology itself or from an unreasoned political reaction against technological innovation—a reaction that could condemn mankind to poverty, frustration and the loss of freedom.

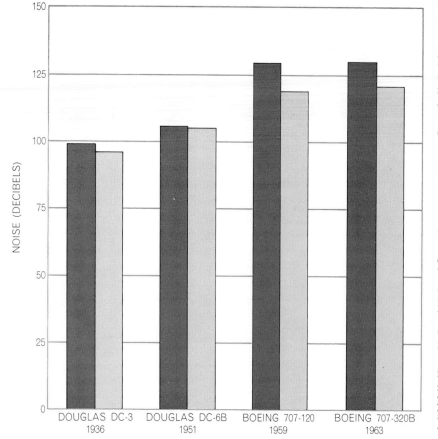

AIRCRAFT NOISE has increased with the weight and propulsive power of transport planes. Dark bars represent noise on takeoff, light bars landing noise. Dates refer to the year when the aircraft was introduced into widespread airline service. The prospect of supersonic transports and the certainty that the airlines will use more planes and make more flights indicate that noise problem will become worse unless an effort is made to reduce it.

SMOKE EMISSION of a Boeing 727 jet aircraft is reduced by the redesign of combustion chambers and fuel nozzles in an experiment undertaken to reduce air pollution. Above is the takeoff of an airplane that has not undergone the smoke-reducing adapta- tions; below, an aircraft of the same type takes off after the adaptations have been made. A number of states and communities have been pressing the airlines to reduce the emission of smoke by jet aircraft by converting engines or installing smokeless ones.

IRRIGATED LAND of small-holders' settlement near Sea of Galilee (*visible through gap in background*) is watered by aluminum sprinkler pipes supplied from wells. Fields are planted to garden crops and to forage for dairy cattle. On slope in foreground, still green from winter rains, is an old olive grove. Land is rented from the state on 49-year leases with rental at 2 per cent of land value.

DESERT LAND in the Negev is made to support forage crops by diversion of flash-flood water, after methods employed by ancient Nabataeans. Water is trapped in basin fields, held long enough to soak the ground and then passed on to the field below over concrete spillways such as that under construction here. Agricultural engineering students inspecting site are armed against border raids.

21

The Reclamation of a Man-Made Desert

WALTER C. LOWDERMILK
March 1960

The State of Israel has undertaken to create a new agriculture in an old and damaged land. The 20th-century Israelites did not find their promised land "flowing with milk and honey," as their forebears did 3,300 years ago. They came to a land of encroaching sand dunes along a once-verdant coast, of malarial swamps and naked limestone hills from which an estimated three feet of topsoil had been scoured, sorted and spread as sterile overwash upon the plains or swept out to sea in flood waters that time after time turned the beautiful blue of the Mediterranean to a dirty brown as far as the horizon. The land of Israel had shared the fate of land throughout the Middle East. A decline in productivity, in population and in culture had set in with the fading of the Byzantine Empire some 1,300 years ago. The markers of former forest boundaries on treeless slopes and the ruins of dams, aqueducts and terraced irrigation works, of cities, bridges and paved highways—all bore witness that the land had once supported a great civilization with a much larger population in a higher state of well-being.

Last year, as a finale to the celebration of the 10th anniversary of the founding of the State of Israel, an international convention brought 485 farmers from 37 countries to see what had been accomplished. They found a nation of two million people, whose numbers had doubled in the decade, principally by immigration. Yet Israel was already an exporter of agricultural produce and had nearly achieved the goal of agricultural self-sufficiency, with an export-import balance in foodstuffs. It had more than doubled its cultivated land, to a million acres. It had drained 44,000 acres of marshland and extended irrigation to 325,000 acres; it had increased many-fold the supply of underground water from wells and was far along on the work of diverting and utilizing the scant surface waters. On vast stretches of uncultivable land it had established new range-cover to support a growing livestock industry and planted 37 million trees in new forests and shelter belts. All this had been accomplished under a national plan that enlisted the devotion of the citizens and the best understanding and technique provided by modern agricultural science. Israel is not simply restoring the past but seeking full utilization of the land, including realization of potentialities that were unknown to the ancients.

For the visiting farmers, many of whom came from the newer and less developed nations of the world, the example of Israel was a proof and a promise. Civilization is in a race with famine. The doubt as to the outcome is due not so much to the limitations of the earth's resources, plundered as they are, but to a lag in the uptake of progressive agricultural practices and failure in the distribution of the present output of food. More than two thirds of the people of the world are undernourished. Most of them live in the lands where mankind has lived longest in organized societies. There, with few exceptions, the soil is in the worst condition. The example of Israel shows that the land can be reclaimed and that increase in the food supply can overtake the population increase that will double the 2,800-million world population before the end of this century. Israel is a pilot area for the arid lands of the world, especially those of her Arab neighbors, who persist in their destitution in the same landscape that Israel has brought into blossom.

The achievement of Israel is the more remarkable for the fact that politics showed little regard for the logic of terrain and watershed in setting the boundaries of the state. The 7,815 square miles allocated to Israel in the 1948 partition of Palestine make a narrow strip of land along the eastern shore of the Mediterranean, roughly 265 miles long and 12 to 70 miles wide. It comprises only part of the Jordan River Valley, the principal watercourse of the region, with its three lakes: Lake Huleh, 230 feet above sea level at the northern end; the Sea of Galilee, nine miles to the south and 680 feet below sea level; and the Dead Sea, 65 miles farther south and 1,290 feet below sea level. More than half of Israel's territory is occupied by true desert or near desert, and the principal agricultural acreage lies on the narrow coastal plain, on the northern uplands and on the western slope of the Jordan Valley from Lake Huleh downstream to 25 miles below the Sea of Galilee, where Israel's boundary comes down to the river. This division of territory and the persistent hostility of Israel's Arab neighbors continue to frustrate programs to realize the full benefits of the water supply to all concerned in a region where water is scarce.

Climatically Israel much resembles California. Rains come in winter, and the summers are long and dry. Moreover, the erratic rainfall varies considerably from one end of the country to the other, from an average of 42 inches in the north, to 26 inches at Jerusalem, to less than two inches at Eilat on the Gulf of Aqaba at the foot of the desert of the Negev. Temperatures range to similar extremes over short distances, being cool at high elevations and hot and tropical in the Jordan Valley. In the spring a hot, dry wind, called the khamsin, may blow for days at a time out of the desert to the east, with calamitous effect upon unprotected crops. Harsh as these conditions are, there has been no significant deterioration in climate since Roman times. The same plants still thrive in protected places, and springs recorded in the Bible still bubble from the ground. The "desert" that took over the once-flourishing land was the work of man, not of nature.

Fortunately one geologic feature operates in favor of the conservation of rainfall; the porous limestone of the landscape absorbs a high percentage of the rain and distributes the water widely from the regions of heaviest fall through labyrinthine aquifers underground. The total discharge from springs exceeds the flow of the Jordan: a single great spring near the foothills of Judea gives rise to the Yarkon River. Another important source of water, the heavy summer dew, helps crops to grow in the uplands.

The agricultural restoration of Israel began in the 1880's, with the arrival of the first immigrants brought by the emergent Zionist movement as refugees from the pogroms of Eastern Europe. They were able to buy "useless" marshland on the coastal plain. These marshes had been created by the shoaling of erosion-laden streams and by the damming effect of the inland march of sand dunes. With heroic labor the early settlers succeeded in draining the marshes and farming them successfully. But until

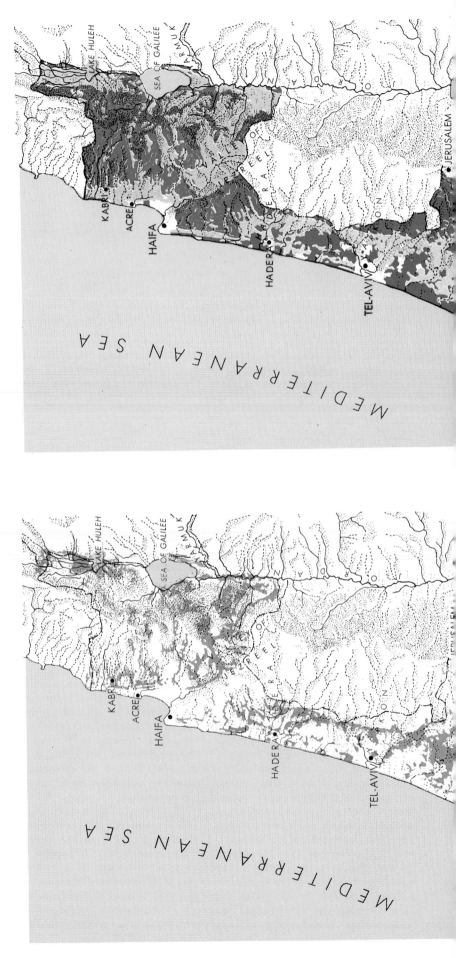

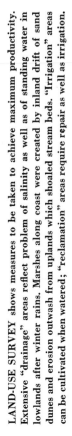

SOIL-RESOURCES SURVEY, covering those areas where water is or can be made available for agriculture, shows the effects of 1,300 years of misuse of the land. Most "very severe" erosion areas are beyond reclamation for cultivation and have been downgraded to forest and pasture or to wasteland. "Severe" erosion areas are reclaimable when watered; "moderate" areas can be restored by using elementary measures of soil management.

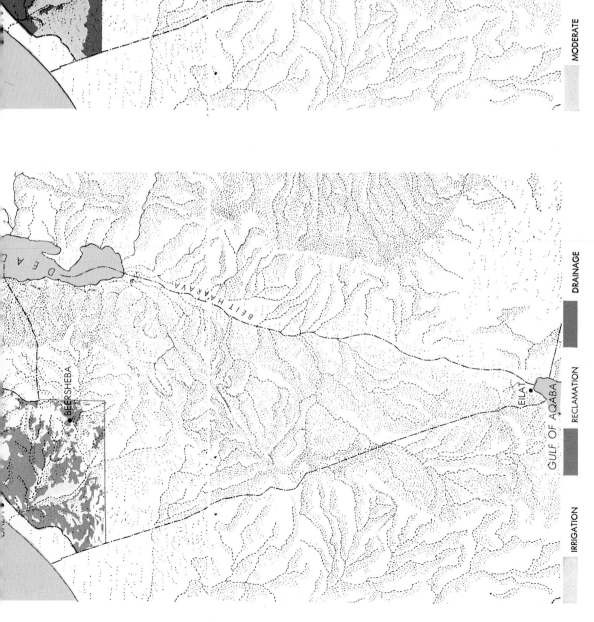

LAND-USE SURVEY shows measures to be taken to achieve maximum productivity. Extensive "drainage" areas reflect problem of salinity as well as of standing water in lowlands after winter rains. Marshes along coast were created by inland drift of sand dunes and erosion outwash from uplands which shoaled stream beds. "Irrigation" areas can be cultivated when watered; "reclamation" areas require repair as well as irrigation.

CONTOUR FARMING in Jezreel Valley is being extended to all slopes that exceed the safe gradient for "safe-line" farming. Steeper slopes are terraced and crops are rotated on contour strips. These practices prevent erosion and conserve the rainfall on fields.

the State of Israel was established, the effort was on a "first aid" basis.

When the new government set out to frame a comprehensive program for the development of the country's soil and water resources, it could call upon a number of outstanding authorities among its own citizens: specialists in forestry, horticulture, soil science, plant breeding and civil engineering who had come as refugees from Germany and Central Europe. But with a major por-

tion of its expanding population coming from the Arab countries of North Africa and the Near East, Israel did not have enough experts in the many disciplines needed to establish a modern agriculture in short order. The government therefore was among the first to draw upon the technical assistance offered by the specialized agencies of the United Nations and by the "Point Four" program of the U. S. I had the rewarding experience of sharing in this work as a

member of missions that served in Israel under the Food and Agriculture Organization of the U.N. from 1951 to 1953, consulting in the establishment of a national program of land development and in building up a staff of men to carry it out; and again from 1955 to 1957 helping to build a department of agricultural engineering at Technion, the Israeli institute of technology.

The first order of business, begun in 1951 and completed in 1953, was the

OLD SETTLEMENT of small-holders at Nahalal is laid out on the eastern European pattern with the village at center, surrounded by individual truck-garden farms, each seven acres in extent.

CITRUS GROVES, managed on a cooperative basis, support a com-

SOIL RECLAMATION has halted gully erosion and brought a limited area of heavily eroded soil under cultivation in the northern Negev. The soils in this region developed a "bad land" topography during centuries in which they were stripped of grass cover.

taking of a comprehensive inventory of the land. This comprises the 2.38 million acres north of the 60th parallel, about half the territory of Israel, where major agricultural development is possible. One of the most thorough inventories of its kind in the world, it furnished a secure foundation for land-use policy and for the immense task of reclamation and water development that has followed. Classification of the inventoried land by end-use shows that,

given adequate water supply, about 40 per cent, or a million acres, can be made suitable for general cultivation; about 15 per cent for orchard, vineyard, pasture and other use that will keep a permanent plant cover on the soil; 20 per cent for natural pasture without irrigation; and 25 per cent for forests, parks and wasteland. Outside the area of detailed survey, in the Negev, an extensive reconnaissance has projected a program for range development and

for the cultivation of forage crops in those areas where the scant winter runoff can be diverted or impounded to support irrigation.

A major feature of the land inventory was the classification of the lands according to their relative exposure to erosion by wind and water. In the hands of the Israeli Soil Conservation Service this has served as a blueprint for measures to preserve the best soils and ultimately to reclaim land now

munity on the Sharon Plain. Taller eucalyptus trees shelter groves.

NEW SETTLEMENT has begun to farm land opened up to cultivation by irrigation and soil-conservation measures. Open center of the village is eventually to be occupied by service buildings.

IRRIGATION BY SPRINKLING is the method that has proved most economical in bringing water to the field in Israel. Aluminum pipes are moved from field to field as needed.

unusable. The hazard of erosion increases in geometrical ratio with increase in the gradient of the soil. The first line of defense is directed against the dynamics of the falling raindrop and includes measures of soil management that are also required for sustained crop yields such as the build-up of organic matter to increase the water-holding capacity of the soil and the use of crop litter to absorb the energy and reduce the splash-erosion of the raindrop. Contour plowing and the planting of crops in strips along the contour provide the second line of defense and usually suffice against the hazards of moderate storms. These defenses can be set up by the individual farmer or farm cooperative and are everywhere encouraged through education and demonstration by the Soil Conservation Service. But rains in Israel characteristically come in downpours, in a few heavy storms during the rainy season and in extreme storms every few years. Where such rains overtax the first two lines of defense, more elaborate and costly measures must be designed and laid out by soil-conservation engineers of the Soil Conservation Service. Slopes must be broken by broadbase terraces to pick up and slow storm runoff and the terraces must be interconnected by waterways to keep the accumulated water from cutting gullies through the fields. Storm waters are then available for storage in surface ponds and reservoirs or to recharge ground waters. This line of defense must be accurately and adequately engineered, for running waters do not forgive a mistake or oversight in design.

One of the effects of man-induced erosion in the past was the creation of marshes on the narrow coastal plain, notably at Hadera, Kabri and in the Jezreel Valley. Carrying through the work started by the early settlers, Israel has now fully reclaimed these lands, draining and planting them to eucalyptus trees in the lowest spots and to citrus groves and crops on the higher ground.

A more substantial engineering challenge was presented by the marshlands of the Huleh basin at the head of the Jordan Valley. In Roman times and before, this region was fertile and thickly populated, but it had become a dismal swamp and a focus of malarial infection to the country at large. Sediments from the uplands to the north had progressively filled in the northern end of Lake Huleh, thus creating a marsh that was overgrown with papyrus. The marshes have now been drained by widening and deepening the mouth of the lake to bring down its water level and by a system of drainage canals. With the papyrus cleared away, the deep deposit of peat beneath yields richly to cultivation, much as do the delta peat-lands at the head of San Francisco Bay. The Huleh Reclamation Authority estimates that this little Garden of Eden will support a population of 100,000 in an intensive agricultural economy, cultivating

vegetables, grapes, fruits, peanuts, grains, sugar cane, rice—even fish (in ponds impounded on the old lake bed). The yield of fruits and vegetables will soon require the installation of processing and canning plants on the spot. Another gain achieved by the reclamation of this land is the conservation of water; the reduction of the evaporation surface of the lake and surrounding marshes will save enough water to irrigate 17,000 to 25,000 acres of land, depending on the rainfall of the district to which these waters will be delivered. The Huleh Drainage and Irrigation Project is not great in size, but it symbolizes the determination of Israel to make the most of its resources.

The development of water supplies and irrigation constitutes the most significant achievement of the new nation and differentiates its agriculture most sharply from that which prevails in all but a few areas in the surrounding Arab countries. Since the time of Abraham, when "there was famine in the land," agriculture in this region has been at the mercy of the variable winter rainfall. In ancient Palestine irrigation was limited to small areas that could be fed by gravity from perennial springs. These works had long since fallen into disuse, and at the beginning of this century very little of the Holy Land was irrigated. In 10 years the State of Israel has quadrupled the acreage under irrigation, from 72,500 to·325,000 acres. It was this achievement that made possible the absorption of the great influx of immigrants. Irrigation has increased yields per acre from three to six times and more over those achieved by dry farming in the region and has secured dependable yields from year to year.

With most of the water coming from wells, irrigation in Israel is accomplished by sprinkling, rather than by furrow or border ditch. The grid of pumps and pipes delivers the water under pressure but at low rates of flow. Irrigation engineers soon found that sprinkling was best adapted to this mode of delivery and for application of the water to sandy soils and to rougher, stony land unsuited for leveling. The high investment in pumps and piping has been more than offset by the intensive year-round cultivation made possible by irrigation and by the urgent need to settle immigrants in self-supporting activity on the lands. Each year from 25,000 to 30,000 additional acres are being brought under irrigation, and the prospect is that this will continue until the limit of water supply is reached.

Meanwhile extensive field research

is devoted to achieving the most efficient use of water. In the northern Negev, for example, it has been found that about six inches of irrigation water, applied just before the winter rains to soak the soil to its water-holding capacity down to a depth of about four feet, will make up the equivalent of 20 inches of rainfall, sufficient for winter grain. In many soils irrigation raises a serious drainage problem. Evaporation from the soil and transpiration by crops in the "consumptive" use of the water leave behind the salts it carries in solution. After a few years the accumulation of salts may reach toxic proportions. Certain crops, such as sugar beets, take up some salts and may be planted in rotation to reduce this accumulation. But whatever the crop, drainage must be provided in time to leach away the salts, and the chemical composition of the soil must be kept under surveillance.

To bring much of the land under irrigation and cultivation has required strenuous repair of the damage done by centuries of erosion. The slopes in stony soils are typically covered by an "erosion pavement" made up of stones too heavy to be moved by rain splash and by the sheet flow of the storm runoff that carried away the topsoil. In some parts of the country, farmers have raked these stones from the fields and piled them into great heaps. Where erosion has exposed the rock or gullied the deep soils beyond plowing, the land has been put to some lower use, such as rough pasture or woodlot. In many parts of the highlands modern farmers have been able to take advantage of the soil-conservation works of the ancient Phoenicians. My own investigations indicate that the Phoenicians, 3,000 to 4,000 years ago, were the first people in the Middle East to clear and cultivate mountain slopes under rainfall agriculture and so were the first to encounter soil erosion. They were also the first to control soil erosion by using the principle of the contour and by building stone walls to convert a slope into a series of level benches. Most of these ancient terraces had been allowed to fall in ruins. Today they are being reconstructed and redesigned. Since the terraces are narrow and so suited only to hand labor, the practice is to collect the stones from old terrace walls and to pile them into ridges spaced more widely apart on the contour, creating terraces with gentle gradients for cultivation by tractor-drawn farm implements. Under sprinkler irrigation the new terraces are proving to be favorable sites for vineyards and orchards.

Over the large stretches of the coun-

SAND DUNES carried inland from coast have been encroaching for centuries upon arable land. Dunes are now being held in place by planting and even reclaimed for cultivation.

FLASH FLOOD from winter downpour rushes over ruins of ancient desert irrigation works in northern Negev. Waterfall in foreground demonstrates gully-cutting action of floods.

PLOWING BY CAMEL in Gaza Strip on Israeli border reflects survival of primitive agricultural practices that over the past millennium have wasted the soil resources of the region.

try that are beyond such reclamation and are too dry for forests, the effort is to develop the land for pasture. Throughout the Near and Middle East and North Africa the land has been overgrazed for more than 1,000 years. What sheep will not eat, goats will, and what the goats leave, camels will graze. By the time these hardy animals have ranged over the land through the long, hot, rainless summer, there is little plant cover left to protect the soil from the winter rains. But if one may judge by the relict species of forage grasses and plants that survive in rocky places and thorn thickets beyond the reach of goats and camels, it may be surmised that this land was once a pastoral paradise. The prompt return of a good cover of grasses and herbs after the goats were removed from the land by the Israeli Government in 1948 confirms this appraisal. The Soil Conservation Service has since been reseeding the range with native plants and with species imported from the U. S. and South Africa. In addition, certain woody bushes and low trees are being planted to hold the soil and furnish browse for livestock; the rich beans of the hardy carob tree, for example, yield as much

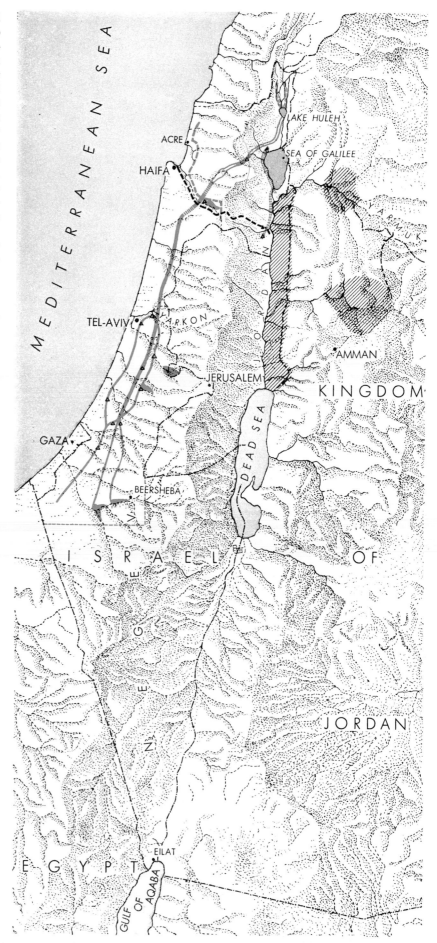

═══ JORDAN-NEGEV CANAL

▒▒▒ JORDAN-NEGEV TUNNEL

▬▬▬ JORDAN-NEGEV PIPELINE

─── YARKON-NEGEV PIPELINE

- - - WESTERN GALILEE PROJECT

▬ ▬ ▬ HULEH DRAINAGE CANALS

▪▪▪▪ OTHER PROJECTS

■ ■ ■ MEDITERRANEAN-JORDAN POWER PROJECT

⌒ DAMS

▨ YARMUK YABOQ SCHEME

▲ POWER PLANT

△ PUMPING PLANT

◆ POWER AND PUMPING PLANT

MASTER WATER PLAN of Israel (*color*) is based upon plan originally designed to maximize water resources for entire Jordan River Valley, including both Israel and what is now the Kingdom of Jordan. Basic scheme calls for diversion of water from the head of the Valley, where rainfall is heaviest, to arid lands in the south. Via the Jordan-Negev canal, a tunnel and a 108-inch pipeline now under construction, water from Lake Huleh region is to be carried to the Negev, with additional water from the Yarkon River being carried by the Yarkon-Negev pipelines. The Mediterranean-Jordan Power Project and Yarmuk-Yaboq scheme await cooperation and action by Jordan.

feed as an equal planting of barley. Measures to divert and spread the storm waters over the pastures are further increasing the yield. Herds of beef and dairy cattle are now beginning to multiply on the restored range.

Early in the Jewish immigration to Israel the planting of trees came to be a symbol of faith in the future. Afforestation now plays a central role in the control of erosion, in reclamation of stony hills and in sheltering orchards and garden plots from the winds, whether from the sea or the desert. Some 250 million trees, both native and imported species selected by the Israeli Forest Experiment Station, are to be planted in the next 10 years. The growing of stock in the nurseries and the planting of trees on uncultivated hillsides, on roadsides, in shelter belts and on sand dunes provides interim employment for new immigrants until they become established. Already the new stands are yielding timber, poles and fuel products—valuable commodities in a deforested land.

The land inventory has served to protect the best agricultural lands from being engulfed by the growing cities and towns of Israel. Along the coast, for example, the communities have been encouraged to expand their boundaries into the sand dunes rather than into surrounding cultivable land. The dunes comprise 10 per cent of the coastal land and, under the drag of the prevailing westerly winds, are overwhelming good land, orchards and even houses. Experiments are under way to hold the shifting dunes by stabilizing the sand surface and by aggregating sand grains into crumb structures. This is accomplished by plantings of hardy shrubs and sand grasses, and of such fibrous-rooted plants as alfalfa, with water supplied to some tracts by sewage effluent and partially rectified sewage water. The rapid growth of the plants where this has been tried converts the sand in a few years into a stable soil-like material suited to the planting of trees and even some crops. But the full reclamation of the dunes to agricultural use is still in the research stage.

Ultimately the expansion of agriculture is limited by the availability of water. The Israeli Water Planning Agency is seeking to double the 1956 water supply by 1966, giving the country a total of 14.5 million acre feet (an acre foot is 12 inches of water per acre) per year. A central feature of the plan derives from a survey that I conducted in 1938

CONCRETE PIPE 70 inches in diameter for Yarkon-Negev pipeline is delivered to location where it is to be set in place in a great trench and buried. This line will carry water from the Yarkon River in the north to the arid lands of the Negev (*see map on page 131*).

and 1939 for the U. S. Department of Agriculture and from the proposal, growing out of that survey, of a Jordan Valley Authority to achieve the fullest development of the surface and underground waters of the valley for the entire original Mandate under the League of Nations, including what is now the Kingdom of Jordan as well as Israel. That proposal called for the development of ground waters and diversion of the upper Jordan waters within Israel to the dry lands in the south and for the diversion of the waters of the Yarmuk River to the eastern side of the Jordan Valley for irrigation of a promising subtropical region in Transjordan. In order to replace the flow of these rivers into the Dead Sea, salt water was to be brought in from the Mediterranean Sea through canals and tunnels to drop through two sets of hydropower stations nearly 1,300 feet below sea level to the Dead Sea. This salt water would not only produce electric power but also would maintain the level of the Dead Sea for the extraction of the minerals and chemicals that are there in fabulous amounts. The plan was declared feasible by an international consulting board of engineers. All parts of the plan that do not require the collaboration of the adjoining Arab states are now being carried out by the Israeli Government. The prestressed-concrete sections of the main 108-inch pipeline that will carry upper Jordan water down as far as the Negev are now being fabri-

cated and set in place in a great trench, and the tunnels to carry it through intervening hills are under construction.

Beyond this major undertaking the country is conserving for use and reuse such minor flows of water as are represented by the sewage of its cities and the runoff of intermittent streams along the coast. In the southern Negev, where the annual rainfall is less than six inches, the Soil Conservation Service is adopting the methods of ancient Nabataeans to impound the waters of flash floods for the irrigation of forage crops.

Prospects for the future have recently been brightened by progress in the desalting of sea water. A new method developed in the laboratories of the Government is about to be tested in two pilot plants, each with an output of 250,000 gallons per day. Success in this undertaking would be a major victory not only for Israel but also for all the other arid-land countries of the world.

On the anvil of adversity the State and people of Israel have been hammering out solutions to problems that other nations must sooner or later face up to. There are no more continents left to explore or to exploit. The best lands of the earth are occupied and in use. All of them, to a greater or lesser extent, need the same measures of reclamation and conservation that have succeeded so well in Israel. The frontiers of today are the lands under our feet.

22

The Rangelands of the Western United States

R. MERTON LOVE
February 1970

The century-old war over the use of the wide-open spaces of the U.S. is now escalating year by year in scope and complexity. In the 19th century it was a relatively simple conflict, mainly between the cattle ranchers and the sheep raisers. Today it has become a huge contest among many interests vying for the space, resources and beauties of our Western rangelands. To the traditional claims on these lands by ranchers, lumbermen, miners, hunters, campers and nature lovers there are now added the demands arising from population growth and the consequent march of urbanization. A creeping encroachment by burgeoning cities and new towns, recreation resorts, highways, communication facilities, industries and intensive farming (displaced by the spreading urbanization of the East and Middle West) is pushing into the ranges and wilds of the West. The resulting pressures, not only for space but also for corollary necessities such as water, obviously make it essential to seek a strategy for management of the rangelands that will reconcile and accommodate the many different interests.

The rangeland region comprises most of the area of the 17 Western states—roughly the portion of the continental U.S. west of Omaha. A tourist roaming this largely wild domain (or seeing it from the air) may well wonder what all the fighting is about. It is a region of mountains, deserts, plateaus and dry basins; of low precipitation, rough topography and shallow, rocky, saline soil; of forests, semiarid grasslands and clumps of inedible shrubs. The terrain seems of little value for anything except the enjoyment of its beauty and the grazing of animals on its meager fare.

The appearance is deceiving. In productivity and economic importance this region, even in the wild state, makes substantial contributions to the national wealth. Its production of meat alone (not to speak of lumber and minerals) is impressive. The Western rangelands, constituting the major portion of the billion acres of range and pasture in the continental U.S., account for more than half of the national production of livestock, which is estimated to total $5 billion to $10 billion a year (compared with $14 billion for all other crops including forest products).

Why not let well enough alone? What could be accomplished by "management" of this beautiful and surprisingly productive region? Should we not restrict ourselves to "conservation" of what nature has wrought?

Experience tells us that we should not take so negative an attitude. The idea that we ought not to meddle with nature arises from several misconceptions.

One misconception is that, by exploitation of nature's productivity (through intensive agriculture, grazing and lumbering), man is ruining the world's wildlands. Admittedly there has been reckless mismanagement in some cases. On the whole, however, the balance is on man's side; if his activities did not help nature more than they hurt, the land could not support the great world population it does today.

The foregoing misconception is based on a more elementary one: that the ecosystem created by nature is the best possible state. Man has shown in his management of agriculture that he can improve on nature; he has overcome its limitations and improved the quality and production of natural grains and other crops. Similarly, he can "farm" for a more productive grazing range, forest, wilderness or watershed. By proper management he can produce plants that are more useful for livestock and game and enable the land to meet the multiple requirements of man for food, water, recreation, mining, grazing, lumbering and so on.

Cecil H. Wadleigh, Director of Soil and Water Conservation in the U.S. Department of Agriculture, has observed that man is engaged in a continual struggle with "the destructive actions of nature." He explains: "If we look at the historical record, one of man's greatest burdens has been that of surviving and progressing under the vicissitudes imposed by the natural environment. This record sends forth a clarion call that we expedite our efforts to protect our watersheds, curb soil erosion, abate floods, conserve soil moisture, improve soil productivity, develop improved varieties of crops and better strains of livestock, wage war on insect enemies, fight diseases of plants and animals, including man, restrict losses due to weeds and brush and continue to develop technology that will ever minimize needed labor efforts."

Consider the rangelands in the context

JACKSON HOLE, at the foot of the Teton mountains in Wyoming (*opposite page*), is typical of the better rangeland in the Northern Rocky Mountain area. Cattle once grazed in the foothills (*foreground*) in spring and fall and in the uplands (*background*) in summer. The harvest of hay from the level valley floor provided winter feed for the stock. The area is now a national elk refuge administered by the U.S. Department of the Interior.

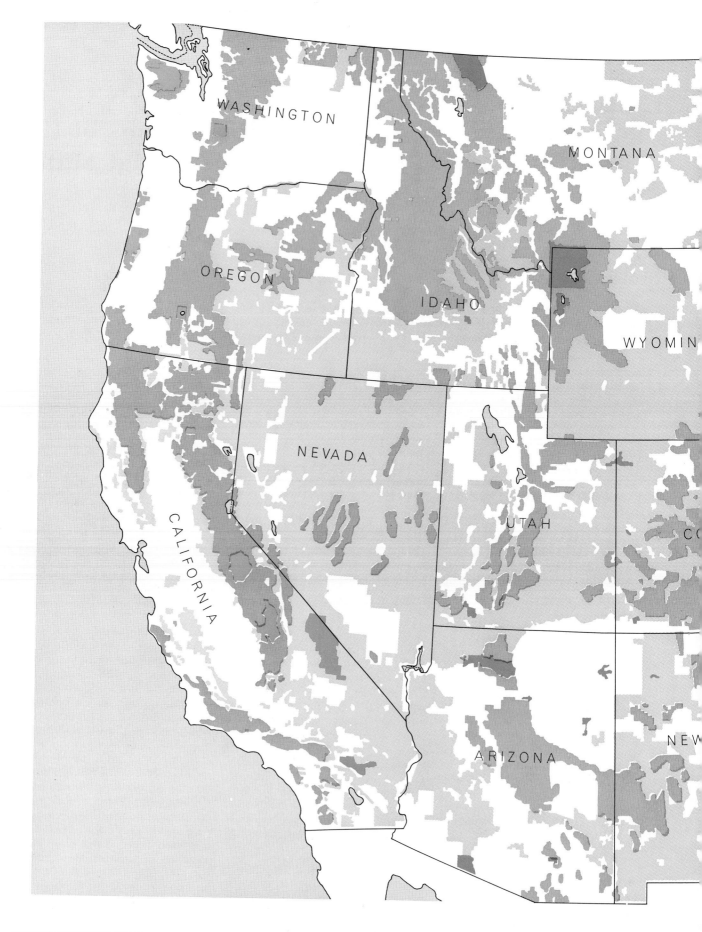

ELEVEN WESTERN STATES of the continental U.S. hold a substantial part of the nation's land that still remains under Federal control. Shown on the map are public lands (*light color*), national parks and monuments (*color*) and national forests (*gray*); wildlife

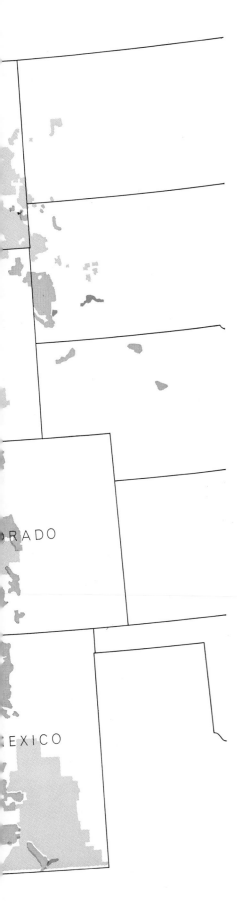

of our growing needs. We are talking mainly about the 11 westernmost states, where almost 54 percent of the land (in contrast to only 4.6 percent in the Eastern states) is Federally owned. The ranges of this vast region can be divided into three distinct types: Northern Rocky Mountain, Intermountain and Southwest. The Northern Rocky Mountain area is characterized by high mountains, plateaus and narrow valleys and by a rugged climate, with sharp seasonal changes. Its plant life is predominantly open forest, bunchgrass, wet meadow grass and sagebrush. The Intermountain area has lower mountains, broad plateaus, deep canyons, extensive valleys, barren salt flats and a somewhat less rigorous climate than the Northern Rockies. Grasslands are rare in this region, and vast areas of it are dominated by shrubs, but there is good grazing in some of the wooded regions. In the Southwest, with its warm, dry climate, deserts and semideserts predominate. There are areas of vegetation, but even in these, unfortunately, grasses and other herbaceous plants tend to lose out to woody plants.

The relatively wild ranges of the Northern Rockies are grazed by migrant herds of sheep and cattle. The cattle use the open range eight months of the year (grazing in the foothills in spring and fall and in the uplands in summer) and return to their home ranches for feeding on hay in winter. The Intermountain ranges similarly provide seasonal grazing for cattle and sheep, as well as for big game. Wide areas of this region, however, are barren wastelands, and from season to season the cattle need to be moved great distances from one range to another. The traditional practice of driving the herds over many miles of trails is now being superseded by transport in trucks.

Needless to say, the vast grazing lands are not used solely for feeding domestic animals. They are shared with hunters and other users. Even where the lands are privately owned by ranchers, the owners commonly sell hunting privileges, and recently hunting clubs have begun to buy large tracts for their own use.

There is growing pressure for the dedication of more lands to recreation. An indication of the proportions this demand is likely to assume in the coming years was given in a 1960 report by the California Public Outdoor Recreation Planning Committee. In that year people in California spent some 235 million person-days in specified outdoor recreational activities, primarily swimming,

picnicking, fishing and boating. By 1980, the committee estimated, such activities are expected to rise tenfold (to nearly 2.5 billion activity-days), with marked increases in camping, winter recreations, riding and hiking. For the nation as a whole Resources for the Future, Inc., predicts that by the year 2000 there will be a fortyfold increase in the patronage of vacation and resort areas in the U.S.

To make appropriate provision of lands for the coming recreation needs we shall need more information than we have at present as to the nature of those needs. A comparison of two resorts in California illustrates this point. Folsom Lake, which is only about 25 square miles in area and is little known outside the state, has twice as many visitor-days per year as the world-renowned Yosemite National Park, which has an area of 1,125 square miles. Obviously the efficient apportionment of lands to needs will require a systematic study of the trends in recreation.

Overall, in considering the impending "civilization" of the rangelands, we need to plan for a total system—not merely for particular uses or areas but for a complex of differing uses, so adjusted to one another that they can live together in harmony. The Federal agencies involved in managing these lands (principally the Department of the Interior and the Department of Agriculture) have adopted a concept of multiple use based on this broad principle. It contemplates applying general improvements that will benefit all users and invoking restrictions that will prevent any single use from unduly interfering with others. In terms of land area, the frame of reference is not particular localities but large areas such as an entire watershed. On this scale things can be done that will be beneficial to all interests.

The central problem in improving the rangelands for everyone's benefit—whether for livestock raising, habitation, recreation or simply enjoyment of the scenery—is that of managing the vegetation. The foremost enemy of the human and animal use of these lands is brush. It drinks up the scarce water, gives rise to devastating fires, makes many areas impenetrable and robs the land of its potential production of useful grasses and other plants. Enormous areas of the Western states are overgrown by the unwanted shrubs. The Intermountain country has 115 million acres of sagebrush. Brush occupies some 24 percent of California's total land area. In Arizona, New Mexico and Texas there are 60 million acres of the spiny shrub

PINE PLANTATION in the southeastern U.S. is an example of "multiple use" rangeland. The cattle feed on the grass that grows abundantly in this open forest environment without disturbing the pine seedlings that will provide a future crop for the plantation.

ROCKY MOUNTAIN UPLANDS also contain vast areas of rangeland with multiple-use potential. They offer good grazing in the summer months, hunting in fall and winter and other recreation the year round, as well as exploitable timber and mineral resources.

mesquite, and millions upon millions of acres of cactus, burroweed and snakeweed. Many species of brush thrive on the soils of the rangelands, and they have proved difficult to eradicate. Year after year the acreage taken over by brush, like the national debt, keeps increasing.

Ten years ago brush fires cost the state of California an average of $25 million per year for fire fighting, and the 250,-000 acres scorched annually by these fires represented an additional loss of $25 million. Today such fires cost about $250 million per year. Ironically the efforts spent to prevent and contain the fires have only increased the hazard! Controlling the fires has enabled the brush to grow more thickly in the forests, with the result that most fires today are big ones. Nature and the aboriginal Indians in California managed better. Frequent fires, ignited by lightning or by man, kept the forest floor clean, so that the fires were small and did not burn the trees. The 19th-century naturalist John Muir, in his famous diaries, told of brush fires in California that consumed everything in their path until they came to the forest; there they subsided to small flames creeping along the ground because there was little combustible material to nourish them. Far from damaging the forest, such burns enriched it. We may be indebted to them for the giant sequoia trees now ennobling California forests; recent research has shown that sequoia seedlings can germinate in ashes but are suppressed under a thick layer of needles such as would cover an unburned forest floor.

To improve the rangelands for all concerned, then, our first step must be to get rid of the brush on selected sites. After this is done, by means of controlled burning, herbicides and uprooting, a good stand of grass can be established. A University of California test of the conversion of brushland to grass on a small watershed of 60 acres showed spectacular results: a dramatic increase in forage for animals, substantial improvement of the available water supply and a drastic reduction of the fire hazard.

Individual livestock operators have obtained similarly striking results. One farmer who burned off 2,400 acres of brush and seeded the area to grass found that within six years this area, which formerly had supported only 20 cows and a few deer and other wild animals, became capable of feeding 150 cows and a large number of deer. Another farmer who converted brushland to grass on a dry range found that streams that had dry range found that streams that had formerly dried up in summer now flowed all year, enabling him to build a reservoir that supplied him with enough water to maintain irrigated pastures. Plant physiologists and hydrologists were not surprised at this seeming miracle. They know that every acre of brush soaks up six more acre-inches of water than herbaceous vegetation does.

Since 1945, under a legislative act permitting livestock ranchers in California to burn off brush under the supervision of the state forester and his deputies, more than two million acres have been burned off and the brush replaced with grass. It is estimated that the water yield from these areas has been increased by about a million acre-feet in the aggregate, and there have been great gains in livestock productivity and in the reduction of fire hazards. Many acres that were once covered with impenetrable brush now look like beautiful parks.

The conversion from brush to grass has been assisted by research and new technology. The Department of Agriculture developed a special tractor-drawn drill for grass-seeding rough terrain. Much study has been given to the various soils of the California rangelands, their fertilizer needs and the types of grass that will do best in these soils. Oddly enough, it has been found that certain imported grasses do much better than the native grasses in California. For example, hardinggrass (from Australia and southern Africa), smilo (from the Mediterranean region), veldtgrass (from southern Africa) and palestine orchard grass (from southwestern Asia) are considerably more productive in California than its native bunchgrasses are. An Australian investigator, William Hartley, concluded from an extensive survey that the pasture grasses most commonly cultivated around the world today originated in Eurasia and parts of Africa. Apparently these grasses, in the course of centuries of heavy grazing in those regions of early herding of livestock, evolved a high degree of vigor.

Man is only at the threshold of the immense exploration that will be necessary to mold the wilderness to his needs. Is the task, after all, too complicated? We can draw some optimism about our ability to master it from what has been accomplished in agriculture. In undertaking to replace the plant communities of nature with single crops of his own, man took on the problem of establishing and maintaining artificial ecosystems whose survival depended on his continuing efforts and ingenuity. In order to perpetuate a crop—a grain such as rice or barley, for example—he has to work at it year by year, seeding it, fertilizing it, fighting off its enemies: weeds, insects, diseases and depletion of the soil. He has found it possible to maintain such systems indefinitely. In the Orient ancient fields that have been cultivated for 40 centuries are still producing, in some cases at ever higher yields, thanks to advancing knowledge and genetic invention. Man has made many mistakes and often been carelessly destructive, to be sure, but through the ages he has steadily enlarged his understanding of nature and moved ahead to increasingly successful control.

Managing the wildlands is of course a vastly more complicated undertaking than growing single crops. A committee of the California Agricultural Experiment Station after a five-year study proposed a program of needed researches that ranges over a great variety of questions, from the interactions between soils and plants to the appropriate diet for each domestic and wild range animal and the interrelations among the various forms of life present in the system (including man). Such studies of ecosystems are really only beginning to get under way. The ecologists engaged in them are enjoying the sense of excitement that is always coupled with new exploration. The investigation has opened new outlooks and generated new concepts.

Among these is a concept called "canopy architecture." It has to do with the photosynthetic response of a community of plants to a given amount of exposure to sunlight for the community as a whole. D. J. Watson, a British ecologist, recently introduced the idea of measuring the production of vegetation in terms of the total leaf area of the plant canopy. It turns out that for subterranean (ground-hugging) clover, for example, the daily production of foliage is highest when the leaf area amounts to about five square feet of leaf surface per square foot of ground area. Presumably when the leaf-area index is less than five some of the available sunlight goes unused and when it is higher than five there is too much shade. The facts suggest that in a pasture of subterranean clover the grazing of animals should be regulated to keep the leaf-area index as close to five as is practical.

Other plants respond differently. Research on white clover and cotton has indicated that the depth of the canopy may be important, which suggests that studies should be made of the flow of sunlight through the foliage of various plant communities and also of the trapping of carbon dioxide within the canopy. The angle of the leaves can have considerable influence. It has been found, for example, that rice plants with erect (mainly vertical) foliage can tolerate a high leaf-area index; consequently such plants could be planted in greater density and produce a greater yield per acre. Breeding programs are under way to develop rice plants, other small grains and millets with an erect leaf habit. Perhaps these findings and ideas will be applicable to the vegetation of grazing ranges as well. Obviously, however, it will be no easy task to apply them to the ranges' multifarious communities, made up of many different species of plants.

Meanwhile we know that the ranges' production of meat could be multiplied, probably to as much as three or four times their present yield, by controlling the brush, planting grass and legumes and fertilizing. Analysis of the present yield of meat from the solar energy received by the rangelands shows that there is a great deal of room for improvement. A typical range in California receives 800,000 kilocalories of sunlight energy per square meter in a year. After deducting what is lost by reflection and

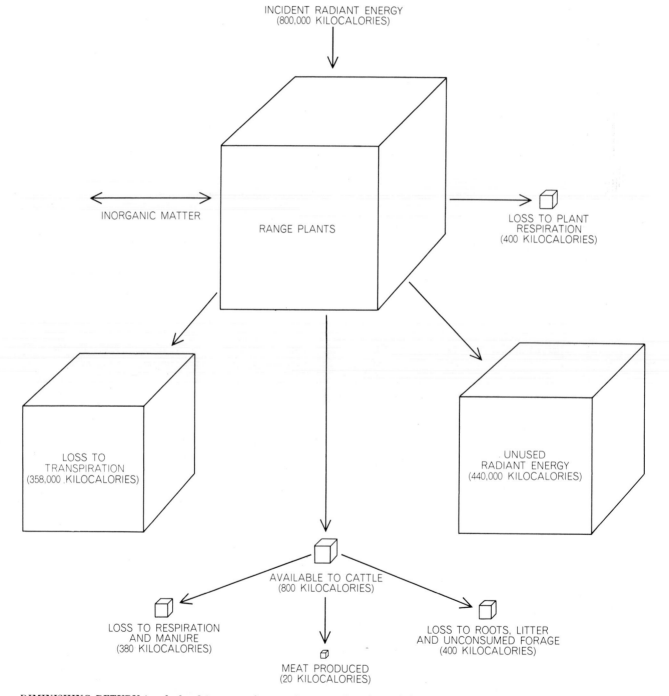

INCIDENT RADIANT ENERGY
(800,000 KILOCALORIES)

INORGANIC MATTER

RANGE PLANTS

LOSS TO PLANT
RESPIRATION
(400 KILOCALORIES)

LOSS TO
TRANSPIRATION
(358,000 KILOCALORIES)

UNUSED
RADIANT ENERGY
(440,000 KILOCALORIES)

AVAILABLE TO CATTLE
(800 KILOCALORIES)

LOSS TO RESPIRATION
AND MANURE
(380 KILOCALORIES)

LOSS TO ROOTS, LITTER
AND UNCONSUMED FORAGE
(400 KILOCALORIES)

MEAT PRODUCED
(20 KILOCALORIES)

DIMINISHING RETURN is calculated in terms of energy input during eight months of meat production on an acre of rangeland in California. The top cube represents the 800,000 kilocalories of radiant energy available per square yard from October to May. Only .1 percent of this energy, or 800 kilocalories, becomes available as food for the cattle grazing the rangeland. Of this amount, no more than 2.5 percent, in the form of 50 pounds of meat on the hoof, is available for human consumption at the end of the eight months.

heating, spent on the plants' requirements for respiration and photosynthesis and drained away into the roots and other unconsumable parts of the plants, we find that only 800 kilocalories are picked up by the grazing animal. The animal in turn spends nearly all this energy unproductively (from man's point of view) in respiration, waste matter and its inedible bones and hide, leaving a net of only 20 kilocalories per square meter, of the original 800,000, that goes into meat. On an acreage basis this represents about 50 pounds of beef on the hoof per acre. The more efficient utilization of sunlight achieved by fertilized legumes can raise this figure to as much as 300 pounds of beef per acre.

The California Highway Commission Budget for 1969–1970 totals $18,945,-000: $8 million for 19 new landscaping projects, $10 million for maintenance and additional planning, $945,000 for maintaining safety roadside rests, plus $2 million for construction of 11 such roadside rests. This totals nearly $21 million, and this is fine. Constructing and landscaping our highways is a never ending task, but we are working at it. Why can we not have such constructive long-term planning programs for reduction of fire hazards and beautification of our watersheds and wildlands?

Private industry, builders, developers, realtors, subdividers and individual homeowners in fire-hazardous wildland areas could hire underemployed agricultural and urban labor, school dropouts and many who are now on welfare rolls to do this work on lands burned by wildfire. Unfortunately little urgency seems to be felt about tackling the preservation and improvement of our forests and brushlands. The Economic Opportunity Act provides an incentive to state and county agencies to put local people to work on this. Local government agencies would pay 25 percent of the labor costs, and the Federal Government 75 percent. (The latter ruling was made in February, 1967.) The state's Resources Agency has work camps for prisoners, but why should one have to commit a crime in order to be put to meaningful work? This would be one work program that would pay for itself as time goes on.

The attitude of those who believe we should become much more active in developing the values of our rangelands has been well stated by Stephen H. Spurr, dean of the School of Graduate Studies at the University of Michigan: "We should be positive and not negative, we should be active and not passive, we should be wilderness managers and not conservationists."

SOUTHWEST RANGELAND is predominantly semidesert and desert, and its areas of vegetation are usually dominated by drought-adapted plants. Cholla cactus and creosote bush are the principal plants in this arid section of San Bernardino County in California.

INTERMOUNTAIN RANGELAND is frequently dominated by shrubs. Here, near Lassen Peak in northern California, the unwanted growth consists of sagebrush and juniper. The Intermountain zone contains more than 100 million acres of such sagebrush-choked grazing.

23

Chemical Fertilizers

CHRISTOPHER J. PRATT
June 1965

Whatever estimate one accepts of the increase of the human population in the finite future, or whatever estimate of how long it will take to bring this increase under control, it is clear that the present rate of increase is alarmingly high. Three centuries ago the number of people in the world was probably about 500 million; now it is more than three billion, and if the current rate of increase holds, it will be six billion by the end of the century and millennium. In some underdeveloped areas, where the rate is highest, the Malthusian prediction that population would eventually outrun food supplies seems close to reality.

Clearly mankind faces a formidable problem in making certain that future populations have enough to eat. Doubtless a partial solution lies in improved technology, which has already done so much to keep the food supply abreast of population, and in the spread of existing technology from the developed to the underdeveloped countries. It should also be possible to bring some new areas under cultivation or grazing, but the opportunities in that direction appear to be limited. Even though only about 2.4 billion acres, or approximately 7 percent of the earth's land area, are used for crop production in any one year, most of the unused land is too dry or too cold for agriculture or is in some other way unsuitable. Neither extensive clearing of forests nor large-scale cultivation of tropical lands offers as much promise as one might think, because much of the soil in such regions is lateritic and turns hard as the result of an oxidizing effect when it is put to the plow [see the article "Lateritic Soils," by Mary McNeil, beginning on page 68].

With huge amounts of capital and carefully planned projects it would be possible to create much new cropland by vast undertakings of irrigation, drainage and other kinds of reclamation. Even if such projects were launched, however, they would take decades to complete. It seems more feasible to look to shorter-range ventures, particularly in those developing areas where famine is an imminent threat.

Of all the short-range factors capable of increasing agricultural production readily—factors including pesticides, improved plant varieties and mechanization—the largest yields and the most substantial returns on invested capital come from chemical fertilizers. The application of these substances to underfertilized soils can have dramatic results. In a typical situation the ratio of the extra weight of grain produced per unit weight of nutrients applied can be as high as 10 to 1. To put it another way, an investment of this kind alone can quickly produce increases in crop yields of 100 to 200 percent.

Today some 30 million tons of the so-called primary nutrients—nitrogen, phosphorus and potassium—are annually supplied to world agriculture by chemical fertilizers. This amount is hardly adequate, for reasons I shall discuss. Moreover, crop yields diminish in proportion to the amount of fertilizer applied. Therefore it can be estimated that a population of six billion in the year 2000 will require at least 120 million tons of primary nutrients. An increase of 90 million tons of nutrients for three billion more people means that 60 pounds of primary nutrients will be needed to help sustain each additional person for a year. This is equivalent to about one 100-pound bag of modern high-analysis chemical fertilizer.

Stated in such a way, the amount of effort required to supply the additional fertilizer may seem modest. Actually the expansion of capacity required is enormous; achieving it may well become a major preoccupation of technology. Fortunately processes for manufacturing the needed substances are already well established on a large scale and are capable of rapid expansion, provided

CHEMICAL FERTILIZER is meticulously placed on a field in Oklahoma by a spreader

that enough capital is made available and the necessary priorities are given. Considering all these factors, it is appropriate to review briefly the fertilizer situation: how plants utilize nutrients, how chemical fertilizers came into use, how they are manufactured, how they are best applied and how the increasing demand for them can be met by chemical technology.

Plants and Nutrients

A growing plant requires most or all of 16 nutrients, nine in large amounts and seven in small. The former are sometimes called macronutrients, the latter micronutrients. Most plants obtain three of the macronutrients—carbon, hydrogen and oxygen—from the air and all the other nutrients from the soil. (A few species, such as clover, are able to fill their nitrogen needs from the air.) The primary soil macronutrients—nitrogen, phosphorus and potassium—are the N, P and K often seen on bags of fertil-

izer; they are also the substances represented by the set of three figures, such as 10-12-8, that normally designates the nutrient content of a fertilizer. Usually these figures respectively denote the percentage in the fertilizer of total nitrogen (N), of phosphorus pentoxide (P_2O_5, often called phosphoric acid or phosphate) in a form available for use by plants and of water-soluble potassium oxide (K_2O, usually called potash).

The three other soil macronutrients—calcium, magnesium and sulfur—are often called secondary. Agricultural lime, limestone and dolomite, which are used to correct soil acidity, also serve as sources of calcium and magnesium. Sulfur deficiencies can be remedied by certain commercial fertilizers. The seven micronutrients, which are sometimes added in traces to fertilizers providing one or more of the primary nutrients, are boron, copper, iron, manganese, zinc, molybdenum and chlorine.

The growth of plants is a highly complicated process that is far from fully

understood. For the purposes of this article it is enough to say that the usual path of mineral nutrients from the soil to the plant is from the solid particles of soil to the water in the soil and thence into the root. The actual transfer of nutrients from soil to root involves the movement of mineral ions. These ions are contained mostly in the soil water, but some of them are adsorbed on solid soil particles.

It follows that nutrients must be in ionic form or capable of transformation to ionic form by soil processes if they are to be of any value to the plant. Hence it is not necessarily a lack of minerals in a soil that causes plants to show signs of nutrient deficiency; the problem can also be that the nutrients are not in a form readily available to the plant. For example, it is quite possible for crops to starve in soils that are amply supplied with phosphorus and potassium if these nutrients are insoluble in water or plant juices. Essentially what the chemical fertilizer industry

34 feet wide. The spreader is of the "drill" type, meaning that it lays fertilizer in precise rows instead of broadcasting it generally over the field as would be done by other types of spreaders. Careful placing is often important for economic or nutritional reasons.

does, in addition to converting inert nitrogen from the air into soluble salts, is employ processes to "open" the molecules containing the vital nutrients so that these molecules form soluble salts that plants can assimilate readily.

One can best grasp the need for mineral nutrients in agriculture by taking account of the nutrients that are removed from the soil by cropping and grazing. A ton of wheat grain is equivalent to about 40 pounds of nitrogen, eight pounds of phosphorus and nine pounds of potassium. If the straw, husks, roots and other agricultural wastes of such a crop are not returned to the soil, they represent additional large losses of nutrients. A ton of fat cattle corresponds to a depletion of about 54 pounds of nitrogen, 15 pounds of phosphorus, three pounds of potassium and 26 pounds of calcium. Such rates of removal will quickly exhaust a typical soil unless the losses are made up by regular additions of suitable fertilizer.

Equivalent additions of fertilizer, however, are not really enough. There are other factors to be taken into account, and they explain why the present consumption of fertilizers is barely adequate. Nutrients are leached from soils by the flow of water; moreover, they are fixed in forms not readily available to plants. As a result of such losses the proportion of soil nitrogen and phosphorus utilized by a crop is rarely more than 75 percent. In some instances the utilization of phosphorus is as low as 10 percent.

Even allowing for losses, the increased crop value resulting from the proper application of fertilizer can be substantial. On a poor soil the gain can approach 10 times the cost of the material applied. Where the soil is good and the crop yields are high the gain from fertilizing is more likely to be three to five times the cost of the fertilizer. Because of this diminishing return there eventually comes a point at which the additional yield no longer

justifies the cost of the corresponding extra fertilizer. There is also an agronomic reason for avoiding the overapplication of fertilizer: ultimately a point can be reached at which the high concentration of nutrient salts in the soil can damage the plants.

The Evolution of Fertilizers

Long before men began to write history they knew about the effects of organic, or natural, fertilizers on growing plants. The effects must surely have been evident in the relatively lush growth induced by animal droppings and carcasses. Eventually farmers began to collect dung and apply it to crops. The first English settlers in North America reported that the Indians substantially increased their yield of maize by burying a fish with each seed they planted. In medieval times farmers in Europe had commonly undertaken to grow nitrogen-converting legumes such as clover and to rotate crops in order to

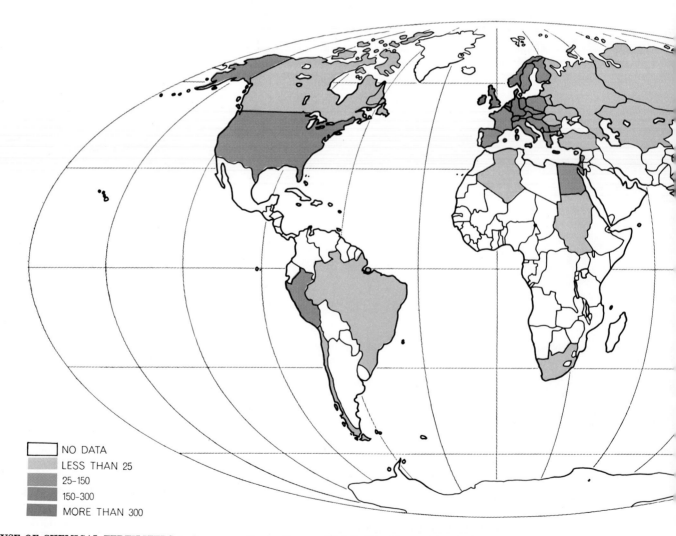

NO DATA
LESS THAN 25
25–150
150–300
MORE THAN 300

USE OF CHEMICAL FERTILIZERS is shown according to data assembled by the Food and Agriculture Organization of the United Nations. Figures give average consumption of fertilizer in metric tons per 1,000 hectares of arable land, defined as land planted to

maintain soil fertility. By the early 19th century the use of farm manure, blood, bones, animal wastes and Peruvian guano became widespread, particularly in England, where the Industrial Revolution had brought about a rapid expansion of population and a simultaneous movement of workers from the land to the manufacturing towns. For a time it appeared that the limited supply of organic fertilizer would be insufficient to meet the rising demand for food in the industrializing countries; it is said that even human bones from the battlefields of Europe were recovered, crushed and used as plant foods.

Although the use of organic fertilizers was well established by the 19th century, the basic reasons for their effectiveness were not understood. This lack of knowledge hampered the discovery of alternative substances that could relieve the pressure on the limited supply of organic matter. Another obstacle was the passionate belief held by many that organic materials had special fertiliz-

crops, in temporary use as meadow for mowing or pasture, or temporarily lying fallow.

ing properties not shared by inorganic substances. Even after the Swiss chemist Nicolas de Saussure demonstrated in 1804 that plants can grow luxuriantly on carbon and oxygen from the air and mineral nutrients from the soil, strong feelings about organic fertilizers persisted. (Today the view is still sometimes expressed that organic fertilizers possess inexplicable virtues unrelated to their content of primary nutrient. Such materials—manure, sewage sludge, compost and the like—are indeed valuable as conditioners of soil and as minor contributors of plant nutrients, but there is not nearly enough organic material to meet present needs, let alone those of the future.)

Gradually the advances of chemistry revealed the processes of plant nutrition and pointed the way toward the substitution of chemical fertilizers for organic fertilizers. In some instances the process was very slow. Nitrogen, for example, was recognized as an important plant nutrient in manures and other organic matter long before anybody understood the complex cycle by which unreactive atmospheric nitrogen is converted by legumes and soil bacteria into ammonia and soluble nitrogen salts. By the time the process was understood, early in this century, conditions were ripe for a rapid evolution of industrial replacements for organic nitrogen in fertilizer. For one thing, ammonia in the form of ammonium sulfate had become available as a by-product of coal-gas works. For another, mine operators in Chile had begun large-scale production and export of sodium nitrate for use in explosives and other chemicals. As a result of their availability these salts rapidly overtook organic nitrogen as an ingredient of fertilizer. The speed of the transformation is indicated by the fact that the proportion of organic nitrogen materials in fertilizers used in the U.S. fell from 91 percent in 1900 to 40 percent in 1913.

Chilean nitrate was not to hold its position for long. A prolonged effort to synthesize ammonia by combining nitrogen with hydrogen succeeded at last in 1910, when the German chemist Fritz Haber found that the reaction would proceed at high pressure (at least 3,000 pounds per square inch) and in the presence of osmium as a catalyst. The achievement gave rise to a revolution in chemical fertilizer technology. In 1913 Haber and Karl Bosch, having worked out many difficult engineering problems, designed a commercial plant that soon produced 20 tons of ammonia a day. The requirements of the two world wars

made ammonia available on a large scale, together with such derivatives as ammonium nitrate and urea. These compounds in time largely replaced Chilean nitrate as a source of nitrogen and also reduced the proportion of fertilizers containing organic nitrogen to a few percent of total fertilizer consumption.

Phosphorus moved from the organic to the chemical stage in fertilizer sooner than nitrogen but by a similarly slow process. The first association of phosphorus with bones was made by the Swedish mineralogist and chemist Johan Gottlieb Gahn in 1769. It took until 1840, however, for chemistry to advance to the stage where it was possible to recognize that phosphorus was the key ingredient in the bone manure that had come into wide use. In that same year the great German chemist Justus von Liebig, who is regarded by many scholars as the founder of agricultural chemistry, put forward the thesis that the action of sulfuric acid on bones would make the phosphorus in the bones more readily available to plants.

This idea was promptly developed in England, where the need for additional sources of fertilizer was acute. In 1842 John Bennet Lawes, a wealthy farmer and industrialist who spent many years conducting agricultural experiments on his estate at Rothamsted, obtained a patent covering the treatment of bones and bone ash with sulfuric acid to make an improved phosphorus-containing fertilizer. Significantly he included "other phosphoritic substances" in his patent, indicating that he foresaw the role of minerals as sources of phosphate. Within 20 years the production in Britain of "chemical manures" made from sulfuric acid, local coprolites (fossil manures) and various phosphatic minerals had risen to a level of 200,000 tons a year. The phosphate fertilizer industry, thus firmly established, spread rapidly to other countries. Toward the end of the 19th century slag removed during the production of iron and steel from high-phosphate ores became another major source of phosphorus for agricultural purposes in Britain and Europe, where even now several million tons of "basic slag" are used annually as a phosphate fertilizer.

As for potassium, the benefits of adding wood ashes ("pot ash") to the soil must have been recognized in ancient times. By early in the 19th century the progress of chemistry was sufficient for a start to be made in the use of potassium chloride deposits in Germany and France as sources of potassium in fertilizer. The first factory producing potash from these deposits was built in 1861. Germany and France continued to be the principal sources of potash until rather recently, when major deposits were developed in the U.S., Israel, the U.S.S.R. and Canada.

Modern Fertilizer Production

Today a farmer can buy a wide variety of chemical fertilizers. If he wants only one nutrient, he can find a fer-

tilizer that provides it; he can also find fertilizers that contain almost any combination of nitrogen, phosphorus, potassium and the micronutrients. The industry that produces them is enormous, having a worldwide output, according to a recent estimate by the Food and Agriculture Organization, of more than 33 million tons a year. I shall briefly describe the processes now involved in producing the primary nutrients.

Synthetic ammonia is firmly estab-

lished as the principal source of nitrogen in fertilizer. Ammonia synthesis remains unchanged in principle from the technique developed by Haber and Bosch. Large-scale production often presents additional problems, however, because of the need to obtain huge supplies of pure gaseous nitrogen and hydrogen at low cost. Pure nitrogen can be produced in quantity with relative ease by removing oxygen and other gases from air through liquefaction or combustion. Hy-

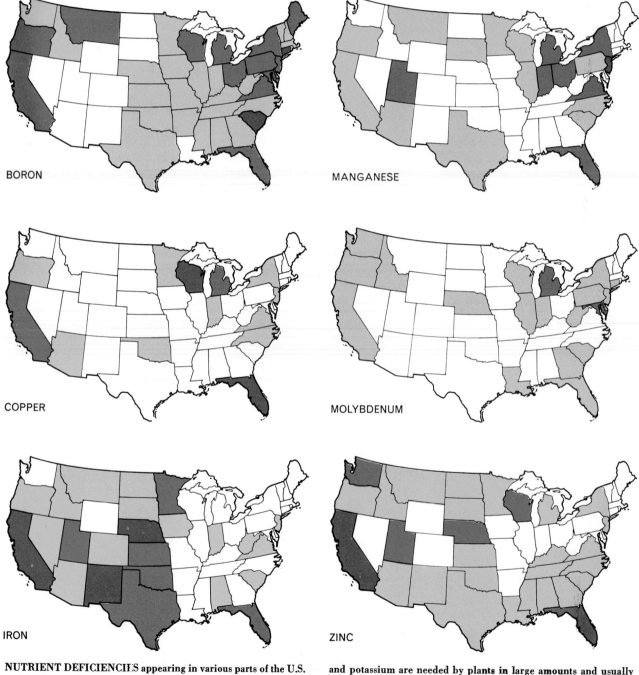

NUTRIENT DEFICIENCIES appearing in various parts of the U.S. mainland are indicated. The findings, based on work done by K. C. Berger of the University of Wisconsin, pertain to several "micronutrients," meaning minerals needed by plants in small but important amounts. "Macronutrients" such as nitrogen, phosphorus

and potassium are needed by plants in large amounts and usually must be supplied wherever commercial crops are grown. The colors indicate the degree of deficiency from modest (*light*) to severe (*dark*) as based on reports of the number of crops affected. The absence of color means that the state has not reported a deficiency.

HELMINTHOSPORIUM BLIGHT

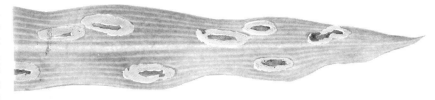

POTASSIUM DEFICIENCY

NITROGEN DEFICIENCY

MAGNESIUM DEFICIENCY

WATER SHORTAGE

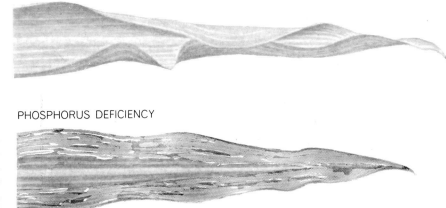

PHOSPHORUS DEFICIENCY

drogen is another matter. Some early ammonia plants used hydrogen made by electrolysis, but the prohibitive cost led to a search for cheaper sources. Methods for producing hydrogen from solid fuels such as coal and lignite were developed in Europe. In the U.S., where natural gas is plentiful, the simpler catalytic re-forming of methane has proved an ideal way of making hydrogen. More recently the catalytic re-forming of light petroleum fractions such as naphtha with the aid of steam and the partial oxidation of heavy oil with oxygen have been widely used in countries that lack natural gas.

Although there is a strong trend, particularly in the U.S., toward injecting ammonia directly into the soil in the form of anhydrous ammonia or aqueous solutions, most agricultural ammonia is still converted into solid derivatives. Ammonium nitrate is a form popular among manufacturers, since the nitric acid needed to produce it is also made from ammonia. Similarly, large amounts of urea are produced by combining ammonia with carbon dioxide derived from oxidation of the raw material used to produce the hydrogen. Ammonium sulfate is also made on a large scale by reacting ammonia with sulfuric acid. In the Far East substantial quantities of ammonium chloride are made from ammonia and salt or hydrochloric acid. Ammonium phosphates and nitrophosphates are additional fertilizers derived from ammonia. A principal advantage of most solid forms of ammonia is the ease with which they can be transported and applied to the soil. The high nitrogen content of urea (46 percent) and ammonium nitrate (33.5 percent) make them particularly advantageous.

Most phosphate fertilizers now come from mineral deposits, chiefly those in Florida, the western U.S., North Africa and parts of the U.S.S.R. Although both igneous and sedimentary phosphate deposits exist, about 90 percent of the world's fertilizer needs are supplied from the sedimentary sources because they are more plentiful than the igneous minerals and also easier to mine and process. The origin of sedimentary phosphates has generated much speculation among geologists. Some of them believe that the minerals were precipitated from seawater after it had been saturated with phosphate and fluorine ions derived from the contact of the water with igneous rocks and gases. It is also possible that these phosphates resulted to some extent from the replacement of calcium carbonate with calcium phos-

CORN-LEAF VARIATIONS directly or indirectly related to the amount of nutrients and water available to the plant are depicted. Gray represents green; the other colors are approximately as they appear in nature. *Helminthosporium* blight is a common fungus disease to which poorly nourished plants are vulnerable. Signs of potassium deficiency usually appear at the tips and along the edges of the lower leaves; of nitrogen deficiency, at the leaf tip, and of phosphorus, on young plants. Water shortage makes leaves a grayish-green.

SOURCES	PROCESS	PRODUCT
PHOSPHATE ROCK	GRIND TO ABOUT .1 MILLIMETER	GROUND PHOSPHATE ROCK (0-35-0)
SULFUR / AIR / WATER	CATALYTIC OXIDATION AND HYDRATION	SULFURIC ACID
PHOSPHATE ROCK / SULFURIC ACID	REACT AND CURE	SINGLE SUPERPHOSPHATE (0-20-0)
PHOSPHATE ROCK / SULFURIC ACID	DISSOLVE AND FILTER	PHOSPHORIC ACID / GYPSUM
PHOSPHATE ROCK / PHOSPHORIC ACID	REACT AND CURE	TRIPLE SUPERPHOSPHATE (0-48-0)
HYDROCARBONS / STEAM / AIR	RE-FORM TO HYDROGEN / SYNTHESIZE / NITROGEN FROM AIR	AMMONIA (82-0-0)
AMMONIA / SULFURIC ACID	REACT AND CRYSTALLIZE	AMMONIUM SULFATE (21-0-0)
AMMONIA / PHOSPHORIC ACID	REACT AND CRYSTALLIZE OR GRANULATE	AMMONIUM PHOSPHATE (18-46-0)
AMMONIA / AIR / WATER	CATALYTIC OXIDATION / ABSORPTION	NITRIC ACID
PHOSPHATE ROCK / NITRIC ACID / AMMONIA	REACT AMMONIATE / FILTER	NITROPHOSPHATES (20-20-0) / CALCIUM NITRATE (15-0-0)
AMMONIA / NITRIC ACID	REACT AND CRYSTALLIZE OR MAKE INTO PELLETS	AMMONIUM NITRATE (33-0-0)
AMMONIA / CARBON DIOXIDE	REACT AND CRYSTALLIZE OR MAKE INTO PELLETS	UREA (46-0-0)
AMMONIA / CARBON DIOXIDE / SALT	CARBONATE AND FILTER / AMMONIATE	SODIUM CARBONATE AMMONIUM CHLORIDE (23-0-0)
COAL / LIMESTONE / NITROGEN	FUSE IN ARC FURNACE / NITRIFY	CALCIUM CYANAMIDE (24-0-0)

BASIC PROCESSES used in manufacturing the major kinds of chemical fertilizers are charted. Each horizontal line shows the flow of the ingredient listed at left opposite the line. A vertical line shows a combining of ingredients. Numbers in parentheses show respectively the typical percentage of nitrogen, phosphorus and potassium materials used as fertilizer. For example, 0-35-0 means no nitrogen, 35 percent phosphorus pentoxide and no potassium oxide. Figures thus show amounts of primary nutrients.

phate in particles of the mineral aragonite on the ocean floor, a slow process that may still be taking place. Marine deposits of this nature may well become future sources of phosphate.

In any event, most of the primary deposits of sedimentary phosphate were laid down on ocean floor that subsequently became dry land. In time the weathering of such areas removed cementing substances such as calcium carbonate and magnesium carbonate, leaving extensive deposits of phosphate in the form of small pellets. Some of these deposits were later moved by surface water and redeposited elsewhere. Because of this extensive redeposition, and because pellet phosphates are insoluble in water, few minerals are found more widely scattered. By the same token, few have been formed over a longer span of time; phosphate minerals were laid down over the 400 million years from the Ordovician period to the Tertiary period and even later.

Often the phosphate pellets are covered by several feet of sand, clay or leached ore that must be taken off by scrapers or draglines before the phosphate matrix can be removed. In the extensive operations in Florida the matrix is excavated, dropped into sumps, slurried with powerful jets of water and then pumped to the processing plants. The material thus obtained may be only about 15 percent phosphate because of the large amounts of sand and clay in the matrix. Much of the sand and clay is removed by various processes to yield concentrates containing 30 to 36 percent phosphate. These concentrates are then blended and dried before further processing or shipment. Somewhat different methods are used in North Africa; there large tonnages of high-grade phosphate rock are mined by underground methods. Often they are only crushed, screened and dried before shipment.

Several types of fertilizer are made from the phosphate rock processed by the methods I have described. The simplest type consists of high-grade rock ground to particles less than .1 millimeter in size. This type is used directly on acid soils, which slowly attack the water-insoluble phosphate to make it available to plants. Next in simplicity is superphosphate, made by mixing ground phosphate rock with sulfuric acid to form a slurry that quickly hardens in a curing pile. After several weeks the hardened superphosphate is excavated and pulverized; often the powder is formed into granules. The pulverized or granulated material is marketed ei-

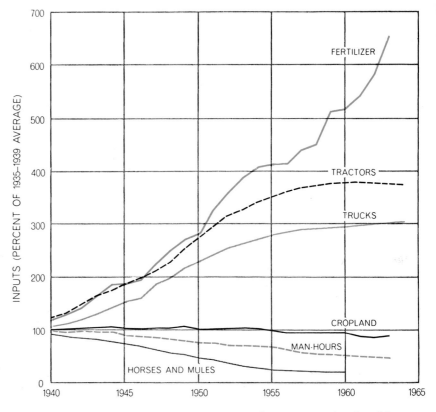

CHANGED TECHNOLOGY of U.S. agriculture over the past 30 years is reflected in a comparison of current inputs with those of 1935 through 1939. The changes are expressed as percentages of the average input in each category for the five-year base period. Concurrent with these changes of input has been a steady rise in the nation's agricultural output.

ther alone, as a phosphate fertilizer containing about 18 percent water-soluble phosphorus pentoxide, or in conjunction with other fertilizer materials. The various processing steps convert insoluble tricalcium phosphate to water-soluble monocalcium phosphate and gypsum.

Gypsum, however, is of little use in soil except when deficiencies in calcium or sulfur exist or when salinity is excessive. It also has a diluting effect on the phosphorus pentoxide content. Therefore it was a substantial advance when methods were devised for producing monocalcium phosphate without gypsum. The technique is to dissolve phosphate rock in a mixture of sulfuric and phosphoric acid to form gypsum and additional phosphoric acid, which can be separated by filtration. Thereafter the gypsum is usually discarded; the phosphoric acid is concentrated and mixed with finely ground phosphate rock to form a slurry that soon hardens into a product known as triple superphosphate. Its content of water-soluble phosphorus pentoxide is about 48 percent. Moreover, the product is cheaper to transport and to apply per unit of phosphorus pentoxide than ordinary superphosphate.

Substantial tonnages of phosphate fertilizers are also made by treating phosphate rock with nitric acid and ammonia to yield a range of materials that contain nitrogen as well as phosphorus. Potash can be added to form high-analysis fertilizers with a content of primary nutrients as high as 60 percent, as for example in a 20-20-20 grade. Another popular fertilizer is diammonium phosphate, which is made by neutralizing phosphoric acid with ammonia to yield a material containing about 20 percent nitrogen and 50 percent water-soluble phosphorus pentoxide. Potash can be added to this product to make another high-analysis mixture containing all the primary nutrients.

Potassium exists in enormous quantities in the rocks and soils of the world. Often, however, it is in the form of insoluble minerals unsuitable for agriculture. Fortunately large deposits of soluble potassium chloride are available, mostly as sylvite and sylvinite or, in conjunction with magnesium, as carnallite and langbeinite. Such deposits are often mixed with sodium chloride in the form of halite, which is toxic to many crops and must be removed.

Extensive supplies of sylvite and

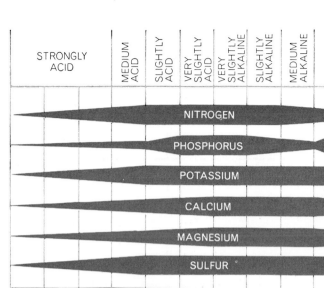

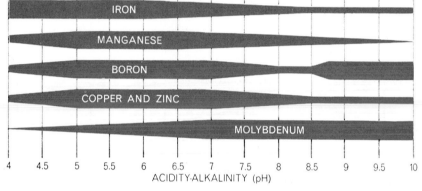

AVAILABILITY OF NUTRIENTS to plants is affected by the condition of the soil. The more soluble a nutrient is under a particular condition of soil acidity or alkalinity, the thicker is the horizontal band representing the nutrient. Solubility in turn is directly related to the availability of the nutrient in an ionic form that is assimilable by the plant.

carnallite were found first in Germany and later in France, the western U.S. and many other countries. Most of these deposits resulted from the evaporation of ancient seas during the Permian period (about 230 to 280 million years ago). In the Canadian province of Saskatchewan huge quantities of sylvite and carnallite were more recently found at depths of 3,000 to 4,000 feet, in the upper portion of a Devonian halite formation. Although these deposits are considerably deeper than U.S. and European potash sources, mining difficulties have now been overcome and the production of several million tons annually of Canadian potash will be of great benefit to world agriculture. Another Canadian development of growing importance is the large-scale production of potash by solution mining, which involves pumping water into the potash beds and bringing the resulting solution to the surface for evaporation and the recovery of potash in solid form.

After solid potash minerals are mined they are sometimes crushed and separated from their impurities by washing and froth-flotation, in which treatment with amine salts and air causes the sylvite particles to float away from the unwanted substances. In other cases potash is recovered by solution and crystallization. The relatively pure product is dried, treated with an amine anticaking agent and sold for agricultural purposes as muriate of potash containing 60 to 62 percent of potassium oxide. Most potash is used in conjunction with nitrogen and phosphorus compounds. Potassium sulfate and potassium nitrate are also used to a limited extent in agricultural situations where the chloride ions of potash would be harmful, as they are to tobacco.

Agronomic Considerations

It is appropriate now to consider the role of nutrients in plant growth, together with some other factors that must be taken into account in the use of fertilizers. As anyone experienced in agronomy or gardening knows, it is wasteful and sometimes even harmful to broadcast fertilizer indiscriminately.

The grower must know the condition of his soil and treat it accordingly. In most cases he must apply the bulk of the treatment before sowing, because as a rule most of the nutrient needed by a plant is taken up in the early stages of its growth. The correct nutrient balance is additionally important because a deficiency of any one plant food in the soil will reduce the effect of others, even if they are in oversupply.

A deficiency of nitrogen usually appears in plants as a yellowing of the leaves, accompanied by shriveling that proceeds upward from the lower leaves. The principal effects of nitrogen on plants include accelerated growth and increased yield of leaf, fruit and seed. Nitrogen also promotes the activity of soil bacteria. Nitrate nitrogen is quickly available to root systems, but it may therefore make the plants grow too rapidly. Moreover, nitrate is easily lost by leaching. Ammoniacal nitrogen, on the other hand, is immediately fixed in the soil by ion-exchange reactions and is released to the plants over a longer period than nitrate nitrogen. For these reasons it is sometimes the practice to inject free ammonia in anhydrous or aqueous form a few inches below the surface of a moist soil. With many crops optimum results are obtained by the proper combination of nitrate nitrogen and ammoniacal nitrogen in either solid or liquid form.

Phosphorus deficiency is often represented by purplish leaves and stems, slow growth and low yields. Phosphorus stimulates the germination of seedlings and encourages early root formation. Since these results are less evident than those induced by applications of nitrogen, many farmers, particularly in the Far East, use insufficient quantities of phosphate fertilizer.

Potassium deficiency can often be detected by a spotting or curling of lower leaves. Additional symptoms are weak stalks and stems, a condition that can cause heavy crop losses in strong winds and heavy rains. The application of potassium improves the yield of grain and seed, and it enhances the formation of starches, sugars and plant oils. It also contributes to the plant's vigor and its resistance to frost and disease.

As for deficiencies of secondary nutrients, a lack of magnesium may cause a general loss of color, weak stalks and white bands across the leaves in corn and certain other plants. A calcium deficiency may give rise to the premature death of young leaves and poor formation of seed. An inadequate supply of sulfur frequently leads to pale leaves, stunted growth and immature fruit.

Typical examples of micronutrient deficiency are heart rot in vegetables and fruits as a result of a shortage of boron and stunted growth of vegetables and citrus plants resulting from insufficient manganese and molybdenum. Micronutrient deficiencies may be hard to detect and even harder to rectify, because the balance between enough of a micronutrient and a toxic oversupply can be delicate.

An important consideration in the use of fertilizers is the acidity of the soil, which considerably influences the availability of many nutrients to the plant [see illustration on opposite page]. To complicate matters, nitrogen fertilizers such as ammonia, urea ammonium nitrate and other ammonia derivatives can

themselves raise the acidity of soils, by means of complex ion-exchange reactions. In most cases the acidity of a soil can be controlled by adding appropriate amounts of lime, ground limestone or other forms of calcium carbonate.

Soil tilth, or structure, is also important. For example, the richer chernozem soils found in the middle of the North American continent and in the Ukraine are in many cases well supplied with organic humus and lime salts and need only regular supplies of plant nutrients to replace those removed by agriculture and leaching. On the other hand, the podzol soils that cover the northeastern U.S., most of Britain and much of central Europe have been intensively leached by centuries of farming and exposure; they need not only

liberal supplies of plant nutrients but also lime and organic humus. Desert soils may be rich in certain minerals and yet lacking in available nutrients and in the organic matter usually necessary to retain moisture and to provide good tilth. Such soils can be made productive, however, as has been amply demonstrated in Israel.

Prospective Developments

In spite of the many improvements made in chemical fertilizers during the past 50 years, several problems still confront the fertilizer industry. One major concern is achieving the controlled release of nutrients so that waste and also damage to young plants can be avoided. Methods now being tested in-

TREATMENT PLANT of the V-C Chemical Company in Florida removes organic material and some carbon dioxide from phosphate rock to provide a raw material for making phosphoric acid, which is used in the manufacture of such chemical fertilizers as triple superphosphate and diammonium phosphate. Piles of phosphate rock as brought from the mine are at top right. Horizontal tube in foreground is a calcine kiln in which rock is given thermal treatment. Treated rock is stored in tanks behind kiln until shipped.

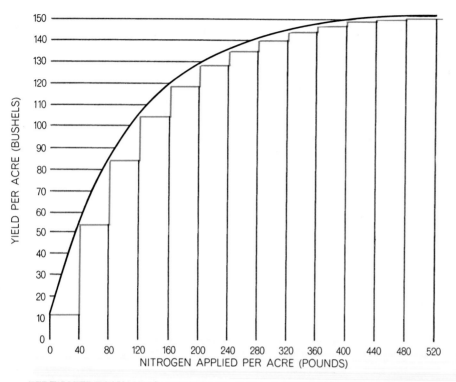

FERTILIZER ECONOMICS are indicated by the curve of yield compared with applications of fertilizer. This curve is based on a crop of irrigated corn grown in the state of Washington. With nitrogen as with other fertilizers, crop yields diminish with increasing applications of nutrients. In time additional increments of fertilizer become uneconomical.

SUBSTANCE	APPROXIMATE POUNDS PER ACRE	SUPPLIED BY
NITROGEN	310	
PHOSPHORUS	120 (PHOSPHATE) 52 (PHOSPHORUS)	1,200 POUNDS OF 25-10-20 FERTILIZER
POTASSIUM	245 (POTASH) 205 (POTASSIUM)	
CALCIUM	58	APPROXIMATELY 150 POUNDS OF AGRICULTURAL LIMESTONE
MAGNESIUM	50	APPROXIMATELY 275 POUNDS OF EPSOM SALT, OR 550 POUNDS SULFATE OF POTASH-MAGNESIA
SULFUR	33	33 POUNDS OF SULFUR
IRON	3	15 POUNDS OF IRON SULFATE
MANGANESE	.45	APPROXIMATELY 1.3 POUNDS OF MANGANESE SULFATE
BORON	.10	APPROXIMATELY 1 POUND OF BORAX
ZINC	TRACE	SMALL AMOUNT OF ZINC SULFATE
COPPER	TRACE	SMALL AMOUNT OF COPPER SULFATE OR OXIDE
MOLYBDENUM	TRACE	VERY SMALL AMOUNT OF SODIUM OR AMMONIUM MOLYBDATE
OXYGEN	10,200	AIR
CARBON	7,800	AIR
WATER	3,225 TO 4,175 TONS	29 TO 36 INCHES OF RAIN

NUTRIENTS REQUIRED to produce 150 bushels of corn are indicated. Most plants take all their nutrients from the soil except carbon, oxygen and hydrogen, obtained from the air.

clude the use of slowly decomposing inorganic materials such as magnesium ammonium phosphate and synthetic organic compounds such as formamide and oxamide. Another technique being studied is the encapsulation of fertilizer particles with sulfur or plastic. Investigators are also exploring the possibilities of producing chemical fertilizers in which a plant nutrient would be "sequestered" in molecules of the chelate type. Chelation involves a tight molecular bonding that would protect the nutrient against rapid attack. In this way the desired plant food would be released slowly and in a prescribed manner by chemical reactions in the soil. An ultimate possibility is the production of "packaged" granules, each containing a seed and whatever substances are needed during the lifetime of the plant. They would be released in the proper amounts and sequence.

A new agricultural technique already in use on a small scale is "chemical plowing." Instead of turning stubble and cover crops into the ground mechanically, the farmer kills them by spraying them with the appropriate herbicides. Eventually the dead plant materials become sources of humus and plant nutrient. Any excess of herbicide is rendered harmless by the action of soil colloids. New seeds and fertilizer are drilled directly through the dead cover material, which also gives protection against erosion, frost and drought.

Efforts are also under way to reduce the cost of transporting fertilizers and their raw materials. The approach here is to try to produce them in highly concentrated liquid or solid form. They are then appropriately diluted or combined at the point of use.

Perhaps the most vital work is the education of farmers—particularly farmers in the developing countries—in modern agricultural methods, including the use of chemical fertilizers. In addition the developing nations must establish low-cost credit plans so that impoverished farmers can buy adequate supplies of fertilizer. Similarly, credit must be extended by the developed nations to the less developed ones on an even bigger scale than at present in order to help the less developed nations obtain the materials, equipment and expert advice they need to build their own chemical fertilizer plants. Until these steps are taken to spread modern agricultural technology, the developing nations will fall far short of the contribution they could make to the intensifying problem of producing enough food for the world's growing population.

24

Third-Generation Pesticides

CARROLL M. WILLAMS
July 1967

Man's efforts to control harmful insects with pesticides have encountered two intractable difficulties. The first is that the pesticides developed up to now have been too broad in their effect. They have been toxic not only to the pests at which they were aimed but also to other insects. Moreover, by persisting in the environment—and sometimes even increasing in concentration as they are passed along the food chain—they have presented a hazard to other organisms, including man. The second difficulty is that insects have shown a remarkable ability to develop resistance to pesticides.

Plainly the ideal approach would be to find agents that are highly specific in their effect, attacking only insects that are regarded as pests, and that remain effective because the insects cannot acquire resistance to them. Recent findings indicate that the possibility of achieving success along these lines is much more likely than it seemed a few years ago. The central idea embodied in these findings is that a harmful species of insect can be attacked with its own hormones.

Insects, according to the latest estimates, comprise about three million species—far more than all other animal and plant species combined. The number of individual insects alive at any one time is thought to be about a billion billion (10^{18}). Of this vast multitude 99.9 percent are from the human point of view either innocuous or downright helpful. A few are indispensable; one need think only of the role of bees in pollination.

The troublemakers are the other .1 percent, amounting to about 3,000 species. They are the agricultural pests and the vectors of human and animal disease. Those that transmit human disease are the most troublesome; they have joined with the bacteria, viruses and protozoa in what has sometimes seemed like a grand conspiracy to exterminate man, or at least to keep him in a state of perpetual ill health.

The fact that the human species is still here is an abiding mystery. Presumably the answer lies in changes in the genetic makeup of man. The example of sickle-cell anemia is instructive. The presence of sickle-shaped red blood cells in a person's blood can give rise to a serious form of anemia, but it also confers resistance to malaria. The sickle-cell trait (which does not necessarily lead to sickle-cell anemia) is appreciably more common in Negroes than in members of other populations. Investigations have suggested that the sickle cell is a genetic mutation that occurred long ago in malarial regions of Africa. Apparently attrition by malaria-carrying mosquitoes provoked countermeasures deep within the genes of primitive men.

The evolution of a genetic defense, however, takes many generations and entails many deaths. It was only in comparatively recent times that man found an alternative answer by learning to combat the insects with chemistry. He did so by inventing what can be called the first-generation pesticides: kerosene to coat the ponds, arsenate of lead to poison the pests that chew, nicotine and rotenone for the pests that suck.

Only 25 years ago did man devise the far more potent weapon that was the first of the second-generation pesticides. The weapon was dichlorodiphenyltrichloroethane, or DDT. It descended on the noxious insects like an avenging angel. On contact with it mosquitoes, flies, beetles—almost all the insects—were stricken with what might be called the "DDT's." They went into a tailspin, buzzed around upside down for an hour or so and then dropped dead.

The age-old battle with the insects appeared to have been won. We had the stuff to do them in—or so we thought. A few wise men warned that we were living in a fool's paradise and that the insects would soon become resistant to DDT, just as the bacteria had managed to develop a resistance to the challenge of sulfanilamide. That is just what happened. Within a few years the mosquitoes, lice, houseflies and other noxious insects were taking DDT in their stride. Soon they were metabolizing it, then they became addicted to it and were therefore in a position to try harder.

Fortunately the breach was plugged by the chemical industry, which had come to realize that killing insects was —in more ways than one—a formula for

248

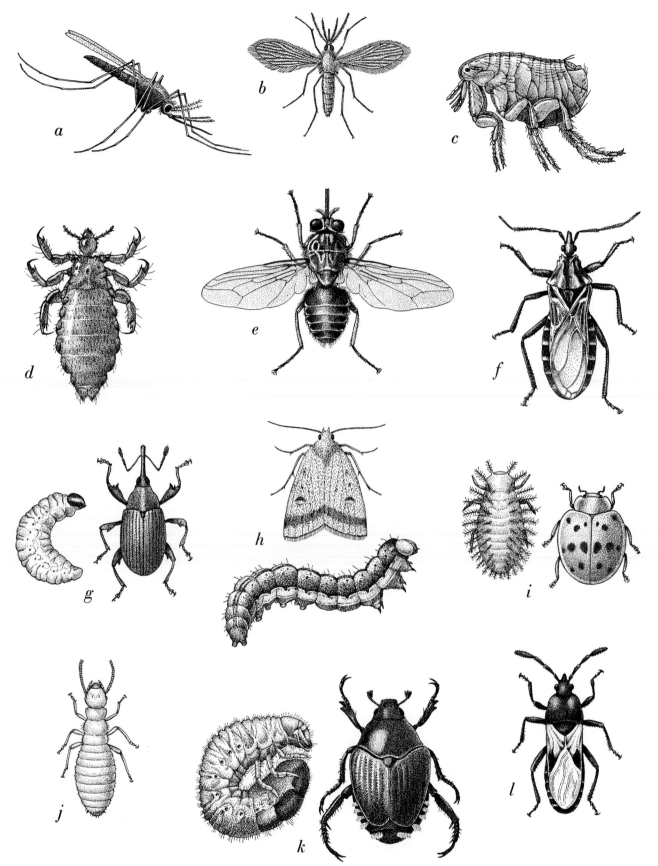

INSECT PESTS that might be controlled by third-generation pesticides include some 3,000 species, of which 12 important examples are shown here. Six (a–f) transmit diseases to human beings; the other six are agricultural pests. The disease-carriers, together with the major disease each transmits, are (a) the *Anopheles* mosquito, malaria; (b) the sand fly, leishmaniasis; (c) the rat flea, plague; (d) the body louse, typhus; (e) the tsetse fly, sleeping sickness, and (f) the kissing bug, Chagas' disease. The agricultural pests, four of which are depicted in both larval and adult form, are (g) the boll weevil; (h) the corn earworm; (i) the Mexican bean beetle; (j) the termite; (k) the Japanese beetle, and (l) the chinch bug. The species in the illustration are not drawn to the same scale.

getting along in the world. Organic chemists began a race with the insects. In most cases it was not a very long race, because the insects soon evolved an insensitivity to whatever the chemists had produced. The chemists, redoubling their efforts, synthesized a steady stream of second-generation pesticides. By 1966 the sales of such pesticides had risen to a level of $500 million a year in the U.S. alone.

Coincident with the steady rise in the output of pesticides has come a growing realization that their blunderbuss toxicity can be dangerous. The problem has attracted widespread public attention since the late Rachel Carson fervently described in *The Silent Spring* some actual and potential consequences of this toxicity. Although the attention thus aroused has resulted in a few attempts to exercise care in the application of pesticides, the problem cannot really be solved with the substances now in use.

The rapid evolution of resistance to pesticides is perhaps more critical. For example, the world's most serious disease in terms of the number of people afflicted continues to be malaria, which is transmitted by the *Anopheles* mosquito—an insect that has become completely resistant to DDT. (Meanwhile the protozoon that actually causes the disease is itself evolving strains resistant to antimalaria drugs.)

A second instance has been presented recently in Vietnam by an outbreak of plague, the dreaded disease that is conveyed from rat to man by fleas. In this case the fleas have become resistant to pesticides. Other resistant insects that are agricultural pests continue to take a heavy toll of the world's dwindling food supply from the moment the seed is planted until long after the crop is harvested. Here again we are confronted by an emergency situation that the old technology can scarcely handle.

The new approach that promises a way out of these difficulties has emerged during the past decade from basic studies of insect physiology. The prime candidate for developing third-generation pesticides is the juvenile hormone that all insects secrete at certain stages in their lives. It is one of the three internal secretions used by insects to regulate growth and metamorphosis from larva to pupa to adult. In the living insect the juvenile hormone is synthesized by the corpora allata, two tiny glands in the head. The corpora allata are also responsible for regulating the flow of the hormone into the blood.

At certain stages the hormone must be

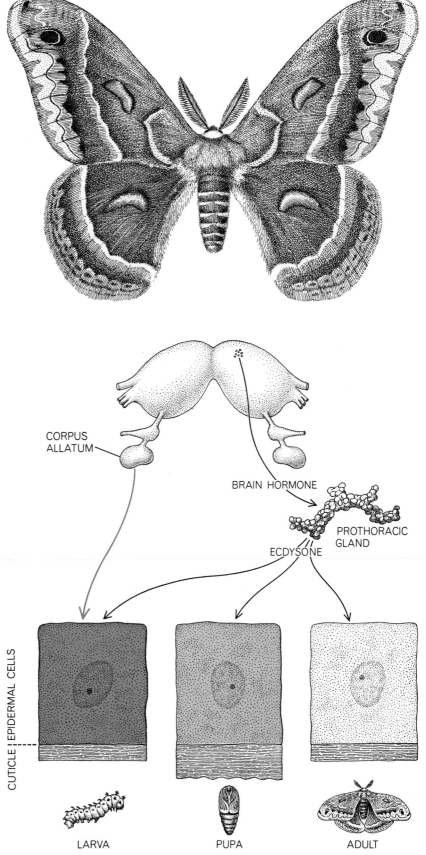

HORMONAL ACTIVITY in a Cecropia moth is outlined. Juvenile hormone (*color*) comes from the corpora allata, two small glands in the head; a second substance, brain hormone, stimulates the prothoracic glands to secrete ecdysone, which initiates the molts through which a larva passes. Juvenile hormone controls the larval forms and at later stages must be in low concentration or absent; if applied then, it deranges insect's normal development. The illustration is partly based on one by Howard A. Schneiderman and Lawrence I. Gilbert.

250

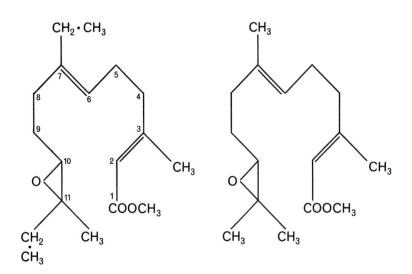

CHEMICAL STRUCTURES of the Cecropia juvenile hormone (*left*), isolated this year by Herbert Röller and his colleagues at the University of Wisconsin, and of a synthetic analogue (*right*) made in 1965 by W. S. Bowers and others in the U.S. Department of Agriculture show close similarity. Carbon atoms, joined to one or two hydrogen atoms, occupy each angle in the backbone of the molecules; letters show the structure at terminals and branches.

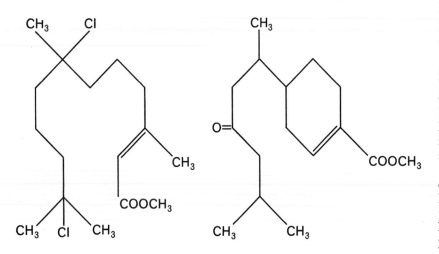

JUVENILE HORMONE ACTIVITY has been found in various substances not secreted by insects. One (*left*) is a material synthesized by M. Romanuk and his associates in Czechoslovakia. The other (*right*), isolated and identified by Bowers and his colleagues, is the "paper factor" found in the balsam fir. The paper factor has a strong juvenile hormone effect on only one family of insects, exemplified by the European bug *Pyrrhocoris apterus*.

secreted; at certain other stages it must be absent or the insect will develop abnormally [*see illustration on preceding page*]. For example, an immature larva has an absolute requirement for juvenile hormone if it is to progress through the usual larval stages. Then, in order for a mature larva to metamorphose into a sexually mature adult, the flow of hormone must stop. Still later, after the adult is fully formed, juvenile hormone must again be secreted.

The role of juvenile hormone in larval development has been established for several years. Recent studies at Harvard University by Lynn M. Riddiford and the Czechoslovakian biologist Karel Sláma have resulted in a surprising additional finding. It is that juvenile hormone must be absent from insect eggs for the eggs to undergo normal embryonic development.

The periods when the hormone must be absent are the Achilles' heel of insects. If the eggs or the insects come into contact with the hormone at these times, the hormone readily enters them and provokes a lethal derangement of further development. The result is that the eggs fail to hatch or the immature insects die without reproducing.

Juvenile hormone is an insect invention that, according to present knowledge, has no effect on other forms of life. Therefore the promise is that third-generation pesticides can zero in on in-

sects to the exclusion of other plants and animals. (Even for the insects juvenile hormone is not a toxic material in the usual sense of the word. Instead of killing, it derails the normal mechanisms of development and causes the insects to kill themselves.) A further advantage is self-evident: insects will not find it easy to evolve a resistance or an insensitivity to their own hormone without automatically committing suicide.

The potentialities of juvenile hormone as an insecticide were recognized 12 years ago in experiments performed on the first active preparation of the hormone: a golden oil extracted with ether from male Cecropia moths. Strange to say, the male Cecropia and the male of its close relative the Cynthia moth remain to this day the only insects from which one can extract the hormone. Therefore tens of thousands of the moths have been required for the experimental work with juvenile hormone; the need has been met by a small but thriving industry that rears the silkworms.

No one expected Cecropia moths to supply the tons of hormone that would be required for use as an insecticide. Obviously the hormone would have to be synthesized. That could not be done, however, until the hormone had been isolated from the golden oil and identified.

Within the past few months the difficult goals of isolating and identifying the hormone have at last been attained by a team of workers headed by Herbert Röller of the University of Wisconsin. The juvenile hormone has the empirical formula $C_{18}H_{30}O_3$, corresponding to a molecular weight of 294. It proves to be the methyl ester of the epoxide of a previously unknown fatty-acid derivative [*see upper illustration on this page*]. The apparent simplicity of the molecule is deceptive. It has two double bonds and an oxirane ring (the small triangle at lower left in the molecular diagram), and it can exist in 16 different molecular configurations. Only one of these can be the authentic hormone. With two ethyl groups ($CH_2 \cdot CH_3$) attached to carbons No. 7 and 11, the synthesis of the hormone from any known terpenoid is impossible.

The pure hormone is extraordinarily active. Tests the Wisconsin investigators have carried out with mealworms suggest that one gram of the hormone would result in the death of about a billion of these insects.

A few years before Röller and his colleagues worked out the structure of the authentic hormone, investigators at several laboratories had synthesized a number of substances with impressive juvenile hormone activity. The most potent of the materials appears to be a crude mixture that John H. Law, now at the University of Chicago, prepared by a simple one-step process in which hydrogen chloride gas was bubbled through an alcoholic solution of farnesenic acid. Without any purification this mixture was 1,000 times more active than crude Cecropia oil and fully effective in killing all kinds of insects.

One of the six active components of Law's mixture has recently been identified and synthesized by a group of workers headed by M. Romaňuk of the Czechoslovak Academy of Sciences. Romaňuk and his associates estimate that from 10 to 100 grams of the material would clear all the insects from 2½ acres. Law's original mixture is of course even more potent, and so there is much interest in its other five components.

Another interesting development that preceded the isolation and identification of true juvenile hormone involved a team of investigators under W. S. Bowers of the U.S. Department of Agriculture's laboratory at Beltsville, Md. Bowers and his colleagues prepared an analogue of juvenile hormone that, as can be seen in the accompanying illustration [*top of opposite page*], differed by only two carbon atoms from the authentic Cecropia hormone (whose structure was then, of course, unknown). In terms of the dosage required it appears that the Beltsville compound is about 2 percent as active as Law's mixture and about .02 percent as active as the pure Cecropia hormone.

All the materials I have mentioned are selective in the sense of killing only insects. They leave unsolved, however, the problem of discriminating between the .1 percent of insects that qualify as pests and the 99.9 percent that are helpful or innocuous. Therefore any reckless use of the materials on a large scale could constitute an ecological disaster of the first rank.

The real need is for third-generation pesticides that are tailor-made to attack only certain predetermined pests. Can such pesticides be devised? Recent work that Sláma and I have carried out at Harvard suggests that this objective is by no means unattainable. The possibility arose rather fortuitously after Sláma arrived from Czechoslovakia, bringing with him some specimens of the European bug *Pyrrhocoris apterus*—a species that had been reared in his laboratory in Prague for 10 years.

To our considerable mystification the bugs invariably died without reaching sexual maturity when we attempted to rear them at Harvard. Instead of metamorphosing into normal adults they continued to grow as larvae or molted into adult-like forms retaining many larval characteristics. It was evident that the bugs had access to some unknown source of juvenile hormone.

Eventually we traced the source to the paper toweling that had been placed in the rearing jars. Then we discovered that almost any paper of American origin—including the paper on which *Scientific American* is printed—had the same effect. Paper of European or Japanese manufacture had no effect on the bugs. On further investigation we found that the juvenile hormone activity originated in the balsam fir, which is the principal source of pulp for paper in Canada and the northern U.S. The tree synthesizes what we named the "paper factor," and this substance accompanies the pulp all the way to the printed page.

Thanks again to Bowers and his associates at Beltsville, the active material of the paper factor has been isolated and characterized [*see lower illustration on opposite page*]. It proves to be the methyl ester of a certain unsaturated fatty-acid derivative. The factor's kinship with the other juvenile hormone analogues is evident from the illustrations.

Here, then, is an extractable juvenile hormone analogue with selective action against only one kind of insect. As it happens, the family Pyrrhocoridae includes some of the most destructive pests of the cotton plant. Why the balsam fir should have evolved a substance against only one family of insects is unexplained. The most intriguing possibility is that the paper factor is a biochemical memento of the juvenile hormone of a former natural enemy of the tree—a pyrrhocorid predator that, for obvious reasons, is either extinct or has learned to avoid the balsam fir.

In any event, the fact that the tree synthesizes the substance argues strongly that the juvenile hormone of other species of insects can be mimicked, and perhaps has been by trees or plants on which the insects preyed. Evidently during the 250 million years of insect evolution the detailed chemistry of juvenile hormone has evolved and diversified. The process would of necessity have gone hand in hand with a retuning of the hormonal receptor mechanisms in the cells and tissues of the insect, so that the use as pesticides of any analogues that are discovered seems certain to be effective.

The evergreen trees are an ancient lot. They were here before the insects; they are pollinated by the wind and thus, unlike many other plants, do not depend on the insects for anything. The paper factor is only one of thousands of terpenoid materials these trees synthesize for no apparent reason. What about the rest?

It seems altogether likely that many of these materials will also turn out to be analogues of the juvenile hormones of specific insect pests. Obviously this is the place to look for a whole battery of third-generation pesticides. Then man may be able to emulate the evergreen trees in their incredibly sophisticated self-defense against the insects.

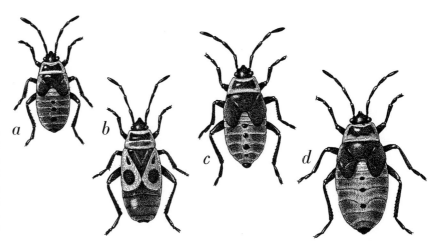

EFFECT OF PAPER FACTOR on *Pyrrhocoris apterus* is depicted. A larva of the fifth and normally final stage (*a*) turns into a winged adult (*b*). Contact with the paper factor causes the insect to turn into a sixth-stage larva (*c*) and sometimes into a giant seventh-stage larva (*d*). The abnormal larvae usually cannot shed their skin and die before reaching maturity.

25

The Prospects of Fusion Power

WILLIAM C. GOUGH AND BERNARD J. EASTLUND
February 1971

The achievement of a practical fusion-power reactor would have a profound impact on almost every aspect of human society. In the past few years considerable progress has been made toward that goal. Perhaps the most revealing indication of the significance of this progress is the extent to which the emphasis in recent discussions and meetings involving workers in the field has tended to shift from the question of purely scientific feasibility to a consideration of the technological, economic and social aspects of the power-generation problem. The purpose of this article is to examine the probable effects of the recent advances on the immediate and long-term prospects of the fusion-power program, with particular reference to mankind's future energy needs.

The Role of Energy

The role of energy in determining the economic well-being of a society is often inadequately understood. In terms of *total* energy the main energy source for any society is the sun, which through the cycle of photosynthesis produces the food that is the basic fuel for sustaining the population of that society. The efficiency with which the sun's energy can be put to use, however, is determined by a feedback loop in which auxiliary energy sources form a critical link [*see illustration, page 254*]. The auxiliary energy (derived mainly from fossil fuels, water power and nuclear-fission fuels) "opens the gate" to the efficient use of the sun's energy by helping to produce fertilizers, pesticides, improved seeds, farm machinery and so on. The result is that the food yield (in terms of energy content) produced per unit area of land in a year goes up by orders of magnitude. This auxiliary energy input, when it is transformed into food energy, enables large populations to live in cities and develop new ways to multiply the efficiency of the feedback loop. If a society is to raise its standard of living by increasing the efficiency of its agricultural feedback loop, clearly it must expand its auxiliary energy sources.

The dilemma here is that the economically less developed countries of the world cannot *all* industrialize on the model of the more developed countries, for the simple reason that the latter countries, which contain only a small fraction of the world's population, currently maintain their high standard of living by consuming a disproportionately large share of the world's available supply of auxiliary energy. Just as there is a direct, almost linear, relation between a nation's use of auxiliary energy and its standard of living, so also there is a similar relation between energy consumption and the amount of raw material the nation uses and the amount of waste material it produces. Thus the more developed countries consume a correspondingly oversized share of the world's reserves of material resources and also account for most of the world's environmental pollution.

In order to achieve a more equitable and stable balance between the standards of living in the more developed countries and those in the less developed countries, only two alternatives exist. The more developed countries could reduce their consumption of auxiliary energy (thereby lowering their standard of living as well) or they could contribute to the development of new, vastly greater sources of auxiliary energy in order to help meet the rising demands for a better standard of living on the part of the rapidly growing populations of the less developed countries.

When one projects the world's long-term energy requirements against this background, another important factor must be taken into account. There are finite limits to the world's reserves of material resources and to the ability of the earth's ecological system to absorb pollutants safely. As a consequence future societies will be forced to develop "looped," or "circular," materials economies to replace their present, inherently wasteful "linear" materials economies [*see bottom illustration on page 263*]. In such a "stationary state" system, limits on the materials inventory, and hence on the total wealth of the society, would be set by nature. Within these limits, however, the standard of living of the population would be higher if the rate of flow of materials were lower. This maximizing of the life expectancy of the materials inventory could be accomplished in two ways: increasing the durability of individual commodities and developing the technological means to recycle the limited supply of material resources.

The conclusion appears radical. Future societies must *minimize* their physical flow of production and consumption. Since a society's gross national product for the most part measures the flow of physical things, it too would be reduced.

But all nations now try to *maximize* their gross national product, and hence their rate of flow of materials! The explanation of this paradox is that in the existing linear economies the inputs for increasing production must come from the environment, which leads to depletion, while an almost equal amount of materials in the form of waste must be returned to the environment, which leads to pollution. This primary cause of pollution is augmented by the pollution that is produced by the energy sources used to drive the system.

In order to make the transition to a stationary-state world economy, the wealthier nations will have to develop the technology—and the concomitant auxiliary energy sources—necessary to operate a closed materials economy. This capability could then be transferred to the poorer nations so that they could develop to the level of the wealthier nations without exhausting the world's supply of resources or destroying the environment. Thus some of the causes of international conflict would be removed, thereby reducing the danger of nuclear war.

Of course any effort to bring about a rapid change from linear economies to looped economies will encounter the massive economic, social and political forces that sustain the present system. The question of how to distribute the stock of wealth, including leisure, within a stationary-state economy will remain. In summary, the world's requirements for energy are intimately related to the issues of population expansion, economic development, materials depletion, pollution, war and the organization of human societies.

The Energy Options

What are the available energy options for the future? To begin with there are the known finite and irreplaceable energy sources: the fossil fuels and the better-grade, or easily fissionable, nuclear fuels such as uranium 235. Estimates of the life expectancy of these sources vary, but it is generally agreed that they are being used up at a rapid rate—a rate that will moreover be accelerated by increases in both population and living standards. In addition, environmental considerations could further restrict the use of these energy sources.

Certain other known energy sources, such as water power, tidal power, geothermal power and wind power are "infinite" in the sense of being continuously replenished. The total useful *amount* of energy available from these sources, however, is insufficient to meet the needs of the future.

Direct solar radiation, resulting from the fusion reactions that take place in the core of the sun, is an abundant as well as effectively "infinite" energy source. The immediate practical obstacle to the direct use of the sun's energy as an effective auxiliary energy source is the necessity of finding some way to economically concentrate the available low energy density of solar radiation. Controlled fusion is another potentially "infinite" energy source; its energy output arises from the reduction of the total mass of a nuclear system that accompanies the merger of two light

U.S. TOKAMAK, a toroidal plasma-confinement machine used in fusion research, was recently put into operation at the Plasma Physics Laboratory of Princeton University. Until about a year ago this machine, formerly known as the Model-C stellarator and now called the Model ST tokamak, had been the largest of the stellarator class of experimental plasma containers developed primarily at the Princeton laboratory. The decision to convert it to the closely related tokamak design followed the 1969 announcement by the Russian fusion-research group of some important new results obtained from their Model T-3 machine, the most advanced of the tokamak class of plasma containers developed mainly at the I. V. Kurchatov Institute of Atomic Energy near Moscow. In large part because of the cooperative nature of the world fusion-research program, this conversion was accomplished quickly and the Model ST has already produced results comparable to those obtained by the Russians. Several other tokamak-type machines are being built in this country.

RUSSIAN STELLARATOR is now the largest representative of this class of experimental plasma containers in the world. It is named the Uragan (or "hurricane") stellarator and is located at the Physico-Technical Institute of the Academy of Sciences of the Ukrainian S.S.R. at Kharkov. In both photographs on this page the large circular structures surrounding and almost completely obscuring the toroidal plasma chambers are the primary magnet coils. The main difference between the tokamak design and the stellarator design is that in a tokamak a secondary plasma-stabilizing magnetic field is generated by an electric current flowing axially through the plasma itself, whereas in a stellarator this secondary magnetic field is set up by external helical coils situated just inside the primary coils and hence not visible.

nuclei. The most likely fuel for a fusion-power energy source is deuterium, an abundant heavy isotope of hydrogen easily separated from seawater.

In addition to these two primary "infinite" energy sources, secondary "infinite" energy sources could be made by using neutrons to transmute less useful elements into other elements capable of being used effectively as fuels. Thus for fission systems the vast reserves of uranium 238 could be converted by neutron bombardment into easily fissionable plutonium 239; similarly, thorium 232 could be converted into uranium 233. For fusion systems lithium could be converted into tritium, another heavy isotope of hydrogen with a comparatively low resistance to entering a fusion reaction and a comparatively high energy output once it does.

The prime hope for extending the world's reserves of nuclear-fission fuels is the development of the neutron-rich fast breeder fission reactors [see "Fast Breeder Reactors," by Glenn T. Seaborg and Justin L. Bloom; SCIENTIFIC AMERICAN, November, 1970]. Another potential source of abundant, inexpensive neutrons is a fusion-fission hybrid system, an

alternative that will be discussed further below.

Fusion Energy

Nuclear fusion, the basic energy process of the stars, was first reproduced on the earth in 1932 in an experiment involving the collision of artificially accelerated deuterium nuclei. Although it was thereby shown that fusion energy could be released in this way, the use of particle accelerators to provide the nuclei with enough energy to overcome their Coulomb, or mutually repulsive, forces was never considered seriously as a practical method for power generation. The reason is that the large majority of the nuclei that collide in an accelerator scatter without reacting; thus it is impossible to produce more energy than was used to accelerate the nuclei in the first place.

The uncontrolled release of a massive amount of fusion energy was achieved in 1952 with the first thermonuclear test explosion. This test proved that fusion energy could be released on a large scale by raising the temperature of a high-density gas of charged particles (a plas-

ma) to about 50 million degrees Celsius, thereby increasing the probability that fusion reactions will take place within the gas.

Coincident with the development of the hydrogen bomb, the search for a more controlled means of releasing fusion energy was begun independently in the U.S., Britain and the U.S.S.R. Essentially this search involves looking for a practical way to maintain a comparatively low-density plasma at a temperature high enough so that the output of fusion energy derived from the plasma is greater than the input of some other kind of energy supplied to the plasma. Since no solid material can exist at the temperature range required for a useful energy output (on the order of 100 million degrees C.) the principal emphasis from the beginning has been on the use of magnetic fields to confine the plasma.

The variety of magnetic "bottles" designed for this purpose over the years can be arranged in several broad categories in order of increasing plasma density [see illustration on pages 258 and 259]. First there are the basic plasma devices. These are low-density, low-temperature systems used primarily to study the fundamental properties of plasmas. Their configuration can be either linear (open) or toroidal (closed). Linear basic-plasma devices include simple glow-discharge systems (similar in operation to ordinary fluorescent lamps) and the more sophisticated "Q-machines" ("Q" for "quiescent") found in many university plasma-physics laboratories. Toroidal representatives of this class include the "multipole" devices, developed primarily at Gulf Energy & Environmental Systems, Inc. (formerly Gulf General Atomic Inc.) and the University of Wisconsin, and the spherator, developed at the Plasma Physics Laboratory of Princeton University.

Next there are the medium-density plasma containers; these are defined as systems in which the outward pressure of the plasma is much less than the inward pressure of the magnetic field. A typical configuration in this density range is the linear magnetic bottle, which is usually "stoppered" at the ends by magnetic "mirrors": regions of somewhat greater magnetic-field strength that reflect escaping particles back into the bottle. In addition extra current-carrying structures are often used to improve the stability of the plasma. These structures were originally proposed on theoretical grounds in 1955 by Harold Grad of New York University. They were first used successfully in an experimental test in 1962 by the Russian physicist M. S. Ioffe.

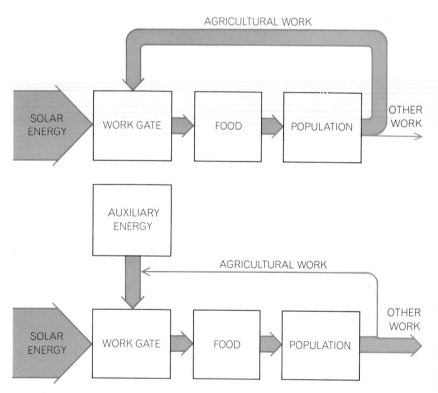

ROLE OF AUXILIARY ENERGY in determining the economic well-being of a society is illustrated by these two diagrams of agricultural feedback loops. In an economically less developed country (*top*) the bulk of the population must be devoted to the agricultural transformation of the sun's energy into food in order to support itself at a subsistence level. In an economically more developed industrial country (*bottom*) auxiliary energy sources "open the gate" to the more efficient utilization of the sun's energy, making it possible for the entire population to maintain a higher standard of living and freeing many people to live in cities and develop new ways to multiply the efficiency of the feedback loop.

		LIFE EXPECTANCY OF KNOWN RESERVES (YEARS)		LIFE EXPECTANCY OF POTENTIAL RESERVES (YEARS)		LIFE EXPECTANCY OF TOTAL RESERVES (YEARS)	
		AT .17Q	AT 2.8Q	AT .17Q	AT 2.8Q	AT .17Q	AT 2.8Q
FINITE ENERGY SOURCES	FOSSIL FUELS (COAL, OIL, GAS)	132	8	2,700	165	2,832	173
	MORE ACCESSIBLE FISSION FUELS (URANIUM AT $5 TO $30 PER POUND OF U_3O_8 BURNED AT 1.5 PERCENT EFFICIENCY)	66	4	66	4	132	8
	LESS ACCESSIBLE FISSION FUELS (URANIUM AT $30 TO $500 PER POUND OF U_3O_8 BURNED AT 1.5 PERCENT EFFICIENCY)	43,000	2,600	129,000	7,800	172,000	10,400
"INFINITE" NATURAL ENERGY SOURCES	WATER POWER, TIDAL POWER, GEOTHERMAL POWER, WIND POWER	INSUFFICIENT		INSUFFICIENT		INSUFFICIENT	
	SOLAR RADIATION	10 BILLION	10 BILLION			10 BILLION	10 BILLION
	FUSION FUELS (DEUTERIUM FROM OCEAN)	45 BILLION	2.7 BILLION			45 BILLION	2.7 BILLION
"INFINITE" ARTIFICIAL ENERGY SOURCES (ELEMENTS TRANSMUTED FROM OTHER ELEMENTS BY NEUTRON BOMBARDMENT)	FISSION FUELS (PLUTONIUM 239 FROM URANIUM 238; URANIUM 233 FROM THORIUM 232)	8.8 MILLION	536,000	21 MILLION	1.3 MILLION	30 MILLION	1.8 MILLION
	FUSION FUELS (TRITIUM FROM LITHIUM) a) ON LAND b) IN OCEAN	48,000 120 MILLION	2,900 7.3 MILLION	UNKNOWN	UNKNOWN	48,000+ 120 MILLION	2,900+ 7.3 MILLION

WORLD ENERGY RESERVES are listed in this table in terms of their life expectancy estimated on the basis of two extreme assumptions, which were chosen so as to bracket a reasonable range of values. First, the assumption was made that the world population would remain constant at its 1968 level of 3.5 billion persons and that the energy-consumption rate of this population would remain constant at the estimated 1968 rate of .17 Q (Q is a unit of heat measurement equal to 10^{18} BTU, or British Thermal Units). Second, the assumption was made that the world population would eventually reach seven billion and that this population would consume energy at a per capita rate of 400 million BTU per year (about 20 percent higher than the present U.S. rate), giving a total world energy-consumption rate of 2.8 Q per year. (A commonly projected world energy-consumption rate for the year 2000 is one Q.) Current fission-converter reactors use only between 1 and 2 percent of the uranium's potential energy content, since the com-

ponent of the ore that is burned as fuel is primarily high-grade, or easily fissionable, uranium 235. The world fission-fuel reserves were derived by multiplying the U.S. reserves times the ratio of world land area to the U.S. land area (approximately 16.2 to one). For fusion-converter reactors lithium-utilization studies show that natural lithium, a mixture of lithium 6 and lithium 7, would be superior to pure lithium 6 in a tritium-breeding reactor "blanket" and would yield an energy output of about 86.4 million BTU per gram. The figure for known world lithium reserves is based on a study carried out last year by James J. Norton of the U.S. Geological Survey. The potential reserves of lithium are unknown, since there has been no exploration program comparable to that undertaken for, say, uranium. Lithium, however, is between five and 15 times more abundant in the earth's crust than uranium. Finally, the life expectancy of the earth—and hence that of potentially useful solar radiation—is predicted to be at most 10 billion years.

The straight rods used by Ioffe in his experiment have come to be called Ioffe bars, but such stabilizing structures can assume various other shapes. For example, in one series of medium-density linear devices they resemble the seam of a baseball; accordingly these devices, developed at the Lawrence Radiation Laboratory of the University of California at Livermore, are named Baseball I and Baseball II.

Medium-density plasma containers with a toroidal geometry include the stellarators, originally developed at the Princeton Plasma Physics Laboratory, and the tokamaks, originally developed at the I. V. Kurchatov Institute of Atomic Energy near Moscow. The only essential difference between these two machines is that in a stellarator a secondary, plasma-stabilizing magnetic field is set up by external helical coils, whereas in a tokamak this field is generated by an electric current flowing through the plasma itself. The close similarity between these two designs was emphasized recently by the fact that the Princeton

Model-C stellarator was rather quickly converted to a tokamak system following the recent announcement by the Russians of some important new results from their Tokamak-3 machine.

The astron concept, also developed at the Lawrence Radiation Laboratory at Livermore, is another example of a medium-density plasma container. In overall geometry it shares some characteristics of both the linear and the toroidal designs.

Higher-density plasma containers, defined as those in which the plasma pressure is comparable to the magnetic-field pressure, have also been built in both the linear and the toroidal forms. In one such class of devices, called the "theta pinch" machines, the electric current is in the theta, or azimuthal, direction (around the axis) and the resulting magnetic field is in the zeta, or axial, direction (along the axis). The Scylla and Scyllac machines at the Los Alamos Scientific Laboratory are respectively examples of a linear theta-pinch design and a toroidal theta-pinch design.

As the density of the plasma is increased further, one reaches a technological limit imposed by the inability of the materials used in the magnet coils to withstand the pressure of the magnetic field. Consequently very-high-density plasma systems are often fast-pulsed and obtain their principal confining forces from "self-generated" magnetic fields (fields set up by electric currents in the plasma itself), from electrostatic fields or from inertial pressures. In this very-high-density category are the "zeta pinch" machines, devices in which the electric current is in the zeta direction and the resulting magnetic field is in the theta direction. An example of this type of configuration is the Columba device at Los Alamos.

Other very-high-density, fast-pulsed systems include the "strong focus" designs, in which a stream of plasma in a cylindrical, coaxial pipe is heated rapidly by shock waves as it is brought to a sharp focus by self-generated magnetic forces, and laser designs, in which a pellet of fuel is ionized instantaneously by a pulse from a high-power laser, producing an "inertially confined" plasma. Still another confinement scheme that has been investigated in this general density range includes an electrostatic device in which the plasma is confined by inertial forces generated by concentric spherical electrodes.

The Fusion-Power Balance

What are the fundamental requirements for a meaningful release of fusion energy in a reactor? First, the plasma must be hot enough for the production of fusion energy to exceed the energy loss due to bremsstrahlung radiation (radiation resulting from near-collisions between electrons and nuclei in the plasma). The temperature at which this transition occurs is called the ignition temperature. For a fuel cycle based on fusion reactions between deuterium and tritium nuclei the ignition temperature is about 40 million degrees C. Second, the plasma must be confined long enough to release a significant net output of energy. Third, the energy must be recovered in a useful form.

In the first years of the controlled-fusion research program one of the major goals was to achieve the ignition temperature in a fairly dense laboratory plasma. Steady progress was made toward this goal, culminating in 1963, when the ignition temperature (for a deuterium-tritium fuel mixture) was reached in one of the Scylla devices at Los Alamos. This test, which was performed in a pure deuterium plasma to avoid the generation of excessive neutron flux, resulted in the release of fusion energy: about a thousandth of a joule per pulse, or 370 watts of fusion power during the three-microsecond duration of the pulse. If the test had been performed using a deuterium-tritium mixture, it would have released approximately a half-joule of fusion energy per pulse, or 180,000 watts of fusion power.

Today a large number of different devices have either achieved the deuterium-tritium ignition temperature or are very close to it [see bottom illustration on opposite page]. The main difficulties encountered in reaching this goal were comparatively straightforward energy-loss processes involving impurity atoms that entered the plasma from the walls of the container. A large research effort in the areas of vacuum and surface technology was a major factor in surmounting the ignition-temperature barrier.

The problem of confining a plasma long enough to release a significant net amount of energy has proved to be even more difficult than the problem of achieving the ignition temperature. Extremely rapid energy-loss processes—known collectively as "anomalous diffusion" processes—appeared to prevent the attainment of adequate confinement times. Plasma instabilities were the primary cause of this rapid plasma leakage [see "The Leakage Problem in Fusion Reactors," by Francis F. Chen; SCIENTIFIC AMERICAN, July, 1967]. Within the past few years, however, several large containment devices have reduced these instabilities to such a low amplitude that other more subtle effects, such as convective plasma losses and magnetic-field imperfections, can be studied. As a result it has been shown that there is no basic law of physics (such as an instability-initiated anomalous plasma loss) that prevents plasma confinement for times long enough to release significant net fusion energy. In fact, "classical," or ideal, plasma confinement has been achieved in several machines; this is the best confinement possible and yields a plasma-loss rate much lower than that required for a fusion reactor.

The twin achievements of ignition temperature and adequate confinement time, it should be noted, have taken place in quite different machines, each

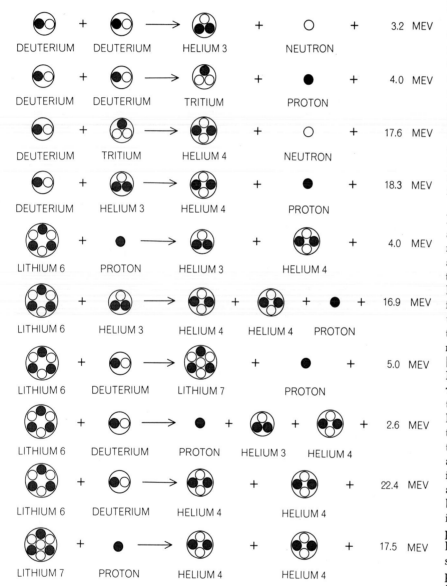

FUSION REACTIONS regarded as potentially useful in full-scale fusion reactors are represented in this partial list. The two possible deuterium-deuterium reactions occur with equal probability. The deuterium-tritium fuel cycle has been considered particularly attractive because this mixture has the lowest ignition temperature known (about 40 million degrees Celsius). Other fuel cycles, including many not shown in this list, have been attracting increased attention lately, since certain plasma-confinement schemes actually operate better at higher temperatures and offer the advantage of direct conversion to electricity. The energy released by each reaction is given at right in millions of electron volts (MeV).

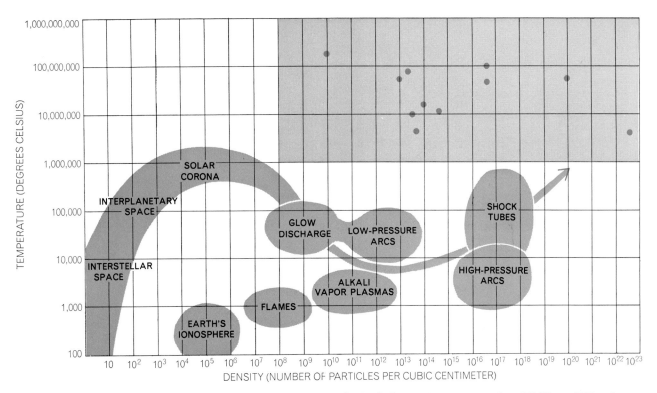

INDUSTRIALLY UNEXPLORED RANGE of plasma temperatures and densities has already been made available by the fusion-power research program. These experimental plasmas (*colored dots*), which range in temperature from 500,000 to a billion degrees C. and in density from 10^9 to 10^{22} ions per cubic centimeter, are compared here with various other industrial and natural plasmas.

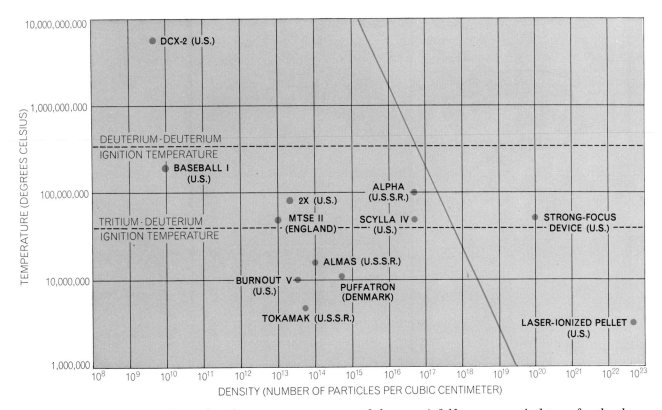

PLASMA EXPERIMENTS that have achieved temperatures near or above the fusion ignition temperatures of a deuterium-tritium fuel (*bottom horizontal line*) and a deuterium-deuterium fuel (*top horizontal line*) are identified by the name of the experimental device and the country in which the experiment took place in this enlargement of the upper right-hand section of the illustration at top. The diagonal colored line represents the limit beyond which the materials used to construct the magnet coils can no longer withstand the magnetic-field pressure required to confine the plasma (assumed to be 300,000 gauss in this case). Beyond this limit only fast-pulsed systems (in which the magnetic fields are generated by intense currents inside the plasma itself) or systems operating on entirely different principles (such as laser-produced, inertially confined plasmas) are possible. The record of six billion degrees C. was achieved with the aid of a high-energy ion-injection system associated with DCX-2 device at the Oak Ridge National Laboratory.

258

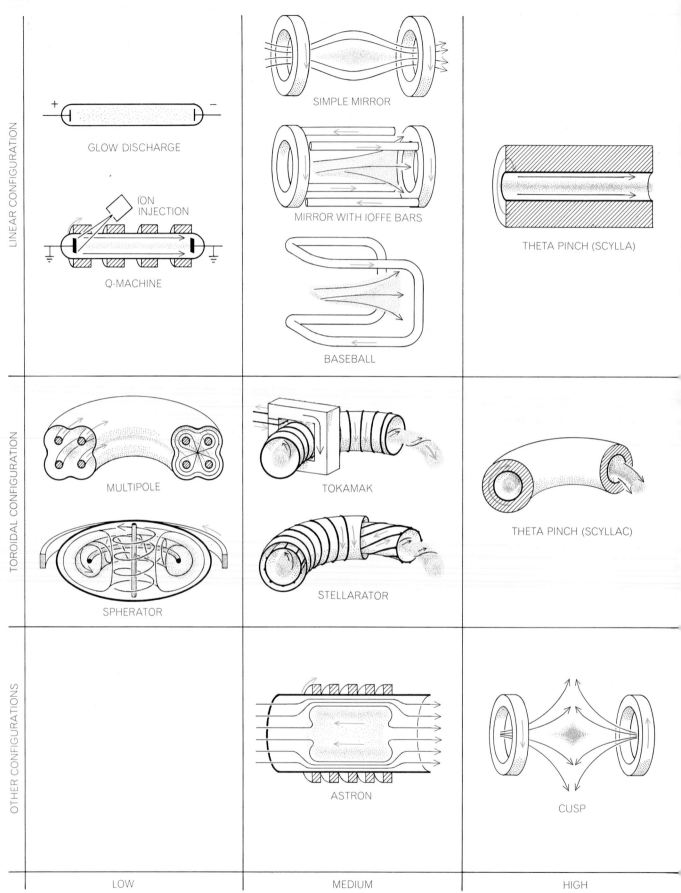

LINEAR CONFIGURATION

GLOW DISCHARGE

ION INJECTION

Q-MACHINE

SIMPLE MIRROR

MIRROR WITH IOFFE BARS

BASEBALL

THETA PINCH (SCYLLA)

TOROIDAL CONFIGURATION

MULTIPOLE

SPHERATOR

TOKAMAK

STELLARATOR

THETA PINCH (SCYLLAC)

OTHER CONFIGURATIONS

ASTRON

CUSP

LOW

MEDIUM

HIGH

PRINCIPAL SCHEMES devised in the past 18 years to confine plasmas for fusion research are arranged in the illustration on these two pages in order of increasing plasma density (*left to right*) and overall geometry (*top to bottom*). Only a few examples are depicted in each category. In every case the plasma is in color, the colored arrows signify the direction of the electric current and the black arrows denote the direction of the resultant magnetic field. Various structural details have been omitted for clarity. For each example shown there are a large number of variations either already in existence or in the conceptual stage. Furthermore, the

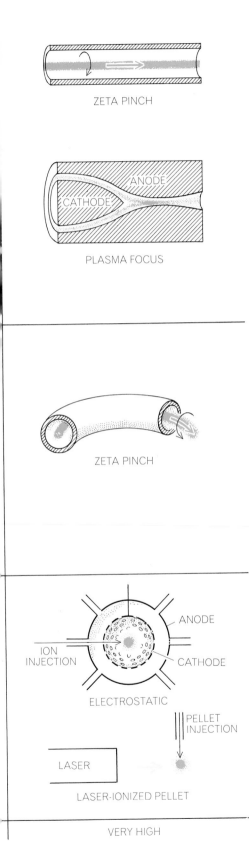

ZETA PINCH

PLASMA FOCUS

ANODE

CATHODE

ZETA PINCH

ANODE

ION
INJECTION

CATHODE

ELECTROSTATIC

PELLET
INJECTION

LASER

LASER-IONIZED PELLET

VERY HIGH

fact that an example is given in one category does not necessarily mean that that configuration is not applicable to some other category; there are, for instance, toroidal Q-machines and medium-density cusp designs.

specially designed to maximize the conditions for reaching one goal or the other. How does one compare the performances of these machines in order to gauge how near one is to the combined conditions needed to operate a practical fusion-power reactor? The basic criterion for determining the length of time a plasma must be confined at a given density and temperature to produce a "break even" point in the power balance was laid down in 1957 by the British physicist J. D. Lawson. Combining data on the physics of fusion reactions with some estimates of the efficiency of energy recovery from a hypothetical fusion reactor, Lawson derived a factor, which he called R, that denoted the ratio of energy output to energy input needed to compensate for all possible plasma losses. Lawson's criterion is still in general use as a convenient yardstick for measuring the extent to which losses must be controlled in order to make possible the construction of a fusion reactor. Although more recent calculations consider many other physical constraints in order to arrive at the break-even power balance, these criteria still give values very close to those derived by Lawson.

For a deuterium-tritium fuel mixture Lawson found that at temperatures higher than the ignition temperature the product of density and confinement time must be equal to 10^{14} seconds per cubic centimeter in order to achieve the break-even condition. This criterion defines a surface in three-dimensional space, the coordinates being the logarithmic values of density, temperature and confinement time [see illustration on page 261]. The goal of a break-even release of energy will have been achieved when the set of conditions for a given machine reaches this surface. It should be emphasized that the exact location and shape of the surface is a function of both the fuel cycle used and the recovery efficiency of the hypothetical reactor system. Fuels other than the deuterium-tritium mixture would increase the temperature needed to achieve a break-even power balance.

The extraordinary progress made recently by various groups in learning how to raise the combination of density, temperature and confinement time to a set of values approaching this break-even surface can be appreciated by referring to the illustration of the Lawson-criterion surface. The several plasma systems shown range in density from about 10^9 ions per cubic centimeter to 5×10^{22} ions per cubic centimeter. (Below a density of about 10^{11} ions per cubic centimeter the power density would be so low that it would require an impractically

large reactor.) The particular density range chosen for investigation in each case is a function of the scientific preferences of the investigators concerning the best route to fusion power and the available technology (magnets, power supplies, lasers and so forth). Thus there are various trajectories to the break-even surface being followed through the three-dimensional "parameter space" of the illustration. Closing the gap between where each trajectory is now and the break-even surface depends in some cases (for example the tokamak devices) on obtaining a better understanding of the physical principles required to develop reliable scaling rules, whereas in other cases (such as the linear theta-pinch devices) all that may be required is an economic solution to the engineering problem of building a large enough system.

Fusion-Reactor Designs

How would a full-scale fusion reactor operate? In the first place fusion reactors, like fission reactors, could be run on a variety of fuels. The nature of the fuel used in the core of a fusion reactor would, however, have a decisive effect on the method used to recover the fusion energy and the uses to which the recovered energy might be put. Most research on reactor technology has centered on the use of a deuterium-tritium mixture as a fuel. The reason is that the mixture has the lowest ignition temperature, and hence the lowest rate of energy loss by radiation, of any possible fusion fuel. Nonetheless, other combinations of light nuclei have been considered for many years as potential fusion fuels. Prominent among these are reactions involving a deuterium nucleus and a helium-3 nucleus and reactions involving a single proton (a hydrogen nucleus) and a lithium-6 nucleus. Because containment based on the magnetic-mirror concept actually operates better at higher temperatures, a number of other fuels have been attracting increased attention [see illustration on page 256].

Depending on the fuel used, a fusion reactor could release its energy in several ways. For example, neutrons, which are produced at various rates by different fusion reactions, can cross magnetic fields and penetrate matter quite easily. A reactor based on, say, a deuterium-tritium fuel cycle would release approximately 80 percent of its energy in the form of highly energetic neutrons. Such a reactor could be made to produce electricity by absorbing the neutron energy in a liquid-lithium shield, circulating the

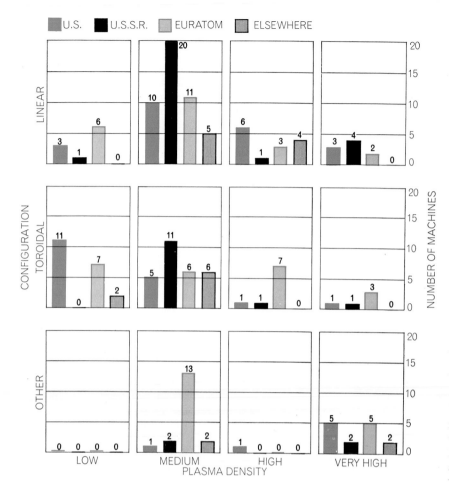

INVENTORY of the number of machines now operating throughout the world in each of the broad categories represented in the illustration on the preceding two pages is given in this table. The total number in each category is broken down into subtotals for the U.S., the U.S.S.R., the European Atomic Energy Community, or Euratom, countries (Belgium, France, Germany, Italy, Luxembourg and the Netherlands) and the rest of the world (principally Japan, Sweden and Australia). Britain, although not officially a member of Euratom, is included in the Euratom subtotal. The figures are drawn mainly from a recent survey compiled by Amasa S. Bishop and published by the International Atomic Energy Commission. The U.S. fusion-power program currently represents about a fifth of the world total.

liquid lithium to a heat exchanger and there heating water to produce steam and so drive a conventional steam-generator electric power plant [see top illustration on page 262].

This general approach could also lead to an attractive new technique for converting the world's reserves of uranium 238 and thorium 232 to suitable fuels for fission reactors—the fusion-fission hybrid system mentioned above. By employing the abundance of inexpensive, energetic neutrons produced by the deuterium-tritium fuel cycle to synthesize fissionable heavy nuclei, a fusion reactor could act as a new type of breeder reactor. This could have the effect of lowering the break-even surface defined by Lawson's criterion, bringing the fusion-breeding scheme actually closer to feasibility than the generation of electricity solely by fusion reactions. Cheap fuel might thus be made for existing fission

reactors in systems that could be inherently safe. A "neutron-rich" economy created by fusion reactors would have other potential benefits. For example, it has been suggested that large quantities of neutrons could be useful for "burning" various fission products, thereby alleviating the problem of disposing of radioactive wastes.

Fuel cycles that release most of their energy in the form of charged particles offer still other avenues for the recovery of fusion energy. For example, Richard F. Post of the Lawrence Radiation Laboratory at Livermore has proposed a direct energy-conversion scheme in which the energetic charged particles produced in a fusion-reactor core are slowed directly by an electrostatic field set up by an array of large electrically charged plates [see bottom illustration on page 262]. By a judicious arrangement of the voltages applied to the

plates such a system could theoretically be made to operate at a conversion efficiency of 90 percent.

J. Rand McNally, Jr., of the Oak Ridge National Laboratory has suggested that a long sequence of fusion reactions similar to those that power the stars could be reproduced in a fusion reactor. The data necessary to evaluate fuel cycles operating in this manner, however, do not exist at present.

The characteristics of a full-scale fusion reactor would depend not only on the fuel cycle but also on the particular plasma-confinement configuration and density range chosen. Thus it is probable that there eventually will exist a number of different forms of fusion reactor. For example, medium-density magnetic-mirror reactors and very-high-density laser-ignited reactors could be expected to operate at power levels as low as between five and 50 megawatts, which could make them potentially useful for fusion-propulsion schemes.

For central-station power generation the medium-density reactors would most likely operate on a deuterium-tritium fuel cycle in order to take advantage of the mixture's low ignition temperature. Because of the high neutron output associated with this fuel, a heat-cycle conversion system would be appropriate.

A reactor of this type would operate most efficiently with a power output in the billion-watt range. Before such a reactor can be built, it will be necessary to prove that the plasma will remain stable as present devices are scaled to reactor sizes and temperatures. Problems likely to be encountered in this effort involve the long-term equilibrium of the plasma, the interaction of the plasma with the walls of the container and the necessity of pumping large quantities of liquid lithium across the magnetic field.

Medium-density linear reactors would be better suited for fuel cycles that yield a major part of their energy output in the form of charged particles, since this approach would allow the direct recovery of the kinetic energy of these reaction products through schemes such as Post's. Such fuel cycles could be based on a deuterium-deuterium reaction, a deuterium-helium reaction or a proton-lithium reaction. A system operating on this principle could be made to produce direct-current electricity at a potential of about 400 kilovolts, which would be ideal for long-distance cryogenic (supercooled) power transmission.

Although the break-even conditions would be lowered in this case (because of the high energy-conversion efficiency), it still remains to be shown that existing experiments can be scaled to large sizes and higher temperatures. Some major technological obstacles that need to be overcome include the construction of large atomic-beam injectors and extremely strong magnetic mirrors.

For reactors operating on the basis of any of the higher-density schemes, such as the theta-pinch machines or the fast-pulsed systems, major technological hurdles include the development of efficient energy-storage and energy-transfer techniques and problems related to heating techniques such as lasers.

In addition to generating electric power and possibly serving in a propulsion system, fusion reactors are potentially useful for other applications. For example, fusion research has already made available plasmas that range in temperature from 500,000 to a billion degrees C. and in density from 10^9 to 10^{22} ions per cubic centimeter. Almost all industrial processes that use plasmas fall outside this range [*see top illustration on page 257*]. In order to suggest how this industrially unexplored range might be exploited, we recently put forward the concept of the "fusion torch." The gen-

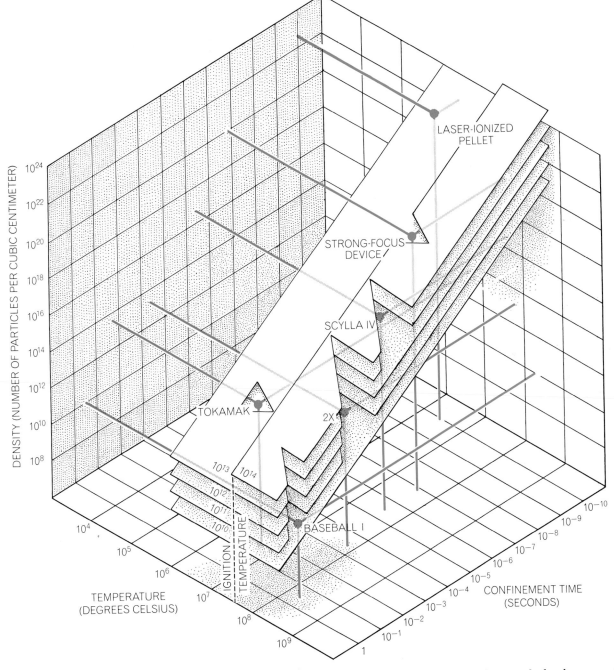

BASIC CRITERION for determining the length of time a plasma must be confined at a given density and temperature to achieve a "break even" point in the fusion-power balance is represented in this three-dimensional graph. The graph is based on a method of analysis devised in 1957 by the British physicist J. D. Lawson. For a deuterium-tritium fuel mixture in the temperature range from 40 million degrees C. to 500 million degrees C., Lawson found that the product of density and confinement time must be close to 10^{14} seconds per cubic centimeter to achieve the break-even condition (based on an assumed energy-conversion efficiency of 33 percent). This criterion corresponds to the top layer in the stack of planes in the illustration. The lower planes, which correspond to successively smaller values of density times confinement time, are included in order to give some idea of the positions of the best confirmed results from several experimental devices with respect to the combination of parameters needed to operate a full-scale fusion reactor.

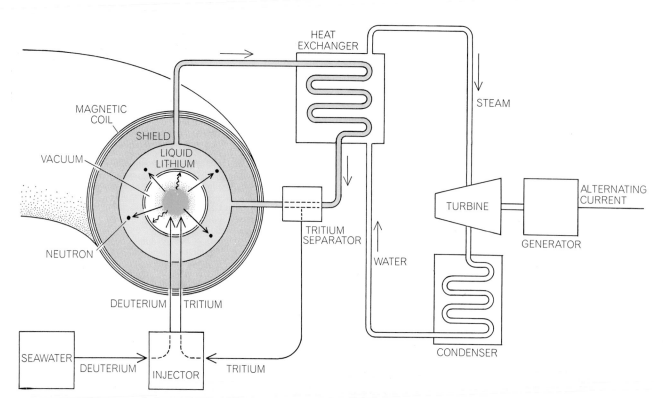

THERMAL ENERGY CONVERSION would be most effective in a fusion reactor based on a deuterium-tritium fuel cycle, since such a fuel would release approximately 80 percent of its energy in the form of highly energetic neutrons. The reactor could produce electricity by absorbing the neutron energy in a liquid-lithium shield, circulating the liquid lithium to a heat exchanger and there heating water to produce steam and thus drive a conventional steam-generator plant. The reactor core could be either linear or toroidal.

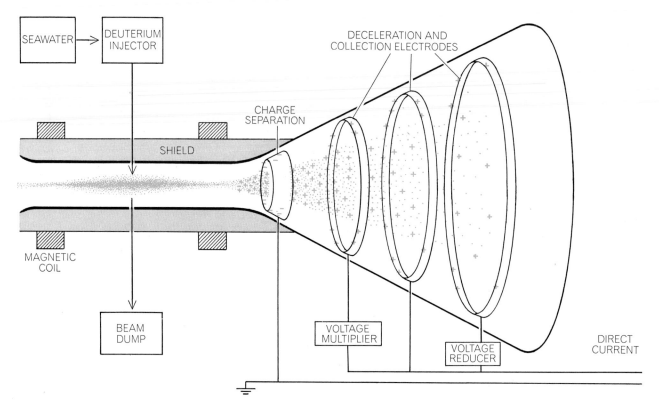

DIRECT ENERGY CONVERSION would be more suitable for fusion fuel cycles that release most of their energy in the form of charged particles. In this novel direct energy-conversion scheme, first proposed by Richard F. Post of the Lawrence Radiation Laboratory of the University of California at Livermore, the energetic charged particles (primarily electrons, protons and alpha particles) produced in the core of a linear fusion reactor would be released through diverging magnetic fields at the ends of the magnetic bottle, lowering the density of the plasma by a factor of as much as a million. A large electrically grounded collector plate would then be used to remove only the electrons. The positive reaction products (at energies in the vicinity of 400 kilovolts) would finally be collected on a series of high-voltage electrodes, resulting in a direct transfer of the kinetic energy of the particles to an external circuit.

eral idea here is to use these ultrahigh-density plasmas, possibly directly from the exhaust of a fusion reactor, to vaporize, dissociate and ionize any solid or liquid material [*see top illustration at right*]. The potential uses of such a fusion-torch capability are intriguing. For one thing, an operational fusion torch in its ultimate form could be used to reduce all kinds of wastes to their constituent atoms for separation, thereby closing the materials loop and making technologically possible a stationary-state economy. On a shorter term the fusion torch offers the possibility of processing mineral ores or producing portable liquid fuels by means of a high-temperature plasma system.

The fusion-torch concept could also be useful in transforming the kinetic energy of a plasma into ultraviolet radiation or X rays by the injection of trace amounts of heavy atoms into the plasma. The large quantity of radiative energy generated in this way could then be used for various purposes, including bulk heating, the desalting of seawater, the production of hydrogen or new chemical-processing techniques. Because such new industrial processes would make use of energy in the form of plasmas rather than in the form of, say, chemical solvents, they would be far less likely to pollute the environment. Although the various fusion-torch possibilities are largely untested and many aspects may turn out to be impractical, the concept is intended to stimulate new ideas for the industrial use of the ultrahigh-temperature plasmas that have already been developed in the fusion program as well as those plasmas that would be produced in large quantities by future fusion reactors.

Environmental Considerations

The environmental advantages of fusion power can be broken down into two categories: those advantages that are inherent in all fusion systems and those that are dependent on particular fuel cycles and reactor designs. Among the inherent advantages, one of the most important is the fact that the use of fusion fuel requires no burning of the world's oxygen or hydrocarbon resources and hence releases no carbon dioxide or other combustion products to the atmosphere. This advantage is shared with nuclear-fission plants.

Another advantage of fusion power is that no radioactive wastes are produced as the result of the fuel cycles contemplated. The principal reaction products would be neutrons, nonradioactive heli-

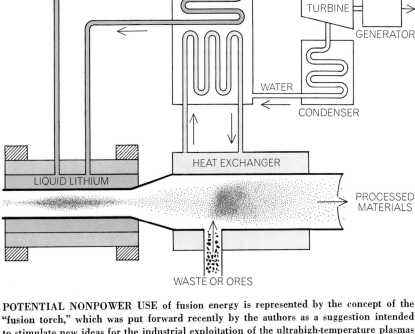

POTENTIAL NONPOWER USE of fusion energy is represented by the concept of the "fusion torch," which was put forward recently by the authors as a suggestion intended to stimulate new ideas for the industrial exploitation of the ultrahigh-temperature plasmas already made available by the fusion-research program as well as those that would be produced by fusion reactors. The general idea is to use some of the energy from these plasmas to vaporize, dissociate and ionize any solid or liquid material. In its ultimate form the fusion torch could be used to reduce any kind of waste to its constituent atoms for separation.

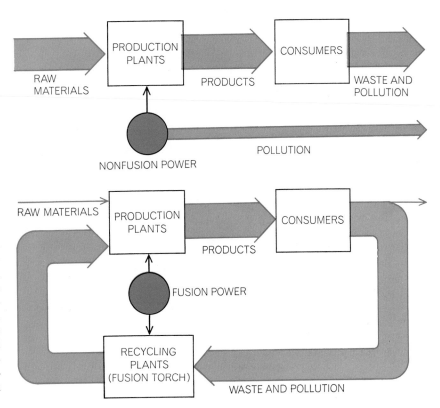

CLOSED MATERIALS ECONOMY could be achieved with the aid of the fusion-torch concept illustrated at the top of this page. In contrast to present systems, which are based on inherently wasteful linear materials economies (*top*), such a stationary-state system would be able to recycle the limited supply of material resources (*bottom*), thus alleviating most of the environmental pollution associated with present methods of energy utilization.

um and hydrogen nuclei, and radioactive tritium nuclei. It is true that tritium emits low-energy ionizing radiation in the form of beta particles (electrons), but since tritium is also a fusion fuel, it could be returned to the system to be burned. This situation is strongly contrasted with that in nuclear fission, which by its very nature must produce a multitude of highly radioactive waste elements.

Fusion reactors are also inherently incapable of a "runaway" accident. There is no "critical mass" required for fusion. In fact, the fusioning plasma is so tenuous (even in the "high density" machines) that there is never enough fuel present at any one time to support a nuclear excursion. This situation is also in contrast to nuclear-fission reactors, which must contain a critical mass of fissionable material and hence an extremely large amount of potential nuclear energy.

Among the system-dependent environmental advantages of fusion power must be counted the fact that the only radioactive fusion fuel considered so far is tritium. The amount of tritium present in a fusion reactor can range from near zero for a proton-lithium fuel cycle to a maximum for a deuterium-tritium cycle, where a "blanket" for the production of tritium must be included. Tritium, however, is one of the least toxic of the radioactive isotopes, whereas the fission fuel plutonium is one of the most toxic radioactive materials known.

The most serious radiological prob-

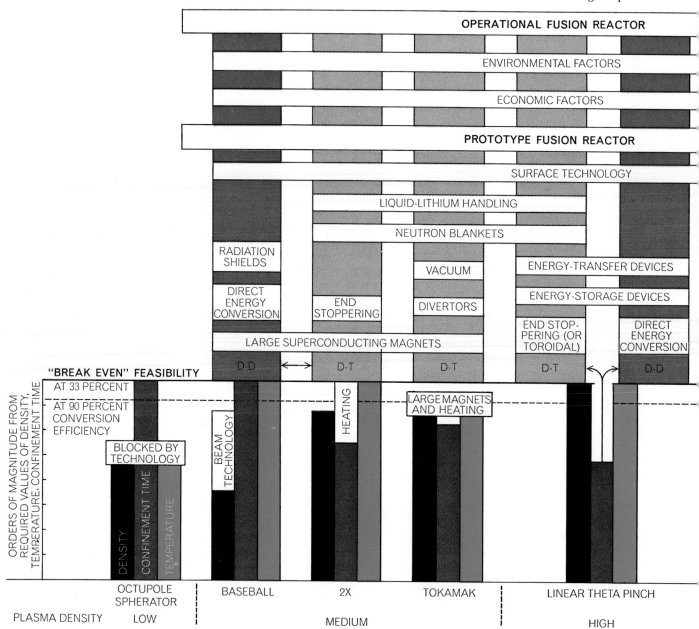

REMAINING PROBLEMS that must be solved before the goal of useful, economic fusion power can be achieved are depicted schematically in this illustration. The major experimental routes to the goal are ordered according to plasma density. Various experimental devices are represented by bars indicating the best combination of plasma density, confinement time and temperature achieved by each device; the logarithmic scale at lower left gauges how far each of these essential parameters is from the values needed to attain break-even feasibility. Technological problems that must be solved in each case are labeled. The achievement of a prototype reactor will be a function not only of plasma technology but also of the fuel cycle and the method of energy conversion chosen. Thus medium-density magnetic-mirror devices could be built to operate with either a deuterium-tritium (D-T) fuel mixture or a deuterium-deuterium (D-D) fuel mixture; the arrows signify these alternatives. If a D-D cycle is chosen, then direct energy conversion is possible, and once the converters are developed very few obstacles would remain to delay the construction of a prototype reactor. If, on the other hand, a D-T cycle is chosen, then conventional thermal energy conversion would be needed, and the listed technological

lems for fusion would exist in a reactor burning and producing tritium. A representative rate of tritium consumption for a 2,000-megawatt deuterium-tritium thermal plant would be about 260 grams per day. Tritium "holdup" in the blanket and other elements of the tritium loop would dictate the tritium inventory. Holdup is estimated to be about 1,000 grams in a 2,000-megawatt plant. If necessary, the doubling time of breeding tritium could be less than two months in order to meet the needs of an expanding

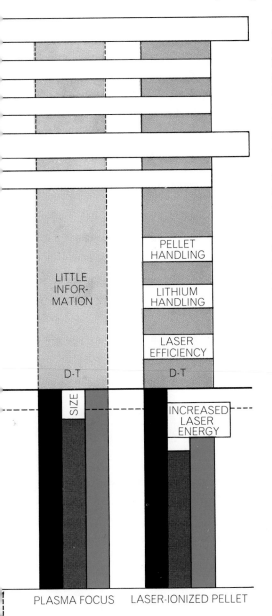

PLASMA FOCUS   LASER-IONIZED PELLET

VERY HIGH

hurdles would have to be overcome. Other systems operating on the D-T cycle would have to climb past similar hurdles. The high-density linear theta-pinch device could take either the thermal-conversion path or the direct-conversion path (arrows). The final step, from a prototype to an operational reactor, would proceed through a region in which economic and environmental considerations can be expected to be paramount.

economy. The amount of tritium produced by the plant is controllable, however, and need not exceed the fuel requirements of the plant.

Careful design to prevent the leakage of tritium fuel from a deuterium-tritium reactor is mandatory. Engineering studies that take into account economic considerations indicate that the leakage rate can be reduced to .0001 percent per day. The conclusion is that even for an all-deuterium-tritium fusion economy the genetic dose rate from worldwide tritium distribution would be negligible.

In fact, for a given total power output the tritium inventory for an all-deuterium-tritium fusion economy (including both the inventory within the plant and that dispersed in the biosphere) would be between one and 100 times what it would be for an all-fission economy. It is true that tritium would be produced in a deuterium-tritium fusion reactor at a rate of from 1,000 to 100,000 times faster than in various types of fission reactor. Since tritium is burned as a fuel, however, it has an effective half-life of only about three days rather than the normal 12 years.

A technology-dependent but possibly serious limitation on deuterium-tritium fusion plants could be the release of tritium to the local environment. The level would be quite low but the long-term consequences from tritium emission to the environment in the vicinity of a deuterium-tritium reactor needs to be explored. In general the biological-hazard potential of the tritium fuel inventory in a deuterium-tritium reactor is lower by a factor of about a million than that of the volatile isotope iodine 131 contained in a fission reactor. Of course there is no expectation in either case that such a release would occur.

The radioactivity induced in the surrounding structures by a fusion reactor is dependent on both the fuel cycle and the engineering design of the plant. This radioactivity could range from zero for a fuel cycle that produces no neutrons up to very high values for a deuterium-tritium cycle if the engineering design is such that the type and amount of structural materials could become highly activated under neutron bombardment. Cooling for "after heat" will be required for systems that have intense induced radioactivity. Even if the cooling system should fail, however, there could be no nuclear excursion that would disperse the radioactivity outside the plant.

Other system-dependent environmental advantages of fusion power include safety in the event of sabotage or natural disaster, reduced potential for the diversion of weapons-grade materials and low

waste heat. In fact, the potential exists for fusion systems to essentially eliminate the problem of thermal pollution by going to charged-particle fuel cycles that result in direct energy conversion. Finally, there is the advantage of the materials-recycling potential of the fusion-torch concept.

The Timetable to Fusion Power

The construction and operation of a power-producing controlled-fusion reactor will be the end product of a chain of events that is already to a certain extent discernible. For controlled fusion, however, there can never be an instant equivalent to the one that demonstrated the "feasibility" of a fission-power reactor (the Stagg Field experiment of Enrico Fermi in 1942). To reach the plasma conditions required for a net release of fusion power it is necessary to first develop many new technologies. In this context the term "scientific feasibility" cannot be precisely defined. To some investigators it means simply the achievement of the basic plasma conditions necessary to reach the break-even surface in the illustration on page 261. To others it represents reaching the same surface—but with a system that can be enlarged to a full-scale, economic power plant. To a few it represents the attainment of a full understanding of all the phenomena involved.

Although these differing interpretations of what is needed to give confidence in our ability to construct a fusion reactor may be somewhat confusing, each interpretation nevertheless contains a modicum of truth. To depict the complexity of this drive toward the goal of fusion power we have prepared the highly schematic illustration on the opposite page. The goal is to achieve useful, economic fusion power. The major routes to the goal are ordered in the illustration according to plasma density. Various individual experiments have climbed past various obstacles to reach positions close to the break-even level. In fact, in some instances two of the three essential parameters (density, temperature and confinement time) have already been achieved. The ignition temperature has been achieved in a number of cases. The rest of the climb to the break-even level in some cases involves a better understanding of the physics of the plasma-confinement system, but in others it may involve only engineering problems. Indeed, the location of the break-even level is a function of the technology used. Direct energy conversion, for example, would lower this level.

The next portion of the climb, the

construction of a prototype reactor, will be a function of the route taken to scientific feasibility. For instance, if a deuterium-tritium mixture is the fuel, this would require the development of components such as lithium blankets, large superconducting magnets, radiation-resistant vacuum liners, fueling techniques and heat-transfer technology. If fuels that release most of their energy in the form of charged particles are considered, however, then in the case of mirror reactors direct-conversion equipment may be part of a device used to demonstrate break-even feasibility. The step from that device to a prototype reactor could then be very short because the conversion equipment would be already developed. Other devices would face similar problems of differing magnitude in prototype construction. The final step from a prototype to an operational reactor would proceed through a much more nebulous region in which economic and environmental considerations would influence the comparative desirability of different power plants.

At present the main factor limiting the rate of progress toward fusion power is financial. The annual operating and equipment expenditures for the U.S.

fusion program, when one uses the consumer price indexes to adjust these dollars for inflation, has remained fairly constant for the past eight years [see illustration below]. The total amount spent on the program since its inception is the cost equivalent of a single Apollo moon shot. The annual funding rate of about $30 million per year is the equivalent of 15 cents per person per year in the U.S.

The road to fusion power is a cumulative one in that successive advances can be built on earlier advances. At present the U.S. has a fairly broad program of investigations approaching the break-even surface for net energy release. It is essential that larger (and thus more expensive) devices be built if the goal of the break-even surface is to be reached. The surface should be broken through in a number of places so that the relative advantages of the possible routes beyond that surface to an eventual fusion-power reactor can be assessed.

Clearly the timetable to fusion power is difficult to predict. If the level of effort on fusion research remains constant or decreases slightly, the requirement for larger devices and advanced engineering will automatically cause a premature

narrowing of the density range under investigation. This increases the risk of reaching the goal in a given time scale. To put it another way, it extends one's estimate of the probable time scale. If the level of fusion research expands sufficiently to maintain a fairly broad program across the entire density range, the probability of success increases and the probable time scale decreases. If fusion power is pursued as a "national objective," expanded programs could be carried out across the entire density range accompanied by parallel strong programs of research on the remaining engineering and materials problems to determine as quickly as possible the best routes to practical fusion-power systems. Therefore, depending on one's underlying assumptions on the level of effort and the difficulties ahead, the time it would take to produce a large prototype reactor could range from as much as 50 years to as little as 10 years.

There is at least one case in which the fusion break-even surface could be reached without making any new scientific advances and without developing any new technologies. This "brute force" approach, which might not be the optimum route to an eventual power reactor, would involve simply extending the length of the existing theta-pinch linear devices. It has been estimated that to reach the break-even surface by this method such a system would have to be about 2,000 feet long—less than a fifth of the length of the Stanford Linear Accelerator. This one fusion device, however, would cost an order of magnitude more than any experimental fusion device built to date. Even though a simple scaling of this type would introduce no new problems in plasma physics, one could not exclude the possibility of unexpected difficulties arising solely from the extended length of the system.

The length of such a device could be shortened by as much as 90 percent by installing magnetic mirrors at the ends, by increasing the diameter of the plasma or by making the system toroidal, but these steps would introduce new physical conditions. The system could also be shortened by the use of a direct energy-conversion approach, but this would introduce an unproved technology. At present a significant portion of the fusion-power program is concentrating on developing the new physics and technology that would reduce the cost of such break-even experiments. This continuing effort is sustained by the growing conviction that the eventual attainment of a practical fusion-power reactor is not blocked by the laws of nature.

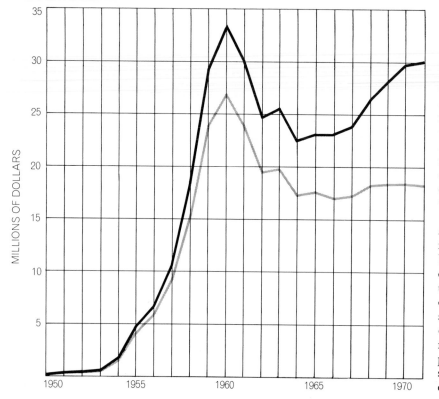

FINANCIAL SUPPORT is currently the main factor limiting the rate of progress toward the goal of fusion power. The solid curve shows the annual operating and equipment expenditures for the U.S. fusion program. The gray curve shows these expenditures adjusted for inflation. The adjustment shows that fusion research has been funded by the Atomic Energy Commission at an essentially constant rate for the past eight years. Smaller research programs have been funded by both private industry and other Government agencies.

26

The Urbanization of the Human Population

KINGSLEY DAVIS

September 1965

Urbanized societies, in which a majority of the people live crowded together in towns and cities, represent a new and fundamental step in man's social evolution. Although cities themselves first appeared some 5,500 years ago, they were small and surrounded by an overwhelming majority of rural people; moreover, they relapsed easily to village or small-town status. The urbanized societies of today, in contrast, not only have urban agglomerations of a size never before attained but also have a high proportion of their population concentrated in such agglomerations. In 1960, for example, nearly 52 million Americans lived in only 16 urbanized areas. Together these areas covered less land than one of the smaller counties (Cochise) of Arizona. According to one definition used by the U.S. Bureau of the Census, 96 million people—53 percent of the nation's population—were concentrated in 213 urbanized areas that together occupied only .7 percent of the nation's land. Another definition used by the bureau puts the urban population at about 70 percent. The large and dense agglomerations comprising the urban population involve a degree of human contact and of social complexity never before known. They exceed in size the communities of any other large animal; they suggest the behavior of communal

insects rather than of mammals.

Neither the recency nor the speed of this evolutionary development is widely appreciated. Before 1850 no society could be described as predominantly urbanized, and by 1900 only one—Great Britain—could be so regarded. Today, only 65 years later, all industrial nations are highly urbanized, and in the world as a whole the process of urbanization is accelerating rapidly.

Some years ago my associates and I at Columbia University undertook to document the progress of urbanization by compiling data on the world's cities and the proportion of human beings living in them; in recent years the work has been continued in our center—International Population and Urban Research—at the University of California at Berkeley. The data obtained in these investigations are reflected in the illustration on the next two pages, which shows the historical trend in terms of one index of urbanization: the proportion of the population living in cities of 100,000 or larger. Statistics of this kind are only approximations of reality, but they are accurate enough to demonstrate how urbanization has accelerated. Between 1850 and 1950 the index changed at a much higher rate than from 1800 to 1850, but the rate of change from 1950 to 1960 was twice that of the preceding 50 years! If the

pace of increase that obtained between 1950 and 1960 were to remain the same, by 1990 the fraction of the world's people living in cities of 100,-000 or larger would be more than half. Using another index of urbanization—the proportion of the world's population living in urban places of all sizes—we found that by 1960 the figure had already reached 33 percent.

Clearly the world as a whole is not fully urbanized, but it soon will be. This change in human life is so recent that even the most urbanized countries still exhibit the rural origins of their institutions. Its full implications for man's organic and social evolution can only be surmised.

In discussing the trend—and its implications insofar as they can be perceived—I shall use the term "urbanization" in a particular way. It refers here to the proportion of the total population concentrated in urban settlements, or else to a rise in this proportion. A common mistake is to think of urbanization as simply the growth of cities. Since the total population is composed of both the urban population and the rural, however, the "proportion urban" is a function of both of them. Accordingly cities can grow without any urbanization, provided that the rural population grows at an equal or a greater rate.

Historically urbanization and the growth of cities have occurred together, which accounts for the confusion. As the reader will soon see, it is necessary to distinguish the two trends. In the most advanced countries today, for example, urban populations are still growing, but their proportion of the total population is tending to remain stable or to diminish. In other words, the process of urbanization—the switch from a spread-out pattern of human settlement to one of concentration in urban centers—is a change that has a beginning and an end, but the growth of cities has no inherent limit. Such growth could continue even after everyone was living in cities, through sheer excess of births over deaths.

The difference between a rural village and an urban community is of course one of degree; a precise operational distinction is somewhat arbitrary, and it varies from one nation to another. Since data are available for communities of various sizes, a dividing line can be chosen at will. One convenient index of urbanization, for example, is the proportion of people living in places of 100,000 or more. In the following analysis I shall depend on two indexes: the one just mentioned and the proportion of population classed as "urban" in the official statistics of each country. In practice the two indexes are highly correlated; therefore either one can be used as an index of urbanization.

Actually the hardest problem is not that of determining the "floor" of the urban category but of ascertaining the boundary of places that are clearly urban by any definition. How far east is the boundary of Los Angeles? Where along the Hooghly River does Calcutta leave off and the countryside begin? In the past the population of cities and towns has usually been given as the number of people living within the political boundaries. Thus the population of New York is frequently given as around eight million, this being the population of the city proper. The error in such a figure was not large before World War I, but since then, particularly in the advanced countries, urban populations have been spilling over the narrow political boundaries at a tremendous rate. In 1960 the New York–Northeastern New Jersey urbanized area, as delineated by the Bureau of the Census, had more than 14 million

people. That delineation showed it to be the largest city in the world and nearly twice as large as New York City proper.

As a result of the outward spread of urbanites, counts made on the basis of political boundaries alone underestimate the city populations and exaggerate the rural. For this reason our office delineated the metropolitan areas of as many countries as possible for dates around 1950. These areas included the central, or political, cities and the zones around them that are receiving the spillover.

This reassessment raised the estimated proportion of the world's population in cities of 100,000 or larger from 15.1 percent to 16.7 percent. As of 1960 we have used wherever possible the "urban agglomeration" data now furnished to the United Nations by many countries. The U.S., for example, provides data for "urbanized areas," meaning cities of 50,000 or larger and the built-up agglomerations around them.

My concern in this article is not with the origin and evolution of cities but with the degree of urbanization in whole societies. It is curious that thousands of years elapsed between the first ap-

MAJOR CITIES OF THE WORLD are depicted as they rank in size according to data on "urban agglomeration" furnished to the United Nations by several countries. The data are intended to take into account not only the population within the political bounda-

pearance of small cities and the emergence of urbanized societies in the 19th century. It is also curious that the region where urbanized societies arose—northwestern Europe—was not the one that had given rise to the major cities of the past; on the contrary, it was a region where urbanization had been at an extremely low ebb. Indeed, the societies of northwestern Europe in medieval times were so rural that it is hard for modern minds to comprehend them. Perhaps it was the nonurban character of these societies that erased the parasitic nature of towns and eventually provided a new basis for a revolutionary degree of urbanization.

At any rate, two seemingly adverse conditions may have presaged the age to come: one the low productivity of medieval agriculture in both per-acre and per-man terms, the other the feudal social system. The first meant that towns could not prosper on the basis of local agriculture alone but had to trade and to manufacture something to trade. The second meant that they could not gain political dominance over their hinterlands and thus become warring city-states. Hence they specialized in commerce and manufacture and evolved

local institutions suited to this role. Craftsmen were housed in the towns, because there the merchants could regulate quality and cost. Competition among towns stimulated specialization and technological innovation. The need for literacy, accounting skills and geographical knowledge caused the towns to invest in secular education.

Although the medieval towns remained small and never embraced more than a minor fraction of each region's population, the close connection between industry and commerce that they fostered, together with their emphasis on technique, set the stage for the ultimate breakthrough in urbanization. This breakthrough came only with the enormous growth in productivity caused by the use of inanimate energy and machinery. How difficult it was to achieve the transition is agonizingly apparent from statistics showing that even with the conquest of the New World the growth of urbanization during three postmedieval centuries in Europe was barely perceptible. I have assembled population estimates at two or more dates for 33 towns and cities in the 16th century, 46 in the 17th and 61 in the 18th. The average rate of growth during

the three centuries was less than .6 percent per year. Estimates of the growth of Europe's population as a whole between 1650 and 1800 work out to slightly more than .4 percent. The advantage of the towns was evidently very slight. Taking only the cities of 100,000 or more inhabitants, one finds that in 1600 their combined population was 1.6 percent of the estimated population of Europe; in 1700, 1.9 percent, and in 1800, 2.2 percent. On the eve of the industrial revolution Europe was still an overwhelmingly agrarian region.

With industrialization, however, the transformation was striking. By 1801 nearly a tenth of the people of England and Wales were living in cities of 100,000 or larger. This proportion doubled in 40 years and doubled again in another 60 years. By 1900 Britain was an urbanized society. In general, the later each country became industrialized, the faster was its urbanization. The change from a population with 10 percent of its members in cities of 100,000 or larger to one in which 30 percent lived in such cities took about 79 years in England and Wales, 66 in the U.S., 48 in Germany, 36 in Japan and 26 in Australia. The close association between economic development and urbanization has persisted; as the bottom illustration on page 272 shows, in 199 countries around 1960 the proportion of the population living in cities varied sharply with per capita income.

Clearly modern urbanization is best understood in terms of its connection with economic growth, and its implications are best perceived in its latest manifestations in advanced countries. What becomes apparent as one examines the trend in these countries is that urbanization is a finite process, a cycle through which nations go in their transition from agrarian to industrial society. The intensive urbanization of most of the advanced countries began within the past 100 years; in the underdeveloped countries it got under way more recently. In some of the advanced countries its end is now in sight. The fact that it will end, however, does not mean that either economic development or the growth of cities will necessarily end.

The typical cycle of urbanization can be represented by a curve in the shape of an attenuated S [see illustrations on page 273]. Starting from the bottom of the S, the first bend tends to come early and to be followed by a long attenuation. In the United Kingdom, for instance, the swiftest rise in the proportion of people living in cities of 100,000 or larger occurred from 1811 to 1851.

RANK	NAME	POPULATION
1	NEW YORK	14,114,927
2	TOKYO	10,177,000
3	LONDON	8,176,810
4	PARIS	7,369,387
5	BUENOS AIRES	7,000,000
6	SHANGHAI	6,900,000
7	LOS ANGELES	6,488,791
8	MOSCOW	6,354,000
9	CHICAGO	5,959,213
10	CALCUTTA	4,518,655
11	BOMBAY	4,422,165
12	PEKING	4,010,000
13	PHILADELPHIA	3,635,228
14	LENINGRAD	3,552,000
15	DETROIT	3,537,309
16	CAIRO	3,418,400
17	RIO DE JANEIRO	3,223,408
18	TIENTSIN	3,220,000
19	SÃO PAULO	3,164,804
20	OSAKA	3,151,000
21	MEXICO CITY	3,050,723
22	SEOUL	2,983,324
23	DJAKARTA	2,906,533
24	DELHI	2,549,162
25	MADRID	2,443,152
26	MANCHESTER	2,442,090
27	BOSTON	2,413,236
28	SHENYANG (MUKDEN)	2,411,000
29	BIRMINGHAM	2,377,230
30	ROME	2,278,882
31	SYDNEY	2,215,970
32	WEST BERLIN	2,176,612
33	MONTREAL	2,156,000
34	WUHAN	2,146,000
35	CHUNGKING	2,121,000
36	KARACHI	2,060,000

ries of a city but also that in the city's metropolitan area. The UN defines an urban agglomeration as the city proper and the "thickly settled territory . . . adjacent" to the city.

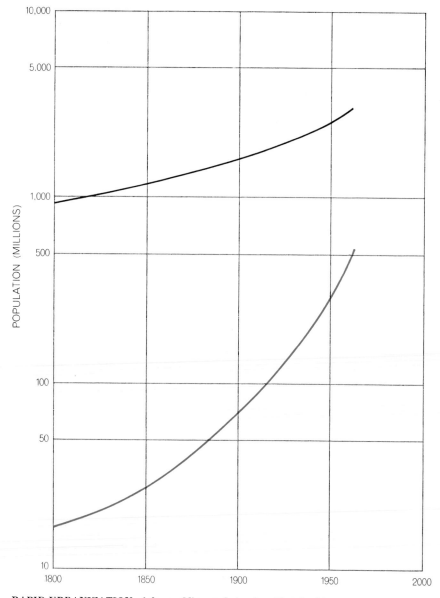

RAPID URBANIZATION of the world's population is evident in this comparison of total population (*black curve*) with the population in cities of more than 100,000 inhabitants (*colored curve*) over more than a century and a half. The use of cities of 100,000 or larger to define an urban population shows a close correlation with other definitions of urbanism.

because the excess of births over deaths is greater in the city than in the country, or because people move from the country to the city.

The first factor has usually had only slight influence. The second has apparently never been the case. Indeed, a chief obstacle to the growth of cities in the past has been their excessive mortality. London's water in the middle of the 19th century came mainly from wells and rivers that drained cesspools, graveyards and tidal areas. The city was regularly ravaged by cholera. Tables for 1841 show an expectation of life of about 36 years for London and 26 for Liverpool and Manchester, as compared to 41 for England and Wales as a whole. After 1850, mainly as a result of sanitary measures and some improvement in nutrition and housing, city health improved, but as late as the period 1901–1910 the death rate of the urban counties in England and Wales, as modified to make the age structure comparable, was 33 percent higher than the death rate of the rural counties. As Bernard Benjamin, a chief statistician of the British General Register Office, has remarked: "Living in the town involved not only a higher risk of epidemic and crowd diseases...but also a higher risk of degenerative disease—the harder wear and tear of factory employment and urban discomfort." By 1950, however, virtually the entire differential had been wiped out.

As for birth rates, during rapid urbanization in the past they were notably lower in cities than in rural areas. In fact, the gap tended to widen somewhat as urbanization proceeded in the latter half of the 19th century and the first quarter of the 20th. In 1800 urban women in the U.S. had 36 percent fewer children than rural women did; in 1840, 38 percent and in 1930, 41 percent. Thereafter the difference diminished.

With mortality in the cities higher and birth rates lower, and with reclassification a minor factor, the only real source for the growth in the proportion of people in urban areas during the industrial transition was rural-urban migration. This source had to be plentiful enough not only to overcome the substantial disadvantage of the cities in natural increase but also, above that, to furnish a big margin of growth in their populations. If, for example, the cities had a death rate a third higher and a birth rate a third lower than the rural rates (as was typical in the latter half of the 19th century), they would re-

In the U.S. it occurred from 1820 to 1890, in Greece from 1879 to 1921. As the proportion climbs above 50 percent the curve begins to flatten out; it falters, or even declines, when the proportion urban has reached about 75 percent. In the United Kingdom, one of the world's most urban countries, the proportion was slightly higher in 1926 (78.7 percent) than in 1961 (78.3 percent).

At the end of the curve some ambiguity appears. As a society becomes advanced enough to be highly urbanized it can also afford considerable suburbanization and fringe development. In a sense the slowing down of urbanization is thus more apparent than real: an increasing proportion of urbanites simply live in the country and are classified as rural. Many countries now try to compensate for this ambiguity by enlarging the boundaries of urban places; they did so in numerous censuses taken around 1960. Whether in these cases the old classification of urban or the new one is erroneous depends on how one looks at it; at a very advanced stage the entire concept of urbanization becomes ambiguous.

The end of urbanization cannot be unraveled without going into the ways in which economic development governs urbanization. Here the first question is: Where do the urbanites come from? The possible answers are few: The proportion of people in cities can rise because rural settlements grow larger and are reclassified as towns or cities;

quire each year perhaps 40 to 45 migrants from elsewhere per 1,000 of their population to maintain a growth rate of 3 percent per year. Such a rate of migration could easily be maintained as long as the rural portion of the population was large, but when this condition ceased to obtain, the maintenance of the same urban rate meant an increasing drain on the countryside.

Why did the rural-urban migration occur? The reason was that the rise in technological enhancement of human productivity, together with certain constant factors, rewarded urban concentration. One of the constant factors was that agriculture uses land as its prime instrument of production and hence

spreads out people who are engaged in it, whereas manufacturing, commerce and services use land only as a site. Moreover, the demand for agricultural products is less elastic than the demand for services and manufactures. As productivity grows, services and manufactures can absorb more manpower by paying higher wages. Since nonagricultural activities can use land simply as a site, they can locate near one another (in towns and cities) and thus minimize the friction of space inevitably involved in the division of labor. At the same time, as agricultural technology is improved, capital costs in farming rise and manpower becomes not only less needed but also economically more

burdensome. A substantial portion of the agricultural population is therefore sufficiently disadvantaged, in relative terms, to be attracted by higher wages in other sectors.

In this light one sees why a large flow of people from farms to cities was generated in every country that passed through the industrial revolution. One also sees why, with an even higher proportion of people already in cities and with the inability of city people to replace themselves by reproduction, the drain eventually became so heavy that in many nations the rural population began to decline in absolute as well as relative terms. In Sweden it declined after 1920, in England and Wales after

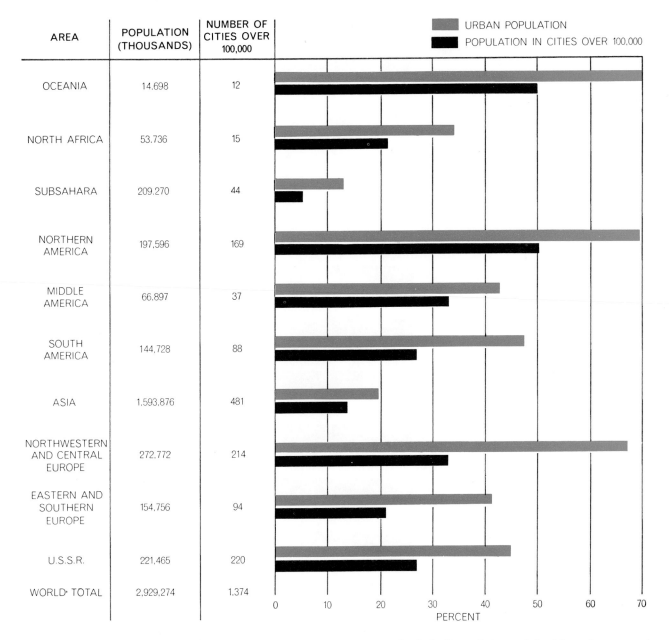

DEGREE OF URBANIZATION in the major regions of the world is indicated according to two different methods of classification.

One uses the "urban" population as defined by each country of a region. The other uses the population in cities of 100,000 or more.

272

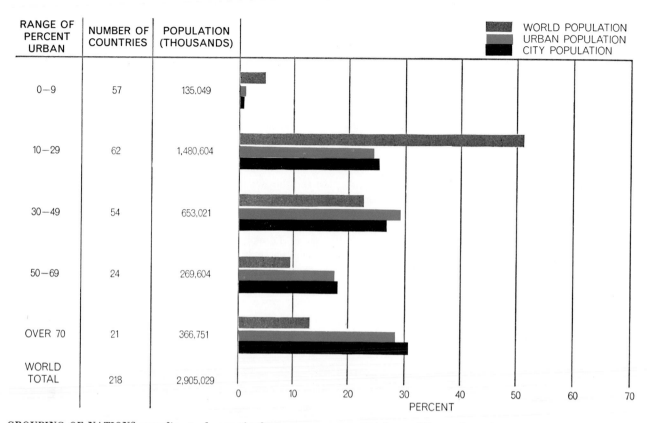

RANGE OF PERCENT URBAN	NUMBER OF COUNTRIES	POPULATION (THOUSANDS)
0—9	57	135,049
10—29	62	1,480,604
30—49	54	653,021
50—69	24	269,604
OVER 70	21	366,751
WORLD TOTAL	218	2,905,029

WORLD POPULATION
URBAN POPULATION
CITY POPULATION

GROUPING OF NATIONS according to degree of urbanization shows that more than half are less than 30 percent urbanized and that 45 are more than 50 percent urbanized. The chart can also be read cumulatively from the bottom to show, for example, that 22 percent of the world's population live in countries that are more than 50 percent urbanized and that those countries have 45 percent of the world's urban people and 48 percent of its city people. The approximate date of the population statistics used is 1960.

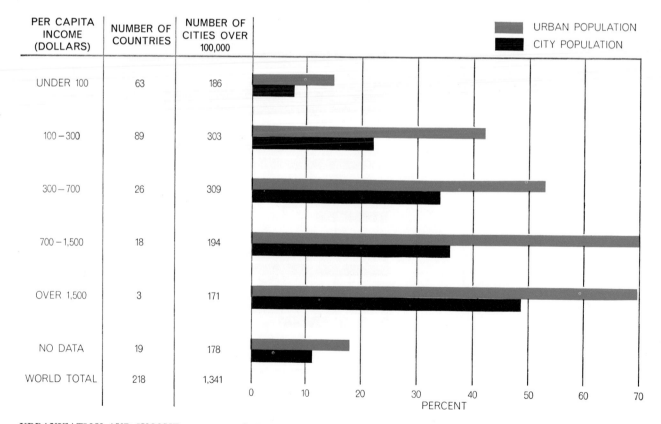

PER CAPITA INCOME (DOLLARS)	NUMBER OF COUNTRIES	NUMBER OF CITIES OVER 100,000
UNDER 100	63	186
100—300	89	303
300—700	26	309
700—1,500	18	194
OVER 1,500	3	171
NO DATA	19	178
WORLD TOTAL	218	1,341

URBAN POPULATION
CITY POPULATION

URBANIZATION AND INCOME are compared. It is apparent that a linear correlation exists between per capita income and degree of urbanization. Thus the three countries with a per capita income of $1,500 or more a year have the highest degree of urbanization—and the 63 countries with per capita income under $100 a year have the lowest degree—by either of two classifications of urbanization: the urban population as defined by each country or the population living in cities of 100,000 or more inhabitants.

1861, in Belgium after 1910.

Realizing that urbanization is transitional and finite, one comes on another fact—a fact that throws light on the circumstances in which urbanization comes to an end. A basic feature of the transition is the profound switch from agricultural to nonagricultural employment. This change is associated with urbanization but not identical with it. The difference emerges particularly in the later stages. Then the availability of automobiles, radios, motion pictures and electricity, as well as the reduction of the workweek and the workday, mitigate the disadvantages of living in the country. Concurrently the expanding size of cities makes them more difficult to live in. The population classed as "rural" is accordingly enlarged, both from cities and from true farms.

For these reasons the "rural" population in some industrial countries never did fall in absolute size. In all the industrial countries, however, the population dependent on agriculture—which the reader will recognize as a more functional definition of the nonurban population than mere rural residence—decreased in absolute as well as relative terms. In the U.S., for example, the net migration from farms totaled more than 27 million between 1920 and 1959 and thus averaged approximately 700,000 a year. As a result the farm population declined from 32.5 million in 1916 to 20.5 million in 1960, in spite of the large excess of births in farm families. In 1964, by a stricter American definition classifying as "farm families" only those families actually earning their living from agriculture, the farm population was down to 12.9 million. This number represented 6.8 percent of the nation's population; the comparable figure for 1880 was 44 percent. In Great Britain the number of males occupied in agriculture was at its peak, 1.8 million, in 1851; by 1961 it had fallen to .5 million.

In the later stages of the cycle, then, urbanization in the industrial countries tends to cease. Hence the connection between economic development and the growth of cities also ceases. The change is explained by two circumstances. First, there is no longer enough farm population to furnish a significant migration to the cities. (What can 12.9 million American farmers contribute to the growth of the 100 million people already in urbanized areas?) Second, the rural nonfarm population, nourished by refugees from the expanding cities, begins to increase as fast as the city popu-

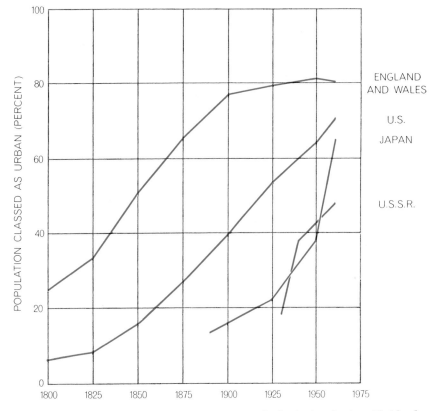

INDUSTRIALIZED NATIONS underwent a process of urbanization that is typified by the curves shown here for four countries. It was closely related to economic development. The figures for 1950 and 1960 are based on a classification that counts as urban the fringe residents of urbanized areas; that classification was not used for the earlier years shown.

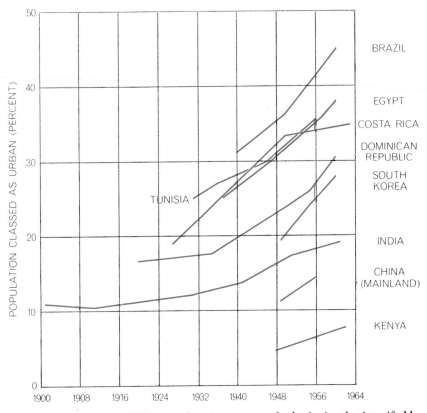

NONINDUSTRIAL NATIONS are undergoing a process of urbanization that is typified by these curves. The process started much later than in the industrialized nations, as can be seen by comparing this chart with the one at the top of the page, and is attributable more to the rapid rise of total population in these countries than to economic development.

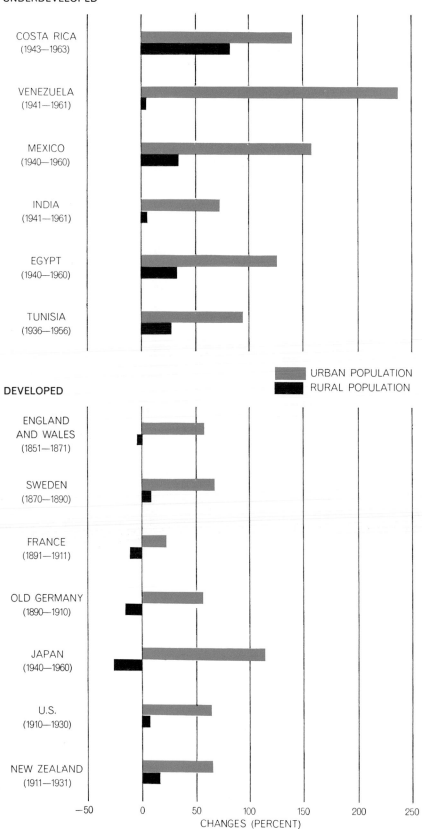

UNDERDEVELOPED

COSTA RICA
(1943—1963)

VENEZUELA
(1941—1961)

MEXICO
(1940—1960)

INDIA
(1941—1961)

EGYPT
(1940—1960)

TUNISIA
(1936—1956)

URBAN POPULATION
RURAL POPULATION

DEVELOPED

ENGLAND
AND WALES
(1851—1871)

SWEDEN
(1870—1890)

FRANCE
(1891—1911)

OLD GERMANY
(1890—1910)

JAPAN
(1940—1960)

U.S.
(1910—1930)

NEW ZEALAND
(1911—1931)

−50   0   50   100   150   200   250
CHANGES (PERCENT)

RURAL AND URBAN POPULATIONS of several underdeveloped countries are compared
with those in the currently developed countries at a time when they were undergoing rapid
urbanization. It is evident that in the underdeveloped countries the rural population is
rising in spite of urbanization, whereas in the earlier period it rose slightly or dropped.

lation. The effort of census bureaus to
count fringe residents as urban simply
pushes the definition of "urban" away
from the notion of dense settlement and
in the direction of the term "nonfarm."
As the urban population becomes more
"rural," which is to say less densely settled, the advanced industrial peoples
are for a time able to enjoy the amenities of urban life without the excessive
crowding of the past.

Here, however, one again encounters
the fact that a cessation of urbanization
does not necessarily mean a cessation
of city growth. An example is provided
by New Zealand. Between 1945 and
1961 the proportion of New Zealand's
population classed as urban—that is, the
ratio between urban and rural residents
—changed hardly at all (from 61.3 percent to 63.6 percent) but the urban population increased by 50 percent. In
Japan between 1940 and 1950 urbanization actually decreased slightly, but
the urban population increased by 13
percent.

The point to be kept in mind is that
once urbanization ceases, city growth
becomes a function of general population growth. Enough farm-to-city migration may still occur to redress the
difference in natural increase. The reproductive rate of urbanites tends,
however, to increase when they live at
lower densities, and the reproductive
rate of "urbanized" farmers tends to decrease; hence little migration is required
to make the urban increase equal the
national increase.

I now turn to the currently underdeveloped countries. With the advanced
nations having slackened their rate of
urbanization, it is the others—representing three-fourths of humanity—that are
mainly responsible for the rapid urbanization now characterizing the world as
a whole. In fact, between 1950 and
1960 the proportion of the population
in cities of 100,000 or more rose about
a third faster in the underdeveloped
regions than in the developed ones.
Among the underdeveloped regions the
pace was slow in eastern and southern
Europe, but in the rest of the underdeveloped world the proportion in cities
rose twice as fast as it did in the industrialized countries, even though the latter countries in many cases broadened
their definitions of urban places to include more suburban and fringe residents.

Because of the characteristic pattern
of urbanization, the current rates of
urbanization in underdeveloped countries could be expected to exceed those

now existing in countries far advanced in the cycle. On discovering that this is the case one is tempted to say that the underdeveloped regions are now in the typical stage of urbanization associated with early economic development. This notion, however, is erroneous. In their urbanization the underdeveloped countries are definitely not repeating past history. Indeed, the best grasp of their present situation comes from analyzing how their course differs from the previous pattern of development.

The first thing to note is that today's underdeveloped countries are urbanizing not only more rapidly than the industrial nations are now but also more rapidly than the industrial nations did in the heyday of their urban growth. The difference, however, is not large. In 40 underdeveloped countries for which we have data in recent decades, the average gain in the proportion of the population urban was 20 percent per decade; in 16 industrial countries, during the decades of their most rapid urbanization (mainly in the 19th century), the average gain per decade was 15 percent.

This finding that urbanization is proceeding only a little faster in underdeveloped countries than it did historically in the advanced nations may be questioned by the reader. It seemingly belies the widespread impression that cities throughout the nonindustrial parts of the world are bursting with people. There is, however, no contradiction. One must recall the basic distinction between a change in the proportion of the population urban, which is a ratio, and the absolute growth of cities. The popular impression is correct: the cities in underdeveloped areas are growing at a disconcerting rate. They are far outstripping the city boom of the industrializing era in the 19th century. If they continue their recent rate of growth, they will double their population every 15 years.

In 34 underdeveloped countries for which we have data relating to the 1940's and 1950's, the average annual gain in the urban population was 4.5 percent. The figure is remarkably similar for the various regions: 4.7 percent in seven countries of Africa, 4.7 percent in 15 countries of Asia and 4.3 percent in 12 countries of Latin America. In contrast, in nine European countries during their period of fastest urban population growth (mostly in the latter half of the 19th century) the average gain per year was 2.1 percent. Even the frontier industrial countries—the U.S., Australia–New Zealand, Can-

ada and Argentina—which received huge numbers of immigrants, had a smaller population growth in towns and cities: 4.2 percent per year. In Japan and the U.S.S.R. the rate was respectively 5.4 and 4.3 percent per year, but their economic growth began only recently.

How is it possible that the contrast in growth between today's underdeveloped countries and yesterday's industrializing countries is sharper with respect to the absolute urban population than with respect to the urban share of the total population? The answer lies in another profound difference between the two sets of countries—a difference in total population growth, rural as well as urban. Contemporary underdeveloped populations have been growing since 1940 more than twice as fast as industrialized populations, and their increase far exceeds the growth of the latter at the peak of their expansion. The only rivals in an earlier day were the frontier nations, which had the help of great streams of immigrants. Today the underdeveloped nations—already densely settled, tragically impoverished and with gloomy economic prospects—are multiplying their people by sheer biological increase at a rate

DENSE URBANIZATION of northeastern U.S. is portrayed in a mosaic of aerial photographs beginning on this page and continued on the next four pages. At left center is the lower part of Manhattan Island. In this and succeeding photographs southwest is to right.

that is unprecedented. It is this population boom that is overwhelmingly responsible for the rapid inflation of city populations in such countries. Contrary to popular opinion both inside and outside those countries, the main factor is not rural-urban migration.

This point can be demonstrated easily by a calculation that has the effect of eliminating the influence of general population growth on urban growth. The calculation involves assuming that the total population of a given country remained constant over a period of time but that the percentage urban changed as it did historically. In this manner one obtains the growth of the absolute urban population that would have occurred if rural-urban migration were the only factor affecting it. As an example, Costa Rica had in 1927 a total population of 471,500, of which 88,600, or 18.8 percent, was urban. By 1963 the country's total population was 1,325,200 and the urban population was 456,600, or 34.5 percent. If the total population had remained at 471,500 but the percentage urban had still risen from 18.8 to 34.5, the absolute urban population in 1963 would have been only 162,700. That is the growth that would have oc-

curred in the urban population if rural-urban migration had been the only factor. In actuality the urban population rose to 456,600. In other words, only 20 percent of the rapid growth of Costa Rica's towns and cities was attributable to urbanization per se; 44 percent was attributable solely to the country's general population increase, the remainder to the joint operation of both factors. Similarly, in Mexico between 1940 and 1960, 50 percent of the urban population increase was attributable to national multiplication alone and only 22 percent to urbanization alone.

The past performance of the advanced countries presents a sharp contrast. In Switzerland between 1850 and 1888, when the proportion urban resembled that in Costa Rica recently, general population growth alone accounted for only 19 percent of the increase of town and city people, and rural-urban migration alone accounted for 69 percent. In France between 1846 and 1911 only 21 percent of the growth in the absolute urban population was due to general growth alone.

The conclusion to which this contrast points is that one anxiety of governments in the underdeveloped nations is mis-

placed. Impressed by the mushrooming in their cities of shantytowns filled with ragged peasants, they attribute the fantastically fast city growth to rural-urban migration. Actually this migration now does little more than make up for the small difference in the birth rate between city and countryside. In the history of the industrial nations, as we have seen, the sizable difference between urban and rural birth rates and death rates required that cities, if they were to grow, had to have an enormous influx of people from farms and villages. Today in the underdeveloped countries the towns and cities have only a slight disadvantage in fertility, and their old disadvantage in mortality not only has been wiped out but also in many cases has been reversed. During the 19th century the urbanizing nations were learning how to keep crowded populations in cities from dying like flies. Now the lesson has been learned, and it is being applied to cities even in countries just emerging from tribalism. In fact, a disproportionate share of public health funds goes into cities. As a result throughout the nonindustrial world people in cities are multiplying as never before, and rural-urban migration is playing a much lesser role.

MOSAIC CONTINUED shows more of the heavily populated area, often called a megalopolis, between New York and Washington.

At left above, about an inch below right-angle bend of Delaware River, is Trenton; at right, where river bends upward, is Phila-

The trends just described have an important implication for the rural population. Given the explosive overall population growth in underdeveloped countries, it follows that if the rural population is not to pile up on the land and reach an economically absurd density, a high rate of rural-urban migration must be maintained. Indeed, the exodus from rural areas should be higher than in the past. But this high rate of internal movement is not taking place, and there is some doubt that it could conceivably do so.

To elaborate I shall return to my earlier point that in the evolution of industrialized countries the rural citizenry often declined in absolute as well as relative terms. The rural population of France—26.8 million in 1846—was down to 20.8 million by 1926 and 17.2 million by 1962, notwithstanding a gain in the nation's total population during this period. Sweden's rural population dropped from 4.3 million in 1910 to 3.5 million in 1960. Since the category "rural" includes an increasing portion of urbanites living in fringe areas, the historical drop was more drastic and consistent specifically in the farm population. In the U.S., although the "rural" population never quite ceased to grow,

the farm contingent began its long descent shortly after the turn of the century; today it is less than two-fifths of what it was in 1910.

This transformation is not occurring in contemporary underdeveloped countries. In spite of the enormous growth of their cities, their rural populations—and their more narrowly defined agricultural populations—are growing at a rate that in many cases exceeds the rise of even the urban population during the evolution of the now advanced countries. The poor countries thus confront a grave dilemma. If they do not substantially step up the exodus from rural areas, these areas will be swamped with underemployed farmers. If they do step up the exodus, the cities will grow at a disastrous rate.

The rapid growth of cities in the advanced countries, painful though it was, had the effect of solving a problem—the problem of the rural population. The growth of cities enabled agricultural holdings to be consolidated, allowed increased capitalization and in general resulted in greater efficiency. Now, however, the underdeveloped countries are experiencing an even more rapid urban growth—and are suffering from urban problems—but urbanization is not solv-

ing their rural ills.

A case in point is Venezuela. Its capital, Caracas, jumped from a population of 359,000 in 1941 to 1,507,000 in 1963; other Venezuelan towns and cities equaled or exceeded this growth. Is this rapid rise denuding the countryside of people? No, the Venezuelan farm population increased in the decade 1951–1961 by 11 percent. The only thing that declined was the amount of cultivated land. As a result the agricultural population density became worse. In 1950 there were some 64 males engaged in agriculture per square mile of cultivated land; in 1961 there were 78. (Compare this with 4.8 males occupied in agriculture per square mile of cultivated land in Canada, 6.8 in the U.S. and 15.6 in Argentina.) With each male occupied in agriculture there are of course dependents. Approximately 225 persons in Venezuela are trying to live from each square mile of cultivated land. Most of the growth of cities in Venezuela is attributable to overall population growth. If the general population had not grown at all, and internal migration had been large enough to produce the actual shift in the proportion in cities, the increase in urban population would have been only 28 percent of

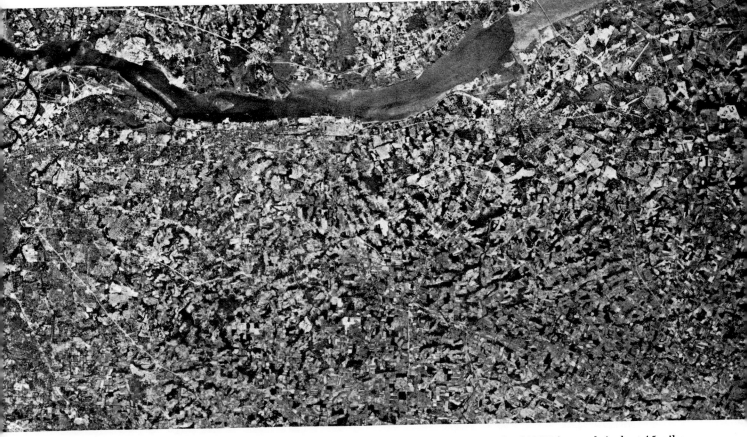

delphia. Near top left on this page the Schuylkill River joins the Delaware; five inches to the right is Wilmington, Del. Photographs were taken from an altitude of 34,000 feet; scale is about 4.5 miles per inch. The dominant checkerboard pattern is made by farms.

what it was and the rural population would have been reduced by 57 percent.

The story of Venezuela is being repeated virtually everywhere in the underdeveloped world. It is not only Caracas that has thousands of squatters living in self-constructed junk houses on land that does not belong to them. By whatever name they are called, the squatters are to be found in all major cities in the poorer countries. They live in broad gullies beneath the main plain in San Salvador and on the hillsides of Rio de Janeiro and Bogotá. They tend to occupy with implacable determination parks, school grounds and vacant lots. Amman, the capital of Jordan, grew from 12,000 in 1958 to 247,000 in 1961. A good part of it is slums, and urban amenities are lacking most of the time for most of the people. Greater Baghdad now has an estimated 850,000 people; its slums, like those in many other underdeveloped countries, are in two zones—the central part of the city and the outlying areas. Here are the *sarifa* areas, characterized by self-built reed huts; these areas account for about 45 percent of the housing in the entire city and are devoid of amenities, including even latrines. In addition to such urban problems, all the countries

struggling for higher living levels find their rural population growing too and piling up on already crowded land.

I have characterized urbanization as a transformation that, unlike economic development, is finally accomplished and comes to an end. At the 1950–1960 rate the term "urbanized world" will be applicable well before the end of the century. One should scarcely expect, however, that mankind will complete its urbanization without major complications. One sign of trouble ahead turns on the distinction I made at the start between urbanization and city growth per se. Around the globe today city growth is disproportionate to urbanization. The discrepancy is paradoxical in the industrial nations and worse than paradoxical in the nonindustrial.

It is in this respect that the nonindustrial nations, which still make up the great majority of nations, are far from repeating past history. In the 19th and early 20th centuries the growth of cities arose from and contributed to economic advancement. Cities took surplus manpower from the countryside and put it to work producing goods and services that in turn helped to modernize agri-

culture. But today in underdeveloped countries, as in present-day advanced nations, city growth has become increasingly unhinged from economic development and hence from rural-urban migration. It derives in greater degree from overall population growth, and this growth in nonindustrial lands has become unprecedented because of modern health techniques combined with high birth rates.

The speed of world population growth is twice what it was before 1940, and the swiftest increase has shifted from the advanced to the backward nations. In the latter countries, consequently, it is virtually impossible to create city services fast enough to take care of the huge, never ending cohorts of babies and peasants swelling the urban masses. It is even harder to expand agricultural land and capital fast enough to accommodate the enormous natural increase on farms. The problem is not urbanization, not rural-urban migration, but human multiplication. It is a problem that is new in both its scale and its setting, and runaway city growth is only one of its painful expressions.

As long as the human population expands, cities will expand too, regard-

MOSAIC COMPLETED begins (*left*) about 30 miles north of Baltimore, which is at right center below an arm of Chesapeake Bay. At right center on opposite page is Washington; the light spot three-quarters of an inch in from the right edge of the photograph, on a

less of whether urbanization increases or declines. This means that some individual cities will reach a size that will make 19th-century metropolises look like small towns. If the New York urbanized area should continue to grow only as fast as the nation's population (according to medium projections of the latter by the Bureau of the Census), it would reach 21 million by 1985 and 30 million by 2010. I have calculated that if India's population should grow as the UN projections indicate it will, the largest city in India in the year 2000 will have between 36 and 66 million inhabitants.

What is the implication of such giant agglomerations for human density? In 1950 the New York–Northeastern New Jersey urbanized area had an average density of 9,810 persons per square mile. With 30 million people in the year 2010, the density would be 24,000 per square mile. Although this level is exceeded now in parts of New York City (which averages about 25,000 per square mile) and many other cities, it is a high density to be spread over such a big area; it would cover, remember, the suburban areas to which people moved to escape high density. Actually, however, the density of the New York urbanized region is dropping, not increasing, as the population grows. The reason is that the territory covered by the urban agglomeration is growing faster than the population: it grew by 51 percent from 1950 to 1960, whereas the population rose by 15 percent.

If, then, one projects the rise in population and the rise in territory for the New York urbanized region, one finds the density problem solved. It is not solved for long, though, because New York is not the only city in the region that is expanding. So are Philadelphia, Trenton, Hartford, New Haven and so on. By 1960 a huge stretch of territory about 600 miles long and 30 to 100 miles wide along the Eastern seaboard contained some 37 million people

Since the whole area is becoming one big polynucleated city, its population cannot long expand without a rise in density. Thus persistent human multiplication promises to frustrate the ceaseless search for space—for ample residential lots, wide-open suburban school grounds, sprawling shopping centers, one-floor factories, broad freeways.

How people feel about giant agglomerations is best indicated by their headlong effort to escape them. The bigger the city, the higher the cost of space; yet, the more the level of living rises, the more people are willing to pay for low-density living. Nevertheless, as urbanized areas expand and collide, it seems probable that life in low-density surroundings will become too dear for the great majority.

One can of course imagine that cities may cease to grow and may even shrink in size while the population in general continues to multiply. Even this dream, however, would not permanently solve the problem of space. It would eventually obliterate the distinction between urban and rural, but at the expense of the rural.

It seems plain that the only way to stop urban crowding and to solve most of the urban problems besetting both the developed and the underdeveloped nations is to reduce the overall rate of population growth. Policies designed to do this have as yet little intelligence and power behind them. Urban planners continue to treat population growth as something to be planned for, not something to be itself planned. Any talk about applying brakes to city growth is therefore purely speculative, overshadowed as it is by the reality of uncontrolled population increase.

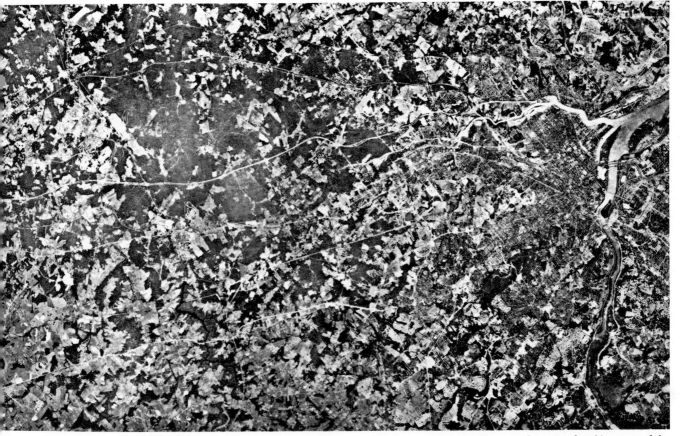

dark point of land adjoining the Potomac River, is the Tidal Basin, with the White House visible in dark spot an eighth of an inch to left of basin. Some 27 million people—more than 14 percent of the U.S. population—live in area between New York and Washington.

27

Military Technology and National Security

HERBERT F. YORK
August 1969

The recent public hearings in the Senate and the House of Representatives on anti-ballistic-missile (ABM) systems have provided an unprecedented opportunity to expose to the people of this country and the world the inner workings of one of the dominant features of our time: the strategic arms race. Testimony has been given by a wide range of witnesses concerning the development and deployment of all kinds of offensive and defensive nuclear weapons; particular attention has been paid to the interaction between decisions in these matters and the dynamics of the arms race as a whole.

In my view the ABM issue is only a detail in a much larger problem: the feasibility of a purely technological approach to national security. What makes the ABM debate so important is that for the first time it has been possible to discuss a major aspect of this larger problem entirely in public. The reason for this is that nearly all the relevant facts about the proposed ABM systems either are already declassified or can easily be deduced from logical concepts that have never been classified. Thus it has been possible to consider in a particular case such questions as the following:

1. To what extent is the increasing complexity of modern weapons systems and the need for instant response causing strategic decision-making authority to pass from high political levels to low military-command levels, and from human beings to machines?

2. To what extent is the factor of secrecy combined with complexity leading to a steadily increasing dominance of military-oriented technicians in some vital areas of decision-making?

3. To what extent do increasing numbers of weapons and increasing complexity—in and of themselves—complicate and accelerate the arms race?

My own conclusion is that the ABM issue constitutes a particularly clear example of the futility of searching for technical solutions to what is essentially a political problem, namely the problem of national security. In support of this conclusion I propose in this article to review the recent history of the strategic arms race, to evaluate what the recent hearings and other public discussions have revealed about its present status and future prospects, and then to suggest what might be done now to deal with the problem of national security in a more rational manner.

The strategic arms race in its present form is a comparatively recent phenomenon. It began in the early 1950's, when it became evident that the state of the art in nuclear weaponry, rocket propulsion and missile guidance and control had reached the point in the U.S. where a strategically useful intercontinental ballistic missile (ICBM) could be built. At about the same time the fact that a major long-range-missile development program was in progress in the U.S.S.R. was confirmed. As a result of

the confluence of these two events the tremendous U.S. long-range-missile program, which dominated the technological scene for more than a decade, was undertaken. The Air Force's Thor, Atlas and Titan programs and the Army's Jupiter program were started almost simultaneously; the Navy's Polaris program and the Air Force's Minuteman program were phased in just a few years later.

More or less at the same time the Army, which had had the responsibility for ground-based air defense (including the Nike Ajax and Nike Hercules surface-to-air missiles, or SAM's), began to study the problem of how to intercept ICBM's, and soon afterward initiated the Nike Zeus program. This program was a straightforward attempt to use existing technology in the design of a nuclear-armed rocket for the purpose of intercepting an uncomplicated incoming warhead. The Air Force proposed more exotic solutions to the missile-defense problem, but these were subsequently absorbed into the Defender Program of the Department of Defense's Advanced Research Projects Agency (ARPA). The Defender Program included the study of designs more advanced than Nike Zeus, and it also incorporated a program of down-range measurements designed to find out what did in fact go on during the terminal phases of missile flight.

By 1960 indications that the Russians were taking the ABM prospect seriously, in addition to progress in our own Nike Zeus program, stimulated our offensive-

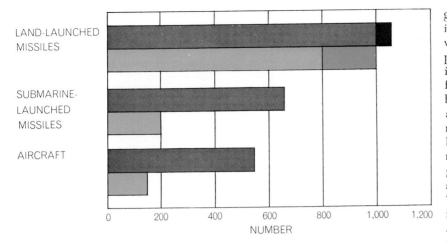

PRESENT STATUS of the deployment of strategic offensive forces by the U.S. (*gray*) and the U.S.S.R. (*color*) shows that the two superpowers are about even in numbers of intercontinental ballistic missiles (ICBM's), and that the U.S. is ahead in both long-range aircraft and submarine-launched ballistic missiles (SLBM's) of the Polaris type. The U.S. ICBM's consist almost entirely of Minutemen (*light gray*), which carry a nuclear warhead with an explosive yield in the megaton range; there currently remain only 54 of the larger Titans (*dark gray*) in our strategic forces. The smaller Russian missiles (*light color*) are mostly SS-11's, which are roughly equivalent in size to our Minutemen. The larger Russian missiles (*dark color*) are SS-9s, which are comparable in size to our Titans. The figures used are from a speech given by Secretary of Defense Melvin R. Laird in March, 1969.

missile designers into seriously studying the problem of how to penetrate missile defenses. Very quickly a host of "penetration aid" concepts came to light: light and heavy decoys, including balloons, tank fragments and objects resembling children's jacks; electronic countermeasures, including radar-reflecting clouds of the small wires called chaff; radar blackout by means of high-altitude nuclear explosions; tactics such as barrage, local exhaustion and "rollback" of the defense, and, most important insofar as the then unforeseen consequences were concerned, the notion of putting more than one warhead on one launch vehicle. At first this notion simply involved a "shotgun" technique, good only against large-area targets (cities), but it soon developed into what we now call MIRV's (multiple independently targeted reentry vehicles), which can in principle (and soon in practice) be used against smaller, harder targets such as missile silos, radars and command centers.

This avalanche of concepts forced the ABM designers to go back to the drawing board, and as a result the Nike-X concept was born in 1962. The Nike-X designers attempted to make use of more sophisticated and up-to-date technology in the design of a system that they hoped might be able to cope with a large, sophisticated attack. All through the mid-1960's a vigorous battle of defensive concepts and designs versus offensive concepts and designs took place. This

battle was waged partly on the Pacific Missile Range but mostly on paper and in committee meetings. It took place generally in secret, although parts of it have been discussed in articles in SCIENTIFIC AMERICAN [see "National Security and the Nuclear-Test Ban," by Jerome B. Wiesner and Herbert F. York, October, 1964; "Anti-Ballistic-Missile Systems," by Richard L. Garwin and Hans A. Bethe, March, 1968; "The Dynamics of the Arms Race," by George W. Rathjens, April, 1969].

This intellectual battle culminated in a meeting that took place in the White House in January, 1967. In addition to President Johnson, Secretary of Defense Robert S. McNamara and the Joint Chiefs of Staff there were present all past and current Special Assistants to the President for Science and Technology (James R. Killian, Jr., George B. Kistiakowsky, Jerome B. Wiesner and Donald F. Hornig) and all past and current Directors of Defense Research and Engineering (Harold Brown, John S. Foster, Jr., and myself). We were asked that simple kind of question which must be answered after all the complicated ifs, ands and buts have been discussed: "Will it work?" The answer was no, and there was no dissent from that answer. The context, of course, was the Russian threat as it was then interpreted and forecast, and the current and projected state of our own ABM technology.

Later that year Secretary McNamara

gave his famous San Francisco speech in which he reiterated his belief that we could not build an ABM system capable of protecting us from destruction in the event of a Russian attack. For the first time, however, he stated that he did believe we could build an ABM system able to cope with a hypothetical Chinese missile attack, which by definition would be "light" and uncomplicated. In recommending that we go ahead with a program to build what came to be known as the Sentinel system, he said that "there are *marginal* grounds for concluding that a light deployment of U.S. ABM's against this possibility is prudent." A few sentences later, however, he warned: "The danger in deploying this relatively light and reliable Chinese-oriented ABM system is going to be that pressures will develop to expand it into a heavy Soviet-oriented ABM system." The record makes it clear that he was quite right in this prediction.

Meanwhile the U.S.S.R. was going ahead with its own ABM program. The Russian program proceeded by fits and starts, and our understanding of it was, as might be supposed in such a situation, even more erratic. It is now generally agreed that the only ABM system the Russians have deployed is an area defense around Moscow much like our old Nike Zeus system. It appears to have virtually no capability against our offense, and it has been, as we shall see below, extremely counterproductive insofar as its goal of defending Moscow is concerned.

Development and deployment of offensive-weapons systems on both sides progressed rapidly during the 1960's, but rather than discuss these historically I shall go directly to the picture that the Administration has given of the present status and future projection of such forces.

Data recently presented by the Department of Defense show that the U.S. and the U.S.S.R. are about even in numbers of intercontinental missiles, and that the U.S. is ahead in both long-range aircraft and submarines of the Polaris type [see illustration on this page]. The small Russian missiles are mostly what we call SS-11's, which were described in the hearings as being roughly the equivalent of our Minutemen. The large Russian missile is what we call the SS-9. Deputy Secretary of Defense David Packard characterized its capability as one 20-megaton warhead or three five-megaton warheads. Our own missiles are almost entirely the smaller Minutemen. There currently remain only 54 of the larger Titans in our strategic forces. Not covered in the table are "extras" such as the U.S.S.R.'s FOBS (fractional orbital bombardment system) and IRBM's (intermediate-range ballistic missiles), nor the U.S.'s bombardment aircraft deployed on carriers and overseas bases in Europe and elsewhere. There are, of course, many important details that do not come out clearly in such a simple tabular presentation; these include payload capacity, warhead yield, number of warheads per missile and, often the most important, warhead accuracy.

In the area of defensive systems designed to cope with the offensive systems outlined above, both the U.S. and the

U.S.S.R. have defenses against bombers that would probably be adequate against a prolonged attack using chemical explosives (where 10 percent attrition is enough) and almost certainly inadequate against a nuclear attack (where 10 percent penetration is enough). In addition the U.S.S.R. has its ineffective ABM deployment around Moscow, usually estimated as consisting of fewer than 100 antimissile missiles.

What all these complicated details add up to can be expressed in a single word: parity. This is clearly not numerical equality in the number of warheads or in the number of megatons or in the total "throw weight"; in fact, given dif-

ferent design approaches on the two sides, simultaneous equality in these three figures is entirely impossible. It is, rather, parity with respect to strategic objectives; that is, in each case these forces are easily sufficient for deterrence and entirely insufficient for a successful preemptive strike. In the jargon of strategic studies either side would retain, after a massive "first strike" by the other, a sufficiently large "assured destruction capability" against the other in order to deter such a first strike from being made.

There is much argument about exactly what it takes in the way of "assured destruction capability" in order to deter, but even the most conservative strategic

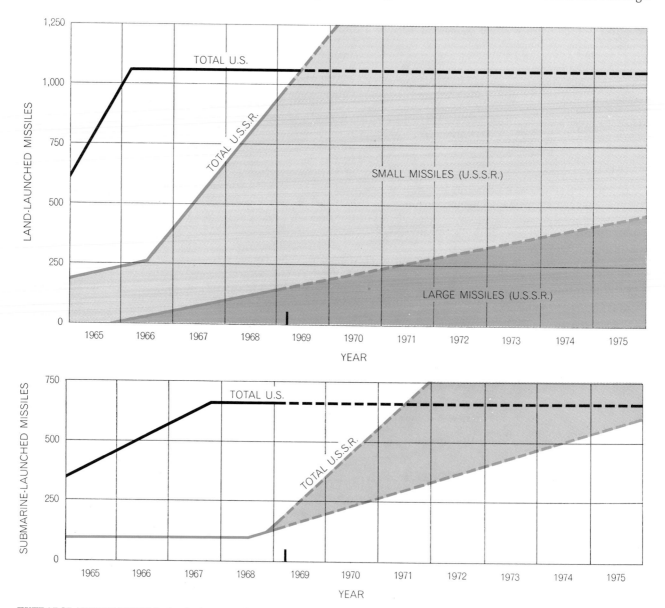

EXTRAPOLATED TRENDS in the deployment of strategic offensive missiles by the U.S. and the U.S.S.R. are indicated by the broken lines in this pair of charts, which are based on a presentation by Deputy Secretary of Defense David Packard to the Senate Foreign Relations Committee in March 1969. The chart at top shows the numbers of deployed ICBM's for both sides during the period 1965–1975. The Russian total is broken down into "small" missiles (the one megaton SS-11's) and "large" missiles (the multimegaton SS-9's). The chart at bottom shows the deployed SLBM's during the same period. The extrapolations suggest that the Russians will be even with us in ICBM's quite soon and will catch up in SLBM's sometime between 1971 and 1977. One important factor omitted from the charts is the imminent deployment by both sides of MIRV's (multiple independently targetable reentry vehicles).

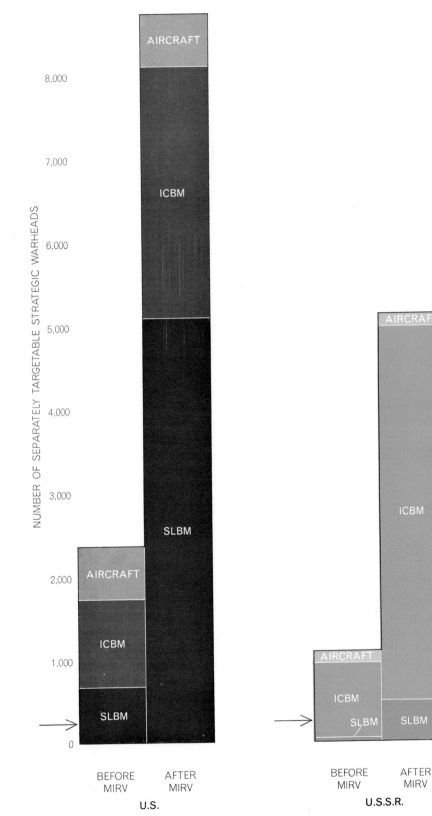

IMPACT OF MIRV on the strategic balance is emphasized in this chart, which is based on one prepared by the staff of the Senate Foreign Relations Committee and presented by Senator Albert Gore of Tennessee in March 1969. The chart depicts the strategic balance in terms of separately targetable strategic warheads before and after MIRVing, which is expected to take place in the next five years. The two black arrows near the bottom indicate the number of warheads that could devastate the 50 largest cities on each side.

planners conclude that the threat of only a few hundred warheads exploding over population and industrial centers would be sufficient for the purpose. The large growing disparity between the number of warheads needed for the purpose and the number actually possessed by each side is what leads to the concept of "overkill." If present trends continue, in the future all or most missiles will be MIRVed, and so this overkill will be increased by perhaps another order of magnitude.

Here let me note that it is sometimes argued that there is a disparity in the present situation because Russian missile warheads are said to be bigger than U.S. warheads, both in weight and megatonnage; similarly, it is argued that MIRVing does not increase overkill because total yield is reduced in going from single to multiple warheads. This argument is based on the false notion that the individual MIRV warheads of the future will be "small" when measured against the purpose assigned to them. Against large, "soft" targets such as cities bombs *very much* smaller than those that could be used as components of MIRV's are (and in the case of Hiroshima were proved to be) entirely adequate for destroying the heart of a city and killing hundreds of thousands of people. Furthermore, in the case of small, "hard" targets such as missile silos, command posts and other military installations, having explosions bigger than those for which the "kill," or crater, radius slightly exceeds "circular error probable" (CEP) adds little to the probability of destroying such targets. Crater radius depends roughly on the cube root of the explosive power; consequently, if during the period when technology allows us to go from one to 10 warheads per missile it also allows us to improve accuracy by a little more than twofold, the "kill" per warhead will remain nearly the same in most cases, whereas the number of warheads increases tenfold.

In any case, it is fair to say that in spite of a number of such arguments about details, nearly everyone who testified at the ABM hearings agreed that the present situation is one in which each side possesses forces adequate to deter the other. In short, we now have parity in the only sense that ultimately counts.

Several forecasts have been made of what the strategic-weapons situation will be in the mid-1970's. In most respects here again there is quite general agreement. Part of the presentation by Deputy Secretary Packard to the Senate Foreign Relations Committee on March

1969 were two graphs showing the trends in numbers of deployed offensive missiles beginning in 1965 and extending to 1975 [see illustrations on page 282]. There is no serious debate about the basic features of these graphs. It is agreed by all that in the recent past the U.S. has been far ahead of the U.S.S.R. in all areas, and that the Russians began a rapid deployment program a few years ago that will bring them even with us in ICBM's quite soon and that, if extended ahead without any slowdown, would bring them even in submarine-launched ballistic missiles (SLBM's) sometime between 1971 and 1977.

One important factor that the Department of Defense omitted from its graphs is MIRV. Deployment plans for MIRV's have not been released by either the U.S. or the U.S.S.R., although various rough projections were made at the hearings about numbers of warheads per vehicle (three to 10), about accuracies (figures around half a mile were often mentioned, and it was implied that U.S. accuracies were better than Russian ones) and about development status (the U.S. was said to be ahead in developments in this field). A pair of charts emphasizing the impact of MIRV was prepared by the staff of the Senate Foreign Relations Committee [see illustration on preceding page].

One could argue with both of these sets of charts. For example, one might wonder why the Senate charts show so few warheads on the Russian Polaris-type submarine and why they show only three MIRV's on U.S. Minutemen; on the other hand, one might wonder whether the Department of Defense's projected buildup of the Russian Polaris fleet could be that fast, or whether one should count the older Russian missile submarines. Nonetheless, the general picture presented cannot be far wrong. Moreover, the central arguments pursued throughout the ABM hearings (in both the Senate Foreign Relations Committee hearings in March and the Senate Armed Services Committee hearings in April) were not primarily concerned with these numerical matters. Rather, they were concerned with (1) Secretary of Defense Melvin R. Laird's interpretation of these numbers insofar as Russian intentions were concerned, (2) the validity of the Safeguard ABM system as a response to the purported strategic problems of the 1970's and (3) the arms-race implications of Safeguard.

As for the matter of intentions, those favoring the ABM concept generally held that the only "rational" explanation of the Russians' recent SS-9 buildup,

coupled with their multiple-warhead development program and the Moscow ABM system, was that they were aiming for a first-strike capability. One must admit that almost anything is conceivable as far as intentions are concerned, but there certainly are simpler, and it seems to me much more likely, explanations. The simplest of all is contained in Deputy Secretary Packard's chart. The most surprising feature of this chart is the fact that the Russians were evidently satisfied with being such a poor second for such a long time. This is made more puzzling by the fact that all during this period U.S. defense officials found it necessary to boast about how far ahead we were in order to be able to resist internal pressures for still greater expansion of our offensive forces.

Another possible reason, and one that I believe added to the other in the minds of the Russian planners, was that their strategists concluded in the mid-1960's that, whatever the top officials here might say, certain elements would eventually succeed in getting a large-scale ABM system built, and that penetration-aid devices, including multiple warheads, would be needed to meet the challenge. Whether or not they were correct in this latter hypothetical analysis is still uncertain at this writing. Let us, however, pass on from this question of someone else's intentions and consider whether or not the proposed Safeguard ABM system is a valid, rational and necessary response to the Russian deployments and developments outlined above.

To many of those who have recently written favorably about ABM defenses or who have testified in their favor before the Congressional committees, Safeguard is supported mainly as a prototype of something else: a "thick" defense of the U.S. against a massive Russian missile attack. This is clearly not at all the rationale for the Safeguard decision as presented by President Nixon in his press conference of March 14, nor is it implied as more than a dividend in the defense secretaries' testimony. The President said that he wanted a system that would protect a *part* of our Minuteman force in order to increase the credibility of our deterrent, and that he had overruled moving in the direction of a massive city defense because "even starting with a thin system and then going to a heavy system tends to be more provocative in terms of making credible a first-strike capability against the Soviet Union. I want no provocation which might deter arms talks." The top civilian defense officials give this same rationale,

although they put a little more emphasis on the "prototype" and "growth potential" aspects of the system. For simplicity and clarity I shall focus on the Administration's proposal, as stated in open session by responsible officials.

From a technical point of view and as far as components are concerned, President Nixon's Safeguard system of today is very little different from President Johnson's Sentinel system [see illustrations on page 287]. There are only minor changes in the location of certain components (away from cities), and elements have been added to some of the radars so that they can now observe submarine-launched missiles coming from directions other than directly from the U.S.S.R. and China. As before, the system consists of a long-range interceptor carrying a large nuclear weapon (Spartan), a fast short-range interceptor carrying a small nuclear weapon (Sprint), two types of radar (perimeter acquisition radar, or PAR, and missile-site radar, or MSR), a computer for directing the battle, and a command and control system for integrating Safeguard with the national command. I shall not describe the equipment in detail at this point but pass on directly to what I believe can be concluded from the hearings and other public sources about each of the following four major questions: (1) Assuming that Safeguard could protect Minuteman, is it needed to protect our deterrent? (2) Assuming that Safeguard "works," can it in fact safeguard Minuteman? (3) Will it work? (4) Anyway, what harm can it do?

First: Assuming that Safeguard could protect Minuteman, is it needed to protect our deterrent?

Perhaps the clearest explanation of why the answer to this first question is "no" was given by Wolfgang K. H. Panofsky before the Senate Armed Services Committee on April 22. He described how the deterrent consists of three main components: Polaris submarines, bombers and land-based ICBM's. Each of these components alone is capable of delivering far more warheads than is actually needed for deterrence, and each is currently defended against surprise destruction in a quite different way. ICBM's are in hard silos and are numerous. Polarises are hidden in the seas. Bombers can be placed on various levels of alert and can be dispersed.

Since the warning time in the case of an ICBM attack is generally taken as being about 30 minutes, the people who believe the deterrent may be in serious danger usually imagine that the bomb-

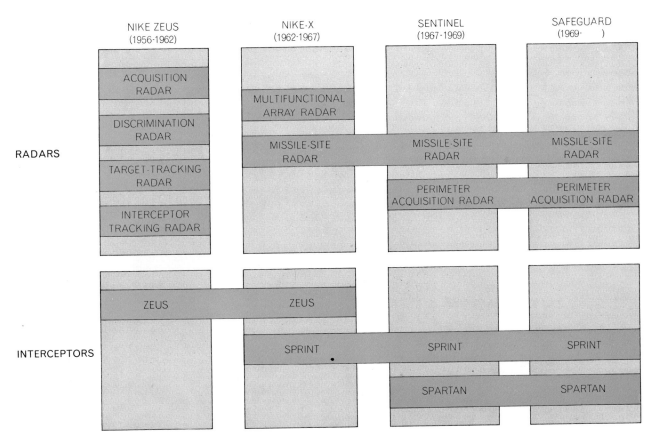

| NIKE ZEUS (1956-1962) | NIKE-X (1962-1967) | SENTINEL (1967-1969) | SAFEGUARD (1969-   ) |

RADARS

- ACQUISITION RADAR
- DISCRIMINATION RADAR
- TARGET-TRACKING RADAR
- INTERCEPTOR TRACKING RADAR
- MULTIFUNCTIONAL ARRAY RADAR
- MISSILE-SITE RADAR
- PERIMETER ACQUISITION RADAR

INTERCEPTORS

- ZEUS
- SPRINT
- SPARTAN

EVOLUTION OF U.S. ABM SYSTEMS is represented in this illustration, adapted from a chart introduced by Daniel J. Fink in his testimony before the Senate Foreign Relations Committee in March 1969. In general the radar components of the successive designs have progressed from slow, mechanically steered, single-function radars to fast, electronically steered, multifunction radars. The slow Zeus ABM missile has been superseded by the short-range Sprint (for terminal defense) and the long-range Spartan (for area defense). The components of the Safeguard system are the same as those that were originally intended for the earlier Sentinel system.

ers are attacked by missile submarines, and therefore have only a 15-minute warning. This is important because a 30-minute warning gives the bombers ample time to get off the ground. In that case, however, an attack on all three components cannot be made simultaneously; that is, if the attacking weapons are launched simultaneously, they cannot arrive simultaneously, and vice versa.

Thus it is incredible that all three of our deterrent systems could become vulnerable in the same time period, and it is doubly incredible that we could not know that this would happen without sufficient notice so that we could do something about it. There is, therefore, no basis for a frantic reaction to the hypothetical Russian threat to Minuteman. Still, it is sensible and prudent to begin thinking about the problem, and so we turn to the other questions. We must consider these questions in the technological framework of the mid-1970's, and we shall do this now in the way defense officials currently seem to favor: by assuming that this is the best of all possible technological worlds, that everything works as intended and that direct extrapolations of current capabilities are valid.

Second: Assuming that Safeguard "works," can it in fact safeguard Minuteman?

One good approach to this problem is the one used by George W. Rathjens in his testimony before the Senate Armed Services Committee on April 23. His analysis took as a basis of calculation the implication in Secretary Laird's testimony that the Minuteman force may become seriously imperiled in the mid-1970's. Rathjens then estimated how many SS-9's would have to be deployed at that time in order to achieve this result. From this number, and the estimate of the current number of SS-9's deployed, he got a rate of deployment. He also had to make an assumption about how many Sprints and Spartans would be deployed at that time, and his estimates were based on the first phase of Safeguard deployment. These last numbers have not been released, but a range of reasonable values can be guessed from the cost estimates given. Assuming that the SS-9's would have four or five MIRV warheads each by that time, Rathjens found that by prolonging the SS-9 production program by a few months the Russians would be able to cope with Safeguard by simply exhausting it and would still have enough warheads left to imperil Minuteman, if that is indeed their intention [see illustration on page 292].

The length of this short safe period does depend on the numbers used in the calculations, and they of course can be disputed to a degree. Thus if one assumes that it takes fewer Russian warheads to imperil Minuteman (it can't be less than one for one!), then the assumed deployment rate is lower and the safe period is lengthened; on the other hand, if one notes that the missile-site radars in our system are much softer than even today's silos, then the first attacking warheads, fired directly at the radars, can be smaller and less accurate, so that a higher degree of MIRVing can be used for attacking these radars and a shorter safe period results. To go further, it was suggested that the accuracy/yield combination of the more numerous SS-11's might be sufficient for attacking the missile-site radars, and therefore, if the Russians were to elect such an option, there would be no safe period at all. In short, the most that Safeguard can do is either delay somewhat the date when Minuteman would be imperiled or cause the attacker to build up his forces at a somewhat higher rate if indeed imperiling Minuteman by a fixed date is his purpose.

In the more general case this problem is often discussed in budgetary terms, and the "cost-exchange ratio" between offense and defense is computed for a wide variety of specific types of weapon. Such calculations give a wide variety of results, and there is much argument about them. However, even using current offense designs (that is, without MIRV), such calculations usually strongly favor the offense. This exchange ratio varies almost linearly with the degree of MIRVing of the offensive missiles, and therefore it seems to me that in the ideal technological future we have taken as our context this exchange ratio will still more strongly favor the offense.

Third: Will it work? By this question I mean: Will operational units be able to intercept enemy warheads accompanied by enemy penetration aids in an atmosphere of total astonishment and uncertainty? I do not mean: Will test equipment and test crews intercept U.S. warheads accompanied by U.S. penetration aids in a contrived atmosphere? A positive answer to the latter question is a necessary condition for obtaining a positive answer to the former, but it is by no stretch of the imagination a sufficient condition.

This basic question has been attacked from two quite different angles: by examining historical analogies and by examining the technical elements of the problem in detail. I shall touch on both here. Design-oriented people who consider this a purely technical question emphasize the second approach. I believe the question is by no means a purely technical question, and I suggest that the historical-analogy approach is more promising, albeit much more difficult to use correctly.

False analogies are common in this argument. We find that some say: "You can't tell me that if we can put a man on the moon we can't build an ABM." Others say: "That's what Oppenheimer told us about the hydrogen bomb." These two statements contain the same basic error. They are examples of successes in a contest between technology and nature, whereas the ABM issue involves a contest between two technologies: offensive weapons and penetration aids versus defensive weapons and discrimi-

nation techniques. These analogies would be more pertinent if, in the first case, someone were to jerk the moon away just before the astronauts landed, or if, in the second case, nature were to keep changing the nuclear-reaction probabilities all during the development of the hydrogen bomb and once again after it was deployed.

Proper historical analogies should involve modern high-technology defense systems that have actually been installed and used in combat. If one examines the record of such systems, one finds that they do often produce some attrition of the offense, but not nearly enough to be of use against a nuclear attack. The most up-to-date example is provided by the Russian SAM's and other air-defense equipment deployed in North Vietnam. This system "works" after a fashion because both the equipment designers and the operating crews have had plenty of opportunities to practice against real U.S. targets equipped with real U.S. countermeasures and employing real U.S. tactics.

The best example of a U.S. system is somewhat older, but I believe it is still relevant. It is the SAGE system, a complex air-defense system designed in the early 1950's. All the components worked on the test range, but by 1960 we came to realize, even without combat testing, that SAGE could not really cope with the offense that was then coming into being. We thereupon greatly curtailed and modified our plans, although we did continue with some parts of the system. To quote from the recent report on the ABM decision prepared by Wiesner, Abram Chayes and others: "Still, after fifteen years, and the expenditure of more than $20 billion, it is generally conceded that we do not have a significant capability to defend ourselves against a well-planned air attack. The Soviet Union, after even greater effort, has probably not done much better."

So much for analogies; let us turn to the Safeguard system itself. Doubts about its being able to work were raised during the public hearings on a variety of grounds, some of which are as follows:

First, and perhaps foremost, there is the remarkable fact that the new Safeguard system and the old Sentinel system use virtually the same hardware deployed in a very similar manner, and yet they have entirely different primary purposes. Sentinel had as its purpose defending large soft targets against the so-called Chinese threat. The Chinese threat by definition involved virtually no sophisticated penetration aids and no

SPRINT ABM MISSILE was photographed during a test flight at the White Sands Missile Range in New Mexico. The photograph, which was released by the U.S. Army's Nike-X Project Office in March, 1966, shows the second stage of the missile heated to incandescence by friction with the atmosphere. Because of the extremely high speed of the Sprint, the missile's skin in places reaches temperatures hotter than inside its rocket motor. The bulges are created by the guidance fins at the rear of the second stage.

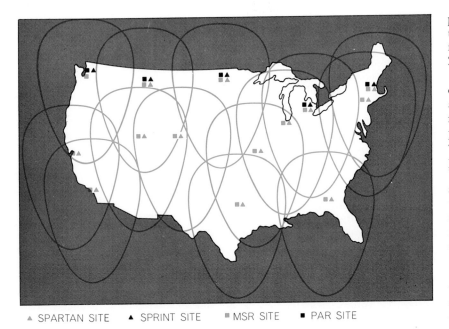

▲ SPARTAN SITE   ▲ SPRINT SITE   ■ MSR SITE   ■ PAR SITE

SENTINEL SYSTEM was described by the Johnson Administration as a "thin" ABM system designed to defend the U.S. against a hypothetical Chinese missile attack in the 1970's. The main defense was to be provided by long-range Spartan missiles. The Spartans would be deployed at about 14 locations in order to provide an area defense of the whole country. The range of each "farm" of Spartans is indicated by the egg-shaped area around it; for missiles attacking over the northern horizon the intercept range of the Spartan is elongated somewhat to the south. The Sentinel system would also include some short-range Sprint missiles, which were originally to be deployed to defend the five or six perimeter acquisition radars, or PAR's, which were to be deployed at five sites located across the northern part of the country. Missile-site radars, or MSR's, were to be deployed at every ABM site.

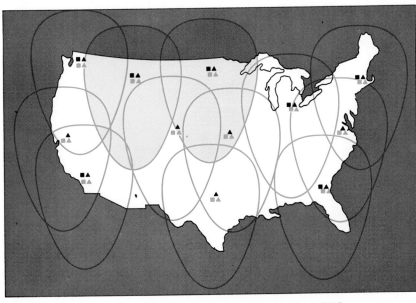

▲ SPARTAN SITE   ▲ SPRINT SITE   ■ MSR SITE   ■ PAR SITE

SAFEGUARD SYSTEM, President Nixon's proposed modification of the Sentinel scheme, uses essentially the same components in a slightly different array to accomplish an entirely different primary purpose: the defense of a part of our Minuteman force against a hypothetical surprise attack by the Russians. Phase I of Safeguard covers the construction of ABM sites at two Minuteman "fields": one near Malmstrom Air Force Base in Montana and the other near Grand Forks Air Force Base in North Dakota (colored areas). The completed system would have a total of 12 sites, each with Sprint and Spartan coverage, located somewhat farther away from the cities. In addition two new PAR sites would be included in order to observe submarine-launched missiles coming from directions other than due north.

possibilities of exhausting the defense; thus were "solved" two of the most difficult problems that had eliminated Nike Zeus and Nike-X.

Safeguard has as its primary purpose defending a part of the Minuteman force against a Russian attack. It is not credible that a Russian attack against the part of the Minuteman force so defended would be other than massive and sophisticated, so that we are virtually right back to trying to do what in 1967 we said we could not do, and we are trying to do it with no real change in the missiles or the radars. It is true that defending hard points is to a degree easier than defending cities because interception can be accomplished later and at lower altitudes, thus giving discrimination techniques more time to work. Moreover, only those objects headed for specific small areas must be intercepted. These factors do make the problem somewhat easier, but they do not ensure its solution, and plenty of room for doubt remains.

Second, there is the contest between penetration aids and discrimination techniques. This was discussed at length by Garwin and Bethe in their March 1968 article in Scientific American and mentioned also in varying degrees of detail by many of those who testified recently concerning the ABM issue. The Russian physicist Andrei D. Sakharov, in his essay "Thoughts on Progress, Coexistence and Intellectual Freedom," put the issue this way: "Improvements in the resistance of warheads to shock waves and the radiation effects of neutron and X-ray exposure, the possibility of mass use of relatively light and inexpensive decoys that are virtually indistinguishable from warheads and exhaust the capabilities of an antimissile defense system, a perfection of tactics of massed and concentrated attacks, in time and space, that overstrain the defense detection centers, the use of orbital and fractional-orbital attacks, the use of active and passive jamming and other methods not disclosed in the press—all of this has created technical and economic obstacles to an effective missile defense that, at the present time, are virtually insurmountable."

I would add only MIRV to Sakharov's list. Pitted against this plethora of penetration aids are various observational methods designed to discriminate the real warheads. Some of the penetration devices obviously work only at high altitudes, but even these make it necessary for the final "sorting" to be delayed, and thus they still contribute to making the defense problem harder. Other devices can continue to confuse the defense even down to low altitudes. Some of the problems the offense presents to the defense can no doubt be solved (and have been solved) when considered separately and in isolation. That is, they can be solved for a time, until the offense designers react. One must have serious reservations, however, whether these problems can ever be solved for any long period in the complex combinations that even a modestly sophisticated attacker can present. Further, such a contest *could* result in a catastrophic failure of the system in which all or nearly all interceptions fail.

Third, there is the unquantifiable difference between the test range and the real world. The extraordinary efforts of the Air Force to test operationally deployed Minutemen show that it too regards this as an important problem. Moreover, the tests to date do seem to have revealed important weaknesses in the deployed forces. The problem has many aspects: the possible differences between test equipment and deployed equipment; the certain differences between the offensive warheads and penetration aids supplied by us as test targets and the corresponding equipment and tactics the defense must ultimately be prepared to face; the differences between the installation crews at a test site and at a deployment site; the differences in attitudes and motivation between a test crew and an operational crew (even if it is composed of the same men); the differences between men and equipment that have recently been made ready and

whom everyone is watching and men and equipment that have been standing ready for years during which nothing happened; the differences between the emotional atmosphere where everyone knows it is not "for real" and the emotional atmosphere where no one can believe what he has just been told. It may be that all that enormously complex equipment will be ready to work the very first time it must "for real," and it may be that all those thousands of human beings have performed all their interlocking assignments correctly, but I have very substantial doubts about it.

Fourth, there is the closely related "hair-trigger/stiff-trigger" contradiction. Any active defense system such as Safeguard must sit in readiness for two or four or eight years and then fire at precisely the correct second following a warning time of only minutes. Furthermore, the precision needed for the firing time is so fine that machines must be used to choose the exact instant of firing no matter how the decision to fire is made. In the case of offensive missiles the situation is different in an essential way: Although maintaining readiness throughout a long, indefinite period is necessary, the moment of firing is not so precisely controlled in general and hence human decision-makers, including even those at high levels, may readily be permitted to play a part in the decision-making process. Thus if we wish to be certain that the defense will respond under conditions of surprise, the trigger of the ABM system, unlike the triggers of

the ICBM's and Polarises, must be continuously sensitive and ready—in short, a hair trigger—for indefinitely long periods of time.

On the other hand, it is obvious that we cannot afford to have an ABM missile fire by mistake or in response to a false alarm. Indeed, the Army went to some pains to assure residents of areas near proposed Sentinel sites that it was imposing requirements to ensure against the accidental launching of the missile and the subsequent detonation of the nuclear warhead it carries. Moreover, Army officials have assured the public that no ABM missiles would ever be launched without the specific approval of "very high authorities."

These two requirements—a hair trigger so that the system can cope with a surprise attack and a stiff trigger so that it will never go off accidentally or without proper authorization—are, I believe, contradictory requirements. In saying this I am not expressing doubt about the stated intentions of the present Army leaders, and I strongly endorse the restrictions implied in their statements. I am saying, however, that if the system cannot be fired without approval of "the highest authorities," then the probability of its being fired under conditions of surprise is less than it would be otherwise. This probability depends to a degree on the highly classified technical details of the Command and Control System, but in the last analysis it depends more on the fact that "the highest authority" is a human being and therefore subject

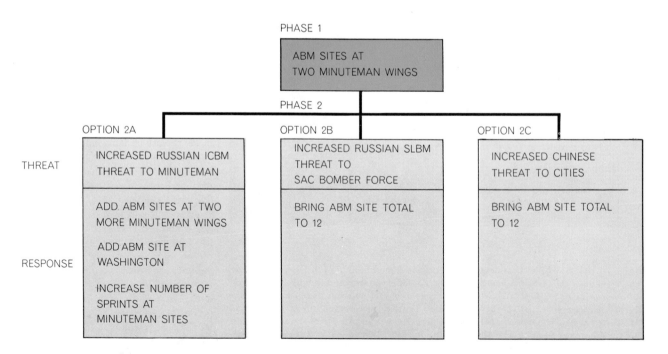

SAFEGUARD PHASE II provides for three different optional responses to various potential threats in the 1970's. A possible fur- ther addition would be sites in Alaska and Hawaii. This chart is adapted from Deputy Secretary Packard's testimony in 1969.

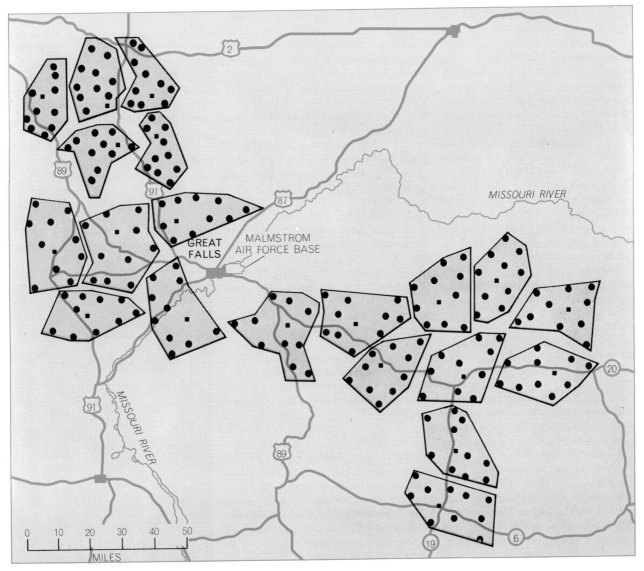

■ CONTROL CENTER   ● MINUTEMAN SILO

MINUTEMAN MISSILE BASE in the vicinity of Malmstrom Air Force Base is shown on this map, which is based on information released by the Department of the Air Force. The Minuteman missiles are grouped in 20 flights of 10 missiles each for a total of 200 missiles. Every flight has its own control center, each of which is capable of launching an entire squadron of 50 missiles.

to all the failures and foibles pertaining thereto.

This brings us to our fourth principal question: Anyway, what harm can it do?

We have just found that the total deterrent is very probably not in peril, that the Safeguard system probably cannot safeguard Minuteman even if it "works," that there is, to say the least, considerable uncertainty whether or not it will "work." Nonetheless, if there were no harm in it, we might be prudent and follow the basic motto of the arms race: "Let us err on the side of military safety." There seem to be many answers to the question of what harm building an ABM system would do. First of all, such a system would cost large sums of money needed for nondefense purposes. Sec-

ond, it would divert money and attention from what may be better military solutions to the strategic problems posed by the Administration. Third, it would intensify the arms race. All these considerations were discussed at the hearings; I shall comment here only on the third, the arms-race implications of the ABM decision.

It is often said that an ABM system is not an accelerating element in the arms race because it is intrinsically defensive. For example, during the hearings Senator Henry M. Jackson of Washington, surely one of the best-informed senators in this field, said essentially that, and he quoted Premier Kosygin as having said the same thing. I believe such a notion is in error and is based on what we may call "the fallacy of the last move." I believe that in the real world of constant

change in both the technology and the deployed numbers of all kinds of strategic-weapons systems, ABM systems are accelerating elements in the arms race. In support of this view let us recall one of the features of the history recited at the start of this article.

At the beginning of this decade we began to hear about a possible Russian ABM system, and we became concerned about its potential effects on our ICBM and Polaris systems. In response the MIRV concept was invented. Today there are additional justifications for MIRV besides penetration, but that is how it started. Now, the possibility of a Russian MIRV is used as one of the main arguments in support of the Safeguard system. Thus we have come one full turn around the arms-race spiral. No one in 1960 and 1961 thought through the potential destabilizing effects of multiple warheads, and certainly no one predicted, or even could have predicted, that the inexorable logic of the arms race would carry us directly from Russian talk in 1960 about defending Moscow against missiles to a requirement for hard-point defense of offensive-missile sites in the U.S. in 1969.

By the same token I am sure the Russians did not foresee the large increase in deployed U.S. warheads that will ultimately result from their ABM deployment and that made it so counterproductive. Similarly, no one today can describe in detail the chain reaction the Safeguard deployment would lead to, but it is easy to see the seeds of a future acceleration of the arms race in the Nixon Administration's Safeguard proposal. Soon after Safeguard is started (let us assume for now that it will be) Russian offense planners are going to look at it and say something such as: "It may not work, but we must be prudent and assume it will." They may then plan further deployments, or more complex penetration systems, or maybe they will go to more dangerous systems such as bombs in orbit. A little later, when some of our optimistic statements about how "it will do the job it is supposed to do" have become part of history, our strategic planners are going to look at Safeguard and say something such as: "Maybe it will work as they said, but we must be prudent and assume it will not and besides, *now* look at what the Russians are doing."

This approach to strategic thinking, known in the trade as "worst-case analysis," leads to a completely hopeless situation in which there is no possibility of achieving a state of affairs that both sides would consider as constituting parity. Unless the arms race is stopped by political action outside the two defense establishments, I feel reasonably sure there will be another "crash program" response analogous to what we had in the days of the "missile gap"— a situation some would like to see repeated.

I also mentioned in my own testimony at the ABM hearings that "we may further expect deployment of these ABM systems to lead to the persistent query 'But how do you know it *really* works?' and thus to increase the pressures against the current limited nuclear-test ban as well as to work against amplifying it." I mentioned this then, and I mention it again now, in the hope that it will become a self-defeating prediction. It is also important to note that the response of our own defense establishment to the

Russian ABM deployment, which I have outlined above, was not the result of our being "provoked," and I emphasize this because we hear so much discussion about what is a "provocative" move and what is not. Rather, our response was motivated by a deep-seated belief that the only appropriate response to any new technical development on the other side is further technical complexity of our own. The arms race is not so much a series of political provocations followed by hot emotional reactions as it is a series of technical challenges followed by cool, calculated responses in the form of ever more costly, more complex and more fully automatic devices. I believe this endless, seemingly uncontrollable process was one of the principal factors President Eisenhower had in mind when he made his other (usually forgotten) warning: "We must be alert to the... danger that public policy could itself become the captive of a scientific-technological elite." He placed this other warning, also from his farewell address, on the same level as the much more familiar comment about the military-industrial complex.

Several alternative approaches to Safeguard for protecting Minuteman have been discussed recently. These include superhardening, proliferation, a "shell game" in which there are more silos than missiles, and land-mobile missiles. Although I was personally hopeful before the hearings that at least one of these approaches would maintain its invulnerability, a review of the recent debates leaves me now with the pessimistic view that none of them holds much promise beyond the next 10 years.

Silo-hardening most probably does work now, in the sense that the combination of SS-11 accuracy and yield and Minuteman silo-hardening works out in such a way that one incoming warhead (and hence one SS-11 missile) has less than a 50-50 chance of destroying a Minuteman. If one considers the technological trends in hardening, yield per unit weight, MIRVing and accuracy, however, it does seem convincing that this is a game in which the offense eventually will win. Albert Wohlstetter, testifying in favor of the Safeguard system before the Senate Armed Services Committee, quoted a paper he wrote with Fred Hoffman in 1954 (long before any ICBM's were actually in place anywhere) predicting that the ability of silo-hardening to protect offensive missiles would run out by the end of the 1960's. That was a remarkably prescient study and is wrong only in numerical detail.

If we take the same rosy view of technology that was taken in almost all the pro-ABM arguments, then hardening will not work for more than another five years. My own view of the technological future is clearly much less rosy, but I do believe that the situation in which hardening is no longer the answer could come by, say, 1980 or, more appropriately, 1984.

Proliferation of Minuteman would have worked in the absence of MIRV. Now, however, it would seem that the ability to MIRV, which no doubt can eventually be carried much further than the fewfold MIRV we see for the immediate future, clearly makes prolifera-

FIRST SALVO LAUNCH of Minuteman ICBM's was made at Vandenberg Air Force Base in California on February 24, 1966. Photograph was released by U.S. Air Force.

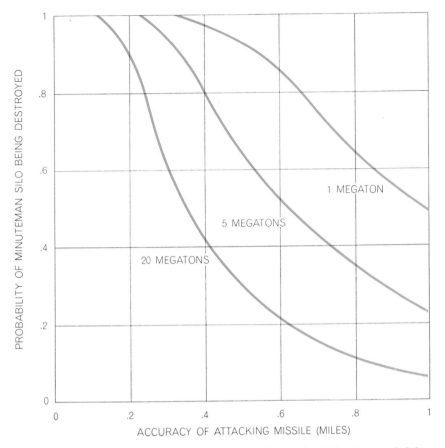

VULNERABILITY OF MINUTEMAN is revealed in this graph, which relates probability of destruction of a hardened Minuteman silo to accuracy for three different sizes of attacking warhead. This graph was interpreted by Deputy Secretary Packard as demonstrating the seriousness of the threat to Minuteman posed by the large Russian SS-9 missile, which he said is capable of carrying either one 20-megaton warhead or three five-megaton warheads.

tion a losing game as well as the dangerous one it always was.

The "shell game" has not in my view been analyzed in satisfactory detail, but it would appear to have a serious destabilizing effect on the arms race. Schemes have been suggested for verifying that a certain fraction of the missile holes are in fact empty, but one can foresee a growing and persistent belief on each side that the "other missiles" must be hidden somewhere.

Road-mobile and rail-mobile versions of Minuteman have been seriously studied for well over a decade. These ideas have always foundered on two basic difficulties: (1) Such systems are inherently soft and hence can be attacked by large warheads without precise knowledge of where they are, and (2) railroads and highways all pass through population centers, and large political and social problems seem unavoidable.

Where does all this leave us insofar as finding a technical solution for protecting Minuteman is concerned? One

and only one technically viable solution seems to have emerged for the long run: Launch on warning. Such an idea has been considered seriously by some politicians, some technical men and some military officers. Launch on warning could either be managed entirely by automatic devices, or the command and control system could be such as to require authorization to launch by some very high human authority.

In the case of the first alternative, people who think about such things envision a system consisting of probably two types of detection device that could, in principle, determine that a massive launch had been made and then somewhat later determine that such a launch consisted of multiple warheads aimed at our missile-silo fields. This information would be processed by a computer, which would then launch the Minutemen so that the incoming missiles would find only empty holes; consequently the Minutemen would be able to carry out their mission of revenge. Thus the steady advance of arms technology may not be leading us to the ultimate

weapon but rather to the ultimate absurdity: a completely automatic system for deciding whether or not doomsday has arrived.

To me such an approach to the problem is politically and morally unacceptable, and if it really is the only approach, then clearly we have been considering the wrong problem. Instead of asking how Minuteman can be protected, we should be asking what the alternatives to Minuteman are. Evidently most other people also find such an idea unacceptable. As I mentioned above, the Army has found it necessary to reassure people repeatedly that ABM missiles would not be launched without approval by "the highest authorities," even though this is clearly a far less serious matter in the case of the ABM missiles than in the case of Minuteman.

The alternative is to require that a human decision-maker, at the level of "the highest authorities," be introduced into the decision-making loop. But is this really satisfactory? We would be asking that a human being make, in just a few minutes, a decision to utterly destroy another country. (After all, there would be no point in firing at *their* empty silos.) If, for any reason whatever, he was responding to a false alarm, or to some kind of smaller, perhaps "accidental," attack, he would be ensuring that a massive deliberate attack on us would take place moments later. Considering the shortness of the time, the complexity of the information and the awesomeness of the moment, the President would himself have to be properly preprogrammed in order to make such a decision.

Those who argue that the Command and Control System is perfect or perfectable forget that human beings are not. If forced to choose, I would prefer a preprogrammed President to a computer when it came to deciding whether or not doomsday had arrived, but again I feel that this solution too is really unacceptable, and that once again, in attempting to defend Minuteman, we are simply dealing with the wrong problem. For the present it would seem the Polarises and the bombers are not, as systems, subject to the same objections, since there are now enough other approaches to the problem of ensuring their invulnerability to sudden massive destruction.

In my view, all the above once again confirms the utter futility of attempting to achieve national security through military technology alone. We must look elsewhere. Fortunately an opportunity does seem to be in the offing. There appears to be real promise that serious strategic-arms-limitation talks will begin soon. The time is propitious. There is in the land a fairly widespread doubt about the strictly military approach to security problems, and even military-minded politicians are genuinely interested in exploring other possibilities. The essay by Academician Sakharov, as well as the statements of Russian officials, indicate genuine interest on the other side. The time is propitious in another sense: both sides will be discussing the matter from a position of parity. Moreover, this parity seems reasonably stable and likely to endure for several years.

Later, however, major deployments of sophisticated ABM systems and, even more important, widespread conversion of present single-warhead systems to MIRV will be strongly destabilizing and will at least give the impression that parity is about to be upset. If so, the motto of the arms race, "Let us err on the side of military safety," will come to dominate the scene on both sides and the present opportunity will be lost. Therefore in the short run we must do everything possible to ensure that the talks not only start but also succeed. Although the ABM decision may not forestall the talks, it would seem that success will be more likely if we avoid starting things that history has shown are difficult to stop once they are started.

Such things surely include deployment of ABM missiles and MIRV's. There have been successes in stopping programs while they were in the development phase, but seldom has anything been stopped after deployment had started. The idea of a freeze on deployment of new weapons systems at this time and for these reasons is fairly widespread already, but achieving it will require concerted action by those believing strongly in the validity and necessity of arms limitations as a means of increasing national security. Thus the principal result of the recent national debate over the ABM issue has been to make it clear that Safeguard will safeguard nothing, and that the right step for the immediate future is doing whatever is necessary (such as freezing present deployments and developments) to ensure the success of the coming strategic-arms-limitation talks.

In addition, the ABM debate has served to highlight more serious issues (for example the implications of MIRV for the arms race) and to raise serious questions about other weapons systems.

For instance, I suggest that we have also found that silo-based missiles will become obsolete. The only sure method for defense of Minuteman beyond, say, the mid-1970's seems to be the unacceptable launch on warning. As long as we must have a strategic deterrent, we must find one that does not force us to turn the final decision over to either a computer or a preprogrammed President. Minuteman was conceived in the 1950's and served its purpose as a deterrent through the 1960's, but it appears that in the 1970's its threat to us will exceed its value, and that it and other silo-based missiles will have to go. The deterrent must have alternatives other than "go/no-go," and for the 1970's at least it would now appear that other strategic weapons (Polaris/Poseidon and bombers) could provide them. I expect, however, that as the continuing national debate subjects the whole matter of strategic arms to further public scrutiny we shall learn that these other alternatives also have dangerous flaws, and we shall see confirmed the idea that there is no technical solution to the dilemma of the steady decrease in our national security that has for more than 20 years accompanied the steady increase in our military power.

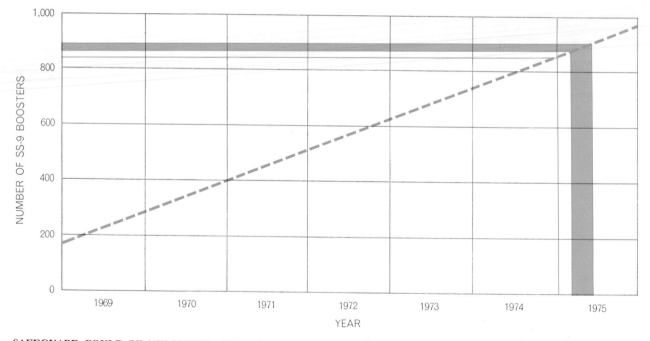

SAFEGUARD COULD BE NULLIFIED within a few months after its Phase I deployment, according to this graph, which is based on calculations presented by George W. Rathjens in his testimony before the Senate Armed Services Committee in April 1969. His analysis took as a basis of calculation the implication in Secretary Laird's testimony that the Minuteman force may become seriously imperiled in the mid-1970's. Assuming that the Russian SS-9s would have four or five MIRV warheads each by that time, Rathjens then estimated that approximately 850 SS-9's would have to be deployed in order to achieve this result. From this, and the estimate of the current number of SS-9's deployed (about 200), he got a rate of deployment (about 100 per year). Making certain assumptions about the numbers and effectiveness of the Spartan and Sprint ABM missiles that would be deployed at that time, Rathjens found that by prolonging the SS-9 production program by two to five months the Russians would be able to cope with Safeguard by simply exhausting it and would still have enough warheads to imperil Minuteman. Recently different numerical assumptions have been made, but they do not change the general conclusion that the proposed Safeguard system is much too thin to safeguard Minuteman.

BIOGRAPHICAL NOTES AND BIBLIOGRAPHIES

I. THE ECOSPHERE AND PREINDUSTRIAL MAN

1. The Ecosphere

The Author

LAMONT C. COLE is professor of zoology at Cornell University. Despite a boyhood passion for snakes, he graduated from the University of Chicago as a physicist. His return to the animal kingdom resulted from a trip down the Colorado River with A. M. Woodbury of the University of Utah, who inspired him to study ecology. Cole's chief interest is now in natural populations. He has taught at Cornell since 1948. Before that he occupied the late Alfred Kinsey's post in entomology at Indiana University, which he had taken over when Kinsey "turned to the study of bigger and better things."

Bibliography

THE ECOLOGY OF ANIMALS. Charles Elton. John Wiley & Sons, Inc., 1950.

ENERGY IN THE FUTURE. Palmer Cosslett Putnam. D. Van Nostrand Company, Inc., 1953.

ELEMENTS OF PHYSICAL BIOLOGY. Alfred J. Lotka. Williams & Wilkins Company, 1925.

FUNDAMENTALS OF ECOLOGY. Eugene P. Odum. W. B. Saunders Company, 1953.

GEOCHEMISTRY. Kalervo Rankama and Th. G. Sahama. The University of Chicago Press, 1950.

THE WEB OF LIFE: A FIRST BOOK OF ECOLOGY. John H. Storer. The Devin-Adair Company, 1953.

2. The Agricultural Revolution

The Author

ROBERT J. BRAIDWOOD is professor in the Oriental Institute and in the department of anthropology at the University of Chicago. He was born in Detroit, Mich., in 1907 and acquired his B.A. and M.A. at the University of Michigan in 1932 and 1933, respectively. He obtained a Ph.D. in archeology at Chicago in 1942, joining the faculty there two years later. Since 1947 he has been field director of a series of archeological expeditions to Iraq and Iran, the results of which are discussed in his article that appears in this volume. This work has been partly financed by the National Science Foundation, the American Philosophical Society and the Wenner-Gren Foundation for Anthropological Research.

Bibliography

ANIMAL DOMESTICATION IN THE PREHISTORIC NEAR EAST. Charles A. Reed in Science, Vol. 130, No. 3,389, pages 1,629–1,639; December 11, 1959.

DOMESTICATION OF FOOD PLANTS IN THE OLD WORLD. Hans Helbaek in Science, Vol. 130, No. 3,372, pages 365–372; August 14, 1959.

NEAR EASTERN PREHISTORY. Robert J. Braidwood in Science, Vol. 127, No. 3,312, pages 1,419–1,430; June 20, 1958.

PREHISTORIC INVESTIGATIONS IN IRAQI KURDISTAN. Robert J. Braidwood and Bruce Howe in Studies in Ancient Civilization, No. 31. University of Chicago Press, 1960.

3. Forest Clearance in the Stone Age

The Author

JOHANNES IVERSEN is head of the Paleobotanical Laboratory of the Geological Survey of Denmark and lecturer at the University of Copenhagen. He took a Ph.D. in biology at the University of Copenhagen in 1936. His principal research has been in plant ecology and vegetational history. While tracing the factors governing the vegetational succession of the past as they are reflected in pollen records, he came upon evidence of large-scale clearances in the Danish forests of Neolithic times. At present he is in the U.S. as a guest of Yale University on a Rockefeller Foundation grant.

Bibliography

THE INFLUENCE OF PREHISTORIC MAN ON VEGETATION. Johs. Iversen in Danmarks Geologiske Undersøgelse, Vol. 4, pages 1–25; 1949.

POLLEN ANALYSES (PALYNOLOGY). H. Godwin in Endeavour, Vol. 10, No. 37, pages 5–16; January, 1951.

4. The Black Death

The Author

WILLIAM L. LANGER is Archibald Cary Coolidge Professor of History at Harvard University. Langer was born in Boston in 1896 and took his degrees at Harvard. He also studied at the University of Vienna in 1921 and 1922. He has been a member of the history department at Harvard since 1926. A veteran of the Saint-Mihiel and Argonne engagements of World War I, Langer served as chief of the Research and Analysis Branch of the Office of Strategic Services during World War II. In 1946 he reorganized the foreign intelligence services of the State Department as Special Assistant to the Secretary of State. From 1950 to 1952 he served as assistant director of the Central Intelligence Agency. He is at present a member of the President's Foreign Intelligence Advisory Board. Langer was director of the Russian Research Center and the Center for Middle Eastern Studies at Harvard from 1954 to 1959. In 1957 he was elected president of the American Historical Association. He spent the academic year 1959–1960 at the Center for Advanced Study in the Behavioral Sciences in Palo Alto, Calif. Langer has written extensively in the fields of European and American diplomatic history; he is also the editor of *An Encyclopedia of World History,* published in 1940, and of the series "The Rise of Modern Europe," of which 13 volumes have appeared to date.

Bibliography

THE BLACK DEATH. G. G. Coulton. Ernest Benn Limited, 1929.

THE BLACK DEATH: A CHRONICLE OF THE PLAGUE. Compiled by Johannes Nohl. George Allen & Unwin Ltd., 1926.

THE BLIGHT OF PESTILENCE ON EARLY MODERN CIVILIZATION. Lynn Thorndike in *The American Historical Review,* Vol. 32, No. 3, pages 455–474; April, 1927.

THE BUBONIC PLAGUE AND ENGLAND. Charles F. Mullett. University of Kentucky Press, 1956.

PLAGUE AND PESTILENCE IN LITERATURE AND ART. Raymond Crawfurd. Oxford University Press, 1914.

II. LIMITS RARELY PERCEIVED

5. The Human Population

The Author

EDWARD S. DEEVEY, JR., is professor of biology and director of the Geochronometric Laboratory at Yale University. Though his researches have centered on paleoecology, he notes that "I seem to be a general ecologist for teaching purposes." A National Science Foundation award for research in the dating of lake sediments enabled him to spend several months recently boring into lake bottoms in the Auvergne and the Jura Mountains. Born in Albany, N.Y., in 1914, he developed an early interest in nature studies which won him 41 Boy Scout merit badges and the Boy Scout Nature Prize in 1928. His major relaxation is scientific field trips; when forced to stay home he enjoys reading and pre-Beethoven chamber music.

Bibliography

THE NEXT HUNDRED YEARS: MAN'S NATURAL AND TECHNICAL RESOURCES. Harrison Brown, James Bonner and John Weir. Viking Press, Inc., 1957.

POPULATION AHEAD. Roy Gustaf Francis. University of Minnesota Press, 1958.

SCIENCE AND ECONOMIC DEVELOPMENT: NEW PATTERNS OF LIVING. Richard L. Meier. John Wiley & Sons, Inc., 1956.

WORLD POPULATION AND PRODUCTION: TRENDS AND OUTLOOK. W. S. Woytinsky and E. S. Woytinsky. Twentieth Century Fund, 1953.

6. Water

The Author

ROGER REVELLE is University Dean of Research at the University of California and director of that university's Scripps Institution of Oceanography. Revelle began his long association with the Scripps Institution in 1931, two years after acquiring an A.B. in geology from Pomona College. He received a Ph.D. from Scripps in 1936 and was professor of oceanography there in 1951, when he became the first alumnus of that institution to be appointed its director. During World War II Revelle served as a commander in the U.S. Navy and immediately after the war joined the Office of Naval Research as head of the Geophysics Branch. In 1946 he organized the oceanographic expedition associated with the atomic bomb test in Bikini Lagoon, measuring the diffusion of radioactive waters and their effects on marine organisms. During the early 1950's he led several other expeditions to the central and southern Pacific, developing new methods for measuring the flow of heat out through the floor of the ocean. He served as president of the first International Oceanographic Congress held by the United Nations in 1959, and in 1961 he became the first man to hold the post of science adviser to the Secretary of the Interior. Revelle is currently president of the Committee on Oceanographic Research of the International Council of Scientific Unions and a member of the U.S. Commission to the UNESCO Office of Oceanography.

Bibliography

DESIGN OF WATER RESOURCES SYSTEMS. Arthur Mass, Maynard Hufschmidt, Robert Dorfman and Harold Thomas. Harvard University Press, 1962.

A HISTORY OF LAND USE IN ARID REGIONS: ARID ZONE RESEARCH, XVII, edited by L. Dudley Stamp. UNESCO, 1961.

MISSION TO THE INDUS. Roger Revelle in *New Scientist*, Vol. 17, No. 326, pages 340–342; February, 1963.

POSSIBILITIES OF INCREASING WORLD FOOD PRODUCTION: BASIC STUDY No. 10. Food and Agriculture Organization of the UN, 1963.

THE VALUE OF WATER IN ALTERNATIVE USES. Nathaniel Wollman. University of New Mexico Press, 1962.

WATER FACTS FOR THE NATION'S FUTURE. W. B. Langbein and W. G. Hoyt. The Ronald Press Company, 1959.

WATER RESOURCES: A REPORT TO THE COMMITTEE ON NATURAL RESOURCES. PUBLICATION 1000-B. National Academy of Sciences–National Research Council, 1962.

7.   Lateritic Soils

The Author

MARY MCNEIL is a geologist on the staff of the Lockheed-California Company, a division of the Lockheed Aricraft Corporation. A graduate of Arizona State University, she obtained an M.A. in geology from the University of California at Los Angeles in 1963; she is currently working for a Ph.D. in geography at U.C.L.A. She has worked for much of the past 12 years as a professional field geologist in Latin America and Africa. From 1952 to 1956 she was employed by the National Economic Council of the Brazilian government. Since joining the Systems Research Division of Lockheed-California in 1960 she has done research in several fields, including oceanography, geophysics and geography.

Bibliography

HUMAN GEOGRAPHY: AN ECOLOGICAL STUDY OF HUMAN SOCIETY. C. Langdon White and George T. Renner. Appleton–Century–Crofts, 1948.

LATERITE. S. Sivarajasingham, L. T. Alexander, J. G. Cady and M. G. Cline in *Advances in Agronomy*, Vol. XIV. Edited by A. G. Norman. Academic Press, 1962.

TROPICAL AND SUBTROPICAL AGRICULTURE. J. J. Ochse, M. J. Soule, Jr., M. J. Dijkman and C. Wehlburg. The Macmillan Company, 1961.

8.   Human Food Production as a Process in the Biosphere

The Author

HARRISON BROWN is professor of geochemistry and of science and government at the California Institute of Technology, where he has been a member of the faculty since 1951. He is also foreign secretary of the National Academy of Sciences and vice-president of the International Council of Scientific Unions. Brown was graduated from the University of California at Berkeley in 1938 and obtained his Ph.D. from Johns Hopkins University in 1941. Before going to Cal Tech he was associated with the U.S. atomic energy program.

Bibliography

THE CHALLENGE OF MAN'S FUTURE. Harrison Brown. The Viking Press, 1954.

THE POSSIBILITIES OF SECURING LONG RANGE SUPPLIES OF URANIUM, THORIUM AND OTHER SUBSTANCES FROM IGNEOUS ROCKS. H. Brown and L. T. Silver in *Proceedings of the International Conference on the Peaceful Uses of Atomic Energy Held in Geneva 8 August–20 August 1955, Vol. VIII: Production Technology of the Materials Used for Nuclear Energy*. United Nations, 1956.

THE NEXT HUNDRED YEARS: A DISCUSSION PREPARED FOR LEADERS OF AMERICAN INDUSTRY. Harrison Brown, James Bonner and John Weir. The Viking Press, 1957.

RESOURCES IN AMERICA'S FUTURE: PATTERNS OF REQUIREMENTS AND AVAILABILITIES 1960–2000. Hans H. Landsberg, Leonard L. Fischman and Joseph L. Fisher. The Johns Hopkins Press, 1963.

MINERALS. Julian W. Feiss in *Scientific American*, Vol. 209, No. 3, pages 128–136; September, 1963.

RESOURCE NEEDS AND DEMANDS. Harrison Brown in *Proceedings of Nobel Symposium 14: The Place of Value in a World of Facts*, edited by Arne Tiselius. Wiley-Interscience, to be published.

9.   The Food Resources of the Ocean

The Author

S. J. HOLT is with the Food and Agriculture Organization of the United Nations, serving temporarily as marine science and fishery coordinator with the United Nations Educational, Scientific and Cultural Organization on leave from his position as director of the Division of Fishery Resources and Exploitation in the Department of Fisheries of the FAO. He was born in London and was graduated from the University of Reading, which in 1966 awarded him a D.Sc. on the basis of his published work. From 1946 to 1953 he was with the British Fisheries Laboratory at Lowestoft, serving also from 1950 to 1953 with the Nature Conservancy in Edinburgh. He has been with the FAO since 1954. Holt writes: "My research has been on animal population dynamics, mainly of fish, with a particular interest in the application of such knowledge to the rational management of international fisheries. I am also concerned with problems of international organization and programming in marine science; with the question of ensuring the participation of small and developing countries in marine research and in its benefits, and with the problems of creating a scientifically competent element in the international civil service."

Bibliography

LIVING RESOURCES OF THE SEA: OPPORTUNITIES FOR RESEARCH AND EXPANSION. Lionel A. Walford. The Ronald Press Company, 1958.

FISHERIES BIOLOGY: A STUDY IN POPULATION DYNAMICS. D. H. Cushing. University of Wisconsin Press, 1968.

MARINE SCIENCE AND TECHNOLOGY: SURVEY AND PROPOSALS. REPORT OF THE SECRETARY-GENERAL. United Nations Economic and Social Council, E/4487, 1968.

THE STATE OF WORLD FISHERIES: WORLD FOOD PROBLEMS, No. 7. Food and Agriculture Organization of the United Nations, 1968.

WORK OF FAO AND RELATED ORGANIZATIONS CONCERNING MARINE SCIENCE AND ITS APPLICATIONS. FAO Fisheries Technical Paper No. 74. Food and Agriculture Organization of the United Nations, September, 1968.

10. The Dimensions of World Poverty

The Author

DAVID SIMPSON is a lecturer in political economy at University College London. He was graduated from the University of Edinburgh in 1959 and then spent five years as a graduate student and teacher at Harvard University, where he served as an assistant to Wassily Leontief in the Harvard Economic Research Project. Simpson prepared for the United Nations a monograph on input-output analysis as an instrument of economic planning. After leaving the U.S. he spent two years at the Economic Research Institute in Dublin. "I think," he writes, "that economic development constitutes the last great economic problem and that small economies make good laboratories for the testing of economic theory."

Bibliography

THE WORLD'S FOOD SUPPLIES. P. V. Sukhatme in *Journal of the Royal Statistical Society*, Series A, Vol. 129, Part 2, pages 222–241; 1966.

THIRD REPORT ON THE WORLD HEALTH SITUATION 1961–1964. No. 155, Official Records of the World Health Organization, 1967.

WORLD ECONOMIC SURVEY 1967 E4488 ADD. 1–5 E4485. United Nations, Department of Economic and Social Affairs, 1968.

11. Human Materials Production as a Process in the Biosphere

The Author

For information on HARRISON BROWN, see the biographical note under Article 8, "Human Food Production as a Process in the Biosphere."

Bibliography

THE CHALLENGE OF MAN'S FUTURE. Harrison Brown. The Viking Press, 1954.

THE POSSIBILITIES OF SECURING LONG RANGE SUPPLIES OF URANIUM, THORIUM AND OTHER SUBSTANCES FROM IGNEOUS ROCKS. H. Brown and L. T. Silver in *Proceedings of the International Conference on the Peaceful Uses of Atomic Energy Held in Geneva 8 August–20 August 1955, Vol. VIII: Production Technology of the Materials Used for Nuclear Energy*. United Nations, 1956.

THE NEXT HUNDRED YEARS: A DISCUSSION PREPARED FOR LEADERS OF AMERICAN INDUSTRY. Harrison Brown, James Bonner and John Weir. The Viking Press, 1957.

RESOURCES IN AMERICA'S FUTURE: PATTERNS OF REQUIREMENTS AND AVAILABILITIES 1960–2000. Hans H. Landsberg, Leonard L. Fischman and Joseph L. Fisher. The Johns Hopkins Press, 1963.

MINERALS. Julian W. Feiss in *Scientific American*, Vol. 209, No. 3, pages 128–136; September, 1963.

RESOURCE NEEDS AND DEMANDS. Harrison Brown in *Proceedings of Nobel Symposium 14: The Place of Value in a World of Facts*, edited by Arne Tiselius. Wiley-Interscience, to be published.

III. THE DIMENSIONS OF INTERVENTION

12. Toxic Substance and Ecological Cycles

The Author

GEORGE M. WOODWELL is an ecologist at the Brookhaven National Laboratory. His original field of study was botany; he received an undergraduate degree in that subject at Dartmouth College in 1950 and master's and doctor's degrees from Duke University in 1956 and 1958 respectively. From 1957 to 1962, when he joined the Brookhaven staff, he taught at the University of Maine. He notes that his article "in no way reflects an official attitude of the U.S. Atomic Energy Commission or Brookhaven National Laboratory."

Bibliography

ENVIRONMENTAL RADIOACTIVITY. Merril Eisenbud. McGraw-Hill Book Company, Inc., 1963.

PESTICIDES AND THE LIVING LANDSCAPE. Robert L. Rudd. University of Wisconsin Press, 1964.

REPORT OF THE UNITED NATIONS SCIENTIFIC COMMITTEE ON THE EFFECTS OF ATOMIC RADIATION. Official Records of the General Assembly, 13th Session, Supplement No. 17, 1958; 17th Session, Supplement No. 16, 1962; 19th Session, Supplement No. 14, 1964.

13. Air Pollution and Public Health

The Author

WALSH MCDERMOTT is Livingston Farrand Professor of Public Health and Preventive Medicine at the Cornell University Medical College. He received a B.A. from Princeton University in 1930 and an M.D. degree from Columbia University in 1934. Tuberculosis interrupted his residency at New York Hospital for a year, and he found that almost the only position available to him at the time was in a newly created syphilis clinic at Cornell. His subsequent work with microbial diseases and the various antimicrobial drugs introduced to combat them gradually led McDermott into the field of public health. For the past 16 years McDermott has been editor of *The American Review of Respiratory Diseases;* for approximately the same length of time he has served as an associate editor of the Cecil-Loeb *Textbook of Medicine,* and more recently, with Paul B. Beeson, as coeditor. For the past year he has also been chairman of the President's Science Advisory Committee Panel on Development Assistance.

Bibliography

AIR POLLUTION ASTHMA AMONG MILITARY PERSONNEL IN JAPAN. H. W. Phelps, G. W. Sobel and N. E. Fisher in *Journal of the American Medical Association,* Vol. 175, No. 11, pages 990–993; March 18, 1961.

PROCEEDINGS, NATIONAL CONFERENCE ON AIR POLLUTION, WASHINGTON, D.C., NOVEMBER 18–20, 1958. Public Health Service Publication No. 654.

14. The Aging Great Lakes

The Authors

CHARLES F. POWERS and ANDREW ROBERTSON are respectively associate research oceanographer and assistant research limnologist with the Great Lakes Research Division of the University of Michigan. Powers received a bachelor's degree in zoology at the University of North Carolina in 1950; while there he developed an interest in water environments. As a graduate student at Cornell University, where he obtained a Ph.D. in 1955, he concentrated on oceanography but also gave attention to limnology and ichthyology. His primary interest is the Great Lakes, but he has also worked on the ecological aspects of small marshes and on coastal oceanography and estuarine processes. Robertson, who majored in chemistry at the University of Toledo, received master's and doctor's degrees in zoology from the University of Michigan.

Bibliography

EUTROPHICATION OF THE ST. LAWRENCE GREAT LAKES. Alfred M. Beeton in *Limnology and Oceanography,* Vol. 10, No. 2, pages 240–254; April, 1965.

GEOLOGY OF THE GREAT LAKES. Jack L. Hough. University of Illinois Press, 1958.

GREAT LAKES BASIN. Edited by Howard J. Pincus. American Association for the Advancement of Science, Publication No. 71. The Horn-Shafer Company, 1962.

GREAT LAKES: SPORT FISHING FRONTIER. Howard A. Tanner in *Michigan Conservation,* Vol. 34, No.6, pages 2–9; November–December, 1965.

THE ST. LAWRENCE GREAT LAKES. Alfred M. Beeton and David C. Chandler in *Limnology in North America,* edited by David G. Frey. The University of Wisconsin Press, 1963.

15. Ionizing Radiation and the Citizen

The Author

GEORGE W. BEADLE, Nobel laureate for his work in biochemical genetics, is head of the division of biology at the California Institute of Technology. For the past year he has been Eastman Visiting Professor at the University of Oxford. He was born in 1903 in Wahoo, Neb., the son of a farmer. Beadle would probably have become a farmer himself but for the influence of a high-school science teacher, Mrs. J. C. Higgins, now of Jackson, Neb., who so fired his imagination that he determined to become a scientist. The late Professor Frank D. Keim at the University of Nebraska introduced him to genetics. After some time at Cal Tech, he went to Paris to work with Boris Ephrussi at the Institut de Biologie Physico-chimique. He returned for a year at Harvard University, and in 1937 went to Stanford University as a professor. There he worked with the chemist Edward L. Tatum. They decided to use the red bread-mold *Neurospora crassa* in genetic experiments, and it was for their work with this organism that they shared half the 1958 Nobel prize in medicine. In 1946 he succeeded Thomas Hunt Morgan, also a Nobel laureate, as head of the Cal Tech biology division.

Bibliography

THE ABC OF NUCLEAR WEAPONS. H. W. B. Skinner in *The New Scientist,* Vol. 5, No. 119, pages 473–475; February 26, 1959.

THE BIOLOGICAL EFFECTS OF ATOMIC RADIATION. National Academy of Sciences, 1956.

GENETIC AND SOMATIC EFFECTS OF CARBON-14. Linus Pauling in *Science,* Vol. 128, pages 1,183–1,186; November 14, 1958.

GENETICS IN THE ATOMIC AGE. Charlotte Auerbach. Oliver and Boyd, 1956.

RECOMMENDATIONS OF THE INTERNATIONAL COMMISSION ON RADIOLOGICAL PROTECTION. *British Journal of Radiology,* Supplement No. 6; 1955.

WORLD-WIDE CAPABILITIES FOR PRODUCTION AND CONTROL OF NUCLEAR WEAPONS. Howard Simons in *Daedalus,* Vol. 88, No. 3, pages 385–409; Summer, 1959.

16. Thermal Pollution and Aquatic Life

The Author

JOHN R. CLARK is assistant director of the Sandy Hook Marine Laboratory of the U.S. Bureau of Sport Fisheries and Wildlife. "My forte," he writes, "has truly been sea work; I've probably spent 1,000 days at sea in the past 20 years, and before that in Seattle I worked summers as a commercial fisherman to get through college." Clark was graduated from the University of Washington in 1949 with a degree in fisheries science. For 10 years after that he worked at the Fisheries Laboratory of the U.S. Bureau of Commercial Fisheries in Woods Hole, Mass. Clark was a founder of the American Littoral Society and is now its president. He wishes to note that his article expresses his personal views and is not to be regarded as an official statement of the U.S. Department of the Interior.

Bibliography

THE PHYSIOLOGY OF FISHES. Edited by Margaret E. Brown. Academic Press, Inc., 1957.

THE PHYSIOLOGY OF CRUSTACEA, VOL. I: METABOLISM AND GROWTH. Edited by Talbot H. Waterman. Academic Press, Inc., 1960.

FISH AND RIVER POLLUTION. J. R. Erichsen Jones. Butterworths, 1964.

A FIELD AND LABORATORY INVESTIGATION OF THE EFFECT OF HEATED EFFLUENTS ON FISH. J. S. Alabaster in Fishery Investigations, Ministry of Agriculture, Fisheries, and Food, Series I, Vol. 6, No. 4; 1966.

THERMAL POLLUTION–1968. Subcommittee on Air and Water Pollution of the Committee on Public Works. U.S. Government Printing Office, 1968.

17. Carbon Dioxide and Climate

The Author

GILBERT N. PLASS is a senior staff member of the Office of Advanced Research of Aeronutronic Systems, Inc. A physics graduate of Harvard College in 1941, he joined in early studies of nuclear reactors for the Manhattan Project at the University of Chicago's Metallurgical Laboratory during World War II, then acquired a Ph.D. from Princeton University and taught physics at Johns Hopkins University. "I spent several years," he says, "studying the dependence of infrared radiation in the atmosphere upon water vapor, carbon dioxide and ozone. This naturally led me to reexamine the old carbon dioxide theory of climatic change. It soon became evident that the usual textbook objections to this theory were invalid. My long-standing interest in geology, biology and chemistry helped me to synthesize the new carbon dioxide theory from these diverse fields."

Bibliography

THE ARTIFICIAL PRODUCTION OF CARBON DIOXIDE AND ITS INFLUENCE ON TEMPERATURE. G. S. Callendar in Quarterly Journal of the Royal Meteorological Society, Vol. 64, No. 275, pages 223–240; April, 1938.

THE CARBON DIOXIDE THEORY OF CLIMATIC CHANGE. Gilbert N. Plass in Tellus, Vol. 8, No. 2, pages 140–153; May, 1956.

THE INFLUENCE OF THE 15μ CARBON-DIOXIDE BAND ON THE ATMOSPHERIC INFRA-RED COOLING RATE. G. N. Plass in Quarterly Journal of the Royal Meteorological Society, Vol. 82, No. 353, pages 310–324; July, 1956.

18. The Climate of Cities

The Author

WILLIAM P. LOWRY is assistant professor of biometeorology at Oregon State University. With a bachelor's degree in mathematics, which he obtained at the University of Cincinnati in 1950, he went to the University of Wisconsin, where he received a master's degree in meteorology in 1955, and to Oregon State University, where in 1962 he was awarded an interdisciplinary doctorate for work done in meteorology, statistics and the physiology and ecology of plants. Lowry was a physicist with the Snow, Ice and Permafrost Research Establishment of the U.S. Army Corps of Engineers from 1951 to 1953, a research associate in meteorology at the University of Wisconsin from 1953 to 1955, a research meteorologist with the Oregon State Board of Forestry from 1955 to 1957 and a research meteorologist with the Oregon Forest Research Center from 1957 to 1961. His first assignment at Oregon State University was as assistant professor of forest meteorology.

Bibliography

THE DONORA SMOG DISASTER–A PROBLEM IN ATMOSPHERIC POLLUTION. Robert D. Fletcher in Weatherwise, Vol. 2, No. 3, pages 56–60; June, 1949.

LOCAL CLIMATOLOGICAL STUDIES OF THE TEMPERATURE CONDITIONS IN AN URBAN AREA. A. Sundborg in Tellus, Vol. 2, No. 3, pages 221–231; August, 1950.

ON THE CAUSES OF INSTRUMENTALLY OBSERVED SECULAR TEMPERATURE TRENDS. J. Murray Mitchell, Jr., in Journal of Meteorology, Vol. 10, No. 4, pages 244–261; August, 1953.

19. Infectious Drug Resistance

The Author

TSUTOMU WATANABE is associate professor of microbiology at the Keio University School of Medicine in Tokyo, where he received his M.D. degree in 1948. He spent a year as an exchange student in radiobiology and bacteriology at the University of Utah in 1951 and 1952 and also worked as a research associate in the department of zoology at Columbia University in 1957 and 1958. He writes that his special field of study is "microbial genetics, particularly the genetics of bacterial drug resistance. Through the studies on infectious drug resistance I have become interested in various episomes and plasmids (parasitic or symbiotic agents) of bacteria and also in the evolution of microorganisms."

Bibliography

EVOLUTIONARY RELATIONSHIPS OF R FACTORS WITH OTHER EPISOMES AND PLASMIDS. T. Watanabe in *Federation Proceedings*, Vol. 26, No. 1, pages 23–28; January–February, 1967.

INFECTIVE HEREDITY OF MULTIPLE DRUG RESISTANCE IN BACTERIA. Tsutomu Watanabe in *Bacteriological Reviews*, Vol. 27, No. 1, pages 87–115; March, 1963.

IV. ON MANAGEMENT AND BUYING TIME

20. The Assessment of Technology

The Authors

HARVEY BROOKS and RAYMOND BOWERS are respectively dean of engineering and applied physics at Harvard University and professor of physics and member of the Laboratory of Atomic and Solid State Physics at Cornell University. Brooks was chairman and Bowers a member of a panel convened by the National Academy of Sciences to examine the assessment of technology; their article is based on the panel's report. Brooks, who was graduated from Yale University in 1937 and obtained his Ph.D. from Harvard in 1940, is chairman of the Committee on Science and Public Policy of the National Academy of Sciences. Bowers, who was born in London, obtained his bachelor's degree at the University of London in 1948 and his Ph.D. from the University of Oxford in 1951. For 14 months in 1966 and 1967 he was a member of the staff of the Office of Science and Technology in the Executive Office of the President.

Bibliography

DESERT AND FOREST: THE EXPLORATION OF ABYSSINIAN DANAKIL. L. M. Nesbitt. Jonathan Cape Ltd., 1934.

GEOLOGIA DELL'AFRICA ORIENTALE. Giotti Dainelli. Reale Accademia d'Italia, 1943.

MAJOR VOLCANO-TECTONIC LINEAMENT IN THE ETHIOPIAN RIFT SYSTEM. P. A. Mohr in *Nature*, Vol. 213, No. 5077. pages 664–665; February 18, 1967.

RELATIONS TECTONIQUES ENTRE L'AFAR ET LA MER ROUGE. Haroun Tazieff in *Bulletin de la Société Géologique de France*, Series 7, Vol. 10, No. 4, pages 468–477; 1968.

TRANSCURRENT FAULTING IN THE ETHIOPIAN RIFT SYSTEM. P. A. Mohr in *Nature*, Vol. 218, No. 5145, pages 938–941; June 8, 1968.

21. The Reclamation of a Man-Made Desert

The Author

WALTER C. LOWDERMILK is a leading conservationist who was associate chief of the Soil Conservation Service in the U.S. Department of Agriculture from 1933 until he retired in 1947. He was also chief of research for the Service from 1937 until 1947. Born in North Carolina in 1888, Lowdermilk acquired his B.A. at the University of Arizona in 1912 and then attended the University of Oxford as a Rhodes scholar. He was in forestry work for many years in this country and in China, where he was associated with the University of Nanking. In 1929 he took his Ph.D. at the University of California. Since 1943 Lowdermilk has been serving as consultant on conservation to many foreign governments as well as to presidential commissions and the Supreme Allied Command of Japan. From 1955 to 1957 he was visiting professor of agricultural engineering at Technion, the Israeli technological institute of Haifa.

Bibliography

PALESTINE, LAND OF PROMISE. Walter Clay Lowdermilk, Harper & Brothers, 1944.

RIVERS IN THE DESERT. Nelson Glueck. Jewish Publication Society of America, 1959.

22. The Rangelands of the Western United States

The Author

R. MERTON LOVE is chairman of the department of agronomy and range science at the University of California at Davis, with which he has been affiliated since 1940. Born in Canada, he was graduated from the University of Saskatchewan in 1932 and obtained his master's degree there in 1933; he took his Ph.D. at McGill University in 1935. His agronomical researches have taken him to many parts of the world, including Australia and New Zealand and a number of countries in Europe. Love writes that "music, travel and photography are my leisure interests."

Bibliography

THE RANGE, A MAJOR RESOURCE. *Grass: The Yearbook of Agriculture 1948*, by United States Department of Agriculture. U.S. Government Printing Office, 1948.

RANGE MANAGEMENT. Laurence A. Stoddart and Arthur D. Smith. McGraw-Hill Book Company, 1955.

THE RANGE—NATURAL PLANT COMMUNITIES OR MODIFIED ECOSYSTEMS? R. Merton Love in *Jour-*

nal of the British Grassland Society, Vol. 1, No. 2, pages 89–99; June, 1961.

WILDERNESS MANAGEMENT: THE HORACE M. ALBRIGHT CONSERVATION LECTURESHIP. Stephen H. Spurr. University of California, School of Forestry, 1966.

23. Chemical Fertilizers

The Author

CHRISTOPHER J. PRATT is manager of international agricultural chemical development for the Mobil Chemical Company. He was born and educated in England, studying industrial chemistry at the Rutherford College of Technology and psychology and music at Goldsmiths' College. For several years before coming to the U.S. in 1953 he was a management consultant to British companies in the field of heavy chemical processing. In his spare time he is a free-lance writer, in which capacity he has written several articles (including the present one) on heavy chemicals and on fertilizer production, and he indulges an interest in baroque music by playing the contrabass—he did so professionally for several years in England—and the organ.

Bibliography

THE CHEMISTRY AND TECHNOLOGY OF FERTILIZERS. Edited by Vincent Sauchelli. Reinhold Publishing Corporation, 1960.

COMMERCIAL FERTILIZERS. G. H. Collings. McGraw-Hill Book Company, Inc., 1955.

FERTILIZER NITROGEN: ITS CHEMISTRY AND TECHNOLOGY. Edited by Vincent Sauchelli. Reinhold Publishing Corporation, 1964.

24. Third-Generation Pesticides

The Author

CARROLL M. WILLIAMS is Bussey Professor of Biology at Harvard University. After his graduation from the University of Richmond in 1937 he went to Harvard and successively obtained master's and doctor's degrees in biology and, in 1946, an M.D. He joined the Harvard faculty in 1946 and became full professor in 1953. From 1959 to 1961 he was chairman of the biology department. He has been a member of the National Academy of Sciences since 1961. Williams' studies of insects have won a number of awards; in 1967 he received the George Ledlie Prize of $1,500, which is given every two years to the member of the Harvard faculty who has made "the most valuable contribution to science, or in any way for the benefit of mankind."

Bibliography

THE EFFECTS OF JUVENILE HORMONE ANALOGUES ON THE EMBRYONIC DEVELOPMENT OF SILKWORMS. Lynn M. Riddiford and Carroll M. Williams in Proceedings of the National Academy of Sciences, Vol. 57, No. 3, pages 595–601; March, 1967.

THE HORMONAL REGULATION OF GROWTH AND REPRODUCTION IN INSECTS. V. B. Wigglesworth in Advances in Insect Physiology: Vol. II, edited by J. W. L. Bement, J. E. Treherne and V. B. Wigglesworth. Academic Press Inc., 1964.

SYNTHESIS OF A MATERIAL WITH HIGH JUVENILE HORMONE ACTIVITY. John H. Law, Ching Yuan and Carroll M. Williams in Proceedings of the National Academy of Sciences, Vol. 55, No. 3, pages 576–578; March, 1966.

25. The Prospects of Fusion Power

The Authors

WILLIAM C. GOUGH and BERNARD J. EASTLUND are with the division of research of the U.S. Atomic Energy Commission. Gough, who obtained his bachelor's and master's degrees in electrical engineering from Princeton University, has been with the AEC since 1953, working mainly on civilian and military power reactor programs. For his work over the past 10 years on the commission's research program in controlled thermonuclear fusion and plasma physics he was awarded the sustained superior performance certificate of the AEC. During the academic year 1966–1967 he held a Government sabbatical at the Kennedy School of Government of Harvard University, where he studied the interaction of science and public policy. Eastlund took his bachelor's degree in physics at the Massachusetts Institute of Technology in 1960 and his Ph.D., also in physics, at Columbia University in 1965. He joined the AEC in 1966.

Bibliography

PROGRESS IN CONTROLLED THERMONUCLEAR RESEARCH. R. W. Gould, H. P. Furth, R. F. Post and F. L. Ribe in Presentation Made before the President's Science Advisory Committee, December 15, 1970, and AEC's General Advisory Committee, December 16, 1970.

WORLD SURVEY OF MAJOR FACILITIES IN CONTROLLED FUSION. Nuclear Fusion, Special Supplement 1970, STI/Pub/23. International Atomic Energy Agency, 1970.

WHY FUSION? William C. Gough in Proceedings of the Fusion Reactor Design Symposium, Held at Texas Tech University, Lubbock, Texas, on June 2–5, 1970. In press.

26. The Urbanization of the Human Population

The Author

KINGSLEY DAVIS is professor of sociology and director of International Population and Urban Research at the University of California at Berkeley. He was born and reared in West Texas, then a highly rural region, where he acquired a strong preference for open spaces rather than cities. He was graduated from the University of Texas and received a master's degree in philosophy there; in 1936 he obtained a Ph.D. in sociology at Harvard University. Later he held a postdoctoral fellowship from the Social Science Research Council for advanced study in demography; more recently he was a fellow at the Center for Advanced Study in the Behavioral Sciences and a senior postdoctoral fellow of the National Science Foundation. His interest in population has taken him to Europe, Latin America, India, Pakistan and 10 countries in Africa; he has also served as U.S. representative to the Population Commission of the United Nations. Davis has been designated as chairman of the National Research Council's newly created Behavioral Sciences Division. Before going to the Oakland–San Francisco metropolitan area in 1955 he taught for seven years at Columbia University, a juxtaposition that moved him to write: "For a man who dislikes large cities, I have spent much of my adult life in major metropolitan areas."

Bibliography

THE GROWTH OF CITIES IN THE NINETEENTH CENTURY: A STUDY IN STATISTICS. Adna Ferrin Weber. Columbia University, 1899.

URBAN RESEARCH METHODS. Edited by Jack P. Gibbs. D. Van Nostrand Company, Inc., 1961.

THE WORLD'S METROPOLITAN AREAS. University of California Press, 1959.

27. Military Technology and National Security

The Author

HERBERT F. YORK is professor of physics at the University of California at San Diego and a member of the general advisory committee of the U.S. Arms Control and Disarmament Agency. York returned to teaching in 1964 after a long career as an administrator and Government official; he was director of the Livermore Laboratory from 1952 to 1958; chief scientist with the Advanced Research Projects Agency of the Department of Defense in 1958; director of defense research and engineering in the office of the Secretary of Defense from 1958 to 1961; chancellor of the University of California at San Diego from 1961 to 1964, and twice a member of the President's Science Advisory Committee, serving as its vice-chairman in the latter years of the Johnson Administration. He was graduated from the University of Rochester in 1942 and received a master's degree there in 1943; he obtained his Ph.D. from the University of California at Berkeley in 1949.

Bibliography

THE ESSENCE OF SECURITY. Robert S. McNamara. Harper & Row, Publishers, 1968.

ABM: AN EVALUATION OF THE DECISION TO DEPLOY AN ANTIBALLISTIC MISSILE SYSTEM. Edited by Abram Chayes and Jerome B. Wiesner, introduction by Edward M. Kennedy. Signet Books, 1969.

STRATEGIC AND FOREIGN POLICY IMPLICATIONS OF ABM·SYSTEMS: HEARINGS BEFORE THE SUBCOMMITTEE ON INTERNATIONAL ORGANIZATION AND DISARMAMENT AFFAIRS OF THE COMMITTEE ON FOREIGN RELATIONS, UNITED STATES SENATE. NINETY-FIRST CONGRESS, FIRST SESSION ON THE STRATEGIC AND FOREIGN POLICY IMPLICATIONS OF ANTIBALLISTIC MISSILE SYSTEMS. U.S Government Printing Office, 1969.

PUBLISHER'S NOTE: These biographies and bibliographies were current at the time of original publication of each article contained in the volume.

Index